PRENTICE HALL STAFF CREDITS

Director of Foreign Languages: Marina Liapunov

Director of Marketing: Karen Ralston

Project Support: Julie Demori

Advertising and Promotion: Carol Leslie, Alfonso Manosalvas, Rip Odell

Business Office: Emily Heins

Design: Jim O'Shea, AnnMarie Roselli

Editorial: Guillermo Lawton-Alfonso, José A. Peláez, Generosa Gina Protano, Barbara T. Stone

Manufacturing and Inventory Planning: Katherine Clarke, Rhett Conklin

Media Resources: Libby Forsyth, Maritza Puello

National Consultants: Camille Wiersgalla, Mary J. Secrest

Permissions: Doris Robinson

Product Development Operations: Laura Sanderson

Production: Janice L. Lalley

Sales Operations: Hans Spengler

Technology Development: Richard Ferrie

3-415670-6

8 9 10 00 99 98 97

ICE HALL
Schuster Education Group
M COMPANY

JUNTOS

PRENTICE
Simon & Schu
A VIACOM C

C
Ne
mitte
recor
from t
ISBN 0-
2 3 4 5 6 7

T2

PRENTI
Simon &
A VIAC

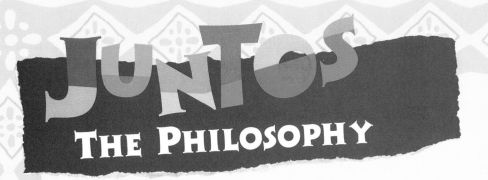

JUNTOS
THE PHILOSOPHY

Juntos reflects the vision and philosophy of the ***Standards for Foreign Language Learning*** developed by the American Council on the Teaching of Foreign Languages, the American Association of Teachers of Spanish and Portuguese, and other second language associations.

"Language and communication are at the heart of the human experience. The United States must educate students who are linguistically and culturally equipped to communicate successfully in a pluralistic American society and abroad. This imperative envisions a future in which ALL students will develop and maintain proficiency in English and at least one other language, modern or classical. Children who come to school from non-English backgrounds should also have opportunities to develop further proficiencies in their first language."

The ***Standards*** identifies five goals of foreign language education: Communication, Cultures, Connections, Comparisons, and Communities. ***Juntos*** is inspired by and organized around these goals.

JUNTOS
THE GOALS

COMMUNICATION

Communication is the central goal of second language learning.

The **Juntos** plan encourages students to use Spanish from the first day! They will understand, speak, read, and write Spanish—quickly taking their first important steps toward developing communicative competence.

CULTURE

Through the study of a second language, students begin to understand and appreciate the diversity of the many cultures of people who speak the language.

In **Juntos**, the relationship between the Spanish language and Spanish-speaking cultures is highlighted through authentic video segments, art, literature, and newspaper and magazine articles.

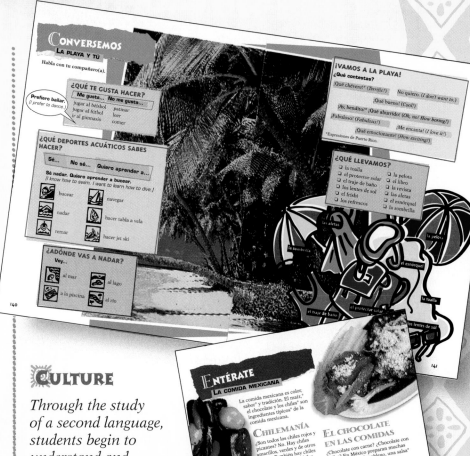

CONNECTIONS

Through the study of a second language, students will access new information and explore issues related to many other subject areas.

In **Juntos**, students investigate content of other subject areas, such as history, social studies, math and science, and the arts.

COMPARISONS

Studying a second language provides insights into other cultures and the nature of language.

In **Juntos**, students directly compare and contrast cultures, customs, literature, and languages, as they reach a better understanding of their own language and culture.

COMMUNITIES

Knowledge of a second language opens doors to a world of other multilingual communities, both at home and elsewhere.

Juntos celebrates the diversity of world communities while encouraging students to use Spanish for lifelong learning.

DEL MUNDO HISPANO

UN PASEO POR CHAPULTEPEC

Chapultepec Mágico
Es el nombre del parque de diversiones de Chapultepec. La montaña rusa° es una de las diversiones favoritas.

◄ La montaña rusa de este parque tiene forma de serpiente.°

► En el parque venden° deliciosas frutas con chile.

Comidas
Chapultepec es un lugar ideal para hacer picnics. Aquí venden comida mexicana deliciosa: tacos, enchiladas y frutas con chile. También venden refrescos, jugos y helados.

Las calles
Como° no hay coches en las calles del parque, patinar es muy divertido.

El Castillo
El Castillo está en la cima° del Monte de Chapultepec. Este edificio° histórico es hoy el Museo Nacional de Historia.

Teatros
En el Auditorio Nacional, la Casa del Lago y el Teatro del Bosque hay conciertos y obras de teatro.°

Muchos jóvenes visitan el zoológico de Chapultepec. ▼

El parque zoológico
En el zoológico ¡hay más de° 2.500 (dos mil quinientos) animales! Es un centro de protección de animales, como el lobo° mexicano, el panda gigante, el orangután, el gorila, el jaguar, el puma y el águila.°

▲ En el zoológico de Chapultepec hay jaguares mexicanos.

como *since*
el edificio *building*
en la cima *on the top*
la montaña rusa *roller coaster*
las obras de teatro *theater plays*
la serpiente *snake*
venden *they sell*

UNIDAD 5

ESTADOS UNIDOS

NUESTRAS COMUNIDADES LATINAS

En lo unidad 5:

Capítulo 9 Los medios de comunicación

Capítulo 10 ¿Vamos de compras?

Adelante

Para leer: Los murales: una tradición hispana

Proyecto: Pintar a la grande

Otras fronteras: Literatura, historia, informática y teatro

Un festival en la Pequeña Habana, en Miami.

De compras en la calle Olvera, en Los Angeles.

Una celebración en Nueva York.

Spanish is spoken in many parts of the U.S. Change the stations on your radio or TV and you're bound to hear Spanish spoken or sung. Look at the stores around you. You may find newspapers or magazines written in Spanish. There are probably Spanish products on your supermarket shelves.

This unit will take you to some Spanish-speaking communities in the United States. You will visit a street fair in a Spanish-speaking neighborhood and do a little shopping. As you walk through the streets of these neighborhood, you'll see Spanish on billboards, movie theatres, signs in stores, and even on street signs. Spanish is read, spoken, and heard in many U.S. neighborhoods — Spanish is all around you!

Colorful murals are a form of expression in many Spanish-speaking neighborhoods. You will learn about the artists who created them, discover the origins and meaning of this kind of art, and understand why it is such an important part of the culture of Spanish-speaking people. Then you and your class can create a mural of your own!

JUNTOS

HOW THE PROGRAM WORKS

Juntos is a multi-media, three-level Spanish program. The plan for the program is based on surveys, conferences, and one-on-one discussions with teachers nationwide.

Juntos Levels One and Two consist of six units, each of which contains two chapters and an *Adelante*—a section which includes a reading on an important cultural aspect of the unit, a hands-on project, information from other subject areas, and writing and reading activities. *Juntos* Level Three consists of ten thematic chapters.

THE UNIT:
THE CULTURAL SETTING

Each unit is based in a country or region where Spanish is spoken. Overall, *Juntos* covers parts of North, Central, and South America, Europe, and the Caribbean. The unit locations are specifically chosen to show the relationship between language and culture.

UNIDAD 3

PUERTO RICO

ISLA DEL ENCANTO
En la unidad 3:

Capítulo 5	Arena, sol y mar
Capítulo 6	¿Cómo te afecta el tiempo?
Adelante	Para leer: El Yunque, un bosque tropical
	Proyecto: Cielo, viento y ¡chiringas!
	Otras fronteras: Ecología, ciencias, arte y música

If you like water sports, you will like Puerto Rico. It has 300 miles of shoreline and just about every water sport from scuba diving to parasailing. And you can enjoy these sports almost every day of the year because Puerto Rico has a tropical climate.

In Puerto Rico you can find colonial-style towns, modern cities, and a tropical rain forest. And there is El Morro, a sixteenth-century fortress that guards San Juan harbor.

The original inhabitants of Puerto Rico were the Taínos, who came to the Caribbean from South America. In 1508 Puerto Rico was colonized by Spain. Today, Puerto Rico is a commonwealth of the United States. This unit will be your guide to Puerto Rico. You will visit the beaches, explore the rainforest, and get plenty of sun. See you at the beach! Terrific! ¡Qué chévere!

El castillo de El Morro en San Juan, Puerto Rico.

137

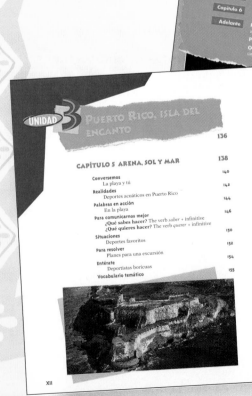

THE CHAPTER:

THE COMMUNICATIVE CORE OF THE PROGRAM

Within each unit, the two chapters are related by a theme—such as, beach sports and weather, news events, foreign exchange programs, and technology. The unit theme provides students a point of departure for learning about the culture, history, and geography of the unit location.

ADELANTE:

AN IMMERSION IN CULTURE

The core of each *Adelante* is *Del mundo hispano*, an article which draws attention to a unique feature of the unit's country or region— for example, the Hispanic influence on music in Texas. The *Adelante* also expands on the communicative objectives of the unit with a cultural hands-on project, reading comprehension strategies and activities, writing suggestions, and short informative readings which provide connections to other subject matters.

FACILITATING SECOND LANGUAGE LEARNING

Facilitating second language learning presents great challenges to the teacher. *Juntos* addresses these challenges directly and effectively.

1 *The challenge:* To foster communication and student involvement in the classroom

Juntos *motivates students by focusing on topics that are part of daily life.*

• The chapter themes in *Juntos* are based on surveys of high school students. When students care about these topics, they will make the effort to communicate.

• From the very beginning, students are asked to respond from their own personal experience, to express their own opinions, and to think critically.

• Every activity is designed specifically to get students to participate and develop a feel for the language.

2 *The challenge:* To have students participate and learn in individual, pair, group, and class settings

Juntos *specifically includes activities that promote learning in all varieties of classroom groupings.*

• A suggested grouping plan is given for each activity.

• Directions are simple and clear so that students can complete the activities without teacher intervention.

• Communicative models are provided to get students started.

• Prompts and hints provide support to students working with each other.

The challenge: *To teach and include students of different backgrounds, abilities, and confidence levels*

Juntos *addresses the individual needs of all students.*

• Every activity is designed to encourage the success of all students.

• For students uncomfortable speaking in a group, paired activities offer a protected setting for developing confidence and competence.

• The Tutor Pages provide a structure for more able students or native speakers to help other students develop vocabulary, structure, and communicative competence.

• This Teacher's Edition suggests specific approaches for students having difficulty.

• Strategies for drawing upon the resources of native speakers are featured in the *Para hispanohablantes* boxes of this Teacher's Edition.

• Spanish speakers and more advanced students can take advantage of *Conexiones*, an illustrated reader, and its accompanying *Cuaderno*, a workbook designed to further develop those students' writing, structure, and study skills.

• More advanced students also benefit from the numerous extension activities provided for them in this Teacher's Edition, the Activity Kit, and the magazines.

The challenge: *To address different learning modalities*

Juntos *provides a full range of activities to accommodate visual, auditory, and kinesthetic learners.*

• Within each unit, the activities provide variety and balance—including dialogs, surveys, roleplaying, writing, hands-on projects, and TPR activities.

• A regular feature of this Teacher's Edition called *Reaching All Students* offers specific guidelines for addressing auditory, kinesthetic, and visual learners.

• The various sections of each chapter and unit are created to support different styles of learning. For auditory learners, *Conversemos* practices vocabulary through discussion. *Realidades* and *Palabras en acción* provide students a visual approach. Finally, the projects in *Para resolver* and *Manos a la obra* are especially effective for students who learn by doing.

The Chapter Organization

Every chapter in Levels One and Two has ten sections:

Objetivos

The objectives in the Chapter Opener provide an overview of the chapter and a basis for evaluating student progress. At a glance, teachers can review how the communicative, cultural, vocabulary, and structure objectives are interrelated.

Conversemos

Students discover the chapter theme and begin to develop proficiency with the chapter vocabulary through a series of discussion activities.

Realidades

Magazine and newspaper articles, journals, and other informative materials link the host country or region to the chapter objectives. Follow-up group activities—including surveys, diagrams, graphic organizers, and debates—give students further opportunities to develop their use of Spanish.

Palabras en Acción

A lively illustration with labeled vocabulary and dialogs in context gives students additional means of working toward the chapter's objectives. A variety of paired and small-group activities offer auditory, visual, and kinesthetic learning through dialogs, collages, and roleplays.

PARA COMUNICARNOS MEJOR (1 AND 2)

Elements of Spanish structure are explained and then illustrated in a series of personalized activities. Students also continue to develop their communicative skills—drawing from their own experiences, making choices, and selecting preferred options.

SITUACIONES

Several realia-based activities develop students' critical thinking skills while integrating the vocabulary and structure that they have learned.

PARA RESOLVER

This group project offers students a chance to explore the culture of a region, to expand their knowledge of the country, and to apply vocabulary and elements of structure from the chapter.

ENTÉRATE

This reading deepens students' knowledge of the culture of the unit's country or region, and offers additional vocabulary-building opportunities.

VOCABULARIO TEMÁTICO

The chapter's vocabulary is organized into thematic categories for handy reference and further practice. *La conexión inglés-español* helps students learn and retain the chapter vocabulary, and reinforces their English skills.

SPECIAL COMPONENTS

- **Activity Magazines**
- **Activity Book**
- **Teaching Resources**
  - **Tutor Pages**
  - **Activity Support Pages**
  - **Classroom Manager**
- **Color Transparencies and Teacher's Guide**
- **Activity Kit and Teacher's Guide**

ACTIVITY MAGAZINES

Six engaging and colorful magazines provide a special spotlight on the countries or regions featured in the student textbooks and videos. Designed to extend students' knowledge of Hispanic customs and cultures and to provide additional reading, the magazines have regular features that motivate students to communicate in Spanish.

ACTIVITY BOOK

The Activity Book is linked directly to the textbook, providing opportunities to reinforce the program's communicative and cultural objectives. Appropriate for either classwork or homework, the Activity Book contains writing activities based on topics presented in the student text, as well as special study guides for the *Adelantes*.

TEACHING RESOURCES: TUTOR PAGES

The Tutor Pages offer a variety of activities to be used by more able students or native speakers in helping classmates who are having difficulty with vocabulary and structure objectives. Sample answers and practical suggestions are provided to the tutor, so that students can work together in a focused and productive manner.

TEACHING RESOURCES: ACTIVITY SUPPORT PAGES

The Teaching Resources Binder includes a section of survey forms, worksheets, and additional cultural information. These pages correlate to the *Actividades* in this Teacher's Edition.

TEACHING RESOURCES: CLASSROOM MANAGER

The Classroom Manager provides teachers with day-to-day lesson plans, suggestions for incorporating components, helpful strategies for including all types of learners, guidance for classrooms using block scheduling, assessment rubrics, and suggestions for Spanish speakers.

COLOR TRANSPARENCIES AND TEACHER'S GUIDE

Transparencies are designed for teachers as supplements to the material in the textbook and as discussion starters. They include project summaries, locator maps, photos, and language activities. The accompanying Guide Book offers suggestions for using the transparencies, as well as pages to be reproduced for student use.

ACTIVITY KIT AND TEACHER'S GUIDE

The Activity Kit makes a variety of realia available to students—including communication cards, menus, telephone guides, maps, schedules, and recipes. The corresponding Guide provides suggestions for incorporating Activity Kit items in the classroom to facilitate group activities.

ASSESSMENT COMPONENTS

JUNTOS

- **Teaching Resources**
  - **Student Evaluation**
  - **Listening Comprehension**
  - **Oral Proficiency**
  - **Portfolio Assessment**
  - **Chapter Tests**
- **Audio CDs/Audio Cassettes**
- **Computer Test Bank (software and booklet)**

STUDENT EVALUATION

These checklists give students the opportunity to improve their self-assessment skills and to take responsibility for evaluating their own progress.

LISTENING COMPREHENSION

To assess students' skills, scripts and activities are included in the Assessment materials.

ORAL PROFICIENCY

The Oral Proficiency section offers teachers strategies for evaluating students' conversational abilities in a series of roleplay activities.

PORTFOLIO ASSESSMENT

Guidelines for helping students select work to include in their Portfolios provide a long-term and qualitative way to evaluate student progress.

CHAPTER TESTS

Listening, reading, writing, and culture tests assess students' understanding of the chapter's objectives.

AUDIO CDs/AUDIO CASSETTES

The listening comprehension activities have been recorded and are available in audio CD and cassette formats. Teachers may wish to use these to narrate the comprehension scripts.

COMPUTER TEST BANK

The Computer Test Bank offers teachers additional options for assessing students' progress in a software format.

SPECIAL COMPONENTS FOR SPANISH SPEAKERS

- **Conexiones**
- **Conexiones Teacher's Guide**
- **Cuaderno**
- **Audio CDs/Audio Cassettes**

CONEXIONES: LECTURAS PARA HISPANOHABLANTES

This illustrated reader is designed for both native speakers and more advanced second language learners. The reader includes short stories, poems, legends, and nonfiction articles that reflect the cultures of Spanish-speaking people. Its twelve chapters mirror the chapters of the student text.

CONEXIONES TEACHER'S GUIDE

The Teacher's Guide provides suggested discussion starters, activities based on the reading selections, and extension activities. Discussion ideas based on chapter themes are also included, along with graphic organizers for students' use in analyzing what they read.

CUADERNO PARA HISPANOHABLANTES

This workbook is designed for native speakers who need support in developing writing, structure, and spelling skills. It provides extension activities for material in the student text, as well as activities intended to improve students' study skills.

AUDIO CDs/ AUDIO CASSETTES

Selected short stories and poems from *Conexiones* are included on these audio components. They are designed to enhance students' appreciation for the beauty of the spoken language.

JUNTOS
TECHNOLOGY COMPONENTS

- Videotapes/Videodiscs
- Video Activity Books
- Audio CDs/Audio Cassettes
- Teaching Resources Audio Scripts and Activities

VIDEOTAPES/VIDEODISCS

Filmed in the locations featured in the student text and hosted by high school students from each of those countries or regions, the videos offer students a look at the culture and lifestyles of young people in each location. The videos also support and expand on the objectives of each unit and chapter. Every video features realia drawn from documentaries, advertisements, news and weather reports, music videos, and sports events. Each video contains five segments:

• the cultural introduction to the host country or region;

• two theme-based segments, one for each of the unit's two chapters;

• a cultural video magazine based on the *Adelante*;

• a feature on the *Manos a la obra* unit project.

VIDEO ACTIVITY BOOKS

The Video Activity Books include transcripts for each of the videos, as well as activity pages for students' use while watching the videos.

AUDIO CDs/AUDIO CASSETTES

The audio components of the program support the communicative, vocabulary, and structure objectives of each level. Readings of stories, articles, and poems give students opportunities to improve their listening comprehension skills.

AUDIO SCRIPTS AND ACTIVITIES

The scripts for the chapter audio tapes are included in the Teaching Resources Binder with specific activities to provide listening comprehension practice.

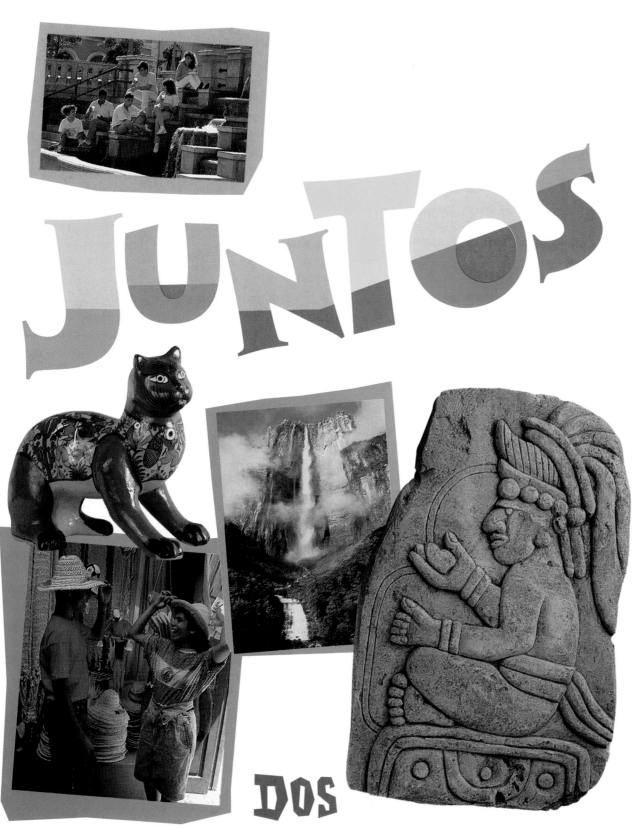

JUNTOS

DOS

PRENTICE HALL
Simon & Schuster Education Group
A VIACOM COMPANY

PRENTICE HALL STAFF CREDITS

Director of Foreign Languages: Marina Liapunov

Director of Marketing: Karen Ralston

Project Support: Julie Demori

Advertising and Promotion: Carol Leslie, Alfonso Manosalvas, Rip Odell

Business Office: Emily Heins

Design: Jim O'Shea, AnnMarie Roselli

Editorial: Guillermo Lawton-Alfonso, José A. Peláez, Generosa Gina Protano,

Barbara T. Stone

Manufacturing and Inventory Planning: Katherine Clarke, Rhett Conklin

Media Resources: Libby Forsyth, Maritza Puello

National Consultants: Camille Wiersgalla, Mary J. Secrest

Permissions: Doris Robinson

Product Development Operations: Laura Sanderson

Production: Janice L. Lalley

Sales Operations: Hans Spengler

Technology Development: Richard Ferrie

PRENTICE HALL
Simon & Schuster Education Group
A VIACOM COMPANY

TEACHER CONSULTANTS

Carol Barnett
Forest Hills High School
Forest Hills, NY

Barbara Bennett
District of Columbia Public Schools
Washington, D.C

Linda Bigler
Thomas Jeffferson High School
Fairfax County, VA

Félix Cortez
The Dalton School
New York, NY

Yolanda Fernandes
Montgomery County Public Schools
Rockville, MD

Cindy Gerstl
Prince George's County Public Schools
Upper Marlboro, MD

Hilda Montemayor Gleason
Fairfax County Public Schools
Alexandria, VA

Leslie Grahn
Prince George's County Public Schools
Upper Marlboro, MD

Mark Grudzien
West Hartford Public Schools
West Hartford, CT

Adriana Montemayor Ivy
Denver Public Schools
Denver, CO

Judith Katzman
West Hartford Public Schools
West Hartford, CT

Delia García Menocal
Emerson High School
Emerson, NJ

Ruth Rivera
Prince George's County Public Schools
Upper Marlboro, MD

CULTURE CONSULTANTS

Mónica Alpacs
Lima, Peru

Virginia Álvarez
Santo Domingo, Dominican Republic

Lola Aranda
Mexico City, Mexico

Gloria Beretervide
Buenos Aires, Argentina

Andrés Chávez
Los Angeles, CA

Chris Chávez
Chicago, IL

Manuel Coronado
Madrid, Spain

Linda Cuéllar
San Antonio, Texas

Eric Delgado
San Juan, Puerto Rico

Carmen Franchi
Miami, FL

José Hernández
San Jose, Costa Rica

Diana Martínez
Los Angeles, CA

Kurt and Christine Rosenthal
Lima, Peru

Lita Vértiz
Mexico City, Mexico

v

CONTENIDO

¡BIENVENIDOS!

SALUDOS

VI

autobús

VII

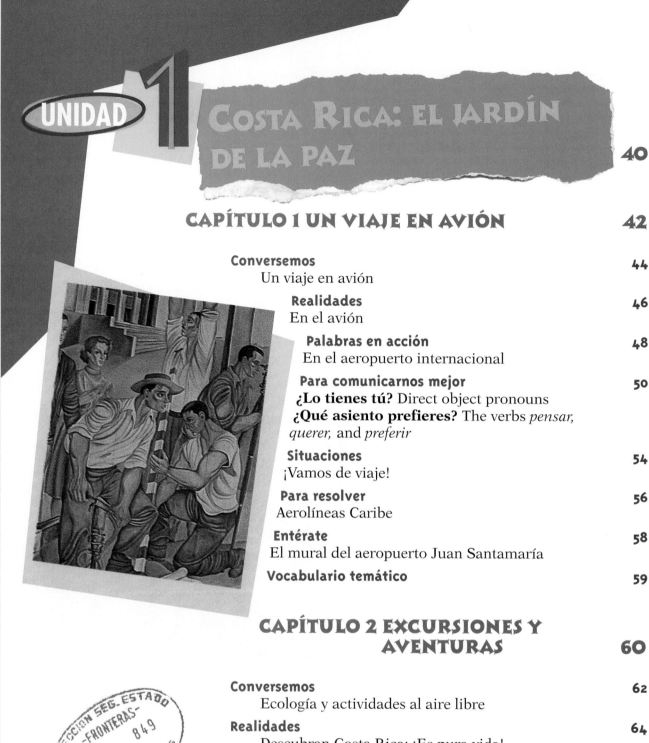

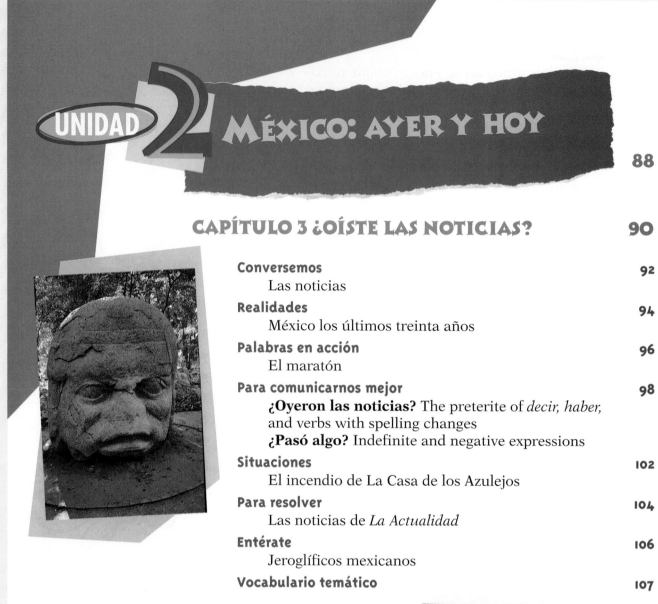

UNIDAD 2 MÉXICO: AYER Y HOY

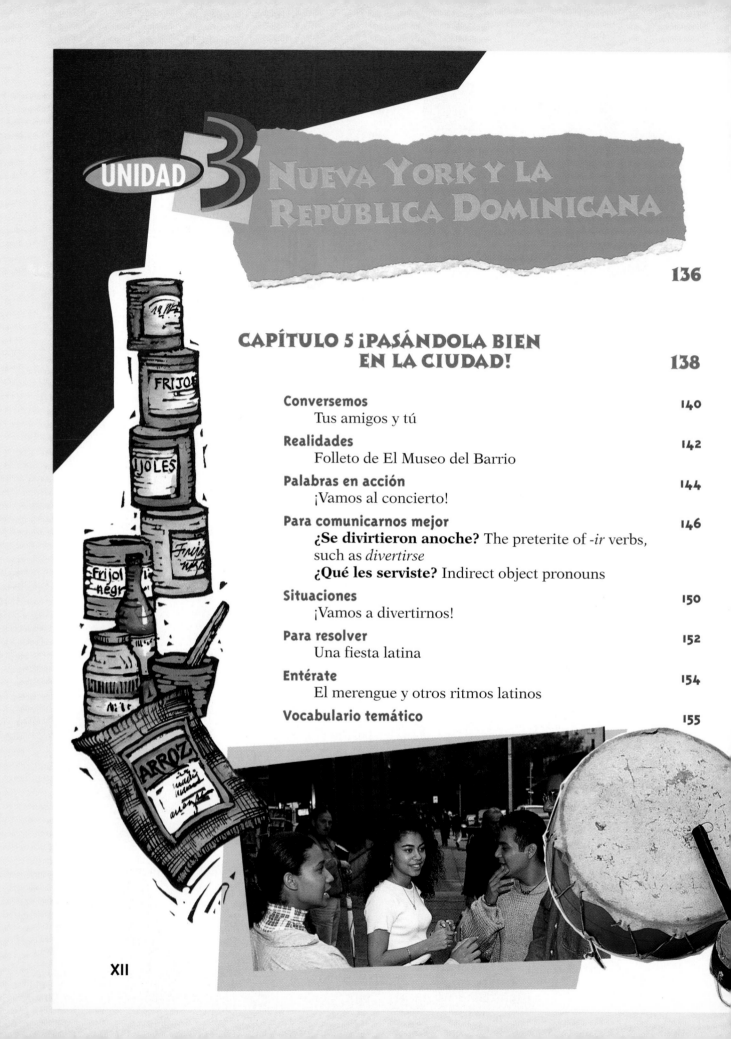

UNIDAD 3 NUEVA YORK Y LA REPÚBLICA DOMINICANA

XII

XV

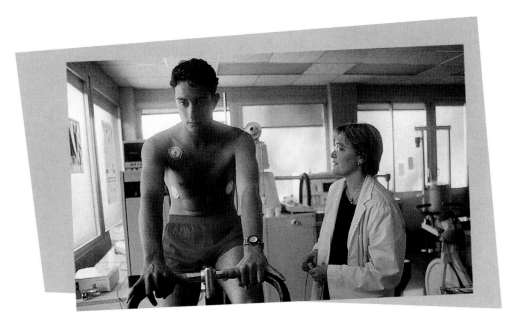

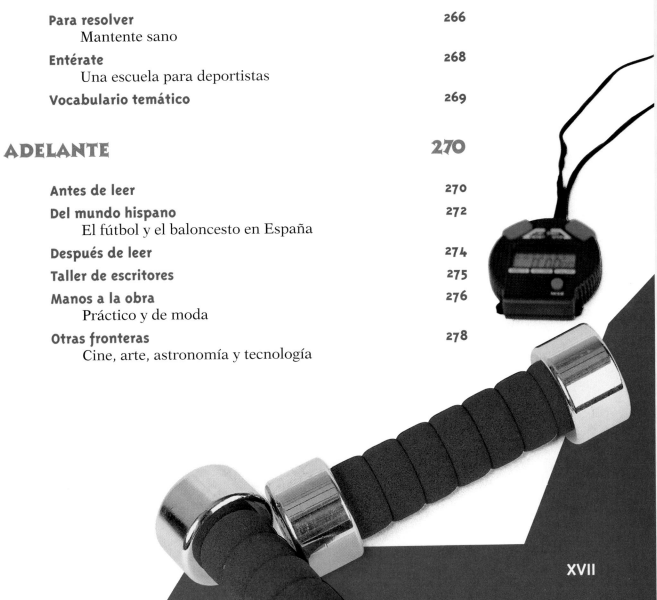

XVIII

BIENVENIDOS AL MUNDO HISPANO

You are about to continue your journey into the language and culture of the Spanish-speaking world to get acquainted with new cities and countries. You'll meet more of the 300 million people who are Spanish speakers. As you gradually become one of them, you may very well find that your new language opens doors to exciting and rewarding opportunities.

¡Buen viaje! Have a good trip!

WHERE IN THE WORLD?

In the section that follows, you will find maps that highlight countries throughout the world where people speak Spanish. These maps will provide you with following information: the name of the country in Spanish, its location, geographic landforms, and the products and wildlife that you will find there. Enjoy studying the maps as you think about where in the world you might want to visit someday.

MAPS AND TABLES
- Population Estimates
- Geographic Landforms Used in the Maps
- Symbols Used in the Maps
- Map of Spain
- Map of South America
- Map of Mexico, Central America, and the Caribbean
- Map of the U.S.
- Map of the World

Population Estimates (Countries where Spanish Is the Primary Language)

Country	Population	Country	Population
Mexico	86,170,000	Bolivia	7,411,000
Spain	39,200,000	Dominican Republic	7,591,000
Colombia	35,600,000	El Salvador	5,635,000
Argentina	34,883,000	Honduras	5,164,000
Peru	23,854,000	Paraguay	5,003,000
Venezuela	19,085,000	Nicaragua	3,932,000
Chile	14,000,000	Puerto Rico	3,500,000
Cuba	10,900,000	Uruguay	3,200,000
Ecuador	11,055,000	Costa Rica	3,300,000
Guatemala	9,705,000	Panama	2,500,000

GEOGRAPHIC LANDFORMS USED IN THE MAPS

On the pages that follow, you will find maps illustrated with geographic landforms. For reference, the landforms that appear in these maps are illustrated below with the name of each feature in Spanish.

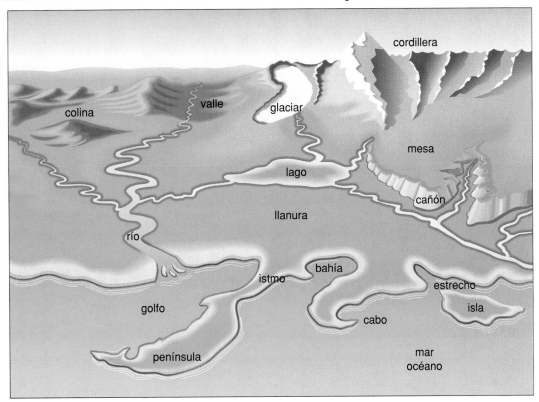

SYMBOLS USED IN THE MAPS

The maps that follow contain symbols that will give you a glimpse of the agricultural products, industries, and animals that you will likely see when you visit the region.

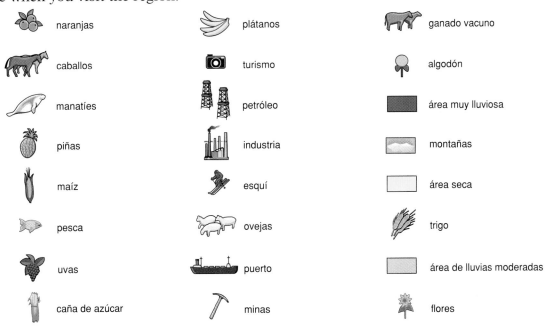

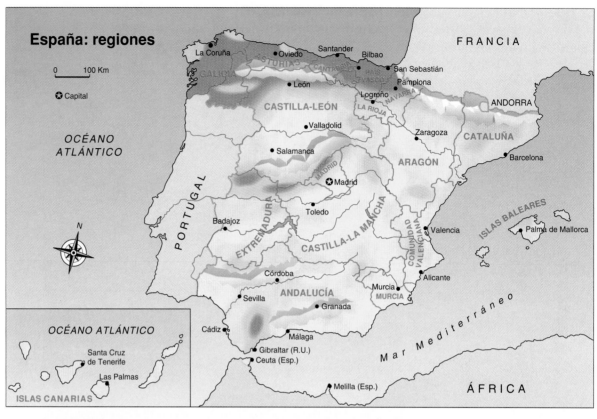

España: regiones

0   100 Km

✪ Capital

FRANCIA

ANDORRA

GALICIA · La Coruña · Oviedo · Santander · Bilbao · San Sebastián · Pamplona

ASTURIAS · CANTABRIA · PAÍS VASCO · NAVARRA

· León · Logroño

LA RIOJA

CASTILLA-LEÓN

· Valladolid

· Zaragoza

CATALUÑA

· Salamanca

ARAGÓN

· Barcelona

MADRID

OCÉANO ATLÁNTICO

PORTUGAL

✪ Madrid

· Toledo

CASTILLA-LA MANCHA

COMUNIDAD VALENCIANA

· Valencia

ISLAS BALEARES

· Palma de Mallorca

· Badajoz

EXTREMADURA

· Alicante

· Córdoba

· Murcia

MURCIA

· Sevilla

ANDALUCÍA

· Granada

· Cádiz

· Málaga

· Gibraltar (R.U.)

· Ceuta (Esp.)

Mar Mediterráneo

· Melilla (Esp.)

ÁFRICA

OCÉANO ATLÁNTICO

· Santa Cruz de Tenerife

· Las Palmas

ISLAS CANARIAS

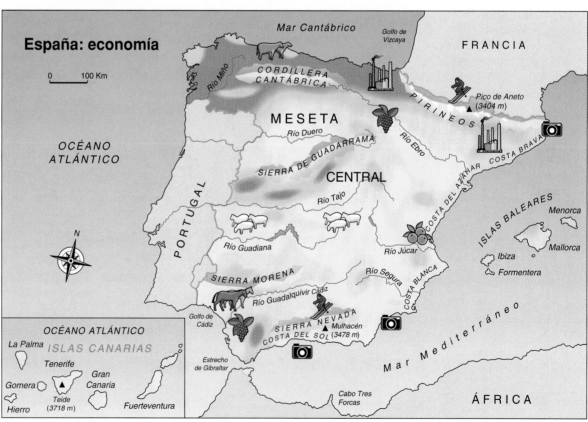

España: economía

0   100 Km

Mar Cantábrico

Golfo de Vizcaya

FRANCIA

Río Miño

CORDILLERA CANTÁBRICA

PIRINEOS

Pico de Aneto (3404 m)

MESETA

Río Duero

Río Ebro

COSTA BRAVA

OCÉANO ATLÁNTICO

SIERRA DE GUADARRAMA

CENTRAL

COSTA DEL AZAHAR

ISLAS BALEARES

Menorca

PORTUGAL

Río Tajo

Río Júcar

Ibiza

Mallorca

Río Guadiana

Formentera

SIERRA MORENA

Río Segura

COSTA BLANCA

Río Guadalquivir Cádiz

Golfo de Cádiz

SIERRA NEVADA

Mulhacén (3478 m)

COSTA DEL SOL

Mar Mediterráneo

Estrecho de Gibraltar

Cabo Tres Forcas

ÁFRICA

OCÉANO ATLÁNTICO

La Palma

ISLAS CANARIAS

Tenerife

Gomera

Gran Canaria

Teide (3718 m)

Hierro

Fuerteventura

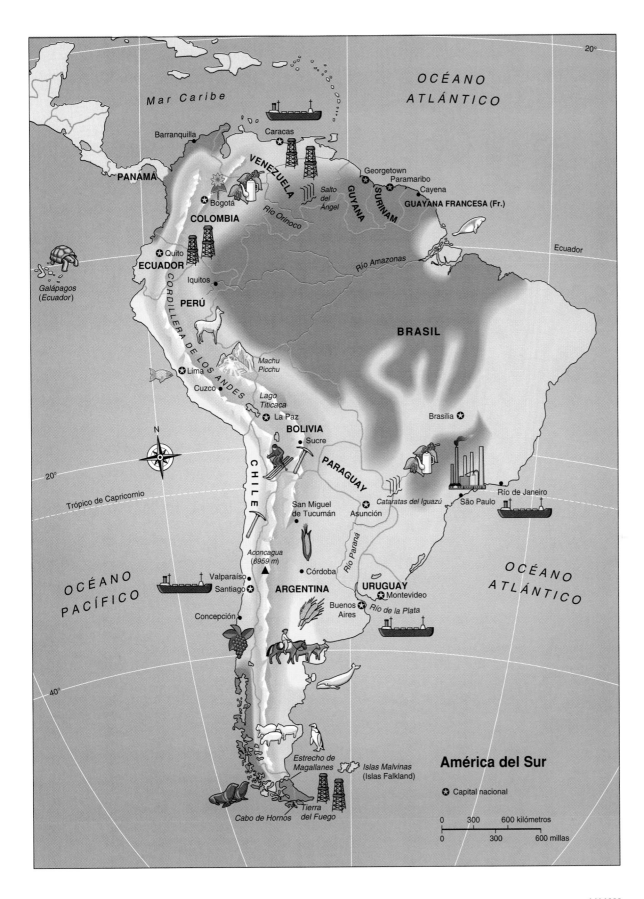

América del Sur

✪ Capital nacional

```
0        300      600 kilómetros
0        300      600 millas
```

OCÉANO ATLÁNTICO

Mar Caribe

OCÉANO PACÍFICO

OCÉANO ATLÁNTICO

PANAMÁ
Barranquilla
Caracas
VENEZUELA
Georgetown
Paramaribo
Cayena
GUAYANA FRANCESA (Fr.)
GUYANA
SURINAM
Bogotá
COLOMBIA
Salto del Ángel
Río Orinoco
Quito
ECUADOR
Ecuador
Río Amazonas
Iquitos
Galápagos (Ecuador)
PERÚ
BRASIL
CORDILLERA DE LOS ANDES
Machu Picchu
Lima
Cuzco
Lago Titicaca
La Paz
Brasilia
BOLIVIA
Sucre
CHILE
PARAGUAY
San Miguel de Tucumán
Asunción
Cataratas del Iguazú
São Paulo
Río de Janeiro
Trópico de Capricornio
20°
Aconcagua (6959 m)
Río Paraná
Córdoba
Valparaíso
Santiago
ARGENTINA
URUGUAY
Montevideo
Concepción
Buenos Aires
Río de la Plata
Estrecho de Magallanes
Islas Malvinas (Islas Falkland)
Cabo de Hornos
Tierra del Fuego
N
20°
40°
```
```

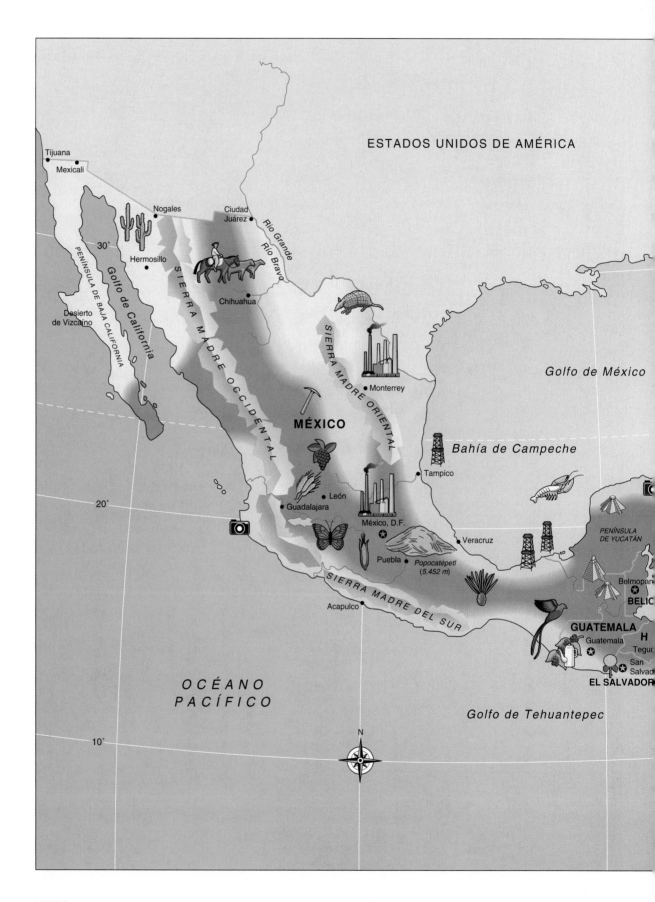

ESTADOS UNIDOS DE AMÉRICA

Tijuana

Mexicali

Nogales

Ciudad
Juárez

Río Grande

Río Bravo

30°

Hermosillo

PENÍNSULA DE BAJA CALIFORNIA

Golfo de California

Chihuahua

*Desierto
de Vizcaíno*

SIERRA MADRE OCCIDENTAL

SIERRA MADRE ORIENTAL

Golfo de México

MÉXICO

Monterrey

Bahía de Campeche

20°

León

Tampico

Guadalajara

México, D.F.

Veracruz

Puebla

*Popocatépetl
(5.452 m)*

*PENÍNSULA
DE YUCATÁN*

Belmopan

BELIC

Acapulco

SIERRA MADRE DEL SUR

GUATEMALA   **H**

Guatemala   Tegu

San
Salvad

EL SALVADOR

OCÉANO
PACÍFICO

Golfo de Tehuantepec

10°

N

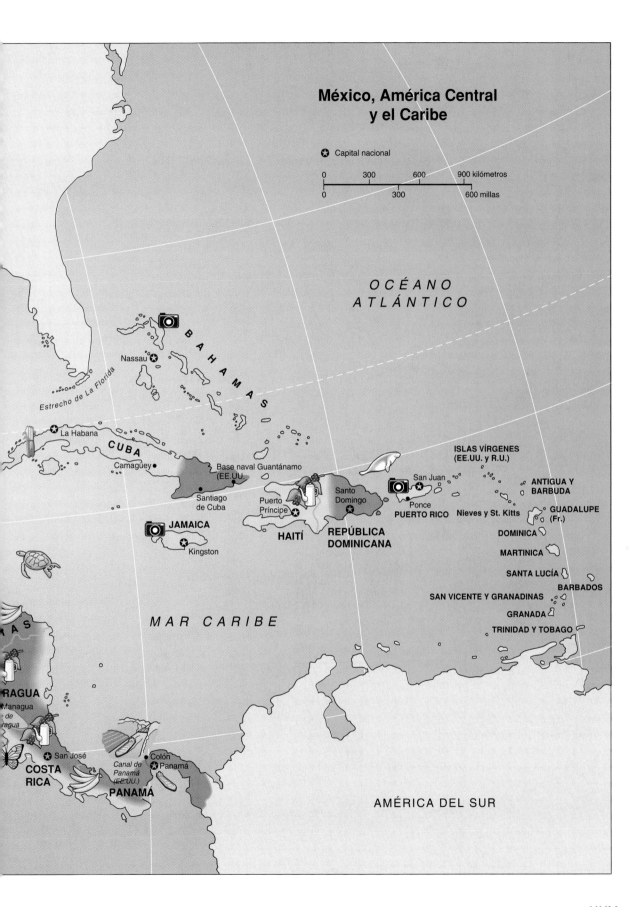

México, América Central y el Caribe

⭐ Capital nacional

0   300   600   900 kilómetros

0   300   600 millas

OCÉANO ATLÁNTICO

B A H A M A S

Nassau ⭐

Estrecho de La Florida

La Habana ⭐

CUBA

Camagüey ●

Base naval Guantánamo (EE.UU.)

Santiago de Cuba ●

JAMAICA

Kingston ●

Puerto Príncipe ⭐

HAITÍ

Santo Domingo ⭐

REPÚBLICA DOMINICANA

San Juan ⭐

Ponce ●

PUERTO RICO

ISLAS VÍRGENES (EE.UU. y R.U.)

ANTIGUA Y BARBUDA

Nieves y St. Kitts

GUADALUPE (Fr.)

DOMINICA

MARTINICA

SANTA LUCÍA

BARBADOS

SAN VICENTE Y GRANADINAS

GRANADA

TRINIDAD Y TOBAGO

MAR CARIBE

...RAGUA

Managua de ...agua

San José ⭐

Colón ●

Panamá ⭐

Canal de Panamá (EE.UU.)

COSTA RICA

PANAMÁ

AMÉRICA DEL SUR

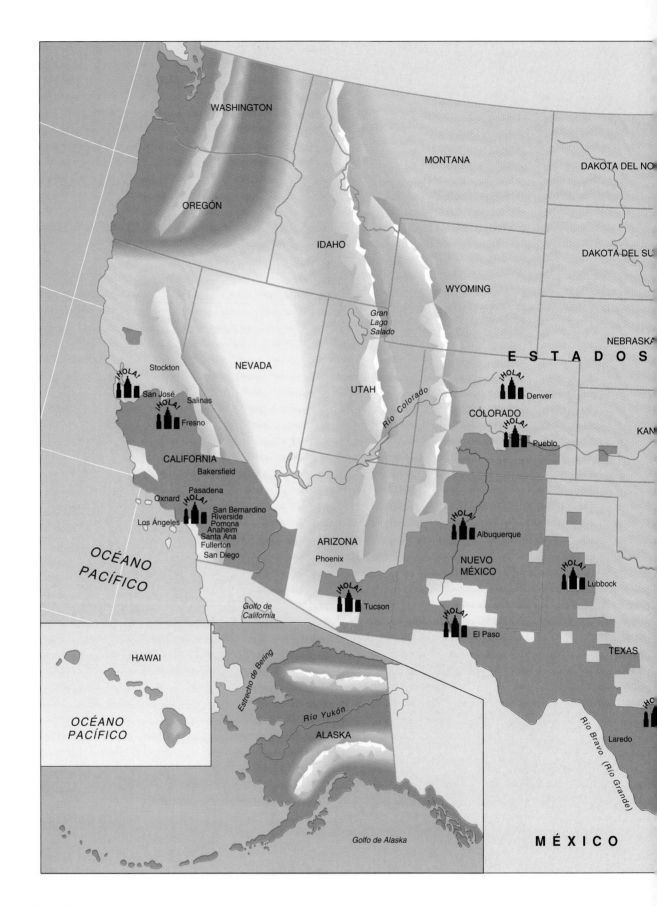

WASHINGTON

OREGÓN

IDAHO

MONTANA

DAKOTA DEL NO

DAKOTA DEL SU

WYOMING

NEBRASKA

*Gran
Lago
Salado*

NEVADA

UTAH

Río Colorado

E S T A D O S

Stockton

¡HOLA!
San José

¡HOLA!
Salinas
Fresno

¡HOLA!
Denver

COLORADO

¡HOLA!
Pueblo

KAN

CALIFORNIA

Bakersfield

Pasadena

Oxnard

¡HOLA!
Los Ángeles

San Bernardino
Riverside
Pomona
Anaheim
Santa Ana
Fullerton
San Diego

ARIZONA

Phoenix

¡HOLA!
Albuquerque

NUEVO
MÉXICO

¡HOLA!
Lubbock

OCÉANO
PACÍFICO

¡HOLA!
Tucson

*Golfo de
California*

¡HOLA!
El Paso

TEXAS

HAWAI

Estrecho de Bering

¡HO

OCÉANO
PACÍFICO

Río Yukón

ALASKA

Río Bravo (Río Grande)

Laredo

Golfo de Alaska

M É X I C O

XXVI

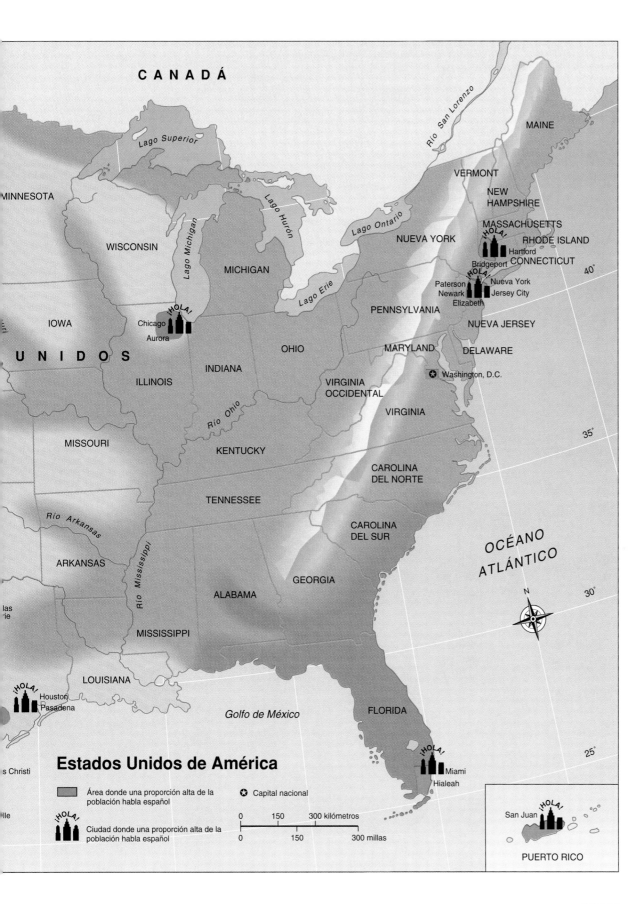

CANADÁ

MINNESOTA

Lago Superior

WISCONSIN

Lago Michigan

MICHIGAN

Lago Hurón

Lago Ontario

Río San Lorenzo

MAINE

VERMONT

NEW HAMPSHIRE

MASSACHUSETTS

¡HOLA!

RHODE ISLAND

Hartford

Bridgeport   CONNECTICUT

NUEVA YORK

Lago Erie

IOWA

¡HOLA!

Chicago

Aurora

U N I D O S

ILLINOIS

INDIANA

OHIO

Río Ohio

PENNSYLVANIA

¡HOLA!

Paterson   Nuéva York

Newark   Jersey City

Elizabeth

NUEVA JERSEY

MARYLAND   DELAWARE

Washington, D.C.

VIRGINIA OCCIDENTAL

VIRGINIA

MISSOURI

KENTUCKY

TENNESSEE

CAROLINA DEL NORTE

Río Arkansas

CAROLINA DEL SUR

OCÉANO ATLÁNTICO

ARKANSAS

Río Mississippi

GEORGIA

ALABAMA

N

MISSISSIPPI

LOUISIANA

¡HOLA!

Houston

Pasadena

s Christi

las rie

Golfo de México

FLORIDA

¡HOLA!

Miami

Hialeah

Estados Unidos de América

| | Área donde una proporción alta de la población habla español |

¡HOLA! Ciudad donde una proporción alta de la población habla español

✪ Capital nacional

0   150   300 kilómetros

0   150   300 millas

40°

35°

30°

25°

San Juan   ¡HOLA!

PUERTO RICO

El Mundo

Países donde el español
es el idioma oficial

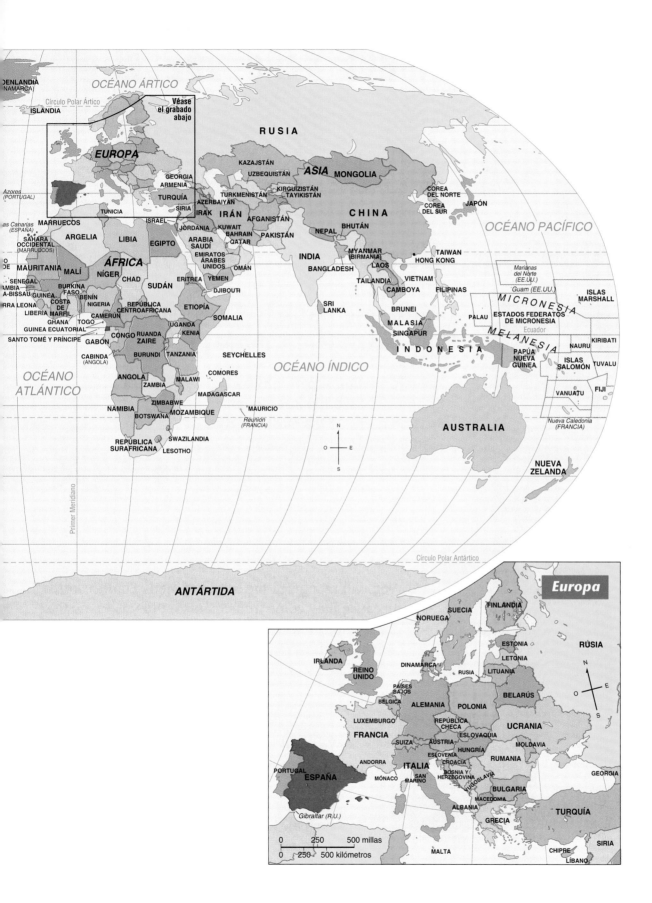

¡Bienvenidos otra vez al ¡español!

¿Por qué aprender todavía más?

(Welcome back to Spanish. Why learn even more?)

- The information superhighway is bringing the world closer together. Spanish is one of the most widely used languages in the world.

- You will recognize the origin of many English words because they come from Spanish. Did you know that *mosquito*, *potato*, and *tornado* are just a few of the words we use every day that are of Spanish origin?

- You will be able to read one of the richest of all European literatures in the original Spanish: *Don Quijote* and *El Cid*—as well as works by contemporary Nobel Prize winners such as Octavio Paz and Gabriel García Márquez.

xxx

- New careers and exciting adventures will open up to you around the world. As the global economy expands, the 18 Spanish-speaking countries of Latin America, Puerto Rico, and Spain will present great job opportunities and markets in the 21st century. You will also enjoy traveling and meeting people in all of these places when you can speak their language!

- You will be better able to communicate with people in your own country. Spanish is the most commonly spoken language in the United States after English. There are Spanish-speaking neighborhoods in many parts of the U.S.

Tips for Learning More Spanish

- **Expand what you already know!** Communicate in Spanish as often as you can. Keep adding the new words and phrases that you learn to those you already know. Remember — the best way to learn to speak Spanish is to do it every day!

- **Listen actively!** Take every opportunity that you can to hear Spanish spoken. Turn on a Spanish station on your radio or TV. Listen to Spanish music — get into the rhythm! Even if you don't understand every word you hear, that's okay. Listen carefully. Spanish is all around you. Take advantage of every chance to surround yourself with the sounds of the language.

- **Be positive!** Remember, you're not exactly a newcomer to this language. You learned a lot of Spanish last year, and there's still more to do, but you are going to succeed! You know how to use ¡JUNTOS! because you've used it before. Look for other ways to practice speaking and reading Spanish. If you didn't find a Spanish-speaking pen pal last year, try to do that this year. Maybe you can even find a Spanish-speaking pal in cyberspace on a World Wide Web site! Go to a Spanish movie and see how much you understand without using the subtitles. Take charge of your own learning!

- **Have fun with language!** Try to use Spanish every day — in and out of the classroom. Tell a joke that has a Spanish punchline. Use your Spanish to order food in a Spanish restaurant or shop in a Spanish store. Speak Spanish to a friend whose first language is Spanish. Don't worry if you don't get everything right. Spanish-speakers will appreciate it if you try to communicate with them in Spanish. They'll even help you out, if you need it!

- **Think about how you learn!** Everybody has a special learning style. Some people learn a language by watching for clues in the way others act when they speak. Some people learn a language by noticing words that sound familiar and making a mental note of them. Still others learn by teaching what they know to others — like a family member or a younger friend. Share your learning style with your classmates. Pick up tips about their learning styles, and try those tips out for yourself.

- **Work together!** Together is what ¡JUNTOS! is all about. It's not just in the classroom, but outside of it as well. Speak Spanish to classmates in the hall, in the lunchroom, over the phone, or even at a football game! Use your new skills together ....¡JUNTOS!

XXXII

SALUDOS

Welcome back to the journey that we began last year! Get ready to visit new places, meet new people, and share exciting experiences. Best of all, we will do all of this together... *¡Juntos!*

This section of your book is called *Saludos,* which means "greetings." It reviews many words and phrases that you already know. As we go on, you will get better and better at communicating and thoroughly enjoy your great adventure in the Spanish-speaking world.

So... *¡Adelante!* Onward!

¿CÓMO SE LLAMAN TUS AMIGOS?

Objectives
- to identify and describe yourself
- to talk about your family

 ARTICULATION

As you cover the material in *Saludos*, work as much as possible on the re-entry of vocabulary and structure from *Juntos* Level One.

 GETTING STARTED

Have students look at the IDs on this page. Tell them that these people are from the same country. Have them identify the country.

¿Cómo te llamas?
If you wish to use Spanish names in the classroom, have students find names that correspond to their own or choose other names. Allow the option of not using the same name as last year.

¿CÓMO SE LLAMAN TUS AMIGOS?

Más nombres

Chicas		Chicos	
Alicia	Guadalupe (Lupe)	Alberto	Javier
Ana	Inés	Alejandro	Jorge
Bárbara	Irene	Alfonso	José (Pepe)
Beatriz	Isabel (Isa,	Alfredo	Juan
Carlota	Chabela)	Andrés	Lorenzo
Carmen (Menchu)	Juana	Antonio (Toni,	Luis
Carolina	Julia	Toño)	Manuel (Manolo)
Catalina	Lucía	Carlos	Martín
Clara	Margarita	Daniel	Miguel
Claudia	Marta	David	Pablo
Cristina (Tina)	Natalia	Eduardo	Pedro
Diana	Pilar	Enrique (Quique)	Rafael (Rafa)
Dolores (Lola)	Sara	Esteban	Ramón (Moncho,
Elena	Susana	Felipe	Mongo)
Elisa	Teresa (Tere)	Fernando (Nano)	Raúl
Estefanía	Virginia	Francisco (Paco)	Roberto (Beto)
Eva		Guillermo	Víctor

2

SALUDOS COMPONENTS

Activity Book	Audio
p. 5-16	Saludos: 1
Audio Book	
Script: p. 5-7	

1 ¿Cómo te llamas?

Pregúntale a tu compañero(a) su nombre y cuántos años tiene.

— ¿Cómo te llamas?
— Me llamo Alicia.
— ¿Cuántos años tienes?
— Tengo 15 años.

 2 Tu familia

Pregúntale a tu compañero(a) sobre su familia.

— ¿Tienes hermanos?
— Sí. Tengo dos hermanos.
— ¿Cómo se llaman?
— Se llaman Jorge y Rosa.
— ¿Tienes mascotas?
— Sí, tengo una tortuga.

3 Tu clase

Pregúntales a tus compañeros de clase.

¿Quién en la clase tiene...?
• un nombre que empieza con L
• un nombre que termina con S
• hermanos
• un nombre con seis letras
• un gato
• un perro

 4 A escribir

Ahora, escribe seis oraciones sobre tu compañero(a). Después, presenta a tu compañero(a) a la clase.

MÁS PREGUNTAS...

¿Cuántos meses / años tiene? ¿Cómo es?

¿Tienes un perro? ¿Cómo se llama?

¿RECUERDAS?

Use the verb **tener** (to have) to talk about your age and what you have or own.

yo	tengo	nosotros(as)	tenemos
tú	tienes	vosotros(as)	tenéis
usted	tiene	ustedes	tienen
él/ella	tiene	ellos/ellas	tienen

¿RECUERDAS?

Use the verb **llamarse** (to be called) to tell your name.

yo	me llamo	nosotros(as)	nos llamamos
tú	te llamas	vosotros(as)	os llamáis
usted	se llama	ustedes	se llaman
él/ella	se llama	ellos/ellas	se llaman

¿SABES QUE...?

In Spanish-speaking countries many people have name combinations that start with *María* or *Mari* for women, such as *María del Carmen* or *María Rosa*, and with *Juan* or *José* for men, such as *José Luis* or *Juan Carlos*.

3

1. ¿Cómo te llamas?
Prepare students by writing a few forms on the board. For example:
Me llamo, te llamas, se llama
Mi, tu, su nombre es...
Mi apellido es....
Yo tengo, tú tienes, él/ella tiene... años
You can review numbers and names of months by having students say when their birthdays are. Write the months on the board and have students raise their hands when you indicate the month of their birthday. Repeat with days.

2. Tu familia
Students will benefit from written examples of possible answers.
Review vocabulary for family members with a family tree, perhaps that of a well-known TV family.
To review animal vocabulary, do a survey of the different kinds of pets students have.
For example: *¿Cuántos tienen un perro? ¿Peces? ¿Tortugas?*

3. Tu clase
Perform this as a class activity. If many students already know each other, have them describe someone's name without saying who it is. The class guesses who is being described.

4. A escribir
Suggest that they write very simple separate sentences.

Questions and Accents
Remind students that question words (*quién, dónde, cómo, qué, cuándo, cuánto, cuál, por qué*) have accents and that questions begin with upside-down question marks.

HOLA, ¿CÓMO ESTÁS?

Objective
- to introduce yourself and others

Introduce a few of those students who have chosen new names to their classmates. Have volunteers read and act out the dialogs on this page. Help students recall other Spanish words and phrases they might use in this situation. Have small groups act out introductions.

DIALOGS

Introduce yourself to and greet the first person in the first row. Have that student introduce you and him or herself to the next student, and so on down the line.

4

¿De dónde eres?

Pregúntale a tu compañero(a) de dónde es.

— *¿De dónde eres?*
— *Soy de Ohio, ¿y tú?*
— *De Illinois.*

 Mucho gusto

En grupos de tres, presenten a sus nuevos(as) compañeros(as). ¡Usen sus nombres españoles!

— *Hola, te presento a mi amigo Pablo.*
— *¿Cómo estás?*
— *Muy bien, ¿y tú?*
— *Estoy bien, gracias.*

 ¿De dónde es? ¿Dónde está?

Pregúntales a tus compañeros(as) de qué ciudad o país son sus familias. ¿Sabes dónde está?

— *¿De dónde es tu familia?*
— *Mis abuelos, los padres de mi madre, son de Bogotá.*
— *¿Dónde está Bogotá?*
— *Está en Colombia.*

 Mi familia

En grupos, hagan una encuesta sobre sus orígenes. Hagan una tabla según el modelo.

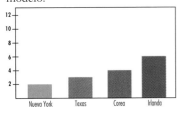

 ¿RECUERDAS?

*Use the verb **ser** (to be) to describe people and things. Use **ser + de** to talk about where somebody is from.*

yo	**soy**	nosotros(as)	**somos**
tú	**eres**	vosotros(as)	**sois**
usted	**es**	ustedes	**son**
él/ella	**es**	ellos/ellas	**son**

¿RECUERDAS?

*Use the verb **estar** (to be) to talk about how you are. Use **estar + en** to indicate location.*

yo	**estoy**	nosotros(as)	**estamos**
tú	**estás**	vosotros(as)	**estáis**
usted	**está**	ustedes	**están**
él/ella	**está**	ellos/ellas	**están**

Te toca a ti

Con tu compañero(a), creen dos diálogos.

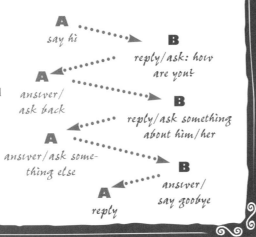

5

Objective
• to talk about food and places to eat

GETTING STARTED

Direct students to the restaurant ads on this page. Ask volunteers to read aloud the ads. Ask which restaurant they would go to if...
1. *Tienes ganas de comer comida picante.*
2. *No tienes mucha hambre pero quieres picar algo.*
3. *Estás con seis amigos y nadie tiene mucho dinero.*
4. *Tienes hambre pero sólo son las 11:20 de la mañana.*
(In some cases there may be more than one appropriate answer.)

¡VAMOS A COMER!

Fonda La Casera
COCINA MEXICANA TRADICIONAL
RESTAURANTE · PIANO · TERRAZA
PLAZA TRES REYES, 31

La Gran Muralla 榮星
Restaurante chino
abierto todos los días del año
de 11 de la mañana
a 2 de la noche

Pizzas Aurelio
Come la mejor pizza de Nueva York.
Gran oferta
Compra dos pizzas medianas y...
¡te damos una gratis!

TAQUERÍA TACOS LOCOS
Tacos   Enchiladas
Burritos
Chiles

Pasteles Aurora
Chocolate · Sándwiches
Batidos naturales

6

1 ¿Adónde te gustaría ir?

Con tu compañero(a), miren los anuncios.
Decidan dónde quieren comer.

— *¿Te gustaría ir a Tacos Locos?*
— *No. ¿Vamos a La Gran Muralla?*
— *Sí. Me gusta mucho la comida china.*

MÁS PREGUNTAS...

¿Es caro?   *¿A qué hora?*

¿Con quién?   *¿Cómo vamos?*

 ### 2 ¿Dónde comes?

Con tu compañero(a), hablen de dónde
comen.

— *Generalmente, ¿dónde comes?*
— *Como en la cafetería de la escuela.*
  ¿Y tú?
— *Yo como en casa.*

MÁS PREGUNTAS...

                  ¿Te gusta?

¿Con quién?   *¿Vas a un restaurante?*

¿Qué tipo de restaurante es?   *¿Cuál te gusta?*

 ### 3 En tu ciudad

Con tu compañero(a), hablen de los
restaurantes y otros lugares de su ciudad
que conocen.

— *¿Conoces el restaurante Tapas?*
— *No, ¿es un restaurante bueno?*
— *Sí, buenísimo. Es un restaurante
  español.*

MÁS PREGUNTAS...

¿Dónde está?   *¿Qué tipo de comida hay?*

¿Comes allí muchas veces?

¿Qué comes allí?   *Generalmente, ¿qué pides?*

  ¿Es caro? ¿Es barato?

             ¿Tienen plato del día?

¿Qué más?
- la plaza
- el centro comercial
- la discoteca
- el gimnasio
- la cafetería
- el cine

1. ¿Adónde te gustaría ir?
After students have interviewed each
other, have them talk about real cafes or
restaurants.

2. ¿Dónde comes?
Take a class survey of the most popular
places for breakfast, lunch, after-school
snacks, and dinner.

3. En tu ciudad
Have students rank local restaurants in
these categories:
para comer una pizza
para comer un postre delicioso
para tomar helado
para comer la mejor hamburguesa
para comer el mejor pollo frito
para comer un sándwich
*para comer comida mexicana (italiana,
china, etc.)*

7

Objective
• to talk about what you eat at different meals

DIALOGS

Poll the class to find the most popular and least popular food for these categories. Write on the board :

	muy popular	poco popular
desayuno	_____	_____
almuerzo	_____	_____
bebida	_____	_____
postre	_____	_____
fruta	_____	_____

Have students raise their hands as a volunteer reads aloud the name of each food or beverage on the page. Tally separately, and write the name in the appropriate place. To provide aural practice, try TPR. Give such commands as:

Marta, come los huevos con jamón.
Sarita, toma un café.
¡Cuidado, el café está muy caliente!
Miguel, prepara un batido.
Susi, come un plátano.

Have students perform the dialogs. To encourage them to express themselves in more specific terms, provide them with the necessary vocabulary. For example: *huevos revueltos, pan integral, jugo de naranja, pollo frito, sopa de tomate, batido de chocolate, helado de fresa.*

¿QUÉ COMES?

¿Qué comes en el desayuno?
● cereales
● huevos con jamón
● mantequilla
● pan
● fruta

¿Qué tomas?
● café
● leche
● café con leche
● té
● jugo
● chocolate caliente

¿Qué comes en el almuerzo?
¿Y en la comida?
● pescado
● verduras
● carne
● arroz
● ensalada
● pollo
● sopa
● frijoles

¿Qué tomas?
● batido
● limonada
● refresco
● agua mineral
● jugo de tomate

¿Y de postre?
● helado
● flan
● pastel
● yogur
● fruta

¿Qué fruta te gusta más?
● la manzana
● el plátano
● la piña
● la naranja
● el melón

8

1 ¿Cuándo...?

Con tu compañero(a), hablen de qué comes y qué tomas en el desayuno, el almuerzo y la cena.
— *En el desayuno, ¿qué comes?*
— *Cereales y fruta.*
— *¿Y qué tomas?*
— *Leche.*

2 En el restaurante

Pregúntale a tu compañero(a) si quiere compartir algo contigo.
— *¿Qué vas a pedir?*
— *No sé. No tengo mucha hambre.*
— *¿Compartimos algo?*
— *Sí. ¿Por qué no compartimos un plato de arroz con frijoles?*
— *Perfecto. ¿Y de postre?*

3 ¿Cuándo dicen...?

Con tu compañero(a), digan cuándo usan las siguientes expresiones.
• ¡Ay, qué rico!
  (*Cuando como helado*)
• ¡Ay, qué horrible!
• ¡Buen provecho!
• ¡Qué buena idea!
• ¡Me encanta!

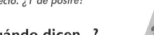

MÁS PREGUNTAS...
¿Y tu hermano(a)?   ¿Y tu mascota?
¿Y los fines de semana?
Generalmente, ¿con quién comes?
¿Comes muchas verduras?

¿RECUERDAS?

To talk about everyday activities in the present you can use many verbs that end in **-ar**, **-er** and **-ir**.

	tomar	comer	compartir
yo	tomo	como	comparto
tú	tomas	comes	compartes
usted	toma	come	comparte
él/ella	toma	come	comparte
nosotros(as)	tomamos	comemos	compartimos
vosotros(as)	tomáis	coméis	compartís
ustedes	toman	comen	comparten
ellos/ellas	toman	comen	comparten

4 Te toca a ti

Con tu compañero(a), imaginen que están en un restaurante. Tienen que decidir qué van a pedir. Creen tres diálogos.

A ask: what do you want to order?
B say you are not sure/ask something about the menu
A suggest something
B reply/ask what you are going to order
A reply/ask what you want to drink
B answer/ask back
A answer

9

1. ¿Cuándo...?
To find out how much students know about nutrition, have pairs or small groups plan a day's meals. They share their menus with the class; the class votes on the best. To review the preterite, have pairs say what they ate and drank yesterday.

2. En el restaurante
As an extension, have each student write four questions. For example:
1. *¿Te gusta la comida italiana?*
2. *¿Comiste pollo ayer?*
3. *¿Te encanta el pescado?*
4. *¿Comes muchas verduras?*
Students circulate, asking their questions. When a student finds someone who answers a question affirmatively, that person signs his or her name next to the question. The first student who gets four signatures wins.

3. ¿Cuándo dicen...?
To practice vocabulary, have students describe their own desserts, salads, soups, or shakes. The recipes could be real or amusing. Students share their recipes with classmates, who respond accordingly. For example:
A: *Mi sopa tiene jamón, leche, arroz, plátano y chocolate caliente. ¿Quién quiere probarla?*
B: *¡Ay, qué horrible!*

4. Te toca a ti
Possible Dialog
A: *¿Qué vas a pedir?*
B: *No sé. ¿Te gusta el arroz con pollo?*
A: *No, pero ¿por qué no lo pides tú?*
B: *Buena idea. ¿Qué vas a pedir?*
A: *Voy a pedir una ensalada de frutas. ¿Qué vas a tomar?*
B: *Agua mineral. ¿Y tú?*
A: *Voy a tomar un jugo de piña.*
As an extension, have students work in groups of three, the third student being the server. Students may enjoy creating humorous conversations (the food is awful, the server spills water on a diner, etc.) and present them to the class.

¿QUÉ TE GUSTA?

Objective

• to talk about daily routines

GETTING STARTED

Direct students to the personality quiz. Have them respond to the questions. Have students work in pairs or small groups to brainstorm vocabulary to answer the following questions.

1. *¿A qué hora te levantas? ¿Y los fines de semana? ¿A qué hora te acuestas? ¿Qué desayunas?*

2. *¿Qué te gusta hacer en tu tiempo libre?*

3. *¿Qué comes de desayuno? ¿Y de almuerzo? ¿Y en la cena?*

4. *¿Cuáles son algunas mascotas populares? ¿Y cuáles son raras?*

---

encuesta

¿Cómo eres?
¿Qué necesitas?

1 **¿Qué es lo primero que haces por la mañana?**
a. Me ducho, me cepillo los dientes, me pongo la ropa, como algo y me cepillo los dientes otra vez.
b. Me ducho y como algo.
c. Veo la televisión.

2 **¿Qué mascota te gusta más?**
a. No me gustan las mascotas.
b. los perros o los pájaros
c. los gatos o los peces

3 **¿Qué comes?**
a. sólo verduras y cereales
b. de todo
c. comida rápida

4 **En tu tiempo libre, ¿qué te gusta hacer?**
a. ir a clases de música y leer
b. practicar deportes y salir con amigos
c. escuchar música y mirar la televisión

5 **¿Cuál es tu materia favorita?**
a. matemáticas, ciencias o historia
b. educación física, español o literatura
c. ninguna

Resultados:
La mayoría a: ¡Atención! ¡Relájate! Eres joven, no necesitas tanto estrés.
La mayoría b: ¡Buenas noticias! ¡Eres una persona equilibrada!
La mayoría c: Compañera, compañero... ¿qué te pasa? ¡Necesitas un poco de salsa en tu vida!

10

Tus costumbres

Pregúntale a tu compañero(a) sobre sus costumbres.

— ¿Qué es lo primero que haces por la mañana?
— Me ducho.
— Y después de ducharte, ¿qué haces?
— Como algo de desayuno.
— ¿Y después?
— Me cepillo los dientes.

¿Qué más?
• bañarse
• ponerse la ropa
• cepillarse el pelo
• lavarse las manos
• peinarse
• secarse el pelo

 ## ¿En cuánto tiempo?

Pregúntale a tu compañero(a) en cuánto tiempo se prepara para ir a la escuela.

— ¿En cuánto tiempo te duchas?
— En siete minutos.
— ¿Y en cuánto tiempo te cepillas los dientes?
— En tres minutos.

MÁS PREGUNTAS...

¿Qué ropa te pones para salir?
¿Y para ir a la escuela?
¿Y para ir a una fiesta?
¿Y para quedarte en casa?
¿Con qué champú te lavas el pelo?

A escribir

Escribe ocho oraciones o más sobre qué haces los fines de semana. Preséntalas a la clase.

El sábado por la mañana me baño y me cepillo el pelo. Por la tarde me encuentro con mis amigos. Generalmente vamos al cine.

¿RECUERDAS?

To talk about daily routines, you can use reflexive verbs. When you use them, you need to include the reflexive pronouns **me, te, se, nos** *and* **os**. *Here are the forms of the verb* **ponerse** *(to put on, to wear):*

yo	**me**	pongo	nosotros(as)	**nos**	ponemos
tú	**te**	pones	vosotros(as)	**os**	ponéis
usted	**se**	pone	ustedes	**se**	ponen
él/ella	**se**	pone	ellos/ellas	**se**	ponen

Other reflexive verbs that you know are: **bañarse** *(to take a bath),* **ducharse** *(to take a shower),* **cepillarse** *(to brush one's hair/teeth),* **encontrarse** *(to meet),* **lavarse** *(to wash one's face/hands),* **peinarse** *(to comb one's hair),* **prepararse** *(to get ready) and* **secarse** *(to dry oneself).*

11

1. Tus costumbres
Remind students that when they use reflexive verbs, they may attach the pronoun to the infinitive or place it before the conjugated verb *(voy a bañarme* or *me voy a bañar).*

2. ¿En cuánto tiempo?
As an extension, have students total the number of minutes in Spanish.

3. A escribir
Review numbers by polling the class to compare and average the amounts of time spent doing such things as combing one's hair.

Objective
• to talk about likes and dislikes

DIALOGS

Have pairs or groups think of additional responses to the questions on this page. Have pairs interview each other using the questions.

Review the preterite tense by asking for occasions when students did something they liked. For example:

Me gusta practicar deportes. La semana pasada jugué al fútbol con mis amigos. Mi equipo ganó.

¿QUÉ MÁS?

¿Qué te gusta?
¿Qué no te gusta?
Me gusta(n)... No me gusta(n)...
• la comida picante
• los conciertos de rock/salsa
• los programas de deportes
• la ciudad
• la escuela
• la playa

Después de la escuela, ¿qué te gusta hacer?

Me gusta... No me gusta...
• pasear por el parque
• bailar
• ir de compras
• hacer la tarea
• hablar por teléfono
• practicar deportes
• trabajar

Los fines de semana, ¿te gusta salir con amigos(as)?

Sí, ¡me encanta!
Sí, a veces.
No, no me gusta nada.
• salir con amigos
• ir al cine
• viajar
• leer
• hacer una barbacoa
• mirar la televisión
• hacer excursiones

12

1 ¿Cuándo?

Pregúntale a tu compañero(a) qué le gusta hacer y cuándo.

— *¿Qué te gusta hacer después de la escuela?*
— *Me gusta jugar con videojuegos.*

MÁS PREGUNTAS...
¿Después del almuerzo?
¿En la clase de educación física?
¿Los fines de semana?
¿Cuando nieva? ¿Cuando hace calor?
¿En las vacaciones de verano?

 2 ¿Y a tus amigos?

Haz a dos de tus mejores amigos(as) cuatro preguntas sobre qué les gusta hacer. Después compara las respuestas con las actividades que a ti te gustan hacer. ¿Son similares las respuestas? Presenta los resultados a la clase.

Cuando llueve, a mí me gusta mirar la televisión, pero a Samuel y a Lisa les gusta ir al cine.

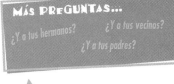

MÁS PREGUNTAS...
¿Y a tus hermanos? *¿Y a tus vecinos?*
¿Y a tus padres?

3 ¿A quién le gusta...?

Pregúntales a tus compañeros(as).

¿A quién...?
• le gusta la comida mexicana
• no le gusta la televisión
• le gusta la música clásica
• no le gustan los deportes
• le gusta mucho la escuela
• no le gustan las telenovelas

 4 Te toca a ti

Con tu compañero(a), crea dos diálogos.

A *greet/ask: how are you?* → B
A ← *reply/ask back* B
A *ask something about likes/dislikes* → B
A ← *answer/ask back something about likes/dislikes* B
A *answer/ask why* → B
reply

¿RECUERDAS?

To talk about things you like or dislike, use the verb **gustar** and a noun. To say that you like or dislike one thing, use **gusta** followed by a singular noun. To say that you like or dislike more than one thing, use **gustan** followed by a plural noun.

(a mí)	**me**	**gusta(n)**	(a nosotros/as)	**nos**	**gusta(n)**
(a ti)	**te**	**gusta(n)**	(a vosotros/as)	**os**	**gusta(n)**
(a usted)	**le**	**gusta(n)**	(a ustedes)	**les**	**gusta(n)**
(a él/ella)	**le**	**gusta(n)**	(a ellos/ellas)	**les**	**gusta(n)**

To talk about activities, use **gustar** + *infinitive* of the verb.

13

1. ¿Cuándo?
If students need a vocabulary review, have them brainstorm activities appropriate for the times in the *Más preguntas...* box. Write these on the board.

2. ¿Y a tus amigos?
Contrast present- and preterite-tense usage by having students mention a specific occasion. For example:
A: *¿Qué te gusta hacer cuando llueve?*
B: *Me gusta mirar la televisión.*
A: *¿Qué miraste la última vez que llovió?*
B: *Miré una pelíclua cómica.*

3. ¿A quién le gusta...?
As an extension, have students pair up and figure out what they would like to do together that evening. For example:
A: *¿Te gusta ir al cine?*
B: *No, no me gusta ir al cine. ¿Te gusta ir al parque?*
Students continue until they find activities that both would enjoy doing.

4. Te toca a ti
Possible Dialog
A: *Hola. ¿Cómo estás?*
B: *Bien, gracias, ¿y tú?*
B: *Bien. ¿Te gusta nadar?*
A: *Sí, pero prefiero el esquí acuático. ¿A ti te gusta el fútbol?*
B: *Sí, pero me gusta más el béisbol. ¿Por qué te gusta el esquí acuático?*
A: *Porque uno puede ir muy rápido.*
As a written extension, have students write down on cards what it is they enjoy doing, and why. Read aloud as many of the cards as possible, and see if the class can figure out who wrote each card.

¿QUÉ HACEMOS HOY?

Objectives
- to talk about plans for the future
- to talk about cultural and sporting events

GETTING STARTED

Direct students to the realia on this page. Have them identify the type of activity and as many countries as they can.

Ask students what kind of event they would recommend to certain individuals.

Examples:

¿Qué le recomiendas a una persona a quien le gustan los deportes?

¿Y a un niño de cinco años?

¿Y a una persona que está interesada en pintura y escultura?

¿Y a una persona a quien le interesan el teatro y la música?

Also ask such questions as:

Estás en Costa Rica y quieres ir al Museo de Arte Costarricense. ¿Es mejor ir el viernes o el domingo? ¿Por qué?

Estás en México y vas a ir al partido de fútbol. ¿A qué hora empieza?

Estás en Madrid y quieres ir al zoo. ¿Puedes ir a las diez de la noche?

 ¿Qué te gustaría hacer?

Con tu compañero(a), habla sobre los espectáculos de los anuncios y sobre qué quieren hacer.

— ¿Qué te gustaría hacer?
— Me gustaría ir a ver el partido de fútbol. ¿Y a ti?
— No sé... ¿Por qué no vamos al zoo?
— ¡Vale!

MÁS PREGUNTAS...
¿Cuándo?   ¿A qué hora empieza?
¿Por qué? ¿Por qué no?

 ¿Y este fin de semana?

Pregúntale a tu compañero(a) sobre sus planes para este fin de semana.

— ¿Qué vas a hacer el sábado?
— Voy a ir a la piscina con mis primos. ¿Y tú?
— Yo voy a ir a la biblioteca. Tengo que estudiar para el examen de historia.

MÁS PREGUNTAS...
¿A qué hora?   ¿Con quién?
¿Y después?   ¿Te gustaría...?

 ¿Y en el futuro?

En grupos pequeños, hablen sobre sus planes para el futuro. ¿Qué quieren hacer? ¿Qué van a hacer algún día?

— Algún día voy a subir al Everest. ¿Y tú?
— Yo voy a estudiar chino. ¿Y tú, Ana?
— Yo quiero viajar por Estados Unidos en autobús.

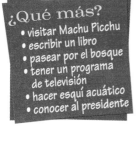

¿Qué más?
• visitar Machu Picchu
• escribir un libro
• pasear por el bosque
• tener un programa de televisión
• hacer esquí acuático
• conocer al presidente

¿RECUERDAS?

Use the verb **ir** (to go) to say that you are going somewhere.

yo	**voy**	nosotros(as)	**vamos**
tú	**vas**	vosotros(as)	**vais**
usted	**va**	ustedes	**van**
él/ella	**va**	ellos/ellas	**van**

Use **ir + a + infinitive** to talk about your plans or what you are going to do in the future.

1. ¿Qué te gustaría hacer?
After students interview each other, have them report their findings to the class. Which activity is the most popular? The least popular?

2. ¿Y este fin de semana?
Give students the options of making up or exaggerating plans. Students report partner's plans to the class; the class decides if they are real, made up, or exaggerated.

3. ¿Y en el futuro?
Have students think more specifically about their goals and hopes for the future by responding to these questions:
¿Qué vas a hacer... ?
1. *después de graduarte*
2. *a los 22 años*
3. *a los 30 años*

15

Objective
• to give directions

DIALOGS

To prepare, have students identify the buildings. Example:
¿Dónde está la biblioteca? (Está al lado de la escuela.)

Next, model the activity. Tell them how to get somewhere on the map—without identifying the place. Example:
Están en la tienda de discos. Salgan de allí. Doblen a la derecha. Ahora, doblen a la izquierda. Doblen a la izquierda en la primera esquina y entren al edificio al lado del teatro. ¿Dónde están?

Working in pairs, students direct each other from one point on the map to another.

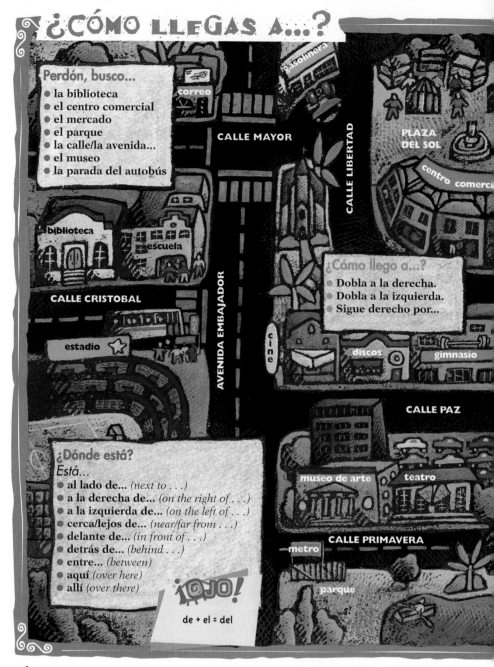

Perdón, …

Con tu compañero(a), miren el mapa. Escojan un lugar. Desde allí, pregunten cómo ir a otros lugares. Creen cuatro diálogos.

> *(Estoy delante de la biblioteca.)*
> — *Perdón, ¿dónde está el museo de arte?*
> — *Sigue derecho por la calle Cristóbal. En la avenida Embajador, dobla a la derecha. En la calle Primavera, dobla a la izquierda.*

 En tu ciudad

Con tu compañero(a), hablen de diferentes lugares de su ciudad.

> — *¿Conoces el restaurante La Bodega?*
> — *No, ¿dónde está?*
> — *Está en la calle Santos, entre el mercado y una tienda de ropa.*

 Está en la ciudad, ¿qué es?

Escoge un edificio del mapa. Tu compañero(a) tiene que hacer preguntas y adivinar cuál es. Tú sólo puedes contestar sí o no.

> — *¿Es una tienda?*
> — *Sí.*
> — *¿Está en una avenida?*
> — *No.*
> — *¿Está en una calle?*
> — *Sí.*

MÁS PREGUNTAS…

¿Es una persona?	*¿Es una cosa?*
¿Está en esta clase?	*¿Es famosa?*
¿Es grande? ¿Es de colores?	
	¿Está cerca de…?

¿Qué más?
- debajo de… (under)
- encima de… (on top of)

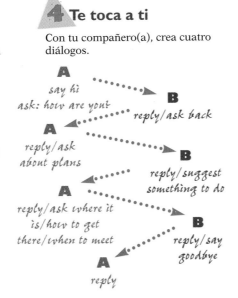 **Te toca a ti**

Con tu compañero(a), crea cuatro diálogos.

A say hi / ask: how are you?

B reply/ask back

A reply/ask about plans

B reply/suggest something to do

A reply/ask where it is/how to get there/when to meet

B reply/say goodbye

A reply

17

1. Perdón…
As an extension, have students direct each other to places in the school. You may need to reintroduce these words:

baja	entra	el salón de clase
el pasillo	sal	sube

You may also have to review the difference between *a la derecha* and *sigue derecho*. Have them practice both by walking up and down the rows.

2. En tu ciudad
As an extension, have students report to the class the locations of these places—without mentioning the name of each place. The class guesses the place. Example:
Este lugar está en la calle Oak, cerca del parque, a la izquierda de la biblioteca.

3. Está en la ciudad, ¿qué es?
As a variation, one student thinks of a Latin American country, and others guess which it is by asking **sí/no** questions. You may wish to review the phrases *al norte, al sur, al este, al oeste de.* For example: *¿El país está lejos de aquí? ¿Está al oeste de Brasil?*

4. Te toca a ti
Possible Dialog
A: *Hola. ¿Cómo estás?*
B: *Bien, ¿y tú?*
A: *Bien, gracias. ¿Qué vas a hacer mañana por la noche?*
B: *Voy a ir a una fiesta en casa de Anita. ¿Quieres venir?*
A: *Sí, gracias. ¿Dónde está su casa? ¿Está lejos? ¿A qué hora es la fiesta?*
B: *Vive en la calle Olmos, en la esquina de la calle Cinco. La fiesta es a las ocho. Hasta mañana.*
A: *Adiós.*
As a written extension, have students write down their dialog on cards (one exchange per card). They scramble the cards with the exchanges, and classmates put exchanges in proper order.

¿QUÉ TAL TUS VACACIONES?

Objective
• to talk about vacations you have taken

GETTING STARTED

Have students look at the three postcards on this page. Have them identify where each person is vacationing.

Have students read the three messages. Ask them which person (Rafa, Sandra, Carolina) each comment refers to:

Esta persona...

1. *viajó con su familia.* (Sandra)

2. *viajó con unos amigos.* (Rafa)

3. *les escribió una postal a unos familiares.* (Rafa)

4. *visitó la capital chilena.* (Sandra)

5. *viajó por el océano Pacífico.* (Sandra)

6. *probablemente sacó muchas fotos del paisaje.* (Carolina)

7. *probablemente llevó un traje de baño.* (Rafa)

Finally, have students locate these places on a map.

1 ¿Adónde fueron?

Con tu compañero(a), hablen sobre dónde fuiste en tus últimas vacaciones.

— ¿Adónde fuiste de vacaciones?
— Fui a California a visitar a mis abuelos. ¿Y tú?
— Fui a la playa.

MÁS PREGUNTAS...

¿Cómo fuiste? ¿En coche? ¿En avión?
¿Cuándo fuiste?
¿En qué mes? ¿Por cuánto tiempo?
¿Con quién? ¿Hizo buen tiempo?
¿Qué tiempo hizo?

 2 ¿Hiciste amigos?

Pregúntale a tu compañero(a) más cosas sobre sus vacaciones.

— ¿Hiciste nuevos amigos?
— Sí. Hice dos amigos. Se llaman Elisa y Felipe.

 3 ¿Qué viste?

Pregúntale a tu compañero(a) qué vio en sus vacaciones.

— ¿Qué viste en tus vacaciones?
— Vi la famosa catedral de Burgos.

MÁS PREGUNTAS...

¿Viste a uno de nuestro compañeros?
¿Cómo es? ¿Dónde está?
¿Qué más viste?
¿Viste a tu familia? ¿Viste una película?

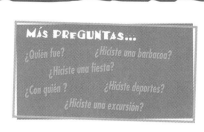

MÁS PREGUNTAS...

¿Quién fue? ¿Hiciste una barbacoa?
¿Hiciste una fiesta?
¿Con quién? ¿Hiciste deportes?
¿Hiciste una excursión?

¿RECUERDAS?

To talk about what you did in the past, you can use the preterite tense. The verbs **ir** (to go), **ver** (to see) and **hacer** (to do) are irregular in the preterite.

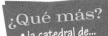

	ir	ver	hacer
yo	fui	vi	hice
tú	fuiste	viste	hiciste
usted	fue	vio	hizo
él/ella	fue	vio	hizo
nosotros(as)	fuimos	vimos	hicimos
vosotros(as)	fuisteis	visteis	hicisteis
ustedes	fueron	vieron	hicieron
ellos/ellas	fueron	vieron	hicieron

¿Qué más?
• la catedral de...
• el castillo de...
• la costa de...
• el valle de...

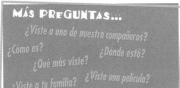

19

Students may need to review regular preterite forms in the ¿Recuerdas? box before doing these activities.

1. ¿Adónde fueron?
After students have interviewed each other, have them report their findings to the class, using third-person singular forms. To practice first and third-person plural forms, have individuals summarize vacations. For example:
Toni y Alberto fueron a Puerto Rico. Susi, Maricarmen y yo no fuimos a ningún lugar.

2. ¿Hiciste amigos?
Have students talk about an aspect of their vacation that they would like to do differently the following year, using the preterite and **me gustaría**. For example:
Este verano fui a la playa. El próximo verano me gustaría ir a las montañas.

Extension: Have students ask each other how things went on their vacation and choose an answer from the preceding page.

3. ¿Qué viste?
Hand out magazine photos and captions for students to use as they speak.

Objective
- to talk about what you did on your vacation

DIALOGS

Have pairs or groups create additional responses to the questions on this page. Then have them tell what the people in each of the photos wrote in their diaries regarding their vacations. For example: *Fuimos a la playa. Compramos libros. Conocí a un chico. Patinamos.*
Students may need to be reminded of the spelling change in the preterite **yo** form of certain -**ar** verbs.
-**gar:** *jugué*
-**car:** *toqué*
-**zar:** *empecé*

¿QUÉ HICISTE?

¿Qué hiciste?
- Nadé en el mar.
- Subí a una montaña.
- Jugué al frisbi.
- Aprendí a hacer surf.
- Escribí un diario.
- Hice un picnic.

¿Compraste alguna cosa?
¿Qué compraste?
Compré...
- una camiseta
- un libro de...
- una tarjeta postal
- una escultura
- No compré nada.

¿Conociste a mucha gente?
- Sí, conocí a una chica de...
- Sí, conocí a mucha gente.
- No, no mucha.

20

¿Qué hicieron?

Pregúntale a tu compañero(a) qué hizo en sus vacaciones.

— ¿Qué hiciste?
— Visité varios museos. ¿Y tú?
— Yo tomé el sol en la playa y nadé en el mar.

 ## Tus experiencias del verano

Pregúntale a tu compañero(a) más cosas sobre sus vacaciones.

¿Cuál fue...?
- la situación más divertida
- el lugar más maravilloso
- la situación más difícil
- la experiencia más emocionante
- el día más divertido
- el día más aburrido
- el paisaje más espectacular

 ## ¿Quién...?

Pregúntales a tus compañeros.

En las vacaciones, ¿quién...?
- fue a un país hispano
- visitó un museo
- nadó en un río/una piscina
- visitó a su familia
- habló español
- viajó en tren

 ## Te toca a ti

Con tu compañero(a), creen tres diálogos.

A ......▶
say hi
            B
        ......▶
        reply/ask: what did you do (sometime)?
A ◀......   B
reply/ask back
            ....▶
            answer/ask with whom, where ...
A ◀......   B
answer/ ask back
        ....▶
            B
        answer

¿RECUERDAS?

To talk about what you did in the past, use the preterite of -ar, -er and -ir verbs.

	hablar	aprender	escribir
yo	hablé	aprendí	escribí
tú	hablaste	aprendiste	escribiste
usted	habló	aprendió	escribió
él/ella	habló	aprendió	escribió
nosotros(as)	hablamos	aprendimos	escribimos
vosotros(as)	hablasteis	aprendisteis	escribisteis
ustedes	hablaron	aprendieron	escribieron
ellos/ellas	hablaron	aprendieron	escribieron

21

---

1. ¿Qué hicieron?
Prior to doing this activity, have the class list Spanish verbs for vacation activities. Write them on the board. Review the preterite paradigms.

2. Tus experiencias del verano
Point out that the verbs **ir** and **ser** have the same preterite conjugation (¿Adónde fuiste? ¿Cómo fue?).
Give students the options of making up or exaggerating experiences.
As an extension to this activity, have each student write down four questions.
Examples:
1. ¿Hablaste español en las vacaciones?
2. ¿Te quedaste en casa todo el verano?
3. ¿Aprendiste a hacer surf?
4. ¿Leiste mucho durante el verano?
Students circulate, asking their questions. When a student finds someone who answers a question affirmatively, that person signs his or her name next to the question. The first student who gets four signatures wins.

3. ¿Quién...?
Have pairs or small groups brainstorm additional questions. For example:
¿Quién aprendió a hacer esquí acuático?
Have students report their findings to the class, and then categorize these as:
divertido, aburrido, or **peligroso.**

4. Te toca a ti
Possible Dialog
A: Hola.
B: Hola. ¿Qué hiciste el sábado?
A: Fui al cine. ¿Y tú?
B: Fui de compras. ¿Con quién fuiste? ¿Qué viste?
A: Fui con Marcos. Vimos la nueva película de Woody Allen. ¿Qué compraste?
B: El nuevo disco de Juan Luis Guerra.
As a written extension, have students write down their dialog on cards (one exchange per card). They scramble the exchanges, and classmates put exchanges in proper order.

¡LLUEVE A CÁNTAROS!

Objectives

- to talk about the weather
- to say what you can or cannot do, using **poder**

GETTING STARTED

Have volunteers read aloud the descriptions on this page.

Have students order these places by:
- most northern to most southern (Los Ángeles, Cumaná, La Paz, Punta Arenas)
- most eastern to most western (Cumaná, La Paz, Punta Arenas, Los Ángeles)
- coolest to warmest (according to text) (Punta Arenas, La Paz, Los Ángeles, Cumaná)
- warmest to coolest (at this time) (Answers will vary.)

Ask volunteers to work out the equivalent temperatures in Fahrenheit.
Ask which place each of these comments refers to: *Esta ciudad...*
1. *es muy alta. (La Paz)*
2. *es muy grande. (Los Ángeles)*
3. *está cerca de la Antártida. (Punta Arenas)*
4. *no está cerca de una playa. (La Paz)*
5. *tiene algunas tormentas. (Cumaná)*

¡LLUEVE A CÁNTAROS!

Cuatro chicos y chicas de diferentes lugares del mundo nos escriben de qué tiempo hace donde ellos viven y qué les gusta hacer.

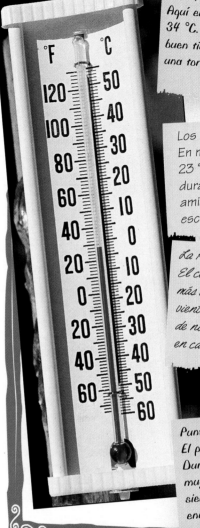

Junio, Cumaná, Venezuela
Aquí en el Caribe hace mucho calor. Hoy en Cumaná hace 34 °C. ¡Está chévere para ir a la playa! Generalmente hace buen tiempo, pero el pronóstico para mañana dice que viene una tormenta. A veces tenemos tormentas con mucho viento.

Los Ángeles, marzo
En mi ciudad hoy hace sol y la temperatura es de 23 °C. En primavera generalmente hace buen tiempo durante el día, pero por la noche hace frío. Mis amigos y yo siempre nos encontramos después de la escuela y vamos a patinar.

La Paz, Bolivia, marzo
El clima aquí es bastante frío. La Paz está en los Andes, a más de 3.000 metros de altura. Hoy hace 14 °C. Hace viento y está lloviendo a cántaros. Generalmente llueve mucho de noviembre a marzo. Nunca salgo cuando llueve. Me quedo en casa y miro la televisión o juego con videojuegos.

Punta Arenas, sur de Chile, abril
El pronóstico dice que va a hacer frío y que va a nevar. Durante todo el año hace mucho frío, porque estamos muy al sur, cerca de la Antártida. La gente dice que aquí siempre hace mal tiempo, ¡pero a mí me gusta! ¡Me encanta la nieve!

¿Qué tiempo hace?

Mira las cartas que chicos y chicas de diferentes países escribieron sobre el tiempo. Describe qué tiempo hace en tu pueblo o ciudad.

 ¿Te gusta la lluvia?

Con tu compañero(a), hablen sobre cómo les afecta el tiempo que hace.

— ¿Te gusta la nieve?

— ¡No, no me gusta! Nunca salgo cuando nieva.

— A mí sí me gusta. Me encanta jugar con la nieve.

— ¿Cuál es tu estación favorita?

— El invierno.

MÁS PREGUNTAS . . .

¿Por qué?   ¿Llueve mucho?

¿Qué te gusta más, ... o ...?

¿Dónde te gustaría vivir?

 ¿Qué puedes hacer?

Con tu compañero(a), hablen de qué actividades pueden hacer y cuáles no pueden hacer según el tiempo que hace.

— ¿Puedes volar chiringas en la playa?

— Sí, cuando hace viento.

— ¿Y si hay una tormenta?

— No, es muy peligroso.

¿Qué más?
- hacer un picnic
- subir a una montaña
- hacer surf
- ver pájaros

¿RECUERDAS?

Use the verb **poder** (to be able to) to talk about what you can or cannot do. Remember it is a stem-changing verb. The vowel in the stem (**pod-**) changes from **o** to **ue** in all forms, except for the **nosotros(as)** and **vosotros(as)** forms.

yo	p**ue**do	nosotros(as)	podemos
tú	p**ue**des	vosotros(as)	podéis
usted	p**ue**de	ustedes	p**ue**den
él/ella	p**ue**de	ellos/ellas	p**ue**den

Other stem changing verbs that you have learned are: **pedir** and **servir** (e > i), **querer**, **preferir** and **nevar** (e > ie), **llover** (o > ue) and **jugar** (u > ue).

1. ¿Qué tiempo hace?
Have students talk about the ways in which climate and weather differs from region to region in the United States, and how the weather in their town is different from that of the students in the book.

2. ¿Te gusta la lluvia?
Have students share with the class what their partner's favorite season is, and why. Help them recall other adjectives or expressions to describe how they feel about different types of weather. (*da igual, me deprime, me encanta, odio, adoro,* etc.)

3. ¿Qué puedes hacer?
Have students practice using preterite forms of **poder** by asking each other what they could or could not do on different days, according to the weather. Example: *¿Pudiste andar en bicicleta ayer? No, no pude, porque llovía.*

23

Objective
• to say what you need

Have students talk about the weather conditions in each photo. Have them describe what the people in the photos are wearing. Then have them talk about different activities the people in each photo can do, using the verb **poder.** Examples: *Pueden esquiar, nadar, hacer surf,* etc.

¿QUÉ NECESITAS?

Cuando vas a la playa, ¿qué necesitas?
Necesito...
● los lentes de sol
● el protector solar
● la sombrilla
● el traje de baño
● la toalla
● el frisbi
● las paletas
● las aletas

¿Y cuando llueve?
Necesito...
● el paraguas
● el impermeable
● las botas

¿Qué ropa llevas cuando nieva?
Llevo...
● el abrigo
● los guantes
● el suéter
● el gorro

24

24

1. ¿Qué necesitas?

Pregúntale a tu compañero(a) qué necesita en las siguientes situaciones.

- Hace sol. ¿Necesitas el protector solar?
  (*Sí, lo necesito.*)
- Estás en la calle. Llueve. ¿Necesitas el paraguas?
- Hace frío y tú estás en casa. ¿Necesitas las botas?
- No sabes qué tiempo va a hacer y quieres salir. ¿Necesitas un periódico para leer el pronóstico del tiempo?
- Viene un huracán. ¿Necesitas la tabla de surf?
- Ahora inventa cuatro situaciones nuevas.

2. ¿Quién?

Pregúntales a tus compañeros(as).

¿A quién...?
- no le gusta la nieve
- no le gusta salir a la calle cuando llueve
- le gusta la primavera

¿Quién...?
- nunca presta atención al pronóstico del tiempo
- sabe el nombre de un huracán
- nunca usa paraguas

3. Te toca a ti

Con tu compañero(a), creen cuatro diálogos.

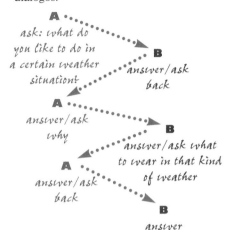

A ask: what do you like to do in a certain weather situation?

B answer/ask back

A answer/ask why

B answer/ask what to wear in that kind of weather

A answer/ask back

B answer

¿RECUERDAS?

*A direct object noun answers the question **what?** or **whom?** To avoid repeating direct object nouns, use direct object pronouns.*

¿Necesitas **el mapa?**   Sí, necesito **el mapa.**
(Sí, **lo** necesito.)

¿Conoces a **esa chica?**   No, no conozco a **esa chica.**
(No, no **la** conozco.)

Here are the direct object pronouns:

me *me*
te *you (informal)*
lo *him, it, you (formal, masc.)*
la *her, it, you (formal, fem.)*
nos *us*
os *you (informal, pl., in Spain)*
los *them (masc., masc. and fem.), you (masc., pl.)*
las *them (fem.), you (fem., pl.)*

ACTIVITIES

1. ¿Qué necesitas?
Have each student name an object from the list on the previous page. His or her partner must respond as to whether it is associated with *la playa, la lluvia,* or *la nieve.*

2. ¿Quién?
Have each student say what he or she likes to do outdoors. The rest of the class must answer by identifying the best season for that activity.
A: *Me gusta patinar y esquiar.*
B: *A ella le gusta el invierno.*

3. Te toca a ti
Possible Dialog
A: *¿Qué te gusta hacer cuando llueve?*
B: *A mí me gusta quedarme en casa y leer un libro. ¿Y a ti?*
A: *A mí me gusta dar un paseo. ¿No te gusta la lluvia?*
B: *No. ¿Qué llevas cuando llueve?*
A: *Llevo un impermeable. ¿Y tú?*
B: *Llevo un traje de baño.*

As a written extension, have students write down what their partner enjoys doing, and read it aloud. For example:
A Fernando le gusta volar chiringas cuando hay mucho viento.

Objectives
- to tell someone what to do
- to talk about parties

GETTING STARTED

Direct attention to the invitations. Tell students that you are going to repeat what some of the people said about the parties after they were over. Ask which party each person attended.

1. *Cuando mi primo entró en la casa, todos salimos corriendo de la cocina. ¡Cuánto le sorprendimos!* (la fiesta sorpresa)

2. *Llegué al salón a las 6:30.* (la fiesta de aniversario)

3. *Yo ayudé a decorar la casa.* (la fiesta sorpresa)

4. *Los maestros nos sirvieron la comida.* (la fiesta de graduación)

5. *Los esposos estaban muy contentos.* (la fiesta de aniversario)

UNA FIESTA

Fiesta del aniversario
de Juan Ramón y Lucía
¡Ven a bailar con nosotros!

Lugar: *salón de fiestas Rotonda*

Fecha: *domingo, seis de mayo*

Hora: *18:00*

¡FIESTA SORPRESA!

Es el cumpleaños de Tomás y vamos a tener una fiesta.

¿cuándo?   ...el sábado
¿a qué hora? ...a las 6 de la tarde
¿dónde?   en su casa

(importante: ¡no debes decirle a Tomás que hay una fiesta!)

Donna te invita a su

Fiesta de graduación

Lugar: Memorial High School

Fecha: 21 de julio

Hora: 4 de la tarde

26

Tu fiesta

En grupos, planeen su fiesta ideal. Decidan qué tipo de fiesta van a hacer, cuándo va a ser, dónde, a quiénes van a invitar y qué van a preparar. Después, diseñen y escriban una invitación.

¿Qué necesitamos?

En grupos, escriban una lista de lo que necesitan. Incluyan el menú, la música, las decoraciones, etc. Anoten quién tiene que hacer o comprar cada cosa.

¿Quién?	¿Qué tiene que hacer?
Rita	comprar decoraciones velas rojas y verdes
Toni	comprar globos de muchos colores
Sofía	hacer una piñata

¿Qué tengo que hacer?

Ahora tienen que decir a cada persona lo que tiene que hacer.

> Toni, compra globos y velas.
> Sofía, haz una piñata.

¿RECUERDAS?

To tell a friend to do something, use the informal **tú** command. Note that the **tú** command forms are the same as the **usted/él/ella** forms of the present tense.

-ar verbs: **-a** ending		**-er/-ir** verbs: **-e** ending	
comprar	compra	comer	come
		escribir	escribe

You can also use **tener que** followed by an infinitive of another verb: **Tienes que escribir una carta.** (You have to write a letter.)

To tell a friend not to do something, you can use **no debes** and an infinitive of another verb: **No debes escribir con lápiz.** (You should not write in pencil.)

Remember that some verbs have an irregular **tú** command.
hacer: **haz**
tener: **ten**
ser: **sé**
decir: **di**
venir: **ven**
ir: **ve**
poner: **pon**
salir: **sal**

1. Tu fiesta
Review the preterite tense by having students imagine that the party is over. Have them describe what it was like and what happened. For example:
¡La fiesta de Navidad fue fantástica! Fue el 20 de diciembre en casa de Lolita. Invitamos a los estudiantes de la clase de español y a nuestros novios. Bailamos salsa. Miguel y Sergio tocaron la guitarra. Miguel invitó a Teresa a bailar cuatro veces.

2. ¿Qué necesitamos?
Have groups say what food and music they are planning to have. The class votes for the best party.

3. ¿Qué tengo que hacer?
Extend this activity by having students pair up and tell each other what each needs to do, using **tener que**, and what each should not do, using **no debes**.

Objectives
• to write about and discuss parties
• to talk about **quinceañeras**

READING

Have volunteers read aloud each paragraph. Ask questions. Ask for comments on the letter. Have pairs create dialogs using a telephone-conversation format. One student has just received the letter from Patricia and calls a classmate to tell him/her about it. The classmate makes appropriate comments and asks questions.

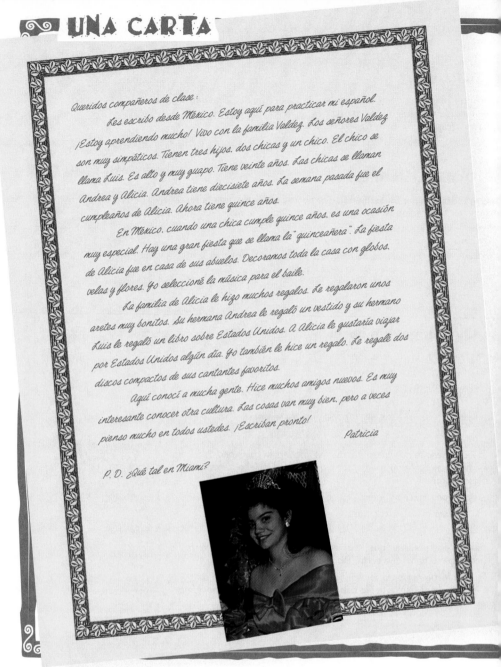

UNA CARTA

Queridos compañeros de clase:

Les escribo desde México. Estoy aquí para practicar mi español. ¡Estoy aprendiendo mucho! Vivo con la familia Valdez. Los señores Valdez son muy simpáticos. Tienen tres hijos, dos chicas y un chico. El chico se llama Luis. Es alto y muy guapo. Tiene veinte años. Las chicas se llaman Andrea y Alicia. Andrea tiene diecisiete años. La semana pasada fue el cumpleaños de Alicia. Ahora tiene quince años.

En México, cuando una chica cumple quince años, es una ocasión muy especial. Hay una gran fiesta que se llama la "quinceañera". La fiesta de Alicia fue en casa de sus abuelos. Decoramos toda la casa con globos, velas y flores. Yo seleccioné la música para el baile.

La familia de Alicia le hizo muchos regalos. Le regalaron unos aretes muy bonitos. Su hermana Andrea le regaló un vestido y su hermano Luis le regaló un libro sobre Estados Unidos. A Alicia le gustaría viajar por Estados Unidos algún día. Yo también le hice un regalo. Le regalé dos discos compactos de sus cantantes favoritos.

Aquí conocí a mucha gente. Hice muchos amigos nuevos. Es muy interesante conocer otra cultura. Las cosas van muy bien, pero a veces pienso mucho en todos ustedes. ¡Escriban pronto!

Patricia

P. D. ¿Qué tal en Miami?

28

La carta de Patricia

Con tu compañero(a), contesten las siguientes preguntas.

- ¿A quién le escribe Patricia una carta? ¿Por qué?
- ¿Qué hace Patricia en México? ¿Con quién vive?
- ¿Cómo es la familia Valdez?
- ¿Sobre qué fiesta escribe Patricia? ¿Por qué?
- ¿Qué regalos le hicieron a Alicia? ¿Quiénes?

Una celebración típica

Con tu compañero(a), piensen en una celebración típica de algún país. Escriban una pequeña descripción.

Celebraciones en familia

Para ti, ¿cuál fue la mejor? ¿Por qué? Escribe seis oraciones describiéndola y preséntalas a la clase.

¿Quién?

Pregúntales a tus compañeros(as).

¿Quién...a quién?

- Muchas veces les hace un pastel de cumpleaños a sus amigos.
- Nunca les escribe una tarjeta de cumpleaños a sus hermanos.
- Le gustan mucho las celebraciones en familia.
- El día de su cumpleaños sus padres le regalaron un reloj.
- Su familia le hizo una fiesta sorpresa.

¿RECUERDAS?

*Indirect object pronouns usually tell **to whom** or **for whom** something is intended.*

me	to/for me
te	to/for you (informal)
le	to/for him, her, it, you (formal)
nos	to/for us
os	to/for you (pl., informal)
les	to/for them, you (pl., formal)

*Some of the verbs you know that can use indirect object pronouns are: **dar** (to give), **decir** (to say) and **pedir** (to ask for).*

MÁS PREGUNTAS...

¿Cuándo es? ¿Con quién?
¿Por qué? ¿Dónde? ¿Te hacen regalos?

Te toca a ti

En parejas, imaginen que están en una fiesta. Creen tres diálogos.

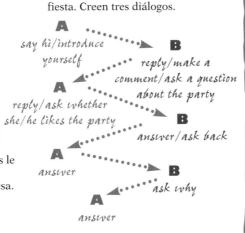

A say hi/introduce yourself
B reply/make a comment/ask a question about the party
A reply/ask whether she/he likes the party
B answer/ask back
A answer
B ask why
A answer

1. La carta de Patricia
Extend by having pairs compose a letter to send to Patricia in Mexico.

2. Una celebración típica
Give students the option of describing the celebration in the present tense or using the preterite to describe a specific occasion, such as last New Year's Eve.

3. Celebraciones en familia
Extend by having students share their descriptions with the class. Ask students to listen carefully to their classmates' descriptions and be prepared to ask questions or make comments about the parties or celebrations.

4. ¿Quién?
Have students make up and answer additional questions.

5. Te toca a ti
Possible Dialog
A: *Hola, soy Maribel López.*
B: *Hola, soy Ricardo Márquez. ¿Te gusta esta música?*
A: *Sí, mucho. ¿Te gusta la fiesta?*
B: *Sí, y tú ¿te diviertes?*
A: *Mucho.*
B: *Por qué?*
A: *Me gusta la gente. Nuestros compañeros son muy simpáticos.*

Have students perform the same activity in front of the class in groups of three or four. Encourage them to improvise, rather than sticking to the model.

¡VAMOS DE VIAJE!

Objectives
- to talk about vacations and trips
- to use superlatives

GETTING STARTED

Ask students which vacation appeals to them the most, and why. Then have them form groups and plan a brochure for a vacation in a Spanish-speaking country or region, including all the things tourists can do. Encourage creativity and make things up.

Ask which place each of these comments refers to: *Puedes...*
1. *ir a Serena Cay.* (el Caribe)
2. *subir montañas.* (Chile)
3. *gastar menos dinero.* (Argentina)
4. *aprender a esquiar.* (Argentina)
5. *quedarte en buenos hoteles.* (España)
6. *viajar en coche.* (Chile)

¡VAMOS DE VIAJE!

En julio y agosto ven a Bariloche, el mejor lugar de Argentina para esquiar.

Si no sabes esquiar, ¡aprende con nosotros!

Ofertas especiales para estudiantes
Avión y una semana ❄ $599
Avión y dos semanas ❄ $899

AVENTURA DE 15 DÍAS EN CHILE
✔ Admira los paisajes naturales
✔ Vive sensaciones emocionantes
✔ Sube a una montaña
✔ Navega los rápidos
✔ Pasea en jeep por el desierto

¡Todo por $ 799!

Ocho días en barco por el Caribe

¡desde $849!
(incluye avión + barco)

San Juan, St. Thomas, St. Marteen, Martinica y Serena Cay

VISITA MADRID, BARCELONA Y SEVILLA

museos   catedrales
ciudades históricas

Dos semanas por sólo $999

Incluye:
Viaje en avión y autobús ☆☆☆☆
Hoteles de cuatro estrellas ☆☆☆☆
Varias excursiones con guías bilingües

30

¿Qué hacemos?

Con tu compañero(a), miren los anuncios. Hagan planes para sus próximas vacaciones y decidan qué necesitan.

— ¿Adónde quieres ir?
— A Bariloche. ¿Y tú?
— Yo también. ¿Necesitamos el pasaporte?
— ¡Sí! El pasaporte es importantísimo.

¿Qué más?
- los esquís
- las aletas
- la cámara
- el protector solar
- la guía turística
- los cheques de viajero
- el traje de baño

 Tus viajes

Pregúntale a tu compañero(a) sobre sus viajes o excursiones.
- ¿Cuál fue su viaje más divertido?
- ¿Y el viaje más aburrido?
- ¿Y el viaje más largo?
- ¿Y el paisaje más espectacular?
- ¿Y un lugar hermosísimo?
- ¿Y un lugar conocidísimo?

 A escribir

Escribe un párrafo sobre tu experiencia más emocionante o increíble. Preséntalo a la clase.

¿RECUERDAS?

To describe a person, place, or thing that stands out from all the rest, use the superlative construction. To form the superlative, use a noun and **más,** *followed by an adjective:* **la montaña más alta** *(the highest mountain).*

Another way to form a superlative is to add the ending **-ísimo(s), -ísima(s)** *to the adjective:* **El pasaporte es importantísimo.** *(The passport is extremely important.)*

31

1. ¿Qué hacemos?
Ask students what the most necessary and the least necessary items would be on each vacation.

2. Tus viajes
Have students use superlatives to talk about classes or places in town. Examples:
El Cybercafé es lo más divertido en la ciudad.
La clase de matemáticas es lo más aburrido para mí.

3. A escribir
Have students exchange their work with each other, and write new versions of the other person's work in which they say that they never had an experience like this one.

Objective
- to say what you or others are doing currently

DIALOGS

Have students come up with additional activities, and talk about them using the present-progressive tense.

VACACIONES IDEALES

Son las vacaciones de invierno. ¿Qué están haciendo?
Están...
- patinando sobre hielo.
- jugando con la nieve.
- abriendo un regalo.

Son las vacaciones de primavera. ¿Qué están haciendo?
Están...
- escribiendo una tarjeta.
- haciendo un picnic.
- montando en bicicleta.

Son las vacaciones de verano. ¿Qué están haciendo?
Están...
- tomando el sol.
- nadando.
- tomando helado.

32

1. **Unas vacaciones ideales**

Imagina unas vacaciones ideales. ¿Dónde estás? ¿Con quién? ¿Qué estás haciendo? Escribe seis oraciones y preséntalas a la clase.

> *Estoy en las montañas de los Andes con mi amiga Rita.*
> *Estamos admirando el paisaje y tomando una taza de chocolate caliente.*

 2. **¿Qué están haciendo?**

Con tu compañero(a), habla de tu familia y amigos. ¿Dónde están ahora? ¿Qué están haciendo?

— ¿Qué está haciendo tu madre?
— Está trabajando en la tienda.

 3. **¿Quién es?**

Pregúntales a tus compañeros(as) si conocen a alguien que siempre está...

- leyendo
- cantando
- bailando
- jugando al béisbol
- mirando la televisión
- jugando al baloncesto

¿RECUERDAS?

To describe an action in progress, use the present progressive tense. To form the present progressive, use a form of the verb **estar** followed by the present participle of the main verb. To form the present participle, replace the **-ar** ending of a verb with **-ando,** and the **-er** and **-ir** ending of a verb with **-iendo**.

visit**ar**	visit**ando**	**Estoy visitando.** (I am visiting.)
com**er**	com**iendo**	**Estás comiendo.** (You are eating.)
escrib**ir**	escrib**iendo**	**Está escribiendo.** (He/She is writing.)

 4. **Te toca a ti**

Con tu compañero(a), crea dos diálogos.

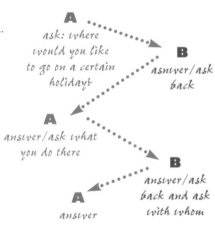

A *ask: where would you like to go on a certain holiday?*

B *answer/ask back*

A *answer/ask what you do there*

B *answer/ask back and ask with whom*

A *answer*

33

---

1. Unas vacaciones ideales
Have students use the preterite to ask each other about their vacations.
Example:
A: *¿Qué hiciste en las montañas?*
B: *Subí dos montañas.*

2. ¿Qué están haciendo?
Have students ask each other what each of the people they spoke about did yesterday.

3. ¿Quién es?
Have students say what each of these people is doing now. Example:
Jorge está leyendo Don Quijote *y los poemas de Stephen King.*

4. Te toca a ti.
Possible Dialog
A: *¿Dónde quieres ir en las vacaciones de invierno?*
B: *Quiero ir a Suiza. ¿Y tú?*
A: *Al Caribe. ¿Qué vas a hacer en Suiza?*
B: *Voy a esquiar. ¿Qué haces en el Caribe y con quién vas?*
A: *Voy con mis tíos. Vamos a nadar y tomar el sol.*

The next four pages of the student text summarize some of the most useful words and phrases introduced in Level One. They are organized by theme, the same approach that is used in the *Vocabulario temático* at the end of each chapter. Encourage students to use this section as necessary and to review it frequently.

Objective

• to talk to others, using common words and phrases

Haciendo amigos

These words and phrases were reviewed on pages 4-5. They are included here for easy reference.

Conociéndose mejor

These words and phrases were reviewed on pages 4-5. They are included here for easy reference.

Por teléfono

These words and phrases were not reviewed, so you may wish to go over them now.

Haciendo planes

These words and phrases were reviewed on pages 14-15. They are included here for easy reference.

ACTIVITIES

1. Have students pair up and write a dialog of six sentences for each category on these two pages.
2. Bring in two toy phones and have students roleplay different phone conversations. Encourage students to incorporate as many of these phrases as possible, without confining themselves to this list entirely.

Haz un diálogo. Haz un diálogo. Haz un diálogo.

Haciendo amigos
Making friends

- **Hola, ¿qué tal?** *(Hello/Hi, what's up?)*
- **Buenos días.** *(Good morning/Hello.)*
- **Buenas tardes.** *(Good afternoon.)*
- **Buenas noches.** *(Good evening / Good night.)*

- **Me llamo..., ¿y tú?** *(My name is . . . What's yours?)*
- **¿Conoces a...?** *(Do you know . . .?)*
- **Te presento a...** *(Let me introduce you to . . .)*
- **Éste(a) es mi amigo(a)...** *(This is my friend . . .)*
- **Mucho gusto.** *(Nice to meet you.)*
- **Encantado(a).** *(Delighted.)*

- **Adiós.** *(Goodbye.)*
- **Chau.** *(Bye.)*
- **Hasta luego.** *(See you later.)*
- **Hasta mañana.** *(See you tomorrow.)*

Conociéndose mejor *Getting to know each other better*

- **¿De dónde eres?** *(Where are you from?)*
- **¿Dónde vives?** *(Where do you live?)*
- **¿Cuántos años tienes?** *(How old are you?)*
- **¿Cuándo es tu cumpleaños?** *(When's your birthday?)*
- **¿Cuál es tu... favorito(a)?** *(What's your favorite . . .?)*

- **¿Cómo estás?** *(How are you?) (familiar)*
- **¿Cómo está?** *(How are you?) (formal)*
- **Muy bien.** *(Very well.)*
- **Bien, gracias.** *(Fine, thanks.)*
- **Regular.** *(So-so.)*
- **Mal, estoy un poco cansado(a).** *(Not well, I'm a little tired.)*

34

Por teléfono *On the phone*

- **¿Puedo hablar con...?** *(May I speak with . . .?)*
- **Un momento, por favor.** *(One moment, please.)*
- **No está.** *(He/She is not in.)*

- **Dígale que me llame, por favor.** *(Tell him/her to call me, please.)*
- **Llama más tarde.** *(Call later.)*
- **¿Quieres dejar un mensaje?** *(Do you want to leave a message?)*
- **Va a volver pronto.** *(He/She will return soon.)*

- **Deja un mensaje en el contestador automático.** *(Leave a message on the answering machine.)*
- **Deja un mensaje después de la señal.** *(Leave a message after the beep.)*
- **Llámame.** *(Call me.)*

Haciendo planes *Making plans*

- **¿Te gustaría ir a patinar?** *(Would you like to go skating?)*
- **¿Vienes a mi fiesta?** *(Are you coming to my party?)*

- **Me encantaría.** *(I'd love to.)*
- **Sí, ¿a qué hora?** *(Yes, at what time?)*
- **¿Dónde nos encontramos?** *(Where shall we meet?)*

- **Lo siento, no puedo.** *(Sorry, I can't.)*
- **¡Qué lástima! Tengo otros planes.** *(What a shame! I have other plans.)*
- **Tal vez otro día.** *(Maybe another day.)*

- **¿Te gustaría ir conmigo?** *(Would you like to go with me?)*
- **¿Adónde te gustaría ir?** *(Where would you like to go?)*
- **¿Qué te gustaría hacer?** *(What would you like to do?)*
- **Me gustaría ir al cine.** *(I'd like to go to the movies.)*

Haz un diálogo. Haz un diálogo. Haz un diálogo. Haz un diálogo. Haz un diálogo.

The following words and phrases were frequently used as instructions in Level One and will be used again in this book. Review them with the students.

Los profesores dicen

Abran el libro en la página
Open your books to page . . .

¡Cierren los libros!
Close your books.

¡Digan/Escriban su nombre!
Say/Write your name.

¡Levanten la mano!
Raise your hand.

¡Saquen un lápiz!
Get a pencil.

¡Saquen un papel!
Get a paper.

¡Señalen la puerta!
Point to the door.

¡Escuchen la cinta!
Listen to the tape.

¡Miren la pizarra!
Look at the blackboard.

¡Pónganse de pie!
Get up.

¡Siéntense!
Sit down.

¡Hablen un poco más alto!
Speak a bit louder.

¡Vamos a hablar en español!
Let's speak Spanish.

Objective

- to talk to others, using common words and phrases

¿Dónde está?

These words and phrases were reviewed on pages 16-17. They are included here for easy reference.

En el restaurante

These words and phrases were reviewed on pages 8-9. They are included here for easy reference.

De compras

These words and phrases were not reviewed, so you may wish to go over them now.

En la escuela

These words and phrases were not reviewed, so you may wish to go over them now.

ACTIVITIES

1. Ask students individually where a room or an object is located within the school. Have them give you directions on how to get there using the phrases on this page.
2. Have students pair up and ask them to act out a scene using the phrases from one of these lists (*¿Dónde está?, En el restaurante,* etc.). Encourage them to use as many of the phrases as possible, without confining themselves to these pages entirely.

Haz un diálogo. Haz un diálogo. Haz un diálogo.

¿Dónde está...? *Where is...?*

- **Perdón, ¿dónde está la estación del metro?** *(Excuse me, where is the subway station?)*
- **Por favor, ¿puede decirme dónde está la salida?** *(Could you tell me where the exit is, please?)*
- **Busco la parada del autobús.** *(I'm looking for the bus stop.)*

- **Dobla a la derecha.** *(Turn right.)*
- **Dobla a la izquierda.** *(Turn left.)*
- **Sigue derecho por la calle...** *(Follow . . . Street.)*
- **Tienes que ir por...** *(You have to go through . . .)*
- **Está cerca de...** *(It's near . . .)*
- **Está al lado de...** *(It's next to . . .)*

- **Gracias.** *(Thank you.)*
- **De nada.** *(You're welcome.)*

En el restaurante *At the restaurant*

- **¿Tienes hambre/sed?** *(Are you hungry/thirsty?)*
- **Tengo mucha hambre/sed.** *(I'm very hungry/thirsty.)*
- **¿Qué vas a pedir?** *(What are you going to order?)*

- **¿Qué desean?** *(What would you like?)*
- **Quiero...** *(I'd like . . .)*
- **No quiero nada.** *(I don't want anything.)*
- **¿Qué quieres tomar?** *(What would you like to drink?)*
- **¿Quieres compartir un postre?** *(Would you like to share a dessert?)*
- **¿Algo más?** *(Anything else?)*
- **¿Es picante?** *(Is it spicy?)*
- **¡Buen provecho!** *(Enjoy your meal!)*

De compras *Shopping*

- **¿Qué desea?** *(What would you like?)*
- **¿En qué le puedo ayudar?** *(How can I help you?)*
- **¿Qué talla tiene(s)?** *(What size are you?)*
- **¿Qué número de zapato tiene(s)?** *(What (shoe) size are you?)*

- **Quiero devolver este suéter.** *(I'd like to return this sweater.)*
- **Quiero cambiar esta corbata.** *(I'd like to exchange this necktie.)*
- **¿Cuánto cuesta(n)?** *(How much does it/do they cost?)*
- **¿Cuánto es?** *(How much is it?)*
- **¿Qué precio tiene?** *(What's the price?)*

- **¿Aceptan tarjetas de crédito/cheques?** *(Do you take credit cards/checks?)*
- **Sólo aceptamos dinero en efectivo.** *(We only take cash.)*
- **Es una ganga.** *(It's a bargain.)*
- **Está en rebaja.** *(It's on sale.)*
- **No funciona.** *(It doesn't work.)*
- **Me queda pequeño/grande.** *(It's small/big on me.)*

En la escuela *At school*

- **¿Cuándo tienes clase de español?** *(When do you have your Spanish class?)*
- **Después.** *(Later.)*
- **Mañana.** *(Tomorrow.)*
- **Todos los días.** *(Every day.)*
- **Los lunes.** *(On Mondays.)*

- **¿Cuándo fue tu examen?** *(When was your exam?)*
- **Ayer.** *(Yesterday.)*
- **La semana pasada.** *(Last week.)*

- **¿Cómo fue tu examen?** *(How was your exam?)*
- **¡Chévere!** *(Great!)*
- **¡Genial!** *(Cool!)*
- **Muy bien, ¡qué suerte!** *(Very well, what good luck!)*
- **¡Qué rollo!** *(What a bore!)*
- **¡Fue fatal!** *(It was awful!)*
- **¡Fue horrible!** *(It was horrible!)*
- **¡Qué mala suerte!** *(What bad luck!)*
- **No fui; estaba enfermo.** *(I didn't go; I was ill.)*

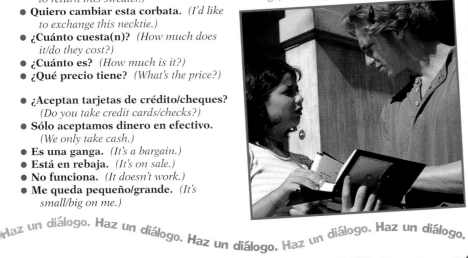

Haz un diálogo. Haz un diálogo. Haz un diálogo. Haz un diálogo. Haz un diálogo.

37

Objectives
- to use cardinal and ordinal numbers
- to discuss dates and seasons

ACTIVITIES

Los números

Números cardinales

1. To review numbers, lead the class in a game of *TENGO* (the Spanish version of BINGO). Have students draw a grid with 25 squares (5x5). At the top of each column they fill in the letters T, E, N, G, and O. They then fill in the 5 squares of column "T" with a random assortment of numbers 1 through 10. Column "E" they fill in with a random assortment of multiples of 10. Column "N" they fill in with multiples of 100, "G" with multiples of 1,000, and "O" with multiples of 1,000,000. (You can vary this, as long as the range of choice for the numbers they pick is no greater than 10.) Then call out numbers randomly from among the possible choices, and have students check off those numbers as they appear on their cards. The first person to get five checks in row (either horizontally, vertically, or diagonally) shouts *"TENGO!"*

2. List numbers by hundreds in a column on the board, and title two other columns *"aguacate"* and *"mariposa,"* or any other two masculine and feminine words. Then fill in the columns under *"aguacate"* and *"mariposa"* with either *"cien,"* *"cientos,"* or *"cientas,"* as students call them out.
Example:

numeros	aguacates	mariposas
100	cien	cien
200	doscientos	doscientas
300	trescientos	trescientas

etc.

3. Pretend that you and the class are trying to open a bicycle lock. Write a series of combinations (*10-25-13, 42-68-7,* etc.) on the board, and have the students write down the word for each number (*diez, veinticinco, trece,* etc.) The first student to finish writing down the words, raise his or her hand, and then successfully call them out wins a point. The first student to receive five points wins.

4. Find a list of the populations of different cities. Write them on the board, and have the students call them out. Then select a few students to go up and write the words out on the board, next to each corresponding number.
Example:

Cleveland	2,759,823	dos millones setecientos cincuenta y nueve mil ochocientos veintitrés
Tulsa	367,302	trescientos sesenta y siete mil trescientos dos

---

LOS NÚMEROS

NÚMEROS CARDINALES

0	cero	19	diecinueve	80	ochenta
1	uno (un, una)	20	veinte	90	noventa
2	dos	21	veintiuno (veintiún,	100	cien (ciento)
3	tres		veintiuna)	101	ciento uno(a)
4	cuatro	22	veintidós	102	ciento dos
5	cinco	23	veintitrés	200	doscientos(as)
6	seis	24	veinticuatro	300	trescientos(as)
7	siete	25	veinticinco	400	cuatrocientos(as)
8	ocho	26	veintiséis	500	quinientos(as)
9	nueve	27	veintisiete	600	seiscientos(as)
10	diez	28	veintiocho	700	setecientos(as)
11	once	29	veintinueve	800	ochocientos(as)
12	doce	30	treinta	900	novecientos(as)
13	trece	31	treinta y uno	1.000	mil
14	catorce	40	cuarenta	1.001	mil uno
15	quince	41	cuarenta y uno	2.000	dos mil
16	dieciséis	50	cincuenta	1.000.000	un millón (de)
17	diecisiete	60	sesenta	2.000.000	dos millones (de)
18	dieciocho	70	setenta		

Notas

- Uno becomes **un** before a masculine noun: **cuarenta y un libros.**
- Uno becomes **una** before a feminine noun: **cuarenta y una camisas.**
- **Cien** is used alone before nouns and before **mil**: **cien pesetas, cien mil pesetas.**
- **Ciento** is used before numbers under 100: **ciento treinta.**
- Numbers from 200 through 999 have a masculine and a feminine form:
  quinientos libros
  cuatrocientas faldas
- The word **y** is used only between the tens and the units in numbers above thirty: **ciento treinta y uno, doscientos cuarenta y dos**
  but: **trescientos uno.**

38

NÚMEROS ORDINALES

1°	primero (primer, primera)	4°	cuarto(a)	9°	noveno(a)
		5°	quinto(a)	10°	décimo(a)
2°	segundo(a)	6°	sexto(a)		
3°	tercero (tercer, tercera)	7°	séptimo(a)		
		8°	octavo(a)		

Notas

- Ordinal numbers are used only through *tenth;* beyond that, cardinal numbers are used: la **Quinta** Avenida, but el **siglo veintiuno**.
- **Primero** and **tercero** drop the final -o before a masculine singular noun: el primer día, el tercer mes.

LA FECHA

Las estaciones (Seasons)

el invierno	winter
la primavera	spring
el verano	summer
el otoño	fall

Los días de la semana (Days of the week)

lunes	Monday
martes	Tuesday
miércoles	Wednesday
jueves	Thursday
viernes	Friday
sábado	Saturday
domingo	Sunday

Los mese del año (Months of the year)

enero	January
febrero	February
marzo	March
abril	April
mayo	May
junio	June
julio	July
agosto	August
septiembre	September
octubre	October
noviembre	November
diciembre	December

Para hablar de la fecha (To talk about the date)

¿Cuál es la fecha de hoy (mañana)?
What is today's (tomorrow's) date?
Es el primero de octubre. *It is October first.*

September 2, 1786	1° de septiembre de 1786	(el dos de septiembre de mil setecientos ochenta y seis)
November 3, 1801	3 de noviembre de 1801	(el tres de noviembre de mil ochocientos uno)
December 8, 1997	8 de diciembre de 1997	(el ocho de diciembre de mil novecientos noventa y siete)
January 10, 2001	10 de enero de 2001	(el diez de enero de dos mil uno)

Números ordinales

1. Draw pictures on the board (or cut them out from magazines) of famous people running in a marathon. Draw or paste them so that there is clearly somebody in first place, second place, third, etc. Then ask the students to write down in which place each has finished.

2. Have students count off in ordinal numbers. Remind them that the eleventh student must switch to cardinal numbers. Any student that makes a mistake must sit behind the last student, so that he or she receives another turn. Continue until each student has given a correct response.

3. Draw a picture of a large store on the board. Place different objects on each floor. Ask students to tell you what each object is, and on which floor it is located.

La Fecha

1. Write a list of dates on the board, and have students call them out. Remind them that in Europe and most Spanish-speaking countries, the day comes before the month.
Example:
30/10/73 El treinta de octubre de mil novecientos setenta y tres.
3/3/75 El tres de marzo de mil novecientos setenta y cinco.

2. Ask students around the room what their favorite day of the week, month of the year, and season are, and why.
Extension: Have students conduct a poll to find out what the most popular responses are, and chart the results on the board.

3. Draw a calendar on the board with certain days of the week and dates (numbers) missing. Have students fill them in.

Tell your students...

In this unit we fly down to Costa Rica, a lush green country that's home to thousands of plant and animal species. Our exploration starts in the Juan Santamaría airport, where we check our surfboards and guitar through customs before driving into the capital (Chapter 1). Then we're off on a whole series of tropical adventures, traveling by bus through dripping jungles and tunneling through clouds along winding stream-crossed roads (Chapter 2). We go whitewater rafting, we climb mountains and volcanoes, we explore rain forests and coffee plantations, and we sing and surf with our Costa Rican friends every chance we get.

Before leaving Costa Rica, we visit a world-famous butterfly farm. Everywhere you look, there are explosions of color! Here we find out that ten percent of the known species of butterflies thrive in tiny Costa Rica. We're also reminded of how important they are to plants, carrying pollen from flower to flower. And speaking of flowers: after jamming with a reggae band on the Caribbean coast, we stop by one of Costa Rica's gorgeous orchid preserves to learn how to grow an orchid on a stand that looks as if it came from the heart of the rain forest. Is anything more beautiful than an orchid?

VIDEO LINKS

Text | **Corresponding Video Segments**

1. Introduction to Costa Rica

Unit Overview
Unit Opener

Costa Rica's natural wonders

2. Un viaje por avion

Chapter 1

Arriving in San José and making plans for the rest of the trip

Grammar: direct object pronouns

3. Excursiones y aventuras

Chapter 2

Rafting the rapids, climbing a volcano, hiking through a rain forest, and visiting a coffee plantation

Grammar: irregular -ar, -er, and -ir verbs

4. Adelante

Adelante

Visiting a butterfly farm; surfing and singing on the Caribbean coast

5. Manos a la obra

Manos a la obra

How to grow an orchid

CULTURAL BACKGROUND: FOR THE TEACHER

Geography and Climate

Costa Rica, with an area of 19,575 square miles (50,700 square kilometers), is the third smallest country in Central America after Belize and El Salvador. It is bordered by Nicaragua to the north, Panama to the south, the Caribbean Sea to the east, and the Pacific Ocean to the west. Most of the country's 3,000,000 inhabitants live on a fertile and temperate central plateau called Meseta Central, but there are mountains over 12,000 feet high (3, 650 meters) where temperatures drop below freezing, and the weather along the coasts can be hot and humid.

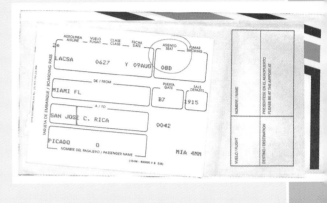

History and Government

The country was named *Costa Rica*—the Rich Coast—because settlers arriving from Spain in 1563 believed that gold jewelry worn by indigenous peoples indicated large deposits of precious metal in the area. This proved to be untrue, and settlers were deceived again when local Indians chose to flee rather than accept slavery.

Costa Rica became independent in 1821 and, after attempting a union with other Central American countries, became a sovereign state in 1838. A democracy almost exclusively since 1889, Costa Rica elects its president to a four-year term.

Remarkably peaceful and stable compared to some of its neighbors, Costa Rica has made a political goal of protecting and developing its natural beauty. Close to twenty percent of the country is national parkland, and its wildlife refuges and protected forests make it a haven not only for plants and animals but also for nature lovers from around the world.

National Flowers

For years Costa Rica has been well known for its coffee and bananas, and now the reputation of Costa Rican orchids is starting to blossom. The Guaria Morada orchid (Cattleya skinneri) is the national flower of this tiny country, which enjoys the largest variety of orchids in the world. Wild native orchids find idea! growing conditions in a landscape covered by dense broadleaf forests that include mahogany and tropical cedar trees. Imported varieties of orchids thrive in plant centers such as the Jardines Lankester and the Robert and Catherine Wilson Botanical Garden. Because Costa Rican orchids are as fragile as they are beautiful, the plants cannot be exported for commercial purposes. To enjoy these flowers, you have to go to Costa Rica in person. Every year more people do.

Costa Rica: el juego

GEOGRAPHY/GAME

Objective
- to play a game about the geography and other attractions of Costa Rica

Use
any time during Unit 1

Materials
- TRB Activity Support Page 1, *Costa Rica: el juego—preguntas* (questions)
- TRB Activity Support Page 2, *Costa Rica: el juego—respuestas* (answers)
- glue stick
- 3" x 5" index cards
- Transparency Unit 1, *Costa Rica* (map)
- overhead projector

Preparation
- Distribute the questions. Make a copy of the answers so you can monitor the game.
- Have students cut questions apart and glue each one on an index card.

Activity
- Project map transparency.
- Shuffle prepared index cards and place them face down on a table.
- Each student draws a card, reads it aloud, and answers the question. If the answer is incorrect, another player tries to answer the question.
- When all questions have been answered, turn off projector and have students ask the class questions from the information they have just heard. For example: *¿Cuál es la capital de Costa Rica?*

Gallo pinto

HANDS ON: COOKING

Objective
- to prepare and eat *gallo pinto,* a popular dish in Costa Rica

Use
any time during Unit 1

Ingredients
- 1 tbs. vegetable oil
- 1 clove crushed garlic
- 1/2 cup chopped onion
- 1/3 cup finely sliced red bell pepper
- 1/4 tsp. ground cumin
- 1 1/2 cups cooked rice
- salt and pepper to taste
- 1 10-oz. can black beans, drained
- Worcestershire sauce

Supplies
- strainer
- frying pan
- serving dish

Preparation
- Heat 1 tbs. oil in frying pan, add garlic and brown a little, then add onions. When onions are soft, add red bell pepper and cumin. Add rice and drained beans. Stir mixture.
- Serve with Worchestershire sauce on the side. Serves 6.

FYI
- Gallo pinto (literally, "spotted rooster," so called because of its speckled appearance) is served at breakfast, or as a snack. Usually made from last night's leftovers, it can be served with fried eggs, sour cream, cheese, and hot *tortillas*. You can spice it up by adding hot sauce. *Ticos* (Costa Ricans) on the Caribbean coast sometimes cook the beans in coconut milk instead of water.

Mariposas y orquídeas

GAME

Objective
- to play a matching game about the flora and fauna of Costa Rica

Use
any time during Unit 1

Materials
- Transparency Unit 1, *Flora y fauna de Costa Rica* (pictures)
- overhead projector
- TRB Activity Support Page 3, *Flora y fauna de Costa Rica* (pictures/descriptions)
- scissors

Activity
- Project transparency and discuss Costa Rican flora and fauna.
- Distribute Activity Support Page. Give students time to match descriptions to the pictures around the border.
- Have each student read one description aloud and match the animal or plant to its numbered picture.
- Go over any Spanish names that students have trouble understanding.

Variations
- After the activity, have each student cut out the picture he/she matched to a description. Collect pictures, shuffle, and redistribute. Have students find descriptions for their new pictures.
- Have students look up more information about Costa Rica and draw or write descriptions of other flora and fauna. Have them present their descriptions and colored drawings to the class.

¡Visiten Costa Rica!

SOCIAL STUDIES CONNECTION

Objective
- to design a travel brochure about Costa Rica

Use
any time during Unit 1

Materials
- Transparency Unit 1, *Costa Rica* (map)
- overhead projector
- reference books (atlas, almanac, encyclopedia, etc.)
- crayons, colored pencils, marking pens
- construction paper, posterboard
- glue sticks

Preparation
- Photocopy reproducible map that accompanies transparency and distribute. Also photocopy photos of Costa Rica and/or have students draw pictures of Costa Rica.
- Have students color the photocopies.

Activity
- Project map transparency
- Students work in pairs to create a travel brochure highlighting facts about Costa Rica. Ask them to stress specific information: flora and fauna, nature reserves, foods, volcanoes, sports, beaches, mountain climbing, camping, etc.
- Ask students to write text for their brochures in short phrases set off with bullets. Have them write on scrap paper first so errors can be corrected before brochures are executed.
- Students present brochures, explaining why they chose to feature one fact instead of others. Class votes on most effective brochure, most artistic brochure, etc. Display brochures.

Variations
- At the end of Chapter 2, have students rewrite brochures using formal *Ud.* and *Uds.* commands.
- Have students design T-shirts that advertise Costa Rica. Ask them to vote for the best design. Have winning T-shirt printed to raise funds for the Spanish Club or for an ecological group helping to preserve the natural beauties of Costa Rica.

COSTA RICA: EL JARDÍN DE LA PAZ

Unit Opener Goal
- to introduce Costa Rica and its ecological diversity

Related Components

Transparencies	Video : Tape/Book
Unit 1: Chapters 1-2	Unit 1: Seg. 1
Transparencies 7-18	

Scan to Unit 1

GETTING STARTED

Ask students to think about the name *Costa Rica*. What does the name imply?

Using the Video

Show Segment 1 of the Unit 1 video, an introduction to Costa Rica.

Using the Transparencies

To help orient students to Costa Rica, use the Locator Map Transparency. You may want to use other Unit 1 transparencies at this time.

DISCUSS

Presenting Costa Rica

For more information about Costa Rica, refer to pages 40A–40D.

Using the Text

English: After students have read the introduction, ask questions. For example:

What kind of plant and animal life would you expect to find in Costa Rica?
What role do national parks have in preserving them?
What image do you now have of the Costa Rican landscape?

Spanish: Ask students to scan the Spanish text for words they recognize. (They should recognize all but **paz.**)
Have them think of other words they associate with the theme, and adjectives to describe the photo.

UNIT COMPONENTS

Activity Book	Audio Book	Conexiones	Tutor Pages
p. 17-40	Script: p. 8-10; 14-16	Chapters 1-2	p. 7-14
Assessment		**Cuaderno**	**Video: Tape/Book**
Oral Proficiency: p. 21-22	Activities: p. 11-13; 17-19	p. 5-20	Unit 1: Segments 1-5
Listening Script: p. 9-10	**Audio**	**Magazine**	
Chapter Tests: p. 45-56	Chapter: 2A, 2B	Juntos en Costa Rica	
Portfolio: p. 33-34	Adelante: 3A, 3B	**Transparencies**	
	Assessment: 14A	Unit 1: Chapters 1-2	
	Conexiones: 16A	Transparencies 7-18	

F asten your seat belts! We're off to Costa Rica, a nation famous for the diversity of its plant and animal life. It is a nation committed to the preservation of its environment. About one-fifth of Costa Rica's land is devoted to national parks and wildlife preserves. It's also a great place for camping, river rafting, and hiking.

Costa Rica is a country of great ethnic diversity. People of European, Middle Eastern, African, and Asian descent, as well as the descendants of the early native populations, make Costa Rica their home. It is one of the few countries in the world without an army. No wonder this country is known as "El jardín de la paz," the garden of peace.

In this unit, you'll learn about Costa Rica's ecological diversity, visit a butterfly farm, and grow orchids. You'll even visit one of Costa Rica's many active volcanos. We're about to land. Get ready for a great adventure. ¡Bienvenidos a Costa Rica!

El Volcán Arenal, uno de los volcanes activos de Costa Rica.

41

ACTIVITIES

INTERDISCIPLINARY CONNECTIONS

To provide other perspectives, have students research questions like these:

Geography

If you were on the Costa Rican shores that face the sunrise, what body of water would you see? (Caribbean Sea)

Economics

Name ways in which the sea can be a resource to this country. (fishing, trade, travel, tourism, cuisine)

Communication

Transportation and tourism require fluency in other languages. What other careers do? Brainstorm a list. (Suggestions: the Peace Corps, U.S. State Department, teaching English as a foreign language, banking, library and information science, journalism and mass communication, health care, translating, interpreting)

Weather

How many seasons are there in Costa Rica? (There are two distinct seasons: a hot, dry season from December to May, and a rainy season from June to November.)

	Objetivos page 43 *Un viaje en avión*	Conversemos pages 44-45 *Un viaje en avión*	Realidades pages 46-47 *En el avión*	Palabras en acción pages 48-49 *En el aeropuerto internacion...*
Comunicación	To talk about: • preparing for a trip	Discuss making a reservation and other preparations for a trip	Read text, answer questions, discuss transportation preferences, survey class	Read cartoon, discuss people, places and things in an airport; create dialogs
	• what to do at the airport	Discuss important activities at the airport		Read cartoon, discuss things you have to do at an airline counter or the baggage claim area; make list; create dialogs
	• safety procedures on an airplane		Read text, answer questions, talk about safety procedures, make list	-
Cultura	To learn about: • the geographical location of Central American countries • the mural in the Juan Santamaría airport in Costa Rica			To learn about: • other words or expressions used by some Spanish speakers for people, places or things in an airport
Vocabulario temático	To know the expressions for: • important people and locations at an airport.	Talk about important people and locations at an airport		Read cartoon, make lists, discuss people at airport
	• items that you use on an airplane	Talk about items used on an airplane	Read text, answer questions, talk about safety procedures, make list	
	• making travel arrangements	Talk about activities related to travel arrangements		Discuss things you have to do at an airline counter or the baggage claim area; make list
Estructura	To talk about: • items that you use and need: direct object pronouns	-	Read text, use direct object pronouns to answer questions, make list	Read cartoon, make list; discuss people at airport
	• travel plans and preferences: the verbs *pensar, querer,* and *preferir*	Discuss making a ticket reservation	Read text, answer questions, discuss transportation preferences, survey class	Read cartoon, call travel agent to buy ticket

Para comunicarnos mejor (1) pages 50-51 *¿Lo tienes tú?*	Para comunicarnos mejor (2) pages 52-53 *¿Qué asiento prefieres?*	Situaciones pages 54-55 *¡Vamos de viaje!*	Para resolver pages 56-57 *Aerolíneas Caribe*	Entérate page 58 *El mural del aeropuerto Juan Santamaría*
Discuss getting ready for trip; talk about who helps during a trip; make list	Talk about travel-related problems; ask about vacation plans; make table of class travel preferences	Role-play ticket sale; discuss future travel plans and report to class; write diary	Discuss, plan, and design an airline ad	Discuss the meaning of the scenes in the mural
Discuss what must be done before, during and after taking a trip; make list	Talk about travel-related problems	Roleplay ticket sale to Costa Rica	Describe an imaginary airline; discuss its advantages	Discuss the history of Costa Rica
	Talk about travel-related problems	Create travel itinerary to Central America		
			Domestic airlines in Spanish-speaking countries of Latin America	
Talk about who helps at the airport	Talk about travel-related problems			
Talk about who helps on the plane	Talk about vacation plans	**Re-entry of vocabulary**		**Extension of vocabulary**
Discuss who helps when you land	Talk about class travel preferences			
Illustrate use of direct object pronouns: *lo, la, los, las*	Talk about travel-related plans using *¿como viajar? ¿por dónde? ¿para hacer qué?*			
	Use all present tense forms of *pensar, querer,* and *preferir.*	**Re-entry of structure**		**Extension of structure**

1 UN VIAJE EN AVIÓN
ACTIVIDADES OPCIONALES DE VOCABULARIO Y ESTRUCTURA

Aeropalabras

GAME

Objective
- to play a memory game, using Chapter 1 *Vocabulario temático*

Use
after *Palabras en acción,* pages 48-49

Materials
- TRB Activity Support Page 4, *Ruleta* (spinner)

Preparation
- Fill in spinner sections with the six categories used in the *Vocabulario temático,* omitting the *Expresiones y palabras* category.

Activity
- Select a scorekeeper.
- Divide class into four groups, and have each group choose a writer.
- Spin the spinner and announce the category.
- Groups have three minutes to write down all the Spanish words they can think of that fit the category. For example, if the category is **En el aeropuerto**, a group might generate the following list: *la aduana, el control de seguridad, restaurantes, la puerta de embarque, la terminal de equipaje, los empleados de las aerolíneas,* etc. Words cannot be repeated from category to category.
- When the time is up, groups take turns reading their lists one word at a time. Groups that have the same word cross it from their lists.
- When a category is exhausted, a tally is taken. The team with the largest number of unique words wins the round and spins for next category.
- Play until all six categories have been used.

Vuelo de primera clase

WRITING CONNECTION

Objective
- to write skits about air travel, using Chapter 1 *Vocabulario temáticio*

Use
after *Palabras en acción,* pages 48-49

Materials
- sentence-strip rolls or posterboard
- thick marking pens
- masking tape
- student-prepared props

Activity
- Have students turn the classroom into an airport and the interior of an airplane. Airport: Students make a *llegadas* and *salidas* board and fill it in with flight numbers and times for airlines flying to cities in the Caribbean, in Central America, and in South America. Airplane: Students set up chairs in rows with aisles and make signs such as *salida de emergencia, prohibido fumar, abróchense los cinturones,* etc.
- Have students roleplay passengers, airport workers, and in-flight personnel. Select groups of three or four to work as *auxiliares de vuelo, piloto, co-piloto, agente de aduana, agente de migración, maletero,* and *pasajeros.* Characters wear identifying badges that also tell their made-up ages and destinations.
- Each group writes a ten-line skit about preparing to fly, the time of the flight, and what happens during the landing. Groups must use three of the lesson verbs (*aterrizar, despegar, pensar, preferir, querer,* and *volver*), two formal imperatives for *Ud.,* and other Chapter 1 vocabulary.
- Present all skits on the same day, so the airport and the airplane interior only have to be simulated once. Videotape if possible.

Bárbara lo pide

GAME

Objective
- to talk about things we want for a trip, using direct object pronouns

Use
after *Para comunicarnos mejor,* pages 50-51

Activity
- Divide the class into three groups. The *antes* group generates a list of things it wants to do before the trip, the *durante* group a list of things to do during the trip, and the *después* group a list of things to do after the trip.
- Groups have ten minutes to generate their lists.
- When time is up, a member of the group that plays first says one thing that he/she wants to do. For example, an *antes* player says: *Quiero comprar un billete de avión.* To continue, a *durante* player must change the sentence to the third person and replace the noun with a direct object pronoun. For example: *Allen quiere comprar un billete de avión; quiere comprarlo.* If the *durante* player is correct, another *durante* player makes a sentence: *Durante el vuelo, pido una manta.* Someone from the *después* group would say: *Durante el vuelo, Barbara pide una manta. Barbara lo pide.* If the *después* player is correct, another *después* player makes a sentence: *Después del vuelo, yo busco un taxi.* Someone from the *antes* group would say: *Después del vuelo, Keith busca un taxi. Keith lo busca.*
- Play continues until a group is stumped. The two remaining groups continue until one group cannot think of a reply. The last group wins.
- No repeated sentences, please.

Variations
- Fill a folder with trip photos and have students take them out one by one, using direct object pronouns for people and things in the pictures.

¿Qué quieres decir?

WRITING CONNECTION

Objective
- to write original sentences, using stem-changing verbs

Use
after *Para comunicarnos mejor,* pages 52-53

Materials
- TRB Activity Support Page 4, *Ruleta* (spinner)

Preparation
- Copy spinner and show class how to use it.

Activity
- Write the subject pronouns on the board and number them: 1) *yo* 2) *tú* 3) *él/ella/Ud.* 4) *nosotros/as* 5) *vosotros/as* 6) *ellos/ellas/Uds.*
- Also write and number the three stem-changing verbs given in the chapter (*querer, preferir, pensar*) plus any three of the following: *cerrar* (to close), *comenzar* (to begin), *despertar* (to wake up), *defender* (to defend), *empezar, negar* (to deny), *perder* (to lose). For example: 1) *pensar* 2) *querer* 3) *preferir* 4) *cerrar* 5) *empezar* 6) *perder.*
- Players come to the front of the classroom and spin the spinner twice; the first number spun is for the subject pronoun, the second number is for the verb.
- Then students make sentences from the words they've spun. For example, John spins a 2 for the subject pronoun *tú* and a 2 for the verb *querer.* He makes the following sentence: *Tú quieres ir a Costa Rica para ver el Volcán Poás, ¿no?* John receives 16 points, 4 for the total of the numbers spun (2+2) and 1 point for each word in the sentence (12).
- Students play until they can make sentences easily.
- Tally points and announce the winner(s).

Variations
- Use the spinner a third time, assigning to the sections time phrases such as: 1) *ayer* 2) *cada dos días* 3) *la semana pasada* 4) *hoy* 5) *esta noche* 6) *todos los días,* etc., so that students can choose between present and preterite tenses.

UN VIAJE EN AVIÓN

Introduce the chapter and its theme by asking students if they have ever traveled on an airplane.

Related Components

Audio Conexiones: 16A	**Video: Tape/Book** Unit 1: Seg. 2
Conexiones Chapter 1	

Scan to Unit 1

GETTING STARTED

Have students look at the photograph. Ask whether they have ever taken an airplane to another country. Ask questions.
Suggestions:
¿Te gustaría volar a Costa Rica? ¿Por qué?

Critical Thinking

Use the following activity to help students discover for themselves what they would need to know in order to take a trip to another country.

Un viaje a otro país
Tell students to think about things they would need to do or take with them if they went to a tropical country. Then assign these activities to groups:

• make a list of things you would take to this country (e.g., which clothes)
• make a list of things you would have to buy and request before flying there (e.g., buy an airline ticket, get a visa)
• make a checklist of things you should do at home before taking a trip (e.g., stop the mail)
• list the things you would see inside an airplane
• list the things you would see and do in an airport

Have each group write its list on the board. Have the class discuss the lists and decide which items from each list are the most essential.
Have each group submit a revised list.
When you finish the chapter, have the class review the lists to see how they compare to what they learned in the chapter.

CAPÍTULO 1

UN VIAJE EN AVIÓN

Aeropuerto Juan Santamaria, en Costa Rica.

42

CHAPTER COMPONENTS

Activity Book p. 17-26	**Audio Book** Script: p. 8-10 Activities: p. 11-13	**Conexiones** Chapter 1	**Transparencies** Chapter 1 Transparencies 7-12

Assessment
Oral Proficiency:
  p. 21
Listening Script: p. 9
Chapter Test:
  p. 45-50
	Audio
	Chapter: 2A
	Assessment: 14A
	Conexiones: 16A
		Cuaderno
		p. 5-12
		Magazine
		Juntos en Costa Rica
			Tutor Pages
			p. 7-10
			Video: Tape/Book
			Unit 1: Seg. 2

Objetivos

COMUNICACIÓN

To talk about:
- preparing for a trip
- what to do at the airport
- safety procedures on an airplane

CULTURA

To learn about:
- the geographic location of Central American countries
- the mural in the Juan Santamaría airport in Costa Rica

VOCABULARIO TEMÁTICO

To know the expressions for:
- important people and locations at an airport
- items that you use on an airplane
- making travel arrangements

ESTRUCTURA

To talk about:
- items that you use and need: direct object pronouns
- travel plans and preferences: the verbs *pensar, querer,* and *preferir*

¿SABES QUE...?

To travel outside the United States, you must have a current passport. Some countries, including Nicaragua and Honduras, require a visa. If you wish to travel to Costa Rica or El Salvador, you must obtain a Tourist Card in the United States before boarding the plane. To travel to the Dominican Republic, you need to obtain a Tourist Card in the airport in Santo Domingo as soon as you land.

Keep in mind that requirements change frequently, so be sure to check with the consulate of the country of your destination when you make plans. *¡Buen viaje!*

43

Here are some additional activities that you may wish to use as you work through this chapter with your students.

Communication

Encourage class and after-class activities that may enhance student interest and proficiency. Some ideas:
- have students request a copy of an airline safety brochure in Spanish and use it to identify parts of the plane and safety measures
- have students ask each other if they have everything they need for class before starting the lesson

Culture

To encourage greater understanding:
- ask students to search for eco-tour information from a tourism office or travel agency
- have them read about Costa Rica in magazines such as *National Geographic*
- show the video that accompanies Unit 1 of this textbook

Vocabulary

To reinforce vocabulary, have students:
- use appropriate vocabulary from this chapter to refer to other forms of transportation
- print signs one might see in an airport in a Spanish-speaking country, and display these in the classroom

Structure

To reinforce the use of direct object pronouns, and the verbs **pensar, querer,** and **preferir:**
- have students identify direct object pronouns in simple Spanish texts
- ask for students' opinions as often as possible

Thinking About Language

After students have finished their list for the previous activity, have them brainstorm cognates. Do they know any travel or tourism words in other languages? Ask students to write them on the board.

Communicative Objective
• to talk about what you do before and during a plane trip

Related Components

Activity Book p. 17	**Cuaderno** p. 5
Audio Book Script: Seg. 1	**Transparencies** Ch. 1: Conversemos Transparency 8
Audio Chapter: 2A, Seg. 1	

☐ GETTING STARTED

Ask students to think of things they might need to say to a flight attendant. Can they think of ways to say them in Spanish?

☐ ACTIVITIES

These activities give students an opportunity to begin communicating with each other and with you, focusing on the theme and objectives of the chapter. The activities can be used as oral class activities, or, if you prefer, you can pair students to achieve more interaction.

¿Qué haces antes de viajar?
Class activity to introduce things one does before traveling. Use gestures and drawings to explain the meaning of each expression.
Have students decide in which order these actions would be done by asking such questions as: *¿Hablo con el/la agente de viajes antes o después de comprar el pasaje?* Say the verbs in random order and ask students to follow them with the appropriate word(s): *sacar (la visa).*

Cuando reservas el pasaje, ¿qué dices?
Class activity to learn how to make plane reservations. Ask students where they would like to go on a trip. Ask questions that would elicit the statements. Example: *¿Necesitas un pasaje de ida y vuelta? ¿Quieres un pasaje con descuento para estudiantes?*

CONVERSEMOS
UN VIAJE EN AVIÓN

Habla con tu compañero(a).

¿QUÉ HACES ANTES DE VIAJAR?

Compro el pasaje.

☐ hablar con el/la agente de viajes
☐ comparar precios y horarios
☐ sacar el pasaporte y la visa
☐ comprar el pasaje
☐ hacer las maletas

CUANDO RESERVAS EL PASAJE, ¿QUÉ DICES?

☐ Necesito un pasaje de ida a...
   (*I need a one-way ticket to . . .*)
☐ Quiero un pasaje de ida y vuelta a...
   (*I want a round-trip ticket to . . .*)
☐ ¿Tiene pasajes con descuento para estudiantes?
   (*Do you have discount tickets for students?*)

☐ Quiero un asiento de ventanilla/de pasillo.
   (*I would like a window/aisle seat.*)
☐ Quiero salir el... y volver el...
   (*I want to leave on . . . and come back on . . .*)
☐ Prefiero un vuelo sin escala.
   (*I prefer a nonstop flight.*)

44

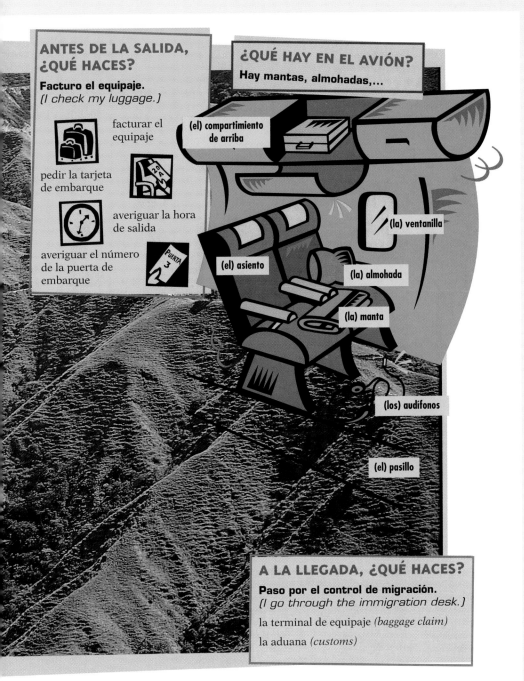

ANTES DE LA SALIDA, ¿QUÉ HACES?

Facturo el equipaje.
(I check my luggage.)

facturar el equipaje

pedir la tarjeta de embarque

averiguar la hora de salida

averiguar el número de la puerta de embarque

¿QUÉ HAY EN EL AVIÓN?

Hay mantas, almohadas,...

(el) compartimiento de arriba

(la) ventanilla

(el) asiento

(la) almohada

(la) manta

(los) audífonos

(el) pasillo

A LA LLEGADA, ¿QUÉ HACES?

Paso por el control de migración.
(I go through the immigration desk.)

la terminal de equipaje *(baggage claim)*

la aduana *(customs)*

Antes de la salida, ¿qué haces?
Class activity to introduce things one does in the airport before getting on the plane. Ask the title question. Model the phrases in sentences while performing each action.

¿Qué hay en el avión?
Class activity to teach vocabulary about places and things on a plane. Read aloud the title question. Have volunteers read aloud the words and identify them. Have pairs make index cards with these words and perform an action they associate with each one.

A la llegada, ¿qué haces?
Class activity to teach the parts of an airport and **pasar por.** Present them by modeling each phrase and performing the activity.

CHECK

- *¿Qué haces antes de subir al avión?*
- *¿Prefieres un asiento de ventanilla o de pasillo?*
- *¿Por dónde tienes que pasar al entrar a un aeropuerto?*

LOG BOOK

Have students write down the phrases or words in this spread that they find most useful.

45

Communicative Objectives
- to talk about airplane safety instructions
- to talk about how you prefer to travel

Related Components

Activity Book p. 18	**Cuaderno** p. 6
Audio Book Script: Seg. 2	**Transparencies** Ch. 1: Realidades Transparency 9
Audio Chapter: 2A, Seg. 2	

GETTING STARTED

Ask students to imagine they are on a plane. Perform the role of the flight attendant before the plane takes off, and explain the *medidas de seguridad*.

DISCUSS

Talk about the airplane safety brochure, and ask questions. Suggestions:

En el avión
¿A quiénes les gusta viajar en avión?
¿Qué medidas de seguridad conocen?

Antes de despegar y de aterrizar
Cuando el avión sale de un aeropuerto, despega. Cuando llega a un aeropuerto, aterriza. La palabra aterrizar *viene de la palabra* tierra, *"earth" o "land".*
¿"Despegar" es ir para arriba o ir para abajo?
¿Y qué es "aterrizar"?
¿Qué tienen que hacer con los cinturones antes de despegar?
¿Dónde tienen que poner el bolso de mano?

You may wish to discuss the reasons for each of these procedures to ensure that students understand what is happening.

En caso de emergencia
¿Qué palabra en inglés es como emergencia?
¿Qué tienen que hacer cuando hay una emergencia?
¿Para qué deportes usamos un chaleco salvavidas?

You may wish to discuss the kinds of emergencies that might take place (e.g., loss of air pressure in the cabin can lead to a shortage of oxygen).

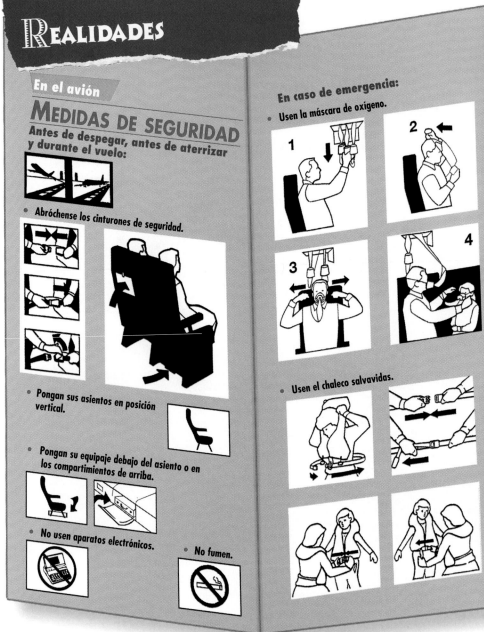

REALIDADES

En el avión

MEDIDAS DE SEGURIDAD
Antes de despegar, antes de aterrizar y durante el vuelo:

- Abróchense los cinturones de seguridad.
- Pongan sus asientos en posición vertical.
- Pongan su equipaje debajo del asiento o en los compartimientos de arriba.
- No usen aparatos electrónicos.

En caso de emergencia:
- Usen la máscara de oxígeno.
- Usen el chaleco salvavidas.
- No fumen.

46

Usen las salidas de emergencia.

HABLA DEL FOLLETO

A. Mira las medidas de seguridad. Haz una lista de las cosas que hay en el avión para la seguridad de los pasajeros.

Los cinturones de seguridad,...

B. ¿Qué dicen las medidas de seguridad?

- *Abróchense los cinturones.*
- *Usen el chaleco salvavidas.*

C. Ahora tú eres el/la auxiliar de vuelo. ¿Qué dices a los pasajeros antes de despegar, de aterrizar o en caso de emergencia? Practica con dos compañeros. Ellos deben hacer lo que tú les dices.

Señoras y señores, vamos a despegar. Pongan sus asientos en posición vertical.

¿QUÉ OPINAS?

Pregunta a cinco compañeros(as): ¿Cómo prefieres viajar: en coche, en tren, en avión, en moto o en bicicleta? ¿Por qué? Haz una tabla y anota los resultados de la encuesta. Usa el modelo.

	Avión	Tren	Coche	Moto	Bicicleta
es más rápido	✓✓✓				
es más cómodo	✓✓		✓✓		
es más barato					✓
es menos peligroso		✓			
quiero hacer ejercicio					✓✓✓
tiene cafetería		✓✓			
conozco mejor el país				✓	

Presenta los resultados a la clase.

Muchos chicos(as) de la clase prefieren viajar en avión porque es más rápido y más cómodo. Otros chicos prefieren viajar en bicicleta porque quieren hacer ejercicio.

47

Habla del folleto

Individual and Group Activities: Summarizing

A. Make a list of objects on an airplane that exist for the safety of the passengers.
Answers:
los cinturones de seguridad, la máscara de oxígeno, el chaleco salvavidas, las salidas de emergencia

B. Write what the safety measures state.
Answers:
Las medidas dicen:
Abróchense los cinturones de seguridad.
Usen el chaleco salvavidas.
Pongan sus asientos en posición vertical.
Pongan su equipaje debajo del asiento o en los compartimientos de arriba.
No usen aparatos electrónicos.
No fumen.

C. You are the flight attendant. What do you say to passengers before taking off, before landing, or during an emergency? Instruct two classmates.
Answers: See model on student page.

¿Qué opinas?

Individual and Group Activity: Taking a Poll

1. Pick one of these: car, train, bicycle, plane, or motorscooter. Write a sentence about why you prefer to travel that way.

2. Compare your answers with those of five classmates, and make a chart like the one in the model. Write a paragraph about the results of your group poll.

Extension: Compare your preferences with those of the other groups. Discuss.

Extension: Poll the class to find out how many have traveled by airplane at least once and how many have flown in the past twelve months.

CHECK

- *¿Qué opinas? ¿Cuál de las medidas de seguridad es la más importante?*
- *¿Dónde debes poner tu equipaje?*
- *En una emergencia, ¿cómo debes salir del avión?*
- *¿Cómo prefieres viajar?*

LOG BOOK

Have students list all of the **Ud.** commands from *Realidades*.

Communicative Objective
• to talk about people, places, and things in an airport

Related Components

Activity Book p. 19-20	Transparencies Ch. 1: Palabras en acción Transparency 10
Cuaderno p. 7-8	Tutor Page p. 7

GETTING STARTED

Ask if any students have traveled to another country. Have them talk about what they had to do after they landed.

DISCUSS

Comment on and ask questions about what the people in the drawing are doing. For example:
¿En qué aeropuerto estamos?
¿A quiénes vemos aquí?
¿Qué hacen las personas que están en el control de migración?

Para hispanohablantes

If you use other words or expressions for some of the ones introduced in this chapter, share them with the class. A few variations:
aterrizar: tomar tierra
los auriculares: los audífonos
el/la auxiliar: la azafata, el/la camarero/a, el/la aeromozo/a
facturar: chequear
la manta: la frisa, la colcha, la cobija
la migración: la inmigración
el pasaje: el boleto
el/la pasajero/a: el/la viajero/a
la reserva: la reservación
la salida de emergencia: la puerta de emergencia

PALABRAS EN ACCIÓN
EN EL AEROPUERTO INTERNACIONAL

1 **¿Qué ves en el dibujo?**

Haz tres listas: una de los lugares que ves en el dibujo, otra de las personas y otra de las cosas.

> Lugares: la terminal de equipaje,...
> Personas: el maletero,...
> Cosas: la tabla de surf,...

2 **Actividades en el aeropuerto**

Con tu compañero(a), hablen de lo que están haciendo las personas del dibujo.

— ¿Qué está haciendo el agente de migración?
— Está mirando el pasaporte del chico.

3 **¿Quién habla?**

Haz tres preguntas. Tu compañero(a) tiene que adivinar quién habla.

— ¿Puedo ver su pasaporte?
— ¡El agente de migración!

4 **¿Qué tienes que hacer?**

Haz una lista de lo que tienes que hacer en el mostrador de la aerolínea.

> Tengo que averiguar el número de la puerta de embarque,...

48

For students having difficulty talking about people, places, things, or activities in an airport, you might consider:
• **The tutor page:** Pair the student with a native speaker or a more able student, using the tutor page.
Optional activity: See page 42C: *Aeropalabras*

5 Llegada y salida de vuelos

Mira el cartel de llegadas y salidas. Tú eres el/la pasajero(a) y tu compañero(a) es el/la empleado(a) de la aerolínea. Pregúntale sobre el horario de los vuelos.

— Perdón, ¿a qué hora llega el vuelo número 51 de Managua?
— A las 3:00 p.m.

6 Miniteatro

Escoge un lugar del aeropuerto y haz un diálogo con tu compañero(a). Representen el diálogo.

— Buenos días. ¿Puedo ver su pasaporte?
— Un momento, por favor. Lo tengo en la mochila. Aquí lo tiene.

7 Un viaje en avión

Tú eres un(a) pasajero(a) que quiere viajar a otro país y tu compañero(a) es el/la agente de viajes.

— Necesito un pasaje de ida y vuelta a...
— ¿Cuándo quiere salir?
— Quiero salir el... y volver el...

8 Tú eres el autor

Estás en la terminal de equipaje y tus maletas no llegan. Haz un diálogo con tu compañero(a). Incluye:

- tu nombre
- tu número de vuelo y de dónde salió
- cómo son las maletas
- qué llevas en ellas

49

ACTIVITIES

1. Individual Activity
Make lists of the places, people, and things in the drawing.

2. Pair Activity
Ask your partner what the people in the drawing are doing. Answer your partner's questions.

3. Individual or Pair Activity
Ask three questions. Your partner should say which person is speaking.
Extension: Answer the questions as if you were the person being asked.

4. Individual Activity
Make a list of the things you have to do at an airline counter.
Extension: Ask if your partner did all the things in your list. For example:
¿Averiguaste el número de la puerta de embarque?

5. Pair Activity
You are a passenger and your partner is an airline employee. Ask about the flights listed on the information board.
Extension: Write complete sentences about each of the flights. Example:
El vuelo número 233 de Guatemala llega a las cuatro y media.

6. Roleplay Activity
Choose a place in the airport. With your partner, create and perform a dialog that takes place there.
Extension: Exchange and perform other pairs' dialogs.

7. Pair Activity
You want to travel to another country. Discuss your trip with your partner, the travel agent.
Extension: Write down everything the travel agent tells you. Write some sentences about your travel schedule.

8. Synthesizing Activity
You are in the baggage claim area, but your luggage is not. Write a dialog between you and your partner, an airline employee. Include:

- your name
- your flight number and point of departure
- what the luggage looks like
- what's in the luggage

CHECK

- ¿Qué dices cuando tu amigo llega a tu ciudad?
- ¿Quién puede ayudarte con tu equipaje?
- ¿En qué lugar del aeropuerto abren las maletas de los pasajeros?

PORTFOLIO
Have students tape their dialogs and include them in their Portfolios.

Communicative Objective

- to talk about people or things, using direct object pronouns

Related Components

Activity Book p. 21-22	**Audio** Chapter: 2A, Seg. 3
Audio Book Script: Seg. 3 Activities: p. 11	**Cuaderno** p. 9
	Tutor Page p. 8

GETTING STARTED

Remind students about direct object pronouns by asking about common items. Example: *Uds. deben tener bolígrafos. ¿Los tienen?*

Language in Context

Direct Object Pronouns

Emphasize the reason for using direct object pronouns by speaking about something in English and repeating the same noun over and over. Demonstrate the same thing in Spanish.

Explain that when you use direct object pronouns to talk about people, **lo** and **la** mean *him* and *her,* and **los** and **las** mean *them.* Point to one student and ask another:

Q: *Laura, ¿lo conoces?*
A: *Sí, lo conozco.*

Placing Direct Object Pronouns

Show that direct object pronouns can be placed in more than one location and still have the same meaning. Example:
Ana, ¿me vas a llamar? ¿Vas a llamarme?

DISCUSS

Review vocabulary from *Saludos* and introduce some of this chapter's vocabulary with questions and statements that incorporate direct object pronouns.
Allí está Juán. ¿Lo viste?
Venden los pasajes en la agencia. ¿Los vas a comprar?
Necesito la maleta. ¿La tienes aquí?
Mis amigas vienen a estudiar. ¿Las conoces?

PARA COMUNICARNOS MEJOR
¿LO TIENES TÚ?

To refer to people and things, use direct object pronouns.

☐ To refer to *him, her, it, you* and *them,* use the direct object pronouns *lo, la, los* and *las.*

— ¿Tienes el pasaporte?	Do you have the passport?
— Sí, lo tengo.	Yes, I have it.

☐ Direct object pronouns must be the same gender and number as the nouns they replace. They usually come before the conjugated verb.

— ¿Ves a las auxiliares de vuelo?	Do you see the flight attendants?
— Sí, las veo.	Yes, I see them.

☐ Sometimes *lo* refers to a complete statement or general idea.

— ¿Para ir a Nicaragua necesitamos una visa?	Do we need a visa to go to Nicaragua?
— No lo sé.	I don't know about that.

☐ To refer to *me, you,* and *us,* use the direct object pronouns *me, te,* and *nos.*

— ¿Me ayudas?	Could you help me?
— Claro que te ayudo.	Of course I'll help you.

Here are all the direct object pronouns.

direct object pronouns

me *me*	**nos** *us*
te *you (informal)*	**os** *you (informal, pl., in Spain)*
lo *him, it, you (formal, masc.)*	**los** *them (masc.), you (masc., pl.)*
la *her, it, you (formal, fem.)*	**las** *them (fem.), you (fem., pl.)*

☐ When the conjugated verb is followed by an infinitive, or by a preposition and an infinitive, as in *voy a comprar*, the direct object pronoun may either come before the conjugated verb or be attached to the end of the infinitive:

— ¿Quieres hacer una reservación?	Do you want to make a reservation?
— Sí, la quiero hacer. (Sí, quiero hacerla.)	Yes, I want to make it.
— ¿Vas a comprar los pasajes?	Are you going to buy the tickets?
— Sí, voy a comprarlos ahora. (Sí, los voy a comprar ahora.)	Yes, I am going to buy them now.

50

For students having difficulty communicating with direct object pronouns, you might consider:

- **The tutor page:** Pair the student with a native speaker or a more able student, using the tutor page.

Optional activity: See page 42D: *Bárbara lo pide*

1 De viaje

Tú y tu compañero(a) van a salir para el aeropuerto en unos minutos. Pregúntale si tiene todo lo que necesita.

— ¿Tienes el pasaporte?
— Sí, lo tengo aquí.
   (No, no lo tengo.)

1. 2. 3. 4. 5. 6.

2 Vuelos internacionales

¿Quién los ayuda? Pregunta a tu compañero(a).

— En el avión, ¿quién te ayuda a poner el bolso en el compartimiento de arriba?
— La auxiliar de vuelo me ayuda.

1. a ti
2. a mi hermano y a mí
3. a los pasajeros
4. a ustedes
5. a los estudiantes
6. y a él, ¿quién lo ayuda?

Nadie lo ayuda.

¿Quién ayuda a...?

- poner el bolso en el compartimiento de arriba
- llevar el equipaje
- facturar la maleta
- hacer una reservación en un hotel
- buscar un taxi
- averiguar la hora de salida

3 Un viaje en avión

A. En grupo, preparen una lista de lo que tienen que hacer antes, durante y después de un vuelo, y anoten quién va a hacer cada cosa.

B. Hablen sobre los resultados.

— ¿Quién va a comprar los pasajes?
— Toni y yo vamos a comprarlos.
— ¿Quién va a facturar las maletas?
— Ana y Lola las van a facturar.

¿Quién va a...?

Antes
- comprar los pasajes: Toni y yo
- facturar las maletas: Ana y Lola

Durante
- poner los bolsos en el compartimiento de arriba: Luis
- pedir las mantas: Ana

Después
- buscar un taxi: Lola y yo
- buscar las maletas: Ana

51

---

3. ¿Tienes el bolso de mano?
   Sí, lo tengo.(No, no lo tengo.)
4. ¿Tienes el mapa de Costa Rica?
   Sí, lo tengo.(No, no lo tengo.)
5. ¿Tienes los pasajes?
   Sí, los tengo.(No, no los tengo.)
6. ¿Tienes la cámara?
   Sí, la tengo.(No, no la tengo.)

Extension: Say that you see something (lo veo), what color it is, the size, and any other characteristics. After each statement, your partner guesses what you see.

2. Pair Activity
Ask your partner who helps various people at the airport.
Possible Answers:
1. See model on student page.
2. ¿Quién nos ayuda a llevar el equipaje?
   El maletero los ayuda.
3. ¿Quién los ayuda a facturar la maleta?
   El/La empleado/a de la aerolínea los ayuda.
4. ¿Quién los ayuda a hacer una reservación de hotel?
   El/La agente de viajes nos ayuda.
5. ¿Quién los ayuda a buscar un taxi?
   El empleado de la aerolínea los ayuda.
6. ¿Quién lo ayuda a averiguar la hora de salida?
   El empleado de la aerolínea lo ayuda.

Extension: Say who helps you do other activities, such as study or clean up.

3. Group Activity
A. Make a list of what you have to do before, during, and after a flight. Write down who is going to do each task.
B. Talk about the results.
Answers: See models on student page.
Extension: Ask if your partner already did each of the activities on the list.

CHECK

- ¿Tienes la maleta?
- ¿Quién te ayuda con la tarea?
- ¿Me vas a llamar?
- ¿Cuándo vas a comprar el pasaje?

LOG BOOK
Have students write a dialog in which they prepare for a plane trip abroad.

ACTIVITIES

Students use direct object pronouns to talk about taking a trip.

1. Pair Activity
You and your partner are about to leave for the airport. Ask if your partner has everything.
Possible Answers:
1. See model on student page.
2. ¿Tienes las dos maletas?
   Sí, las tengo aquí. (No, no las tengo.)

Para hispanohablantes

Tell the class who helps who do chores around your house. Use several direct object pronouns.

Communicative Objectives
• to talk about plans, using **pensar**
• to say what you want, using **querer**
• to say what you prefer, using **preferir**

Related Components

Activity Book p. 23-24	**Cuaderno** p. 10
Audio Book Script: Seg.4 Activities: p. 12	**Transparencies** Ch. 1: Para comunicarnos mejor
Audio Chapter: 2A, Seg. 4	Transparency 11
	Tutor Page p. 9

GETTING STARTED

Ask students to discuss differences in the meanings of these phrases:
I want to go to the movies on Monday.
I prefer to go to the movies on Monday.
I plan to go to the movies on Monday.

Language in Context

Querer and *Preferir*
Review **querer** and **preferir** by talking about situations in the classroom:
¿Quieres ayudarme?
¿Prefieres hacer algo diferente?
Ask what the title question means. Review the -**ie**- changes in the paradigm.

Pensar
Explain that **pensar** means "to think," but that when it is used with an infinitive it means "to plan or intend." Examples:
Yo pienso mucho.
Yo pienso viajar a Costa Rica.
Review the -**ie**- changes in the paradigm.

DISCUSS

Review vocabulary from *Saludos* and introduce some of this chapter's vocabulary with questions and statements that incorporate **querer, pensar,** and **preferir**.
¿Quieres hacer un viaje en avión?
¿Adónde quieres ir?
¿Quieres comprar un pasaje de ida o de ida y vuelta?
¿Cuándo piensas ir?
¿Piensas ir hoy o mañana?
En el avión, ¿dónde prefieres sentarte?

¿QUÉ ASIENTO PREFIERES?

To talk about your plans, things you want to do, and your preferences, use the verbs *pensar, querer,* and *preferir*.

Prefiero un asiento de ventanilla.	I prefer a window seat.
Queremos ir a Costa Rica.	We want to go to Costa Rica.
Pienso salir en mayo.	I plan to leave in May.

Pensar, querer, and ***preferir*** are stem-changing verbs. In the present tense, the **-e-** in the stem changes to **-ie-** in all forms, except ***nosotros(as)*** and ***vosotros(as)***.

	pensar (ie) (to intend, to think)	querer (ie) (to want)	preferir (ie) (to prefer)
yo	pienso	quiero	prefiero
tú	piensas	quieres	prefieres
usted	piensa	quiere	prefiere
él/ella	piensa	quiere	prefiere
nosotros(as)	pensamos	queremos	preferimos
vosotros(as)	pensáis	queréis	preferís
ustedes	piensan	quieren	prefieren
ellos/ellas	piensan	quieren	prefieren

For students having difficulty talking about their plans, things they want to do, or preferences, you might consider:
• **The tutor page:** Pair the student with a native speaker or a more able student, using the tutor page.

Optional activity: See page 42D: *¿Qué quieres decir?*

1 Problemas en el viaje

Tu familia tiene problemas durante un viaje. ¿Con quién quiere hablar cada uno para resolver su problema?

Mi hermana y yo necesitamos pasajes con descuento. Queremos hablar con la empleada de la aerolínea.

1. Mi hermana y yo necesitamos pasajes con descuento.
2. Mis primos no tienen las tarjetas de embarque.
3. Mis tíos viajan con 10 maletas y 15 bolsos de mano.
4. No puedo poner el bolso debajo del asiento.
5. Mi madre no sabe el número de la puerta de embarque.

¿Con quién quiere(n) hablar?
con el / la empleado(a) de la aerolínea
con el maletero
con el / la auxiliar de vuelo

2 De vacaciones

¿Qué piensan hacer en las próximas vacaciones? Pregunta a tu compañero(a).

— *¿Qué piensan hacer tú y tus compañeros(as) en las vacaciones?*
— *Pensamos ir a América Central.*

1. tú y tus compañeros(as)
2. tus padres
3. tus amigos(as)
4. tus primos
5. tu profesora
6. tus hermanos

Planes y más planes
- ir a América Central
- visitar a mis tíos en California
- navegar en bote
- ir a esquiar
- alquilar muchos videos
- hacer una excursión en bicicleta

3 Preferencias

A. ¿Cómo prefieren viajar? ¿Por dónde? ¿Para hacer qué?

		yo	Pedro	Juana
cómo viajar	• en avión		✓	✓
	• en barco			
	• en coche	✓		
por dónde	• por Estados Unidos		✓	
	• por otro país			✓
para hacer qué	• ir a la playa			
	• ir a las montañas	✓		
	• conocer otras culturas			

B. Informen a la clase de los resultados.

Pedro y Juana prefieren viajar en avión. Pedro prefiere viajar por Estados Unidos. Juana prefiere ir a otro país. Yo prefiero hacer un viaje en coche a las montañas.

53

Para hispanohablantes

Write your resolutions for the upcoming school year.

ACTIVITIES

Students use the verbs **pensar**, **querer**, and **preferir** with infinitives to talk about plans, wishes, and preferences.

1. Individual or Pair Activity
Your family has problems during a trip. Which person does each family member want to speak with to solve his or her problem?
Possible Answers:
1. See model on student page.
2. *Quieren hablar con el empleado de la aerolínea.*
3. *Quieren hablar con el maletero.*
4. *Quiero hablar con el/la auxiliar de vuelo.*
5. *Quiere hablar con el/la empleado(a) de la aerolínea.*

2. Pair Activity
Ask your partner what these people plan to do on their next vacation.
Possible Answers:
1. See model on student page.
2. *¿Qué piensan hacer tus padres?*
   Piensan visitar a mis tíos en California.
3. *¿Qué piensan hacer tus amigos(as)?*
   Piensan hacer una excursión en bicicleta.
4. *¿Qué piensan hacer tus primos?*
   Piensan ir a esquiar.
5. *¿Qué piensa hacer tu profesora?*
   Piensa alquilar muchos videos.
6. *¿Qué piensan hacer tus hermanos?*
   Piensan navegar en bote.

3. Group Activity
A. How and where do you prefer to travel, and what do you prefer to do? Make a chart like the model.
B. Write a statement for the class in which you describe the results of your survey.
Answer: See model on student page.
Extension: Ask other groups why they want, plan, or prefer to go to these places.

CHECK

- *¿Quieres viajar en avión?*
- *¿Adónde piensas viajar?*
- *¿Prefieres quedarte en casa?*

LOG BOOK
Have students write a dialog in which they and a partner talk about how, where, and why they want to travel.

SITUACIONES

Objectives
Communicative: to talk about Central America
Cultural: to learn about Central America

Related Components

Assessment Oral Proficiency: p. 21	Conexiones: 16A **Conexiones** Chapter 1
Audio Book Script: Seg. 5 Activities: p. 13	**Magazine** Juntos en Costa Rica
Audio Chapter: 2A, Seg.5	**Tutor Page** p. 10

GETTING STARTED

Students should now be able to use **pensar, preferir, querer**, direct object pronouns, and all of the chapter vocabulary correctly.
Ask if any students have traveled to Costa Rica or to other parts of Central America. What were their reactions to that part of the world? How was it different from other places they have lived in or visited?

APPLY

In Activity 1, make sure that all countries shown on the map are included.

1. Group Activity
A. Look at the map and decide which country you want to go to and which places you want to visit.
Answers: See model on student page.
B. Explain why you prefer to travel to that country and visit those places.
Possible Answer:
Preferimos viajar a Panamá porque queremos ver el canal de Panamá.

2. Pair Activity
You want to travel to one of the countries shown on the map. Your partner is an airline employee who answers your questions. The questions:
• How much does a round-trip ticket to [Costa Rica] cost?
• Do you have student-discount tickets?
• Is this flight direct or does it have a stopover?
• I plan to stay there two weeks. Can I return on [the 15th]?
• When is the departure? And the arrival?

SITUACIONES
¡VAMOS DE VIAJE!

1. Un viaje por América Central

A. En grupo, miren el mapa y decidan a qué país quieren ir y qué lugares piensan visitar allí.

> *Queremos ir a Costa Rica. Allí pensamos visitar el volcán Arenal y puerto Limón.*

B. Expliquen por qué prefieren viajar a ese país y visitar esos lugares.

2. En el aeropuerto

Quieres viajar a uno de los países del mapa. Tu compañero(a) es el/la empleado(a) de la aerolínea y contesta tus preguntas.

• ¿Cuánto cuesta un pasaje de ida y vuelta a...?
• ¿Tiene pasajes con descuento para estudiantes?
• ¿Es un vuelo con o sin escala?
• Pienso quedarme dos semanas. ¿Puedo volver el...?
• ¿A qué hora es la salida? ¿Y la llegada?

54

Possible Answers:
• *Un pasaje de ida y vuelta a Costa Rica cuesta quinientos dólares.*
• *No, no hay pasajes con descuento para estudiantes.*
• *Es un vuelo sin escala.*
• *Sí, puede volver el sábado 15 de agosto.*
• *La salida es a las seis de la tarde. La llegada es a las diez de la noche.*

For students having difficulty talking about travel, you might consider:
• **The tutor page:** Pair the student with a native speaker or a more able student, using the tutor page.
Optional activity: See page 42C: *Vuelo de primer clase*

¡Visítenos!

HONDURAS
Conozca las ruinas mayas de Copán. Tegucigalpa, la capital, está en un lugar increíble: entre el río Choluteca y el monte El Picacho.

NICARAGUA
El lago de Nicaragua es el único lugar del mundo donde viven tiburones de agua dulce. Cerca del lago está la bellísima ciudad colonial de Granada, fundada en 1524.

GUATEMALA
Si le gusta la aventura, visite el bosque tropical de Petén. Si prefiere algo más tranquilo, visite los museos y las iglesias de la Ciudad de Guatemala.

COSTA RICA
Este maravilloso país tiene de todo: volcanes, playas, flora y fauna tropicales, y verdes montañas. Visite las playas de puerto Limón y el volcán Arenal.

EL SALVADOR
Es el país más pequeño de América Central, pero sus playas son las mejores para hacer surf. Por todas partes hay mercados indígenas y fiestas populares.

PANAMÁ
La atracción principal es el famoso Canal, pero si le gusta la naturaleza no deje de visitar el Parque Nacional de Portobelo.

---

3 Minidiálogos

Con tu compañero(a), crea diálogos para las siguientes situaciones.

1. Estás en el aeropuerto antes de la salida del avión y no sabes el número de la puerta de embarque.

2. Estás en el avión y tienes sed.

3. Estás en la terminal de equipaje y tu maleta no llega.

4 Tu diario

Escribe en tu diario qué viaje te gustaría hacer.

1. ¿Adónde quieres ir? ¿Por qué prefieres ir a ese lugar?

2. ¿Qué lugares piensas visitar allí?

> **PARA TU REFERENCIA**
>
> **el monte** *hill*
> **no deje de** *don't fail to*
> **los tiburones de agua dulce**
> *fresh-water sharks*

55

---

3. Pair Activities
Create dialogs for the following three situations:
1. You are at the airport before the plane's departure and you don't know your boarding gate.
2. You are on the plane and you are thirsty.
3. You are at the baggage terminal and your baggage doesn't arrive.

4. Homework or Classwork
Write in your diary about a trip you would like to take.
1. Where would you like to go? Why?
2. What places do you plan to visit there?
Extension: Dictate a paragraph of your writing to a partner as he/she transcribes it.

CHECK

- *¿A qué países de América Central prefieres ir?*
- *¿Qué lugares piensas visitar allí?*
- *¿Cuándo quieres ir?*

PORTFOLIO
Have students copy the map of Central America and label the places they want to visit. They can also make a list of phrases to use at the airport.

> **Para hispanohablantes**
>
> Write a list of useful phrases for a tourist going to Central America.

Communicative Objective
- to discuss, plan, and design an airline advertisement

Related Components

Video: Tape/Book
Unit 1: Seg. 2

Search to frame 1012901

GETTING STARTED

Ask students to list what they would look for when choosing an airline. What can make a flight more comfortable and enjoyable?

APPLY

Form groups. Each will design an advertisement for a new airline.

PASO 1: Nuestra aerolínea
Decide:
- the name and logo of the airline
- what color you prefer for the planes and the flight attendants' uniforms
- how many seats the planes will have
- where you will fly

Extension: Think of at least five words to describe your airline. Use them in the following *Pasos.*

PASO 2: ¡Buen viaje!
Explain what makes your airline better than the others.
Answers: See model on student page.
Extension: Find an ad for an airline in the newspaper. Say why you prefer your airline to the one in the ad.

PASO 3: ¡Bienvenidos!
Make a list of things your airline will offer.
Answers: See model on student page.
Extension: Five students draw cards, each with a job on it (*maletero/a, empleado/a de la aerolínea, agente de aduana, agente de migración*). The class tries to guess each one's job by asking **sí/no** questions.

PASO 4: El anuncio
Prepare the final version of your ad, using the answers from the previous activities.
Extension: Present the ads to the class. Class members write which airline they prefer and why.

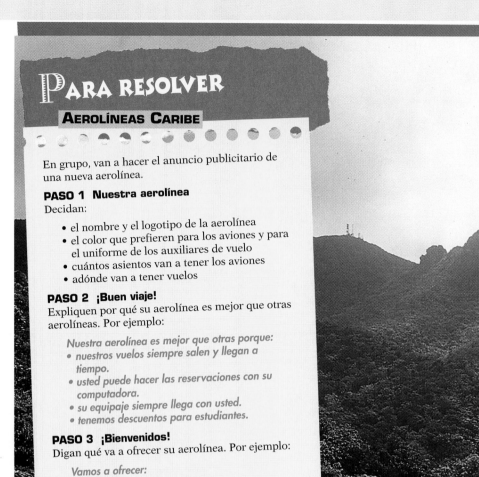

PARA RESOLVER

AEROLÍNEAS CARIBE

En grupo, van a hacer el anuncio publicitario de una nueva aerolínea.

PASO 1 Nuestra aerolínea
Decidan:
- el nombre y el logotipo de la aerolínea
- el color que prefieren para los aviones y para el uniforme de los auxiliares de vuelo
- cuántos asientos van a tener los aviones
- adónde van a tener vuelos

PASO 2 ¡Buen viaje!
Expliquen por qué su aerolínea es mejor que otras aerolíneas. Por ejemplo:

Nuestra aerolínea es mejor que otras porque:
- *nuestros vuelos siempre salen y llegan a tiempo.*
- *usted puede hacer las reservaciones con su computadora.*
- *su equipaje siempre llega con usted.*
- *tenemos descuentos para estudiantes.*

PASO 3 ¡Bienvenidos!
Digan qué va a ofrecer su aerolínea. Por ejemplo:

Vamos a ofrecer:
- *una película.*
- *periódicos y revistas en inglés y en español.*
- *una computadora y videojuegos para cada pasajero(a).*
- *mantas, almohadas, audífonos, refrescos y dulces. ¡Todo gratis!*

PASO 4 El anuncio
Con las respuestas de los pasos anteriores, hagan la versión final de su anuncio publicitario.

56

AEROLÍNEAS CARIBE

Vuelos diarios a todos los países del Caribe

- Usted puede comprar pasajes por medio de su computadora
- Videojuegos en cada asiento
- Comidas vegetarianas
- Las últimas películas

Nuestros precios
y horarios son los mejores.

¿SABES QUE...?

Each of the nations of Latin America and Puerto Rico has at least one domestic airline. Some have many more. As of January 1996, there were a total of 57 domestic airlines in all of the Spanish-speaking countries of Latin America.

57

- ¿Cómo se llama tu aerolínea?
- ¿Adónde van los vuelos de tu aerolínea?
- ¿Qué va a ofrecer tu aerolínea?
- ¿Cuáles son los colores de tu aerolínea?
- ¿Por qué es mejor tu aerolínea?

PORTFOLIO

Encourage students to add their airline advertisements to their Portfolios.

Background

Travel Words

Here are additional words that students may be interested in knowing:

air traffic control tower *torre control de tráfico aéreo, torre de mando, torre de control*
baggage claim *recogida/llegada de equipajes*
baggage lockers *consigna de equipaje*
car rental *alquiler de automóviles*
currency exchange *cambio de divisas (de moneda)*
first aid *primeros auxilios, enfermería*
gift shop *tienda de regalos*
lost and found *objetos perdidos*
no entry *prohibida la entrada*
no parking *prohibido aparcar*
parking *aparcamiento, estacionamiento*
ramp *rampa de acceso*
runway *pista de aterrizaje*
short-term parking *estacionamiento de tiempo limitado*

Research Project

Have students research one of the cities in their airline's itinerary. Then have them organize the information they obtain into categories, such as: *"Información general," "Vistas," "Alojamiento," "Restaurantes," "Sitios historicos," "Paseos interesantes,"* etc. Then, students select one category they find interesting and dictate it to a partner.

MEETING INDIVIDUAL NEEDS

Reaching All Students

For Auditory Learners
Create a radio announcement for your airline. Tape the final version and play it for the class.

Para hispanohablantes

Find out what airlines your family or friends prefer and why they like them.

Objectives

Communicative: to talk about a mural
Cultural: to learn about the history of Costa Rica

Related Components

Audio	Magazine
Conexiones: 16A	Juntos en Costa Rica
Conexiones	
Chapter 1	

GETTING STARTED

Ask students to comment on this mural.

DISCUSS

Using the Realia

Have volunteers read the text aloud. After each paragraph, ask questions. Suggestions:

El mural
¿Dónde puedes ver este mural?
¿Cuántas escenas tiene?
¿Cuántas partes tiene un tríptico?

La primera escena
¿Qué hay en la primera escena?
¿Qué simbolizan los libros?
¿Qué simbolizan las herramientas?
¿Prefieres las herramientas o los libros?

La segunda escena
¿Qué hay en la segunda escena?
¿Qué simboliza el hombre con el rifle?
¿De dónde es el otro hombre?
¿Cuál de los hombres representa el pasado?
¿Y cuál representa el presente?

La tercera escena
¿Dónde están las personas en esta escena?
¿Qué hacen allí?
¿Crees que es una escena de la vida de hace muchos años o de ahora?

ENTÉRATE

EL MURAL DEL AEROPUERTO JUAN SANTAMARÍA

El turista que viaja a Costa Rica por avión puede admirar un impresionante mural en la sala de espera° del aeropuerto Juan Santamaría.

El mural tiene tres partes. Cada parte constituye una escena distinta. La primera escena ocurre° en la ciudad. En ella, un grupo de personas lleva libros para simbolizar la importancia que tiene la educación. Otro grupo de personas lleva herramientas° para representar la importancia que tiene el trabajo.

En la segunda escena se unen° el pasado y el presente de Costa Rica. El hombre con el rifle simboliza la guerra civil° de 1948. El hombre vestido como los españoles del siglo XVI representa el pasado colonial del país.

La tercera escena ocurre en el campo. En ella hay un grupo de campesinos° trabajando la tierra.

el campesino *peasant*	la sala de espera *waiting room*
la escena *scene*	ocurre *takes place*
la guerra civil *civil war*	se unen *unite*
la herramienta *tool*	

TE TOCA A TI

Completa las oraciones.

1. El turista que viaja a Costa Rica por avión...
2. En la escena del campo hay...
3. El hombre con el rifle representa...
4. En la escena de la ciudad hay...
5. El mural está en...

58

CHECK

Te toca a ti
Possible Answers:
1. ...puede admirar un impresionante mural.
2. ...un grupo de campesinos trabajando la tierra.
3. ...la guerra civil de 1948.
4. ...un grupo de personas llevando libros y otro grupo con herramientas.
5. ...la sala de espera del aeropuerto Juan Santamaría.

PORTFOLIO

Have students write phrases about one section of this mural and what it symbolizes.

Para hispanohablantes

Explain the mural to the class as if you were a tourist guide. Use the information in the reading.

VOCABULARIO TEMÁTICO

Antes de viajar en avión
Before traveling by plane

comparar precios/horarios
to compare prices/schedules

comprar un pasaje de ida/de ida y vuelta *to buy a one-way/round-trip ticket*

hacer una reservación
to make a reservation

pedir un pasaje con descuento *to ask for a discount ticket*

pedir un vuelo con escala/sin escala *to ask for a stopover/nonstop flight*

reservar *reserve*

En el aeropuerto
At the airport

la aduana *customs*

el control de migración *immigration desk*

el control de seguridad *security check*

el mostrador de la aerolínea *airline ticket counter*

el/la pasajero(a) *passenger*

la puerta de embarque *boarding gate*

la terminal de equipaje *baggage claim*

En el mostrador de la aerolínea
At the airline counter

averiguar el número de la puerta de embarque *to find out the gate number*

averiguar la hora de salida/de llegada *to find out the departure/arrival time*

averiguar si el vuelo está retrasado *to find out if the flight is delayed*

facturar el equipaje *to check the luggage*

pedir la tarjeta de embarque *to ask for the boarding pass*

Los empleados del aeropuerto
Airport employees

el/la agente de aduanas *customs officer*

el/la agente de migración *immigration officer*

el/la auxiliar de vuelo *flight attendant*

el/la empleado(a) de la aerolínea *airline representative*

el maletero *baggage handler*

En el avión
On the plane

la almohada *pillow*

el asiento de pasillo *aisle seat*

el asiento de ventanilla *window seat*

los audífonos *headphones*

el compartimiento de arriba *overhead compartment*

la manta *blanket*

la salida de emergencia *emergency exit*

Las medidas de seguridad
Safety measures

Abróchense los cinturones. *Fasten your seat belts.*

En caso de emergencia
In an emergency

No usen aparatos electrónicos. *Don't use electronic equipment.*

Pongan sus asientos en posición vertical. *Put your seat in the upright position.*

Pongan su equipaje debajo del asiento. *Put your luggage under the seat.*

Usen el chaleco salvavidas. *Use the life jacket.*

Usen la máscara de oxígeno. *Use the oxygen mask.*

Usen las salidas de emergencia. *Use the emergency exits.*

Expresiones y palabras

a tiempo *on time*

¿Cuál es el motivo de su viaje? *What's the purpose of your trip?*

¿Cuánto tiempo piensa quedarse? *How long do you plan to stay?*

aterrizar *to land*

despegar *to take off*

durante *during*

pasar por *to go through*

pensar (e>ie) *to think, to intend*

preferir (e>ie) *to prefer*

quedarse *to stay*

retrasado(a) *delayed*

volver (o>ue) *to come back*

LA CONEXIÓN INGLÉS-ESPAÑOL

Can you find the common origins of Spanish and English words? Here are some examples:

avión	*aviation*
seguridad	*security*
aterrizar → **tierra** →	*territory*

Look at the vocabulary list above. What other connections can you make?

VOCABULARIO TEMÁTICO

Objective
• to review vocabulary

Related Components

Activity Book	**Cuaderno**
Chapter Review:	p. 11-12
p. 25-26	**Transparencies**
Assessment	Ch. 1: Dibujos y
Listening Script: p. 9	palabras
Chapter Test:	Transparency 12
p. 45-50	
Audio	
Assessment: 14A	

Vocabulary

Point out that this list is organized by themes. Use the headings to review vocabulary. You may wish to ask Spanish speakers to share variations on these words and phrases with the class.

	Objetivos page 61 *Excursiones y aventuras*	Conversemos pages 62-63 *Ecología y actividades al aire libre*	Realidades pages 64-65 *Descubran Costa Rica*	Palabras en acción pages 66-67 *Excursión a una reserva natural*
Comunicación	To talk about: • what you can see and do outdoors	Discuss sites for outdoor adventures	Read text, answer questions, discuss sites in Costa Rica, talk about outdoor activities, make table	Read cartoon, discuss camping; create dialog; talk about visits to nature preserves; act out an outdoor activity; invent directions
	• items needed for outdoor activities	Discuss ecological and outdoor activities	Read text, answer questions, discuss outdoor activities, make table	Read cartoon, discuss visits to nature preserves
	• how to care for the environment	Discuss items needed for camping	Read text, answer questions, discuss items to take to Costa Rica	Read cartoon, make lists; act out an outdoor activity; invent directions
Cultura	To learn about: • ecotourism in Costa Rica • the geography of Costa Rica • national parks of Costa Rica		Article on ecotourism in Costa Rica; information on cultural diversity	
Vocabulario temático	To know the expressions for: • outdoor and ecological activities	Talk about outdoor and ecological activities	Read text, answer questions, discuss sites in Costa Rica, talk about outdoor activities, make table	Read cartoon, discuss camping; create dialog; talk about visits to nature preserves; act out an outdoor activity; make collage; invent directions
	• outdoor equipment and supplies	Discuss equipment and supplies needed for camping	Read text, answer questions, discuss items to take to Costa Rica	Read cartoon, discuss visits to nature preserves
	• cardinal points on a compass	Discuss cardinal points	Read text, answer questions, discuss sites in Costa Rica	Read cartoon, discuss camping; make collage; invent directions
Estructura	To talk about: • what others should do: *Usted* and *Ustedes* commands	Use singular *Ud.* commands to tell others how to protect the environment	Read text, answer questions, discuss items to take to Costa Rica	Create dialog; invent directions
	• activities that you have done: the preterite of *-ar*, *-er*, and *-ir* verbs and *hacer* and *ir*		Read text, answer questions, discuss sites in Costa Rica, talk about outdoor activities, make table	Discuss visits to nature preserves

EXCURSIONES Y AVENTURAS

Para comunicarnos mejor (1) pages 68-69 ¡No acampen aquí!	Para comunicarnos mejor (2) pages 70-71 ¿Qué hiciste en el verano?	Situaciones pages 72-73 Una excursión de un día	Para resolver pages 74-75 ¡Visítenos!	Entérate page 76 Parques nacionales de Costa Rica
Give advice about outdoor adventures	Discuss an imaginary trip in Costa Rica	Read ad, answer questions, discuss Tortuguero, give advice	Look at map, describe Costa Rica's geography; list things to do; talk about home and make a map; write invitation to visit your state	Discuss conservation and Costa Rica's national parks
	Discuss outdoor activities in nature preserves; make table; talk about an imaginary trip in Costa Rica	Discuss Tortuguero; talk about field trip; write in diary		
Give advice to friends and teacher about outdoor adventures	Discuss outdoor activities in nature preserves; talk about an imaginary trip in Costa Rica	Give advice to people who want to visit Tortuguero	Make list of things to do in Costa Rica; talk about home	
	Discuss an imaginary trip to Costa Rica	Read an advertisement about a visit to a turtle farm in Costa Rica	Examine a map of Costa Rica	Article on national parks in Costa Rica and environmental policy; information about the Costa Rican expression, *pura vida*
Give advice about outdoor adventures; role-play giving directions	Discuss outdoor activities in nature preserves; make table; talk about an imaginary trip in Costa Rica			
Give advice about outdoor adventures	Discuss outdoor activities in nature preserves; talk about an imaginary trip in Costa Rica	**Re-entry of vocabulary**		**Extension of vocabulary**
Roleplay giving directions				
Give advice about outdoor adventures; role-play giving directions		**Re-entry of structure**		**Extension of structure**

Al aire libre

GAME

Objective
- to play a game about camping, using Chapter 2 *Vocabulario temático*

Use
after *Palabras en acción,* pages 66–67

Materials
- 3" x 5" index cards

Preparation
- Form two teams.
- Distribute index cards.
- Beginning with the first letter of the Spanish alphabet, have each player on Team 1 name an item or phrase beginning with that letter that has to do with camping. (For example: *acampar, animal, al noreste, al noroeste*)
- Each player writes his or her word on an index card, before passing the card to the next player.
- When Team 1 exhausts all of its possible words, Team 2 does the same with next letter of the alphabet.
- At the end of the game the teams count the number of words they came up with.
- The team with the most words wins.

(Note: the article does not count as an initial letter)

Variation:
Make index cards with the names of outdoor activities, such as: *pescar, montar a caballo, observar a los animales* Have groups choose a card at random and name items needed for such an activity.

¿Qué prefieres llevar?

GAME

Objective
- to play a game about packing for a camping trip, using Chapter 2 *Vocabulario temático* and vocabulary from other chapters.

Use
after *Palabras en acción,* pages 66–67

Activity
- Have the class generate a list of 20 to 25 things to take on a camping trip. Write them on the board. For example: *la tienda de campaña, una brújula, el saco de dormir, el chaleco salvavidas, la mochila, el protector solar, los tenis, un casco, un mapa, una cantimplora, el repelente de insectos, los lentes de sol, una gorra, agua, el pasaporte, los cheques de viajero, el traje de baño, una toalla, un libro,* etc.
- Have students copy the list.
- Have each student circle five things essential to him/her without showing the circled items to anyone.
- Pair students and have them take turns trying to guess an item circled. For example: *¿Prefieres llevar una mochila?* or *¿Quieres llevar una mochila?* If the partner has that item circled, he/she says: *Sí, quiero llevar una mochila.* Or if not: *No, no quiero llevar una mochila.*
- To avoid repetitions, students mark X next to items as they are mentioned.
- The first to guess all five of a partner's items wins.

Variations
- Play with places to go, outdoor sports, after-school activities, etc.

SOCIAL STUDIES CONNECTION

Objective
- to discuss protecting the environment, using formal commands for **Ud.** and **Uds.**

Use
after *Para comunicarnos mejor,* pages 68–69

Materials
- 3" x 5" index cards

Preparation
- On each card write the name of an environment. For example: *la playa, el campo, el bosque tropical, el parque nacional, la ciudad, el hogar, la escuela,* etc. Shuffle and place cards face down on table.
- Divide class into as many groups as there are environments. Each group picks a card.

Activity
- For 15 minutes each group brainstorms ways to improve their environment. They write formal commands with **Ud.** or **Uds.** for slogans telling people how to improve the environment.
- Each group presents its slogans to the rest of the class. For example, the school group might say: *No escriba en las mesas. No tire basura. Recicle los papeles.*
- The class votes on each group's top slogans.
- Groups design and present posters of their top slogan.
- Display the posters. Have students present their slogan to another Spanish class, or explain them to an English class.

Variations
- Groups exchange brainstorming lists. Students change each **Ud.** imperative to its plural **Uds.** form and each **Uds.** imperative to its singular **Ud.** form.

FYI
Since 1989 schoolchildren in 37 countries have contributed to the purchase of land in Costa Rica's *Bosque Eterno de los Niños.* Thousands of acres of lush vegetation are protected, along with endangered quetzals, monkeys, umbrella birds, ocelots, jaguars, and tapirs. To find out how your students can help, contact: Monteverde Conservation League, Apartado 10581-1000, San José, Costa Rica.

WRITING CONNECTION

Objective
- to tell a class story, using the preterite of **hacer** and of -**ar**, -**er**, and -**ir** verbs, as well as stem-changing -**ar** and -**er** verbs

Use
after *Para comunicarnos mejor,* pages 70–71

Materials
- an oversized pad or posterboard
- thick black and red marking pens

Preparation
- Have student pairs write down a noun, a verb, and an adjective from Chapter 2.

Activity
- Have each pair pass their paper to the pair behind them. (Last pair gives first pair their sheet.)
- Select the order in which pairs will tell the story.
- Begin by giving some suggestions as to the type of story and/or the characters involved. For example: *Era un día de mucho calor...* Have pairs continue by using the three words on their sheets. For example, the first pair has *noreste, acampar, cantimplora.* So: *Mi amiga Jenny, nuestro guía Juan y yo acampamos en el noreste del parque natural. Gracias a una cantimplora, bebimos agua.* One member of the pair reads the previous installment of the story, and the other their newly written addition. They may write as many sentences as they like, but their contribution must further the storyline or it will be excluded from the story.
- Once an addition is accepted, one of the pair writes it on posterboard and underlines the three words used.
- When the group story is complete, read it from beginning to end. And hold on for laughter.

Variations
- Give the class thematically linked characters, setting, and verbs so that students have greater control of their stories. For example: *un monitor y varios estudiantes/campamento de verano/comer, dormir, nadar, tener miedo, reír,* etc.

EXCURSIONES Y AVENTURAS

Introduce the chapter and its theme by asking students to share their outdoor activities with the class. They may also describe movies that depict outdoor adventures.

Related Components

Audio	**Video: Tape/Book**
Conexiones: 16A	Unit 1: Seg. 3
Conexiones	
Chapter 2	

Scan to Chapter 2

GETTING STARTED

Have students look at the photo. Ask questions like these:
¿Qué hacen los chicos de la foto?
¿Te gustaría hacer esta actividad?
¿Qué otras actividades puedes hacer en un río?

Critical Thinking

Use the following activity to help students discover for themselves what they would need to know in order to go on an outdoors trip.

Tell students to think about what they would need and what they could do if they went camping in a park in a tropical country. Assign groups to make lists of:

- things they would need on a camping trip
- things they could do or see there
- animals and plants they might expect to see in a tropical forest

Have each group write its list on the board. Have the class discuss the lists and suggest additions or other changes.

Have each group submit a revised list. When you finish the chapter, have the class review the lists to see if they learned those words in the chapter.

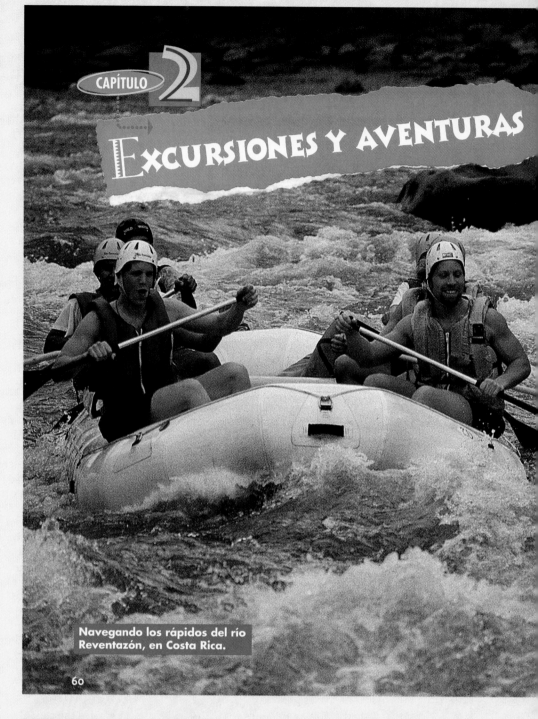

CAPÍTULO 2

EXCURSIONES Y AVENTURAS

Navegando los rápidos del río Reventazón, en Costa Rica.

60

CHAPTER COMPONENTS

Activity Book p. 27-36	**Audio Book** Script: p. 14-16 Activities: p. 17-19	**Conexiones** Chapter 2	**Transparencies** Chapter 2 Transparencies 13-16
Assessment Oral Proficiency: p. 22 Listening Script: p. 10 Chapter Test: p. 51-56	**Audio** Chapter: 2B Assessment: 14A Conexiones: 16A	**Cuaderno** p. 13-20 **Magazine** Juntos en Costa Rica	**Tutor Pages** p. 11-14 **Video: Tape/Book** Unit 1: Seg. 3

Objetivos

COMUNICACIÓN
To talk about:
- what you can see and do outdoors
- items needed for outdoor activities
- how to care for the environment

CULTURA
To learn about:
- ecotourism in Costa Rica
- the geography of Costa Rica
- national parks of Costa Rica

VOCABULARIO TEMÁTICO
To know the expressions for:
- outdoor and ecological activities
- outdoor equipment and supplies
- animals and plants
- cardinal points of a compass

ESTRUCTURA
To talk about:
- what others should do: formal commands
- what you have done: the preterite of regular -ar, -er, and -ir verbs and of the irregular verbs *hacer* and *ir*

¿SABES QUE...?
Costa Ricans have set aside a quarter of their land for national parks and nature preserves. These areas are teeming with some 750 species of birds, as well as with jaguars, crocodiles, tapirs, peccaries, otters, monkeys, armadillos, and many other animals. Protected areas include steaming volcanoes, undisturbed tropical forests, lakes, islands, dry grasslands, beaches, mountains, and pre-Columbian ruins.

61

OPTIONAL CHAPTER ACTIVITIES

Here are some additional activities that you may wish to use as you work through the chapter with your students.

Communication
Encourage after-class activities that may enhance student interest and proficiency. You may want to:
- organize a trip to a nature reserve or local park
- suggest that students read a travel guide on Costa Rica
- have students determine the compass points and post them around the classroom in Spanish

Culture
The written word can only hint at what life is like in other lands. To encourage greater understanding:
- have students create a bilingual campaign for the environment
- ask students to bring in Costa Rican products that are sold in the United States, such as coffee and bananas
- show the video that accompanies Unit 1 of this textbook

Vocabulary
To reinforce vocabulary, have students:
- create a picture dictionary using photos or magazine pictures
- decorate the classroom with words, pictures, and objects related to the chapter's vocabulary

Structure
To reinforce the use of the preterite:
- have students begin each class by saying what they did the day before

Thinking About Language
Point out to students the cognates in the chapter title. Explain to students that **excursión** comes from the Latin *excursio*, "a running out or forth", and that **aventura** also has a Latin root, *adventura*, which means "a happening."

▶▶▶ INTERNET LINK
About Costa Rica's Parks http://www. centralamerica.com/cr/parks/index.htm

Communicative Objectives
- to talk about outdoor activities
- to talk about animals and plants

Related Components

Activity Book p. 27	**Cuaderno** p. 13
Audio Book Script: Seg. 1	**Transparencies** Ch. 2: Conversemos Transparency 13
Audio Chapter: 2B, Seg. 1	

GETTING STARTED

Ask students to name things to do and see when camping or visiting a national park.

ACTIVITIES

These activities give students an opportunity to begin communicating with each other and with you, focusing on the theme and objectives of the chapter. The activities can be used as oral class activities, or, if you prefer, you can pair students to achieve more interaction.

¿Dónde te gustaría pasar una semana al aire libre?
Class activity to review **gustaría** and introduce compass directions.
Use a map to present compass directions.
Examples:
Alaska está al noroeste de nuestro estado.
¿Dónde está Texas? ¿Está al norte de qué país?
Ask volunteers variations on the title question: *¿Dónde te gustaría pasar una semana?*

¿Qué vas a llevar?
Class activity to introduce camping vocabulary and review **tener que**.
Have students explain why they have to bring each of these things (e.g., *Tenemos que llevar la brújula para saber donde estamos*).
Extend this activity by playing a word association game. Begin with an environmental condition (such as rain) or an object (such as a raincoat). Have students list all the vocabulary words or phrases associated with the initial word that they can think of. Then have them list those associated with the opposite condition or type of object.
Example:
impermeable:
- *llueve a cántaros, paraguas*
- *sol, protector solar, traje de baño*

CONVERSEMOS

ECOLOGÍA Y ACTIVIDADES AL AIRE LIBRE

¿DÓNDE TE GUSTARÍA PASAR UNA SEMANA AL AIRE LIBRE?

Me gustaría pasar una semana en el parque nacional Yellowstone. Está al norte del parque nacional Grand Teton.

en el parque...
en la costa de...
en las playas de...
en las montañas...
cerca de un río...
cerca de un lago...
en la reserva natural...

NORTE
NOROESTE
NORESTE
OESTE
ESTE
SUROESTE
SURESTE
SUR

¿QUÉ VAS A LLEVAR?

Voy a llevar el repelente de insectos.
(I am going to take insect repellent.)

la tienda de campaña
las botas de montaña
la brújula
el saco de dormir
los binoculares
la cantimplora

62

MEETING INDIVIDUAL NEEDS

Reaching All Students

For Visual Learners
Make Spanish ecology signs like the ones in the book for the classroom. Make the most important word the largest (or a different color).

¿QUÉ ACTIVIDAD AL AIRE LIBRE TE GUSTA HACER?

Me gusta...

observar los animales

mirar las flores

No me gusta...

pescar

hacer caminatas

montar a caballo

acampar

PARA EXPLICAR CÓMO LLEGAR A UN LUGAR, ¿QUÉ DICES?

Siga el sendero hasta el volcán.
[Follow the path until you reach the volcano.]

Siga la señal hacia el noreste.
[Follow the sign towards the northeast.]

PARA CONSERVAR EL MEDIO AMBIENTE, ¿QUÉ CONSEJOS DAS?
[To preserve the environment, what advice do you give?]

No moleste a los animales

RECICLE LAS LATAS

Mantenga limpio el aire

No tire basura al mar

No dé comida a los animales

RECICLE los periódicos y las revistas

63

¿Qué actividad al aire libre te gusta hacer?
Class activity to introduce vocabulary for outdoor activities. Model each of the statements, and comment on the activities. For example: *No me gusta montar a caballo porque es peligroso.*
Ask individuals the title question. Poll the class for preferences.

Para explicar cómo llegar a un lugar, ¿qué dices?
Class activity to introduce **seguir** and **Ud.** commands. Ask the title question, and model both statements. Make drawings on the board to demonstrate **hasta** and **hacia**.

Para conservar el medio ambiente, ¿qué consejos das?
Class activity to practice **Ud.** commands. Read aloud the title and explain **medio ambiente**. Ask students to read aloud the signs. Have them infer the meaning by looking at the cognates and drawings. Some commands, such as **mantenga** and **dé**, will be difficult. Have students try to figure out the infinitive of each.

CHECK

- *¿Dónde está el parque nacional que prefieres?*
- *¿Por qué te gustaría ir allí?*
- *¿Qué tienes que llevar?*
- *¿Qué actividades te gustaría hacer allí?*

LOG BOOK
Have students write down the three pieces of environmental advice they consider to be most important.

Environmental/Community Link
Write to the following address to request information in English and Spanish on how you can help the environment:
Environmental Protection Agency
401 M St. SW
Washington, DC 20460

Communicative Objectives
- to talk about eco-tourism in Costa Rica
- to talk about outdoor activities

Related Components

Activity Book p. 28	**Audio** Chapter: 2B, Seg. 2
Audio Book Script: Seg. 2	**Cuaderno** p. 14

GETTING STARTED

Ask if anyone knows what eco-tourism is. Ask students to comment on the usefulness of eco-tourism.

DISCUSS

Talk about the photographs and captions, and ask questions. Sample questions:

Descubran Costa Rica
¿Qué hicieron esta persona y sus amigos el verano pasado?
¿Les gustó a ellos ir a Costa Rica? ¿Cómo sabemos que les gustó?
¿Por qué dice "Es pura vida"?

¡Observen la naturaleza!
¿Dónde pueden Uds. observar la naturaleza?
¿Qué dicen sobre el quetzal?
¿Qué animales hay en la reserva natural?
¿Qué deben llevar a este lugar?

¡Naveguen sus ríos!
¿Qué río visitaron?
¿Qué hicieron allí?
¿Qué consejos nos dan?

¡Conozcan su música y su gente!
¿Adónde fueron los chicos?
¿Qué hicieron allí?
¿Saben Uds. cómo cantar "La Bamba"?
¿A quiénes conocieron?
¿De qué hablaron?

REALIDADES NATURALEZA

Descubran Costa Rica
¡Es pura vida!

El verano pasado hice ecoturismo en Costa Rica con un grupo de amigos. Costa Rica es el país del mundo que más cuida el medio ambiente. El 28% del territorio del país son parques nacionales. Mis amigos y yo la pasamos pura vida:* visitamos las reservas naturales, observamos animales y flores, e hicimos muchas actividades al aire libre. Aquí tienen algunos de nuestros recuerdos y consejos.

* Expresión de Costa Rica. En otros países: la pasamos muy bien.

¡OBSERVEN LA NATURALEZA!
En la reserva natural de Monteverde vimos un quetzal, un pájaro en peligro de extinción. También vimos monos, serpientes, tucanes y muchas mariposas. Lleven sus binoculares y ¡no se olviden del repelente de insectos!

¡NAVEGUEN SUS RÍOS!
Hicimos una excursión al río Reventazón y navegamos los rápidos en balsa. ¡Fue muy divertido! Si van, usen chalecos salvavidas y cascos, y sigan las indicaciones del guía.

¡CONOZCAN SU MÚSICA Y SU GENTE!
En las playas al sur de puerto Limón fuimos a una fiesta caribeña. Bailamos reggae y cantamos canciones populares como *La bamba*. Conocimos a jóvenes de la región y todos hablamos de nuestras experiencias.

64

CULTURE NOTE

Although Costa Rica comprises only 0.5% of the world's surface, it is home to 8% of all plant species and 10% of all animal species.
Costa Rica has done much to protect its environment and to develop eco-tourism. The tourist industry there ranks as the third largest source of foreign currency, after coffee and bananas.
The Monteverde reserve is a cloud forest. The town there was originally settled by Quakers from the United States.

HABLA DE LA REVISTA

A. Haz una lista de los lugares que visitó el grupo de amigos y otra lista de las actividades que hicieron en cada lugar.

En...	Actividades
las playas al sur de puerto Limón	bailaron reggae
la reserva natural de Monteverde	vieron un quetzal

B. Tus compañeros van a viajar a Costa Rica. Diles qué cosas deben llevar.

— *Vamos a navegar los rápidos en balsa.*
— *Lleven cascos, impermeables...*

¿QUÉ OPINAS?

A. ¿Qué actividades al aire libre hiciste alguna vez?

Pesqué y saqué fotos.

B. Ahora haz una encuesta en la clase. Anota los resultados en una tabla. Usa el modelo.

Actividades	Yo	La clase
saqué fotos	I	IIIII
navegué en balsa		
monté a caballo		
pesqué		
acampé cerca del río		
hice caminatas		
observé animales		

C. Según la encuesta, ¿cuál es la actividad al aire libre más popular? ¿Y la menos popular?

¿SABES QUE...?

The majority of people of African descent live along the east coast of Costa Rica, particularly in the area south of puerto Limón. Many arrived in Costa Rica from Jamaica and other Caribbean Islands at the beginning of the nineteenth century. The sounds of reggae music that abound in this southeast region of the country are a reminder of Costa Rica's rich African heritage.

65

Para hispanohablantes

Create a script for a Spanish public service announcement about a national park.

Habla de la revista

Individual or Pair Activity: Categorizing

A. Make two lists: one of the places in Costa Rica that the group of friends visited, and another of what they did in each place.

Possible Answers:

En las playas al sur de Puerto Limón: fueron a una fiesta caribeña, bailaron reggae, cantaron canciones populares, conocieron a jóvenes, hablaron de sus experiencias en la reserva natural de Monteverde: observaron el quetzal, vieron monos, serpientes, tucanes y mariposas en el río Reventazón: navegaron en balsa

B. Your classmates are traveling to Costa Rica. Tell them what they should bring.

Possible Answers:

Vamos a una reserva natural.
Lleven binoculares y repelente de insectos.
Vamos a la playa.
Lleven trajes de baño, toallas, protector solar y un frisbi.

¿Qué opinas?

Individual or Group Activity: Description

A. Name outdoor activities you have done.
Answers: See model on student page.

Class Activity: Taking a Poll

Make a chart like the model and mark the activities you and others have done.

Class Activity: Evaluation

According to your survey, which outdoor activity is the most popular? Which is the least popular?
Extension: Write a few sentences, saying which activities were the most and least popular, and explaining why.

CHECK

- *¿Qué puedes hacer en Costa Rica?*
- *¿Qué consejos le das a un(a) amigo(a) que va a Costa Rica?*
- *¿A qué lugar de las fotos de estas páginas te gustaría ir? ¿Por qué?*

LOG BOOK

Have students write five sentences about endangered animal or plant species.

Communicative Objectives
- to talk about camping
- to tell people what they can and cannot do, using **Ud.** commands
- to give directions

Related Components

Activity Book p. 29-30	Transparencies Ch. 2: Palabras en acción Transparency 14
Cuaderno p. 15-16	**Tutor Page** p. 11

GETTING STARTED

Ask if anyone has ever gone on an overnight camping trip. What advice would students give for this type of trip?

DISCUSS

Ask a few questions about the drawing. Examples:
¿Cuántas personas hay en el dibujo?
¿Qué animales ven aquí?
¿Se puede pescar allí?
¿Cómo saben que no se puede pescar?
¿Cuántas señales hay?

Para hispanohablantes

If you use other words or expressions for some of the ones introduced in this chapter, share them with the class. A few variations:
al aire libre: a la intemperie
los binoculares: los anteojos
el impermeable: la capa
el mono: el macaco
la planta: la mata
el saco de dormir: el talego para dormir
el sendero: el camino
la serpiente: la culebra
sureste: sudeste
suroeste: sudoeste
la tienda de campaña: la casa de campaña
la tortuga: la jicotea

PALABRAS EN ACCIÓN
EXCURSIÓN A UNA RESERVA NATURAL

1 ¿Qué ves en el dibujo?

Haz tres listas: una de cosas, otra de animales y flores, y otra de lugares.

> *Cosas: la tienda de campaña...*
> *Animales y flores: el tucán...*
> *Lugares: la selva tropical...*

2 ¿Dónde quieres acampar?

Mira el dibujo. Con tu compañero(a), haz planes para acampar.

> — *¿Dónde quieres acampar?*
> — *Al noroeste del río. Es un lugar hermosísimo, con muchas mariposas. ¿Y tú?*
> — *Yo prefiero acampar al...*

3 ¿Qué te gustaría hacer?

Haz tres diálogos con tu compañero(a). Hablen de las actividades que les gustaría hacer en una reserva natural.

> — *¿Qué te gustaría hacer?*
> — *Me gustaría navegar en balsa.*

4 ¡Pesquen en el lago!

Hagan una lista de las cosas que pueden o no pueden hacer en una reserva natural.

> • *Podemos mirar los quetzales, acampar...*
> • *No podemos hacer fogatas, tirar basura...*

66

For students having difficulty talking about camping, you might consider:
• **The tutor page:** Pair the student with a native speaker or a more able student, using the tutor page.
Optional activity: See page 60C: *Al aire libre*

el volcán

¿Adónde van?

Vamos de excursión al río.

la tienda de campaña

Mire, un quetzal.

Sí, es increíble.

la palmera

el guía

el tucán

el saco de dormir

los binoculares

PROTEJA LAS ESPECIES EN PELIGRO DE EXTINCIÓN

la serpiente

NO HAGA FOGATAS

NO TIRE BASURA

la señal

el mono

la selva tropical

5 ¿Adónde fuiste? ¿Qué hiciste?

Imagina que fuiste a una reserva natural. Dile a tu compañero(a) qué lugares visitaste y qué hiciste en cada lugar.

— ¿Adónde fuiste?
— Fui a la selva tropical, a la montaña y al volcán.
— ¿Qué hiciste en cada lugar?
— En la selva observé las plantas,...

6 Miniteatro

Representa una actividad al aire libre. La clase tiene que adivinar qué actividad es.

7 Un cartel

Con fotos de revistas, haz el cartel de una reserva natural, real o imaginaria.

8 Tú eres el autor

Con tu compañero(a), haz un diálogo para pedir información a un guía turístico sobre cómo llegar a un lugar.

— Queremos explorar el volcán. ¿Cómo llegamos allí?
— Sigan por ese sendero hacia el noroeste hasta el volcán.

67

ACTIVITIES

1. Individual Activity

Make three lists: one of things, one of animals and flowers, and one of places in the drawing.

Extension: List three actions in the drawing. List the things you associate them with. Example: *nadar, lago*

2. Pair Activity

Look at the drawing and make plans to go camping.

3. Pair Activity

Create three dialogs about what you would like to do at a nature reserve.

Extension: Pretend you did these things last weekend. Example:
Navegué en balsa el fin de semana pasado.

4. Pair Activity

Make a list of things you can and cannot do at a nature reserve.

5. Pair Activity

Pretend you went to a nature reserve. Tell your partner which places you visited and what you did in each place.

Extension: For each of these places, tell your partner what items to take along. Use **Ud.** commands.

6. Roleplay Activity

Mime an outdoor activity. The class must guess what it is.

7. Hands-On Activity

Homework or classwork for individuals or small groups.

With magazine pictures, make a poster for a real or imaginary nature reserve.

Extension: Exchange posters with another group and talk about what you see.

8. Writing Activity

With your partner, create a dialog in which you ask a tour guide for directions to a place you'd like to visit.

Extension: Pairs read their dialogs to other pairs.

CHECK

- *¿Qué puedes hacer en una reserva natural? ¿Qué no puedes hacer?*
- *¿Qué animales hay en este parque?*
- *¿Cómo llegas a tu parque favorito?*
- *Da tres mandatos a tu compañero(a).*

LOG BOOK

Have students make a list of at least ten animals and plants they would like to be able to name in Spanish, then have them look up the words in a bilingual dictionary.

Communicative Objectives
- to tell someone what to do
- to suggest what someone should do

Related Components

Activity Book p. 31-32	**Audio** Chapter: 2B, Seg. 3
Audio Book Script: Seg. 3 Activities: p. 17	**Cuaderno** p. 17
	Tutor Page p. 12

GETTING STARTED

Ask whether English-language signs that state rules, such as *No Smoking,* are formal or informal. How could we tell?

Language in Context

Remind students that Spanish has two forms of "you," a formal one (**Ud.**) and an informal one (**tú**). Explain that the same is true of commands. Ask why signs that state rules are usually formal.

Ask students to compare the command form of the first three verbs here with the present-tense **Ud.** form (i.e., *hable/habla, coma/come, comparta/comparte*). What difference do they note? (The command form of the **-ar** verb has the same ending as the present-tense form of an **-er** or **-ir** verb, and vice versa.)

DISCUSS

Review vocabulary from previous sections and introduce some of this chapter's vocabulary with questions and statements that incorporate **Ud.** or **Uds.** commands.

No hable en la clase.
Comparta el libro con su compañero(a).
No coma en la clase.
Escriban en sus cuadernos.
Estén aquí mañana temprano.
Pongan sus tareas en sus escritorios.
Hable con su compañera ahora.

PARA COMUNICARNOS MEJOR

¡NO ACAMPEN AQUÍ!

To give directions and make suggestions, you may use the *Ud.* (usted) or the *Uds.* (ustedes) form of the command.

Acampen cerca del río.	Camp near the river.
Para llegar al lago, siga el sendero.	To get to the lake, follow the path.

To form the ***usted*** formal command of regular **-ar** verbs, add **-e** to the verb stem. For regular **-er** and **-ir** verbs, add **-a** to the verb stem.

To form the plural ***ustedes*** form, add **-n** to the ***usted*** formal command.

	hablar	comer	compartir
stem	habl-	com-	compart-
Ud.	hable	coma	comparta
Uds.	hablen	coman	compartan

☐ Most verbs that are irregular in the ***yo*** form of the present tense show the same irregularity in the formal commands.

	pensar (ie)	tener	volver (ue)	seguir (i)
yo	pienso	tengo	vuelvo	sigo
Ud.	piense	tenga	vuelva	siga
Uds.	piensen	tengan	vuelvan	sigan

☐ A few verbs have irregular **Ud.** and **Uds.** command forms. For example:

ir *vaya / vayan*   **dar** *dé / den*

☐ Verbs ending in **-car (pescar)**, **-gar (navegar)**, **-zar (empezar)**, and **-ger (proteger)** have a spelling change in the **Ud.** and **Uds.** forms of the command.

No pesque en el lago.	*Empiecen a caminar ahora.*
Naveguen los rápidos.	*Proteja el medio ambiente.*

☐ Direct and indirect object pronouns are attached to the end of the affirmative formal command. With negative formal commands, they are placed between the ***no*** and the verb.

Denle la brújula al guía.	*No les den comida a los animales.*

68

For students having difficulty using the preterite to talk about saying what they did in school, you might consider:
- **The tutor page:** Pair the student with a native speaker or a more able student, using the tutor page.

Optional activity: See page 60D: *Piense en su planeta*

Los consejos de un(a) amigo(a)

Tus amigos van a pasar el fin de semana al aire libre.
¿Qué consejos les das?

Saquen muchas fotos.

 Vamos de campamento

El/la profesor(a) de español va de campamento por
primera vez. ¿Qué consejos le das?

Lleve una brújula.

Consejos
* *sacar muchas fotos*
* *proteger el medio ambiente*
* *acampar cerca del lago*
* *llevar sacos de dormir*
* *no navegar los rápidos sin el casco*
* *no ir de noche al río*

✔ **llevar una brújula**

✔ **no pescar especies en peligro de extinción**

✔ **llena de agua la cantimplora**

✔ **no tirar basura**

✔ **seguir las indicaciones del guía**

✔ **no hacer fogatas**

 ¿Por dónde voy?

Estás caminando por el bosque y una persona
que no conoces te pregunta qué tiene que hacer
para volver a la ciudad. Practica con tu compañero(a).

— ¿Por dónde voy?
— *Siga el sendero de la derecha.*

¡Por allí!
* *seguir el sendero de la derecha*
* *volver al río y caminar hacia el noroeste*
* *ir al lago y doblar a la izquierda*
* *seguir la señal*

69

Para hispanohablantes

You are a guide at a national forest.
Advise the tourists on what they can
and cannot do.

ACTIVITIES

Students use formal commands to talk
about outdoor activities.

1. Individual Activity
Give advice to friends who are going to
spend their weekend outdoors.
Possible Answers:
1. See model on student page.
2. *Protejan el medio ambiente.*
3. *Acampen cerca del lago.*
4. *Lleven sacos de dormir.*
5. *No naveguen los rápidos sin el casco.*
6. *No vayan de noche al río.*

2. Individual Activity
The Spanish teacher is going camping for
the first time. What advice can you give?
Possible Answers:
1. See model on student page.
2. *No pesque especies en peligro de extinción.*
3. *Ponga agua en la cantimplora.*
4. *No tire basura.*
5. *Siga las indicaciones del guía.*
6. *No haga fogatas.*
Extension: Give the same advice to two
teachers who will be camping together.

3. Pair Activity
You are walking in the woods. Someone
asks you how to return to the city.
Answers:
• See model on student page.
• *Vuelva al río y camine hacia el noroeste.*
• *Vaya al lago y doble a la izquierda.*
• *Siga la señal.*
Extension: Give the same directions to a
group of people.

CHECK

Ask students to give you advice using **Ud.**
commands:
• *¿Dónde puedo acampar?*
• *¿Es necesario llevar una brújula?*
• *¿En qué parte del río puedo pescar?*
• *Para llegar al lago, ¿qué sendero sigo?*
• *¿Qué debo hacer con estas latas?*

LOG BOOK
Have students write what happens to
different verbs when they are conjugated
in the **Ud.** and **Uds.** command forms.

Communicative Objective
• to say what you did in the past, using the preterite tense

Related Components

Activity Book p. 33-34	**Cuaderno** p. 18
Audio Book Script: Seg. 4 Activities: p. 18	**Transparencies** Ch. 2: Para comunicarnos mejor Transparency 15
Audio Chapter: 2B, Seg. 4	**Tutor Page** p. 13

GETTING STARTED

The preterite tense was introduced in Level 1, Chapter 7; the preterite of **ir** was introduced in Level 1, Chapter 10.

Language in Context
Review the idea of the past with a series of statements about past, present, and future actions. Example:
Ayer leí un libro. Hoy leo el periódico. Mañana voy a leer un poema.

DISCUSS

Review vocabulary from previous sections and introduce some of this chapter's vocabulary with questions and statements that use the preterite.
¿Visitaste a tu mejor amiga?
¿Hiciste la tarea de ayer?
¿Hizo Juan su informe para la clase?
¿Hicieron un viaje el verano pasado?
¿Adónde fueron?
¿Visitaron muchos lugares?
¿Navegaron en balsa?
¿Pescaron en el lago?
¿Observaron los animales?
¿Qué hiciste?

PARA COMUNICARNOS MEJOR

¿QUÉ HICISTE EN EL VERANO?

To say what you or someone else did, you can use the preterite tense.

— *Pasé un mes en Costa Rica.*	I spent a month in Costa Rica.
— *¿Y qué hiciste allí?*	And, what did you do there?
— *Aprendí a navegar en balsa.*	I learned to go rafting.

Here are the forms of regular *-ar*, *-er*, and *-ir* verbs in the preterite, along with the forms of the irregular verbs *hacer*, *ir*, and *ser*.

	visitar	aprender	vivir	hacer	ir/ser
yo	visité	aprendí	viví	hice	fui
tú	visitaste	aprendiste	viviste	hiciste	fuiste
usted	visitó	aprendió	vivió	hizo	fue
él/ella	visitó	aprendió	vivió	hizo	fue
nosotros(as)	visitamos	aprendimos	vivimos	hicimos	fuimos
vosotros(as)	visitasteis	aprendisteis	vivisteis	hicisteis	fuisteis
ustedes	visitaron	aprendieron	vivieron	hicieron	fueron
ellos/ellas	visitaron	aprendieron	vivieron	hicieron	fueron

☐ Regular verbs ending in *-gar (navegar)*, *-car (pescar)*, and *-zar (empezar)* have a spelling change in the *yo* form of the preterite:

navegar > nave**gu**é   pescar > pes**qu**é   empezar > empe**c**é

70

For students having difficulty using the preterite to say what they did in the past, you might consider:
• **The tutor page:** Pair the student with a native speaker or a more able student, using the tutor page.
Optional activity: See page 60D: *Y además…*

1 Una excursión

Tu compañero(a) hizo una excursión a una reserva natural. Pregúntale qué hizo allí.

— ¿Montaste a caballo?
— Sí, monté a caballo y saqué muchísimas fotos. Fue maravilloso.

De excursión

* montar a caballo
* sacar fotos
* navegar en balsa
* observar los animales
* acampar cerca del río
* aprender a remar

2 El fin de semana pasado...

A. En grupo, hablen de qué hizo cada uno(a) durante el fin de semana pasado. Anoten las respuestas en una tabla.

— Yo visité una reserva natural y vi muchas especies de mariposas. Y tú, Mark, ¿qué hiciste?
— Yo jugué al béisbol.

	yo	Lila	Mark	Pedro
pescar en el lago		✓		
jugar al béisbol			✓	✓
visitar una reserva natural	✓			
ir a un concierto				
hacer una caminata				
escribir cartas				

B. Informen a la clase de los resultados.

Lila pescó en el lago. Mark y Pedro jugaron un partido de béisbol.

3 Un viaje maravilloso

Tu compañero(a) y tú vuelven de Costa Rica. Un grupo de amigos les preguntan sobre el viaje.

— ¿Nadaron en el océano Pacífico?
— ¡Claro! Nadamos en el océano Pacífico y en el mar Caribe también.

Al aire libre

* nadar en el océano Pacífico
* ir a la costa atlántica
* visitar el Parque Nacional Braulio Carrillo
* cantar La bamba
* bailar reggae en la playa
* hacer tabla a vela
* navegar los rápidos en balsa

71

Students use the preterite to talk about things they have done.

1. Pair Activity
Ask what your partner did on a trip to a nature reserve.
Answers: See model on student page.
Extension: Ask what places your partner visited during other trips.

2. Group Activity
A. Talk about what you did last weekend. Write the answers on a chart.
Extension: Encourage students to add topics to the list. Examples: *hacer la tarea, limpiar la casa, mirar la televisión.*
B. Share your results with the class.
Answers: See model on student page.

3. Pair Activity
You and your partner arrive from Costa Rica. Friends ask you about your trip.
Possible Answers:
• See model on student page.
• ¿Fueron a la costa atlántica? No, nos quedamos en la costa pacífica.
• ¿Visitaron el Parque Nacional Braulio Carrillo?
  Sí, vimos muchas especies de pájaros.
• ¿Cantaron "La Bamba"?
  ¡Sí, fue pura vida!
• ¿Bailaron reggae en la playa?
  Sí, bailamos reggae en la playa.
• ¿Hicieron tabla a vela?
  No, no hicimos tabla a vela.
• ¿Navegaron los rápidos en balsa?
  Sí, navegamos los rápidos en balsa.
Extension: Exchange your answers with other groups. Report what the pairs did. Example:
Mercedes nadó en el océano Pacífico. Larry no acampó cerca del río.

CHECK

• ¿Qué lugares visitaste el verano pasado?
• ¿Hizo tu clase una excursión a una reserva natural?
• ¿Visitaron ustedes otro país en el verano?
• ¿Quién visitó tu casa la semana pasada?
• ¿Qué actividades de esta página no hiciste nunca?

LOG BOOK
Have students write five sentences saying what they did last weekend.

Para hispanohablantes

Tell the class what you did yesterday from the time you woke up until you went to sleep.

Objectives

Communicative:
• to talk about things you did on a trip
• to give environmental advice
Cultural: to learn about Tortuguero, a nature reserve in Costa Rica

Related Components

Assessment	Conexiones: 16A
Oral Proficiency: p. 22	**Conexiones** Chapter 2
Audio Book Script: Seg. 5 Activities: p. 19	**Magazine** Juntos en Costa Rica
Audio Chapter: 2B, Seg. 5	**Tutor Page** p. 14

GETTING STARTED

Students should now be able to correctly use formal commands, the preterite tense, and all of the chapter vocabulary. Review formal commands and the preterite by handing out index cards with verbs from this chapter. Students go to the board, write the infinitive, one formal command, and one form of the preterite.

APPLY

1. Individual or Class Activities
A. Read the advertisement and answer the questions.
Possible Answers:
• *En Tortuguero hay playas llenas de tortugas marinas, bosques de orquídeas y pájaros tropicales.*
• *La excursión sale a las ocho de la mañana.*
• *La excursión cuesta $75 por persona.*
B. Ask what your partner did during a trip to Tortuguero.
Answers: See model on student page.
C. Your friends are going on a trip to Tortuguero. Make a list of suggestions.
Possible Answers:
Lleven impermeables.
Usen botas de montaña o tenis.
Pónganse repelente de insectos.
Pónganse protector solar.
Lleven binoculares y cámaras.
Extension: With a partner, take turns dictating your lists to each other.

SITUACIONES

UNA EXCURSIÓN DE UN DÍA

Excursiones de un día a Tortuguero

Visite sus famosas playas, llenas de tortugas marinas y sus bosques de orquídeas y pájaros tropicales. Navegue por sus canales y vea una de las regiones más espectaculares del mundo.

$75 por persona
Salidas diarias a las ocho de la mañana

Programa: • Visita al Parque Nacional Braulio Carrillo
• Desayuno y almuerzo incluidos
• Paseo por los canales

Recomendaciones
Lleve: • Impermeable y ropa cómoda
• Botas de montaña o tenis
• Repelente de insectos
• Protector solar
• Binoculares y cámara fotográfica

1 Un día en Tortuguero

A. Lee el anuncio y contesta las preguntas.

• ¿Qué hay en Tortuguero?
• ¿A qué hora sale la excursión?
• ¿Cuánto cuesta?

B. Tu compañero(a) fue de excursión a Tortuguero. Pregúntale qué hizo allí.

— ¿Qué hiciste en Tortuguero?
— Navegué por los canales...

C. Tus amigos(as) van a ir de excursión a Tortuguero. Haz una lista de recomendaciones para ellos/as.

Lleven ropa cómoda...

> **PARA TU REFERENCIA**
>
> **incluidos** *included*
> **canales** *channels*
> **llenas de** *full of*

72

✓ CULTURE NOTE

The Spanish word *tortuguero* means "turtle catcher," but the 80 kilometers (50 miles) of beaches where green, hawksbill, leatherback, and loggerhead turtles come to lay their eggs are now part of a national park, and the animals are protected.

For students having difficulty talking about preparing for a camping trip, you might consider:
• **The tutor page:** Pair the student with a native speaker or a more able student, using the tutor page.
Optional activity: See page 60C: *¿Qué prefieres llevar?*

2 **Una excursión**

Pregúntale a tu compañero(a) si alguna vez fue de excursión.

— ¿Fuiste alguna vez de excursión?
— Sí, fui a una reserva natural.
— ¿Y qué hiciste allí?
— Exploré volcanes.
— ¿Qué animales viste?
— Vi mariposas...

 3 **Consejos para conservar el medio ambiente**

¿Qué consejos le das a una persona que va de excursión a un parque?

No tire basura.
No corte las flores.

 4 **Entrevista**

Entrevista a un(a) compañero(a). Pregúntale qué hace para ayudar a conservar el medio ambiente. Informa a la clase.

Azucena Vidal hace mucho para conservar el medio ambiente. En su casa, ella recicla periódicos, revistas, latas y botellas. En la calle no tira basura. En la escuela... En el parque...

 5 **Tu diario**

Escribe un párrafo en tu diario sobre una excursión a un parque. ¿Cuándo y con quién fuiste? ¿Qué viste? ¿Qué hiciste?

2. Pair Activity
Ask if your partner ever went on a camping trip.
Answers: See model on student page.
Extension: One of you pretends to be a famous person. The other interviews him or her about a recent vacation. Use **Ud.**

3. Individual Activity
Give advice to someone who is going to a nature park.
Possible Answers:
Mantenga limpio el lago.
No moleste a los animales.
No haga fuego.
Siga las indicaciones.
No corte las flores.

4. Pair Activity
Interview your partner to find out what he or she does to preserve the environment. Report to the class.
Answers: See model on student page.
Extension: Create a class bulletin board on ways to help protect the environment. Have three groups profile one area: **aire**, **tierra**, or **océano**.

5. Homework or Classwork
Write a paragraph in your diary about a day in a park. When and with whom did you go? What did you see? What did you do?
Extension: Make a list of things you can find in a local park. If you don't know a word, look it up in the dictionary.

CHECK

- ¿Qué hay en Tortuguero?
- ¿Qué necesitas para ir a Tortuguero?
- ¿Qué hiciste la última vez que fuiste a un parque nacional?
- ¿Qué debes hacer para conservar el medio ambiente?

LOG BOOK
Have students make a list of things they should bring with them on their next trip to the park.

Para hispanohablantes

Change all of the sentences in the text to the preterite.

PARA RESOLVER

Objectives
Communicative: to talk about geography
Cultural: to learn about the geography of Costa Rica

Related Components

Video: Tape/Book
Unit 1: Seg. 3

Scan to Chapter 2

GETTING STARTED

Ask students to look at the key to the map of Costa Rica. How many national parks are there? How many volcanos?

APPLY

In groups, students will make a map of their state or country. Students may have to consult reference books to gather the necessary information about their state or country's geography, animals, plants, etc.
Note: For purposes of comparison, you may want to assign other states or countries to some groups.

PASO 1: La geografía
Decide if you want to make a map of your state or of your country. Describe its location with respect to other places, and discuss its topography (physical features).
Answers: See model on student page.
Extension: Look at the map of Costa Rica and find similarities between its geography and that of the United States. Example:
En el centro de Costa Rica hay montañas. También hay montañas en el estado de Colorado.
En el norte de Costa Rica hay volcanes. También hay volcanes en el estado de Hawai.

PASO 2: Animales y plantas
Make a list of animals and another list of plants found in your state or country.
Answers: See model on student page.
Extension: Say which animals or plants you can find in your state or country that cannot be found in Costa Rica.

₽ARA RESOLVER
¡VISÍTENOS!

En grupo van a hacer un mapa de su estado o país.

PASO 1 La geografía

Decidan si prefieren hacer un mapa de su estado o de su país. Describan su situación geográfica con respecto a otros lugares y digan qué accidentes geográficos hay.

Vamos a hacer un mapa de nuestro país: Costa Rica.

Al norte está Nicaragua, al sur el océano Pacífico y al sureste Panamá y el mar Caribe. En el norte, centro y sur, hay volcanes y montañas. En la costa hay playas y selvas tropicales.

PASO 2 Animales y plantas

Hagan una lista de animales y otra de plantas.

Animales: murciélagos, pelícanos, flamencos...

Plantas: orquídeas, palmeras...

PASO 3 Las actividades

Hagan una lista de las actividades que pueden hacer.

Podemos observar las tortugas, pescar, hacer caminatas...

PASO 4 Recomendaciones

Hagan una lista de recomendaciones para las personas que quieran visitar su estado o país.

- *No pesquen en el río.*
- *Protejan los animales en peligro de extinción.*
- *No hagan fogatas.*
- *Sigan las indicaciones de las señales.*

PASO 5 El mapa

Hagan un mapa. Escriban en el mapa el nombre de los estados, océanos o países que rodean su estado o país. Dibujen los animales y las plantas que hay. Representen con símbolos qué actividades pueden hacer. Presenten el mapa a la clase.

74

el murciélago

el flamenco

el pelícano

los peces

N
O   E
S

OCÉANO PACÍFICO

PASO 3: Las actividades
Make a list of the activities you can do in your state or country.
Answers: See model on student page.
Extension: With a partner, take turns dictating the list to each other and correcting each other's work.

PASO 4: Recomendaciones
Make a list of recommendations for visitors to your state or country.
Answers: See model on student page.

PASO 5: El mapa
Make a map. Label the states, bodies of water, or countries that surround your state or country. Draw the animals and plants you can find there. Create symbols for the activities you can do. Present the map to the class.
Extension: Exchange maps with another group and write down descriptions of each other's maps. Ask questions about things you don't understand.

SÍMBOLOS

Parque nacional

Navegación

Pesca

Buceo

Área para acampar

Surf

NICARAGUA

la serpiente

la orquídea

la tortuga

el mono

la mariposa

la vaca

el quetzal

el tucán

el perezoso

la palmera

el jaguar

MAR CARIBE

PANAMÁ

PARA TU REFERENCIA

los accidentes geográficos
  topographical features

el buceo *snorkling*

el flamenco *flamingo*

la navegación *sailing*

el perezoso *sloth*

la pesca *fishing*

rodean *surround*

la vaca *cow*

75

PORTFOLIO

Students may want to include their map from *Paso 5* in their Portfolios.

Thinking About Language

Write on the board the question: *¿Cómo es el lugar donde tú vives?*

Ask if students notice anything unusual about the spelling in this sentence. (They may be used to seeing an accent on question words like **dónde**.) Ask how this is different from other questions.

Explain that **dónde** is accented only when it is used to ask the question, "Where?" In this case, however, the question is **cómo**, "how," and **donde** is used as an adverb.

Background

Tropical Animal Names

Here are additional words that students may be interested in knowing:

BIRDS
heron *la garza*
hummingbird *el picaflor, el colibrí*
macaw *el guacamayo*
parakeet *el periquito*
parrot *la cotorra*
spoonbill *el ave de cuchara*
stork *la cigüeña*

OTHER ANIMALS
alligator *el lagarto*
anteater *el oso hormiguero*
armadillo *el armadillo*
cayman *el caimán*
crocodile *el cocodrilo*
deer *el venado*
iguana *la iguana*
otter *la nutria*
peccary *el pecarí*
tapir *el tapir*
tarantula *la tarántula*

Para hispanohablantes

Write several sentences that describe the geography and climate of one part of the United States. Other students will try to guess which region it is.

Objectives

Communicative: to talk about conservation
Cultural: to learn about Costa Rica's national parks

Related Components

Audio	Conexiones
Conexiones: 16A	Chapter 2
	Magazine
	Juntos en Costa Rica

 GETTING STARTED

Ask students if national parks are important. Why or why not?

 DISCUSS

Using the Text

Have volunteers look at the photo and read aloud the text. After reading, ask some questions. Suggestions:

¿Hay muchas especies de animales en Costa Rica?
¿Dónde hay más especies de animales y plantas, en Estados Unidos y Canadá o en Costa Rica?
¿Qué es la ecología? (It is the branch of biology that deals with relations between living organisms and their environment.)
¿Cuántos años tiene el movimiento ecologista de Costa Rica? (In 1996, around forty years.)
¿Cuántos parques tiene Costa Rica?
¿Cuáles son algunos de los parques de Costa Rica?

CHECK

Te toca a ti
Answers:
1. *Falsa. En Costa Rica hay más especies de mariposas que en toda África.*
2. *Cierta.*
3. *Falsa. Hay más especies de animales que en Europa.*
4. *Falsa. El Sistema Nacional de Áreas de Conservación se inició en los años cincuenta.*

ENTÉRATE
PARQUES NACIONALES DE COSTA RICA

¿Sabías que en Costa Rica hay más diversidad biológica° que en Estados Unidos y Canadá juntos, más especies de animales que en Europa y más especies de mariposas que en África?

Costa Rica es el único país de América Latina que tiene un Sistema Nacional de Áreas de Conservación para proteger y estudiar el medio ambiente. Este movimiento ecologista se inició° en los años cincuenta.

Hoy día Costa Rica tiene más de 30 parques y reservas naturales. Dos de sus parques más famosos son el Parque Nacional Corcovado y el Parque Nacional Santa Rosa.

¿SABES QUE...?

Pura vida is the expression most used by Costa Ricans to describe their country. They say that their air is the cleanest and their forests the greenest of all the Central American countries. **Pura vida** is such a positive expression that Costa Ricans use it to greet each other and to describe all good things.

la diversidad biológica
  biological diversity
se inició *began*

TE TOCA A TI

Di qué oraciones son ciertas y cuáles son falsas. Corrige las falsas.

1. En África hay más especies de mariposas que en Costa Rica.
2. El Sistema Nacional de Áreas de Conservación protege el medio ambiente.
3. Hay 30 especies de animales en Costa Rica.
4. El Sistema Nacional de Áreas de Conservación se inició en los años noventa.

 CULTURE NOTE

The **Parque Nacional Corcovado,** on the Osa peninsula in the southeast, is Costa Rica's last great wilderness. It has more than 100,000 acres of tropical forest and beaches.
The **Parque Nacional Santa Rosa,** by the ocean in the northwest corner, contains the type of dry tropical forest that was once typical of much of Central America's coastline. Olive ridley turtles lay their eggs on the park's beaches.

VOCABULARIO TEMÁTICO

Actividades al aire libre
Outdoor activities
acampar *to camp out*
explorar volcanes
to explore volcanos
hacer caminatas *to hike*
ir de campamento
to go camping
montar a caballo
to horseback ride
observar los animales
to watch animals
pescar *to fish*
**visitar las reservas
naturales/los parques
nacionales** *to visit natural
reserves/national parks*

Equipo para acampar
los binoculares *binoculars*
las botas de montaña
hiking boots
la brújula *compass*
la cantimplora *canteen*
el repelente de insectos
insect repelent
el saco de dormir *sleeping bag*
la tienda de campaña *tent*

**Para navegar (los
rápidos) en balsa**
To go (white water) rafting
la balsa *raft*
el casco *helmet*

Animales y plantas
el flamenco *flamingo*
la mariposa *butterfly*
el mono *monkey*
el murciélago *bat*
la palmera *palm tree*
el pelícano *pelican*
el perezoso *sloth*
la orquídea *orchid*
el quetzal *quetzal*
la serpiente *snake*
el tucán *toucan*
la vaca *cow*

**Consejos para
conservar el medio
ambiente**
To preserve the atmosphere
Mantenga limpio el aire.
Keep the air clean.
No corte las flores.
Don't cut the flowers.
No haga fogatas.
Don't make bonfires.
**No dé comida a los
animales.**
Don't feed the animals.
No moleste a los animales.
Don't bother the animals.
No tire basura. *Don't litter.*
**Proteja las especies en peligro
de extinción/la selva tropical.**
*Protect endangered species/the
rainforest.*

**Recicle los periódicos/las
revistas/las latas/las botellas.**
*Recycle newspapers/
magazines/cans/bottles.*
Siga las indicaciones/las señales.
*Follow the instructions/
the signs.*
Siga el sendero. *Follow the path.*

**Expresiones y
palabras**
Al noreste (de)...
To the northeast (of) . . .
Al noroeste (de)...
To the northwest (of) . . .
Al sureste (de)...
To the southeast (of) . . .
Al suroeste (de)...
To the southwest (of) . . .
En el centro... *In the center . . .*
Ir de excursión.
To go on an outing.
hacia *towards*
hasta *to, as far as (destination)*
proteger *to protect*
seguir (e>i) *to follow*
la señal *sign*

Expresión de Costa Rica
¡Pura vida! *Cool!/Great!*

LA CONEXIÓN INGLÉS-ESPAÑOL

Look for infinitives in the *Vocabulario temático* that have English
cognates. Do they mean the same thing? Examples: ***acampar,
explorar.***

77

VOCABULARIO TEMÁTICO

Objectives
• to review vocabulary

Related Components

Activity Book	Audio
Chapter Review: p. 35-36	Assessment: 14A
Assessment	**Cuaderno**
Listening Script: p. 10	p. 19-20
Chapter Test: p. 51-56	**Transparencies** Ch. 2: Dibujos y palabras Transparency 16

Vocabulary
Point out that this list is organized by
themes. Use the headings to review
vocabulary. You may wish to ask Spanish
speakers to share variations on these words
and phrases with the class.

La conexión inglés-español
The rule in Chapter One for discovering
English cognates is to consider the stem
of the Spanish infinitive and possibly add
the English letter "e." Verbs in this chapter that clearly follow that rule are
explorar, observar, and *visitar.*

ADELANTE

Objectives

Prereading Strategy: to determine the main idea of a reading based on photo captions

Cultural: to learn about the ethnic, ecological, and geographic diversity of Costa Rica

Related Components

Magazine	Video: Tape/Book
Juntos en Costa Rica	Unit 1: Seg. 4

Scan to Adelante

GETTING STARTED

Using the Video

Show Segment 4 of the Unit 1 video, an introduction to Costa Rica.

Antes de leer

Have students read the paragraph and answer the question. (Answer: b)

About Costa Rica's Geography

Costa Rica has a tropical climate. The dry season runs from December to May; the wet season lasts from June to November. The terrain is diverse. The coastal plains on the Caribbean and the Pacific are separated by mountains and volcanoes.

Costa Rica's environment is threatened by deforestation—largely a result of clearing land for cattle ranching—and resultant soil erosion. The small Central American nation is also subject to a variety of natural disasters: occasional earthquakes, hurricanes on the Caribbean coast, flooding of lowlands at the onset of the rainy season, and volcanic eruptions.

ADELANTE

ANTES DE LEER

Costa Rica limita° al norte con Nicaragua y al sureste con Panamá y es uno de los países más pequeños de América Latina. Tiene una gran diversidad étnica,° biológica y geográfica.

Mira las fotos de las páginas 78–81.

¿Cuál es el tema principal?

    a. La diversidad de América Central.

    b. La diversidad étnica de Costa Rica.

    c. Los volcanes de Costa Rica.

la diversidad étnica *ethnic diversity*   limita *borders on*

78

ADELANTE COMPONENTS

Activity Book	Audio	Transparencies
p. 37-40	Adelante: 3A, 3B	Unit 1: Adelante
Assessment	**Magazine**	Transparencies 17-18
Portfolio: p. 33-34	Juntos en Costa Rica	**Video: Tape/Book**
		Unit 1: Seg. 4-5

◄ Costa Rica tiene miles de especies de orquídeas. La *guaria morada* es la flor nacional.

◄ En la cordillera Central hay volcanes activos.°

◄ Una de las riquezas° de Costa Rica es su diversidad étnica y cultural.

activos *active*   las riquezas *riches*

79

Using the Photos

Guaria Morada
There are more than 1,400 species of orchids in Costa Rica.
¿Qué es la guaria morada?
¿Qué tipo de clima crees que necesitan las orquídeas?
¿Cuál creen Uds. que debe ser la flor nacional de Estados Unidos?
Botany Link: Do you know the state flower of your state? Why do you think states have official flowers?

Cordillera Central
Central America was formed in large part by volcanoes, and Costa Rica is still one of the world's most active volcanic zones. Dust and ashes from Irazú's eruptions in the early sixties seriously disrupted the economy.
¿Dónde está la cordillera en Costa Rica, en la costa o en el centro del país?
¿Cómo son los volcanes en la cordillera?
¿Conoces volcanes en otros países?
Geography Link: Locate Costa Rica's central mountain range on a map.

Diversidad étnica
Compared to other Latin American countries, Costa Rica's population is very diverse. Because intermarriage between Europeans and Native Americans took place from the beginning of the colonial period, most Costa Ricans are **mestizos**, or of European descent. Native Americans comprise 1% of the population, and Jamaicans, who arrived in the late 1800s, 2%. Costa Rica's current population is about 3,500,000.
¿Qué ven en la foto?
¿De dónde son estas personas?
¿Por qué dice que hay diversidad étnica en Costa Rica?

Para hispanohablantes

Talk with the class about the geography and climate of countries you have visited. If you have not been to another country, talk, in Spanish, about the geography and climate where you live.

▶▶▶ INTERNET LINK

Pictures of Costa Rica http://www.hip.atr.co.jp/~ray/cr.html

Objectives

Reading Strategy: to elicit meaning from context; to use photos to facilitate reading comprehension
Cultural: to learn about ecological, geographical, and ethnic diversity of Costa Rica

Related Components

Activity Book	Audio
p. 37	Adelante: 3A

GETTING STARTED

Ask students if they have ever visited a country with a tropical climate like that of Costa Rica. What sorts of places and things would they expect to find there?

Background

Costa Rica is one of the world's most ecologically conscious nations. A large part of the country has been set aside as natural reserves. There is at least one park area for every type of ecosystem in the country, from volcanic summits to wet lowlands. Although eco-tourists from all over the world come to admire the parks, there are no lodges or hotels there. Little of the park budget goes into tourism facilities; most is spent on protecting the plants and animals.

Identifying Main Ideas and Details

Have students notice that the subheadings in the text identify main ideas. With your students, construct a chart showing the main ideas and details of the passage.

Reading Aloud

Have volunteers take turns reading aloud paragraphs from the article.

LA DIVERSIDAD DE
Costa Rica

▲ El volcán Arenal es uno de los volcanes más activos del mundo.

Costa Rica está entre el océano Pacífico y el mar Caribe, y es el puente° natural entre América del Norte y América del Sur. Su paisaje, su flora y su fauna son muy diversos.

El paisaje

La cordillera Central está situada entre las tierras bajas° del Caribe y las playas del Pacífico. Esta cadena° de montañas tiene volcanes activos, como el volcán Irazú, el volcán Poás y el volcán Arenal. Allí también hay grandes valles donde se cultiva° café. En estos valles vive la mayor parte de la población. En el valle Central está San José, la capital de Costa Rica.

La flora

Costa Rica es un país relativamente pequeño, pero tiene varios climas y ecosistemas. Tiene bosques tropicales secos° y lluviosos. En estos bosques hay más de 13.000 especies de plantas. Esta diversidad de hábitats permite° una gran diversidad de fauna.

▲ La piña es una de las frutas que puedes encontrar en los bosques tropicales.

▲ San José está en el valle Central.

la cadena *chain*	secos *dry*
permite *allows*	se cultiva *is grown*
el puente *bridge*	las tierras bajas *lowlands*

80

▲ **El quetzal.**

El tigrillo ▼

La fauna

En Costa Rica hay muchísimas especies de insectos, reptiles, mamíferos y aves.

¿Sabes que allí hay más especies de mariposas que en África? El tipo de mariposa más conocido es la mariposa celeste común, que vive en la costa atlántica.

En las montañas puedes ver el quetzal. Su nombre viene de una palabra azteca que significa "hermoso" o "precioso". Este pájaro tiene plumas° de colores vivos y una larga cola que puede medir hasta 1 metro.

Uno de los reptiles más conocidos es la iguana verde. También hay mamíferos como el puma, el tigrillo, el ocelote, el mono ardilla° y el mono congo.°

Una de las atracciones más grandes de Costa Rica es su variedad de tortugas marinas. Miles de tortugas anidan en las playas del Atlántico y del Pacífico.

La gente

La población de Costa Rica es muy diversa. Gran parte de la población de Costa Rica es de origen español y mestiza°. Un pequeño porcentaje de la población costarricense es de origen africano, asiático o del medio oriente. En las regiones norte y sur del país hay indígenas que aún hablan dialectos nativos.

En las calles de San José. ▼

mestiza *of Spanish and indigenous descent*
el mono ardilla *squirrel monkey*

el mono congo *black monkey*
las plumas *feathers*

81

DISCUSS

Suggestions for discussion:

El paisaje

¿Cuál es la capital de Costa Rica?
¿Dónde está San José?
¿Qué es Irazú?
¿Hay volcanes activos en Costa Rica?
¿Qué se cultiva en Costa Rica?

La flora

Costa Rica tiene árboles muy altos. ¿En qué parte del país crees que se encuentran, en bosques secos o lluviosos?

La fauna

¿La mariposa es insecto, reptil o ave?
¿De qué reptil se habla en esta sección?
¿Puedes nombrar un mamífero que se encuentra en Costa Rica?
¿De qué ave se habla? Descríbela.
De todos los animales de que se hablan en esta sección, ¿cuáles te gustaría observar?

Biology Link: What are some examples of the fauna where you live?

La gente

¿Cuál es la composición étnica de gran parte de la población de Costa Rica?
¿Qué tipo de lenguajes se hablan en el norte y el sur del país?

Ethnology Link: In Costa Rica, as in the US, some indigenous people live in reservations. Today there are about 75,000 indigenous people who speak *guatuso, cabécar,* and *bribrí.* Courses in these languages are offered in Costa Rican universities.

CHECK

- *Vas a pasar dos días en Costa Rica. ¿Qué parte del país quieres visitar? ¿Por qué?*
- *¿A quién le interesaría visitar Costa Rica, a un arqueólogo, a un botánico, a un médico o a un químico? ¿Por qué?*

LOG BOOK

Have students imagine that they are visiting one of Costa Rica's parks. Ask them to describe some of the things they saw today.

These activities can be done as classwork or as homework.

Objectives

Organizing Skills: to categorize key information in a reading

Communication Skills: to develop vocabulary

Related Components

Activity Book p. 38	Assessment Portfolio: p. 33-34

ACTIVITIES

1. La diversidad de Costa Rica

Individual Activity Write about the diversity of Costa Rica. You may want to consult your library for additional information on Costa Rica's diversity.

Possible Answers: *Paisaje: Porque hay playas, tierras bajas, valles, una cordillera central y volcanes. Flora: Porque hay más de 13.000 especies de plantas. Fauna: Porque hay muchísimas especies de insectos, reptiles, mamíferos y aves.*

2. Doce preguntas

Group Activity Form two groups. Each group must think of six questions about the reading to ask the other group. Write down their answers.

• if you answer correctly, you get a point
• if you can't answer, you lose a turn

Answers: Answers will vary.

3. Clasifica los animales

Individual Activity Classify each animal.

Answers: *Insectos: las mariposas; Aves: los quetzales; Reptiles: las iguanas verdes y las tortugas marinas; Mamíferos: los pumas, tigrillos, ocelotes, y los monos ardilla y congo*

4. ¿Cierto o falso?

Individual Activity Say whether each statement is true or false.

Answers: **1.** *falso* **2.** *cierto* **3.** *cierto* **4.** *falso* **5.** *cierto*

---

❶ La diversidad de Costa Rica

Escribe una oración usando cada categoría para explicar por qué decimos que en Costa Rica hay mucha diversidad.

❷ Doce preguntas

Formen dos grupos. Cada grupo escribe seis preguntas sobre Costa Rica y le hace las preguntas al otro grupo. Anoten las respuestas. Los grupos ganan un punto por cada respuesta correcta. Si un grupo no sabe la respuesta, pierde su turno.

❸ Clasifica los animales

Mira las páginas anteriores. Haz una lista de los animales que puedes encontrar en Costa Rica y clasifícalos.

❹ ¿Cierto o falso?

Di si las oraciones son ciertas o falsas. Corrige las oraciones falsas.

1. Costa Rica es un país muy grande.
2. Costa Rica tiene gran diversidad de flora, fauna, paisajes y población.
3. La cordillera Central tiene volcanes activos.
4. En Costa Rica no hay bosques tropicales.
5. El nombre *quetzal* viene de una palabra azteca que significa hermoso o precioso.

TALLER DE ESCRITORES

1. ESCRIBE DESDE SAN JOSÉ

San José, la capital de Costa Rica, tiene un sistema de direcciones muy original: muchas veces no aparece el nombre de la calle o el número de la casa. Simplemente indica a cuántos metros está (al este, oeste, norte o sur) de otro lugar.

Mira los anuncios:

¿Cuáles son las direcciones?

> MUSEO LA SELVA
> TROPICAL
>
> Visite nuestra famosa colección de mariposas y otros artrópodos de todo el mundo.
>
> 300 metros al oeste del puente sobre el río Virilla.
>
> Abierto todos los días de 9 a.m. a 6 p.m.

> ¡Hola! Sandra
> Te escribo desde San José.
> Me estoy divirtiendo muchísimo.
> Besos.
>
> Teo
>
> Sandra Pórtoles
> 25 metros al norte de la Avenida Central.
> Número 324 San José.
> Costa Rica

> Alquiler de motos
> **Oasis, S.A.**
> *¡Disfruta de Costa Rica en moto!*
> 25 metros al este de
> Autos la Castellana
> Avenida 10,
> Número 272,
> San José
> Teléfono: (506)23-2736

Imagínate que estás de viaje en Costa Rica. Escríbeles una postal a tus padres o a tus amigos(as) contándoles todo lo que hiciste y viste. Pero, ¡atención! Vas a escribir su dirección como se hace en Costa Rica.

> ¡OJO!
>
> 1 METRO = ALGO MÁS DE 3 PIES,
> **39,37 pulgadas°**

2. ¿ADÓNDE QUIERES IR?

Escoge un país de América Latina que te gustaría visitar. Escribe cuatro oraciones explicando por qué quieres viajar allí.

Quiero ir a Costa Rica para observar los animales y navegar los rápidos del río Reventazón.

3. UN CARTEL DEL MEDIO AMBIENTE

Haz un cartel para poner en tu escuela o en tu comunidad. Escribe cinco consejos para conservar el medio ambiente.

una pulgada *inch*

83

TALLER DE ESCRITORES

Objectives
- to practice writing
- to use vocabulary and structures from this unit

Related Components

Activity Book	Assessment
p. 39	Portfolio: p. 33-34

ACTIVITIES

1. Escribe desde San José
Individual Activity
A. Students will look at the pictures and write what the addresses are.
Suggest that students answer the first question by making a drawing.
B. Students will write a postcard to parents or friends about what they did and saw. They should write the recipient's address in the same style as that used in Costa Rica. Encourage the use of direct-object pronouns through such phrases as: *la visité el sábado* or *el guía nos llevó.*

2. ¿Adónde quieres ir?
Individual Activity Students will select a Latin American country and write why they would like to travel there.

3. Un cartel del medio ambiente
Individual Activity Students will make a poster for the school or community. It will include five pieces of advice for protecting the environment.
Offer examples like these to encourage the use of direct-object pronouns:
El medio ambiente—debemos cuidarlo.
Las tortugas marinas—hay que protegerlas.

PORTFOLIO
Have students select one of these assignments for their Portfolios.

Para hispanohablantes

Write a letter to a friend in another country. Tell that person about what you have been doing here in the United States.

Objectives

Communicative: to listen to and understand directions

Cultural: to learn how orchids grow in their natural environment

• to make "orchid trees"

Related Components

Assessment	Video: Tape/Book
Portfolio: p. 33-34	Unit 1: Seg, 5
Transparencies	
Unit 1: Project	
Transparency 17	

Scan to La obra

Materials

• orchids
• a bag of moss
• a branch of a tree
• a wooden board
• a saw
• a spray bottle
• a hammer
• nails
• scissors
• string

GETTING STARTED

In this exercise, encourage students to use their eyes more than their ears. They should concentrate on the actions and listen only for clues, not for each and every word.

Have students look at the photographs on these two pages to get an idea of the nature of the project.

DISCUSS

Have students read the introductory paragraph. Make sure they understand that, in their natural environment, orchids attach themselves to trees and form vines. Ask questions, such as:

¿En qué tipo de clima crecen las orquídeas?
¿Podrían las orquídeas existir en un clima frío?
¿Son las orquídeas plantas trepadoras o árboles?

ÁRBOLES DE ORQUÍDEAS

La orquídea es una planta con flores muy delicadas que crece° en lugares húmedos. En los bosques tropicales lluviosos, las orquídeas trepan° por los árboles y cubren sus troncos° con flores. A estos árboles se les llama *árboles de orquídeas*. En los bosques tropicales de América Central y del Sur crece gran parte de las orquídeas de todo el mundo.

TE TOCA A TI

Escoge una o varias orquídeas pequeñas para hacer tu árbol de orquídeas. Puedes usar un bulbo o una flor en una maceta°.

Materiales

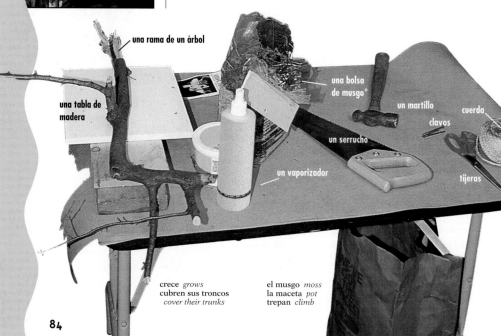

una rama de un árbol
una tabla de madera
una bolsa de musgo°
un martillo
cuerda
clavos
un serrucho
un vaporizador
tijeras

crece *grows*
cubren sus troncos *cover their trunks*
el musgo *moss*
la maceta *pot*
trepan *climb*

84

Research Project

Have students use the library to research information on orchids and other exotic plants. Ask them to organize what they learn according to what region of the world the various plants can be found.

Students will probably do this project as homework. To be sure they understand the directions, lead them through the various steps of the project.
1. Act out the process as you or a volunteer read aloud the instructions. (If you do not have orchids, use paper flowers or similar materials.)
2. After you have done this several times, invite volunteers to do it as you read aloud the instructions.
3. Do this as TPR with the whole class.

Have students perform the process of making an orchid tree as you narrate, but give the instructions in a different order.

LOG BOOK
Write down all the verbs that describe essential actions in making an orchid tree.

Para hispanohablantes

Use your own words to demonstrate each step to the class.

Con el martillo y los clavos clava la rama a la tabla de madera.

Si tu orquídea está en una maceta, sácala° con cuidado. Quítale la tierra° y corta las raíces.° Tienen que medir una o dos pulgadas.

Envuelve° las raíces con musgo húmedo. Después pon la orquídea sobre la rama del árbol. Con la cuerda, ata° la orquídea al árbol. Decora el árbol y la base con más musgo.

Pon tu árbol de orquídeas al lado de una ventana que dé° al sur. No lo pongas muy cerca de la calefacción.° La temperatura no debe bajar° de los 55 °F. Con el vaporizador, moja° tu árbol de orquídeas dos o tres veces al día.

ata *tie*
bajar *to drop*
la calefacción *heater*
envuelve *wrap*
moja *wet*

que dé *that faces*
quítale la tierra *clean off the compost*
las raíces *roots*
sácala *take it out of*

85

Thinking About Language
Ask students, particularly Spanish speakers, to think of flower and plant names they know in Spanish. They may come up with **rosa** (rose), **girasol** (sunflower), **margarita** (daisy), and **crisantemo** (chrysanthemum). Do students know any other names which are cognates?

Objectives

Communicative: to expand reading comprehension
Cultural: to relate the study of Spanish to other subject areas

Related Components

Activity Book p. 40	**Transparencies** Unit 1: Adelante Transparency 18
Assessment Portfolio: p. 33-34	**Video: Tape/Book** Unit 1: Seg. 4
Audio Adelante: 3B	

Scan to Adelante

El jardín Gaia

Possible Answers:

• *El jardín Gaia es un centro en Costa Rica que protege animales y plantas que están en peligro de extinción.*
• *Ayudan a animales del bosque que están enfermos.*
• *Cultivan plantas que están en peligro de extinción.*

Activity

Ask students to identify whether these comments were made by people who work in **jardín Gaia** or by people who work in a zoo.
1. *Muchas personas visitaron la jaula de los quetzales hoy.*
2. *Hoy les expliqué a unos niños qué animales están en peligro de extinción.*
3. *Hoy llevamos a una tortuga marina a la playa.*
4. *Los osos polares jugaron toda la tarde.*

El enigma de las esferas

About the Spheres

The spheres—some of which weigh more than a ton—were carved from basalt, a volcanic rock.

Possible Answers:

• *Porque no sabemos cómo los indígenas hicieron esferas de piedra con una circunferencia casi perfecta.*
• *Las piedras de Stonehenge, en Inglaterra; las estatuas de la Isla de Pascua, en Chile; las líneas de Nazca, Perú.*

ECOLOGÍA

EL JARDÍN GAIA

El jardín Gaia es un centro dedicado a la conservación de animales y plantas en peligro de extinción. Tiene dos proyectos principales: uno para la fauna y otro para la flora. En el primero, los científicos° ayudan a los animales enfermos del bosque tropical. En el proyecto dedicado a la flora, los científicos cultivan orquídeas y otras especies de plantas. El jardín Gaia también le enseña a la población a conservar el medio ambiente.

• ¿Qué es el jardín Gaia?
• ¿Qué hacen los científicos en el proyecto para la fauna?
• ¿Qué hacen en el proyecto para la flora?

ARQUEOLOGÍA

EL ENIGMA DE LAS ESFERAS°

Hace más de mil años, los indígenas de Costa Rica hicieron varias esferas de piedra° en Palmar Sur, cerca de la frontera con Panamá. Estas esferas son un enigma. ¿Cómo hicieron los indígenas esferas tan grandes y tan precisas? Nadie lo sabe. Algunos creen que no las hicieron los indígenas, sino extraterrestres; otros, que los indígenas las hicieron por medios mágicos.° Hoy día, los científicos todavía investigan este misterio.

• ¿Por qué son un enigma estas esferas?
• ¿Conoces otros misterios de la historia?

los científicos *scientists*	la piedra *stone*
las esferas *spheres*	por medios mágicos *with magic*

Activity

Ask whether these statements are true or false, or if the information is not provided in the reading.
1. *Los indígenas fabricaron las esferas de piedra con las manos.* (not provided)
2. *Algunos piensan que seres de otros planetas hicieron las esferas.* (true)
3. *Las esferas son de colores muy vivos.* (false, they are black)

Reading Aloud

Have volunteers take turns reading aloud the selections in *Otras fronteras*.

POLÍTICA

COSTA RICA, TIERRA DE PAZ

Costa Rica es el único país de América que no tiene ejército.° En 1948, después de una sangrienta° revolución, este país abolió° el ejército. En 1987 Oscar Arias, presidente de Costa Rica, y los presidentes de otros cuatro países centroamericanos firmaron° un acuerdo° de paz para América Central. Ese mismo año, Arias recibió el premio Nobel de la Paz. Con el dinero del premio creó la Fundación Arias para fomentar° la paz y el desarrollo° de América Central.

• ¿Por qué decimos que Costa Rica es la tierra de la paz?

• ¿Qué recibió Oscar Arias?

BIOLOGÍA

UNA GRANJA DE MARIPOSAS

Cerca de San José, Costa Rica, hay una granja de mariposas. Allí puedes ver más de 1.000 mariposas de 36 especies diferentes. En esta granja también puedes observar la metamorfosis de las mariposas. Te enseñan sus hábitos de alimentación° y reproducción. Costa Rica tiene un clima tropical perfecto para el desarrollo de las mariposas.

• ¿Cuántas especies de mariposas hay en la granja?

• ¿Qué puedes observar en la granja?

abolió *abolished*	el desarrollo	firmaron *signed*
el acuerdo *treaty*	*development*	fomentar *to promote*
la alimentación *feeding*	el ejército *army*	sangrienta *bloody*

87

Research Project

Form groups and ask each group to do additional research on one of the selections on pages 86 and 87. Students should use the library, as well as other sources such as interviews with teachers or classmates, if possible. Ask each group to write a report and to organize their findings according to the sources used.

Costa Rica, tierra de paz

About Peace in Costa Rica
Costa Rica does have a National Guard (*la Guardia Nacional*) that is apolitical and functions as a civil police corps. Oscar Arias was Costa Rica's president from 1986 to 90.
Answers:
• *Porque ese país no tiene ejército.*
• *Oscar Arias recibió el Premio Nóbel de la Paz en 1987.*

Activity
Ask whether these statements are true or false, or if the information is not provided in the reading.
1. *Se abolió el ejército costarricense después de una guerra con Nicaragua y Panamá.* (False, *después de la revolución*)
2. *Oscar Arias fue vicepresidente de Costa Rica.* (False, *fue presidente*)
3. *Arias recibió el Premio Nóbel de Economía en 1987.* (False, *recibió El Premio Nóbel de la Paz.*)
4. *Arias creó una fundación para la paz en Costa Rica.* (False, *es para la paz y el desarrollo de América Central.*)

Political Link: Have students talk about what would happen if all nations abolished their armed forces.

Una granja de mariposas

About the Farm
The butterfly farm is in La Guácima de Alajuela, a short ride from the city of San José. The tours offer information about bees and butterflies.
Possible Answers:
• *Hay 36 especies.*
• *Puedes observar muchas especies de mariposas y aprender sobre la metamorfosis de las mariposas y sus hábitos de alimentación y reproducción.*

Activity
Ask whether these statements are true or false, or if the information is not provided in the reading.
1. *La granja de las mariposas está cerca de San Juan.* (False, *San José*)
2. *En la granja puedes ver las mariposas más grandes del mundo.* (Not provided)
3. *En la granja puedes aprender qué comen las mariposas.* (True)
4. *En Costa Rica viven más mariposas que en cualquier otro país.* (Not provided)
5. *El clima de Costa Rica es bueno para las mariposas.* (True)

Tell your students...

In this unit we roam around Mexico, exploring highlights of the past and scenes from an energetic present that promises an even brighter future. First we check out a few headlines from Mexico's recent history (Chapter 3). We then look into today's technological advances and their effect on Mexican life (Chapter 4). In quick succession, we visit the sites of the terrible 1985 earthquake, the 1968 Olympic Games, and the economy-boosting 1970 discovery of vast oil reserves. We meet the great marathon runner Germán Silva, take classes via satellite in Monterrey, and, finally, design a house for the 21st century. Imagine what the Aztecs would say about a Mexico City in which there are more office buildings than parks, and in which the only canals left in Xochimilco are tourist attractions.

Before leaving Mexico, we visit Teotihuacán, an ancient city that was already in ruins when the Aztecs discovered it. They named it "the city of the gods," believing that only gods were worthy of a place so large and beautiful. After marveling at the Pyramid of the Sun and the Pyramid of the Moon, we take off for Toluca, where a master craftsman helps us make a Tree of Life.

VIDEO LINKS

Corresponding Video Segments

Text

**Unit Overview
Unit Opener**

1. Introduction to Mexico

A whirlwind tour of Mexico today and yesterday

Chapter 3

2. ¿Oíste las noticias?

Mexican news stories from the recent past and the present, including an interview with champion marathon runner Silva

Grammar: preterite of **-ir** verbs with spelling changes; indefinite and negative words

Chapter 4

3. La tecnología de hoy

How modern technology has changed Mexico, and especially Mexico City, the largest city in the world

Grammar: imperfect tense; comparatives (**más/menos... que, tan... como, tanto/a/os/as... como; más/menos que..., tanto como...**)

Adelante

4. Adelante

Teotihuacán: home to 250,000 people 3,000 years ago, "city of the gods" to Aztecs 500 years ago, and a fascinating archaeological site today

Manos a la obra

5. Manos a la obra

How to make a Tree of Life

Geography and Climate

Two mountain ranges, the Sierra Madre Oriental and the Sierra Madre Occidental, run from north to south and divide Mexico into three sections: the Pacific coast, with beautiful beach towns such as Ensenada and Acapulco; the oil-rich tropical Gulf coast, stretching from Matamoros to the Yucatán peninsula; and the historic heart of Mexico, the central plateau. Almost half of Mexico's 90 million people live on this temperate plateau, which covers only 10% of the country's land mass.

History and Government

Indigenous Mexicans began to farm land over 8,000 years ago, and by 1200 BC the first of many advanced civilizations had developed. Among these were the Olmecs, Zapotecs, Teotihuacanos, Mayans, and Toltecs. The last and most powerful of these pre-Columbian peoples were the Aztecs. In 1519, the Spanish conquistador Hernan Cortés and his army arrived on the Gulf coast. Two years later, Cortés had overthrown the Aztec empire and made Mexico a Spanish colony.

Great instability followed the withdrawal of Spanish forces in 1821. US forces invaded in 1846 and took all Mexican territory north of the Rio Grande. In 1876 Porfirio Díaz established a dictatorship which ended only with the Mexican Revolution of 1910. By 1920 one million Mexicans, including revolutionary general and folk hero Emiliano Zapata, had lost their lives in the conflict.

Since World War II the population has more than quadrupled, and Mexico has transformed itself into a modern industrialized nation.

The Mayan Past

The Mayan civilization that flourished on the Yucatán peninsula from about 250 to 950 AD was probably the greatest of Mexico's pre-Columbian civilizations. The Mayans had a 365-day calendar, based on the earth's orbit around the sun. In addition to being sophisticated astronomers and mathematicians, they were superb architects whose ceremonial centers featured tall pyramids of limestone with small temples on top.

Polvorones de nuez*

HANDS ON: COOKING

Objective
• to prepare and taste *polvorones,* traditional Mexican Christmas cookies

Use
any time during Unit 2

Ingredients
• 1 stick of softened butter
• 2 tbs. powdered sugar, plus more sugar for dusting
• 1 pinch of salt
• 1/2 tsp. pure vanilla extract
• 1 cup all-purpose flour
• 3/4 cup finely chopped walnuts

Supplies
• bowl
• large fork or pastry cutter
• cookie sheet
• wire rack
• colored tissue

Preparation
• Preheat oven to 375°F.
• Cream butter until light and fluffy.
• Add 2 tbs. powdered sugar, salt, and vanilla; beat for 2 minutes or more until light.
• Gradually beat in flour.
• Add walnuts.
• Shape into balls, using 1 tbs. of batter for each, and place them about an inch apart on the ungreased cookie sheet.
• Bake 15 minutes in oven preheated to 375°F, turning cookie sheet once.
• Cool on rack and dust with sifted extra sugar.
• Wrap each *polvorón* in colored tissue, per inset. Makes 24 *polvorones.*

FYI
A Christmas treat, *polvorones* have changed very little since they were brought to Mexico from Spain. They can also be made with almonds, pecans, or other nuts.

nuez—walnut

Las mañanitas* del Rey David*

MUSIC CONNECTION

Objective
• to sing a traditional Mexican birthday song

Use
any time during Unit 2

Materials
• TRB Activity Support Page 6, *Las mañanitas del Rey David*

Activity
• Distribute song sheet and read FYI below.
• Go over words that are new to students. Those who read music can lead the class as it sings.

King David's Morning Songs (Anonymous)

These are the morning songs
That King David sang,
And to each pretty girl
He sang them like this:
(Chorus) Wake up, my love, wake up,
Look, it's already dawn;
The birds are singing
And the moon is gone.

If the watchman on the corner
Would do me a favor,
He'd turn off his lantern
While my love passes by.
(repeat chorus)
And now, mister watchman,
Thank you for the favor;
You can turn on your light again,
My love has passed by.
(repeat chorus)

FYI
In Mexico, your birthday celebration starts with family members standing around your bed and singing *Las mañanitas del Rey David.* Later there's a party with presents, cake, and the traditional *piñata* filled with sweets and mementos.

mañanitas—morning songs
Rey David—King David of Israel: statesman, poet, musician

Calaveras* y calacas*

ART CONNECTION

Objectives
- to discuss the life of Mexican artist José Guadalupe Posada
- to generate original writing from some of Posada's most famous images

Use
any time during Unit 2

Materials
- TRB Activity Support Page 7, *Calaveras y calacas*

Preparation
- Distribute activity support page.
- Discuss FYI and the *Día de los Muertos* celebration.

Activity
- Have each student write talk bubbles and/or captions for two *calaveras*. The skeletons can be Mexicans or Americans talking about a past event or reacting to a news story. Or the skeletons can be classmates talking about classmates. Ask students not to use proper names.
- Have students read aloud what they write. Does anyone recognize the people portrayed?
- Display the skeletons with the most effective talk bubbles and captions—whoever they are!

FYI
In the stark, powerful lithographs* of José Guadalupe Posada (1852–1931), joking figures of death make fun of political events, sensational murder trials, and everyday human weakness and glory. Published in newspapers and broadsheets, Posada's lithographs circulated all over Mexico in the late nineteenth and early twentieth-centuries. The broadsheets for the *Día de los Muertos* (Day of the Dead) were especially popular. Posada's humor is black, his lines hard, and his contrasts sharp.

*calavera—skull
*calaca—Mexican slang for skeleton
*lithograph—print made on paper from an engraved stone or metal surface coated with ink

Televisión azteca

MEDIA/ART CONNECTION

Objective
- to explore a unique form of Aztec communication

Use
any time during Chapter 4

Materials
- TRB Activity Support Page 5, *Televisión azteca*
- pens, pencils, or markers
- large stick-on notes

Preparation
- Distribute storyboard.

Activity
- Share the FYI below, plus anything else you may know about Aztec news artists.
- Have students think of a story to tell with pictures—something that happened at home, at school, or on television.
- After they draw their stories on the storyboards, have students write captions for the stories and cover the captions with stick-on notes.
- Divide the class into pairs and have them exchange news pictures. Each writes new captions on the notes covering the original captions. No peeking!
- Students remove the stick-on notes to compare their captions with the original captions.

FYI
When Cortés and his army arrived in Mexico in 1519, Montezuma sent ambassadors to talk with the Spaniards, and artists to paint pictures of them. The artists worked on sheets of henequen, a quick-drying paper made from the maguey plant. Couriers then relayed the pictures to Montezuma, who was several hundred miles away and received them in two or three days. These artists were predecessors of our own courtroom artists, photojournalists, and television camera operators.

MÉXICO: AYER Y HOY

Unit Opener Goals
• to introduce Mexico and its history
• to discuss the influence of technology

Related Components

Transparencies	Video: Tape/Book
Unit 2: Chapters 3-4	Unit 2: Seg. 1
Transparencies 19-31	

Scan to Unit 2

GETTING STARTED

Distribute articles from newspapers or magazines about business and technology in Mexico today. After students have examined this material, ask if it contradicts images students have of Mexico.

Using the Video

Show Segment 1 of the Unit 2 video, an introduction to Mexico.

Using the Transparencies

To help orient students to Mexico, use the Locator Map Transparency. You may want to use other Unit 2 transparencies at this time.

DISCUSS

Presenting Mexico

For more information about Mexico's past and present, refer to pages 88A—88D.

Using the Text

English: Have students read the English introduction, then ask questions, such as: What are some examples of "modern technology"?
How does technology affect our everyday lives?
What everyday technologies did not exist when your parents were growing up?
Spanish: ¿Qué ves en las fotos?¿Cuál foto representa el México de ayer?
¿Qué tecnologías se utilizaron para construir el templo?
¿Qué hay en la foto pequeña?

UNIDAD 2

MÉXICO

AYER Y HOY

En la unidad 2:

Capítulo 3	¿Oíste las noticias?
Capítulo 4	La tecnología de hoy
Adelante	**Para leer:** Las pirámides del antiguo México
	Proyecto: Tu árbol de la vida
	Otras fronteras: Literatura, baile, deporte y ecología

Centro arqueológico maya de Uxmal, en Yucatán. Catedral y torre en Monterrey.

88

UNIT COMPONENTS

Activity Book
p. 41-64

Assessment
Oral Proficiency:
 p. 23-24
Listening Script:
 p. 11-12
Chapter Tests:
 p. 57-68
Portfolio: p. 35-36

Audio Book
Script: p. 25-22;
26-29
Activities: p. 23-25;
 30-32

Audio
Chapter: 4A, 4B
Adelante: 5A, 5B
Assessment:
 14A, 14B
Conexiones: 16B

Conexiones
Chapters 3-4

Cuaderno
p. 21-36

Magazine
Juntos en México

Transparencies
Unit 2: Chapters 3-4
Transparencies 19-31

Tutor Pages
p. 15-22

Video: Tape/Book
Unit 2: Segments 1-5

odern Mexico is as vital and current as today's headlines. As our nearest neighbor to the south, news about Mexico is reported in our newspapers and nightly news programs. You probably already know about some of the people and events that are part of Mexico's recent history.

In this unit, you will also learn about Mexico's aspirations as you unite its past, present, and future to form a picture of today's Mexico! Your picture will include the influence of technology on Mexico's present and future. It will also include many great treasures of Mexico's past.

That past will be found at the centuries-old pyramids of Chichén Itzá and Teotihuacán, the Zapotec pyramids at Monte Albán, the massive Olmec sculptures, and the Mayan ruins of Bonampak. You will take part in an ancient Mexican tradition by making a clay sculpture of a tree of life. These activities will give you a new appreciation of the rich culture of the Mexican people as they look toward the twenty-first century. Join them.

¡Únete a ellos!

89

 CULTURE NOTE

The Faro del Comercio (Lighthouse of Commerce) pictured above is a large concrete tower in the Plaza Zaragoza of Monterrey. At night, a laser beam from the tower sweeps across the city.

ACTIVITIES

INTERDISCIPLINARY CONNECTIONS

To provide other perspectives, have students research questions like these:

Technology

What makes Mexico City more vulnerable to earthquakes than other major cities? (The city was built on the site of several lakes, and the Valley of Mexico does not have natural drainage. The soil, therefore, is spongy and has a high water content. Parts of the city sink as much as one foot per year. Special foundations are created for new buildings, to prevent both shrinking and earthquake damage.)

Social Studies

Approximately how many Mexicans emigrate to the United States each year?

Economics

Find out what NAFTA stands for. What countries are involved and when did it go into effect? (North American Free Trade Agreement)

Para hispanohablantes

What cultures exist or once existed in the country your family came from? Share what you know about them with the class.

 **INTERNET LINK**

For a broad collection of WWW links from the University of Guadalajara:
http://mexico.udg.mx:80/grafica.html

	Objetivos page 91 ¿Oíste las noticias?	Conversemos pages 92-93 Las noticias	Realidades pages 94-95 México, los ultimos treinta años	Palabras en acción pages 96-97 El maratón
Comunicación	To talk about: • people and events that made the news	Discuss people and events that made news	Read text, answer questions, discuss news events, revise descriptions, make table	Read cartoon, make list; talk about characters; discuss yesterday's news; create dialog; design poster; write about this week's news and report to class
	• reactions to news events	Discuss reactions to news events		Read cartoon, create dialog; discuss news events; role play news scene
	• responses to emergency situations	Discuss responses to emergency situations	Read text, answer questions, make table	Read cartoon, make list; discuss yesterday's news; design poster; write about this week's news and report to class
Cultura	To learn about: • recent events in Mexico • the history of a famous landmark in Mexico City • the victory of the Mexican runner, Germán Silva		Timeline of 30 years of Mexican history; information about Mexico and Mexico City	
Vocabulario temático	To know expressions for: • typical news events	Talk about news events	Read text, answer questions, discuss news events and revise descriptions; make table	Read cartoon, make list; talk about characters; discuss yesterday's news; create dialog; design poster; write about this week's news and report to class
	• reactions to events	Talk about reactions to events		Read cartoon, create dialog; discuss news events; role play news scene
	• people who respond to emergencies/news events	Talk about people who respond to emergencies/ news events	Read text, answer questions, make table	Read cartoon, make list; discuss yesterday's news; design poster; write about this week's news and report to class
Estructura	To talk about: • past events; the preterite of decir, haber, and verbs with spelling changes	Discuss past news events	Read text, answer questions, discuss news events and revise descriptions; make table	Read cartoon, discuss yesterday's news; create dialog; discuss news events; role play news scene; write about this week's news and report to class
	• indefinite and negative words			

Para comunicarnos mejor (1) pages 98-99 ¿Oyeron las noticias?	Para comunicarnos mejor (2) pages 100-101 ¿Pasó algo?	Situaciones pages 102-103 El incendio de la Casa de los Azulejos	Para resolver pages 104-105 Las noticias de La Actualidad	Entérate page 106 Jeroglíficos mexicanos
Discuss news events; make up a news report; discuss yesterday's news	Discuss news events; talk about news events and news media	Read text, role-play interview with soccer player; write in diary	Make list of news stories; write and illustrate cover story; write up other news stories; list and describe your newspaper's sections; present front page to class	Discuss ancient Mexican civilization and its art
Discuss news events; talk about yesterday's news		Read text, make list; role play interview with soccer player; write in diary	Present front page to class	
Discuss news events; make up a news report	Discuss news events	Read text, answer questions; make list; write in diary	Make list of news stories; write and illustrate cover story; write up other news stories; present front page to class	
		La casa de los Azulejos, a famous Mexican restaurant in Mexico	Mexican runner wins the New York City marathon	Olmec hieroglyphics in Veracruz, Mexico
Discuss news events; make up a news report; discuss yesterday's news	Discuss news events; talk about news events and news media			
Discuss news events; talk about yesterday's news		**Re-entry of vocabulary**		**Extension of vocabulary**
Discuss news events; make up a news report	Discuss news events			
Use preterite of decir, haber, and verbs with spelling changes. Discuss news events; make up a news report; discuss yesterday's news	Discuss news events; talk about news events and news media	**Re-entry of structure**		**Extension of structure**
	Use indefinite and negative words. Discuss news events; talk about news events and news media			

Verdugo*

GAME

Objective
• to play Spanish Hangman, using Chapter 3 *Vocabulario temático*

Use
after *Palabras en acción,* pages 96–97

Activity

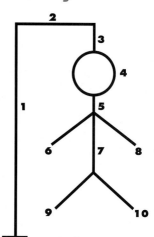

• Pair students.
• Player A chooses a word from the *Vocabulario temático* and writes a blank for each letter without identifying the word. For example, **preocuparse:**

— — — — — — — — — — —

• Player B tries to guess Player A's word in as few tries as possible. He/she might begin:
¿Hay una "a"?
A: *Sí, hay una "a".* (Player A fills in the letter *a*:

— — — — — — — a— — —)
B: *¿Hay una "d"?*
A: *No, no hay ninguna "d".* (Player A draws stroke 1 of the hanged man.)
B: *¿Hay una "t"?*
A: *No, no hay ninguna "t".* (Player A draws stroke 2 of the hanged man.)
• Play continues until Player B guesses Player A's word or the hanged man is completed. Then Player B chooses a new word and writes a blank for each letter.
• Players record the number of strokes on the hanged man for each word played. They must play an even number of words, and the winner is the player with the smallest total number of strokes. (See inset.)

*****verdugo**—hangman

¿Cómo te sientes?

ART CONNECTION

Objective
• to discuss emotional reactions, using Chapter 3 *Vocabulario temático*

Use
after *Palabras en acción,* pages 96–97

Materials
• drawing paper
• colored pencils, markers, crayons
• magazines
• scissors
• posterboard
• glue sticks

Activity
• On the board write verbs from Chapter 3 that refer to the emotions (*alegrarse, asustarse, emocionarse, preocuparse, sorprenderse*) and add others, such as *enamorarse, entristecerse, enfadarse, enojarse,* etc.
• Divide the class into as many groups as there are verbs. Give each group a piece of posterboard.
• On the posterboard, one member of each group draws a large face depicting his/her group's emotion. Other members of the group look for photos or draw pictures of a person or persons displaying that emotion.
• Group members give their characters names and write a few sentences using the group verb and other words from the *Vocabulario temático.* For example: Julie, from the *alegrarse* group, has a photo of a woman smiling at a bouquet of flowers. Julie says: *La señora Reyes se alegra porque su marido recordó su aniversario de boda.*
• Each group makes a poster with the group verb as its title. On the poster is the large face drawn by one group member, plus the pictures that the other group members found or drew.
• Groups trade posters and write first-person talk bubbles to accompany the cut-out poster pictures. For example, the person assigned Julie's picture of *la señora Reyes* might write: *Me alegra que mi marido recordó nuestro aniversario de boda.*
• Display the posters and use them for review.

¿Qué noticias hubo?

WRITING CONNECTION

Objective
- to write a news article from photographs, using the preterite of **-ir** verbs with spelling changes

Use
after *Para comunicarnos mejor,* pages 98–99

Materials
- photos from news magazines

Preparation
- Have each student bring in two or three color photos from a single news story. Make sure they cut off the captions.

Activity
- Display photo sets and have each pair of students select one to work with. First they write individual captions for the photos and then an article about the sequence of events, using the preterite of **-ir** verbs with spelling changes, such as **oír, destruir,** and **decir,** plus other verbs with spelling changes in the preterite, such as **leer, caerse,** and **haber.** For example: *El domingo pasado, durante la noche, un incendio destruyó una fábrica de cartón. Hubo que emplear más de 20 bomberos y 5 coches de bomberos para apagar el fuego. Un bombero se cayó de una escalera y lo llevaron al hospital. Los vecinos estuvieron muy asustados cuando oyeron las sirenas de los bomberos.* etc.
- Ask the students who brought the photographs to describe the actual events so that the class can compare the real story to the student article.
- Display articles with the photos.

Variation
- Have student pairs adapt their articles for television. One is the anchorperson in the news studio and the other is a reporter on the scene. Give them time to write questions and answers from the original article. For example: *Ahora vamos a hablar con el bombero Mario Rodríguez. ¿Cuántas víctimas hubo?,* etc.

A nadie le amarga un dulce*

GAME

Objective
- to create original sentences using negative words and other Chapter 3 *Vocabulario temático*

Use
after *Para comunicarnos mejor,* pages 100–101

Preparation
- Walk around the classroom and whisper one of these negative words or constructions to each student: **nada, nadie, ni... ni..., ningún, ninguna, tampoco.**

Activity
- Select a scorekeeper and divide the class into Teams A and B. Each Team A player thinks of a sentence that can be changed to accommodate his/her negative word. Each player from Team B thinks of a sentence using the negative word that can be converted to an affirmative sentence.
- Students go in row order, Team A players alternating with players from Team B. For example, a Team A player might say: *En mi casa no comemos carne.* Then he/she would say the negative word: *Nadie.* Opponent: *Nadie en la casa de Karen come carne.* This correct answer would give Team B a turn: *Ni el reportero ni el policía se preocuparon al oír el reportaje del incendio.* The second Team A person responds: *El reportero y el policía no se preocuparon al oír el reportaje del incendio.*
- Teams receive 1 point for each vocabulary word, as well as 1 point for each correct sentence. For example, the sentence *Ni el reportero ni el policía se preocuparon al oir el reportaje del incendio* receives 6 points: 1 point for a correct sentence with **ni...ni...,** 5 points for **reportero, policía, se preocuparon, el reportaje, incendio.**
- If a team cannot make a sentence, it loses its turn. No sentence can be repeated.

*A nadie le amarga un dulce—Nobody minds something sweet.

¿OÍSTE LAS NOTICIAS?

Introduce the chapter and its theme by asking students to think of some recent news events. Discuss what happened, who was involved, and what students' reactions are. Why is it important to read or watch the news?

Related Components

Audio	Video: Tape/Book
Conexiones: 16B	Unit 2: Seg. 2
Conexiones	
Chapter 3	

Scan to Chapter 3

GETTING STARTED

Have students look at the photo and ask questions like these:
¿A qué juegan los hombres en esta foto?
¿Qué relación tiene este deporte con México?
Ask if anything that happened in Mexico has been in the news recently. What was the story about? Why is it important to people in the United States?

Critical Thinking

Use the following activity to help students discover for themselves what they would need to know in order to talk about the news and emergency situations.
Ask students to think about typical news stories. Then have groups make lists of:
• natural disasters, such as hurricanes, and other emergencies
• events other than disasters or emergencies that we often see on the TV news, such as elections
• the kinds of people who often appear in the news
• reactions people may have to all kinds of news reports
• the workers involved in rescues
• what you might say if someone tells you about a news event
Have each group write its list on the board. Have the class discuss the lists and decide which items from each list are the most essential.
Have each group submit a revised list. When you finish the chapter, have the class review the lists to see how they compare to what they learned in the chapter.

CAPÍTULO **3**
¿OÍSTE LAS NOTICIAS?

Campeonato Mundial de fútbol, Ciudad de México.

90

CHAPTER COMPONENTS

Activity Book	Audio Book	Conexiones	Transparencies
p. 41-50	Script: p. 20-22	Chapter 3	Chapter 3
Assessment	Activities: p. 23-25	**Cuaderno**	Transparencies 20-23
Oral Proficiency:	**Audio**	p. 21-28	**Tutor Pages**
p. 23	Chapter: 4A	**Magazine**	p. 15-18
Listening Script: p. 11	Assessment: 14A	Juntos en México	**Video: Tape/Book**
Chapter Test:	Conexiones: 16B		Unit 2: Seg. 2
p. 57-62			

Objetivos

COMUNICACIÓN
To talk about:
- people and events that made the news
- reactions to news events
- responses to emergency situations

CULTURA
To learn about:
- recent events in Mexico
- the history of a famous landmark in Mexico City
- the victory of the Mexican runner, Germán Silva

VOCABULARIO TEMÁTICO
To know the expressions for:
- typical news events
- reactions to events
- people who respond to emergencies or news events

ESTRUCTURA
To talk about:
- past events: the preterite of *decir, haber,* and verbs with spelling changes
- actions: indefinite and negative expressions

¿SABES QUE...?
Mexico, our neighbor to the south, is never far from the eyes and ears of Americans eager for some extraordinary news. The event could be an Olympic competition or a World Cup soccer match. It could be a discovery by archaeologists about the mysterious civilization of the ancient Mayas, or hurricanes that meteorologists are tracking via satellite.

91

Here are some additional activities that you may wish to use as you work through the chapter with your students.

Communication

Encourage after-class activities that may enhance student interest and proficiency. Some ideas:
- compare a Spanish-language newspaper with one in English; see which news stories appear in both and which do not
- have students make lists of words they see in the Spanish newspaper that are cognates of English words. For example, they may find: *gobierno* (government), *presidente* (president), *clasificados* (classifieds)
- have students find an interesting news story about a Spanish-speaking country and follow that story in the papers or on TV during the course of this chapter

Culture

To encourage greater understanding:
- make a timeline of events in Mexico in the last twenty years
- invite a bilingual reporter, firefighter, police officer, or photographer to speak about his or her job—prepare questions for the guest speaker in advance
- show the video that accompanies Unit 2 of this textbook

Vocabulary

To reinforce vocabulary, have students:
- draw pictures of faces to represent reactions to news events (e.g., *asustarse, emocionarse*)
- collect photos from newspapers and, in Spanish:
  -label the people
  -make talk balloons
  -write captions

Structure

To reinforce this chapter's structures:
- Play *Viajeros* (materials: world map and self-adhesive notes in two colors). On index cards, write questions that can be answered with this chapter's structures (or vocabulary). Divide the class into two teams that take turns answering questions. If a team answers correctly, members choose a country, say its name in Spanish, and stick their color on that country. The team that "visits" the most countries wins the game.

 **INTERNET LINK**

Mexican Newspapers http://www.media info.com:80/edpub/e-papers.mexico.html

Communicative Objectives
- to talk about the news
- to say how you reacted to the news

Related Components

Activity Book p. 41	**Cuaderno** p. 21
Audio Book Script: Seg. 1	**Transparencies** Ch. 3: Conversemos Transparency 20
Audio Chapter: 4A, Seg. 1	

GETTING STARTED

Ask what the headlines or top stories were yesterday or this morning. How did students react?

ACTIVITIES

These activities give students an opportunity to begin communicating with each other and with you, focusing on the theme and objectives of the chapter. The activities can be used as oral class activities, or, if you prefer, you can pair students to achieve more interaction.

¿Cómo te enteraste de la noticia?
Class activity to review the names of media and introduce **enterarse**. Name a recent event and ask the title question. Have volunteers read aloud each answer.
Ask what verbs they could use to talk about these media. Examples:
encontrar, escuchar, leer, mirar, oír, ver

¿Qué oíste en el noticiero? ¿Cómo reaccionaste?
Class activity to introduce news vocabulary and the preterite of verbs that undergo spelling changes.
Ask students to identify the words through the logos. Rather than give a translation, they should give an example or description in English (e.g., "when the ground shakes violently").
Have volunteers read aloud and act out each reaction. Ask the question in the title for each of the events. Have volunteers select an appropriate response.
Have volunteers make sentences that name other situations, and have others react to each one. Example:
Hay mucha nieve y van a cerrar la escuela.

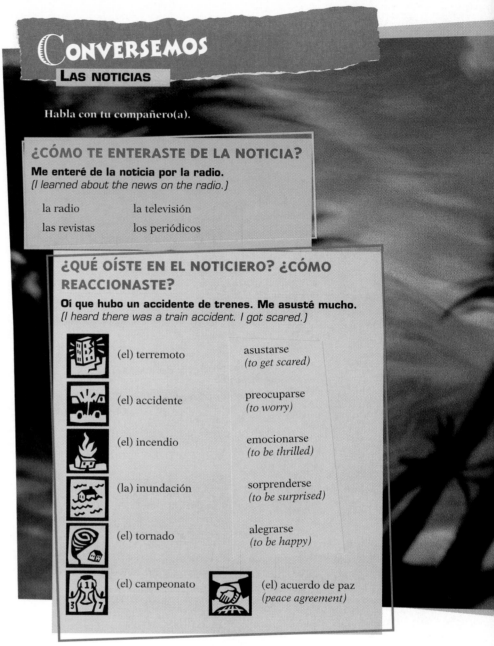

CONVERSEMOS

LAS NOTICIAS

Habla con tu compañero(a).

¿CÓMO TE ENTERASTE DE LA NOTICIA?

Me enteré de la noticia por la radio.
(I learned about the news on the radio.)

la radio	la televisión
las revistas	los periódicos

¿QUÉ OÍSTE EN EL NOTICIERO? ¿CÓMO REACCIONASTE?

Oí que hubo un accidente de trenes. Me asusté mucho.
(I heard there was a train accident. I got scared.)

(el) terremoto	asustarse *(to get scared)*
(el) accidente	preocuparse *(to worry)*
(el) incendio	emocionarse *(to be thrilled)*
(la) inundación	sorprenderse *(to be surprised)*
(el) tornado	alegrarse *(to be happy)*
(el) campeonato	(el) acuerdo de paz *(peace agreement)*

92

MEETING INDIVIDUAL NEEDS

Reaching All Students

For Visual Learners
Look through newspapers and magazines to find photos that illustrate the words learned in this lesson. Write a comment to go with each photo.

For Kinesthetic Learners
Prepare a pantomime of one of these situations. The class discusses what happened after each performance.

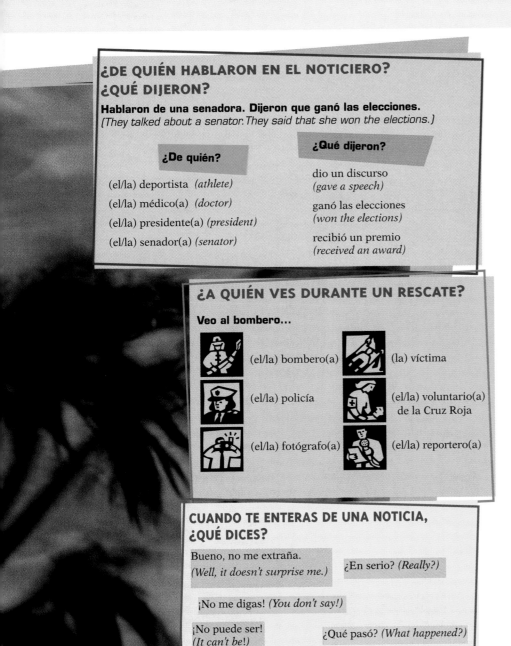

¿DE QUIÉN HABLARON EN EL NOTICIERO? ¿QUÉ DIJERON?

Hablaron de una senadora. Dijeron que ganó las elecciones.
(They talked about a senator. They said that she won the elections.)

¿De quién?

(el/la) deportista *(athlete)*

(el/la) médico(a) *(doctor)*

(el/la) presidente(a) *(president)*

(el/la) senador(a) *(senator)*

¿Qué dijeron?

dio un discurso
(gave a speech)

ganó las elecciones
(won the elections)

recibió un premio
(received an award)

¿A QUIÉN VES DURANTE UN RESCATE?

Veo al bombero...

(el/la) bombero(a)

(el/la) policía

(el/la) fotógrafo(a)

(la) víctima

(el/la) voluntario(a)
de la Cruz Roja

(el/la) reportero(a)

CUANDO TE ENTERAS DE UNA NOTICIA, ¿QUÉ DICES?

Bueno, no me extraña.
(Well, it doesn't surprise me.)

¿En serio? *(Really?)*

¡No me digas! *(You don't say!)*

¡No puede ser!
(It can't be!)

¿Qué pasó? *(What happened?)*

¡Qué horror! *(How awful!)*

93

Class activity to introduce types of public figures and reasons why we hear about them. Ask the title questions and have students match each person with an event. Then have students think of real-life examples.

¿A quién ves durante un rescate?
Class activity to introduce the names of the professions of people who are usually present at a rescue scene (or disaster). Have volunteers read aloud the name of each person and say or act out an example of what that person does. Name the disasters in *¿Qué oíste en el noticiero?* and ask *¿A quiénes ves después de (durante) un(a)...?*
Language Note: Point out that either **el** or **la** precedes the word **policía** when referring to individual police officers. When referring to the police in general, **la policía** is used. Explain that the word is derived from Latin and Greek words that referred to the state (as *politics* does).

Cuando te enteras de una noticia, ¿qué dices?
Class activity to introduce phrases used to respond to events. Model the phrases and then ask questions. Use the events in *¿Qué oíste...?* to elicit responses. Make up weather reports, descriptions of great or terrible meals, the imaginary weddings of famous people, and similar events to review vocabulary while working on these expressions.

CHECK

- *¿Cómo te enteraste de las noticias ayer?*
- *¿Qué oíste? ¿Cómo reaccionaste?*
- *¿A quiénes viste en el noticiero?*

LOG BOOK

Have students write a summary of who and what they saw on last night's news, and how they reacted to it.

REALIDADES

Communicative Objective
• to discuss events in Mexican history

Related Components

Activity Book p. 42	Audio Chapter: 4A, Seg. 2
Audio Book Script: Seg. 2	Cuaderno p. 22

GETTING STARTED

Ask students to name some important events of the past few years. Why are they important?

DISCUSS

Talk about the photographs and captions, and ask questions. Sample questions:

1968
¿Cuál es la capital mexicana?
¿Qué juegos organizaron allí?
¿Qué quiere decir anfitriona?

1970
¿Qué encontraron en México?
¿Qué es exportar?
¿Qué exporta Estados Unidos? (Examples: películas, discos, computadoras)

1978
¿Quiénes encontraron las ruinas del templo?
¿Qué es un metro?
¿De qué año son las ruinas?

1985
¿Cuántos edificios destruyó el terremoto?
¿Qué quiere decir México D.F.? (See the ¿Sabes que...? inset)

1986
¿Qué es el Mundial de Fútbol?
¿En qué año se jugó el Mundial en los Estados Unidos? (1994)

1994
¿Quién es Ernesto Zedillo?
¿Qué ganó?

MÉXICO DÍA A DÍA

REALIDADES

México LOS ÚLTIMOS TREINTA AÑOS

1965   1975   1985   1995

1968 Juegos Olímpicos. Por primera vez en la historia, un país latinoamericano organizó los Juegos Olímpicos. La capital mexicana fue la anfitriona.

1994 Zedillo, nuevo presidente de México. Ernesto Zedillo ganó las elecciones.

1978 Encuentran las ruinas de un templo azteca. Unos trabajadores del metro de México, D.F. encontraron las ruinas de un templo azteca del año 1428.

1970 Petróleo mexicano. Encuentran grandes reservas de petróleo. El país es ahora uno de los mayores exportadores del mundo.

1985 Un terremoto destruye muchos edificios. Un terremoto destruyó más de 1.100 edificios en México, D.F.

1986 Mundial de Fútbol. México organizó el Mundial de Fútbol. Argentina ganó el campeonato.

94

✔ CULTURE NOTE

Ernesto Zedillo was born in Mexico City in 1952 and educated at Yale University. He is a member of the PRI (Institutional Revolutionary Party).
The World Cup Tournament, the world championship of soccer, is held every four years.
The pyramid in the metro was once an altar in a large religious sanctuary.

HABLA DE LA REVISTA

A. Con tu compañero(a), habla de cada una de las noticias.

— *¿Qué pasó en 1970?*
— *Encontraron petróleo en México.*

B. Con tu compañero(a) corrige las oraciones según la revista.

1. Unos bomberos descubrieron las ruinas de un templo azteca.
2. Un tornado destruyó muchos edificios en México, D.F.
3. México organizó el Mundial de Fútbol de 1968.
4. En 1990 encontraron petróleo en México, D.F.
5. Argentina ganó los Juegos Olímpicos en 1968.

¿QUÉ PASÓ?

En grupo, escojan una de las noticias de la página anterior. Busquen más información sobre la noticia y hagan una tabla con la información obtenida.

¿Qué pasó?	¿Quiénes?	¿Cuándo?	¿Dónde?
Hubo un Mundial de Fútbol	Equipos de muchos países	En 1986	En México

Luego, informen a la clase.

¿SABES QUE...?

Like the United States, Mexico is a federation formed by many states. In fact, the correct name of the country is ***Estados Unidos Mexicanos*** (United Mexican States). Like Washington, D.C., the Mexican capital (Mexico City) has a special status and is not part of any state. It is a district in itself and is called ***México, Distrito Federal***, which usually is abbreviated as ***México, D.F.***

95

Communicative Objectives

To talk about:
- people and events that make news
- people who respond to news events
- how you feel about news events

Related Components

Activity Book p. 43-44	Transparencies Ch. 3: Palabras en acción
Cuaderno p. 23-24	Transparency 21
	Tutor Page p. 15

GETTING STARTED

Ask students to look at the drawing. How many different reactions can they find? What are the people reacting to in each case?

DISCUSS

Discuss ways to organize the activities that are going on in this drawing. What is the central event? Why are the reporters and photographers there? Why are there so many of them? Why are the firefighters there? Why is the ambulance there? What is the doctor doing? The volunteers? What is happening at the far right of the drawing? What does that have to do with what is going on elsewhere in the drawing?

Para hispanohablantes

If you use other words or expressions for some of the ones introduced in this chapter, share them with the class. For example, you may use some of the following:

el camión de bomberos: el coche de los bomberos
el campeonato: el torneo
el/la congresista: el/la diputado/a
decir un discurso: dar un discurso, hacer un discurso, pronunciar un discurso
el/la deportista: el/la atleta
¿En serio?: ¿De veras?, ¿De verdad?
el incendio: el fuego
el médico: el/la doctor/a, el galeno
el terremoto: el sismo

PALABRAS EN ACCIÓN

EL MARATÓN

el carro de bomberos
la bombera
el policía
el periodista
la reportera
el fotógrafo
META

 ¿Qué ves en el dibujo?

Haz una lista de las cosas que ves en el dibujo.

La ambulancia...

 En el maratón

Haz una lista de las personas que ves en el maratón.

El médico, el fotógrafo...

 ¿Qué hace...?

Habla con tu compañero(a) sobre cuatro personas del dibujo. ¿Qué hace cada persona?

— ¿Qué hace el fotógrafo?
— Está sacando fotos.

4 ¿Qué oíste en el noticiero?

Haz un diálogo con tu compañero(a) sobre las noticias de la última semana.

— ¿Qué oíste en el noticiero?
— Oí que Brasil ganó el campeonato de fútbol.
— ¿En serio? ¡Qué bien!

96

For students having difficulty talking about people and events in the news, as well as their reactions to the news, you might consider:
- **The tutor page:** Pair the student with a native speaker or a more able student, using the tutor page.

Optional activity: See page 90C: *Verdugo*

¿Pasó algo? — **Sí, hubo un accidente.**

los voluntarios de la Cruz Roja
la ambulancia

¡Felicidades, Roca!

¿Qué pasó? — **Alguien se cayó.**

el médico

¿Quién ganó? — **Ganó Roca.**

---

⑤ ¿Cómo reaccionaste cuando...?

Habla con tu compañero(a) sobre una noticia que oíste y di cómo reaccionaste.

— ¿Cómo reaccionaste cuando el presidente ganó las elecciones?
— Me sorprendí mucho.

⑥ Miniteatro

Eres un(a) reportero(a). Tu compañero(a) es una víctima, un(a) bombero(a), o un(a) voluntario(a) de la Cruz Roja. Pregúntale cómo reaccionó y qué hizo.

— ¿Cómo reaccionaste cuando empezó el terremoto?
— Me asusté mucho.
— ¿Y qué hiciste?
— Salí de mi cuarto.

⑦ Cartel

Diseña un cartel sobre las noticias más importantes de esta semana. Usa dibujos o fotos de revistas y periódicos. Escribe un pie de foto para cada ilustración. Presenta el cartel a la clase.

⑧ Tú eres el autor

Escribe un párrafo sobre una noticia importante ocurrida esta semana donde vives. Luego lee el párrafo a la clase.

Un terremoto destruyó un edificio de la avenida Colón. Hubo tres víctimas. La ambulancia llevó a las víctimas al hospital.

97

---

3. Pair Activity
Talk about what four people in the drawing are doing.
Extension: Do the same activity using the preterite tense.

4. Pair Activity
Create a dialog in which you and your partner discuss the news of the past week.
Extension: Exchange dialogs with another pair and edit each other's work.

5. Pair Activity
Talk about a news story you heard recently and say how you reacted to it.
Extension: Make flashcards for various reactions to news events (make drawings on the other side). With a partner, use the flashcards to test your vocabulary.

6. Roleplay Activity
Act out an interview in which you are a reporter and your partner is an accident victim, firefighter, or Red Cross volunteer. Ask how your partner reacted and what he or she did.
Extension: Write up your report.

7. Hands-On Activity
Homework or classwork for individuals or small groups. Design a poster of the most important news of the week. Use drawings and photos. Write captions for each. Present the poster to the class.

8. Synthesizing Activity
Write a paragraph about an important local news story from the past week. Read your paragraph to the class.
Extension: In a group of four, create a news story about an imaginary event. Each person takes the role of one person who was there (reporter, firefighter, etc.). Work together to create four accounts of what happened. (Remember, each person may have perceived this in a slightly different way.) Have each group member present his or her character's account to the class.

ACTIVITIES

1. Individual Activity
Make a list of the things you see in the drawing.
Extension: Write an adjective for each word on your list.

2. Individual Activity
Make a list of the people you see at the marathon.
Extension: Divide the list into masculine and feminine nouns.

CHECK

- *¿Viste las noticias del incendio en el noticiero de anoche?*
- *¿Qué oíste en el noticiero de ayer?*
- *¿Cómo reaccionaste cuando oíste qué equipo ganó el partido de fútbol?*

PORTFOLIO
Encourage students to include their poster or one of the scripts in their Portfolios.

Communicative Objective
• to say what happened in the past, using verbs whose spelling changes in the preterite

Related Components

Activity Book p. 45-46	**Cuaderno** p. 25
Audio Book Script: Seg. 3 Activities: p. 23	**Transparencies** Ch. 3: Para comunicarnos mejor Transparency 22
Audio Chapter: 4A, Seg. 3	**Tutor Page** p. 16

GETTING STARTED

Ask *¿Qué pasó en las noticias de ayer?* Ask about the people and the events that made news yesterday.

Language in Context

Use gestures to explain the meaning of each verb. Model the paradigms. Point out the spelling change in the third-person singulars and plurals. Draw attention to the fact that **caerse** is a reflexive verb.

DISCUSS

Review vocabulary from previous chapters and introduce some of this chapter's vocabulary with questions and statements that incorporate the preterite forms on this page.
Me caí de una escalera el sábado pasado.
El libro se cayó de la mesa.
¿Leyeron noticias importantes en el periódico?
¿Destruyeron edificios en tu ciudad?
¿Qué noticias oyeron en la radio ayer?
¿Qué dijeron?
La periodista dijo que hubo un terremoto en México. ¿Qué pasó después?
¿Hubo un incendio en tu ciudad? ¿Qué hicieron los bomberos?

PARA COMUNICARNOS MEJOR

¿OYERON LAS NOTICIAS?

¡OJO!

The preterite of **hay** *(there is / there are)* is **hubo** *(there was / there were).* **Hubo una inundación.**

To talk about news events, you can use the preterite tense.

Dijeron que el terremoto destruyó un edificio.	They said that the earthquake destroyed a building.

☐ Some verbs such as **destruir**, **leer**, **oír** and **caerse** have a spelling change in the preterite. This change takes place in the **usted/él/ella** and **ustedes/ellos/ellas** forms.

	destruir (to destroy)	leer (to read)	oír (to hear)	caerse (to fall)
yo	destruí	leí	oí	me caí
tú	destruiste	leíste	oíste	te caíste
usted	**destruyó**	**leyó**	**oyó**	**se cayó**
él/ella	**destruyó**	**leyó**	**oyó**	**se cayó**
nosotros(as)	destruimos	leímos	oímos	nos caímos
vosotros(as)	destruisteis	leísteis	oísteis	os caísteis
ustedes	**destruyeron**	**leyeron**	**oyeron**	**se cayeron**
ellos/ellas	**destruyeron**	**leyeron**	**oyeron**	**se cayeron**

☐ Another verb that follows the pattern of **destruir** is **construir** *(to build)*. **Creer** *(to believe)* follows the pattern of **leer**.

☐ To talk about what you or somebody else said, use the preterite of **decir**. Note that the stem of **decir** in the preterite is **dij-**.

Dijeron que hubo un incendio.	They said there was a fire.

decir (to say)			
yo	**dije**	nosotros(as)	**dijimos**
tú	**dijiste**	vosotros(as)	**dijisteis**
usted	**dijo**	ustedes	**dijeron**
él/ella	**dijo**	ellos/ellas	**dijeron**

For students having difficulty using verbs with a spelling change in the preterite, you might consider:
• **The tutor page:** Pair the student with a native speaker or a more able student, using the tutor page.
Optional activity: See page 90D: *¿Qué noticias hubo?*

¿Dónde lo leíste?

Tu compañero(a) te habla de las siguientes noticias. Pregúntale dónde oyó, vio o leyó cada una.

> — El senador José Caminos dijo unas palabras sobre el medio ambiente.
> — ¿En serio? ¿Dónde lo leíste?
> — No lo leí. Lo oí por la radio.

1. El senador José Caminos dijo unas palabras sobre el medio ambiente.
2. Hubo un incendio y los bomberos lo apagaron.
3. La periodista Lola Figueroa hizo un documental sobre los tornados.
4. Un policía recibió el premio Nobel de la Paz.
5. El periodista Zenón Zarabia ganó el premio Pulitzer.
6. Se cayó un edificio y hubo dos víctimas.

 ¿Qué pasó ayer?

Con tu compañero(a), forma oraciones.

> — ¿Qué pasó ayer?
> — Un terremoto destruyó el antiguo cine Variedades.

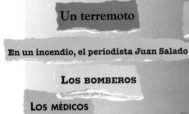

Un terremoto

AYUDARON A LAS VÍCTIMAS.

En un incendio, el periodista Juan Salado

APAGARON EL INCENDIO.

LOS BOMBEROS

RECIBIÓ UN PREMIO.

LOS MÉDICOS

se cayó de una escalera.

Una periodista

destruyó el antiguo cine Variedades.

 Las noticias de ayer

Habla con tu compañero(a) sobre las noticias de ayer. Pregúntale cómo reaccionó.

> — Ayer leí en el periódico que hubo un acuerdo de paz en...
> — ¡No me digas! ¿Y cómo reaccionaste?
> — Me emocioné mucho.

99

ACTIVITIES

Students use verbs with a spelling change in the preterite to talk about yesterday's events.

1. Pair Activity
Your partner tells you about a news story. Ask where he or she heard, saw, or read about it.

Possible Answers:
1. See model on student page.
2. ¡No me digas! ¿Dónde lo leíste? Lo leí en El Nuevo Herald.
3. ¿En serio? ¿Dónde lo leíste? No lo leí. Lo vi por la televisión.
4. ¡No puede ser! ¿Dónde lo viste? No lo vi. Lo oí por la radio.
5. Bueno, no me extraña. ¿Dónde lo oíste? Lo leí en una revista.
6. ¡Qué horror! ¿Dónde lo oíste? Lo oí por la radio.

Extension: Make up statements of your own for your partner to react to.

2. Pair Activity
Ask your partner what happened yesterday.
Answers:
1. See model on student page.
2. En un incendio, el periodista Juan Salado se cayó de una escalera.
3. Los bomberos apagaron el incendio.
4. Los médicos ayudaron a las víctimas.
5. Una periodista recibió un premio.

Extension: Make up sentences like these, write half of each on a different card, and have others try to recreate the sentences.

3. Pair Activity
Talk about yesterday's news. Ask how your partner reacted.
Answers: See model on student page.
Extension: Report to the class how your partner reacted. Example:
Yo dije que hubo un incendio en el centro comercial. Lorrie dijo que se asustó porque ella y sus amigas van allí todos los días.

CHECK

- ¿Leíste el periódico anoche?
- ¿Oíste las noticias por la radio?
- ¿Hubo un huracán? ¿Qué destruyó?
- ¿Viste una noticia importante en la televisión?
- ¿Cómo reaccionaste a las noticias?

LOG BOOK
Have students write sentences with the third-person singular and plural forms of the preterite of the verbs in the paradigm.

Para hispanohablantes
Ask other Spanish speakers what kinds of things they say when they hear about surprising or frightening news items.

Communicative Objectives
• to say that something did not happen, using words that mean *nothing, never, no one, none,* and *neither*

Related Components

Activity Book p. 47-48	**Audio** Chapter: 4A, Seg. 4
Audio Book Script: Seg.4 Activities: p. 24	**Cuaderno** p. 26
	Tutor Page p. 17

GETTING STARTED

Ask students for sentences that use the words *everything, always, someone, something,* and *all.* Write these on the board. Then ask what the opposite of each of those five words is, and use the opposites to replace the words. Example: *All of us went.* —> *None of us went.*

Language in Context

Go through the examples on the student page. After asking the question at the left, answer it with an affirmative (e.g., *Sí, pasó algo*) before modeling the two negative phrases.
Discuss the use of double negatives in both languages. Point out that in English a second negative is considered to negate the first one (e.g., "I did **not** do **nothing**" means "I did do something"). In Spanish, however, a second (or even a third) negative is seen as emphasizing or reinforcing the first (Yo **no** hice **nada**.)

DISCUSS

Review vocabulary from previous chapters and introduce some of this chapter's vocabulary with questions and statements that use indefinite and negative words and expressions.
¿Qué oíste en el noticiero? (No oí nada.)
¿De quién hablaron en la clase? (No hablaron de nadie.)
¿Ves a alguien en esta escena? (No veo a nadie.)
¿Qué pasó? (No pasó nada or Nada pasó.)
¿Qué te gusta más, Nueva York o Los Ángeles? (No me gustan ni NYC ni LA.)
¿Hubo algún problema con este ejercicio? (No, no hubo ningún problema.)

PARA COMUNICARNOS MEJOR
¿PASÓ ALGO?

To answer a question or to state something in the negative, you can use a number of different negative expressions.

No pasó nada.	Nothing happened.
No se cayó ningún edificio.	None of the buildings collapsed.
No hubo víctimas tampoco.	There were no victims either.

Note that in the examples, *no* comes before the verb and *nada, ningún/ninguna,* and *tampoco* follow it.

☐ Sometimes you can put the negative word before the verb and leave out the word *no.*

Ningún edificio se cayó.	None of the buildings collapsed.
Tampoco hubo víctimas.	There were no victims either.

☐ Note that negative words have contrasting indefinite expressions.

¡OJO!

The negative words *ningún* and *ninguna* have only singular forms and are always used with singular nouns.

Hoy no leí ninguna revista.

indefinite and negative words

indefinite word	no + verb + negative word	negative word + verb
¿Pasó **algo**?	**No** pasó **nada**.	**Nada** pasó.
¿**Alguien** visitó a las víctimas?	**No** las visitó **nadie**.	**Nadie** las visitó.
¿Se cayó **alguna** casa?	**No** se cayó **ninguna** casa.	**Ninguna** casa se cayó.
Yo **siempre** leo el periódico.	Yo **no** lo leo **nunca**.	Yo **nunca** lo leo.
Yo lo leo **también**.	Yo **no** lo leo **tampoco**.	Yo **tampoco** lo leo.
¿Juan **y** tú lo leyeron?	**No** lo leímos **ni** Juan **ni** yo.	**Ni** Juan **ni** yo lo leímos.
¿Lo dijo la radio **o** la televisión?	**No** lo dijo **ni** la radio **ni** la televisión.	**Ni** la radio **ni** la televisión lo dijo.

☐ Use the shortened forms of *alguno* and *ninguno (algún* and *ningún)* before a masculine singular noun.

¿Hiciste algún cambio?	Did you make any changes?

For students having difficulty communicating with negative words and indefinite expressions, you might consider:
• **The tutor page:** Pair the student with a native speaker or a more able student, using the tutor page.
Optional activity: See page 90D: *A nadie le amarga un dulce*

Los terremotos de Ciruelos

Los terremotos de Ciruelos nunca son graves. Pregunta a tu compañero(a) qué pasó en el último terremoto.

— *¿Qué pasó en el último terremoto?*
— *No pasó nada. Todo está bien.*

1. ¿Qué pasó en el último terremoto?
2. ¿Destruyó algún edificio?
3. ¿Hubo alguna víctima?
4. ¿Fue algún periodista?
5. ¿Fueron los bomberos o la policía?

 ¿Qué pasó?

Tu compañero(a) nunca lee las noticias. Pregúntale qué pasó y vas a ver qué dice.

— *¿Te enteraste del campeonato de ajedrez?*
— *¿Qué campeonato? ¿Hubo algún campeonato?*

1. el campeonato de ajedrez
2. el terremoto
3. el accidente
4. el acuerdo de paz
5. las inundaciones
6. la entrevista con el presidente

 Un periódico muy bueno

La voz de Ciruelos es un periódico muy bueno, pero a veces no da muchos detalles.

— *¿Leíste La voz de Ciruelos hoy?*
— *Sí, lo leí.*
— *¿Dice algo del incendio del cine Variedades?*
— *No, no dice nada.*

1. ¿Dice algo del incendio del cine Variedades?
2. ¿Hay alguna entrevista con alguien interesante?
3. ¿Qué te gusta más, la sección de noticias locales o la sección de deportes?
4. ¿Tú lo lees siempre?
5. ¿También ves las noticias por televisión?

101

ACTIVITIES

Students use indefinite expressions and negative words to talk about news items.

1. Pair Activity
The earthquakes in Ciruelos are never very serious. Ask your partner what happened in Ciruelos' last earthquake.
Note: Ciruelos is a fictional town.

Possible Answers:
1. See model on student page.
2. *No, no destruyó ningún edificio.*
3. *No hubo ninguna víctima. (or No, ninguna.)*
4. *No, no fue ningún periodista. (or No, ninguno.)*
5. *No, no fueron ni los bomberos ni la policía. No fue necesario.*

2. Pair Activity
Your partner never reads the news. Ask what happened and hear the response.
Possible Answers :
1. See model on student page.
2. *¿…del terremoto de ayer?*
¿Qué terremoto? ¿Hubo algún terremoto?
3. *¿…del accidente?*
¿Qué accidente? ¿Hubo algún accidente?
4. *¿…del acuerdo de paz?*
¿Qué acuerdo de paz? ¿Hubo algún acuerdo de paz?
5. *¿…de las inundaciones?*
¿Qué inundaciones? ¿Hubo algunas inundaciones?
6. *¿…de la entrevista con el presidente?*
¿Qué entrevista? ¿Hubo alguna entrevista?

3. Pair Activity
La voz de Ciruelos is a good newspaper, but it doesn't always include details. Answer these questions using negative words and phrases.
Possible Answers:
1. See model on student page.
2. *No, no hay ninguna entrevista a nadie interesante.*
3. *No me gusta ni la sección de noticias locales ni la sección de deportes.*
4. *No, no lo leo nunca.*
5. *No, tampoco veo las noticias por televisión.*

CHECK

- *¿Te enteraste de qué pasó ayer?*
- *¿Qué pasó?*
- *¿Qué te gusta más, la clase de matemáticas o la clase de español?*
- *Yo nunca veo la televisión. ¿Y tú?*
- *¿Llegó tarde algún estudiante?*

LOG BOOK
Have students make a list of positive words and their negative equivalents.

Para hispanohablantes

Think of a recent news event in the country your family came from, and share it with the class.

Objectives

Communicative: to talk about things that happened in the past
Cultural: to learn about a Mexico City landmark

Related Components

Assessment	Conexiones: 16B
Oral Proficiency: p. 23	**Conexiones** Chapter 3
Audio Book Script: Seg. 5 Activities: p. 25	**Magazine** Juntos en México
Audio Chapter: 4A, Seg.5	**Tutor Page** p. 18

GETTING STARTED

Students should now be able to correctly use indefinite expressions and negative words, several verbs that have spelling changes in the preterite, and the chapter vocabulary.

Ask students to skim through the title and article for words they recognize. What do they think this section will be about? Remind them of the things they learned about Andalusian **azulejos** in Level One.

APPLY

1. Individual or Class Activity

Read the brochure and answer the questions.
Answers:
1. *Construyeron La Casa de los Azulejos en el siglo XVI.*
2. *Decoraron la fachada con azulejos en el siglo XVIII.*
3. *La familia Iturbe vivió allí hasta 1891.*
4. *Sanborns compró la casa en 1919.*
5. *Hubo un accidente con el gas que causó un incendio.*
6. *Los bomberos y voluntarios ayudaron a apagar el incendio.*
7. *No, no hubo ninguna víctima.*

Extension: Make statements about the article and have others guess if they are true or false. Correct the false statements.

2. Pair Activity

Choose an emergency situation (an earthquake, for example). Make a list of things you should and should not do.
Answers: See model on student page.

3. Pair Activity

You are a journalist and your partner is a soccer player whose team just won the world championship. Interview the soccer player and then share with the class.
Answers: See models on student page.

4. Homework or Classwork

Write a paragraph in your journal about a news story you saw on television. What happened? How did you react?

Dictation

Dictate some phrases or words from the brochure to the class.

For students having difficulty talking about emergency situations and their reactions to them, you might consider:
• **The tutor page:** Pair the student with a native speaker or a more able student, using the tutor page.
Optional activity: See page 90C: *¿Cómo te sientes?*

SITUACIONES

EL INCENDIO DE LA CASA DE LOS AZULEJOS

EL RESTAURANTE LA CASA DE LOS AZULEJOS

reabre hoy sus puertas para dar la bienvenida a todos los mexicanos.

La Casa de los Azulejos fue construida en el siglo XVI. En el siglo XVIII decoraron la fachada con azulejos blancos de dibujos azules y amarillos. Hacia 1870 la familia Iturbe compró el edificio y vivió allí hasta 1891. En el siglo XX, el artista José Orozco decoró las paredes de la Casa con un mural. En 1919, la cadena de restaurantes Sanborns compró la Casa. El 25 de agosto de 1994, un accidente con el gas causó un incendio. El fuego no destruyó todo el edificio gracias a los bomberos y a los voluntarios que ayudaron a apagar el incendio. No hubo ninguna víctima. Después del incendio, se hicieron

cambios para restaurar la apariencia original del edificio.

PARA TU REFEREN

la apariencia original *original lo*
la cadena *chain*
causó *(it) caused*
dar la bienvenida *to welcome*
la fachada *facade*
fue construida *(it) was built*
reabre *(it) reopens*
se hicieron *were made*
restaurar *to restore*

102

La Casa de los Azulejos

Lee el anuncio del periódico y contesta las preguntas:

1. ¿En qué siglo construyeron la Casa de los Azulejos?
2. ¿Cuándo decoraron la fachada con azulejos?
3. ¿Hasta qué año vivió allí la familia Iturbe?
4. ¿Cuándo compró Sanborns la Casa?
5. ¿Qué pasó el 25 de agosto de 1994?
6. ¿Quiénes ayudaron a apagar el incendio?
7. ¿Hubo alguna víctima?

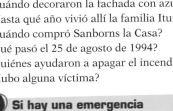

2 Si hay una emergencia

Escoge una situación de emergencia (un terremoto, una inundación, un incendio...). Con tu compañero(a) haz una lista de cosas que tienes que hacer y otra lista de cosas que no debes hacer.

— *Tengo que llamar por teléfono a la policía o a los bomberos, usar la escalera de incendios...*
— *No debo asustarme, ni usar el ascensor del edificio...*

3 Entrevista

Eres un(a) periodista y tu compañero(a) es un(a) jugador(a) del equipo de fútbol que ganó el Campeonato Mundial. Hazle una entrevista.

— *¿Cómo reaccionó cuando su equipo ganó el campeonato?*
— *Me alegré muchísimo.*

Luego, informa a la clase.

Juan García se alegró muchísimo cuando su equipo ganó el campeonato.

 Tu diario

Escribe un párrafo en tu diario sobre una noticia que viste en la televisión. ¿Qué pasó? ¿Cómo reaccionaste?

103

Communicative Objectives
- to write like a journalist
- to discuss the news

Related Components

Video: Tape/Book
Unit 2: Seg. 2

Scan to Chapter 3

GETTING STARTED

Ask students what kinds of news usually appear on the front page of a newspaper. How do they think the editors decide what is to go there?

APPLY

Form groups. Students will write and design the front page of a newspaper.

PASO 1: ¿Qué noticias hay?
Make a list of stories (true or invented) to include in your newspaper. Choose the most important as the cover story, and three others as front-page stories.
Answers: See model on student page.
Extension: Write questions about each news story to use as a guide for the following activities.

PASO 2: La noticia del día
Write the headline and text for the cover story. Find a photo and write a caption.
Answers: See model on student page.
Extension: Write a cover story about a famous event from the past.

PASO 3: Otras noticias
Write a headline and a short paragraph for each of the other news stories.
Answers: See model on student page.
Extension: Create advertisements for your newspaper.

PASO 4: Resumen
Make a list of your newspaper's sections. Make a table of contents.

PASO 5: Nuestro periódico
Present your work to the class.
Extension: Compare your work with that of other groups. Find three similarities and three differences.

PARA RESOLVER

LAS NOTICIAS DE LA ACTUALIDAD

En grupo, van a escribir la primera plana de un periódico.

PASO 1 ¿Qué noticias hay?

Hagan una lista de las noticias (verdaderas o inventadas) que quieren poner en su periódico. Escojan el tema más importante para ponerlo como noticia del día. Luego, escojan tres noticias más para la primera plana.

Noticias: *las elecciones para senador, el accidente en la autopista central, Silva ganó el maratón de Nueva York...*

La noticia del día va a ser que Silva ganó el maratón.

Las tres noticias van a ser: las elecciones para senador...

PASO 2 La noticia del día

Escriban el titular y el texto de la noticia del día. Luego, busquen una fotografía y escriban el pie de foto.

Titular: *Silva ganó el maratón*

Texto: *Éste es el segundo año que el mexicano Germán Silva...*

Pie de foto: *Germán Silva llega a la meta.*

PASO 3 Otras noticias

Escriban un titular y un pequeño párrafo para las otras noticias de su lista.

Titular: *García, senadora*

Texto: *Ana García ganó las elecciones para senadora. La nueva senadora se emocionó profundamente...*

PASO 4 Resumen

Hagan una lista de las secciones que va a tener su periódico. Luego, escriban un resumen.

PASO 5 Nuestro periódico

Presenten la portada de su periódico a la clase.

104

PARA TU REFERENCIA

chocó con *crashed into*

la meta *finish line*

la noticia del día *cover story*

otros(as) *others*

la primera plana *front page*

el resumen *news summary*

el titular *headline*

Dictation

Ask one or two volunteers to read aloud some phrases from the newspaper article while the rest of the class transcribes them.

LA ACTUALIDAD

Sollangos, lunes 13 de noviembre

SILVA GANÓ EL MARATÓN

Germán Silva llega a la meta.

Éste es el segundo año que el mexicano Germán Silva gana el maratón de Nueva York. El año pasado hizo un calor increíble y este año un frío impresionante. Pero Silva no se asustó ni del frío ni del calor. (Pasa a la página 14.)

GARCÍA, SENADORA

Ana García ganó las elecciones para senadora. La nueva senadora se emocionó profundamente al enterarse de la noticia. Después leyó un discurso. (Pasa a la página 5.)

ACCIDENTE EN LA AUTOPISTA CENTRAL

Ayer sábado hubo un accidente en la autopista central. Un carro de bomberos chocó con un camión. Hubo tres víctimas. Los voluntarios de la Cruz Roja llevaron a las víctimas al hospital de Guadalupe. (Pasa a la página 9.)

EL PREMIO LIBRO DE ORO PARA ROJAS

El escritor Alberto Rojas ganó el premio Libro de Oro. Rojas se sorprendió mucho cuando se enteró de la noticia y dijo: "Estoy muy contento porque…" (Pasa a la página 7.)

RESUMEN

Política	pág. 5	Arte	pág. 17
Cultura	pág. 7	Espectáculos	pág. 19
Deportes	pág. 14		

105

Objective
Cultural: to learn about an ancient Mexican civilization and its art

Related Components

Audio	Conexiones
Conexiones: 16B	Chapter 3
	Magazine
	Juntos en México

GETTING STARTED

Ask students what hieroglyphics are. What purpose did they serve? Why did ancient peoples use hieroglyphics instead of an alphabet?

DISCUSS

Using the Text
After reading each paragraph, ask a few questions. Suggestions:
¿De quién habla este texto?
¿Qué pasó después de su muerte?
¿Qué es una estela? (Miren la foto.)
¿Cómo son las esculturas de los olmecas?

Thinking About Language
Remind students of the importance of using context clues. Point out that it is difficult, but not impossible, to translate a written language that no living person knows.
¿Por qué no comprendieron nada de la estela los arqueólogos?
¿Por qué son importantes los jeroglíficos?
Could you teach yourself Spanish without a teacher by reading Spanish newspapers? How would you figure out what words meant?

CHECK

Te toca a ti
Possible Answers:
1. *Se olvidó por completo.*
2. *La descubrieron en 1986.*
3. *Es importante porque cuenta la historia del rey. (Or …porque nos ayudó a descifrar los jeroglíficos de los Olmecas.)*
4. *Descifraron los jeroglíficos en 1993.*
5. *Son conocidos por sus misteriosas esculturas de grandes cabezas.*

106

ENTÉRATE

JEROGLÍFICOS° MEXICANOS

Hace más de 1.800 años vivía un rey olmeca en la costa del Golfo de México. Después de su muerte° la historia del rey se olvidó° por completo. En 1986, los arqueólogos descubrieron una estela° que tenía esculpida una gran figura y jeroglíficos. Los arqueólogos ignoraban lo que decían los jeroglíficos y no fue hasta 1993 que los descifraron.°

La estela cuenta la historia de ese rey olmeca. Los olmecas vivieron en la zona de Veracruz, en el Golfo de México.

En el arte olmeca podemos ver muchos símbolos y temas que reaparecen° en civilizaciones más recientes. Por ejemplo,° el calendario y la figura del jaguar, que son muy importantes en el arte olmeca, también aparecen entre° los aztecas. Los olmecas son especialmente conocidos por sus misteriosas esculturas de cabezas° colosales con labios gruesos° y expresiones solemnes. Con la información de los jeroglíficos va a ser posible conocer mejor esta antigua civilización.

TE TOCA A TI

1. ¿Qué pasó con la historia del rey olmeca?
2. ¿Cuándo descubrieron la estela?
3. ¿Por qué es importante esta estela?
4. ¿Cuándo descifraron los jeroglíficos?
5. ¿Por qué son conocidos los olmecas?

las cabezas *heads*
descifrar *to decipher*
entre *among*
la estela *stele (stone monument)*
los jeroglíficos *hieroglyphics*

los labios gruesos *full lips*
la muerte *death*
por ejemplo *for example*
reaparecen *(they) reappear*
se olvidó *(it) was forgotten*

106

✓ CULTURE NOTE

Hieroglyphics use symbols to represent words or sounds. Pictographic styles of writing were found in Egypt, Asia Minor, and Crete as well as Central America. The word is from the Greek *hieros*, "sacred" or "priestly," and *glyphe*, "carving."

Para hispanohablantes

Explain the reading to the class in your own words.

VOCABULARIO TEMÁTICO

Las noticias
The news

el accidente *accident*
el acuerdo de paz
  peace agreement
el campeonato *championship*
las elecciones *elections*
el incendio *fire*
la inundación *flood*
el maratón *marathon*
el rescate *rescue*
el terremoto *earthquake*
el tornado *tornado*

En el noticiero
In the news report

el/la bombero(a) *firefighter*
el/la deportista *athlete*
el/la fotógrafo(a) *photographer*
el/la médico(a) *doctor*
el/la periodista *journalist*
el/la policía *police officer*
el/la presidente(a) *president*
el/la reportero(a) *reporter*
el/la senador(a) *senator*
la víctima *victim*
**el/la voluntario(a) de la Cruz
  Roja** *Red Cross volunteer*

Reacciones
Reactions

alegrarse *to be happy*
asustarse *to get scared*
emocionarse *to be thrilled*
preocuparse *to worry*
reaccionar *to react*
sorprenderse *to be surprised*

¿Qué oyes en el noticiero?
What do you hear in the news report?

apagar un incendio
  to put out a fire
caerse *to fall, to collapse*
construir *to build*
dar un discurso
  to give a speech
destruir *to destroy*
encontrar (o>ue) *to find*
recibir *to receive*

Cuando te enteras de una noticia, ¿qué dices?
When you find out about a news event, what do you say?

Bueno, no me extraña.
  Well, it doesn't surprise me.
¿En serio? *Really?*
¡No me digas! *You don't say!*
¡No puede ser! *It can't be!*
¡Qué horror! *How awful!*
¿Qué pasó? *What happened?*

Expresiones y palabras

algo *something*
alguien *someone*
alguno(a)/algún *some*
la ambulancia *ambulance*
el carro de bomberos *firetruck*
el ascensor *elevator*
enterarse *to learn about*
el hospital *hospital*
hubo *there was/there were*
la meta *finish line (in a race)*
oír *to hear, to listen*
el premio *award, prize*
la reacción *reaction*
nadie *no one*
ni... ni... *neither . . . nor . . .*
ninguno(a)/ningún *none*
el pie de foto *caption*

LA CONEXIÓN INGLÉS-ESPAÑOL

In this chapter, you have learned several words that are spelled the same way in English and Spanish and have the same meaning: *hospital, tornado, horror*. The only difference is in the pronunciation of the words in the two languages.

What do these English words mean?

incendiary— inundate—encounter

Find your clues from the meaning of Spanish words in the *Vocabulario temático*.

	Objetivos page 109 *La tecnología de hoy*	Conversemos pages 110-111 *El pasado y el presente*	Realidades pages 112-113 *El presente y el pasado de Monterrey*	Palabras en acción pages 114-115 *La gran ciudad*
Comunicación	To talk about: • advantages and disadvantages of city life	Discuss advantages and disadvantages of life in today's cities	Read text, make list, survey class about changes in the community, report results	Read cartoon, discuss the neighborhood's past; write article
	• comparisons between the past and present	Compare life today and life in the past	Read text, answer questions; make list; survey class about changes in the community; report results	Read cartoon, discuss technology; the neighborhood's past
	• modern technology	Discuss modern technology	Read text, make list; survey class about changes in the community; report results	Read cartoon, discuss characters; create dialogs; discuss technology; neighborhood; roleplay phone conversation; make poster
Cultura	To learn about: • the present and past of Monterrey, Mexico • using the Internet to learn more about Mexican writers • hidden treasures in the Gulf of Mexico		Monterrey, Mexico: culture, history, and industry	
Vocabulario temático	To know the expressions for: • modern technological innovations	Talk about modern technological innovations	Read text, make list, survey class about changes in the community, report results	Read cartoon, discuss characters; create dialogs; discuss technology; talk about the neighborhood's past; roleplay phone conversation; make poster
	• yesterday's technology	Talk about innovations of yesterday		Read cartoon, discuss technology; the neighborhood's past
	• features of today's cities	Talk about features of today's cities	Read text, answer questions, make list, survey class about changes, report results	Read cartoon, make list; write article
Estructura	To talk about: • how life used to be: the imperfect tense	Discuss how life used to be	Read text, answer questions	Read cartoon, discuss technology; the neighborhood's past
	• comparisons between people and things: *más/menos... que, tan... como, tanto... como*, etc.	Compare life today and life in the past	Read text, make list, survey class about changes in the community, report results	Read cartoon, discuss technology; the neighborhood's past

LA TECNOLOGÍA DE HOY

Para comunicarnos mejor (1) pages 116-117 ¿Qué usaban antes?	Para comunicarnos mejor (2) pages 118-119 ¿Qué es más rápido?	Situaciones pages 120-121 Bienvenidos a la Enciclopedia electronica	Para resolver pages 122-123 Una casa más cómoda	Entérate page 124 Tesoros en el Golfo de México
Discuss life before modern technology; compare world today and when grandparents were young	Compare present and past	Discuss computer encyclopedias; create dialog; conduct interview; write E-mail		Discuss sunken treasures and modern technology
Discuss life before modern technology; compare past and present; talk about life as a child	Compare present and past; discuss the town; compare childhood to now	Discuss computer encyclopedias; create dialog; conduct interview; write E-mail	Read text, make list of home innovations	
Discuss life before modern technology; compare past and present	Compare present and past; discuss the town; compare childhood to now	Talk about using a computer encyclopedia; create dialog; conduct interview; write E-mail	Read text, make list of home innovations; discuss la casa del futuro; design and explain 3 innovations; make poster	
		Latin American literature via computer	Read about la casa del futuro.	Article about sunken ships in the Gulf of Mexico
Discuss life before modern technology; compare past and present	Compare present and past; discuss the town; compare childhood to now	**Re-entry of vocabulary**		**Extension of vocabulary**
Discuss life before modern technology; compare past and present	Compare present and past; discuss the town; compare childhood to now			
Use all regular forms of imperfect tense. Activities 1-3: Discuss life before modern technology	Compare life today and in the past			
Discuss life before modern technology; compare past and present; talk about life as a child	Compare present and past; discuss the town; compare childhood to now	**Re-entry of structure**		**Extension of structure**
	Compare present and past; discuss the town; compare childhood to now			

Palabras en palabras

GAME

Objective

- to play a word game using Chapter 4 *Vocabulario temático*

Use

after *Palabras en acción*, pages 114–115

Materials

- a bilingual dictionary for each group

Activity

- Select one of the longer words from the *Vocabulario temático—cinematográfica,* for instance.
- Give players 10 minutes to generate as many words as they can from the original word.
- When time is up, a student from one group reads the Spanish words and the corresponding English words. For example: *cama* (bed), *cine* (movies), *metro* (subway, meter), *gato* (cat), *cámara* (camera), *arte (art)*, *mí* (my), *mía* (mine), *mío* (mine), *nota* (grade), *toma* (take), *tango* (dance from Argentina), *tráfico* (traffic), *camión* (bus), *cero* (zero).
- When the player reaches the end of his/her group's list, a player from another group reads any words that weren't on the first list.
- The winning group is the one that generates the most words.

Variations

- Score words by the number of letters in each. A group would get 6 points for *cámara,* 4 points for *mata,* etc.
- Words with multiple meanings, like *metro,* can be used more than once if a different meaning is given each time the word is repeated.

Ahora soy reportero

WRITING CONNECTION

Objective

- to conduct an interview using Chapter 4 *Vocabulario temático*

Use

after *Palabras en acción,* pages 114–115

Materials

- English- and Spanish-language newspapers and news magazines about modern Mexico

Preparation

- Pair students and have each pair choose a person, topic, or news event to research.

Activity

- Have each pair read articles about their choice, using both English- and Spanish-language publications. After reading the articles, each member of the pair should assume a role. One student interviews the other in front of the class.
  For example: One pair's article is about new technology. One student acts as the *reportero* who wrote the article; the other as the *inventor* who designed the new machine.
  Reportero: *¿Cuándo decidió Ud. inventar esta nueva computadora?*
  Inventor: *Una noche, estaba en mi oficina y mi computadora era muy lenta. Decidí inventar una computadora más rápida.*

Había una vez

HISTORY CONNECTION

Objective
- to talk about historic people, places, and things, using the imperfect tense

Use
after *Para comunicarnos mejor,* pages 116–117

Materials
- reference books (encyclopedia, bilingual dictionary, almanac, etc.)

Preparation
- Review words that deal with continuous, customary, or habitual actions, and list them on the chalkboard. For example: *siempre, a veces, muchas veces, cada año/día/mes, todos los días.*

Activity
- Have each student choose a figure from Hispanic history.
- Each student writes a five-sentence description of his/her character's life and times, using the imperfect tense (and preterite tense, if necessary) and related expressions. Students also list five things that existed and five things that did not exist during their characters' lifetimes. For example: *Vivió hace más de quinientos años. Era explorador y trabajaba al servicio de los Reyes Católicos de España. Hizo varias expediciones en México y Guatemala. Buscaba oro. Empezó como ayudante del gobernador de Cuba. Antes de su llegada los indígenas no tenían armas de fuego, ni conocían la pólvora, ni la religión católica. Europa no tenía ni maíz, ni tomates, ni chocolate,* etc.
- Each student presents his/her character without revealing the character's name.
- The first student to guess the character goes next.
- When all the characters have been identified, the class can decide which presentation was cleverest, funniest, most unusual, etc.

Tan bonita como tú

GAME

Objective
- to play a game comparing people, places, and things, using the comparatives *más/menos... que, tan... como, tanto (a/as/os)... como, más/menos que,* and *tanto como*

Use
after *Para comunicarnos mejor,* pages 118–119

Materials
- pictures supplied by students

Preparation
- Have students bring in drawings or photographs of two people, places, or things.

Activity
- Students form two teams.
- Have each student from Team A pair up with someone from Team B. Without using the same comparatives twice, both students must come up with as many sentences contrasting the other student's pictures as possible.
- Each student then shows his or her pictures to the rest of the class, giving each team a second chance to come up with additional sentences.
- The team with the most sentences wins.

LA TECNOLOGÍA DE HOY

Introduce the chapter and its theme by asking students how the world has changed since their grandparents were young. Have them name some inventions that have made people's lives easier since then. Do they think they would be able to survive without these things?

Related Components

Audio	Video: Tape/Book
Conexiones: 16B	Unit 2: Seg. 3
Conexiones	
Chapter 4	

Scan to Chapter 4

GETTING STARTED

Ask students if they use the technology shown in the picture. How is it useful to them? Ask questions. For example: *¿Qué hacen los chicos de la foto? ¿Dónde están? ¿Cómo te va a ayudar en tu futuro profesional conocer la tecnología?*

Critical Thinking

Use the following activity to help students discover what they need to know in order to talk about life today and in the past. Have students think about the words they use when comparing the way things are now and the way they used to be. Then have groups make lists of a few:
- reasons why they would or would not like to live in a big city
- things that have changed in the past one hundred years
- new technologies that replaced traditional things (e.g., cars replaced wagons)
- ways to send information

Have each group write its list on the board. Have the class discuss the lists and decide which items are the most essential.

Have each group submit a revised list. When you finish the chapter, have the class review the lists to see how they compare to what they learned in the chapter.

CAPÍTULO 4

LA TECNOLOGÍA DE HOY

Dos jóvenes mexicanos diseñando una computadora.

108

CHAPTER COMPONENTS

Activity Book	Audio Book	Conexiones	Transparencies
p. 51-60	Script: p. 26-29	Chapter 4	Chapter 4
Assessment	Activities: p. 30-32	**Cuaderno**	Transparencies 24-29
Oral Proficiency:	**Audio**	p. 29-36	**Tutor Pages**
p. 24	Chapter: 4B	**Magazine**	p. 19-22
Listening Script:	Assessment: 14B	Juntos en México	**Video: Tape/Book**
p. 12	Conexiones: 16B		Unit 2: Seg. 3
Chapter Test:			
p. 63-68			

Objetivos

COMUNICACIÓN
To talk about:
- advantages and disadvantages of city life
- comparisons between the past and present
- modern technology

CULTURA
To learn about:
- the present and past of Monterrey, Mexico
- using the Internet to find out more information about Mexican writers
- sunken treasures in the Gulf of Mexico

VOCABULARIO TEMÁTICO
To know the expressions for:
- modern technological innovations
- yesterday's technology
- features of today's cities

ESTRUCTURA
To talk about:
- how life used to be: the imperfect tense
- comparisons between people and comparisons between things: *más/menos... que, tan... como, tanto(a/os/as)... como*

¿SABES QUE...?

Using computer technology in the classroom has become increasingly popular in Mexico, as it has in the United States. Even small cities have received grants to purchase computers for classroom use. Recently, in Tlaxcala, the capital city of the state of the same name (located just east of Mexico City), about 45,000 students in 74 secondary schools benefited from the installation of 1,700 computers.

109

Here are some additional activities that you may wish to use as you work through this chapter with your students.

Communication

Encourage after-class activities that may enhance student interest and proficiency. Some ideas:
- have students videotape or record an interview with a Spanish speaker about ways in which his or her life has changed from past years

Culture

To encourage greater cultural understanding, have students:
- surf the Internet to find out about present-day Mexico
- invite as a guest speaker someone who is from or has been to Mexico
- show the video that accompanies Unit 2 of this textbook

Vocabulary

To reinforce vocabulary, have students:
- do a photo essay about changes in technology
- use magazine photos to make flashcards of past and present innovations
- make a vocabulary timeline that includes past and present items
- Ask students to think about the word *tecnología* and its English cognate, "technology." Explain that both words come from the Greek *techne*, "science" or "skill," and *logos*, "study" or "writing."

Structure

To reinforce the imperfect tense and comparisons, have students:
- write a sentence about their childhood and share it with the class. Have the class help correct sentences.
- say what activities they used to do as children; compare their responses with others in the class. For example: *Peter iba al cine menos que yo cuando éramos niños.*

▶▶▶ INTERNET LINK

Monterrey http://www.mexguide.net:80/monterrey/

CONVERSEMOS

Communicative Objectives

To talk about:
- the advantages of living in a city
- life today and life in the past
- modern means of sending information

Related Components

Activity Book p. 51	**Cuaderno** p. 29
Audio Book Script: Seg. 1	**Transparencies** Ch. 4: Conversemos Transparency 24
Audio Chapter: 4B, Seg. 1	

GETTING STARTED

Ask students to think of things that were once used but are now obsolete. What replaced them?

ACTIVITIES

These activities give students an opportunity to begin communicating with each other and with you, focusing on the theme and objectives of the chapter. The activities can be used as oral class activities, or, if you prefer, you can pair students to achieve more interaction.

Donde tú vives, ¿cómo eran las cosas antes?
Class activity to introduce the imperfect tense and city vocabulary and to review comparisons. Point out that **había**, like **hay**, is used to mean both "there was" and "there were."
Do a quick review of comparisons with classroom objects. Ask the title question, emphasizing the words **antes** and **ahora** to elicit past and present tenses. Expand the activity by asking for examples from school. For example:
Antes había más estudiantes que ahora.

¿Cuáles son las ventajas de vivir en una ciudad?
Class activity to review **hay** and introduce more city vocabulary. Ask students *¿Qué hay en una ciudad?* Have them use vocabulary from previous chapters to name and describe things in a city. Examples:
centro comercial, cine, concierto, discoteca, edificio, interesante, metro, mucha gente, museo, restaurante, taxi, teatro

CONVERSEMOS

EL PASADO Y EL PRESENTE

Habla con tu compañero(a).

DONDE TÚ VIVES, ¿CÓMO ERAN LAS COSAS ANTES?

Antes había menos contaminación que ahora.
(In the past, there was less pollution than now.)

Antes había más parques que ahora.
(In the past, there were more parks than now.)

(el) parque

menos... que

más... que

(el) tráfico

En mi pueblo nada ha cambiado mucho.
(In my town, nothing has changed much.)

(la) fábrica

(el) edificio de oficinas

(el) ruido

(el) rascacielos

¿CUÁLES SON LAS VENTAJAS DE VIVIR EN UNA CIUDAD?
(What are the advantages of living in a city?)

Hay muchos cines y transporte público.

(los) cines   (las) tiendas

(el) transporte público *(public transportation)*

(los) eventos deportivos *(sports events)*

¿Y las desventajas?
(And the disadvantages?)

110

MEETING INDIVIDUAL NEEDS

Reaching All Students

For Auditory Learners
Read aloud vocabulary and have others say if it belongs with **antes** or **ahora**.

For Kinesthetic Learners
Mime ways to send information. Have others guess what they are.

110

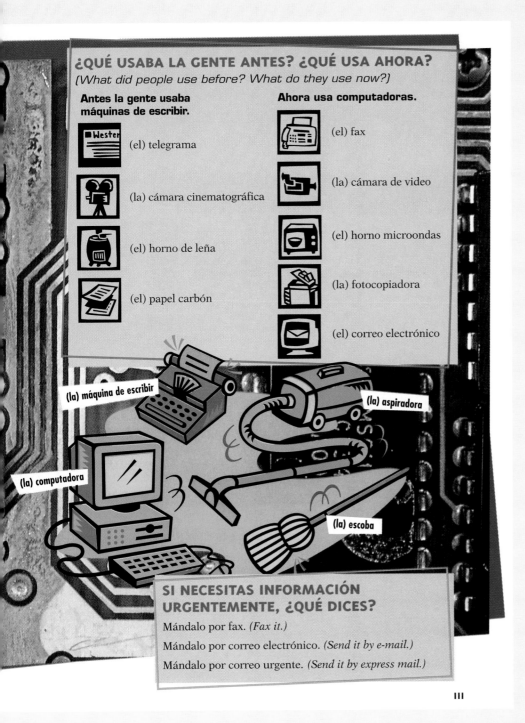

¿QUÉ USABA LA GENTE ANTES? ¿QUÉ USA AHORA?

[What did people use before? What do they use now?]

Antes la gente usaba máquinas de escribir.

(el) telegrama

(la) cámara cinematográfica

(el) horno de leña

(el) papel carbón

Ahora usa computadoras.

(el) fax

(la) cámara de video

(el) horno microondas

(la) fotocopiadora

(el) correo electrónico

(la) máquina de escribir

(la) aspiradora

(la) computadora

(la) escoba

SI NECESITAS INFORMACIÓN URGENTEMENTE, ¿QUÉ DICES?

Mándalo por fax. *(Fax it.)*

Mándalo por correo electrónico. *(Send it by e-mail.)*

Mándalo por correo urgente. *(Send it by express mail.)*

III

¿Qué usaba la gente antes? ¿Qué usa ahora?
Class activity to introduce the imperfect tense to talk about what people used to do. Model the questions and sentences, and have students read them aloud. Emphasize **antes** and **ahora** as you repeat or correct student responses. Extend by substituting **haber** for **usar.** For example: *¿Qué había antes? ¿Qué hay ahora? Antes había telegramas. Ahora hay faxes.*

Si necesitas información urgentemente, ¿qué dices?
Class activity to introduce vocabulary for different ways of corresponding. Model the sentences and suggest alternatives. Example: *Tengo que mandar una carta muy importante. La voy a mandar por correo urgente.*

CHECK

- *¿Cuáles son las ventajas de vivir en una ciudad?*
- *¿Cómo eran las cosas antes en tu ciudad?*
- *¿Qué usábamos antes de la computadora?*
- *¿Mandas muchas cosas por fax? ¿Cómo las mandas?*

LOG BOOK

Have students think of five things people use today as much as they did many years ago. Have them find out what the Spanish words for these items are. (This information can be used in *Para comunicarnos mejor,* pp. 118-119.)

REALIDADES

Objectives

Communicative: to talk about the past, using the imperfect tense

Cultural: to learn about the past and present of Monterrey, Mexico

Related Components

Activity Book p. 52	**Audio** Chapter: 4B, Seg. 2
Audio Book Script: Seg. 2	**Cuaderno** p. 30

GETTING STARTED

Ask students what "Out with the old, in with the new" means to them. Is it always a good idea? When is it a bad idea?

DISCUSS

After reading the title, ask students to identify the photos for which they would use the word *presente* or *pasado*. Ask questions. Suggestions:

Monterrey
¿Qué hay en Monterrey?

La Gran Plaza
¿En qué parte de la ciudad está la Gran Plaza?
¿Qué hay en la plaza de Monterrey?
¿Qué es un ejemplo del presente de México?
¿Qué es un ejemplo del pasado?

El Instituto Tecnológico
¿Cuál fue el modelo para el Instituto Tecnológico de Monterrey?
¿Qué es SEIS?
Si vas a una universidad, ¿te gustaría tomar clases de otras?

Los productos industriales
¿Los productos industriales son cosas o ideas?
¿Por qué es importante Monterrey?
¿Qué porcentaje de los productos industriales de México se hacen en Monterrey?
¿Cuántas fábricas hay?
¿Qué fabrican?

Language Note
You can use this opportunity to model the pronunciation of percentages for students. Make sure that students understand that "25%" is *veinticinco por ciento*, but that "a percentage" is *un porcentaje.*

El Obispado
¿El Obispado es del presente o del pasado?
¿Qué era el Obispado?
¿Qué es hoy?
¿Dónde está situado?
¿Qué es una vista panorámica?

REALIDADES

¡VISITA MONTERREY, LA TERCERA CIUDAD MÁS GRANDE DE MÉXICO!

Monterrey

EL PRESENTE Y EL PASADO SE ENCUENTRAN EN

Un ejemplo del encuentro del presente y el pasado de Monterrey es la Gran Plaza, que está en el centro de la ciudad. En esta plaza hay una catedral colonial y, al lado, una escultura modernísima de Rufino Tamayo, uno de los artistas más famosos de México.

El Instituto Tecnológico y de Estudios Superiores de Monterrey se creó siguiendo el modelo del *Massachusetts Institute of Technology* (MIT) de Cambridge. El Instituto forma parte del Sistema de Educación Interactiva por Satélite (SEIS). Desde allí, puedes tomar clases de otras universidades, vía satélite.

Monterrey produce el 25% de los productos industriales de México y el 50% de los productos de exportación. Monterrey es famosa por sus fundiciones de acero. Hay más de 500 fábricas en Monterrey que producen ropa, cemento, jabón y plásticos.

El Obispado es uno de los mejores ejemplos de arquitectura colonial de Monterrey. A principios del siglo XVIII era la residencia del obispo. Hoy es un museo. Está situado en un cerro, con vistas panorámicas de la ciudad.

112

✓ CULTURE NOTE

Rufino Tamayo (1899-1991) was one of the most important modern artists of Mexico. He used his personal collection to create Mexico City's Tamayo Museum, which is probably the best collection of twentieth-century art in Mexico.

HABLA DEL FOLLETO

Mira el folleto sobre Monterrey.

A. Haz una lista con ejemplos del pasado y otra con ejemplos del presente de Monterrey.

pasado	*presente*
la catedral	*la escultura de Tamayo*

B. Habla con tu compañero(a) del folleto.

— *¿De qué siglo es el Obispado?*
— *Es del siglo XVIII. ¿De quién es la escultura de la Gran Plaza?*

¿QUÉ OPINAS?

1. En grupo, hablen de cómo ha cambiado su comunidad en los últimos 50 años. Hagan una lista de cinco o seis cambios.

2. ¿Qué cambios creen que fueron buenos y cuáles no? Hagan una encuesta en el grupo. Usen el modelo.

	buenos	*malos*
más coches	///	////
teléfonos celulares	////	
correo electrónico	////	
fotocopiadoras	////	
fax		
más tráfico		
más transporte público		

Comparen los resultados con otros grupos.

¿SABES QUE...?

Monterrey is the third largest city in Mexico, with approximately 2.5 million inhabitants. Monterrey's strong industrial base has made it an important commercial city in Mexico. It is located about 450 miles from Mexico City and only 150 miles from Laredo, Texas. Although known for its industry and commerce, Monterrey is an old city. It was founded by the Spaniard Diego de Montemayor in 1560 and incorporated as a city in 1596.

113

113

Communicative Objectives

To talk about:
• how technology affects us
• how we use technology every day

Related Components

Activity Book p. 53-54	**Transparencies** Ch. 4: Palabras en acción Transparency 25
Cuaderno p. 31-32	**Tutor Page** p. 19

GETTING STARTED

Ask students to say which of the objects in the drawing they or their families use at home. Which ones have been in most homes for many years? Which ones were invented recently?

DISCUSS

Model the statements that people in the drawing are making. Comment on and ask questions about them. For example:
¿Qué hacen las personas en las oficinas?
¿Quién está hablando por teléfono celular?
¿Tenemos que estar en un coche para usar un teléfono celular?

Para hispanohablantes

If you use other words or expressions for some of the ones introduced in this chapter, share them with the class. For example, you may use some of the following:

la autopista: la carretera, la pista
la cámara cinematográfica: la cámara de cine
los comercios: los negocios, las tiendas
el correo urgente: el correo inmediato
el horno de leña: la cocina de leña, el fogón
mandar: enviar
el papel carbón: el papel de calco, el papel para calcar
el tráfico: el tránsito
el ventilador: el abanico (eléctrico)

¿Qué ves en el dibujo? Haz una lista de las cosas que ves en la ciudad.

La fábrica, la autopista...

¿Qué hacen? Habla con tu compañero(a) sobre tres personas del dibujo.

— *¿Qué hace el hombre del apartamento D?*
— *Está hablando por teléfono.*

114

¿Qué dicen? Haz tres diálogos entre las personas del dibujo.

— *¿Tienes el número de fax del Sr. García?*
— *Sí, es el 555-2211.*

La tecnología Habla con tu compañero(a) sobre la tecnología que la gente usaba antes y la tecnología que usa ahora.

— *Antes la gente usaba ventiladores. Ahora usa aire acondicionado.*
— *Antes la gente usaba escobas. Ahora usa aspiradoras.*

For students having difficulty talking about technology and differences between the past and present, you might consider:
• **The tutor page:** Pair the student with a native speaker or a more able student, using the tutor page.
Optional activities: See page 108C: *Palabras en palabras* and *Ahora soy reportero*

5 Hace muchos años

¿Cómo eran las cosas antes en tu vecindario? Habla con tu compañero(a).

— ¿Cómo eran las cosas antes en tu vecindario?
— Antes había menos ruido y más parques que ahora.

6 Miniteatro

Llama por teléfono para pedir información sobre productos electrónicos. Haz un diálogo.

— Buenos días. ¿Me puede mandar por fax información acerca de una fotocopiadora?
— Sí. Deme su número de fax, por favor.

7 Cartel

Diseña un cartel con anuncios sobre la tecnología de hoy. Usa dibujos y fotos de revistas y periódicos. Escribe un pie de foto para cada ilustración. Presenta el cartel a la clase.

8 Tú eres el autor

Escribe un artículo sobre las ventajas y las desventajas de vivir en tu ciudad o en tu pueblo.

Ventajas: En mi ciudad hay muchas tiendas y muchos restaurantes. El transporte público es moderno y rápido.
Desventajas: Hay mucho ruido.

115

ACTIVITIES

1. Individual and Group Activity
Make a list of things you see in the city.

2. Pair Activity
Speak about three people in the drawing.
Extension: Pretend what they are doing took place yesterday.
A: ¿Qué hizo el hombre en el dormitorio?
B: Habló por teléfono.

3. Individual or Pair Activity
Create three new dialogs between people in the drawing.
Extension: Discuss what you could do to make your home more modern.

4. Pair Activity
Talk about the technology people used in the past and what they use today.
Extension: Say a word from this page. Your partner must say either *Es de antes* or *Es de ahora.*

5. Pair Activity
Speak about the way things used to be in your neighborhoods.
Extension: With a partner, write three sets of sentences about now and before. Leave out one word. Exchange sets with other partners and try to solve. Example:
Antes no había aire acondicionado. Usaban...

6. Roleplay Activity
Write and act out a dialog in which you ask for information over the telephone about electronic devices.

7. Hands-On Activity
Homework or classwork for individuals or small groups. Design a poster about today's technologies. Use drawings and photos. Write captions for each. Share with the class.
Note: You may wish to get students started by eliciting a list of advantages and disadvantages. Write the list on the board. Students can then select two advantages and two disadvantages to write about.

8. Writing Activity
Write an article about the advantages and disadvantages of living in your town or city.
Note: You may wish to get students started by eliciting a list of advantages and disadvantages. Write the list on the board. Students can then select two advantages and two disadvantages to write about.

CHECK

- ¿Qué hacen las personas en el dibujo?
- ¿Qué cosas usaba la gente antes? ¿Qué usa la gente ahora?
- ¿Cómo puedes mandar información?
- ¿Había muchas computadoras cuándo tenías siete años?
- ¿Usaste el aire acondicionado el verano pasado?

PORTFOLIO
Suggest that students include their articles from *Tú eres el autor* in their Portfolios.

Communicative Objectives

• to talk about how things used to be, using the imperfect tense
• to talk about what people used to do, using the imperfect tense

Related Components

Activity Book p. 55-56	**Cuaderno** p. 33
Audio Book Script: Seg. 3 Activities: p. 30	**Transparencies** Ch. 4: Para comunicarnos mejor
Audio Chapter: 4B, Seg. 3	Transparency 26
	Tutor Page p. 20

GETTING STARTED

Ask students to think of things they often did when they were very young.

Language in Context

Write these sentences on the board:
  We went to the swimming pool.
  We used to go to the swimming pool.
Ask which sentence could end:
  . . . last Tuesday.
  . . . every Saturday.
  . . . when we were in grammar school.
  . . . but it was raining.

Establish the difference between an action that took place once and one that took place a number of times. Point out that in English "used to" is the main way we express an action that took place a number of times. The imperfect tense is the main way we express this kind of action in Spanish.
Use the paradigm to review the imperfect tense forms of -ar, -er, and -ir verbs. Ask which forms have an accent.

DISCUSS

Review vocabulary from previous chapters and introduce some of this chapter's vocabulary with questions and statements that use the imperfect of -ar, -er, and -ir verbs. For example:
Cuando eras pequeño, ¿qué hacías los fines de semana?
¿Ibas a la playa?
¿Escribías cartas a tus abuelos?
¿Montabas a caballo?
¿Escuchabas bien a tus padres?

116

To talk about how things used to be and what people used to do, use the imperfect tense.

Cuando tu abuelo y yo éramos jóvenes, no había computadoras. Mandábamos telegramas o escribíamos cartas.

When your grandfather and I were young, there weren't any computers. We sent telegrams or wrote letters.

To form the imperfect tense of **-ar** verbs and **-er** and **-ir** verbs, add the appropriate endings to the stem of the verb.

imperfect tense	usar	leer	escribir
yo	us**aba**	le**ía**	escrib**ía**
tú	us**abas**	le**ías**	escrib**ías**
usted	us**aba**	le**ía**	escrib**ía**
él/ella	us**aba**	le**ía**	escrib**ía**
nosotros(as)	us**ábamos**	le**íamos**	escrib**íamos**
vosotros(as)	us**abais**	le**íais**	escrib**íais**
ustedes	us**aban**	le**ían**	escrib**ían**
ellos/ellas	us**aban**	le**ían**	escrib**ían**

There are only three irregular verbs in the imperfect: *ver*, *ser* and *ir*.

imperfect tense	ver	ser	ir
yo	ve**ía**	era	**iba**
tú	ve**ías**	eras	**ibas**
usted	ve**ía**	era	**iba**
él/ella	ve**ía**	era	**iba**
nosotros(as)	ve**íamos**	éramos	**íbamos**
vosotros(as)	ve**íais**	erais	**ibais**
ustedes	ve**ían**	eran	**iban**
ellos/ellas	ve**ían**	eran	**iban**

The imperfect form of **hay** is **había** (there was, there were.)

Antes no había hornos microondas.

116

Yo leía mucho los fines de semana, ¿y tú? Cuando eras joven, ¿preferías helado de chocolate o de vainilla?

For students having difficulty using the imperfect to say what they used to do or how things were, you might consider:

• **The tutor page:** Pair the student with a native speaker or a more able student, using the tutor page.

Optional activity: See page 108D: *Había una vez*

1 En el pasado

Pregunta a tu compañero(a) qué hacían sus abuelos.

— ¿Qué hacían tus abuelos cuando todavía no había computadoras?
— Usaban una máquina de escribir.

1.   3.   5.

2.   4.   6.

2 ¿Cómo era antes? ¿Cómo es ahora?

Habla con tu compañero(a) sobre cómo era la vida antes y cómo es ahora.

— Antes la gente iba a la oficina a pie.
— Ahora va en coche, en autobús o en metro.

	Antes	Ahora
ir a la oficina	a pie	en coche, en autobús o en metro
mandar	cartas	fax y correo electrónico
escuchar	discos	discos compactos
cocinar	en hornos de leña	en hornos microondas
usar	papel carbón	la fotocopiadora

3 Cuando eras pequeño(a), ¿qué hacías?

Pregunta a tus compañeros qué hacían cuando eran pequeños. Anota las respuestas en una tabla.

	Esteban	Raúl	Laura
¿Adónde ibas de vacaciones?	a la playa	a la playa	a la montaña
¿A qué jugabas?			
¿Qué leías?			

Presenta los resultados a la clase.

Esteban y Raúl iban de vacaciones a la playa.
Laura iba a la montaña.

117

ACTIVITIES

Students use the imperfect tense to talk about the past.

1. Pair Activity
Ask what your partner's grandparents used to do.
Possible Answers:
1. See model on student page.
2. ...televisión?
   Escuchaban la radio.
3. ...cámaras de video?
   Sacaban fotos.
4. ...hornos microondas?
   Usaban hornos de leña.

5. ...aire acondicionado?
   Usaban el ventilador.
6. ...fotocopiadora?
   Usaban papel carbón.
Extension: Pretend that you are old, and say what you used to do when you were young. Example:
Mi novia y yo paseábamos en bote.

2. Pair Activity
Compare how life used to be and how it is today.
Answers:
1. See model on student page.
2. ...mandaba cartas.
   Ahora manda información por fax y correo electrónico.
3. ...escuchaba discos.
   Ahora escucha discos compactos.
4. ...cocinaba en hornos de leña.
   Ahora cocina en hornos microondas.
5. ...usaba el papel carbón.
   Ahora usa la fotocopiadora.

3. Group Activity
Ask what members of your group used to do when they were children. Complete the chart together. Share it with the class.
Answers: See models on student page.
Extension: Answer these questions again. Say things you did not used to do.

CHECK

• ¿Usaba una computa

117

Communicative Objective
• to make comparisons, using comparative expressions

Related Components

Activity Book p. 57-58	**Audio** Chapter: 4B, Seg. 4
Audio Book Script: Seg.4 Activities: p. 31	**Cuaderno** p. 34
	Tutor Page p. 21

GETTING STARTED

Ask students to name and compare two devices, such as rotary phones and digital phones. Is one better than the other? Why?

Language in Context

Draw several lines of different lengths. Compare the lines using the structures: **más largo que, menos largo que,** and **tan largo como.** Ask students to identify the lines from your descriptions.

DISCUSS

Review vocabulary from previous chapters and introduce some of this chapter's vocabulary with questions and statements that use **más/menos que, más/menos... que, tan/tanto(a/os/as)... como,** and **tanto como.**
¿Un teléfono celular es más barato que una aspiradora?
¿Mirar la televisión te emociona tanto como leer una novela?
¿Es nuestra ciudad tan grande como Los Ángeles?
¿Te gusta el baloncesto más que el fútbol?

PARA COMUNICARNOS MEJOR

¿QUÉ ES MÁS RÁPIDO?

To compare people or things using adjectives, use *más* **or** *menos* **followed by an adjective and** *que.*

El correo electrónico es más rápido que el fax.	E-mail is faster than a fax.

To show equality, use *tan* **followed by an adjective and** *como.*

Este teléfono es tan antiguo como esa máquina de escribir.	This telephone is as old as that typewriter.

To compare people or things using nouns, use *tanto(a/os/as)* **followed by a noun, and then** *como* **followed by the second term of the comparison.**

Yo tengo tantos discos compactos como cintas.	I have as many CDs as cassettes.
Mi hermano compra tantos discos compactos como yo.	My brother buys as many CDs as I do.

To compare people or things using verbs, use *más/menos que* **or** *tanto como* **followed by the second term of the comparison.**

Los coches contaminan el aire más que las fábricas.	Cars pollute the air more than factories do.
Esa computadora cuesta tanto como esta cámara de video.	That computer costs as much as this videocamera.

¡OJO!

Tanto, tanta, tantos, tantas are adjectives and must have the same number and gender as the nouns they modify.

Antes, esta calle no tenía tantos cines ni tantas tiendas.

118

For students having difficulty comparing people or things, using **más que, menos...que, tan...como,** and **tanto como,** you might consider:
• **The tutor page:** Pair the student with a native speaker or a more able student, using the tutor page.
Optional activity: See page 108D: *Tan bonita como tú*

Antes, ahora

Con tu compañero(a), compara cómo eran las cosas antes y cómo son ahora.

Antes el transporte público no era tan rápido como ahora.

¿Cómo era(n)...?

el transporte público	contaminado(a)
las ciudades	grande
los aparatos electrónicos	rápido(a)
los edificios	moderno(a)
el aire	alto(a)
	cómodo(a)

 ¿Había más o menos?

Con tu compañero(a), compara cómo era tu pueblo o ciudad antes y cómo es ahora. ¿Qué cosas no han cambiado?

Antes había menos rascacielos que ahora.

Había...
tráfico
ruido
aparatos electrónicos
escobas
hornos de leña

 ¿Cómo cambió tu vida?

Con tu compañero(a), comparen las cosas que hacían cuando eran pequeños(as) con las cosas que hacen ahora.

Antes yo jugaba con videojuegos más que ahora. ¿Y tú?

1. jugar con videojuegos
2. hablar por teléfono
3. jugar en el parque
4. ir al centro comercial
5. escribir en la computadora

119

ACTIVITIES

Students use **más/menos... que, más/menos que, tan... como, tanto(a/os/as)... como,** and **tanto como** to compare people or things.

1. Pair Activity
Compare how things used to be with how they are now.
Possible Answers:
1. See model on student page.
2. *Antes las ciudades no eran tan grandes como ahora.*
3. *Antes los aparatos electrónicos no eran tan modernos como ahora.*
4. *Antes los edificios no eran tan altos como ahora.*
5. *Antes el aire era tan contaminado como ahora.*

2. Pair Activity
Compare how your town or city used to be with the way it is today. What hasn't changed?
Possible Answers:
1. See model on student page.
2. *Antes había tanto tráfico como ahora.*
3. *Antes había menos ruido que ahora.*
4. *Antes había menos aparatos electrónicos que ahora.*
5. *Antes había tantas escobas como ahora.*
6. *Antes había más hornos de leña que ahora.*

3. Pair Activity
Compare the things you did as children with the things you do now.
Possible Answers:
1. See model on student page.
2. *Antes hablaba por teléfono tanto como ahora.*
3. *Antes jugaba en el parque más que ahora.*
4. *Antes iba al centro comercial más que ahora.*
5. *Antes escribía en la computadora menos que ahora.*

CHECK

• *Compara dos cosas en este salón de clases.*
• *¿Cómo eran las computadoras de antes, ¿más rápidas que las de ahora?*
• *¿Hay una persona en la clase tan alta como tú? ¿Quién es?*
• *Alquilar un video cuesta tanto como ir al cine, ¿no?*

LOG BOOK
Have students write comparisons of five of this year's classes. Which are more interesting? More boring? More fun?

Para hispanohablantes

Compare the weather in the country that your family is from with that of your town or city.

Communicative Objective
• to talk and write about past and present technology

Related Components

Assessment Oral Proficiency: p. 24	**Conexiones** Chapter 4
Audio Book Script: Seg. 5 Activities: p. 32	**Magazine** Juntos en México
Audio Chapter: 4B, Seg. 5 Conexiones: 16B	**Tutor Page** p. 22

GETTING STARTED

Students should now be able to make comparisons, and use the imperfect tense and all of the chapter vocabulary correctly. Ask students if they have ever used a CD-ROM encyclopedia.

APPLY

1. Pair Activity
You are going to use an electronic encyclopedia for the first time. Say what steps you have to follow to do research on Hispanic-American literature.
Answers: See model on student page.

2. Pair Activity
Speak about the advantages of using an electronic encyclopedia and of how you used to get information.
Answers: See model on student page.
Extension: Compare two other sources of information *(el diccionario, el Internet, la biblioteca, el noticiero, la televisión, la radio).*

SITUACIONES

BIENVENIDOS A LA *ENCICLOPEDIA ELECTRÓNICA*

HISPANOAMÉRICA Obras Autores Historia Países Ayuda

LITERATURA México

OCTAVIO PAZ (Ciudad de México, 1914) poeta y ensayista. Obras: Máscaras mexicanas, Libertad bajo palabra, Puertas al campo, Vueltas, El laberinto de la soledad...
Biografía Texto 1 Texto 2

ELENA PONIATOWSKA (París, Francia, 1933) Narradora y periodista. Obras: La noche de Tlatelolco, Fuerte es el silencio, De noche vienes, Querido Diego, te abraza Quiela...
Biografía Texto 1 Texto 2

SOR JUANA INÉS DE LA CRUZ (San Miguel de Neplanta, 1651 - Ciudad de México, 1695) Poeta. Obras: Inundación Castálida, Primero sueño, El divino Narciso, Respuesta, Carta atenagórica...
Biografía Texto 1 Texto 2

120

Background
Octavio Paz (b. 1914) is a poet, essayist, and diplomat. In 1990, he won the Nobel Prize for Literature. One example of his work is: *Mexican Masks.*
Elena Poniatowska (b. 1933) was born in France and later became a Mexican citizen. She is a well-known novelist, essayist, screenwriter, and journalist. Works: *Night of Tlatelolco, Strong is Silence, You Come at Night, Dear Diego.*
Sor Juana Inés de la Cruz (1651-1695) was a child prodigy who became a nun in order to devote her life to learning. She wrote poems, plays, and satires. Works: *Flood from the Muses' Springs, First Dream, Divine Narcise, Reply.*

For students having difficulty talking about technology, you might consider:
• **The tutor page:** Pair the student with a native speaker or a more able student, using the tutor page.

1 **Un paseo por la *Enciclopedia electrónica***

Tú y tu compañero(a) van a usar la *Enciclopedia electrónica* por primera vez. Digan qué pasos tienen que seguir para hacer una investigación sobre la literatura hispanoamericana.

> *Primero tenemos que escoger un tema del menú principal. Luego tenemos que seleccionar un autor...*

 2 **¿Qué ventajas tiene?**

Con tu compañero(a), habla de las ventajas que tiene una enciclopedia electrónica y de cómo buscaban datos antes.

> — *Yo antes buscaba datos en las enciclopedias. ¿Y tú?*
> — *Yo también, pero una enciclopedia electrónica es más rápida.*

 3 **¿Qué usaba antes?**

Eres el/la vendedor(a) de una tienda de aparatos electrónicos y tu compañero(a) viene a comprar algo. Hagan un diálogo.

> — *Buenos días. Quiero comprar el último modelo de computadoras.*
> — *¿Qué usaba usted antes?*
> — *Antes usaba una máquina de escribir.*

 4 **Entrevista**

Entrevista a un familiar. Pregúntale cómo eran las cosas cuando él/ella tenía tu edad. Informa a la clase.

> — *¿Cómo era antes la vida en el pueblo?*
> — *Antes había menos tráfico que ahora.*

 5 **Tu diario**

Por primera vez vas a escribir a un amigo una carta usando el correo electrónico. Explícale qué te parece este sistema de comunicación y cómo te comunicabas antes.

> *www.mark.mcs.@hrc.sp.*
> *Querido Andrés:*
>
> *Es la primera vez que mando una carta por correo electrónico. Antes mandaba cartas por correo urgente o llamaba por teléfono. Pero el teléfono es más caro que el correo electrónico y el correo urgente es más lento. Contesta pronto.*
>
> *Tu amiga,*
> *cristina.es@nca.stl*

121

3. Pair Activity

You're the salesperson in an electronics store and your partner is a customer. Create a dialog.
Answers: See model on student page.
Extension: Create a dialog in which a customer describes a product without saying what it is. A salesperson tries to guess what the product is.

4. Individual Activity

Interview one of your relatives. Ask what things were like when he or she was your age. Report what you find out to the class.
Answers: See model on student page.
Extension: Compare your interview with those of other students. Find two similarities and two differences.

5. Homework or Classwork

You are sending e-mail for the first time. Tell the friend you write to what you think about e-mail and how you used to communicate.
Answers: See model on student page.
Note: You may want to get students started by eliciting various possibilities, according to the model. Students can then select two or three sentences for their own letter.

Dictation

Students should read their letters aloud while their partners transcribe them. Switch roles and repeat. Compare the transcriptions with the originals and correct each other's work.

CHECK

- ¿Cómo es la *Enciclopedia electrónica*?
- ¿Por qué debo tener una computadora?
- ¿Qué es más caro, un horno microondas o una computadora?

PORTFOLIO

Students may want to include the report of their interview from Activity 4 in their Portfolios.

Para hispanohablantes

Find a song or poem in Spanish that talks about the way life used to be. Explain the meaning to the class.

Communicative Objectives
- to talk about houses
- to talk about technology

Related Components

Transparencies	Video: Tape/Book
Ch. 4: La casa del futuro	Unit 2: Seg. 3
Transparency 27	

Scan to Chapter 4

GETTING STARTED

Ask students what types of appliances they expect to have in their homes in the year 2020.

APPLY

Form groups. Explain that each will design the house of the future. Refer to the article.

PASO 1: En la casa del futuro
Make a list of the things from page 123 you would like to have in the house of the future. Then, include your own inventions in the list and choose two of them to talk about.
Answer: See model on student page.
Extension: "Necessity is the mother of invention." What do you think that expression means?

PASO 2: Ventajas
Talk about the advantages of the two things that you chose.
Answer: See model on student page.
Extension: Pretend you are living in the year 2050. Say what you used to do before these inventions were available.

PASO 3: Desventajas
Talk about the disadvantages.
Answer: See model on student page.
Extension: Compare the two inventions you selected.

PASO 4: El mejor invento
Decide which is your best invention. Make a poster with a drawing of the invention you selected and lists of its advantages and disadvantages. Present the poster to the class. Choose the best invention.
Extension: Imagine you are living in the house with all the inventions that the class presented. Compare that house with today's houses.

122

PARA RESOLVER
UNA CASA MÁS CÓMODA

En grupo, van a diseñar la casa del futuro.

PASO 1 En la casa del futuro

Hagan una lista de las cosas de la página 123 que les gustaría tener en la casa del futuro. Luego, pongan en la lista sus propios inventos y escojan dos cosas para hablar sobre ellas.

Una tarjeta de identificación para abrir la puerta, ropa de cama resistente al fuego...

Vamos a hablar sobre una computadora que... y sobre...

PASO 2 Ventajas

Digan cuáles son las ventajas de las dos cosas que escogieron.

Una computadora que llama a los bomberos sirve cuando hay un incendio y no hay nadie en casa...

PASO 3 Desventajas

Ahora, digan cuáles son las desventajas.

Si no hay nadie en casa y la computadora no funciona, nadie va a llamar a los bomberos...

PASO 4 El mejor invento

Decidan cuál es el mejor invento. Después hagan un cartel con un dibujo y las ventajas y desventajas del invento que seleccionaron.

Presenten el cartel a la clase. Escojan el mejor invento de la clase.

122

PARA TU REFERENCIA

cerrar (e>ie) *to close*
conectadas *connected*
empañar(se) *to fog up*
entrar *to enter*
el invento *invention*
la película especial *a special coating*
las tarjetas de identificación *identification cards*
el tejado *roof*

Architecture Link
Have students research Mexican architecture and make lists of famous Mexican architects and their work.

EN LA CASA DEL FUTURO

Éstos son algunos inventos que ya existen y que van a cambiar nuestras casas.

La casa del futuro va a ser de plástico, porque el plástico es más barato que los materiales tradicionales.

Para entrar a la casa, no vamos a necesitar llaves. Vamos a usar tarjetas de identificación conectadas a una computadora. En caso de incendio, la computadora cierra automáticamente el gas y llama a los bomberos. Las computadoras también nos van a poder leer los periódicos.

Otros inventos son la ropa de cama resistente al fuego y unos espejos para el baño con una película especial para que no se empañen. También vamos a poder abrir y cerrar el techo de nuestras casas con un control remoto.

Todos estos inventos van a hacer de nuestras casas lugares más cómodos.

123

Dictation

Select one paragraph from the reading and dictate it to the class.

123

Objectives

Communicative: to talk about the past and about modern technology

Cultural: to learn about the Spanish ships that were carrying treasure from Peru and Mexico to Spain

Related Components

Audio	Magazine
Conexiones: 16B	Juntos en México
Conexiones	
Chapter 4	

GETTING STARTED

Ask students what they know about recent discoveries of sunken ships that were buried for hundreds of years.

DISCUSS

Using the Text

After each paragraph, ask questions, such as:

¿Qué eran los galeones?
¿Dónde están los galeones hundidos?
¿Qué llevaban? ¿Adónde lo llevaban?
¿De qué países eran los piratas?
¿Cómo se hundieron la mayoría de los barcos?
¿Qué significa la expresión "hoy día"?
(nowadays)
¿Qué cognados hay en el tercer párrafo?
(robots, cámaras, video, rayos, láser, instrumentos, detectar, galeones, expediciones, marinas, usan, acuáticos)
Point out the imperfect in the last sentence: *llevaba el tesoro.* This means "was carrying" rather than "used to carry."

CHECK

Te toca a ti
Possible Answers:

1. *oro, plata y joyas.*
2. *protegerse de los piratas.*
3. *huracanes y tormentas tropicales.*
4. *robots, cámaras de video, rayos láser y otros instrumentos.*
5. *el tesoro más grande que se ha encontrado.*

ENTÉRATE
TESOROS° EN EL GOLFO DE MÉXICO

En el Golfo de México hay muchos galeones hundidos° con tesoros de la época colonial (del siglo XVI al XVIII). Estos galeones llevaban oro, plata y joyas de Perú y México a España. Pero por alguna razón° no llegaron nunca a su destino.

Los barcos generalmente viajaban juntos para protegerse° de los piratas ingleses, franceses y holandeses°. Algunos de estos galeones se hundieron° a causa de° los ataques de los piratas, pero la mayoría se hundió a causa de los huracanes y tormentas tropicales, que son muy comunes en el Golfo.

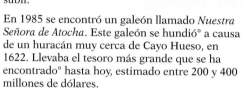

Hoy día, hay robots con cámaras de video, rayos láser y otros instrumentos para detectar dónde están los galeones hundidos. También, las expediciones marinas usan ascensores° acuáticos para ayudar a los buzos° a bajar y a subir.

En 1985 se encontró un galeón llamado *Nuestra Señora de Atocha.* Este galeón se hundió° a causa de un huracán muy cerca de Cayo Hueso, en 1622. Llevaba el tesoro más grande que se ha encontrado° hasta hoy, estimado entre 200 y 400 millones de dólares.

a causa de *because of*	protegerse *to protect themselves*
los buzos *divers*	la razón *reason*
Cayo Hueso *Key West*	se ha encontrado *has been found*
el destino *destination*	se hundió/se hundieron *sank*
holandeses *Dutch*	los restos *wreckage*
hundidos *sunken*	los tesoros *treasures*

124

TE TOCA A TI

Completa las oraciones.

1. Los galeones de la época colonial llevaban...
2. Los barcos viajaban juntos para...
3. Algunos galeones se hundieron a causa de...
4. La tecnología moderna usa...
5. El *Nuestra Señora de Atocha* llevaba...

✓ CULTURE NOTE

Galleons were large Spanish sailing ships built for transport and war. Their route to Spain was determined by prevailing currents and the need to avoid the Atlantic's winter storms and the Caribbean's summer hurricanes.
Pirates and privateers (state-sponsored pirates like Sir Walter Raleigh) attacked Spanish ships in the Caribbean mainly in the 1600s.

PORTFOLIO

Have students make a treasure map and write directions for finding the treasure.

Para hispanohablantes

Tell the class a story about pirates of the Caribbean.

VOCABULARIO TEMÁTICO

Antes
la cámara cinematográfica
movie camera
la escoba *broom*
el horno de leña
wood burning stove
la máquina de escribir
typewriter
el papel carbón *carbon paper*
el telegrama *telegram*
el ventilador *electric fan*

Ahora
el aire acondicionado
air conditioner
la aspiradora *vacuum cleaner*
la cámara de video
video camera
el correo electrónico *e-mail*
el correo urgente *express mail*
el fax *fax*

la fotocopiadora
photocopying machine
el horno microondas
microwave oven
el teléfono celular
cellular phone
el transporte público
public transportation

En las grandes ciudades
la autopista *expressway*
la contaminación *pollution*
el edificio de oficinas
office building
el evento deportivo
sports event
la fábrica *factory*
el rascacielos *skyscraper*
el ruido *noise*
el tráfico *traffic*

Expresiones y palabras
Mándalo por... *Send it by . . .*
Mándalo por fax. *Fax it.*
cómodo(a) *comfortable*
la desventaja *disadvantage*
la exportación *export trade*
limpio(a) *clean*
mandar *to send*
el/la oficinista *office worker*
producir *to make, to produce*
tan... como *as . . . as*
tanto(a)... como
as much . . . as
tantos(as). . . como
as many . . . as
la tecnología *technology*
urgentemente *urgently*
la ventaja *advantage*

Estas personas clasifican los restos de galeones hundidos. ▼

LA CONEXIÓN INGLÉS-ESPAÑOL

In the preceding chapter we learned that an English cognate can be discovered by dropping the final vowel (or diphthong) of a Spanish word and adding a silent *e* when appropriate. How many words can you find in the *Vocabulario temático* that follow this rule?

Sometimes the final diphthong *-ia* can be replaced by a **y** (instead of a silent *e*) in order to discover the English cognate:
memoria → *memor* → **memory**

Find another word in the *Vocabulario temático* that conforms to this rule.

Objectives
• to review vocabulary

Related Components

Activity Book	Audio
Chapter Review: p. 59-60	Assessment: 14B
Assessment	**Cuaderno**
Listening Script: p. 12	p. 35-36
Chapter Test: p. 63-68	**Transparencies** Ch. 4: Dibujos y palabras Transparencies 28-29

Vocabulary

Point out that this list is organized by themes. Use the headings to review vocabulary. You may wish to ask Spanish speakers to share variations on these words and phrases with the class.

La conexión inglés-español

Cognates for *aire, cinematográfica, electrónico, urgente, público, evento,* and *tráfico* can be found by dropping the final vowel of each word. Cognates for *teléfono* and *tecnología* can be discovered by dropping the final vowel(s) of each word and adding an "e" and a "y," respectively.

ADELANTE

Objectives
Prereading Strategy: to gain meaning from photographs and captions
Cultural: to learn about Mexico's pre-Columbian civilizations.

Related Components

Magazine	Video: Tape/Book
Juntos en México	Unit 2: Seg. 4
Transparencies	
Unit 2: Adelante	
Transparency 30	

Search to frame 1212900

GETTING STARTED

Using the Video
Show Segment 4 of the Unit 2 video, an introduction to Mexico's pre-Columbian civilizations.

Antes de leer
Have students read the *Antes de leer* and suggest words that one might expect to appear in this section.
A few words: *años, centro, construir, cultura, destruir, escultura, espectacular, kilo, máscara, metro, moderno, mural, piedra, pirámide, rey, siglo, templo*
Ask such questions as:
¿Cuál fue la primera civilización? ¿Y la última?
¿Cómo terminó el imperio azteca?

About Mexico's Indigenous Peoples
About 90% of Mexico's people can trace their roots to pre-Columbian civilizations. **Mestizos,** people of mixed European and indigenous heritage, account for nearly two-thirds of the population. Another 30% are of purely or predominantly indigenous heritage. Only 9% are Caucasian or predominantly Caucasian.
Spanish is Mexico's official language, but many indigenous dialects are still spoken. Among the largest groups are variations of the Nahuatl language (est. 1.7 million speakers).

ADELANTE

ANTES DE LEER

Desde el 1200 a.C.,° grandes civilizaciones surgieron° en lo que es hoy México. La primera° fue la olmeca. Después vinieron la zapoteca, la teotihuacana, la maya, la tolteca, y otras. La última gran civilización del antiguo México fue la azteca. Los aztecas fundaron el imperio más poderoso° de la época. En 1525, los españoles conquistaron este imperio.

En grupos, miren las fotos de las páginas 126–129 y hagan una lista de las obras de arte y construcciones que dejaron estas civilizaciones.

Los teotihuacanos construyeron la gran Pirámide del Sol hacia° el año 200 a.C.

a.C. (antes de Cristo) *BC (before Christ)*   hacia *around*   la primera *the first one*
poderoso *powerful*   surgieron *arose*

126

ADELANTE COMPONENTS

Activity Book	Audio	Transparencies	Video: Tape/Book
p. 61-64	Adelante: 5A, 5B	Unit 2: Adelante	Unit 2: Seg. 4-5
Assessment	**Magazine**	Transparencies	
Portfolio: p. 35-36	Juntos en México	30-31	

◄ Nadie sabe cómo los olmecas hicieron estas cabezas° colosales. Cada una mide tres metros y pesa miles de kilos.

◄ Los mayas decoraron con pinturas las paredes interiores de muchos edificios. Este mural está en el templo de Bonampak.

◄ Los teotihuacanos hicieron hermosas máscaras de distintos materiales. Muchas de ellas están adornadas con gemas.°

las cabezas *heads*   las gemas *gems*

127

Using the Photos

Pyramid of the Sun

Although its base is the same size as that of the Pyramid of Cheops in Egypt, the Pyramid of the Sun is only half as tall.
¿Cuánto tiempo hace que fue construida la Pirámide del Sol?

Extension: What is the largest pyramid in the world? (the Pyramid of Quetzalcóatl in Cholula)

The Olmecs

The Olmecs were the first group in Mexico to engage in large-scale building and to develop the arts and sciences. It was their civilization which formed the basis for all other advanced pre-Columbian civilizations in Mesoamerica.
¿Quiénes hicieron las cabezas colosales?
¿Qué piensas de las cabezas?

Extension: *Las cabezas miden tres metros. ¿Cuántos pies miden?* (about 12′ 10″)

The Maya

Mayan civilization began about 200 A.D. Their system of mathematics was unequaled in Europe at that time, and their calendar provided not just an accurate measure of the year but exact predictions of solar eclipses.
¿Cómo decoraron los mayas sus edificios?
¿Qué hacen los hombres de la foto del mural?

Teotihuacán

Teotihuacán, about 30 miles northeast of Mexico City, was the first great city of the Americas—a cultural and religious center for the continent. The population exceeded 125,000.
¿Quiénes hicieron máscaras de piedra?
¿De qué colores es esta máscara?

Para hispanohablantes

Tell the class what you know about indigenous societies in the country of your ancestors.

 ►►►▶ **INTERNET LINK**

Maya/Aztec/Inca Exchange
http://www.realtime.net/maya/

Objectives

Reading Strategy: to identify main ideas and details

Cultural: to learn about Mexico's pre-Columbian civilizations

Related Components

Activity Book p. 61	Audio Adelante: 5A

GETTING STARTED

Ask if anyone has been to a pyramid. If so, ask where it was and what it was like. If not, ask what they think it would be like.

Background

The **valle de México** is the central part of the country and contains Mexico City. The valley is formed by three surrounding Sierra Madre mountain ranges: *Oriental, Occidental,* and *del Sur.*

The **Zapotecs** are believed to be descendants of the Olmecs, who moved from the Gulf coast to south central Mexico. **Monte Albán** is located near Oaxaca, southeast of Mexico City.

Chichén Itzá is located near Merida, at the tip of the Yucatan.

Teotihuacán is located about 30 miles northeast of Mexico City. Teotihuacán is a Nahuatl word for "place where one becomes a god." Impressed by the magnificence of Teotihuacán, the Aztecs believed that its people had become gods after their deaths.

The **Toltecs** gained supremacy in the Valley of Mexico (the region of present-day Mexico City) after the decline of Teotihuacán. They established their capital at **Tula,** which is about 50 miles north of Mexico City.

The **Aztecs** reached the Valley of Mexico early in the 14th century A.D., and soon became the most powerful society of Mesoamerica. Mexico City was built over the ruins of **Tenochtitlán.**

DEL MUNDO HISPANO

Las pirámides
del antiguo México

Desde hace más de tres mil años, varias civilizaciones habitaron el valle de México. Allí dejaron testimonios° de su presencia: esculturas, palacios, estadios para el juego de pelota y, especialmente, pirámides.

Las civilizaciones del antiguo México construyeron pirámides muy peculiares. Eran escalonadas° y terminaban en una plataforma donde había un templo. Algunos templos eran de madera y otros de piedra.

La pirámide de Monte Albán está en una gran plaza y es más ancha° que alta. ▼

Los zapotecas

Los zapotecas construyeron la ciudad de Monte Albán hacia el año 500 a.C. En el año 600 d.C.,° Monte Albán era el centro de un gran imperio. Está entre tres valles y es la ciudad más impresionante del antiguo México.

▲ La pirámide de Chichén Itzá es un ejemplo típico de la arquitectura maya.

Los mayas

Los mayas eran muy buenos astrónomos y arquitectos. Hicieron ciudades enteras sin conocer la rueda° y sin la ayuda de animales o herramientas de metal. Las pirámides mayas son más altas y empinadas° que las de otras civilizaciones.

Los teotihuacanos

Hacia el siglo I d.C., Teotihuacán era la ciudad más importante del continente. Tenía entre 125.000 y 200.000 habitantes. Los teotihuacanos la abandonaron entre los años 650 d.C. y 700 d.C., después de un incendio. Ochocientos años después, cuando los aztecas la encontraron, se quedaron maravillados° y la llamaron *la ciudad donde nacen° los dioses.°*

Teotihuacán es famosa por sus pirámides. Las más conocidas son la pirámide

ancha *wide*
d.C. (después de Cristo) *A.D. (after Christ)*
los dioses *gods*
empinadas *steep*
escalonadas *with steps*
las herramientas *tools*
nacen *are born*
la rueda *wheel*
se quedaron maravillados *they were astonished*
los testimonios *evidence*

128

Identifying Main Ideas and Details

Have students notice that the subheadings in the text identify main ideas. With your students, construct a chart showing the main ideas and details of the passage.

◄Hoy puedes visitar las ruinas de Tula en la región de Hidalgo, al norte de la Ciudad de México.

Los aztecas

Los aztecas construyeron Tenochtitlán, la capital de su imperio, en el año 1325 d.C. Doscientos años más tarde el imperio azteca llegaba° hasta Yucatán y América Central.

En el centro de Tenochtitlán había un templo y una gran pirámide de más de cien metros de altura. En la cima° de esta pirámide estaba la piedra del sol, que era un calendario. Hernán Cortés destruyó Tenochtitlán y muchos de los edificios aztecas. Con sus piedras construyó los primeros edificios coloniales de la Ciudad de México.

del Sol y la pirámide de la Luna.

Los toltecas

Los toltecas fueron grandes arquitectos y construyeron la ciudad de Tula. La pirámide de Tula está rodeada° de columnas. Sobre la plataforma de esta pirámide hay esculturas muy grandes.

CIVILIZACIÓN	ZAPOTECA	TEOTIHUACANA	MAYA	TOLTECA	AZTECA
CIUDADES	Monte Albán	Teotihuacán	Chichén Itzá, Tulum, Uxmal y otras	Tula	Tenochtitlán
ANIMALES SAGRADOS	jaguar	serpiente con plumas°	jaguar y serpiente	serpiente con plumas	águila° y serpiente
GOBIERNO	rey	rey	rey°	rey y sacerdote°	emperador
PIRÁMIDES	las que tenían las bases más grandes	la más grande es la del Sol	las más altas y empinadas	con esculturas muy grandes	la gran pirámide de Tenochtitlán (la destruyó Cortés)

águila *eagle*　la cima *the top*　llegaba *reached*　las plumas *feathers*　el rey *king*　rodeada *surrounded*　el sacerdote *priest*

129

Reading Aloud

Have students take turns reading aloud sections of the article.

DISCUSS

Suggestions for discussion:

Las pirámides

Aquí vemos tres pirámides. ¿A qué civilizaciones pertenecen?
¿En cuál de ellas se ve gente?
¿Cuál les gusta más?
¿Prefieres las pirámides altas o anchas?
¿Qué había encima de algunas pirámides?

Los zapotecas

¿Dónde vivieron los zapotecas?
¿En qué año se construyó la ciudad zapoteca de Monte Albán?
¿Qué era esta ciudad en el año 600 d.C.?
¿Les gusta Monte Albán? ¿Por qué?

Los mayas

¿Por qué eran conocidos los mayas?
¿Les sorprenden las grandes ciudades que los mayas construyeron? ¿Por qué?
¿Cómo son las pirámides de los mayas?
¿En qué son diferentes las pirámides mayas de las zapotecas?

Los teotihuacanos

¿Cuántos habitantes había en Teotihuacán?
Cuando la descubrieron los aztecas, ¿qué les pareció? ¿Cómo la llamaron?
¿Cómo se llaman las dos grandes pirámides de Teotihuacán?

Los toltecas

¿Cómo se llama la ciudad que construyeron los toltecas?
Miren la foto de la página 129. ¿Qué les parece la arquitectura tolteca?

Los aztecas

¿Qué construyeron los aztecas?
¿Qué había en el centro de la ciudad?
¿Qué hizo Hernán Cortés en Tenochtitlán?

CHECK

• *¿Qué dejaron las culturas antiguas de México?*
• *¿Cómo son las pirámides de cada cultura?*
• *¿Quién destruyó Tenochtitlán?*

LOG BOOK

Have students write their impressions of the pyramids of different Mexican civilizations in their Log Books.

These activities can be done as classwork or as homework.

Objectives
Organizing Skills: to establish a chronology
Communication Skills: to write sentences

Related Components

Activity Book p. 62	Assessment Portfolio: p. 35-36

ACTIVITIES

1. Historia del antiguo México
Individual Activity Place these events in Mexican history in chronological order. Remind students about the meaning of **a.C.** and **d.C.**
Answers:
1200 a.C. *la civilización Olmeca*
500 a.C. *la civilización Zapoteca*
400 a.C. *fin de la civilización Olmeca*
200 a.C. *la civilización Teotihuacana*
1 *comienzo de la era cristiana*
200 d.C. *la civilización Maya, edad de oro de la civilización Teotihuacana*
600 d.C. *edad de oro de la civilización Zapoteca*
700 d.C. *fin de la civilización Teotihuacana*
900 d.C. *la civilización Tolteca, fin de la civilización Zapoteca*
950 d.C. *fin de la civilización Maya*
1300 d.C. *la civilización Azteca, fin de la civilización Tolteca*
1492 d.C. *Llegada de los españoles a América*
1520 d.C. *Conquista de Tenochtitlán por Hernán Cortés, fin de la civilización Azteca*

2. Contesta las preguntas
Individual Activity Using the information from Activity 1, answer the questions.
Answers:
• *la civilización Olmeca*
• *la civilización Zapoteca, la civilización Azteca*
• *600 d.C.*
• *1492*

3. Compruébalo
Individual Activity Choose the correct ending for each sentence.
1. b
2. e
3. a
4. c
5. d

❶ Historia del antiguo México
Aquí tienes varios datos sobre la historia de las civilizaciones del antiguo México. Haz una tabla y ponlos en orden cronológico.

200 a.C.	la civilización teotihuacana
600 d.C.	edad de oro° de la civilización zapoteca
1520 d.C.	Conquista de Tenochtitlán por Hernán Cortés.
	fin de la civilización azteca
950 d.C.	fin de la civilización maya
1	comienzo de la era cristiana
1200 a.C.	la civilización olmeca
500 a.C.	la civilización zapoteca
400 a.C.	fin de la civilización olmeca
1300 d.C.	la civilización azteca
	fin de la civilización tolteca
900 d.C.	la civilización tolteca
	fin de la civilización zapoteca
1492 d.C.	Llegada de los españoles a América.
700 d.C.	fin° de la civilización teotihuacana
200 d.C.	edad de oro de la civilización teotihuacana, la civilización maya

❷ Contesta las preguntas
Contesta las siguientes preguntas.

- ¿Cuál es la civilización más antigua?
- ¿Qué civilización duró° más? ¿Qué civilización duró menos?
- ¿Cuándo fue la edad de oro de la civilización zapoteca?
- ¿En qué año llegaron los españoles a América?

❸ Compruébalo
Une elementos de las dos columnas para hacer oraciones.

1. El águila y la serpiente
2. Las pirámides mayas
3. Los toltecas
4. Los teotihuacanos
5. La civilización azteca

a. construyeron la ciudad de Tula.
b. son los animales sagrados de los aztecas.
c. construyeron la pirámide del Sol.
d. fue la civilización más corta.
e. son altas y empinadas.

duró *lasted*
la edad de oro *golden age*
el fin *end*

TALLER DE ESCRITORES

1. TU ABUELO Y TÚ

Toma notas sobre la vida de tu abuelo o abuela, cuando era adolescente. Después, escribe ocho oraciones comparando su vida° con tu vida.

Mi abuelo
1. Mi abuelo usaba una máquina de
escribir.
2.
3.

Yo
Yo escribo en la computadora.

2. ENTREVISTA

Usa una enciclopedia y busca datos sobre la civilización azteca. Ahora, prepara cinco preguntas para entrevistar al emperador Moctezuma.

3. EL MEJOR INVENTO°

¿Qué invento es tan importante en tu vida que no podrías° vivir sin él? En grupos, decidan cuál es el mejor invento del siglo.° Después escriban cinco oraciones explicando por qué escogieron este invento y por qué es tan importante. Presenten los resultados a la clase.

POR EJEMPLO

la radio	el correo electrónico
la calculadora	el aire acondicionado
la computadora	la televisión
el avión	el horno microondas

UN SISTEMA DE LA COMPUTADORA INDICA QUIÉN VA A CLASE Y QUIÉN NO VA.

Marcelo Santos, un estudiante de 17 años, sorprendió a profesores y estudiantes de su escuela con su original invento, que presentó al público ayer. Marcelo hizo un sistema para la computadora para controlar quién va a clase y quién no va. Los estudiantes se preocuparon un poco al enterarse de la noticia. Los profesores se alegraron mucho.

4. ESCRIBE PARA EL PERIÓDICO

Escribe algo sobre tu escuela para un periódico. Puede ser un pequeño artículo con una noticia, una entrevista o una carta al director del periódico con una sugerencia.°

el invento *invention*
no podrías *you couldn't*
el siglo *century*

la sugerencia *suggestion*
la vida *life*

131

Para hispanohablantes

For the *Entrevista,* interview a Spanish speaker, using a tape or video recorder. Play the tape for the class.

TALLER DE ESCRITORES

Objectives
• to practice writing
• to use vocabulary from this unit

Related Components

Activity Book p. 63	Assessment Portfolio: p. 35-36

ACTIVITIES

1. Tu abuelo y tú
Individual Activity Students will take notes about their grandfather or grandmother's adolescence. Then, they will write eight sentences comparing their lives to that person's life.

2. Entrevista
Individual Activity Students will use an encyclopedia to gather information about the Aztec civilization. Then they will prepare five questions to ask the Emperor Moctezuma.

3. El mejor invento
Group Activity Students will identify an invention they couldn't do without. They will then write five sentences explaining why they chose it and why it is important.

4. Escribe para el periódico
Individual Activity Students will write something about their school for a newspaper. It can be a news item, a description of a sports event, an interview, or a letter to the editor with a suggestion. Have them use the library to gather the information that they need. They can also interview faculty or alumni.
Edit: Students exchange, review, and edit each other's work. They should circle words they think are misspelled, make notes about possible grammar errors, and help each other prepare final drafts.
Present: Students read their final drafts aloud to another person or the class.

PORTFOLIO
Have students select one of these assignments for their Portfolios.

MANOS A LA OBRA

Objectives
Communicative: to listen to and understand directions
Cultural: to learn about the Mexican tradition of trees of life
• to make a tree of life

Related Components

Assessment	Video: Tape/Book
Portfolio p. 35-36	Unit 2: Seg. 5
Transparencies	
Unit 2: Project	
Transparency 31	

Scan to La obra

Materials

- air-dry clay
- a cardboard tube
- acrylic paints
- adhesive tape
- brushes
- a candle
- acrylic glaze
- aluminum foil
- paper or plastic soup bowl
- a knife
- a plastic glass
- wire
- pliers (or a wire cutter)

GETTING STARTED

Encourage students to use their eyes more than their ears. Rather than try to understand every word, they should concentrate on the images and listen only for clues. Show the tree of life segment of the Unit 2 video.

DISCUSS

Have volunteers read aloud the paragraphs. Make sure students understand the various functions of trees of life, as well as what they look like. Ask questions, such as:
¿Qué es un árbol de la vida?
¿Para qué lo usan los mexicanos?
¿De qué formas pueden ser?

MANOS A LA OBRA

TU ÁRBOL DE LA VIDA

El árbol de la vida es una antigua tradición mexicana. Es una escultura de barro° en forma de árbol que representa la vida. En muchos pueblos mexicanos todavía usan el árbol de la vida en ceremonias y celebraciones. Los mexicanos también lo usan para decorar sus casas.

Hay muchos tipos de árboles de la vida. Generalmente tienen adornos de colores en forma de hojas,° frutas, flores, personas, pájaros y otras cosas.

TE TOCA A TI

Ahora tú vas a hacer tu árbol de la vida. Piensa en algo que para ti representa la vida y que quieres incluir en tu árbol. El árbol de la vida que vamos a hacer es de barro y va a servir de° candelero.°

Materiales

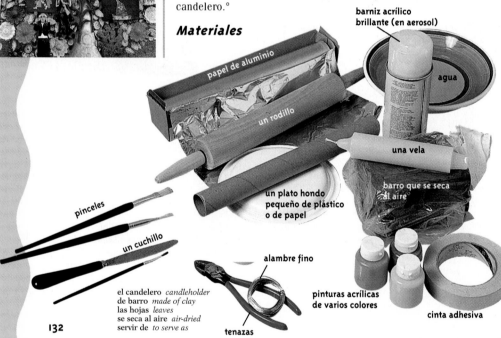

barniz acrílico brillante (en aerosol)
papel de aluminio
agua
un rodillo
una vela
pinceles
barro que se seca al aire
un cuchillo
un plato hondo pequeño de plástico o de papel
alambre fino
pinturas acrílicas de varios colores
cinta adhesiva
tenazas

el candelero *candleholder*
de barro *made of clay*
las hojas *leaves*
se seca al aire *air-dried*
servir de *to serve as*

132

Language in Context

Ask students to think of the word *vida* and some related words in English, such as "vital" and "vitamin." Explain that they all come from the Latin *vita:* "life."

132

1 Pon el plato boca abajo.° Haz un agujero° en el centro del plato. Pon el tubo en el agujero. Pégalo con cinta adhesiva.

2 Con el papel de aluminio, haz dos rollos.° Con la cinta adhesiva, pega los rollos al tubo en forma de círculo o de corazón.°

3 Cubre° todo con una capa° de barro de 1/4". Humedécete° los dedos° en agua para moldear el barro más fácilmente. Déjalo secar° durante 24 horas.

4 Con el rodillo, haz una capa de barro de 1/4". Ahora usa el cuchillo para cortar° el barro y formar hojas y flores. También puedes hacer figuras humanas, pájaros, frutas y otras cosas.

5 Con el alambre fino, haz agujeros pequeños en el árbol y en las figuras. Pinta el árbol y las figuras de colores. Con el pegamento o los alambres, pega las figuras al árbol.

6 Deja secar la pintura y aplica barniz. Pon la vela en su lugar y... ¡ya tienes tu árbol de la vida!

el agujero *hole*
boca abajo *upside down*
la capa *layer*

el corazón *heart*
cortar *to cut*
cubre *cover*

los dedos *fingers*
deja secar... *let ... dry*

humedécete *dampen*
los rollos *rolls*

Objectives

Communicative: to expand reading comprehension

Cultural: to relate the study of Spanish to other subject areas

Related Components

Activity Book p. 64	Audio Adelante: 5B
Assessment Portfolio: p. 35-36	Video: Tape/Book Unit 2: Seg. 4

Search to frame 1270820

Un gran poeta mexicano

About Octavio Paz

Octavio Paz has written essays, short stories, and poetry. A constant theme in his work is our sense of identity and ability—or inability—to communicate with others. *El laberinto de la soledad,* his most famous collection of essays, was published in 1950 and brought him immediate international fame.

Have volunteers read and answer the questions on the student page.

Possible Answers:

• *A los 17 años.*

• *Recibió el Premio Nobel de literatura.*

Activity

Ask questions:

Octavio Paz tiene muchos talentos. ¿Cuáles son algunos?

¿De qué habla en sus poemas?

¿Cuál es su obra más famosa?

Literature Link

Have students look up in the library other works by Octavio Paz, and organize them according to their genre.

INTERNET LINKS

Pok-a-lok http://mexico.udg.mx:80/Deporte/pelota.html

Whale Watching Web: http://www.physics.helsinki.fi:80/whale/

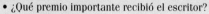

LITERATURA

UN GRAN POETA MEXICANO

El gran poeta y escritor Octavio Paz nació en México en 1914. A los diecisiete años empezó a escribir poesía.° Años después, Paz fue diplomático, traductor° y profesor. En 1990 recibió el premio Nobel de literatura. En sus poemas, Octavio Paz habla del amor,° de la vida, de la soledad° y de la muerte.° Pero sobre todo, habla del mundo mexicano. Su obra en prosa° más conocida es *El laberinto de la soledad.*

• ¿Cuándo empezó Octavio Paz a escribir poesía?

• ¿Qué premio importante recibió el escritor?

BAILE

EL BALLET FOLKLÓRICO DE MÉXICO

Para conocer bien México tienes que oír su música y ver sus bailes. La mexicana Amalia Hernández fundó° el Ballet Folklórico de México en 1952. En 1961, este ballet ganó el primer premio del Festival de las Naciones, en París. Desde entonces, el Ballet Folklórico lleva las canciones y los bailes mexicanos por todo el mundo. El colorido° de los trajes, la música y el ritmo de sus espectáculos fascina a todos.

• ¿Cuándo se hizo famoso el Ballet Folklórico de México?

• ¿Por qué a todo el mundo le gustan los espectáculos de este ballet?

el amor *love*	la muerte *death*	la soledad *solitude*
el colorido *colors*	la poesía *poetry*	el traductor *translator*
fundó *founded*	la prosa *prose*	

134

El Ballet Folklórico de México

About the Company

The Ballet Folklórico de México has two troupes, one that performs in Mexico and another that gives performances around the world. The company performs dances from many regions of Mexico, as well as dances from Mexico's history.

Possible Answers:

• *En 1961, cuando ganó el primer premio del Festival de las Naciones, en París.*

• *Por el colorido de los trajes, la música y el ritmo de sus espectáculos.*

Activity

Have students say whether the following statements are **cierto** or **falso**.

1. *La méxicana Amalia Hernández fundó el Ballet Forklórico de México en 1961.* (falso)

2. *El Ballet baila en muchos países.* (cierto)

3. *Amalia Hernández nació en 1952.* (falso)

DEPORTE

LOS ANTIGUOS FUTBOLISTAS°

El pok-a-tok era un deporte muy popular entre los antiguos mexicanos. Dos equipos de siete jugadores cada uno jugaban con una pelota de caucho.° La pelota sólo se podía tocar con los codos°, las caderas° y los pies, y había que meterla° en un aro° de piedra. Los historiadores creen que el pok-a-tok puede ser el origen del fútbol y de otros juegos de pelota.

- ¿Qué era el pok-a-tok?
- ¿Con qué podían tocar la pelota los jugadores?

ECOLOGÍA

EL SANTUARIO DE LAS BALLENAS° GRISES

El desierto Vizcaíno está en la península mexicana de Baja California. En este desierto hay dos lagunas saladas° —conectadas al Océano Pacífico—que se llaman Ojo de Liebre y San Ignacio. Cada año, las ballenas grises llegan a estas lagunas desde el océano. Las ballenas se quedan en las lagunas varios meses. Allí se reproducen y cuidan° a sus crías.° Allí también pasan el invierno otros animales marinos, como la ballena azul, el elefante marino,° la foca° leopardo y el león marino de California. En febrero, todos estos animales vuelven al norte.

- ¿Qué hacen las ballenas grises en las lagunas saladas de Baja California?
- ¿Qué otros animales marinos van también allí?

el aro *ring*	cuidan *care for*	las crías *offspring*	los futbolistas *football players*
las ballenas *whales*	el caucho *rubber*	el elefante marino *elephant seal*	meter *to put*
las caderas *hips*	los codos *elbows*	la foca *seal*	salada *salt*

135

Reading Aloud
Have students take turns reading aloud from *Otras Fronteras.*

Los antiguos futbolistas

About the Sport
The game was played in a narrow, paved gallery with a wider area at each end. The rings were on either side of the center— sometimes at the top of a ramp. In the *Popol Vuh*, which contains creation stories of the Maya, two heroes play a game of pok-a-tok to determine the destiny of the human race.
Have volunteers read and answer the questions on the student page.

Possible Answers:
- *Era un deporte muy popular entre los antiguos mexicanos.*
- *Podían tocarla sólo con los codos, las caderas y los pies.*

Activity
Ask questions:
¿Cuántos jugadores jugaban en cada partido?
¿Qué tenían que hacer con la pelota?
¿Cómo es el pok-a-tok similar al fútbol? ¿Al baloncesto?
¿Te gustaría jugar al pok-a-tok?

El santuario de las ballenas grises

About Whale Migration
Most whales migrate between tropical and Arctic waters. They spend summers in the Arctic, where the waters are rich in plankton. In the winter they move to tropical waters, where pregnant females give birth to babies. The warm waters provide a comfortable environment for babies, but food is scarce, so adults must live off their blubber.

Possible Answers:
- *Pasan el invierno, se reproducen y cuidan a sus crías.*
- *La ballena azul, el elefante marino, la foca leopardo y el león marino.*

Activity
Have students say whether the following statements are **cierto** or **falso.**
1. *Baja California es parte de Estados Unidos.* (falso)
2. *Las ballenas grises van a los desiertos de Ojo de Liebre y San Ignacio.* (falso)
3. *Las ballenas crían en los meses de invierno.* (cierto)

3 NUEVA YORK Y LA REPÚBLICA DOMINICANA

UN PUENTE CULTURAL

 Tell your students...

In this unit we discover the many things you can do in New York City to enjoy Dominican culture (Chapter 5), before visiting the beautiful Caribbean island itself (Chapter 6). After gasping at the New York skyline and sightseeing at Lincoln Center and Central Park, we eat lunch at a Dominican restaurant, listen to a hot *merengue* band practicing, watch a few Dominican New York Yankees play, and hang out in the Dominican neighborhood of Washington Heights. In the Dominican Republic, we thread our way through the historic streets of Santo Domingo, home of the Western Hemisphere's oldest Roman Catholic cathedral and European-style university, before catching a jitney bus to the fishing village of La Romana. Then, we make our way to a stone amphitheater—just the place to prime us for a night of dancing the *merengue*.

Before leaving the island, we talk to a young Dominican baseball player and go deep-sea fishing. Many Dominicans eat, sleep, and breathe baseball, and the results are evident in ballparks all over the island country, and on the rosters of every pro team in the United States. Finally, we visit a professional *maracas* maker who helps us make *maracas* that any *merenguero* would be proud to shake.

VIDEO LINKS

Corresponding Video Segments

Text	
Unit Overview Unit Opener	**1. Introduction to New York and the Dominican Republic** A quick glimpse of the island city and the island country
Chapter 5	**2. Pasándola bien en Nueva York** Sightseeing and listening to Dominican style music in New York City Grammar: the preterite of stem-changing **-ir** verbs
Chapter 6	**3. ¡Recuerdos de la isla!** Discovering the Dominican Republic: historic Santo Domingo, the lovely fishing village of La Romana, the echoing amphitheater at Vila del Rio Chávon, and *el merengue* Grammar: indirect object pronouns
Adelante	**4. Adelante** Pro baseball and deep-sea fishing in the Dominican Republic
Manos a la obra	**5. Manos a la obra** How to make *maracas*

NUEVA YORK Y LA REPÚBLICA DOMINICANA: UN PUENTE CULTURAL

New York City is the largest city in the United States, and in recent years natives of the Dominican Republic have made up the fastest-growing segment of the city's large Hispanic population. In the 1990 census, 500,000 Dominicans accounted for 22 percent of the city's total Hispanic population of 1,780,000. Most of us know a great deal about New York City, our country's multicultural capital; but apart from its incredible output of first-class baseball players, most people know little about the Dominican Republic.

Dominican Republic: Geography and Climate

The Dominican Republic takes up the eastern two-thirds of the Caribbean island of Hispaniola, which is about 600 miles (1,000 kilometers) southeast of Florida, with Cuba to the west and Puerto Rico to the east. The Dominican Republic's 20,000 square miles (50,000 square kilometers) include a wide variety of mountains, valleys, rivers, and coast line. At 10,417 feet (3,175 meters), Pico Duarte is the highest mountain in the West Indies. Santo Domingo, the country's capital, is on the island's southern coast. The climate is subtropical; temperatures average 77°F (25°C) with little variation. The rainy season lasts from May to November.

Dominican Republic: History and Government

Originally inhabited by Taino Indians, Hispaniola is where Christopher Columbus first set foot in the New World in 1492. The city of Santo Domingo, founded in 1496, is the oldest extant colonial settlement in the Western Hemisphere. During the 16th century, French settlers landed on the western part of the island, and in 1697 Spain was forced to officially recognize the colony, which eventually became Haiti.

The Dominican Republic, then called Santo Domingo like its capital city, achieved independence from Spain in 1821. The new country fell under the influence first of Haiti and then of the United States, which came close to annexing the debt-ridden nation in 1870. Forty years later, following a rebellion that threatened US economic interests, the United States invaded and set up a protectorship which lasted for eight years (1916–1924).

The history of the Dominican Republic has been marked by civil strife, military rule, dictatorships, and assassinations; but in recent years the country has become more democratic. A president and national assembly are elected every four years.

Dominican Republic: The Other Side of the Island

The Dominican Republic and Haiti share the island of Hispaniola, but very little else. Different languages and European traditions are barriers by themselves. They are heightened, however, by Dominican memories of Toussaint-L'Ouverture's bloody overthrow of the Spanish colonists after the successful 1795 slave revolt in Haiti, and of Haitian president Jean Pierre Boyer's invasion of the Dominican Republic following the Spanish withdrawal in 1821. The subsequent occupation lasted from 1822 to 1844 and left deep scars. Today the two countries coexist side by side, but warily.

Enriquillo

HISTORY CONNECTION

Objective
- to explore the life and times of Enriquillo, the Dominican Republic's first national hero

Use
any time during Unit 3

Activity
- Have the class brainstorm heroic qualities and list them on the board. For example: *valiente, arriesgado, listo, ingenioso*, honesto, independiente,* etc. Help them with difficult Spanish words.
- Read the FYI and have the class discuss Enriquillo's heroic qualities.
- Have students create an Enriquillo poster that includes a list of his heroic qualities.
- Display the poster.

FYI
Born the son of a Taino chief, Enriquillo was captured by Spaniards when he was a boy and educated by Franciscan monks. He labored under the colonial system of *repartimiento** until, after a series of run-ins with the authorities, he escaped and in 1520 led a Taino revolt against the Spaniards. From their mountain strongholds, Enriquillo and his men held off the colonists for 13 years. In 1533 the Spaniards were forced to allow Enriquillo to form an independent community of escaped Tainos. Enriquillo died a free man in 1538.

Variation
- Columbus and Enriquillo were on the island of Hispaniola at the same time. Have the class compare them by discussing their similarities and differences. For example, someone listing the similarities might say: *Vivían en la misma época, eran bilingües, sabían leer y escribir, sufrían injusticias, recibían títulos de la corona española,* etc.

***valiente** *courageous, brave*
***arriesgado** *bold, daring*
***listo** *smart, clever (a person)*
***ingenioso** *ingenious, resourceful*
***repartimiento** *forced labor and payment in exchange for protection*

Juguemos al béisbol

GAME

Objective
- to play a baseball game and to explore the popularity of baseball in the Dominican Republic

Use
any time during Unit 3

Materials
- TRB Activity Support Page 8, *Juguemos al béisbol*
- scissors, pen

Activity
- Share the FYI, and talk about why baseball is so popular in the Dominican Republic. Have students brainstorm names of pro baseball players from the Dominican Republic. List names on the board.
- Have students form pairs. Distribute one activity support page to each pair. Students should then cut page into squares, number the backs consecutively, and line them up 4 x 4, numbers up.
- One player calls two numbers, turns squares over, reads the information, and decides whether or not the squares match. For example, they might read *nueve* and *¿Cuántas entradas hay en un partido de béisbol?* If it's a match, the player calls two more numbers and reads the information to his/her partner. If not, the player puts back the squares and the partner selects two new ones.
- Play continues until all questions and answers are matched. The player who makes the most matches wins.

FYI
Baseball is an obsession in the Dominican Republic, where it is also called *pelota.* It was brought to the island by U.S. troops at the end of the 19th century, though a ball game had been played by indigenous Tainos centuries before. There are more players from the Dominican Republic on U.S. pro teams than from any U.S. state or from any other Latin American nation. Some of the better-known players: Felipe Alou, Orlando Cepeda, Pedro Guerrero, José de León, Manny Mota, José Rijo, Juan Samuel, and the great Juan Marichal, pitcher and 1983 Hall of Famer.

Entre tres mundos

HISTORY CONNECTION

Objective
• to explore the Dominican Republic's role in a historically important and infamous trade triangle

Use
any time during Unit 3

Materials
• TRB Activity Support Page 9, *Un triángulo comercial* (map)
• TRB Activity Support Page 10, *Palabras claves* (word grid)

Activity
• Make one copy of *Palabras claves*. Cut along the lines and place face down in a box or on a plate.
• Divide the class into two teams.
• Read the FYI and distribute *Un triángulo comercial*.
• Teams alternate, each picking a word or phrase and discussing it in relationship to the map and the FYI. For example, Team A picks *Cristóbal Colón* and comes up with this sentence: *Cristóbal Colón llegó a la isla de La Española en 1492.*
• If the information is correct, the team picks a new word or phrase; if incorrect, Team B can either correct the information or pick a new word. If Team B is correct, they pick a new slip. If Team B is incorrect, Team A can either try the first word again or use the new Team B word.
• Continue until all key words are discussed.

FYI
Welcomed by Taino natives who spoke of gold, the Spaniards who followed Christopher Columbus to Hispaniola founded towns and cultivated sugarcane and cacao. By the early 1500s, the indigenous population had dwindled and the Spaniards needed a new source of cheap labor. This led to the beginning of the African slave trade. Iron, guns, gun powder, textiles, and liquor were shipped from Europe to Africa, where they were exchanged for slaves who were brought to Hispaniola to work on plantations whose owners exported products to Europe. Millions of Africans were brought to the New World during the next 350 years. Millions are estimated to have died in transit.

*claves key

Bai-la-la-lar el merengue

HANDS ON: DANCING

Objective
• to learn the steps of the *merengue,* the Dominican Republic's best-known dance

Use
any time during Unit 3

Materials
• TRB Activity Support Page 11, *Pasos del merengue*
• TRB Activity Support Page 12, *Pasos del merengue* (female footprints)
• TRB Activity Support Page 13, *Pasos del merengue* (male footprints)
• audiocassette player
• *merengue* music

Preparation
• Make copies of both sets of footprints—enough for the basic steps on *Pasos del merengue.*
• Distribute *Pasos del merengue.*

Activity
• Share and discuss the FYI below.
• Have students form mixed pairs.
• Tape footprints to floor to form the basic steps shown on *Pasos del merengue.*
• Pick a couple to serve as models. They follow the steps in front of the class, and the other pairs follow the models.
• When everyone has mastered the steps, put on a tape and turn up the volume.

FYI
The *merengue* is the Dominican Republic's unique contribution to Hispanic music. Played on an assortment of indigenous and African instruments dominated by the accordion–like European *melodeón, merengues* are played in lively 2/4 time, danced mostly from the waist down, and sung either solo or by call-and-response. In newer songs, you'll hear saxophones and electric guitars. Some famous *merengue* artists are Wilfrido Vargas, Johnny Ventura, La Coco Band, José Estefan y la Patrulla 15, Juan Luis Guerra, Luis Días, Sergio Vargas, and Anthony Santos.

*huellas tracks

NUEVA YORK Y LA REPÚBLICA DOMINICANA: UN PUENTE CULTURAL

Unit Opener Goal

Communicative: to talk about the Dominican Republic and New York City
Cultural: to develop cross-cultural awareness

Related Components

Transparencies Unit 3: Chapters 5-6 Transparencies 32-41	**Video: Tape/Book** Unit 3: Seg. 1

Scan to Unit 3

GETTING STARTED

Ask students why they think New York City and the Dominican Republic are discussed in the same unit. How are these two places related?

Using the Video

Show Segment 1 of the Unit 3 video, an introduction to New York City and the Dominican Republic.

Using the Transparencies

To help orient students, use the Locator Map Transparency. You may want to use other Unit 3 transparencies at this time.

DISCUSS

Presenting New York and the Dominican Republic
For more information about New York and the Dominican Republic, refer to pages 136A–136D.

Using the Text

English: After students have read the introduction, ask questions. For example:

Where are some Spanish-speaking communities in our area?

What countries are the people in those communities from?
Spanish: ¿Qué es un "puente cultural"?
¿Qué hay en la foto? ¿Está foto esta tomada en Nueva York o en la República Dominicana? ¿Cómo lo sabes?

UNIDAD 3

NUEVA YORK

Y LA REPÚBLICA DOMINICANA

UN PUENTE CULTURAL

En la unidad 3:

Capítulo 5	¡Pasándola bien en la ciudad!
Capítulo 6	Recuerdos la isla
Adelante	**Para leer:** El béisbol dominicano de ayer y de hoy
	Proyecto: Al ritmo de maracas
	Otras fronteras: Arte, mineralogía, biología y economía

UNIT COMPONENTS

Activity Book
p. 65-88
Assessment
Oral Proficiency:
  p. 25-26
Listening Script:
  p. 13-14
Chapter Tests:
  p. 69-80
Portfolio: p. 37-38

Audio Book
Script: p. 33-45;
  39-41
Activities: p. 36-38;
  42-44
Audio
Chapter: 6A, 6B
Adelante: 7A, 7B
Assessment: 14B
Conexiones: 17A

Conexiones
Chapters 5-6
Cuaderno
p. 37-52
Magazine
Juntos en República
  Dominicana

Transparencies
Unit 3: Chapters 5-6
Transparencies
  32-41
Tutor Pages
p. 23-30
Video: Tape/Book
Unit 3: Segments 1-5

Mural de homenaje a la música latina.

You do not need to travel outside the United States to use your Spanish. Many parts of this country have thriving communities where Spanish is spoken.

In this unit, you will visit Spanish-speaking communities in New York City and take part in activities with young people who live in the city's diverse neighborhoods. You will go to a Latino concert, learn about a museum that celebrates Hispanic culture, and plan your own excursion.

After you visit New York City, you will explore the Dominican Republic. There you will visit a small village and share memories of its past. You'll even get to play a typical island game and learn about the Domincan celebration of *¡Carnaval!*

Finally, you will learn about the national Dominican sport — *béisbol.* You will find it very familiar! You may even recognize some of the players. There are over 100 Dominicans in the major leagues today.

Then you will learn how to make maracas, a musical instrument used in the dance of the Domincan Republic — *el merengue.* *¡Bailemos!*

137

■ ACTIVITIES

INTERDISCIPLINARY CONNECTIONS

To provide other perspectives, have students research questions like these:

History

In which Dominican city are Christopher Columbus' remains buried? Where are they in that city? (See Culture Note below.) The Dominican Republic won its independence in 1844. What was going on that year in the United States? (A few facts: James K. Polk was elected President, Samuel F. B. Morse sent the first telegraph message, and Florida and Texas were about to become the 27th and 28th states.)

Geography

The Dominican Republic is the second-largest nation in the West Indies. What is the first? What island groups make up the West Indies? (Cuba is the largest. The four main island groups are the Greater Antilles—Cuba, Jamaica, Hispaniola, and Puerto Rico—the lesser Antilles, the Dutch West Indies, and the Bahamas.)

Language

What is the difference between *migration, immigration,* and *emigration?* (*Migration* refers to movement from one region to another within a country, immigration to the movement of people into a country, and emigration to the movement of people out of a country. For example, someone *emigrates* from Spain and *immigrates* to Argentina.)

	Objetivos page 139 ¡Pasándola bien en la ciudad!	Conversemos pages 140-141 Tú y tus amigos	Realidades pages 142-143 Folleto de El Museo del Barrio	Palabras en acción pages 144-145 ¡Vamos al concierto!
Comunicación	To talk about: • what you and your friends like to do	Discuss typical teen activities	Read text, discuss El Museo del Barrio, make table	Read cartoon, make list; discuss ad, characters, weekend activities, show; design poster; write invitation
	• favorite entertainers	Discuss types of entertainers	Read text, discuss El Museo del Barrio, make table	Read cartoon, make list; discuss ad, characters, weekend activities, show; design poster; write invitation
	• reactions to recent entertainment events	Discuss reactions to entertainment events		Read cartoon; talk about characters; discuss weekend activities; talk about show
	• how to meet other teens	Discuss how to meet other teens	Read text, discuss El Museo del Barrio, make table	Read cartoon; write invitation
Cultura	To learn about: • El Museo del Barrio in New York City • typical activities for Latin American teens in New York City • merengue: a Dominican dance		Pamphlet about El Museo del Barrio in New York City	
Vocabulario temático	To know the expressions for: • typical teen activities and favorite places	Talk about typical teen activities and favorite places	Read text, discuss El Museo del Barrio, make table	Read cartoon, make list; discuss ad, characters, weekend activities, show; design poster; write invitation
	• types of entertainers	Talk about types of entertainers	Read text, discuss El Museo del Barrio, make table	Read cartoon, make list; discuss ad; characters; weekend activities; show; design poster; write invitation
	• introductions and asking about introductions	Talk about introductions		Read cartoon, discuss how to meet another teen; write invitation
Estructura	To talk about: • past activities: preterite of -ir verbs, such as divertirse	Discuss past activities		Read cartoon, talk about characters; discuss weekend activities; talk about show
	• for whom or to whom something is done: indirect object pronouns		Read text, answer questions, discuss El Museo del Barrio	Read cartoon, write invitation
	• generalizations without using a subject: se come, se busca, se necesitan			

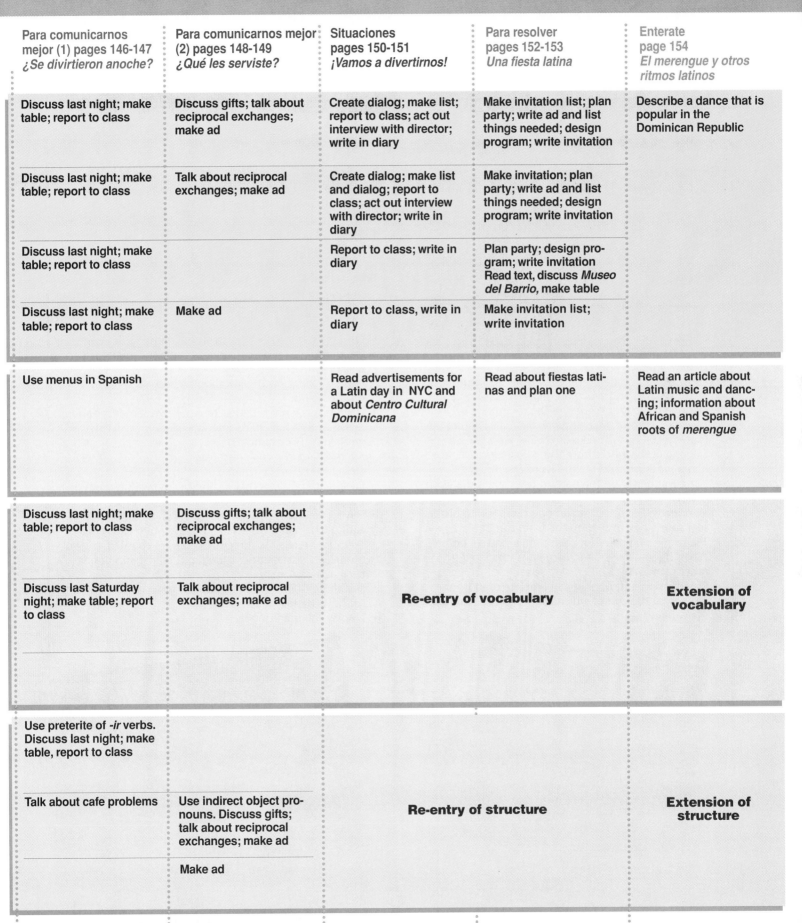
Para comunicarnos mejor (1) pages 146-147 *¿Se divirtieron anoche?*	Para comunicarnos mejor (2) pages 148-149 *¿Qué les serviste?*	Situaciones pages 150-151 *¡Vamos a divertirnos!*	Para resolver pages 152-153 *Una fiesta latina*	Enterate page 154 *El merengue y otros ritmos latinos*
Discuss last night; make table; report to class	Discuss gifts; talk about reciprocal exchanges; make ad	Create dialog; make list; report to class; act out interview with director; write in diary	Make invitation list; plan party; write ad and list things needed; design program; write invitation	Describe a dance that is popular in the Dominican Republic
Discuss last night; make table; report to class	Talk about reciprocal exchanges; make ad	Create dialog; make list and dialog; report to class; act out interview with director; write in diary	Make invitation; plan party; write ad and list things needed; design program; write invitation	
Discuss last night; make table; report to class		Report to class; write in diary	Plan party; design program; write invitation Read text, discuss *Museo del Barrio,* make table	
Discuss last night; make table; report to class	Make ad	Report to class, write in diary	Make invitation list; write invitation	
Use menus in Spanish		Read advertisements for a Latin day in NYC and about *Centro Cultural Dominicana*	Read about fiestas latinas and plan one	Read an article about Latin music and dancing; information about African and Spanish roots of *merengue*
Discuss last night; make table; report to class	Discuss gifts; talk about reciprocal exchanges; make ad			
Discuss last Saturday night; make table; report to class	Talk about reciprocal exchanges; make ad	**Re-entry of vocabulary**		**Extension of vocabulary**
Use preterite of *-ir* verbs. Discuss last night; make table, report to class				
Talk about cafe problems	Use indirect object pronouns. Discuss gifts; talk about reciprocal exchanges; make ad	**Re-entry of structure**		**Extension of structure**
	Make ad			

Partido de béisbol

¿Qué hiciste?

SPORTS CONNECTION

Objective
• to have a baseball spelling bee, using the Chapter 5 *Vocabulario temático*

Use
after *Palabras en acción,* pages 144–45

Activity
• Review the FYI for *Juguemos al béisbol* on page 136C.

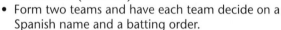

• Select a scorekeeper and draw a scorecard on the chalkboard (see inset).
• Form two teams and have each team decide on a Spanish name and a batting order.
• Designate the four corners of the room *base del bateador, primera base, segunda base,* and *tercera base* (see inset). Choose one team to bat first.
• Say one of the words from the *Vocabulario temático,* use it in a sentence, and say the word again.
• If the first player on the batting team spells the word correctly, he/she goes to first base. If the word is spelled incorrectly, the player strikes out, returning to his/her seat so the next player on the team can bat.
• Teams get one point for each runner batted home.
• When three players on a team have struck out, the other team gets to bat.
• Play continues through nine complete rounds, or innings, at the end of which the scorekeeper announces the winning team.

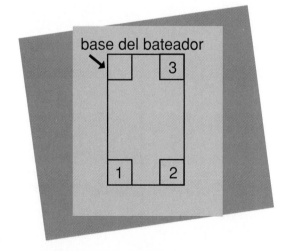

MATH CONNECTION

Objective
• to graph and discuss weekend leisure activities using the preterite of stem-changing **-ir** verbs.

Use
after *Para comunicarnos mejor,* pages 146–147

Materials
• graph paper

Activity
• On the board, write a list of stem-changing **-ir** verbs in the preterite. For example: *dormirse, pedir, preferir, servir, divertirse, reírse, decir, ir.*
• Form 3 teams. Each team should choose 2 of the verbs on the board.
• Have teams work together to write two sentences about activities that they participated in during the last few weekends. For example:
Me divertí mucho en la discoteca.
Dormí todo el fin de semana.
• Each team presents their sentences by writing them on the board.
• Have a volunteer poll the class by a show of hands indicating which of the six activities described each class member prefers. As students' votes are counted, the volunteer or class recorder should put tally marks beside each activity.
• Distribute graph paper. Have each group create a graph to show the tally results.
• Display the graphs.

Le compré...

SOCIAL STUDIES CONNECTION

Objective
- to describe in cartoons activities one might do in the Dominican Republic.

Use
after *Para comunicarnos mejor,* pages 148–149

Materials
- 8 1/2" x 11" drawing paper
- magic markers, crayons, colored pencils
- newspaper, magazine, and personal photos

Activity
- Ask students to think of something they might do during a visit to the Dominican Republic (learn the merengue; go fishing; play baseball).
- Have students either draw a cartoon or use pictures from newspapers or magazines to depict themselves borrowing, buying, or renting something from a local person. Use talk balloons.
- Have drawings placed in front of the room.
- Ask volunteers to choose a partner and make up sentences about each cartoon. For example: (a cartoon of someone shopping) *¿Me puede vender ese pescado? Claro que sí.* (a cartoon about baseball) *¿Me puede dar aquel guante de béisbol? No, lo necesito yo ahora.* (a fishing cartoon) *¿Qué le compraste a tu hijo? Le compré una caña de pescar.*

¿Qué se debe hacer?

ENVIRONMENTAL CONNECTION

Objective
- to play a game about quality-of-life issues, using the impersonal **se**

Use
after *Para comunicarnos mejor,* pages 148–149

Materials
- large writing pad
- marking pen

Activity
- Divide class into teams A, B, C, and D. Select a score-keeper and a spokesperson for each team.
- Give teams ten minutes to list problems that exist in their town or nearby, and to jot down their solutions to the problems.
- When time is up, the spokesperson for one team uses the impersonal *se* to present the problem. For example, team A might say: *Se necesita limpiar mejor las calles.* Other teams then present their solutions. Team B: *Se necesitan grupos de voluntarios para limpiarlas.*
- After teams present their solutions, a vote is taken and five points are given to the team with the best solution. If two teams tie, each gets five points. The scorekeeper writes winning solutions on the pad.
- Play at least four rounds so that each team has a chance to present a problem. The team that scores the most points wins.

PASÁNDOLA BIEN EN NUEVA YORK

Introduce the chapter and its theme by asking students what they do to have fun. Do they think that young people do the same things in other countries? What makes them think so?

Related Components

Audio	**Video: Tape/Book**
Conexiones: 17A	Unit 3: Seg. 2
Conexiones	
Chapter 5	

Scan to Chapter 5

GETTING STARTED

Ask students to talk about the scene in the photograph. What places can they identify? Ask questions. Suggestions:
¿De qué cosas en la foto conoces el nombre?
¿Qué está haciendo la gente?

Critical Thinking

You can use this opportunity to help students discover for themselves what they would need to know in order to have a conversation with Spanish-speaking teenagers.

Pasarla bien con los amigos

Ask students to think about the words that are used to talk about meeting people in social situations. Then assign these activities to groups:

• make a list of places you would go to on weekends
• make a list of activities you would do on weekends
• list the types of performers you would find in the entertainment world
• list the reactions you would have to performers and performances
• list the things you would say when introducing friends

Have each group write its list on the board. Have the class discuss the lists and decide which items are the most essential.
Have each group submit a revised list.
When you finish the chapter, have the class review the lists to see how they compare to what was learned in the chapter.

CAPÍTULO 5

¡PASÁNDOLA BIEN EN LA CIUDAD!

Calle 175 en Washington Heights, Nueva York.

138

CHAPTER COMPONENTS

Activity Book	**Audio Book**	**Conexiones**	**Transparencies**
p. 65-74	Script: p. 33-35	Chapter 5	Chapter 5
Assessment	Activities: p. 36-38	**Cuaderno**	Transparencies 32-35
Oral Proficiency:	**Audio**	p. 37-44	**Tutor Pages**
p. 25	Chapter: 6A	**Magazine**	p. 23-26
Listening Script:	Assessment: 14B	Juntos en República	**Video: Tape/Book**
p. 13	Conexiones: 17A	Dominicana	Unit 3: Seg. 2
Chapter Test:			
p. 69-74			

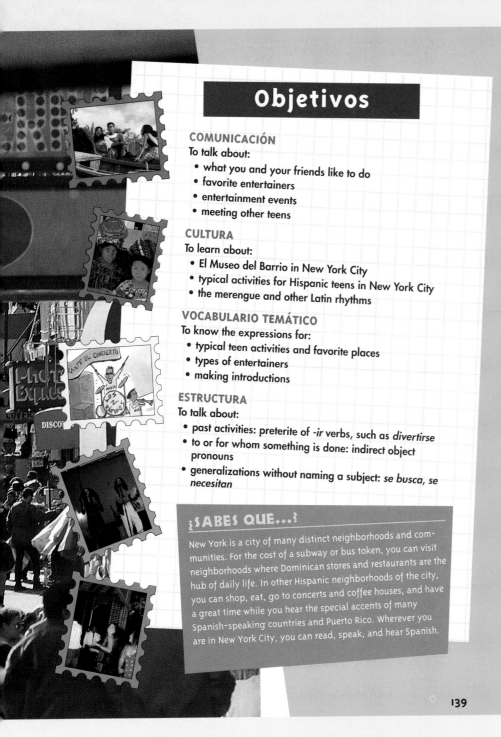

Objetivos

COMUNICACIÓN
To talk about:
- what you and your friends like to do
- favorite entertainers
- entertainment events
- meeting other teens

CULTURA
To learn about:
- El Museo del Barrio in New York City
- typical activities for Hispanic teens in New York City
- the merengue and other Latin rhythms

VOCABULARIO TEMÁTICO
To know the expressions for:
- typical teen activities and favorite places
- types of entertainers
- making introductions

ESTRUCTURA
To talk about:
- past activities: preterite of -ir verbs, such as *divertirse*
- to or for whom something is done: indirect object pronouns
- generalizations without naming a subject: *se busca, se necesitan*

¿SABES QUE...?

New York is a city of many distinct neighborhoods and communities. For the cost of a subway or bus token, you can visit neighborhoods where Dominican stores and restaurants are the hub of daily life. In other Hispanic neighborhoods of the city, you can shop, eat, go to concerts and coffee houses, and have a great time while you hear the special accents of many Spanish-speaking countries and Puerto Rico. Wherever you are in New York City, you can read, speak, and hear Spanish.

139

Here are some additional activities that you may wish to use as you work through this chapter with your students.

Communication

Encourage after-class activities that may enhance student interest and proficiency. Some ideas:
- have students find a Dominican pen pal in a New York City school
- inform the class in Spanish about events and shows of interest

Culture

To encourage greater cultural understanding:
- have students collect information on Latino artists, authors and musicians living in New York
- show the video that accompanies Unit 3 of this textbook

Vocabulary

To reinforce vocabulary, have students:
- keep track of unusual words or phrases they come across on TV, at home, or at school
- use photos or drawings to create a picture dictionary

Structure

To reinforce the preterite of **-ir** verbs, indirect-object pronouns, and generalizations (using **se** and a verb):
- have students say what they did yesterday or make a generalization as they enter class each day

Thinking About Language

Have students look at the lists they wrote for the *Critical Thinking* activity. Do they know any of those words in Spanish? How many do they know? Are any of them cognates? Ask speakers of other languages to volunteer any words they know that are related to the theme of cities.

INTERNET LINK

Republica Dominicana http://spin.com. mx.:80/~hvelarde/RepublicaDominicana/

Communicative Objectives
To talk about:
- going out with friends
- what you do, see, and feel when you go out with friends

Related Components

Activity Book p. 65	**Cuaderno** p. 37
Audio Book Script: Seg. 1	**Transparencies** Ch. 5: Conversemos Transparency 32
Audio Chapter: 6A, Seg. 1	

GETTING STARTED

Ask students what the most popular after-school or weekend activities are. Why are these activities important for them?

ACTIVITIES

These activities give students an opportunity to begin communicating with each other and with you, focusing on the theme and objectives of the chapter. The activities can be used as oral class activities, or, if you prefer, you can pair students to achieve more interaction.

¿Adónde fueron tú y tus amigos el fin de semana?
Class activity to review the preterite and to introduce vocabulary for places to go. Ask the title question. Ask: *¿Y después?* Ask when they went to these places.

¿Qué hicieron?
Class activity to review and introduce vocabulary for weekend activities. Ask the title question. Encourage the use of alternative answers. Extend by asking with whom they did these things. Ask: *¿Y después?* Use TV or movie characters. Ask where they went and what they did. Example: *Juan, ¿adónde fue Rosanne el fin de semana y qué hizo?*

Si quieres presentar a alguien, ¿qué dices?
Class activity to practice how to introduce people. After modeling the activity and the phrases, have pairs practice with other pairs.

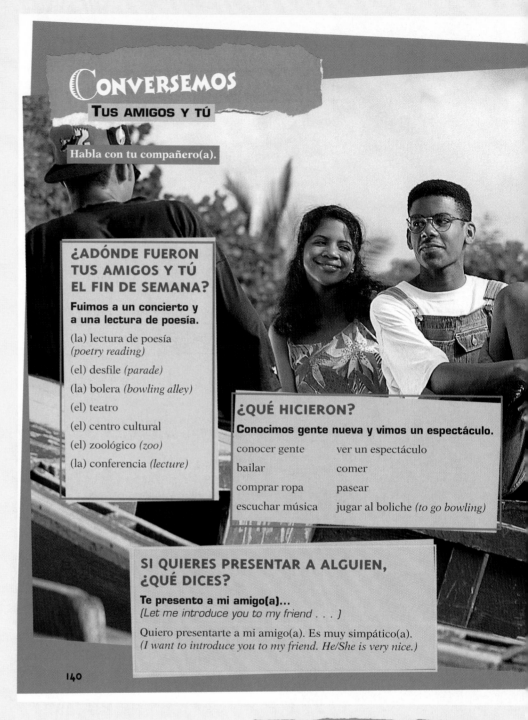

CONVERSEMOS
TUS AMIGOS Y TÚ

Habla con tu compañero(a).

¿ADÓNDE FUERON TUS AMIGOS Y TÚ EL FIN DE SEMANA?

Fuimos a un concierto y a una lectura de poesía.

(la) lectura de poesía *(poetry reading)*

(el) desfile *(parade)*

(la) bolera *(bowling alley)*

(el) teatro

(el) centro cultural

(el) zoológico *(zoo)*

(la) conferencia *(lecture)*

¿QUÉ HICIERON?

Conocimos gente nueva y vimos un espectáculo.

conocer gente	ver un espectáculo
bailar	comer
comprar ropa	pasear
escuchar música	jugar al boliche *(to go bowling)*

SI QUIERES PRESENTAR A ALGUIEN, ¿QUÉ DICES?

Te presento a mi amigo(a)...
[Let me introduce you to my friend . . .]

Quiero presentarte a mi amigo(a). Es muy simpático(a).
(I want to introduce you to my friend. He/She is very nice.)

140

MEETING INDIVIDUAL NEEDS

Reaching All Students

For Auditory and Kinesthetic Learners
Have groups create a series of sentences using the words in the *¿Cómo la pasaron?* box. Have them use sounds or actions they associate with each sentence. For example, a student can say, *Nos aburrimos mucho* and group members can yawn to "illustrate" the phrase *nos aburrimos*.

¿QUÉ VIERON?

Vimos a un músico que tocó el saxofón.

Vimos a una poeta que leyó unos poemas muy buenos.

ver...

 (el) conjunto musical

 (el/la) poeta

 (el/la) cómico(a)

 (el) actor / (la) actriz

 (el/la) músico(a)

 (el/la) cantante

tocar...

 el bajo

 la guitarra eléctrica

 la batería

 el saxofón

que...

actuar en una obra *(to act in a play)*

contar chistes *(to tell jokes)*

cantar sus canciones más conocidas
(to sing his/her/their most popular songs)

leer unos poemas muy buenos
(to read some very good poems)

¿CÓMO LA PASARON?

Nos divertimos mucho en la lectura de poesía.

Nos aburrimos mucho en el concierto.

aburrirse *(to get bored)*   divertirse *(to have fun)*

quedarse hasta tarde *(to stay late)*   reírse *(to laugh)*

SI QUIERES CONOCER A UN(A) CHICO(A), ¿QUÉ DICES?

¿Es tu amigo(a)?

¿Me puedes presentar a ese(a) chico(a)?

¿Quién es ese(a) chico(a) tan guapo(a)? ¿Tiene novio(a)?

141

¿Qué vieron?
Class activity to introduce vocabulary for people and things that are part of weekend activities.
Ask the question in the title with places taught earlier, for example, *¿Qué vieron en el concierto?* Say what you saw in any of the previous places, but make up unlikely combinations, such as *Fui al boliche y vi una obra de teatro.* Ask students to correct your sentences.

¿Cómo la pasaron?
Class activity to introduce vocabulary for responses and reactions to events and activities.
Have the class rate all the activities in these pages using **aburrido** or **divertido**. See *Meeting Individual Needs.*

Si quieres conocer a un(a) chico(a), ¿qué dices?
Class activity to learn how to ask who a person is. Model the activity and the text.
Extension: Model how to make introductions. Have pairs create dialogs that begin by asking about other people and continue through introductions.

CHECK

* *¿Adónde fuiste con tus amigos?*
* *¿Qué vieron?*
* *¿Qué hicieron allí?*
* *¿Cómo la pasaron?*
* *¿Quién es ese(a) chico(a) tan guapo(a)?*
* *¿Me puedes presentar a ese(a) chico(a)?*

LOG BOOK
Have students write down three phrases they would teach a friend if they were both going to a concert where they knew a lot of people.

Communicative Objective

• to talk about museums

Related Components

Activity Book p. 66	**Audio** Chapter: 6A, Seg. 2
Audio Book Script: Seg. 2	**Cuaderno** p. 38

GETTING STARTED

Ask students to talk about the most interesting museums they have been to. What made them interesting?

DISCUSS

Ask questions about New York's Museo del Barrio brochure. Suggestions:

El Museo del Barrio
¿Por qué es importante el Museo del Barrio?
¿Cuántos objetos hay en el museo?
¿Qué tipos de objetos hay?
¿Te gustaría visitarlo?

¡En las fiestas latinas!
¿En qué fiestas participa El Museo del Barrio?
¿Cuáles de estas fiestas conoces?
¿En qué fecha es el día de los Reyes Magos?
¿Y el día de Puerto Rico? ¿Y el Día de los Muertos? (Jan. 6; second Sunday in June; Nov. 2)

¡Se necesitan socios!
¿Qué palabras en inglés se parecen a la palabra socio? (social, society, associate)
¿Qué le dan los socios al museo? (Le dan dinero.)
¿Qué les da el museo a los socios?
¿Qué títulos tienen los socios que dan más dinero? ¿Y los que dan menos dinero?
¿Cuánto dinero da un benefactor?

El Museo del Barrio

El Museo del Barrio en Nueva York tiene una colección permanente de casi 8.000 objetos: cuadros, esculturas, dibujos y fotografías. Incluye obras precolombinas y contemporáneas, caribeñas y latinoamericanas, tradicionales y de vanguardia. Hay exposiciones, conferencias y presentaciones de música, teatro y danza.

¡En las fiestas latinas!

El Museo del Barrio también participa en algunas celebraciones tradicionales latinas, muy populares en la ciudad:

• el desfile del Día de los Reyes Magos
• el desfile del Día de Puerto Rico
• el Día de los Muertos

El Museo del Barrio • 1230 Fifth Avenue
New York, N.Y. 10029
tel. (212) 831-7272

142

¡Se necesitan socios!

El Museo del Barrio necesita dinero para seguir su trabajo de difusión de la cultura latina. Su contribución nos ayuda. Por favor, hágase socio del museo. ¡Le vamos a dar un título muy especial!

Título	Contribución
Vecino(a)	$20
Amigo(a)	$30
Familiar	$50
Padrino/Madrina	$100
Ángel	$500
Benefactor(a)	$1.000
Corporación	$5.000

✔ CULTURE NOTE

El Museo del Barrio was founded in 1969 by a group of teachers, activists, parents, and artists to collect, preserve, and disseminate the artistic heritage of Latin America. In addition to the exhibitions, lectures, and special events, it offers educational programs for students and the general public. The museum is at 1230 Fifth Avenue, New York, NY 10029.

HABLA DEL FOLLETO

A. Di tres cosas importantes sobre El Museo del Barrio.

El Museo del Barrio participa en celebraciones latinas.

B. Di qué títulos da el museo a las personas que dan dinero.

Una contribución de 30 dólares les da el título de "Amigo(a)".

¿QUÉ OPINAS?

¿En qué actividad de El Museo del Barrio te gustaría participar? Pregunta a tres compañeros(as). Anota los resultados en la tabla. Usa el modelo.

	yo	Elvira	Natacha	Agustín
una exposición de fotografía	✓	✓	✓	✓
el desfile del Día de Puerto Rico			✓	✓
una exposición de arte latino de vanguardia				
el Día de los Muertos				
una exposición de arte precolombino				
el desfile del Día de los Reyes Magos				

Compara tu tabla con la de tus compañeros(as).

▲ Este cuadro de Eric Guttelewitz está en El Museo del Barrio.

¿SABES QUE...?

- El Museo del Barrio is one of many New York City institutions that shares Latin American culture with the community.
- The Ballet Hispánico of New York performs dances based on Spanish and Latin American traditions.
- The Hispanic Society of America is a museum and reference library of art and history.
- El Repertorio Español is a theater that presents performances of plays by Spanish and Latin American playwrights.

El Museo del Barrio, esculturas.

ACTIVITIES

Habla del folleto

Individual Activities: Comprehension

A. Say three important things about El Museo del Barrio.

Posssible Answers:

- *Tiene una colección de casi 8,000 objetos*
- *Organiza exposiciones, conferencias y presentaciones de música, teatro y danza.*
- *Incluye obras precolombinas y contemporáneas de artistas latinoamericanos, tradicionales y de vanguardia.*

B. Say what titles the museum offers people who contribute money.

Answers: See model on student page. See list on student page for amounts.

Extension: Your class needs contributions to make an art exhibit. Make a list of categories of membership. Give them special titles.

¿Qué opinas?

Group Activity: Taking a Poll

Form groups of four. Discuss which of the Museo del Barrio's activities you'd like to take part in. Record your answers on a chart like the one on page 143.

Class Activity: Evaluation

- Have a volunteer list activities on the board as a representative of each group calls them out.
- Have another volunteer add the numbers for each activity.
- Rank the popularity of the activities and discuss reasons for the rankings.

Extension: Use the results of the survey to design a brochure for a Latino art museum in your area.

CHECK

- *¿Qué hay en El Museo del Barrio?*
- *¿Qué fiestas latinas celebra el museo?*
- *¿Qué contribución das para ser* Padrino *o* Madrina *del museo?*

LOG BOOK

Have students write why they would or would not like to become members of El Museo del Barrio.

Para hispanohablantes

You are a representative of El Museo del Barrio. Tell the class about the museum and tell them why they should become members.

Communicative Objectives

To talk about:
- things and people you see at a concert
- what people do at a concert
- someone you would like to meet

Related Components

Activity Book	Transparencies
p. 67-68	Ch. 5: Palabras en acción
Cuaderno	Transparency 33
p. 39-40	**Tutor Page**
	p. 23

☐ GETTING STARTED

Ask students why they like to go to concerts. What are some of the things they feel during a concert? How do they feel at a concert they do not like?

☐ DISCUSS

Comment on and ask questions about the drawing. For example:
¿Qué pasa en la primera escena?
¿Y en la segunda escena?
¿Cómo se llama el grupo?
¿Qué tocan los miembros del grupo?
¿De qué hablan los chicos que escuchan el concierto?
¿Es guapo el cantante?

Para hispanohablantes

If you use expressions other than the ones introduced in this chapter, share them with the class. A few variations:
el/la comediante: el cómico
el chiste: el cuento
jugar al boliche: jugar a los bolos
el escenario: la tarima
los parlantes: las bocinas, los altavoces
hacer cola: hacer fila
guapo(a): bien parecido(a), buen(a) mozo(a)

PALABRAS EN ACCIÓN
¡VAMOS AL CONCIERTO!

1 **¿Qué ves en el dibujo?**

Haz una lista de las cosas que ves en el dibujo.

> *La batería, el escenario...*

2 **El tour de Los Rápidos**

Habla con tu compañero(a) sobre el cartel que anuncia el tour de Los Rápidos.

> — ¿Cómo se llama el último álbum de Los Rápidos?
> — Se llama Magia.
> — ¿A qué hora empieza el concierto en Nueva York?

3 **¿Qué hicieron?**

Escoge tres personas del dibujo. Pregunta a tu compañero(a) qué hicieron durante el concierto.

> — ¿Qué hizo Marta?
> — Se aburrió.

4 **El fin de semana**

Habla con tu compañero(a) sobre lo que hicieron tus amigos y tú el fin de semana pasado.

> — ¿Qué hicieron el fin de semana pasado tus amigos y tú?
> — Fuimos a un concierto de rock. Nos divertimos mucho. ¿Y ustedes?

144

For students having difficulty talking about things they see and do at a concert or on weekends, you might consider:
- **The tutor page:** Pair the student with a native speaker or a more able student, using the tutor page.

Optional activity: See page 138C: *Partido de béisbol.*

5 ¿Qué vieron?

Habla con tu compañero(a) sobre el espectáculo que vieron tus amigos y tú.

— ¿Qué espectáculo vieron la semana pasada?
— Vimos a una cómica. Contó chistes y nos reímos mucho. ¿Y ustedes?

6 Miniteatro

Habla con tu compañero(a) sobre una persona que quieres conocer.

— ¿Esa chica tan guapa es tu amiga?
— Sí, es mi mejor amiga.
— ¿Tiene novio?
— No. ¿Te gustaría conocerla?
— Sí, me encantaría.

7 Cartel

Diseña un cartel para un conjunto musical (real o imaginario) que va a presentar su nuevo álbum. Di qué instrumentos tocan los músicos, el título del álbum, dónde va a ser el concierto y cuánto cuesta el disco y la entrada. Usa dibujos y fotos de revistas y periódicos.

8 Tú eres el autor

Invita a un(a) amigo(a) a ir a un espectáculo. Usa el correo electrónico.

elisa@usol.com
El conjunto Marcha va a dar un concierto en el Estadio Municipal el 20 de noviembre. ¿Quieres venir? Te voy a presentar a mi amigo Pablo. Escríbeme pronto.

anaida@colo.com

145

ACTIVITIES

1. Individual and Group Activity
Make a list of the things you see in the drawing.
Extension: Make a list of all the verbs used in the labels and the talk balloons in the drawing.

2. Pair Activity
Talk about the poster that advertises the Los Rápidos tour.
Extension: Ask your partner about his or her favorite groups.

3. Pair Activity
Choose three people in the drawing. Ask your partner what each of these people did during the concert.

4. Pair Activity
Talk about what you and your friends did last weekend.
Extension: Say what you want to do next weekend.

5. Pair Activity
Talk to your partner about a show you and your friends saw. (You may want to talk about a TV show.)

6. Roleplay Activity
Act out a dialog in which you talk about someone you'd like to meet.
Extension: Introduce your partner to the person he or she would like to meet.

7. Hands-On Activity
Homework or classwork for individuals or small groups. Design a poster for a real or imaginary musical group that is coming out with a new album. Decide the type of music and the instruments each one plays, what the title of the album is, where the concert will be, and how much the album and a ticket cost. Use photos and drawings.

8. Writing Activity
Send e-mail to invite a friend to a show. Say where you are going, when it will be, and who else will be there.
Extension: Exchange letters and respond to each other.

CHECK

- ¿Dónde están los chicos en cada escena?
- ¿Quieres conocer al chico que toca el bajo? ¿No? ¿A cuál de ellos?
- ¿Qué instrumentos tocan los músicos?
- ¿Dónde va a ser el primer concierto de Los Rápidos?

LOG BOOK
Have students clip an article from a magazine in Spanish, and look up in the dictionary any words they don't know.

Communicative Objective
• to talk about things you did, using stem-changing -ir verbs in the preterite

Related Components

Activity Book p. 69-70	**Cuaderno** p. 41
Audio Book Script: Seg. 3 Activities: p. 36	**Transparencies** Ch. 5: Para comunicarnos mejor Transparency 34
Audio Chapter: 6A, Seg. 3	**Tutor Page** p. 24

 GETTING STARTED

Ask students to list all the Spanish verbs they know that end in **-ir,** and the actions those verbs denote. (A few: *abrir, compartir, escribir, vivir, salir, pedir, decir, dormir, destruir, recibir.*)

Language in Context

Use the paradigm to present **pedir** and **dormirse,** and have students note the changes that occur in the verbs. Have students identify the changes and test this with **divertirse** and **servir.** Point out that not all verbs ending in **-ir** are stem-changing.
Make sure students are aware of the reflexive verbs.

 DISCUSS

Review vocabulary from previous chapters and introduce some of this chapter's new words with questions that incorporate **-ir** verbs with stem changes in the preterite.
¿Quién pidió una pizza por teléfono anoche?
¿Quién se durmió temprano?
¿Me pidieron un examen?
¿Se rieron cuando sacaron mala nota en el examen?

PARA COMUNICARNOS MEJOR

¿SE DIVIRTIERON ANOCHE?

To talk about actions in the past, use the preterite. Verbs that end in *-ir* and have a stem change in the present also have a stem change in the preterite.

— *Sí, nos divertimos mucho.* Yes, we had a lot of fun.

— *¿A qué hora se durmieron?* What time did you fall asleep?

— *Yo me dormí a las doce.* I fell asleep at 12:00.
Eleanor se durmió antes. Eleanor fell asleep before.

☐ *Pedir* has a stem change from *-e-* to *-i-* in the *usted/él/ella* and *ustedes/ellos/ellas* forms of the preterite. *Dormirse* has a stem change from *-o-* to *-u-*.

preterite tense	pedir (to ask for)	dormirse (to fall asleep)
yo	pedí	me dormí
tú	pediste	te dormiste
usted	**pidió**	**se durmió**
él/ella	**pidió**	**se durmió**
nosotros(as)	pedimos	nos dormimos
vosotros(as)	pedisteis	os dormisteis
ustedes	**pidieron**	**se durmieron**
ellos/ellas	**pidieron**	**se durmieron**

☐ Some other verbs that have the same stem change as *pedir* in the preterite are *servir (to serve)*, *divertirse (to have fun)*, *reírse (to laugh)*, and *sonreír (to smile)*.

146

For students having difficulty using the preterite of -ir verbs with stem changes, you might consider:
• **The tutor page:** Pair the student with a native speaker or a more able student, using the tutor page.
Optional activity: See page 138C: *¿Qué hiciste?*

1 El sábado por la noche

¿Adónde fueron estas personas el sábado? ¿Se divirtieron? Pregunta a tu compañero(a).

¿Adónde fueron el sábado?
¿A qué hora se durmieron?
¿Dónde comieron? ¿Qué pidieron?
¿Se divirtieron? ¿Se rieron mucho?

— ¿Adónde fueron tus padres
el sábado por la noche?
— Fueron a un concierto y se divirtieron mucho.

1. tus padres
2. tus mejores amigos(as)
3. tú y tus amigo
4. ¿Y tú? ¿Adónde fuiste?

2 Cafetería En la luna

En la cafetería En la luna siempre hay problemas entre los meseros y los clientes. Pregunta a tu compañero(a) qué pasó en cada mesa.

— ¿Qué pasó en la mesa uno?
— El hombre pidió un flan y el mesero le sirvió un pastel de manzana.

Mesa 1. el hombre **Mesa 3.** los chicos
Mesa 2. la mujer **Mesa 4.** tú y tu amiga

CAFETERÍA EN LA LUNA

COMIDAS	
Hamburguesa	$2.50
Sándwich de jamón y queso	$2.50
Huevos con jamón	$1.99
Papas fritas	$1.50

POSTRES	
Helados de piña, chocolate y vainilla	$1.99
Pasteles de manzana, queso y chocolate	$2.99
Flan	$1.50

BEBIDAS	
Refrescos de papaya y de naranja	$0.75
Agua mineral	$1.00
Limonada natural	$1.25
Jugo de naranja	$1.50
Batidos de chocolate, vainilla y frutas	$2.00

3 El viernes pasado

A. En grupo, hagan una tabla de las cosas que hicieron el viernes pasado.

	yo	Alma	Sandra	Ezequiel
¿Adónde fueron?	a una discoteca	a una lectura de poesía	a una lectura de poesía	a un partido de baloncesto
¿Se divirtieron?	sí, mucho	sí, mucho	sí, mucho	no, me aburrí muchísimo
¿A qué hora llegaron a su casa?				

B. Informa a la clase de los resultados.

El viernes pasado yo fui a una discoteca y me divertí mucho.
Alma y Sandra fueron a una lectura de poesía y se divirtieron
mucho. Ezequiel fue a un partido de baloncesto, pero se aburrió.

147

Para hispanohablantes

Choose at least five stem-changing verbs ending in **-ir**. Use them to write sentences about several classmates and share them with the class.

ACTIVITIES

Students use preterite forms of stem-changing -ir verbs to talk about what they did in the past.

1. Pair Activity
Ask your partner where these people went on Saturday.
Possible Answers:
1. See model on student page.
2. ¿Dónde comieron tus mejores amigos(as) el sábado?
Comieron en un restaurante y pidieron tamales.
3. ¿Adónde fueron tú y tus amigos el sábado?
Fuimos a una lectura de poemas y nos aburrimos muchísimo.
4. Y tú, ¿adónde fuiste el sábado?
Fui al cine con María.
Extension: One partner asks about a member of the other's family. The other answers that that person went to a party. They talk about what the family member did at the party.

2. Pair Activity
At the cafetería En la Luna there are always problems between waiters and clients. Ask your partner what happened at each table.
Possible Answers:
1. See model on student page.
2. ¿Qué pasó en la mesa 2?
La mujer pidió pastel y el mesero le sirvió helado.
3. ¿Qué pasó en la mesa 3?
Los chicos pidieron hamburguesas y el mesero les sirvió huevos con jamón.
4. ¿Qué pasó en la mesa 4?
Tú y tu amiga pidieron flan y el mesero les sirvió refrescos.
Extension: Act out the answers. Have the class say what happened.

3. Group Activity
A. Make a list of what you did last Friday.
B. Share your list with the class.
Answers: See models on student page.

CHECK

- ¿Qué pediste en la cafetería de la escuela?
- ¿A qué hora se durmieron anoche?
- ¿Qué comieron tus padres anoche?
- ¿Pidieron una pizza por teléfono?
- ¿Se rió mucho tu amigo cuando vio la última película de Jim Carrey?

LOG BOOK

Have students write down five things they did yesterday, and say whether these things amused or bored them.

Communicative Objectives

- to say to whom you give something, using indirect object pronouns
- to make generalizations, using **se** and a verb

Related Components

Activity Book p. 71-72	**Audio** Chapter: 6A, Seg. 4
Audio Book Script: Seg.4 Activities: p. 37	**Cuaderno** p. 42
	Tutor Page p. 25

GETTING STARTED

Ask students what they would write on a sign if they were trying to hire a Spanish tutor.

Language in Context

Indirect Object Pronouns

Warm up and review by making statements and having students ask you questions. For example:

T: *Le doy buena nota.*
S: *¿A quién le das buena nota?*
T: *A él, a Celestino.*

Point out that the third-person singular form of indirect object pronouns is only **le**, not **lo** and **la**, as is the case with direct object pronouns.

Generalizations

Introduce the concept with a few examples in English that use the "one" form, such as: What does one do when one is introduced? Point out that "one" is used in the same way as the third-person singular form **le**, but does not refer to a specific person.

DISCUSS

Review vocabulary from previous chapters and introduce some of this chapter's new vocabulary with questions and statements that use indirect object pronouns and **se**.

¿Quién le regaló una joya a su madre?
¿Quién te prestó el reloj?
¿Quiénes me dieron las manzanas?
¿Qué se necesita en un restaurante que no tiene meseros?
Aquí se habla español, ¿verdad?
¿Se habla español en México también?

To tell to or for whom something is done, use indirect object pronouns.

— *¿Qué serviste a tus amigos?*	What did you serve your friends?
— *Les serví arroz y frijoles.*	I served them rice and beans.

☐ Note that when you use an indirect object formed by *a* plus a noun (*a mis amigos*) or *a* plus a name (*a Juan*), you must also include the indirect object pronoun before the verb.

Le compré un boleto a Juan.	I bought a ticket for Juan.

Here are the indirect object pronouns.

indirect object pronouns	
singular	**plural**
me to/for me	**nos** to/for us
te to/for you (informal)	**os** to/for you (informal)
le to/for him, her, it, you (formal)	**les** to/for them, you (formal)

To make generalizations or to talk about actions without naming a specific subject, use *se* followed by the third-person singular or plural of the verb.

Se busca actor.	Actor wanted.
Se necesitan cómicos.	Comedians needed.

☐ Note that the verb agrees in number with the noun that follows it. If there is no noun following the verb, use the singular form.

Aquí se habla español.	Spanish is spoken here.
En ese restaurante se come muy bien.	In that restaurant, you can eat very well.

148

For students having difficulty using indirect object pronouns and **se**, you might consider:

- **The tutor page:** Pair the student with a native speaker or a more able student, using the tutor page.

Optional activity: See page 138D: *Le compré*

Entradas y más entradas

Pregunta a tu compañero(a).

— *¿Quién le regaló entradas a tu amigo?*
— *Su abuela le regaló entradas.*

1. a tu amigo
2. a tus compañeros
3. a tu hermano y a ti
4. a tus amigas
5. a tu papá
6. ¿y a mí?

 Intercambios

Pregunta a tu compañero(a).

— *¿Quién te prestó discos compactos?*
— *Mi amigo me prestó discos compactos.*
— *Y tú, ¿a quién le prestaste discos compactos?*
— *Yo le presté discos compactos a mi hermano.*

1. prestar discos compactos
2. regalar entradas para conciertos
3. presentar a sus amigos
4. prestar la bicicleta
5. comprar refrescos en el cine
6. contar chistes
7. mandar cartas

 El centro cultural

La clase está organizando un centro cultural para la escuela. Se necesitan muchas cosas y muchos voluntarios. En grupo, hagan carteles sobre lo que se necesita.

Se buscan actrices.

Se necesita(n)...

1. parlantes
2. equipo de sonido
3. micrófonos
4. conjunto musical

Se busca(n)...

5. actrices
6. cómicos
7. cantante
8. poetas

149

ACTIVITIES

Students use indirect object pronouns to indicate to or for whom something is intended, and use **se** plus a verb to make generalizations.

1. Pair Activity
Ask your partner who gives tickets to these people.

2. Pair Activity
Ask who does things for your partner and for whom your partner does the same.

3. Group Activity
Make posters to announce what the school's new cultural center needs.

CHECK

- *¿Qué anuncio pones en un restaurante que no tiene meseros?*
- *¿Qué les regalaron los Reyes Magos el año pasado?*
- *¿Nos vas a comprar entradas para ir a un concierto?*
- *¿Te cuentan chistes tus hermanos?*

149

Objectives

Communicative: to talk about and plan an excursion
Cultural: to talk about cultural activities

Related Components

Assessment
Oral Proficiency:
  p. 25
Audio Book
Script: Seg. 5
Activities: p. 38
Audio
Chapter: 6A, Seg. 5
Conexiones: 17A
	Conexiones
	Chapter 5
	Magazine
	Juntos en República
	  Dominicana
	Tutor Page
	p. 26

GETTING STARTED

Students should now be able to correctly use stem-changing -**ir** verbs in the preterite, indirect object pronouns, **se** with a verb, and all of the chapter vocabulary. Review grammar and vocabulary by asking such questions as:
¿Fueron a ver un concierto el año pasado?
¿Se necesitan entradas para ir a un teatro?
¿Quién les compró las entradas?
¿Quién se durmió en el concierto?

APPLY

1. Pair Activity
You are going to go on an excursion in New York. Create a dialog about the trip.
Answers: See model on student page.
Extension: Ask your partner when your group is going to do specific activities.
Example: *¿A qué hora vamos a patinar?*

2. Individual and Pair Activity
Make a list of things you will need for the trip. Talk about them with your partner.
Answers: See model on student page.
Extension: Dictate your list as a partner transcribes it.

3. Pair Activities
It's Friday night and you're getting together with a group of your friends at a restaurant. You see a friend in another group. Introduce that friend to your group.
Answers: See model on student page.

SITUACIONES

¡VAMOS A DIVERTIRNOS!

Excursión sólo para jóvenes

Un día latino en Nueva York

■ De 9:00 a 12:00 del mediodía
Paseo por Manhattan en un autobús de dos pisos
■ De 12:30 a 2:00 de la tarde
Picnic en Central Park
■ De 2:30 a 4:30 de la tarde
Visita a El Museo del Barrio

■ De 5:00 a 7:30 de la tarde
Patinaje en Skate Key (se alquilan patines)
■ De 8:00 a 9:30 de la noche
Cena y lectura de poesía en el Nuyorican Poet's Café
■ De 10:00 a 12:00 de la noche
Concierto del conjunto de merengue Eco Cumbé

1 ¿Hacemos la excursión?

Tu compañero(a) y tú van a hacer la excursión por Nueva York. Hagan un diálogo.

— *¿Tienes los boletos para la excursión por Nueva York?*
— *Sí, los compré ayer.*
— *¿Para quién compraste boletos?*
— *Compré uno para mí y también le compré un boleto a mi amigo Juan.*

2 ¿Qué se necesita para la excursión?

Haz una lista de las cosas que se necesitan para la excursión. Luego, haz un diálogo con tu compañero(a).

— *¿Se necesitan patines?*
— *No. En Skate Key se alquilan patines.*
— *¿Qué se necesita para el picnic en Central Park?*

3 Presenta a tus amigos

Es viernes por la noche y estás en un restaurante con un grupo de amigos. Ves a una amiga en otro grupo. Haz las presentaciones con tu compañero(a).

— *Quiero presentarte a una amiga. Nacho, te presento a Matilda.*
— *Encantado.*

150

For students having difficulty talking about going on a trip or introducing people, you might consider:
• **The tutor page:** Pair the student with a native speaker or a more able student, using the tutor page.
Optional activity: See page 138D: *¿Qué se debe hacer?*

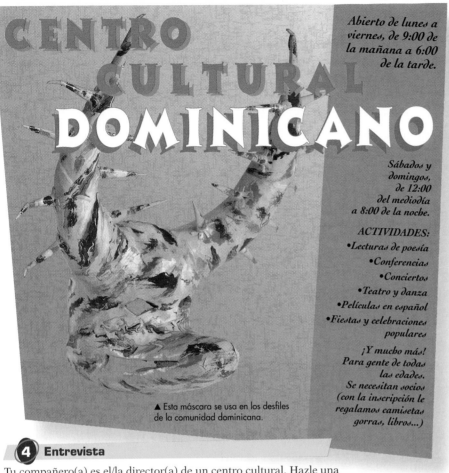

CENTRO CULTURAL DOMINICANO

Abierto de lunes a viernes, de 9:00 de la mañana a 6:00 de la tarde.

Sábados y domingos, de 12:00 del mediodía a 8:00 de la noche.

ACTIVIDADES:
- *Lecturas de poesía*
- *Conferencias*
- *Conciertos*
- *Teatro y danza*
- *Películas en español*
- *Fiestas y celebraciones populares*

¡Y mucho más! Para gente de todas las edades. Se necesitan socios (con la inscripción le regalamos camisetas gorras, libros...)

▲ Esta máscara se usa en los desfiles de la comunidad dominicana.

 Entrevista

Tu compañero(a) es el/la director(a) de un centro cultural. Hazle una entrevista sobre las actividades del centro. Informa a la clase.

— *¿Qué actividades hay en el centro cultural?*
— *Hay conferencias, lecturas de poesía...*
— *¿Qué les regalan a los socios con la inscripción?*

5 **Tu diario**

Escribe un párrafo sobre las actividades que hiciste este fin de semana y di cómo la pasaste.

El sábado por la mañana fui al zoológico con mi primo. Me aburrí mucho. Por la tarde, salí con mis amigos. Vimos una obra de teatro. Fue muy divertida y nos reímos mucho. El domingo...

PARA TU REFERENCIA

la inscripción *membership*
el patinaje *skating*
los patines *skates*
los socios *members*

151

---

4. Pair Activity
Your partner is the director of a cultural center. Interview your partner about the activities at the center. Tell the class what you found out.
Answers: See model on student page.
Extension: Think of activities you would enjoy, and ask if the center offers them.

5. Homework or Classwork
Write a paragraph for your diary about your weekend activities. Say what they were like.
Answers: See model on student page.
Extension: Make a list of the good deeds you did this weekend. For example: *Le di comida a mi perro.*

CHECK

- *¿Qué regalos les diste a tus amigos?*
- *¿Qué hiciste en Nueva York?*
- *¿Te divertiste en Central Park?*

PORTFOLIO
Students may wish to add their diary entries to their Portfolios.

Para hispanohablantes

Introduce a Spanish-speaking friend to the class.

PARA RESOLVER

Objectives
Communicative: to say what you need for a party
Cultural: to talk about a party

Related Components

Video: Tape/Book
Unit 3: Seg. 2

Scan to Chapter 5

GETTING STARTED

Ask students if they have ever been to a Latino party or any party with a cultural theme. What activities did they do there? What would they expect to do?

APPLY

Form groups. Each group will plan part of the party. If they need ideas, they can borrow library books and magazines on Latino music, cooking, dancing, and so on. Have them organize the information they obtain according to these and other categories they find interesting.

PASO 1: Actividades
Make a list of activities you would like to have at the party and a list of people you are going to invite.
Extension: You have attended a party that you did not enjoy. Tell why. Example: *En esa fiesta no se bailó…*

PASO 2: Los preparativos
Present your list of activities to the class. As a class, choose which ones will be included in the party's program.
Decide what each group is going to do.
Extension: Make a schedule to follow on the date of the party. For example:
A las 8:00 AM se limpia la sala.

PARA RESOLVER
UNA FIESTA LATINA

La clase va a preparar una fiesta latina.

PASO 1 Actividades

En grupos, hagan una lista de actividades para la fiesta.

> *Tocar música, contar chistes, leer poemas, cocinar…*

PASO 2 Los preparativos

Presenten su lista a la clase y escojan las actividades que van a incluir en el programa de la fiesta.

> *Vamos a tener música latina, una obra de teatro en español y chistes en español y en inglés.*

Después decidan qué va a hacer cada grupo.

> *El grupo 1 va a contar chistes. El grupo 2 va a pedir las cosas que se necesitan para la obra de teatro.*

PASO 3 Se necesita…

Ahora trabajen en grupos.

Grupo 1: Decidan si van a pedir chistes o van a escribirlos ustedes. Si van a pedirlos, hagan un anuncio.

> *Se necesitan chistes. Si sabes un chiste divertido, mándalo por correo electrónico a…*

Grupo 2: Hagan una lista de las cosas que se necesitan y otra de las personas a quienes tienen que pedir lo que necesitan.

> *Se necesita un lugar con escenario para la fiesta…*
> *Se necesitan sillas para los invitados, micrófonos…*
> *Le tenemos que pedir la sala a… las sillas a…*

PASO 4 El programa

Hagan el programa.
Incluyan fotos o dibujos.

PASO 5 ¡Los invitamos!

Escriban la invitación.

152

Invitación
LA CLASE DE ESPAÑOL 2
LOS INVITA A UNA ESPECTACULAR

Fiesta Latina

el sábado 16 de diciembre a las 7:00 de la tarde
en el gimnasio
¡Vengan todos!
¡La vamos a pasar muy bien!

PASO 3: Se necesita…
Form groups.
Group One: Decide whether to look for jokes or to write them. If you are going to look for them, make an ad. (See model.)
Group Two: Make a list of the things you need, and another list of the people you need to borrow them from. (See model.)
Extension: Exchange lists and revise the other group's work. Suggest anything that they might have left out.

Dictation
Ask volunteers to read aloud the jokes they wrote or found as the class writes them down.

PASO 4: El programa
Present the results to the class and make a program for the party. Include photos or drawings and when each activity will begin.

PASO 5: ¡Los invitamos!
Write the invitation.
Extension: Have each student write an invitation and exchange it with a partner for review and editing.

7:00
La poeta
Mary Braun va a leer
sus poemas más conocidos.

7:30
El divertido cómico John Aristeo va a
contar sus mejores chistes.

8:00
El famoso conjunto Eco Cumbé va a
tocar música caribeña.

153

PORTFOLIO

Suggest that students add their work from *PASO 4* and *PASO 5* to their Portfolios.

Background

Party Words

Here are some additional words that students may be interested in knowing:

MUSIC
accordion *el bandoneón*
accordionist *el/la bandoneonista*
rattles *las maracas*
drums *el tambor, el bongó*
percussionist *el/la percusionista*
guitar *la guitarra*
trumpet *la trompeta*
saxophone *el saxofón*
tune *la melodía*
rhythm *el ritmo*
beat *el compás*

DANCE
tap-dance *zapatear*
to turn *girar, dar vueltas*
to dance in couples *bailar en parejas*
the dance floor *la pista de baile*

PEOPLE AT A PARTY
the host/ess *el anfitrión/la anfitriona*
the guest *el/la invitado(a)*
the dancer *el bailarín, la bailarina*
the waiter *el/la mesero(a), el/la mozo(a)*
the master of ceremony *el maestro de ceremonias*

ORNAMENTS AND PARTY FAVORS
wreath *la guirnalda*
streamer *la serpentina*
candle *la vela*
whistle *el silbato*
cornet *el cornetín*
straw *la pajita, el sorbete*

FOOD
appetizers *los entremeses*
sandwich(es) *bocadito(s)*
drinks *los refrescos*
soda *la soda-pop, la gaseosa*
potato chips *papas fritas, patatas fritas*
fried plantains *tostones, plátanos fritos*
cake *el pastel, la torta*

 CULTURE NOTE

Jokes are an important part of Latino parties. Usually towards the end of a party, people get together to tell jokes. There are usually only one or two people who tell most of the jokes as everyone else listens and laughs, but all guests may contribute their own.

Para hispanohablantes

Ask people to tell you jokes in Spanish that you can share with the class.

Objectives
Communicative: to describe a dance that is popular in the Dominican Republic
Cultural: to learn about the *merengue,* a very popular dance

Related Components

Audio	Magazine
Conexiones: 17A	Juntos en República
Conexiones	Dominicana
Chapter 5	

GETTING STARTED

Ask students to mention any Latino dances they know of. What dances do they know how to dance?

DISCUSS

Using the Text

Have volunteers read aloud each section. Ask questions. Suggestions:

El merengue
¿De qué país es el merengue?
¿Qué raíces tiene?

El conjunto de merengue
¿Cuál de los instrumentos del merengue tiene raíces españolas? (melodeón)
¿Qué raíces crees que puede tener el güiro?
¿Cuál de los bailes típicos dominicanos es el más rápido? (Demonstrate **rápido** *and* **lento**)

Los cantantes
¿Quién es un cantante muy famoso de merengue?
¿Qué artista representa a los más jóvenes?

CHECK

Te toca a ti
Answers:
1. *moviendo las caderas de lado a lado, a la vez que los pies.*
2. *Wilfrido Vargas y Juan Luis Guerra.*
3. *africanas y españolas.*
4. *la tambora, el melodeón y el güiro.*
5. *perfecta para bailar.*

ENTÉRATE
EL MERENGUE Y OTROS RITMOS LATINOS

La música latina, especialmente la caribeña, tiene mucho ritmo y es ideal para bailar. La salsa, el merengue, la cumbia, la bachata y también el reggae (en la zona atlántica de América Central) son los ritmos favoritos de jóvenes y viejos.

El merengue y la bachata son los dos bailes típicos dominicanos. El merengue es también muy conocido en toda América Latina. Tiene raíces° africanas y españolas.

Generalmente, un conjunto de merengue toca tres instrumentos: la tambora (un tambor pequeño), el melodeón (parecido° a un acordeón) y el güiro (un instrumento de percusión).

El ritmo del merengue es rápido y la letra° de las canciones es graciosa° y satírica. El merengue se baila moviendo las caderas° de lado a lado,° a la vez que° los pies. Muchas veces se baila en parejas, pero también puedes bailar merengue solo o sola.

Wilfrido Vargas es uno de los cantantes más famosos de este estilo. Juan Luis Guerra es el representante más conocido de la nueva generación de merengue.

TE TOCA A TI
Completa las oraciones según el artículo.

1. El merengue se baila...
2. Los cantantes de merengue más conocidos son...
3. El merengue tiene raíces...
4. Los instrumentos de un conjunto de merengue son...
5. La música latina es...

a la vez que *at the same time as*	**la letra** *lyrics*	**parecido** *similar*
de lado a lado *from side to side*	**moviendo las caderas**	**las raíces** *roots*
graciosa *funny*	*moving the hips*	

154

✔ CULTURE NOTE

The merengue dates from the 1840s, but was little known outside the Caribbean before the 1950s. It has had a renaissance recently, in large part due to Guerra and the Dominicans of New York City.
The *güiro,* often made from a kitchen grater, is played by scraping it with a wire. The *tambora* is a double-headed drum beaten with both hand and stick.

LOG BOOK
Have students describe their favorite dance.

Para hispanohablantes

Write a paragraph about your favorite Latino dance.

VOCABULARIO TEMÁTICO

Lugares y actividades
la bolera *bowling alley*
el centro cultural *cultural center*
la conferencia *lecture*
el desfile *parade*
la lectura de poesía
  poetry reading
el zoológico *zoo*

Personas
el actor/la actriz *actor/actress*
el/la cantante *singer*
el/la cómico(a) *comedian*
el conjunto musical *musical group*
el/la músico(a) *musician*
el poeta *poet*

¿Qué hicieron?
actuar en una obra *to act in a play*
contar chistes *to tell jokes*
jugar al boliche *to go bowling*
tocar el bajo *to play the bass guitar*
  la batería *the drums*
  la guitarra eléctrica
    the electric guitar
  el saxofón *the saxophone*
  la trompeta *the trumpet*

¿Cómo la pasaron?
How was it?
aburrirse *to get bored*
divertirse (e>ie) *to have fun*
quedarse hasta tarde *to stay late*
reírse (e>i) *to laugh*

En el concierto
el equipo de sonido
  sound equipment
el escenario *stage*
el micrófono *microphone*
los parlantes *speakers*

Expresiones y palabras
hacer cola *to stand in line*
¿Me puedes presentar a ese(a)
chico(a)? *Can you introduce me
  to that boy/girl?*
pasarla bien/mal *to have a
  good/bad time*
Quiero presentarte a...
  I want to introduce you to . . .
Te presento a...
  Let me introduce you to . . .
la canción *song*
el chiste *joke*
dormirse (o>ue) *to fall asleep*
presentar a *to introduce*
prestar *to lend*
servir (e>i) *to serve*

LA CONEXIÓN INGLÉS-ESPAÑOL

For English words that contain the letter *ph* and are pronounced like the *f* in *fox*, cognates in Spanish are always written with an *f*.

teléfono → telephone
telegráfico → telegraphic

Find more examples in the *Vocabulario temático*.

¿SABES QUE...?
Because New York is fairly close to the Caribbean, it has long been a center for Caribbean music. Besides the merengue, Caribbean music styles that have been popular in New York include the mambo and rumba from Cuba, and the salsa, a blend of many lively styles of Afro-Cuban and Puerto Rican origin, influenced by jazz and rock. Caribbean musicians such as Tito Puente and Celia Cruz have a large following in New York.

155

VOCABULARIO TEMÁTICO

Objective
• to review vocabulary

Related Components

Activity Book	Audio
Chapter Review: p. 73-74	Assessment: 14B
Assessment	**Cuaderno**
Listening Script: p. 13	p. 43-44
Chapter Test: p. 69-74	**Transparencies** Ch. 5: Dibujos y palabras Transparency 35

Vocabulary
Point out that this list is organized by themes. Use the headings to review vocabulary. You may wish to ask Spanish speakers to share variations on these words and phrases with the class.

Language Note
In some countries (like Puerto Rico), the rr is pronounced like the English h in "hill," but more strongly.

LOG BOOK
Have students copy and read aloud the following tongue-twister:

Erre con erre, guitarra.
Erre con erre, carril.
Erre con erre,
ruedan los carros
del ferrocarril.

(R with R, guitar.
R with R, the tracks.
R with R,
roll the railroad cars.)

La conexión inglés-español
Vocabulary words in this chapter that clearly follow the cognate-finding rule are: *(poet)* and *cómico* (comedian or comic). Following the rule can also help remember the meaning of the words: *centro* (center or "centre" in British spelling), *trompeta* (trumpet), *conferencia* (conference, but meaning "lecture"), and *lectura* (lecture, but meaning "reading").

	Objetivos page 157 *¡Recuerdos de la isla!*	Conversemos pages 158-159 *Mis recuerdos*	Realidades pages 160-161 *El álbum de fotos de mi familia*	Palabras en acción pages 162-163 *¡Vamos al pueblo!*
Comunicación	To talk about: • childhood memories and recent times	Discuss childhood memories and recent times	Read text, answer questions, create dialog, discuss siblings, make table	Read cartoon, discuss characters; talk about home towns; discuss collections and toys; act out interview; write in diary
	• relationships among people	Discuss relationships among people	Read text, answer questions, create dialog, discuss siblings, make table	Read cartoon, discuss characters; talk about home towns; write in diary
Cultura	To learn about: • everyday life in the Dominican Republic • *el matao,* a typical game of the Dominican Republic • *carnaval* in the Dominican Republic		Review Dominican family photographs and history, learn about Dominican holidays	Passport stamps from Latin American countries
Vocabulario temático	To know the expressions for: • childhood games	Talk about childhood games	Read text, answer questions, create dialog	Read cartoon, make list; discuss characters, collections, and toys; act out interview; make poster; write in diary
	• collections and toys	Talk about some collections and toys	Read text, answer questions, create dialog, discuss siblings, make table	Read cartoon, make list; discuss characters; talk about collections and toys; make poster; write in diary
	• relationships	Talk about relationships	Read text, answer questions, create dialog, discuss siblings, make table	Read cartoon, discuss characters; talk about home towns; write in diary
Estructura	To talk about: • how people interact, using reciprocal verbs	Use reciprocal verbs to discuss how people interact	Read text, answer questions, create dialog, discuss siblings, make table	Read cartoon, discuss characters; write in diary
	• events in the past, using the preterite or the imperfect tense	Use the preterite and imperfect tenses to discuss events in the past	Read text, answer questions, create dialog	Read cartoon, discuss characters; talk about home towns; discuss collections and toys; act out interview; write in diary

¡RECUERDOS DE LA ISLA!

Para comunicarnos mejor (1) pages 164-165 *¿Dónde se conocieron?*	Para comunicarnos mejor (2) pages 166-167 *¿Qué hacían cuando llegaste?*	Situaciones pages 168-169 *Los juegos de tu niñez*	Para resolver pages 170-171 *Una historieta*	Entérate page 172 *El carnaval dominicano*
Discuss where people meet; talk about friendship; discuss childhood relationships	Discuss yesterday; talk about childhood; discuss time and place of birth	Discuss childhood games and anecdotes; talk about old photos; act out interview with Dominican writer; write in diary	Choose type of story; discuss characters and plot; write and illustrate text, present to class	Discuss the *carnaval* in the Dominican Republic
Discuss where people meet; talk about friendship; discuss relationships	Talk about childhood; discuss time and place of birth	Discuss childhood games and anecdotes; talk about old photos; act out interview with Dominican writer; write in diary	Choose type of story; discuss characters and plot; write and illustrate text, present to class	
Culture note about the pronouns *os* and *se*	Note about a Dominican neighborhood in New York City	Read about children's games from the Dominican Republic		
Discuss childhood relationships	Talk about childhood			
	Talk about childhood		**Re-entry of vocabulary**	**Extension of vocabulary**
Discuss where people meet; talk about friendship; discuss childhood relationships	Talk about childhood; discuss time and place of birth			
Discuss where people meet; talk about friendship; discuss childhood relationships	Talk about childhood; discuss time and place of birth		**Re-entry of structure**	**Extension of structure**
Discuss where people meet; talk about friendship; discuss childhood relationships	Discuss yesterday; talk about childhood; discuss time and place of birth			

La vida era un juego

WRITING CONNECTION

Objective
• to write about childhood toys and games, using Chapter 6 *Vocabulario temático*

Use
after *Palabras en acción,* pages 162-163

Activity
• Divide the class into groups.
• Have the class brainstorm a list of childhood toys and games. Write these on the board.
• Assign one to each group. Have groups write collectively a paragraph describing the toy or game. For example: *Cuando yo era pequeña, tenía una muñeca favorita. Se llamaba Cookie. Tenía el pelo largo y rubio y los ojos azules. Cuando le daba un beso, decía "mamá". Mi abuela diseñó muchos vestidos para Cookie, y yo la cambiaba de ropa todas las mañanas para vestirla igual que yo. Por las noches, le ponía un pijama y, después de cenar, Cookie y yo dormíamos juntas. Siempre quería llevarla a la escuela conmigo, pero mi mamá no quería.*
• When students have finished, have one member from each group read the paragraph to the class.

¿Nos conocemos?

WRITING CONNECTION

Objective
• to describe actions, using reciprocal verbs and pronouns

Use
after *Para comunicarnos mejor,* pages 164-165

Activity
• Ask students to think of a famous romantic movie that they have seen. Each student writes (in first person) the plot of the movie, without naming the title. For example: *Yo estaba enamorada de Ashley, pero él y mi prima Melanie se casaron. Entonces Rhett y yo nos conocimos y nos gustamos. Al principio no nos llevábamos bien, pero luego nos enamoramos y nos casamos.*
• Each student reads his/her story to the class, as others guess what movie they have described. For example, John says: Es Gone with the Wind. If John is right, the writer replies: *Sí, tienes razón.* And John goes next.
• Students take turns reading their stories aloud until each story is identified.

NOTE: To avoid repetition, you may wish to make a list of appropriate movies for students to choose from.

Rápida—¡mente!

GAME

Objective

- to play a fast-moving word game, using adjectives that can be converted to adverbs

Use

after *Para comunicarnos mejor,* pages 164-165

Activity

- Select a recorder for each team. Divide the class into four teams, and decide on a playing order.
- Give teams five minutes to list all the adverbs they can think of that are formed by adding the **-mente** suffix to an adjective. For example: *inteligentemente, felizmente, fácilmente, especialmente, estupendamente, cuidadosamente, enormemente, positivamente, alegremente, antiguamente, maravillosamente.*
- Teams list their adverbs—one at a time, in playing order.
- The next team uses the adverb in a sentence. For example: *El niño lloraba fácilmente cuando su padre lo miraba.* Because the sentence is acceptable, the recorder of that team gives a new adverb to the next team in the playing order. If the adverb were *absolutamente,* the next team might say: *Estoy absolutamente segura de que no sabe nada de la lección de ayer.*
- Play continues until all the adverbs have been used. Teams receive one point for each adverb they listed and another for each sentence they made with another team's adverb.

Mundo imperfecto

GAME

Objective

- to play a question-and-answer game, using verbs in the imperfect tense

Use

after *Para comunicarnos mejor,* pages 166-167

Materials

- 3" x 5" index cards, cut in half
- small paper bag

Activity

- Give each student two halves of an index card and ask him/her to write a question in the imperfect tense on one half and an answer in the imperfect tense on the other. Questions can be funny, outlandish, or serious. For example: *¿Cuánta leche bebías cuando eras bebé? Cuando era bebé no bebía leche. Bebía refrescos y ahora tengo sólo once dientes.*
- Place answers in bag and mix them up.
- Each student selects a card from the bag without showing it to classmates.
- Students decide on a playing order.
- The first player reads his/her question aloud while students listen to see if the answer is on the card they drew. A student who thinks he/she has the correct answer reads it to the class. If correct, this student reads the next question. An incorrect answer gives another player a chance to read an answer. If, after three tries, no one presents the correct answer, the player who wrote the original question and answer says the correct answer and chooses someone to read the next question.
- The game is over when all questions and answers have been matched.

¡RECUERDOS DE LA ISLA!

Introduce the chapter and its theme by asking students to think about childhood memories. How do they think their lives would be different if they had been born in another country?

Related Components

Audio	Video: Tape/Book
Conexiones: 17A	Unit 3: Seg. 3
Conexiones	
Chapter 6	

Scan to Chapter 6

GETTING STARTED

Ask students to discuss the scene in the photo. Have any of them visited a place like this? Ask questions. Suggestions:
¿Dónde está la playa de la foto?
¿Visitaste alguna ves un lugar similar?

Critical Thinking

Use the following activity to help students discover for themselves what they would need to know in order to talk about childhood memories.
Tell students to think about what they did when they were little. Then assign these activities to groups:
- make a list of games you played when you were little
- make a list of things you collected, for example: stickers, toy trucks
- list words that express how you got along with others
- list verbs that express physical or emotional contact

Have each group write its list on the board. Have the class discuss the lists and decide which items are the most useful.
Have each group submit a revised list.
When you finish the chapter, have the class review the lists to see how they compare to what they learned in the chapter.

CAPÍTULO **6**

¡RECUERDOS DE LA ISLA!

Bayahibe, un pueblo pesquero en la República Dominicana.

156

CHAPTER COMPONENTS

Activity Book	Audio Book	Conexiones	Transparencies
p. 75-84	Script: p. 39-41	Chapter 6	Chapter 6
Assessment	Activities: p. 42-44	**Cuaderno**	Transparencies 36-39
Oral Proficiency:	**Audio**	p. 45-52	**Tutor Pages**
p. 26	Chapter: 6B	**Magazine**	p. 27-30
Listening Script:	Assessment: 14B	Juntos en República	**Video: Tape/Book**
p. 14	Conexiones: 17A	Dominicana	Unit 3: Seg. 3
Chapter Test:			
p. 75-80			

Objetivos

COMUNICACIÓN
To talk about:
- childhood memories and recent times
- relationships among people

CULTURA
To learn about:
- everyday life in the Dominican Republic
- *el matao*, a typical game of the Dominican Republic
- *Carnaval* in the Dominican Republic

VOCABULARIO TEMÁTICO
To know the expressions for:
- childhood games
- collections and toys
- relationships

ESTRUCTURA
To talk about:
- how people interact: reciprocal verbs
- how something is done: adverbs
- events in the past: the preterite or the imperfect tense

¿SABES QUE...?
The Dominican Republic covers two-thirds of the island of Hispaniola, which it shares with Haiti. One of the world's most geographically diverse nations, it consists of more than 20 different geographic regions. Tropical forests, deserts, fertile agricultural land, and bustling towns are all found in the Dominican Republic. Along the coastline, you will find dozens of private resorts, public beaches, and quiet fishing villages such as the one pictured here.

157

Here are some additional activities that you may wish to use as you work through the chapter with your students.

Communication
Encourage after-class activities that may enhance student interest and proficiency. Some ideas:
- have students conduct an interview with a Spanish speaker about where he or she was born and grew up
- create a lending library of information and resources—music, magazines, radio programs, video

Culture
To encourage greater cultural understanding:
- show slides or photos to introduce the landscape of the Dominican Republic
- have students organize a carnival with flags, masks, music and food of the Dominican Republic.
- show the video that accompanies Unit 3 of this textbook

Vocabulary
To reinforce vocabulary, have students:
- make reflexive verb flashcards with a picture of the action on one side, and the Spanish word on the other
- make a bulletin board of students' childhood memories

Structure
To reinforce reciprocal pronouns and the imperfect and preterite tenses:
- have groups present a review of this chapter's grammar
- give simple quizzes, and have students correct each other's answers

Thinking About Language
Ask students to look at the lists they created for the *Critical Thinking* activity on page 156. Do they know how to say any of the words or phrases in Spanish? Are any of those words cognates? Ask speakers of other languages to share expressions from those languages that relate to childhood.

▶▶▶ INTERNET LINK
Dominican Music http://www.mind spring.com:80/~adiascar/musica/

Communicative Objectives

• to talk about where you were born and where you grew up
• to talk about childhood memories
• to answer questions about the past

Related Components

Activity Book p. 75	**Cuaderno** p. 45
Audio Book Script: Seg. 1	**Transparencies** Ch. 6: Conversemos Transparency 36
Audio Chapter: 6B, Seg. 1	

GETTING STARTED

Ask students to think back to their earliest childhood memories. What are they and where did they take place?

ACTIVITIES

These activities give students an opportunity to begin communicating with each other and with you, focusing on the theme and objectives of the chapter. The activities can be used as oral class activities, or, if you prefer, you can pair students to achieve more interaction.

¿Dónde naciste?

Class activity to learn to say where you were born. Ask the title question. Answer it with the country you were born in. Ask again, and answer with the state, then the city. Follow with *¿Cuándo naciste?* Arrange students' seats in a circle. Assign each student a country or city. Clockwise, have students go around the circle asking where the next person was born, and answering. Have them select new places to be from each time around.

Extension: You may want to extend this activity by using the maps at the beginning of this textbook.

¿Dónde creciste?

Class activity to learn to say where you grew up. Have students identify the logos. Ask the title question. Have students choose the place that best matches where they grew up. On later rounds, assign locations or let them invent new ones. Ask them to think of words they associate with each of these places.

CONVERSEMOS

MIS RECUERDOS

Habla con tu compañero(a).

¿DÓNDE NACISTE?

Nací en la República Dominicana.
[I was born in the Dominican Republic.]

¿DÓNDE CRECISTE?

Crecí en una ciudad, en Santo Domingo.
[I grew up in a city, in Santo Domingo.]

	una ciudad		un pueblo pesquero
	el campo		un pueblo costero
	una granja		un pueblo en las montañas

158

MEETING INDIVIDUAL NEEDS

Reaching All Students

For Auditory Learners
Name childhood games, collections and toys. Others say *jugaba* or *coleccionaba*.

For Visual Learners
Make drawings of childhood activities and use as flashcards.

For Kinesthetic Learners
Act out one of the childhood activities for others to guess.

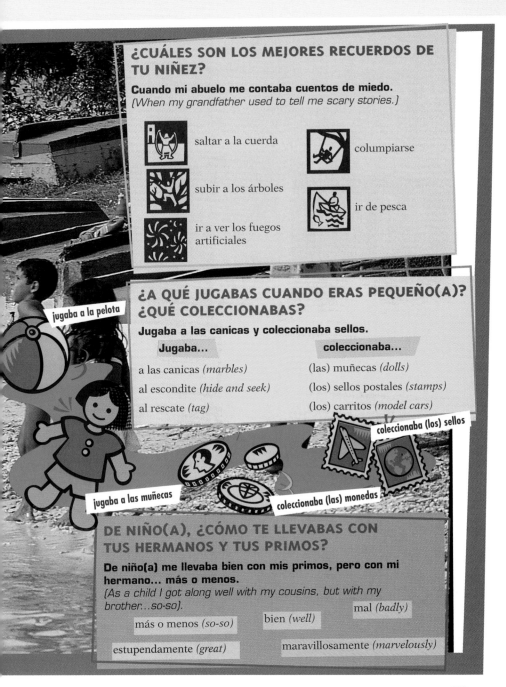

¿CUÁLES SON LOS MEJORES RECUERDOS DE TU NIÑEZ?

Cuando mi abuelo me contaba cuentos de miedo.
(When my grandfather used to tell me scary stories.)

saltar a la cuerda

columpiarse

subir a los árboles

ir de pesca

ir a ver los fuegos artificiales

¿A QUÉ JUGABAS CUANDO ERAS PEQUEÑO(A)? ¿QUÉ COLECCIONABAS?

Jugaba a las canicas y coleccionaba sellos.

Jugaba...	coleccionaba...
a las canicas *(marbles)*	(las) muñecas *(dolls)*
al escondite *(hide and seek)*	(los) sellos postales *(stamps)*
al rescate *(tag)*	(los) carritos *(model cars)*

jugaba a la pelota

coleccionaba (los) sellos

jugaba a las muñecas

coleccionaba (las) monedas

DE NIÑO(A), ¿CÓMO TE LLEVABAS CON TUS HERMANOS Y TUS PRIMOS?

De niño(a) me llevaba bien con mis primos, pero con mi hermano... más o menos.
(As a child I got along well with my cousins, but with my brother...so-so).

más o menos *(so-so)*

bien *(well)*

mal *(badly)*

estupendamente *(great)*

maravillosamente *(marvelously)*

¿Cuáles son los mejores recuerdos de tu niñez?
Class activity to introduce vocabulary related to childhood memories. Review the imperfect with a drill. Ask the title question and have volunteers read aloud the answers. Encourage alternative responses.

¿A qué jugabas cuando eras pequeño(a)? ¿Qué coleccionabas?
Class activity to introduce vocabulary related to childhood pastimes and to review the imperfect. Use gestures and body language to explain each activity. Remind students of the **a** that goes with **jugaba**.
Extension: Ask, *¿Con quién jugabas cuando eras pequeño(a)?*

De niño(a), ¿cómo te llevabas con tus hermanos y tus primos?
Class activity to talk about relationships with family members. Demonstrate the meaning of these words with facial expressions and gestures. Have pairs ask each other the title question. Ask about their relationships with other people, such as neighbors, teachers and friends.

CHECK

- *¿Dónde naciste y creciste?*
- *¿Jugabas al escondite cuando eras pequeño?*
- *¿Cómo te llevabas con tus hermanos?*

LOG BOOK
Have each student write down vocabulary and expressions that specifically relate to his or her childhood, and look up in a bilingual dictionary any words he or she doesn't know.

Objectives
Communicative: to talk about a photo album
Cultural: to talk about families and relationships in the Dominican Republic

Related Components

Activity Book p. 76	**Audio** Chapter: 6B, Seg. 2
Audio Book Script: Seg. 2	**Cuaderno** p. 46

GETTING STARTED

Ask whose families take lots of photos. Why do they do that? Do they ever look at the photos?

DISCUSS

Talk about the photographs and captions, and ask questions. Suggestions:

Mi abuelo
¿Dónde estaba el abuelo cuando le tomaron esta foto?
¿Cómo se llamaba su barco?
¿Qué pasaba cuando no podía ir a pescar?

Mi padre
¿Cuántos años tenía el padre en la foto?
¿Qué hacían frecuentemente los hermanos?
¿Dónde nació el padre?

Mis padres
¿Desde cuándo se conocían los padres?
¿Qué hacían los padres en esta escuela?

Todo el pueblo
¿Qué celebraba todo el pueblo?
¿Cómo lo celebraban?
¿De qué día es la foto?
¿Qué hicieron los padres enseguida?
¿Y qué hicieron poco después?

REALIDADES

El álbum de fotos de mi familia

Mi abuelo José Luis en su barco pesquero <u>El pescador.</u> Se enojaba cuando hacía mal tiempo y no podía ir de pesca.

Mi padre, el día que cumplió quince años, con sus hermanos. Se peleaban con frecuencia pero se querían mucho. Mi padre nació en esta casa.

Mis padres se conocían desde niños. Ésta es la escuela donde estudiaban.

Todo el pueblo celebraba el aniversario de la fundación de Santo Domingo con un festival de merengue. Éstos son mis padres el día de su primera cita. Se enamoraron enseguida y poco después se casaron.

160

Reaching All Students

For Auditory Learners
Record the photo captions, leaving out two words from each. Exchange tapes with others and figure out which words are missing.

For Kinesthetic Learners
Act out skits of brothers and sisters getting along: *estupendamente, bien,* and *no muy bien.*

¿QUÉ DICES?

A. Di qué hace la gente en cada foto.

> *El abuelo José Luis está preparándose para salir de pesca.*

B. Haz un diálogo con tu compañero(a) sobre el álbum de fotos.

> — *¿Qué hacía el abuelo José Luis?*
> — *Iba de pesca en su barco El pescador.*
> — *¿Y cómo era la casa de... ?*

¿QUÉ OPINAS?

¿Cómo te llevas con tus amigos? Pregunta a tres compañeros(as) y anota los resultados en una tabla. Usa el modelo.

Me llevo...	yo	Jorge	Martín	Nieves
estupendamente				
bien		✓	✓	
más o menos				✓
nos queremos mucho pero a veces nos peleamos	✓			

Compara tu tabla con la de otros(as) compañeros(as).

¿SABES QUE...?

Fireworks are an important part of the festivities for both Dominican Independence Day and for New Year's Eve. In Santo Domingo, crowds gather on the boulevard of the Malecón, listening to merengue music, to usher in the *Día de año nuevo*. The partying lasts until sunrise.

161

Individual and Pair Activities: Writing and Conversing
A. Say what the people in each photo are doing.
B. With a partner, create a dialog about the photo album.
Answers: See models on student page.
Extension: Bring in photos from your own album. Follow the same directions.

¿Qué opinas?

Group Activity: Taking a Poll
In groups of four, say how each of you gets along with your brothers and sisters. Put your answers in a chart like the one on page 161.

Class Activity: Evaluation
Have a volunteer write in the numbers for each answer as representatives of each group take turns reporting on their polls.
Extension: Compare the results, write a few sentences about your findings, and talk about them.

CHECK

- *¿Por qué se enojaba el abuelo?*
- *¿Quiénes se peleaban mucho?*
- *¿Cuándo se enamoraron los padres?*

LOG BOOK
Have students list all the reflexive verbs from the photo album.

Para hispanohablantes

Tell the class about the relationship you have with your brothers and sisters.

161

Communicative Objectives

• to talk about games and childhood activities
• to talk about childhood memories

Related Components

Activity Book p. 77-78	Transparencies Ch. 6: Palabras en acción Transparency 37
Cuaderno p. 47-48	Tutor Page p. 27

GETTING STARTED

Ask what differences students can find between the left and right sides of the drawing on pages 162 and 163.

DISCUSS

Read aloud the talk balloons. Comment on and ask questions about what the people are doing. Examples:
¿Qué juegos ves en el dibujo?
¿De qué hablan Rafael y su familia?
¿Qué pasa en la tienda de frutas?

Para hispanohablantes

If you use words or expressions other than the ones introduced in this chapter, share them with the class. A few variations:
enojarse: enfadarse
la costumbre: el hábito
jugar a las canicas: jugar a las bolas, ...a las bolitas, jugar corote
el pueblo pesquero: el pueblo de pescadores, el pueblo pescador
recuerdo: me acuerdo de
saltar a la cuerda: saltar a la comba, ...a la suiza, brincar cuica
¿Dónde creciste?: ¿Dónde te criaste?

PALABRAS EN ACCIÓN

¡VAMOS AL PUEBLO!

Vamos a jugar al rescate.

Me gusta mucho saltar a la cuerda.

las canicas

la cuerda

el columpio

la muñeca   el muelle

el carrito

el muñequito

el pescador

De niño yo iba de pesca.

Yo navegaba con mi abuelo.

la caña de pescar

 1 ¿Qué ves en el dibujo?

Haz una lista de las cosas que ves en el dibujo.

> *La caña de pescar, la piña...*

 2 ¿Qué hacen?

Escoge tres personas o grupos de personas del dibujo. Pregunta a tu compañero(a) qué están haciendo.

> — *¿Qué está haciendo el pescador de la camiseta roja?*
> — *Está limpiando el barco.*
> — *¿Qué están haciendo las niñas en el parque?*
> — *Están saltando a la cuerda.*

 3 La familia de Rafael

Habla con tu compañero(a) sobre lo que hacían de niños tres personas del dibujo.

> — *¿Qué hacía el primo de Rafael?*
> — *Escuchaba los cuentos de miedo que le contaba su abuela.*

 4 ¿De dónde eres?

Pregunta a tres compañeros dónde nacieron y dónde crecieron.

> — *¿Dónde naciste?*
> — *En Argentina.*
> — *¿Dónde creciste?*
> — *En el campo, cerca de Buenos Aires.*

162

For students having difficulty talking about childhood memories or activities, you might consider:
• **The tutor page:** Pair the student with a native speaker or a more able student, using the tutor page.
Optional activity: See page 156C: *La vida era un juego*

Speech bubbles in drawing:
- **Aquí nos besamos por primera vez.**
- **Ese día nos enamoramos.**
- **Cuando era pequeño iba de pesca con el abuelo.**
- **De niña me subía a los árboles.**
- **La abuela nos contaba cuentos de miedo.**

Labels: la piña · la novia · el novio · Rafael · la abuela · la tía · el primo · el abuelo

5 Juegos y colecciones

Habla con tu compañero(a) y pregúntale a qué jugaba y qué coleccionaba cuando era pequeño(a).

— ¿A qué jugabas cuando eras pequeño?
— Jugaba a las canicas.
— ¿Qué coleccionabas?
— Coleccionaba sellos postales.

6 Miniteatro

Imagina que tu compañero(a) es un(a) pescador(a). Hazle una entrevista.

— ¿Es peligroso el trabajo de pescador?
— No, si prestas atención al pronóstico del tiempo.

7 Cartel

De niño, ¿cuál era tu juego favorito? Haz un cartel. Incluye: cómo se llama, cómo se juega, qué se necesita para jugarlo y cuántas personas pueden jugar. Usa fotos o dibujos de revistas o periódicos.

8 Tú eres el autor

Escribe un párrafo en tu diario sobre tus mejores recuerdos.

> Querido diario:
> Cuando tenía ocho años fui a Puerto Rico a visitar a la familia de mi mamá. Cuando llegué a la casa de mis abuelos, todos nos abrazamos y nos besamos. Me llevé maravillosamente con el tío Juan.

163

ACTIVITIES

1. Individual Activity
Make a list of the things in the drawing.
Extension: Make a list of the activities.

2. Pair Activity
Choose three people or groups in the drawing. Ask what they are doing.
Extension: Change the verbs in these sentences to the imperfect.

3. Pair Activity
Talk about what three people in the drawing used to do as children.
Extension: Talk about something you used to do when you were young.

4. Group Activity
Ask three classmates where they were born and where they grew up.
Extension: Write a report about what you learned. Example: *Mónica nació en Minnesota y creció en California.*

5. Pair Activity
Talk with your partner about things you used to collect and games you used to play when you were younger.
Extension: Talk about the same activities as if you had played them yesterday. Example: *Ayer jugué a las canicas.*

6. Roleplay Activity
Imagine that your partner is a fisherman. Ask questions.
Extension: Write down your interview and exchange it with another pair. Read it aloud.

7. Hands-On Activity
Make a poster for your favorite childhood game. Include:
- what it is called
- how it is played
- what is needed to play it
- how many people can play

Use illustrations from magazines or newspapers.
Extension: Exchange posters with someone who illustrated a different game. Write a few sentences about that game, based on the poster.

8. Writing Activity
Write a paragraph in your diary about your fondest childhood memories.
Note: You can help students get started by copying the model on the board and underlining those words which students will replace. Elicit suggestions, write them on the board, and have students choose some for their paragraphs.

CHECK

- ¿Qué coleccionabas cuando eras pequeño(a)?
- ¿Dónde nacieron y crecieron tus compañeros de clase?
- ¿Qué querías ser cuando eras pequeño(a)?

LOG BOOK
Have students write a few sentences about real or imaginary places they visited when they were young.

Communicative Objectives

- to talk about reciprocal actions, using **nos** and **se**
- to say how something is or was done, using adverbs

Related Components

Activity Book p. 79-80	**Audio** Chapter: 6B, Seg. 3
Audio Book Script: Seg. 3 Activities: p. 42	**Cuaderno** p. 49
	Tutor Page p. 28

Language in Context

Reciprocal Pronouns
Write a short love story on the board:
Ellos se vieron. Se enamoraron. Se casaron.
Emphasize the repetition of **se**.
Write the same story in English:
> They saw each other. They fell in love with each other. They married each other.

Emphasize the use of "each other."

Adverbs
Remind students of the role of adverbs by comparing a few sentences. Example:
> José plays marvelous music.
> (The music is great.)
> José plays marvelously.
> (The way he plays is great.)

Show how these work in Spanish:
José toca música maravillosa.
José toca maravillosamente.
Ask for other sentences about the way people do things.

Review vocabulary from previous chapters and introduce some of this chapter's new vocabulary with questions and statements that use adverbs and reciprocal verbs and pronouns.
¿Se conocen bien Uds.?
¿Se ayudan con la tarea?
¿Se ven mucho después de la clase?
Nos llamamos continuamente.
¿Cómo se conocieron? ¿Dónde se conocieron?
¿Cómo te llevas con tus padres?
¿Dónde se casaron? ¿Cuándo?

PARA COMUNICARNOS MEJOR

¿DÓNDE SE CONOCIERON?

The reciprocal pronoun *os* is used only in Spain.

Y vosotros, ¿dónde os conocisteis?

To say that two or more people do something that affects each other, use the reciprocal pronouns *nos* and *se*.

Se conocieron en un concierto. Se vieron y enseguida se enamoraron.	They met at a concert. They saw each other and immediately fell in love.
Mi hermana y yo nos llevamos muy bien.	My sister and I get along very well.

Some verbs often used as reciprocals are:

reciprocal verbs

abrazarse to hug each other	**enojarse** to get angry with each other
besarse to kiss each other	**llevarse (bien, mal) con...** to get along (well, badly) with . . .
contarse (cuentos) to tell each other (stories)	**pelearse** to fight with each other
enamorarse to fall in love with each other	**quererse** to love each other

□ Many verbs that you have already learned can be used as reciprocals: *conocerse* (to know each other, to meet each other), *ayudarse* (to help each other), *escribirse cartas* (to write each other letters), *llamarse por teléfono* (to call each other on the phone), *verse* (to see each other) and *visitarse* (to visit each other).

To say how or in what manner something is or was done, you may use adverbs.

Se llevan maravillosamente.	They get along marvelously.

□ You have already used some adverbs, such as *mucho* and *bien*. To form adverbs from adjectives, add *-mente* to the feminine form of the adjective. If the adjective ends in *-e* or in a consonant, just add *-mente*:

continua	**continuamente**	general	**generalmente**
enorme	**enormemente**	lenta	**lentamente**
estupenda	**estupendamente**	rápida	**rápidamente**

For students having difficulty using adverbs or reciprocal verbs and pronouns, you might consider:
- **The tutor page:** Pair the student with a native speaker or a more able student, using the tutor page.

Optional activities: See page 156C: *¿Nos conocemos?* and page 156D: *Rápida-¡mente!*

Recuerdos de familia

Pregunta a tu compañero(a).

— *¿Dónde se conocieron tu mamá y tu papá?*
— *Se conocieron en la piscina. A los dos les gustaba nadar.*

1. tu mamá y tu papá
2. tus abuelos
3. tú y tu mejor amigo(a)
4. tu hermana(o) y su novio(a)
5. tu mamá y su mejor amigo(a)
6. tus dos mejores amigos(as)

2 **Amigos(as) de muchos años**

Pregunta a tu compañero(a) sobre su relación con su mejor amigo(a).

— *¿Cuándo se conocieron tú y tu mejor amigo(a)?*
— *Nos conocimos en 1992, en una fiesta en casa de mis primos.*

1. ¿Cuándo se conocieron?
2. ¿Con qué frecuencia se ven?
3. ¿Se visitan siempre?
4. ¿Se escriben por correo electrónico o se hablan por teléfono?
5. ¿Se ayudan?
6. ¿Se cuentan todos sus secretos?

3 **¿Cómo te llevabas con...?**

Pregunta a tu compañero(a) cómo se llevaba con otras personas cuando era pequeño(a).

— *¿Cómo te llevabas con tu hermano(a)?*
— *Muy mal. Nos peleábamos continuamente.*

1. con tu hermano(a)
2. con tus padres
3. con tus compañeros(as) de clase
4. con tus primos(as)
5. con tus tíos(as)
6. con tu abuelo(a)

Maravillosamente
Estupendamente
Mal
Muy mal
Muy bien
Más o menos

165

ACTIVITIES

Students use adverbs, reciprocal verbs, and pronouns to talk about the past and about relationships.

1. Pair Activity
Ask each other where these people met. If you don't know, make something up.
Possible Answers:
1. See model on student page.
2. *¿Dónde se conocieron tus abuelos?*
Se conocieron en un baile. A los dos les gustaba bailar.
3. *¿Dónde se conocieron tú y tu mejor amigo?*

Nos conocimos en el equipo de fútbol. A los dos nos gustaban los deportes.
4. *¿Dónde se conocieron tu hermano y su novia?*
Se conocieron en el boliche. A los dos les gustaba jugar al boliche.
5. *¿Dónde se conocieron tu mamá y su mejor amiga?*
Se conocieron en la escuela de teatro. A las dos les gustaba actuar.
6. *¿Dónde se conocieron tus dos mejores amigas?*
Se conocieron en una lectura de poemas. A las dos les gustaba la poesía.

2. Pair Activity
Ask and answer questions about your relationship with a best friend.
Possible Answers:
1. See model on student page.
2. *Nos vemos casi todos los días.*
3. *Sí, nos visitamos siempre.*
4. *Nos hablamos por teléfono.*
5. *Sí, nos ayudamos siempre con la tarea.*
6. *No, no nos contamos todos nuestros secretos.*

3. Pair Activity
Ask how your partner got along with others when he or she was younger.
Possible Answers:
1. See model on student page.
2. *¿...con tus padres?*
Muy bien. No nos peleábamos mucho.
3. *¿...con tus compañeros de clase?*
Nos llevábamos estupendamente. Nos ayudábamos mucho con la tarea.
4. *¿...con tus primos(as)?*
Nos llevábamos más o menos. No nos visitábamos mucho.
5. *¿...con tus tíos?*
Mal. Nunca nos llamábamos.
6. *¿...con tu abuelo?*
Nos llevábamos maravillosamente. Nos queríamos mucho.

CHECK

- *¿Dónde se conocieron tus padres?*
- *¿Cuándo se conocieron tú y tu mejor amiga?*
- *¿Cómo te llevabas con tus hermanos?*

165

Communicative Objectives
- to talk about what you used to do, using the imperfect
- to talk about what you did, using the preterite

Related Components

Activity Book p. 81-82	**Cuaderno** p. 50
Audio Book Script: Seg.4 Activities: p. 43	**Transparencies** Ch. 6: Para comunicarnos mejor Transparency 38
Audio Chapter: 6B, Seg. 4	**Tutor Page** p. 29

GETTING STARTED

Language in Context

Preterite and Imperfect
Remind students that, as a general rule, the preterite is used to refer to a specific moment while the imperfect is used to refer to an ongoing action.
Say several sentences in English that offer striking contrasts between the ongoing and the specific. Example:
Last night we ate dinner ar 6 o'clock.
We were eating when he called.
Invite students to suggest sentences with stronger contrasts.
Contrast the situations:
Anoche comimos. Anoche él nos llamó.
Anoche comíamos cuando él nos llamó.

DISCUSS

Review vocabulary from previous chapters and introduce this chapter's new vocabulary with questions and open-ended statements that use the preterite and imperfect tenses. Invite students to complete the sentences.
María leía cuando... sonó el teléfono.
Mientras esperábamos el autobús... vimos un accidente.
Jugábamos al escondite cuando... llegó mi abuela.
La profesora me dijo la frase otra vez porque... no entendía.
Sam comió mucho porque... tenía hambre.
Empezó a llover mientras... nosotros pescábamos.
¿Sabes qué pasó cuando... estábamos en el cine?

166

PARA COMUNICARNOS MEJOR

¿QUÉ HACÍAN CUANDO LLEGASTE?

The preterite and the imperfect are both past tenses. However, each one is used differently.

Use the preterite to talk about:

Completed actions in the past, especially if the beginning or the end of the activity is given.	**Anoche comimos a las 8:00.** Last night we ate at 8:00.
An action that changed or interrupted a situation.	**En 1993 mi familia se mudó a California.** In 1993 my family moved to California.
Actions in the past, when accompanied by some expressions such as **ayer, anoche, el lunes pasado, el año pasado, nunca, todo el día, una vez, dos veces.**	**Ayer pasé el día con mis abuelos.** Yesterday, I spent the day with my grandparents. **Hoy estudié todo el día.** Today I studied all day long.

Use the imperfect to talk about:

Actions in the past, which were ongoing when another action occurred.	**Nosotros estábamos allí cuando él llegó.** We were there when he arrived.
Physical or emotional descriptions and references to time and age.	**Era la primavera de 1957. Mi mamá tenía dos años. Era muy feliz.** It was spring 1957. My mother was two years old. She was very happy.
Actions in the past, when accompanied by some expressions such as **todos los días, todos los lunes, siempre, con frecuencia, de niño(a).**	**Cuando era joven, mi abuelo iba de pesca todos los domingos.** When he was young my grandfather went fishing every Sunday. **De niño, mi padre vivía en una casa en las montañas.** As a child, my father lived in a house in the mountains.

166

For students having difficulty using the preterite and imperfect tenses, you might consider:
- **The tutor page:** Pair the student with a native speaker or a more able student, using the tutor page.

Optional activity: See page 156D: *Mundo imperfecto*

1 Nada especial

Pregunta a tu compañero(a) qué hizo ayer.

— *Dime todo lo que hiciste ayer.*
— *Me levanté a las ocho de la mañana, me duché y desayuné. Después fui a... ¿Y tú?*

2 Costumbres de familia

Pregunta a tu compañero(a) qué costumbres tenía su familia cuando él/ella era pequeño(a).

— *¿Qué costumbres tenía tu familia cuando tú eras pequeño(a)?*
— *Los domingos por la mañana mi familia y yo íbamos a visitar a mis abuelos. Luego íbamos a comer a un restaurante, y después, mi papá, mi hermano y yo nos quedábamos en el parque y jugábamos a la pelota.*

3 Cuando tú naciste

Haz preguntas a tu compañero(a) sobre su familia.

— *¿Dónde vivía tu familia cuando tú naciste?*
— *Cuando yo nací, mi familia vivía en Washington Heights, un vecindario de Nueva York donde hay una comunidad dominicana muy grande.*

1. ¿Dónde vivía tu familia cuando tú naciste?
2. ¿Cómo era el vecindario/el pueblo/la ciudad?
3. ¿Había en la familia otros chicos de tu edad? ¿Quiénes eran? ¿Cómo eran?
4. El año en que tú naciste, ¿qué otras cosas importantes pasaron?

Para hispanohablantes

Tell the class about something that happened to you a few years ago. Have them put their right hands on their heads every time you use the preterite and wave their left hands when you use the imperfect tense.

ACTIVITIES

Students use the imperfect and the preterite to talk about actions in the past.

1. Pair Activity
Ask your partner to tell you everything that he or she did yesterday.
Answers: See model on student page.
Extension: Write a report about what your partner did.

2. Pair Activity
Ask your partner what routines his/her family had when he/she was young.
Answers: See model on student page.
Extension: Write five sentences about ongoing actions in the past. Use a different time expression for each.
Todos los lunes, Manuel nadaba en la piscina.

3. Pair Activity
Ask your partner questions about his/her family.
1. Where was your family living when you were born?
2. What was your neighborhood (town, city) like?
3. Were there other kids your age in your family? Who were they? What were they like?
4. What other important events happened the year you were born?
Answers: See model on student page.
Extension: Write five open-ended sentences for your partner to complete.
El lunes pasado, mi novia y yo estábamos en la playa cuando....

CHECK

- *¿Qué hicieron Uds. ayer?*
- *¿Cuál era tu canción favorita cuando eras pequeño?*
- *¿Dónde estaban Uds. cuándo llegué?*
- *Cuándo eras pequeño, ¿qué hacías los domingos?*

LOG BOOK
Have students write five sentences in which an ongoing action is interrupted.

Objectives

Communicative: to talk about childhood games and things that happened when you were young

Cultural: to learn about children's games in the Dominican Republic

Related Components

Assessment Oral Proficiency: p. 26 **Audio Book** Script: Seg. 5 Activities: p. 44 **Audio** Chapter: 6B, Seg.5 Conexiones: 17A	**Conexiones** Chapter 6 **Magazine** Juntos en República Dominicana **Tutor Page** p. 30

GETTING STARTED

Students should now be able to correctly use adverbs, reciprocal verbs and pronouns, the preterite and imperfect tenses, and all of the chapter vocabulary. Have students read aloud the steps to play the *matao* game. After each step, ask questions. For example:
¿Qué se necesita para jugar al "matao"?

APPLY

1. Pair Activity

Talk about the *matao* game.
Answers: See model on student page.
Extension: Say whether or not you and your friends would like to play the *matao* game.

2. Pair Activity

Talk about the games you used to play as children and the rules of those games.
Answers: See model on student page.
Extension: Write a brief set of instructions on how to play one of the games. With your partner, take turns dictating your instructions to each other.

SITUACIONES

LOS JUEGOS DE TU NIÑEZ

¿A qué jugabas cuando eras pequeño(a)? Aquí tienes las reglas de uno de los juegos más conocidos entre los niños de la República Dominicana.

El "matao"

Número de jugadores: cuatro o más **Qué se necesita:** una pelota **Dónde se juega:** al aire libre

1. Se dibuja una línea en medio de la zona donde se va a jugar. Se forman dos equipos y cada uno juega a un lado de la línea.

2. Alguien de un equipo tiene que tirar la pelota y tocar con ella a otro del equipo contrario.

3. Si la pelota toca a alguien y cae al suelo, esa persona no puede jugar más. Si el/la jugador(a) ataja la pelota antes de que ésta toque el suelo, ese(a) jugador(a) trata de tocar con la pelota a alguien del otro equipo.

4. Gana el equipo que elimina a todos los jugadores del equipo contrario.

1 ¿A qué jugaban?

Con tu compañero(a), habla del juego *el matao*.

— *¿Cuántos jugadores se necesitan?*
— *Cuatro o más.*

PARA TU REFERENCIA

ataja *catches*
esconderse *to hide*
golpear *to hit*
el suelo *ground*
tirar *to throw*
tocar *to touch*

For students having difficulty talking about childhood games or activities, you might consider:

• **The tutor page:** Pair the student with a native speaker or a more able student, using the tutor page.

¿A qué jugabas tú?

Con tu compañero(a), di a qué jugabas cuando eras pequeño(a) y cuáles eran las reglas del juego.

— *Cuando yo era pequeño jugaba al escondite.*
— *¿Cómo jugabas al escondite?*
— *Un niño o una niña se cubría los ojos y contaba hasta 20. Los otros niños se escondían. Luego, la persona que contaba tenía que ir a buscarlos. Y tú, ¿a qué jugabas?*

 Tus fotos

Escoge dos fotos de cuando eras pequeño(a): una sobre algo especial que pasó o que hiciste; la otra, sobre algo que hacías todos los días. Explica las fotos a tu compañero(a).

Esta foto es de un viaje a Disneylandia. Mi padre nos llevó el día que cumplí diez años. Mi hermano y yo nos divertimos mucho.

En esta foto estoy en la clase de baile. Iba a tomar clases tres veces a la semana. Mi profesora se llamaba Antonia. Me llevaba estupendamente con ella.

 Entrevista

Tu compañero(a) es un(a) famoso(a) escritor(a) dominicano(a) que ahora vive en Estados Unidos. Hazle una entrevista.

— *¿Cuáles son los mejores recuerdos de su niñez?*
— *Vivía en un pueblo pesquero de la República Dominicana. Me gustaba ir a la playa todos los días. Mi abuelo me regaló una caña de pescar el día que cumplí siete años y todos los sábados iba de pesca con él.*

Tu diario

Escribe un párrafo sobre los recuerdos de tu niñez y di cómo te llevabas con los otros niños de tu familia.

Me llevaba estupendamente con mis primos, pero mi hermano se llevaba muy mal con ellos. Los fines de semana íbamos de excursión juntos y saltábamos a la cuerda. Mi hermano nunca quería jugar con nosotros y a veces nos peleábamos.

3. Pair Activity
Choose two photos of yourself as a kid: one that was taken on a special occasion, another that was taken when you were doing something that you often did. Tell your partner about them.
Answers: See model on student page.
Extension: Display some of the photos for the class. Try to match the stories with the photos.

4. Pair Activity
Interview your partner, who is a famous Dominican writer now living in the United States.
Answers: See model on student page.
Extension: Record interviews and exchange with other pairs. Listen to their tapes and write down what you hear.

5. Homework or Classwork
Write a paragraph about your childhood memories and how you got along with other kids in your family.
Answers: See model on student page.
Note: Have students follow the model, changing words as necessary. Help students by copying the paragraph on the board, underlining the words to be changed.

CHECK

• *¿A qué jugabas cuando eras pequeño(a)?*
• *¿Cuáles son los mejores recuerdos de tu niñez?*
• *Describe una foto de tu compañero(a).*

LOG BOOK
Have students write a few sentences about a funny anecdote from their childhood.

Para hispanohablantes

Write the instructions to a game.

Communicative Objective
• to write and design a comic strip

Related Components

| Video: Tape/Book |
| Unit 3: Seg. 3 |

Scan to Chapter 6

☐ GETTING STARTED

Ask students to recall favorite stories from childhood. What was it about those stories that made them memorable?

☐ APPLY

Form groups. Have each group write and illustrate a short story.

PASO 1: Preparativos para la historieta
Decide what kind of short story it will be—love, horror, travel, adventure… Where and when does it take place?
Answers: See model on student page.

PASO 2: Los personajes
Decide how many characters your story will have. What are the characters' names and ages? What do they look like?
Answers: See model on student page.

PASO 3: El argumento
Think about the story. Why are the characters where they are? What is the story about, and what will happen?
Answers: See model on student page.

PASO 4: Nuestra historieta
Draw pictures for the story, write the dialog and text, and choose a title. Present your story to the class.
Answers: See model on student page.
Extension: Ask each of the other groups three questions about their story.

Extension: Telling stories is an age-old way to pass on information and traditions. Ask your parents or grandparents about a story that has been passed down through your family.

PARA RESOLVER
UNA HISTORIETA

En grupo, van a escribir y dibujar una historieta. Si prefieren, pueden representar una obra de teatro o hacer un video.

PASO 1 Preparativos para la historieta
Decidan qué tipo de historieta va a ser (de amor, de miedo, de viajes, de aventuras...), cuándo y dónde va a pasar.

Va a ser una historieta de amor muy romántica. Va a pasar en el muelle de un pueblo pesquero, durante el verano.

PASO 2 Los personajes
Decidan cuántos personajes va a tener su historieta, cómo se van a llamar y cómo van a ser.

Nuestra historieta tiene dos personajes. Se llaman Alina y Ramiro. Alina tiene 16 años y Ramiro 15. Alina tiene el pelo negro, corto y rizado. Ramiro tiene el pelo...

PASO 3 El argumento
Piensen en los detalles de la historieta. ¿Por qué están en ese lugar los personajes? ¿Cuál va a ser el argumento y cómo termina?

Alina va de vacaciones a un pueblo pesquero. Allí vive Ramiro. Ellos se conocen en el muelle y se enamoran enseguida. El día de su cumpleaños, Ramiro le regala a Alina un sombrero que tiene una pluma de tucán. Pero Ramiro no sabe que Alina es ecologista...

PASO 4 Nuestra historieta
Dibujen la historieta, escriban los diálogos y el texto, y escojan un título. Luego, preséntenla a la clase.

PARA TU REFERENCIA

el argumento *plot*
los detalles *details*
empezó a llorar *started to cry*
la historieta *short story*
los personajes *characters*
la pluma *feather*
se sintió *he felt*

170

Una

—Hola, me llamo Alina, ¿y tú?
—Ramiro. ¿Vives aquí?

Ramiro y Alina se conocieron en un muelle un pueblo pesquero. Era verano.

—¡Oh, pobre tucán!
—¡Lo siento! No sabía que eras ecologista.

Pero en la fiesta de cumpleaños de Alina, el empezó a llorar porque Ramiro le regaló u sombrero que tenía una pluma de tucán.

Research Project
Have students use library reference sources and interviews to research information on different cultures' use of illustrations to tell stories (e.g., cave drawings and hieroglyphics). Ask students to classify their findings either by source or by culture.

historia de amor

> No, estoy de vacaciones.

> Yo vivo aquí.

Y enseguida se enamoraron.

> ¿Quieres ver los fuegos artificiales?

> ¡Claro que sí!

Alina y Ramiro se llevaban estupendamente y nunca se peleaban.

> Sí, ahora mismo.

> Quiero cambiar este sombrero.

Ramiro cambió el regalo.

Alina y Ramiro se besaron y se abrazaron.

171

LOG BOOK

Have students write down all examples of the preterite and the imperfect in *Una historia de amor.*

Background

Story Words

Here are additional words that students may be interested in knowing:

TYPES OF STORIES

adventure *el libro de aventuras*
biography *la biografía*
children's book *el cuento infantil*
comic book *la historieta, el cómic*
essay *el ensayo*
fairy tale *el cuento de hadas*
fiction *la ficción*
history *la historia*
legend *la leyenda*
mystery *el libro de misterio*
myth *el mito*
novel *la novela*
picture book *el libro de láminas*
romance *la novela romántica*
science fiction *la ciencia ficción*
short story *el cuento*

Para hispanohablantes

Assist other students with their stories.

MEETING INDIVIDUAL NEEDS

Reaching All Students

For Auditory Learners

One student reads aloud *Una historia de amor* and another writes it down. Correct each other's work.

For Visual Learners

Show other groups your story drawings. Have them figure out the plot without showing them the texts.

Objectives
Communicative: to talk about holidays
Cultural: to learn about *carnaval* in the Dominican Republic

Related Components

Audio	Magazine
Conexiones: 17A	Juntos en República
Conexiones	Dominicana
Chapter 6	

 **GETTING STARTED**

Ask students to think of famous carnival celebrations. Ask if anyone has been to one and can describe it.

DISCUSS

Using the Text
Have volunteers read aloud both paragraphs. Ask questions. Suggestions:

El carnaval
¿Qué se celebra en febrero en la República Dominicana?
¿Cómo se celebra?
Da ejemplos de distintas máscaras que se usan para el carnaval.

Día de la Independencia
¿Cuál es el día más importante del carnaval?
¿Cuándo se celebra?
¿Cuántos dominicanos participan en esta fiesta?
¿Cómo son los trajes?

CHECK

Te toca a ti
Possible Answers:
1. *El carnaval se celebra en febrero.*
2. *Es el día más importante porque se celebra el Día de la Independencia.*
3. *Hay un gran desfile.*
4. *La gente se viste con trajes vistosos y divertidos.*
5. *En Santiago se usan las máscaras de lechones. En Montecristi hay máscaras de toros.*

ENTÉRATE
EL CARNAVAL DOMINICANO

En la República Dominicana el carnaval se celebra en febrero. El carnaval es la fiesta más concurrida° del año y se celebra con desfiles y ferias callejeras°. Cada pueblo o ciudad participa en las festividades con máscaras típicas. En Santiago, por ejemplo, se usan las máscaras de lechones° y en Monte Cristi se usan las máscaras de toros°.

Hay muchas fiestas y desfiles; pero la fiesta más importante es la del Día de la independencia, que se celebra el 27 de febrero. Ese día hay un gran desfile por el Malecón° de Santo Domingo, en el que participan más de 30.000 personas disfrazadas con trajes vistosos° y divertidos.

TE TOCA A TI

Contesta las preguntas:

1. ¿Cuándo se celebra el carnaval en la República Dominicana?
2. ¿Por qué el 27 de febrero es el día más importante?
3. ¿Qué hay en el Malecón ese día?
4. ¿Cómo se viste la gente?
5. ¿Cómo son las máscaras de carnaval?

concurrida(o)	*well attended*	los protagonistas	*main figures*
ferias callejeras	*street fairs*	los toros	*bulls*
los lechones	*suckling pigs*	el traje	*costume*
el Malecón	*jetty*	vistosos(as)	*colorful*

172

✓CULTURE NOTE

Carnival is held just before the beginning of Lent. Because Easter is a moveable feast, Carnival usually—but not always—takes place in February. Mardi Gras (Fat Tuesday) is the last time for partying and eating fat until after Holy Week. Among the better-known carnivals are those of Cadiz, Cologne, Munich, New Orleans, Nice, Rio de Janeiro, Seville, and Venice.

Para hispanohablantes

Describe a *carnaval* or other community celebration that you have been to.

VOCABULARIO TEMÁTICO

Lugares
el muelle *dock*
el pueblo costero *beach village*
el pueblo en el campo
  country village
el pueblo pesquero
  fishing village
el puerto *seaport*

Juegos y actividades
Games and activities
coleccionar *to collect*
columpiarse *to swing*
contar cuentos de miedo
  to tell scary stories
ir de pesca *to go fishing*
jugar a las canicas
  to play marbles
jugar al escondite
  to play hide and seek
jugar a las muñecas
  to play with dolls
jugar al rescate *to play tag*
saltar a la cuerda *to jump rope*
ver los fuegos artificiales
  to watch fireworks

Colecciones
Collections
los carritos *toy cars, model cars*
las monedas *coins*
los muñequitos *action figures*
los sellos postales *stamps*

Relaciones
Relationships
Llevarse... *To get along...*
  bien *well*
  estupendamente
    wonderfully, great
  mal *badly*
  maravillosamente
    marvelously
  más o menos *so-so*

Entre amigos
abrazarse *to hug each other*
besarse *to kiss each other*
contarse (o>ue) cuentos
  to tell each other stories
enamorarse *to fall in love*
enojarse
  to get angry with each other
pelearse *to fight with each other*
quererse (e>ie) *to love each other*

Expresiones y palabras
Cuando era pequeño(a)...
When I was little . . .
De niño(a)... *As a child . . .*
¿Dónde creciste?
Where did you grow up?
¿Dónde naciste?
  Where were you born?
Me llevaba... *I got along . . .*
la caña de pescar *fishing pole*
con frecuencia *frequently*
el columpio *swing*
continuamente *continually*
la costumbre *habit*
crecer *to grow up*
cumplir ... años
  to turn... years old
enormemente *enormously*
enseguida
  immediately, at once
el juego *game*
lentamente *slowly*
nacer *to be born*
la niñez *childhood*
pasar *to happen*
el/la pescador(a)
  fisherman,
  fisherwoman
el recuerdo
  memory

LA CONEXIÓN INGLÉS-ESPAÑOL

Spanish words ending in ***-mente*** typically correspond to English words ending in *-ly*:

rápidamente → *rapidly*

Many adverbs that end in *-ly* in English can be formed in Spanish by adding ***-mente*** to the feminine form of the adjective:

ruidosa → ***ruidosamente***

Find the words in the **Vocabulario temático** that follow to this rule.

173

VOCABULARIO TEMÁTICO

Objective
• to review vocabulary

Related Components

Activity Book	Audio
Chapter Review: p. 83-84	Assessment: 14B
Assessment	**Cuaderno**
Listening Script: p. 14	p. 51-52
Chapter Test: p. 75-80	**Transparencies** Ch. 6: Dibujos y palabras Transparency 39

Vocabulary

Point out that this section is organized by themes. Use the headings to review vocabulary. You may wish to ask Spanish speakers to share variations on these words and phrases with the class.

La conexión inglés-español

Some words in the list that end in *-mente* and correspond to English words ending in **-ly** are: *continuamente* (continually), *enormemente* (enormously), *estupendamente* (stupendously, or wonderfully), and *maravillosamente* (marvelously).

ADELANTE

Objectives

Prereading Strategy: to gain meaning from photographs and captions
Cultural: to learn about the popularity of baseball in the Dominican Republic

Related Components

Magazine	Video: Tape/Book
Juntos en República Dominicana	Unit 3: Seg. 4

Scan to Adelante

GETTING STARTED

Ask students where, besides the United States, baseball is popular. Do they know if there are baseball leagues in other countries? (Dominican Republic, Mexico, Venezuela, Puerto Rico, Japan, Taiwan, South Korea, Australia, Holland, and Italy have them.)

Using the Video

Show Segment 4 of the Unit 3 video, an introduction to baseball in the Dominican Republic.

Antes de leer

Have a volunteer read aloud the first paragraph; ask questions.
¿Cuál es el deporte más popular en la República Dominicana?
¿Ese país produce jugadores buenos?
¿Cómo se llama el béisbol en la República Dominicana?

Have students read the second paragraph and make two lists of words: one for sports in general, one for baseball.
Sports List: *jugadores, pelota, posiciones, partido, jugadas, juego, estrella, ligas, equipo, profesional, club(es), jugar, temporadas, récords, campo*
Baseball List: *lanzador, lanzar, base (primera, segunda y tercera), bateador, batear, ponchar, guante, lanzamiento, bate, jonrón, batazo, doblematanza, turnos, "catcher", receptor*

ADELANTE

ANTES DE LEER

Si le preguntas a un dominicano qué es lo mejor de su país, es muy posible que te dé° una lista de jugadores° de pelota. La pelota, o béisbol, es el deporte nacional de la República Dominicana y muchos de sus jugadores están entre los mejores del mundo.

Mira las páginas 174–177. Piensa en las palabras en inglés que relacionas con° el béisbol: los nombres de los jugadores, las posiciones, las jugadas...° Lee el artículo y busca los equivalentes de estas palabras en español. Haz una lista de palabras que tienen relación con los deportes en general y otra lista de palabras que son específicamente del béisbol.

las jugadas *plays*
los jugadores *players*
relacionas con *(you) relate to*
te dé *he/she will give you*

174

ADELANTE COMPONENTS

Activity Book p. 85-88 Assessment Portfolio: p. 37-38	Audio Adelante: 7A, 7B	Magazine Juntos en República Dominicana	Transparencies Unit 3: Adelante Transparencies 40-41 Video: Tape/Book Unit 3: Seg. 4-5

About Sports

Baseball may be the Dominican Republic's national sport, but basketball, boxing, tennis, golf, hunting, fishing, and scuba diving are also popular. The Pablo Duarte Olympic Center is one of the Caribbean's best-equipped sports facilities.

◄Un bateador° se prepara para batear la pelota. Es un momento decisivo del partido: hay un jugador en la segunda base y otro en la tercera.

◄Jugadores del equipo miran el partido desde el banquillo.°

◄Para muchos jóvenes, el béisbol es mucho más que un juego. Ser una estrella del béisbol es un sueño° que comparten muchos niños de la República Dominicana.

el banquillo	ponchar *strike out*
dugout	la segunda/tercera base *second/third base*
el bateador *batter*	el sueño *dream*
la estrella *star*	

175

DISCUSS

Using the Photos

El bateador
¿Qué está haciendo el bateador?
¿Qué pasa si el lanzador poncha a tres bateadores?

En el banquillo
¿Qué miran los jugadores?
¿Dónde están?

Los jóvenes
¿Con qué sueñan muchos jóvenes dominicanos?
¿Sueñas tú con ser una estrella de béisbol? ¿De fútbol? ¿De cine?

Extension: Have students locate the Dominican Republic on a map of the Caribbean. Have them note the country's proximity to the United States.

Para hispanohablantes

Talk about sports played in the country your family came from. Try to find out about some of that country's best-known athletes.

►►►INTERNET LINK

Baseball Links http://www.nando.net:80/SportServer/baseball/

175

Objectives

Reading Strategy: to gain meaning from context

Cultural: to learn about the origins of baseball in the Dominican Republic
• to learn about some famous Dominican baseball players

Related Components

Activity Book p. 85	Audio Tapes Adelante: 7A

GETTING STARTED

Ask students to name some Hispanic professional baseball players.

Background

The influence of Hispanic baseball players on professional baseball in the United States is greater than ever. When the Cleveland Indians went to the World Series in 1995, the team was dominated by Hispanic players: Dominicans Jose Mesa, Tony Peña, Manny Ramirez, and Julian Tavarez; Puerto Ricans Sandy Alomar Jr. and Carlos Baerga; Venezuelans Alvaro Espinoza and Omar Vizquel; and Nicaraguan Dennis Martinez.

Batting championships have been won recently by Julio Franco of the Dominican Republic (1991, American League), Andres Galarraga of Venezuela (1993, National League), and Edgar Martinez, a Hispanic American (1992 and 1995, American League).

Other Hispanic players include: Jose Rijo, Sammy Sosa, and brothers Ramon and Pedro Martinez (D. R.); Roberto Alomar, Juan Gonzalez, Ivan Rodriguez, and Ruben Sierra (Puerto Rico); Jose Canseco and Rafael Palmeiro (Cuba); and Bobby Bonilla and Moises Alou (Hispanic American). Alou's father, Felipe, a Dominican, is currently manager of the Montreal Expos and was voted Manager of the Year in 1994.

Identifying Main Ideas and Details

Have students notice that the subheadings in the text identify main ideas. With your students, construct a chart showing the main ideas and details of the passage.

EL BÉISBOL dominicano
DE AYER Y DE HOY

▲ **Aunque° la República Dominicana es relativamente pequeña, tiene muchos jugadores de béisbol. En las grandes ligas norteamericanas la mayoría de los jugadores extranjeros son dominicanos.**

San Pedro de Macorís es un pueblecito ubicado en el sureste de la República Dominicana. De San Pedro de Macorís han salido muchas de las grandes estrellas del béisbol.

Así° empezó...

Los norteamericanos introdujeron° el béisbol en Cuba en 1860. En 1891 los hermanos Aloma, dos cortadores de caña° cubanos, llevaron el béisbol a la República Dominicana.

El béisbol dominicano empezó en los campos de caña de azúcar. Cuando terminaba la temporada° de la corta de la caña, se jugaba al béisbol. En 1907 se formó° el primer equipo profesional dominicano, el Licey.

La "invasión" dominicana

En 1956 los Gigantes de San Francisco contrataron° a Osvaldo Virgil, el primer jugador de béisbol dominicano en formar parte de las grandes ligas norteamericanas. En 1980, cuarenta y nueve

dominicanos jugaban en Estados Unidos. Entre 1980 y 1990, los clubes norteamericanos contrataron a más de cien jugadores dominicanos, entre ellos a Gerónimo Peña, Tony Peña, José Luis Vizcaíno, Félix José Fermín y Julio César Franco.

Un personaje de ayer: Juan Marichal

Juan Marichal empezó a jugar en las grandes ligas en 1960. Los periodistas lo llamaban el Caballo de

así *this way*	los cortadores de caña *sugar cane cutters*	la temporada *season*
aunque *although*	introdujeron *introduced*	se formó *was formed*
contrataron *signed up*	nace *is born*	

176

Thinking About Language

Point out the suffixes of **lanzador** and **receptor**. Ask students to think of words with this ending. (A few: *matador, actor, jugador, vendedor, refrigerador, escritor, borrador*) Ask what the suffixes **-or** and **-ador** seem to mean. ("Doer [of whatever the stem means]" is one possibility.)

✓ CULTURE NOTE

San Pedro de Macorís (pop. 140,000) is sometimes called "The Cradle of Short-stops." The town has sent 12 of them to the US major leagues in the last 25 years, including Tony Fernandez, an All-Star and Gold Glove winner. Other major leaguers include Joaquín Andújar, George Bell, Julio Franco, Dámaso García, Alfredo Griffin, Pedro Guerrero, Rafael Ramírez, and Juan Samuel.

hierro.° Marichal jugó durante catorce temporadas con los Gigantes de San Francisco y estableció° grandes records, que todavía nadie ha podido batir.° Su nombre está en la lista de los mejores jugadores de la historia.

Un jugador del futuro

El bateador dominicano Miguel Rodríguez nació en Seibo en 1974. Actualmente juega en las grandes ligas de Estados Unidos con los Cerveceros de Milwaukee. En invierno, Rodríguez juega en su país con el equipo de los Azucareros de la Romana.

▲Muchas grandes estrellas de las ligas de Estados Unidos juegan en la liga de invierno de la República Dominicana. Miguel Rodríguez es uno de ellos.

El idioma del béisbol

Como el béisbol se originó en Estados Unidos, en español muchos de sus términos son derivaciones directas del inglés. Fíjate en la siguiente tabla y en la ilustración. ¿Qué palabras no son derivadas del inglés?

el bate	bat
el guante	glove
la pelota	ball
el jonrón	home run
el batazo	hit
la doblematanza	double play
ponchar	to strike out
el campo	baseball diamond
turnos al bate	times at bat

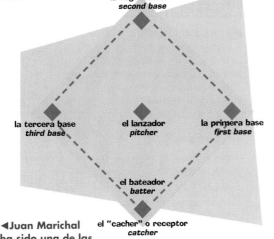

la segunda base
second base

la tercera base
third base

el lanzador
pitcher

la primera base
first base

el bateador
batter

el "cacher" o receptor
catcher

◄Juan Marichal ha sido una de las grandes figuras de la historia del béisbol. Sus trece variedades de lanzamiento° son muy famosas.

el Caballo de hierro *Iron Horse*
estableció *established*
el lanzamiento *throw*

177

DISCUSS

Suggestions for discussion:

El béisbol dominicano

Busca San Pedro de Macorís en un mapa de la República Dominicana.

Así empezó...

¿Dónde está la República Dominicana? ¿Está cerca de Cuba? Busca los dos países en un mapa.
¿Dónde se jugaba el béisbol, en las ciudades o en el campo?

Extension: When is baseball played in the Dominican Republic? (Baseball season in Latin America is generally from November to January. U.S. major leaguers often refer to it as "winter baseball.")

La "invasión" dominicana

¿En qué año jugó Osvaldo Virgil en una liga norteamericana? ¿En qué equipo? ¿Cuántos dominicanos jugaron en Estados Unidos en 1980?
¿Cuántos dominicanos jugaron en Estados Unidos entre 1980 y 1990?

Un personaje de ayer: Juan Marichal

¿Cuándo empezó Marichal a jugar en las grandes ligas?
¿En qué equipo jugaba?
¿Cómo lo llamaban los periodistas?

Un jugador del futuro

¿Cuántos años tiene Miguel Rodríguez?
¿Te gusta su equipo en Estados Unidos? ¿Por qué?
¿Conoces su otro equipo?
¿Qué equipos dominicanos conoces?

El idioma del béisbol

¿De qué idioma derivan muchas palabras del béisbol en español?

CHECK

- *¿Quiénes introdujeron el béisbol en la República Dominicana? ¿En qué año?*
- *¿Quién es Osvaldo Virgil?*
- *¿Quiénes son otros jugadores dominicanos famosos?*

LOG BOOK

Have students describe baseball in Spanish, including how many players are on a team, the names of the positions, and various plays.

These activities can be done as classwork or as homework.

Objectives
Organizing Skills: to use lists and tables to organize information
Communication Skills: to develop vocabulary

Related Components

Activity Book	Assessment
p. 86	Portfolio: p. 37-38

ACTIVITIES

1. Deportes en español
Individual Activities
A. Use the baseball information on the preceding pages to complete the chart.
Answers:
Número de jugadores: *nueve*
Posiciones: *lanzador; receptor; primera, segunda y tercera base; jardinero corto; jardineros izquierdo, central y derecho.*
¿Qué necesitas?: *un bate, un guante, una pelota y un campo*
Otras palabras: *bateador, ponchar, lanzamiento, jonrón, batazo, doblematanza, turno*
B. Use a dictionary or encyclopedia, or consult your teacher to create a similar chart for another sport you enjoy.
Answers: Answers will vary.

2. Tu diccionario
Individual Activity In Spanish, many sports words come from English. Make a list of sports words. What do they mean? Start your own Spanish dictionary of sports terms.
Answers: record, champion, soccer ball, tennis racquet, golf, ice hockey

3. Compruébalo
Individual Activity Say which are true or false. Correct the false statements.
Possible Answers:
1. *Cierta.*
2. *Cierta.*
3. *Falsa. Juan Marichal no juega actualmente.*
4. *Cierta*
5. *Falsa. En esos años contrataron a más de cien jugadores dominicanos.*

---

❶ Deportes en español

A. Completa la tabla según la información del artículo.

NÚMERO DE JUGADORES

POSICIONES
primera base

béisbol

¿QUÉ NECESITAS?
un bate

OTRAS PALABRAS
el jonrón
el batazo

B. Escoge un deporte que te guste. Con la ayuda de un diccionario y tu profesor(a), completa la tabla. También puedes buscar información en la enciclopedia.

BALONCESTO			
NÚMERO DE JUGADORES	POSICIONES	¿QUÉ NECESITAS?	OTRAS PALABRAS
12 (5 en la cancha)	*defensor, aleros*	*la canasta*	*la cancha*

❷ Tu diccionario

En español, muchas palabras relacionadas con los deportes provienen del inglés. Haz una lista de palabras usadas en los deportes. ¿Qué significan? Haz tu propio minidiccionario de deportes.

el récord
el campeón/la campeona
el balón de fútbol
la raqueta de tenis
el golf
el hockey sobre hielo

❸ Compruébalo

Según el texto, di cuáles de las siguientes oraciones son ciertas o falsas. Corrige las oraciones falsas.
1. El Licey fue el primer equipo profesional dominicano.
2. Los dominicanos jugaban al béisbol en los campos de caña de azúcar.
3. Actualmente, Juan Marichal juega con los Gigantes de San Francisco.
4. En las grandes ligas de béisbol norteamericanas la mayoría de los jugadores extranjeros son dominicanos.
5. Entre 1980 y 1990 los clubes americanos contrataron a 100 jugadores dominicanos.

Research Project
Have students choose a sport to research. They should various reference sources—such as, encyclopedias, newspapers, documentaries, etc.—to gather information. Ask them to organize that information in categories (e.g., *historia del deporte, jugadores(as) famosos(as), campeonatos,* etc.).

TALLER DE ESCRITORES

1. TU JUGADOR DE BÉISBOL FAVORITO

Haz una tarjeta de béisbol en español sobre tu jugador favorito. Incluye el nombre, dónde nació, con qué equipo juega, qué récords tiene y toda la información que puedas encontrar.

2. ENTREVISTA

Entrevista a un familiar. Puede ser uno de tus padres o de tus abuelos: tiene que ser mayor que tú. Pregúntale cómo eran las cosas cuando era joven. Antes de hacer la entrevista prepara una lista de preguntas.

- ¿Dónde creció?
- ¿A qué jugaba cuando era pequeño(a)?
- ¿Le gustaba la escuela?

3. LA ANÉCDOTA MÁS DIVERTIDA

Escribe una anécdota de tu vida o de alguien que conoces, en seis oraciones (más o menos). Lee tu anécdota a la clase. La clase vota por la anécdota más divertida.

4. ESCRIBE UNA CARTA

Escribe una carta a un(a) estudiante de otro país describiéndole las actividades extraescolares o deportes que ofrece tu escuela. Cuéntale qué haces generalmente después de la escuela.

Querida Ana:
Mi escuela tiene varios equipos deportivos. Puedes jugar al fútbol americano, al béisbol, al baloncesto... Yo juego al baloncesto. Todos los sábados tenemos un partido contra equipos de otras escuelas.

179

Para hispanohablantes

Tell the class what you admire about your favorite Hispanic athlete or public figure.

TALLER DE ESCRITORES

Objectives
- to practice writing
- to use vocabulary from this unit

Related Components

Activity Book	Assessment
p. 87	Portfolio: p. 37-38

ACTIVITIES

1. Tu jugador de béisbol favorito
Individual Activity Students will create a baseball card of a favorite player. They should include the player's name, birthplace, team, records, and any other useful information they find.

2. Entrevista
Individual Activity Students will interview an older person about his or her childhood. Questions should include:
- Where did you grow up?
- What games did you play as a child?
- Did you like school?

3. La anécdota más divertida
Individual and Pair Activity Students will write six sentences, more or less, about an anecdote from their own life or a friend's life.
Edit: Pairs exchange stories, and review and edit each other's work. They should circle words they think are misspelled, and make notes about possible errors. Together, they will check spelling and grammar, and prepare final drafts.
Present: Students read their final drafts aloud to the class. The class votes on the funniest anecdote.

4. Escribe una carta
Individual Activity Students write a letter to a student abroad describing their school's extracurricular activities or sports. Students should include what activities they generally take part in after school. (Ask students to use the impersonal **se** form where possible.)

PORTFOLIO
Have students select one of these assignments to add to their Portfolios.

Objectives
Communicative: to listen to and understand directions
Cultural: to learn about the role of maracas in Hispanic culture and music
• to make maracas

Related Components

Assessment	Video: Tape/Book
Portfolio: p. 37-38	Unit 3: Seg. 5
Transparencies	
Unit 3: Project	
Transparency 40	

Scan to La obra

Materials
• 2 small, empty cereal boxes (you can also use two small plastic bottles)
• 2 wood sticks
• beans
• a saw
• glue or masking tape
• scissors
• colored paper or paint
• a ruler and a pencil

GETTING STARTED

Encourage students to use their eyes more than their ears. Rather than try to understand every word, they should focus on the actions and listen only for clues.
If possible, show the maracas-making segment of the Unit 3 video.

DISCUSS

Have students read aloud the two paragraphs. Ask questions, such as:
¿Son las maracas un instrumento moderno?
¿Qué encontraron los arqueólogos?
¿Con qué estaban relacionadas las maracas?
¿En qué tipo de música se usan maracas?
¿Les gusta oír las maracas?

MANOS A LA OBRA

AL RITMO° DE MARACAS

¿Sabías que las maracas son uno de los instrumentos más antiguos del mundo? Los arqueólogos encontraron objetos prehistóricos similares a las maracas. Muchas culturas relacionaban las maracas con los poderes° sobrenaturales. Por eso, eran un elemento muy importante en las ceremonias religiosas. Hoy las maracas son sólo un instrumento de percusión que da ritmo y alegría° a la música que acompañan.°

TE TOCA A TI

Las maracas se usan° en casi todos los ritmos latinos: en la salsa, el mambo, la cumbia, la guaracha, el merengue, el chachachá, el jazz afrocubano y muchos más. Vamos a hacer unas maracas. ¡Pon tu cinta de música latina favorita!

Materiales
• dos cajitas de cereales vacías° (también puedes usar dos botellas pequeñas de plástico)
• dos palos de madera
• frijoles
• una sierra°
• pegamento o cinta adhesiva
• tijeras
• papel de colores o pinturas
• una regla y un lápiz

acompañan *they accompany*   se usan *are used*
la alegría *joy*   la sierra *saw*
los poderes *powers*   vacías *empty*
el ritmo *rhythm*

180

Research Project
Have students think of a musical instrument they would like to know more about. Ask them to do research on the instrument, using the library and other sources. Have them organize their information in categories such as *historia, intérpretes famosos,* etc.

1 Abre las cajas y vacíalas.° (Guarda los cereales.) Pégalas° con la cinta adhesiva.

2 Haz un agujero° en cada caja.

3 Mete° los frijoles dentro de las cajas. Después ciérralas. Pégalas con la cinta adhesiva.

4 Con la sierra corta los palos. Deben medir unas nueve pulgadas. Mete un palo por el agujero de cada caja y sujétalo con cinta adhesiva.

5 Envuelve° las cajas con papel de colores.

6 Decora las maracas a tu gusto. ¡Y ya puedes tocarlas!

el agujero *hole*	**pégalas** *seal them*
envuelve *wrap*	**vacíalas** *empty them*
mete *place*	

Objectives

Communicative: to expand reading comprehension
Cultural: to relate the study of Spanish to other subject areas

Related Components

Activity Book p. 88	Transparencies Unit 3: Adelante Transparency 41
Assessment Portfolio: p. 37-38	Video: Tape/Book Unit 3: Seg. 4
Audio Adelante: 7B	

Scan to Adelante

El arte naïf de la República Dominicana

About Naive Art

Naive art, also known as primitive art, is known for bright colors and a literal-minded vision. Interest in the freshness and directness of naive art was prompted by exhibitions of art from Africa and the South Pacific at the turn of the century. The French painters Paul Gauguin and Henri Rousseau, and the Spaniard Pablo Picasso were among the first to recognize the originality of art from other traditions. Have volunteers read aloud and answer the questions on the student page.
Answers:
• *Es sencilla.*
• *Pintan paisajes del campo, la costa y escenas de la vida cotidiana.*

Activities

A. Have students say whether the following statements are true or false.
1. *Los pintores naïf dominicanos estudian en la Galería de Arte Moderno. (Falso)*
2. *La vida cotidiana es un tema muy común de la pintura naïf. (Cierto)*
B. Encourage students who have artistic interests to do paintings in this style.

Language Note

Art naïf is a French art term that describes a particular style. There is no Spanish cognate for *naive*.

 ARTE

EL ARTE NAÏF DE LA REPÚBLICA DOMINICANA

En la República Dominicana al igual que en Haití, el arte naïf o primitivista tiene gran aceptación. Por lo general los artistas naïf no tienen educación formal y han aprendido a pintar solos°. Muchos son campesinos° o hijos de campesinos que viven en la ciudad. Sus pinturas tienden a ser sencillas. Algunos pintan paisajes de la costa y el campo. Otros pintan escenas de la vida cotidiana°.

• ¿Cómo es la pintura naïf?
• ¿Qué pintan los artistas naïf?

 MINERALOGÍA

EL ÁMBAR°

¿Sabías que las minas de ámbar más importantes y grandes del mundo están en el norte de la República Dominicana, en la Costa del Ámbar?

El ámbar es resina fosilizada° de árboles que vivieron hace más de cuarenta millones de años. A veces esta resina contiene plantas o insectos. Los indígenas de la República Dominicana creían° que el ámbar era la luz° del sol convertida en° piedra. Para ellos el ámbar era una piedra mágica y la usaban como amuleto.°

• ¿Dónde están las minas de ámbar más importantes del mundo?
• ¿Qué creían que era el ámbar los indígenas de la República Dominicana?

el ámbar *amber*	creían *believed*	sencilla *simple*
el amuleto *charm*	la luz *light*	solos *on their own*
los campesinos *peasants*	la resina fosilizada *fossilized resin*	la vida cotidiana *everyday life*
convertida en *turned into*		

182

El ámbar

About Amber

Resins are gummy materials mixed with oils in trees. When the resins become hard, they form amber. Amber is primarily used to make jewelry. The insects often found inside amber were trapped there when the material was still sticky, and were eventually covered.

Have volunteers read aloud and answer the questions on the student page.
Answers:
• *Están en el norte de la República Dominicana, en la Costa del Ámbar.*
• *Creían que era la luz del sol convertida en piedra.*

Activity

Read aloud the paragraph and ask questions:
¿Qué es el ámbar?
¿Qué puede contener?
¿Has visto ámbar alguna vez? ¿Cómo es?
¿Por qué hay insectos en el ámbar?

BIOLOGÍA

Paraíso° de coral

Bajo las aguas marinas de la República Dominicana el paisaje es tan hermoso como en la superficie.° Hay corales de diferentes tipos y colores. Los más conocidos son los de color blanco, rojo y negro, que es muy escaso.° Cuando un coral muere, sus restos° forman las playas de arena blanca de la costa dominicana.

- ¿De qué color es el coral?
- ¿Qué pasa cuando un coral muere?

ECONOMÍA

La pesca, tradición y deporte

La pesca es una actividad tradicional en la República Dominicana. Allí hay una gran variedad de peces y muchos mariscos. Los indígenas° fueron los primeros pescadores. Antes de la llegada de los españoles, el pescado era el alimento° principal de los indígenas.

El pescador dominicano usa la red, las trampas metálicas° y la caña. También usa anzuelos° con espejos para atraer° a los peces. Los dominicanos son grandes aficionados° a la pesca de caña.° Este deporte es muy común en todo el país.

- ¿Quiénes fueron los primeros pescadores de la República Dominicana?
- ¿Para qué ponen espejos en los anzuelos los pescadores?

los aficionados *fans*	la caña *fishing rod*	los peces *fish (alive)*
el alimento *food*	escaso *scarce*	los restos *remains*
los anzuelos *hooks*	los indígenas *original inhabitants*	la superficie *surface*
atraer *to attract*	el paraíso *paradise*	las trampas metálicas *metal traps*

183

Paraíso de coral

About Coral
Coral is a limestone formation created by the skeletons of millions of tiny marine animals. Sometimes formations build up enough to form coral islands.
Coral cannot exist in water colder than 65 degrees Fahrenheit.
Have volunteers read aloud and answer the questions on the student page.
Answers:
- *Puede ser de diferentes colores. Los colores de coral más conocidos son blanco, rojo y negro.*
- *Forma playas de arena blanca.*

Activity
Have students say whether the following statements are true or false.
1. *El paisaje submarino de la República Dominicana es muy bonito. (Cierto)*
2. *Sólo existe un tipo de coral. (Falso)*
3. *Hay mucho coral negro. (Falso)*

La pesca, tradición y deporte

About Food Production
Although the Dominican Republic is almost completely surrounded by water, fishing is not the main source of food. Sugar, coffee, cocoa, corn, rice, beans, tomatoes, and plantains are the most important crops.
Meat and dairy production are increasing.
Have volunteers read aloud and answer the questions on the student page.
Answers:
- *Los indígenas.*
- *Los ponen para atraer a los peces.*

Activity
Have students say whether the following statements are true or false.
1. *La pesca es algo nuevo en la República Dominicana. (Falso)*
2. *Antes de la llegada de los españoles, los indígenas no comían mucho pescado. (Falso)*
3. *Los españoles introdujeron la pesca en la República Dominicana. (Falso)*

Research Project
Have students do additional research on one of the selections in *Otras fronteras*. Help students information categories relevant to their topic of choice. Then have students organize their findings according to those categories.

ARGENTINA
DOS ESCENAS DE LA VIDA COTIDIANA

Tell your students...

In this unit we travel to Argentina, the second largest country in Latin America. One-third of the population lives in Buenos Aires, and our trip begins with a week in this vibrant capital (Chapter 7). Then we're off for a week on an *estancia*, one of the huge grassland estates that are half ranch, half farm (Chapter 8). In Buenos Aires, we sample some regional delicacies, visit a fascinating flea market, and buy supplies for a home cookout. The next day, we're on the *estancia*, where life's a lot different than in Buenos Aires. We watch *gauchos* as they tame wild horses. We go for a horse-and-buggy ride and try a *danza criolla*. We're certainly ready for the barbecue afterwards!

Before leaving Argentina, we take a whirlwind tour of the country, admiring its wide variety of climates and landscapes. We travel from the roar of the falls in tropical Iguazu to the ferocious surf in frigid Tierra del Fuego. We see icebergs and the peaks of Aconcagua and Mount Fitz Roy. Hungry again, we make our own *empanadas* and wash them down with some *mate*.

VIDEO LINKS

Corresponding Video Segments

Text	
Unit Overview Unit Opener	**1. Introduction to Argentina** Argentina and its people from the Andes to the Pampas to Tierra del Fuego
Chapter 7	**2. Un fin de semana en Buenos Aires** Pool party, shopping for food, patio cookout, dancing the tango Grammar: irregular preterites; past participles
Chapter 8	**3. Una semana en una estancia** Farm life, swimming and boating, watching *gauchos* tame wild horses, rounding up cattle on horseback Grammar: **tener que** + infinitive; **es** + adjective + infinitive; **por** and **para**
Adelante	**4. Adelante** The Palermo zoo: llamas, snakes, penguins, and other Argentinean animals
Manos a la obra	**5. Manos a la obra** How to make an Argentinean *empanada*

Geography and Climate

The second largest South American country after Brazil, Argentina covers an area of 1.07 million square miles (2.8 million square kilometers). It takes up most of the southern tip of the continent, except for the long sliver of Chile on the west coast. In the north, a wooded subtropical region borders Bolivia, Paraguay, Uruguay, and Brazil. In the west are the Andes mountains. The Pampas, an enormous grassy plain ideal for cattle grazing, takes up most of the country's center. In the south, Patagonia's windy barren plateaus give way to icy lakes and snow-capped peaks; even farther south are the island of Tierra del Fuego and the Argentine Antarctic. Argentina's climate varies greatly: rainy and hot in the north, temperate in the center, cold and windy in the south.

History and Government

Much of Argentina's history revolves around its capital, Buenos Aires. First settled by the Spanish in 1580, when Argentina was part of the colony of Peru, it became the capital of the viceroyalty of Río de la Plata in 1776. Buenos Aires was also the first Latin American city to rebel against Spain. General José de San Martín successfully defended the city and led the country to independence in 1816.

Argentina prospered from about 1880 until the start of the great depression in the 1930s. Rich grazing land and fertile farmlands helped to make it a major agricultural exporter. Immigrants, mostly from Spain and Italy, came in great numbers. During this period, stylish and culturally oriented Buenos Aires became known as the "Paris of South America."

In 1944 Juan Perón seized power in a military coup and for the next 11 years ran the country as a dictator. He and his charismatic wife Eva were revered by their supporters, including those Eva called her *descamisados,* or "shirtless ones"—destitute Argentines who benefited from the social programs put in place by the Peróns. Eva, called Evita by adoring crowds, died at the age of 31 in 1952. Perón was soon ousted and took refuge in Spain, though he returned to power in 1973. A year later he died at the age of 79.

A military reign of terror followed soon after, and thousands who resisted the regime were killed. Argentine politics improved greatly when a democratically elected civilian government came to power in 1983.

Jorge Luis Borges

Dancers and music lovers know Argentina's tangos. Cowboy buffs have probably heard of Argentina's *gauchos.* Historians and playgoers can't get enough of the Peróns. But many readers with an intimate sense of Argentina learned what they know from the brilliant work of Jorge Luis Borges (1899–1986). Tangos and *gauchos* figure prominently in Borges's poems and stories.

Gauchos y vaqueros*

SOCIAL STUDIES CONNECTION

Objective
- to compare the Argentine *gaucho* and the North American cowboy

Use
any time during Unit 4

Materials
- bilingual dictionary
- TRB Activity Support Page 15, *Gauchos y vaqueros**

Activity
- Share the FYI and compare the Argentine *gaucho* with the North American cowboy (Canada, US, Mexico). Ask students to contribute information.
- On the chalkboard have students list characteristics that a *gaucho* and a cowboy might share, first in English and then in Spanish, looking up words in a bilingual dictionary. For example: solitary/*solitario,* rough/*rudo,* impulsive/*impulsivo,* strong/*fuerte,* brave/*valiente,* wanderer/*itinerante,* expert horseman/*gran jinete.*
- Distribute Activity Support Page. Have students fill in blanks and compare the outfits and equipment used by *gauchos* and cowboys. For example: *Los dos usan sombreros de ala* ancha para protegerse del sol. Los dos llevan botas.*

FYI
Argentina's cowhands on horseback appeared on the *pampas* and in Argentine folklore during the 18th and 19th centuries, when large herds of Spanish horses and cattle roamed the expansive rolling grasslands near Buenos Aires. Today *gauchos* still wear a wide belt/*cinturón,* a woolen poncho, pleated pants/ *bombachas,* and high leather boots. They still carry a lasso, a knife/*facón,* and connected leather cords weighted at the ends which they throw at animals' legs to stop them/*boleadoras.* But while *gauchos* of 150 years ago herded cattle, repaired fences, and tamed horses, modern *gauchos,* like today's cowboys, also repair engines and vaccinate cattle. The old customs are still evident, though, when they gather around the campfire after a hard day's work and eat grilled beef/*asado,* drink *mate,* play guitar, and sing about love and the *gaucho* code of honor.
  *****ala** brim; literally, wing
  *****vaqueros** cowboys

Mate

HANDS ON: COOKING

Objective
- to prepare and drink *mate,* the Argentine national beverage

Use
any time during Unit 4

Ingredients
- 1/2 oz. *mate* powder (see FYI)
- 1 cup water, hot but not boiling
- pinch of sugar

Supplies
- TRB Activity Support Page 16, *Mate*
- *pava* (kettle)
- *mate* gourd or large cup; small paper cups
- *bombilla* (silver sipping straw with strainer at bottom) or paper straws

Preparation
- Put *mate* and sugar in the *mate* gourd (or cup) and add a cup of hot water.
- Let the *mate* powder steep for 3–5 minutes before drinking through a *bombilla* or a straw. Keep straws away from the grounds at bottom.
- Argentines sit in a circle and pass the *mate* clockwise. When more water is needed, the *cebador* (server) adds it from the *pava* always on the stove in Argentine homes. Tell students this as you pour their *mate* into small paper cups.
- Half an ounce of good *mate* can produce five or six excellent large-cup infusions, which should be enough for 30 students.

FYI
Mate is the dried and powdered leaves of a wild holly found in Uruguay, Paraguay, and Argentina. In Argentina *mate* drinking is an elaborate ritual. The *mates* are either simple gourds or made of carved wood, engraved and chased silver, or aluminum. The *cebador* puts the mate into the gourd and slowly pours hot water over the powder. *Mate* can be drunk *dulce* (with sugar) or *amargo* (without sugar). It can also be served with milk or lemon juice. In the US *mate* is available in health food stores and in specialty stores, such as Argentine bakeries.

Antártida Argentina

GAME

Objective
- to play a game about an almost unknown region of Argentina—in Antarctica

Use
any time during Unit 4

Materials
- TRB Activity Support Page 17, *Antártida Argentina* (map)

Activity
- Share the FYI and give Spanish equivalents for words students don't know, e.g., *Antártida, continente, siglo,* etc. Write facts on chalkboard, erasing them after they have been discussed.
- Select a scorekeeper, and form two teams that will trade facts about the Argentine Antarctic. For example, the first person on Team A might say: *La Antártida es un continente al sur del mundo.* Team B might follow with: *James Cook exploró la Antártida en el siglo dieciocho.*
- If someone can't remember a fact or says something incorrect, his/her team has one minute to come up with another fact. If the team can't, it loses a turn.
- The game continues until neither team can come up with a new fact. Then the scorekeeper tallies each team's facts and announces the winner.

FYI
Most people don't know it, but Argentina's national boundaries include a 400,000-square-mile sector of Antarctica, the gigantic continent around the South Pole. Antarctica's ice cap, 10,000 feet thick, hides abundant mineral resources, and Argentina claims a wedge between longitudes 25°W and 74°W that overlaps Chilean and British claims. The Argentine mining business is not yet fully developed there, but already tourists brave rough seas and mountainous icebergs to visit scientific research stations and to see the breeding grounds of seals, wild geese, ducks, and penguins.

¿Qué es un argentino?

SOCIAL STUDIES CONNECTION

Objective
- to explore and graph the composition of Argentina's population

Use
at the end of Unit 4

Materials
- reference books on Argentina
- posterboard
- crayons, markers, colored pencils
- magazine photos

Activity
- Form small groups and share the FYI below.
- Have a student write facts and statistics on the chalkboard as they are discussed.
- Each group plans a poster that shows the national backgrounds of Argentina's population, using a pie chart, a bar graph, or flags to represent the different countries, while others write a paragraph based on facts gathered from the text or reference books. For example: *Argentina es una nación de inmigrantes europeos. Los argentinos hablan español, pero el 45 por ciento son de origen italiano,* etc.
- Groups illustrate, label, and display the posters.

FYI
Like the US, Argentina is a nation of immigrants. The original inhabitants were spread across the land in small tribes, and for 300 years foreign settlers were mostly Spanish. This led to a *mestizo* population (Indian, Spanish) and, when African slaves came, to a *mulato* population (black, indigenous, white). Then, between 1857 and 1939, more than 3,500,000 European workers immigrated to Argentina—Italian (45%), Spanish (30%), French, Polish, Russian, Swiss, Welsh, German, Danish, and British. In some cities the immigrants outnumbered native Argentines. Of the 33,000,000 Argentines today, 85% are of European descent and the remaining 15% are of Indian, *mestizo,* Asian, and Arab descent. No wonder some Argentines ask: Are we Europeans or Latin Americans?

ARGENTINA: DOS ESCENAS DE LA VIDA COTIDIANA

Communicative Objectives
- to introduce Argentina
- to talk about city and country life

Related Components

Transparencies	Transparencies
Unit 4: Chapters 7-8	42-54
	Video: Tape/Book
	Unit 4: Seg. 1

Scan to Unit 4

GETTING STARTED

Before students open their books, ask them what they know about Argentina. Write their comments on the board.
If no one has any thoughts on the matter, ask them to comment on the photos on these pages.

Using the Video

Show Segment 1 of the Unit 4 video, an introduction to Argentina.

Using the Transparencies

To help orient students, use the Locator Map Transparency. You may want to use other Unit 4 transparencies at this time.

DISCUSS

Presenting Argentina

For more information about Argentina, refer to pages 184A–184D.

Using the Text

English: After students read the introduction, ask questions. For example:
Which would you prefer to visit: a city like Buenos Aires or the grassy plains of the pampas? Why?
Spanish: Have students scan the lefthand page for unfamiliar words.
¿Qué es la vida cotidiana? Es lo que hacemos cada día, ¿no?
¿Qué palabra en inglés es como gastronomía?

UNIDAD 4

ARGENTINA

DOS ESCENAS DE LA VIDA COTIDIANA

En la unidad 4:

Capítulo 7	¡Un fin de semana en Buenos Aires!
Capítulo 8	Una semana en una estancia
Adelante	**Para leer:** Argentina, tierra de contrastes
	Proyecto: Empanadas argentinas
	Otras fronteras: Deporte, gastronomía, arte y cine

Caballos en Patagonia, en el sur de Argentina.
Calle Florida, una calle en el centro de Buenos Aires.

184

UNIT COMPONENTS

Activity Book p. 89-112	**Audio Book** Script: p. 45-47; 51-53	**Conexiones** Chapters 7-8	**Transparencies** Unit 4: Chapters 7-8
Assessment Oral Proficiency: p. 27-28	Activities: p. 48-50; 54-56	**Cuaderno** p. 53-68	**Transparencies** 42-54
Listening Script: p. 15-16	**Audio** Chapter: 8A, 8B	**Magazine** Juntos en Argentina	**Tutor Pages** p. 31-38
Chapter Tests: p. 81-92	Adelante: 9A, 9B Assessment: 15A		**Video: Tape/Book** Unit 4: Segments 1-5
Portfolio: p. 39-40	Conexiones: 17B		

Welcome to Argentina, the second largest country in South America. In this land of vivid contrasts, 86% of the population lives in cosmopolitan cities that are centers of industry, trade, and culture. Other Argentines live on huge *estancias,* or ranches, either in the pampas, a large area of grassy plains, or in the southern region known as Patagonia.

In this unit, you will experience daily life in two areas of Argentina. In the capital, Buenos Aires, you will join a family to shop and prepare food for a holiday celebration. Then you will travel to the pampas and take part in life on an *estancia.*

Your stay in Argentina will also include a visit to some of its exciting landscapes: the spectacular Iguazú Falls on the border of Argentina and Brazil, the snowcapped Andes mountains separating Argentina and Chile, and the glaciers of the island of Tierra del Fuego. Finally, you will learn to make a traditional Argentinian dish— *empanadas.*
¡Buen provecho!

185

INTERDISCIPLINARY CONNECTIONS

To provide other perspectives, have students research questions like these:

History

What island group has been a source of conflict between Argentina and England since 1833?
(The Falkland Islands, located 250 miles off the Argentine coast and known as *Las Islas Malvinas* to Argentines. The dispute flared as recently as 1982, when Argentina assumed military control of the islands, only to have them retaken by British troops.)

Arts

What Broadway musical dealt with an Argentinian political figure?
(The political and personal life of Eva Duarte de Perón, the wife of former Argentine president Juan Perón, was brought to the stage in Andrew Lloyd Webber's 1978 musical *Evita.*)

	Objetivos page 187 *¡Un fin de semana en Buenos Aires!*	Conversemos pages 188-189 *Las celebraciones y tú*	Realidades pages 190-191 *Mapa gastronómico de Argentina*	Palabras en acción pages 192-193 *¡Es hora de comer!*
Comunicación	To talk about: • planning and preparing for holiday celebrations	Discuss plans and preparations for special holiday events	Read map, discuss holiday foods, make table	Read cartoon, discuss characters; talk about special dish; make poster
	• cooking special meals	Discuss cooking special dishes	Read map, talk about eating in Argentina, create dialog, discuss holiday foods, make table	Read cartoon, discuss characters; talk about special dish; make poster
Cultura	To learn about: • the agriculture of Argentina • weekend activities in Buenos Aires • the use of *vos* in Argentina		Map of Argentina with foods from different regions; descriptions of regional specialties	
Vocabulario temático	To know expressions for: • certain holiday foods	Talk about holiday foods	Read map, talk about eating in Argentina, create dialog, discuss holiday foods, make table	Read cartoon, discuss characters; talk about special dish; make poster
	• cooking and recipes	Talk about cooking and recipes	Read map, talk about eating in Argentina	Read cartoon, make list; discuss characters; talk about kitchen items; discuss favorite dish; make poster; write paragraph
	• how to prepare a meal	Talk about preparing a meal	Read map, talk about eating in Argentina	Read cartoon, discuss characters; discuss favorite dish; make poster; write paragraph
Estructura	To talk about: • how long you have been doing something: *hace...que* + verb	Use *hace...que* + verb to discuss how long ago something was done	Read map, create dialog	Read cartoon, discuss characters
	• what you or someone else did: verbs with an irregular stem in the preterite	Use verbs with irregular stem in preterite to discuss what someone did	Read map, talk about eating in Argentina, create dialog	Read cartoon, discuss characters; talk about special dish; create dialog
	• food and other party preparations, using past participles	Use past participles to discuss food and other party preparations	Read map, talk about eating in Argentina, create dialog, discuss holiday foods, make table	Read cartoon, discuss favorite dish; talk about special dish; write paragraph

Para comunicarnos mejor (1) pages 194-195 ¿Cuánto tiempo hace que viven en Buenos Aires?	Para comunicarnos mejor (2) pages 196-197 ¿Está puesta la mesa?	Situaciones pages 198-199 Guía para el fin de semana	Para resolver pages 200-201 ¡Es hora de comer!	Enterate page 202 ¿Che, tenés hambre?
Discuss previous weekend	Act out preparations for a New Year's meal	Read text, create dialog; act out interview; write in diary	Make lists; write recipe steps; present recipe to class	Discuss the different ways people speak Spanish
Discuss previous weekend	Act out preparations for a New Year's meal; discuss making *flan;* make table, report to class	Read text, discuss things to do in Buenos Aires; create dialog; act out interview; write in diary	Make lists; write recipe steps; present recipe to class	
	Create a dialog about New Year's dinner in Buenos Aires.	Announcements about weekend activities in Buenos Aires; information on cosmopolitian Buenos Aires	Infomation about popular desserts in Argentina; recipe for *flan*	Cultural note on the use of *vos, che,* and other Argentine vocabulary
Discuss previous weekend	Act out preparations for a New Year's meal			
Discuss previous weekend	Act out preparation for a New Year's meal; discuss making *flan;* make table, report to class	**Re-entry of vocabulary**		**Extension of vocabulary**
Discuss previous weekend	Act out preparations for a New Year's meal; discuss making *flan;* make table, report to class			
Read text, answer questions; discuss lapsed time				
Read text, answer questions; discuss lapsed time; discuss previous weekend	Act out preparations for a New Year's meal	**Re-entry of structure**		**Extension of structure**
Discuss previous weekend	Act out preparations for a New Year's meal; discuss making flan; make table, report to class			

Pruébalo

ACTIVITY

Objective
- to discuss where foods come from, how they're sold, and the recipes that make them taste best, using Chapter 7 *Vocabulario temático*

Use
after *Palabras en acción,* pages 192-193

Materials
- food pictures from magazines and newspapers
- large manila envelope
- masking tape
- posterboard

Preparation
- Have students bring in pictures of food items mentioned in Chapter 7.

Activity
- Place pictures in envelope, making sure there's one picture per student, and have each student select one without showing it to classmates.
- Each student writes a description of his/her food item, telling where it comes from, how it is sold, and the recipes that make it taste best. For example, Student A selects *aceite de oliva* and writes a description without mentioning it by name: *Está hecho en Europa y en América Latina. Se compra en botella por litro o cuarto de galón.* Se usa para preparar comida frita y para ensaladas. ¿Qué es?*
- A student who identifies an item presents the next item. But if his/her identification is incorrect, select another volunteer.
- When all food items have been identified, students tape the pictures to the chalkboard for other students to name and discuss. For instance, Student C points to a picture of onions. Another student says: *Son cebollas, se compran por kilo o por libra. También hay paquetes de 5 libras o 5 kilos. En los Estados Unidos, muchas vienen de California. Se usan en ensaladas y con hamburguesas. A mí me gustan mucho.*
- Use pictures for a classroom poster that incorporates the written descriptions.

***cuarto de galón** quart

¿Cuánto tiempo hace?

GAME

Objective
- to discuss ongoing actions using **hace** + expression of time + **que** + verb in present or present progressive tense

Use
after *Para comunicarnos mejor,* pages 194-195

Materials
- one 3" x 5" index card, cut in half, per student pair

Activity
- Have each student pair select an occupation—a *panadero,* for example, or a *cocinero.* It can also be someone from public life, such as a politician, an actor, or a singer.
- The pair writes one occupation/person on a card half. These card halves are collected and redistributed.
- On the remaining card half, the student pair writes five questions about the person and his/her profession that can be answered by using the **hace...que** construction. For example: *¿Cuántos años hace que vives en la misma casa? ¿Cuánto tiempo hace que tienes la misma ocupación? ¿Cuánto tiempo hace que nació su hija? ¿Cuánto tiempo hace que haces footing* por las mañanas? ¿Cuánto tiempo hace que tocas el saxofón?*
- The pair that receives the card half with *el presidente de los Estados Unidos* answers the questions prepared by the pair who wrote them.
- Classmates listen carefully to guess the person interviewed.
- After all interviews have been presented, students decide which one they like best.

***footing** jogging

Del dicho al hecho*

WRITING CONNECTION

Objective
- to write and tell a story, using verbs with irregular stems in the preterite

Use
after *Para comunicarnos mejor,* pages 194-195

Materials
- writing pads
- 8 3" x 5" index cards, cut in half

Activity
- Divide the class into groups of eight and give each group a writing pad.
- Have someone from each group write the infinitive of one of the eight irregular-stem preterite verbs on an index-card half: **estar, poder, poner, querer, saber, tener, traer, venir.**
- Group members choose a playing order, shuffle their cards, and pick one card each.
- They decide on a title and a plot for a story set in Argentina with Argentine characters. The main character could be a *gaucho,* a tango interpreter, a soccer player, a wine producer, a meat packer, a *pato* player, the owner of an *estancia,* etc.
- Each group member works his/her irregular-stem verb into the story. For example, one group chooses the title *El tango era mi baile: Soy Ana Estrella, argentina de descendencia italiana. Era intérprete de tango cuando era joven. No podía ser otra cosa porque vengo de una familia de bailarines de tango. Aprendí a bailar a los cuatro años. Quise ser bailarina desde siempre. Tuve los mejores profesores—mis padres,* etc.
- Groups read their stories to the class, each writer reading his/her portion.
- The class votes for the group that used the verbs to create the funniest story, the most interesting story, etc.

Variation
- After each story is presented, have listeners retell it in the third person to practice using another form of irregular-stem preterite verbs. For example: *Ana Estrella dijo que era intérprete de tango. Dijo que aprendió a bailar a los cuatro años,* etc.

*__Del dicho al hecho__ from word to deed

¿Cómo está preparado?

ACTIVITY

Objective
- to discuss food preparation, using past participles

Use
after *Para comunicarnos mejor,* pages 196-197

Materials
- 3" x 5" index cards

Preparation
- Review regular and irregular participles on page 196 of *Juntos,* and present a few new ones. Write these new ones on the chalkboard: *cocido en el horno*/baked in the oven, *asado*/roasted, *puesto al horno*/put in the oven, *gratinado*/baked with a crust of bread crumbs or grated cheese, *pasado por agua*/soft-boiled, *batido*/beaten, *salado*/salty, *insípido*/lacking salt.

Activity
- Divide the class into two teams that will go in row order. Instruct students to use food items from the *Vocabulario temático* plus any others they know.
- Each student receives an index card, thinks about how a food is prepared, writes the question on one side of an index card and the answer on the back. For example: *Pongo huevos en agua muy caliente. Después de 10 minutos, ¿cómo están los huevos?* The opponent on Team B answers: *Los huevos están hervidos (cocidos).* If the anwer is correct, that student continues: *Pongo el pavo al horno por dos horas, ¿cómo está el pavo?* And the second player from Team A might respond: *El pavo está asado.* If the answer is incorrect, the next person from Team B reads a clue: *Cuando hago un flan, ¿cómo están los huevos? Los huevos están batidos,* etc.
- Teams alternate until everyone has had a turn.

Variation
- Play with past participles that refer to people. For example: *Trabajé 12 horas seguidas hoy. Cuando llego a casa, ¿cómo estoy?* The opponent might answer: *Estás cansado.*

¡UN FIN DE SEMANA EN BUENOS AIRES!

Introduce the chapter and its theme by asking students what holidays are special to them or their families. Do students associate any types of food with those events? Why?

Related Components

Audio	**Video: Tape/Book**
Conexiones: 17B	Unit 4: Seg. 2
Conexiones	
Chapter 7	

Scan to Chapter 7

GETTING STARTED

Have students look at the photographs. Ask questions. Suggestions:
¿Piensas que la comida de la foto es una comida especial?
¿Qué piensas que están celebrando?

Critical Thinking

Use the following activity to help students discover for themselves what they would need to know in order to talk about cooking and festivities.

Cocinas en tu casa
Tell students to think about what events they celebrate at home and what special meals they identify with these celebrations. Then ask each group to make a list of one of the following:

- events that your families celebrate together
- list things from the supermarket you would need for a very special meal
- things you would need to do before sitting down to eat
- what you would have to do after eating
- ways you can cook foods

Have each group write its list on the board. Have the class discuss the lists and decide which items are the most essential.
Have each group submit a revised list.
When you finish the chapter, have the class review the lists to see how they compare to what they learned in the chapter.

CAPÍTULO 7

¡UN FIN DE SEMANA EN BUENOS AIRES!

Una fiesta en Buenos Aires, Argentina.

186

CHAPTER COMPONENTS

Activity Book	**Audio Book**	**Conexiones**	**Transparencies**
p. 89-98	Script: p. 45-47	Chapter 7	Chapter 7
Assessment	Activities: p. 48-50	**Cuaderno**	Transpariencies 43-47
Oral Proficiency:	**Audio Tapes**	p. 53-60	**Tutor Pages**
p. 27	Chapter: 8A	**Magazine**	p. 31-34
Listening Script:	Assessment: 15A	Juntos en Argentina	**Video: Tape/Book**
p. 15	Conexiones: 17B		Unit 4: Seg. 2
Chapter Test:			
p. 81-86			

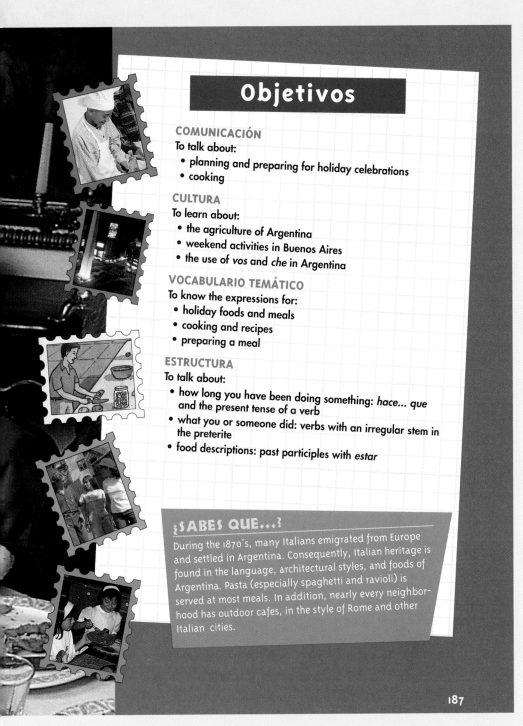

Objetivos

COMUNICACIÓN

To talk about:
- planning and preparing for holiday celebrations
- cooking

CULTURA

To learn about:
- the agriculture of Argentina
- weekend activities in Buenos Aires
- the use of *vos* and *che* in Argentina

VOCABULARIO TEMÁTICO

To know the expressions for:
- holiday foods and meals
- cooking and recipes
- preparing a meal

ESTRUCTURA

To talk about:
- how long you have been doing something: *hace... que* and the present tense of a verb
- what you or someone did: verbs with an irregular stem in the preterite
- food descriptions: past participles with *estar*

¿SABES QUE...?

During the 1870's, many Italians emigrated from Europe and settled in Argentina. Consequently, Italian heritage is found in the language, architectural styles, and foods of Argentina. Pasta (especially spaghetti and ravioli) is served at most meals. In addition, nearly every neighborhood has outdoor cafes, in the style of Rome and other Italian cities.

187

Here are some additional activities that you may wish to use as you work through this chapter with your students.

Communication

Encourage after-class activities that may enhance student interest and proficiency. Some ideas:
- organize a trip to a restaurant that specializes in Latin American or Spanish cuisine
- have them find out and report about special dishes prepared in Hispanic countries

Culture

The written word can only hint at what life is like in other lands. To encourage greater understanding:
- have students read a book about Argentina
- show the video that accompanies Unit 4 of this textbook

Vocabulary

To reinforce vocabulary, have students:
- demonstrate the preparation of a meal for the class
- make a cookbook of holiday recipes, including detailed instructions

Structure

To reinforce the use of **hace... que** and a verb, the preterite of irregular verbs, and past participles:
- have students write down five after-school activities they are involved in, one per flashcard. Students exchange cards and ask ¿*Cuánto hace que...*? questions
- read aloud a list of infinitives and have students write down the past participle of each

✔ CULTURE NOTE

The Spanish settlers that colonized the territories of South America in the eighteenth century believed there were large silver reserves waiting to be exploited. The Vicerroyalty was named "Virreinato del Río de la Plata" after the river whose course—they thought— would lead them to the mines. The name **Argentina** comes from the Latín **argentum**: "silver."

▶▶▶ INTERNET LINK

Gardel, an unoffical site http://www. informatik.uni-muenchen.de/rec/ argentina/argentina.html

Communicative Objectives

- to talk about holidays
- to talk about what you bought
- to describe how meals are prepared
- to say how long ago something happened

Related Components

Activity Book p. 89	**Cuaderno** p. 53
Audio Book Script: Seg. 1	**Transparencies** Ch. 7: Conversemos Transparency 43
Audio Chapter: 8A, Seg. 1	

GETTING STARTED

Ask students to name foods they associate with holiday celebrations.

ACTIVITIES

These activities give students an opportunity to begin communicating with each other and with you, focusing on the theme and objectives of the chapter. The activities can be used as oral class activities, or, if you prefer, you can pair students to achieve more interaction.

¿Cuándo hiciste la última fiesta en tu casa? ¿Qué celebraste?
Class activity to introduce holidays and **hacer** with time expressions. Say aloud combinations of **hacer** and expressions for years, months, weeks, days, and hours. Ask the questions in the title. Expand by asking students the date of each holiday.

¿Qué compraste para la fiesta?
Class activity to introduce food vocabulary. Have students run through the list, and identify the words with the logos. Ask them the title question. Vary by specifying the *fiesta* and by asking questions that elicit direct or indirect object pronouns.
¿Cuándo compraste las aceitunas?
Las compré ayer.

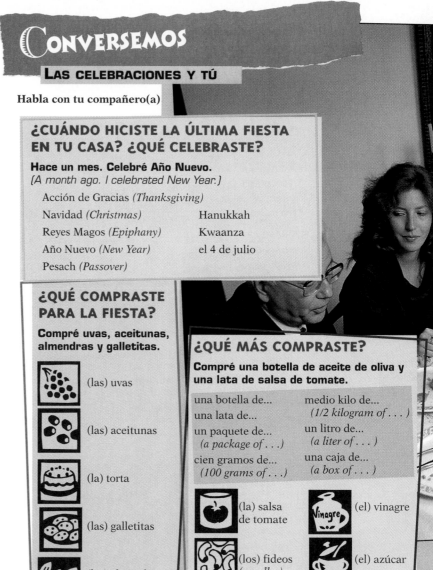

CONVERSEMOS

LAS CELEBRACIONES Y TÚ

Habla con tu compañero(a)

¿CUÁNDO HICISTE LA ÚLTIMA FIESTA EN TU CASA? ¿QUÉ CELEBRASTE?

Hace un mes. Celebré Año Nuevo.
(A month ago. I celebrated New Year.)

Acción de Gracias *(Thanksgiving)*	
Navidad *(Christmas)*	Hanukkah
Reyes Magos *(Epiphany)*	Kwaanza
Año Nuevo *(New Year)*	el 4 de julio
Pesach *(Passover)*	

¿QUÉ COMPRASTE PARA LA FIESTA?

Compré uvas, aceitunas, almendras y galletitas.

(las) uvas

(las) aceitunas

(la) torta

(las) galletitas

(las) almendras

 Y... ¿qué más?

¿QUÉ MÁS COMPRASTE?

Compré una botella de aceite de oliva y una lata de salsa de tomate.

una botella de...	medio kilo de... *(1/2 kilogram of . . .)*
una lata de...	
un paquete de... *(a package of . . .)*	un litro de... *(a liter of . . .)*
cien gramos de... *(100 grams of . . .)*	una caja de... *(a box of . . .)*

 (la) salsa de tomate

 (el) vinagre

 (los) fideos *(noodles)*

(el) azúcar

(el) cordero *(lamb)*
(el) aceite de oliva *(olive oil)*
(las) pasas *(raisins)*
(la) carne picada *(ground meat)*

188

¿Qué más compraste?
Class activity to introduce more foods and food measurements. Model the question and answers. Have students associate foods with each measurement. Have them mention dishes that include these ingredients.

¿QUÉ COMIDA PREPARASTE?

Hice torta de nueces.

(la) torta de nueces
(walnut cake)

(el) pollo asado
(roast chicken)

(la) carne a la parrilla
(grilled meat)

(la) tortilla
(omelette)

(el) pavo
(turkey)

(el) asado
(barbecue)

(las) verduras al vapor
(steamed vegetables)

(las) empanadas
*(small vegetable or
meat pies)*

(los) huevos revueltos
(scrambled eggs)

 huevos duros

huevos fritos

ANTES DE COMER, ¿QUÉ HICISTE?

Barrí la cocina.
(I swept the kitchen.)

Me lavé las manos.

Calenté la comida.
(I heated the food.)

Puse la mesa.
(I set the table.)

DESPUÉS DE COMER, ¿QUÉ HICISTE?

Recogí la mesa.
(I cleared the table.)

Limpié la mesa.
(I cleaned off the table.)

Lavé los platos.
(I washed the dishes.)

Saqué la basura.
(I took out the garbage.)

189

¿Qué comida preparaste?

Class activity to introduce ways that foods are prepared and more food vocabulary. Model the question and answers. Have students mention, in English, other foods that are prepared *asado, a la parrilla,* or *al vapor.* Ask: *¿Qué preparaste para la fiesta?* or *Si compraste [huevos], ¿qué preparaste?*

Antes de comer, ¿qué hiciste?

Class activity to introduce things to do before eating. Act out each sentence as you model it, and then have students do the same. Expand by replacing *comer* with such words as *la fiesta, la cena, el almuerzo,* etc.

Después de comer, ¿qué hiciste?

Class activity to introduce things to do after eating. Point out the sound at the end of each verb (e.g., **lavé**), similar to the long **a** sound in English. Ask why all these words have this sound. (All are preterite forms of **-ar** verbs.) Expand by asking what students do, did, and will do after dinner at home.

CHECK

- ¿Qué comida compraste para tu última fiesta?
- ¿Qué comiste?
- ¿Qué hicieron tus hermanos y tú después de comer en la última celebración?

PORTFOLIO

Have students find a magazine photo of a holiday meal. Have them identify the food and the way it was prepared.

MEETING INDIVIDUAL NEEDS

Reaching All Students

For Visual Learners

Use the letters of food words to make a *sopa de letras* (wordsearch), and give them to others to figure out.

For Kinesthetic Learners

Act out sentences and have others say if the actions occur *antes o después de comer.*

189

Objectives
Communicative: to talk about food
Cultural: to identify regional delicacies in Argentina

Related Components

Activity Book p. 90	Cuaderno p. 54
Audio Book Script: Seg. 2	**Transparencies** Ch. 7: Realidades Transparency 44
Audio Chapter: 8A, Seg. 2	

GETTING STARTED

Comment on the Argentinian foods that appear on the map. Compare them to foods in the United States. For example: *Las manzanas de Río Negro son tan deliciosas como las del estado de Washington.*

DISCUSS

Talk about the drawings and captions, and ask questions. Suggestions:

Mapa gastronómico de Argentina
¿Qué comidas hay en el mapa?
¿En qué regiones están?
¿Qué comida crees que es la más deliciosa?
¿Qué comidas no te gustan?
¿Qué lugar es famoso por el pescado?
¿Qué hay en Mendoza?

Background

Alfajores are biscuits with a layer of marmalade or **dulce de leche** (a very sweet, caramel-like paste made from condensed milk).
An **asado** consists of beef grilled over coals or a wood fire.
Chipá is a cheese bread, generally in sconelike form.
Chocolate blanco con almendras is a white milk chocolate, with almonds.
Chorizos are spicy pork sausages.
Cordero asado is grilled lamb.
Dulce de cayote is a marmalade made from the Argentinian fruit, **cayote**, which is too bitter to be eaten fresh.
Empanadas are savory turnovers, usually filled with chopped beef, potatoes, raisins, olives, hard-boiled eggs, and **ají**, a name for Andean chilis.

190

Locro is a soup made of potatoes and corn, sometimes served with avocado slices.
Mate is a tealike beverage made by steeping holly-bush leaves in water.

HABLA DEL MAPA GASTRONÓMICO

A. Con tu compañero(a), habla de la comida, bebida o postre típicos de cada lugar.

— *¿Qué es típico de Buenos Aires?*
— *Los alfajores. ¿Qué es típico de Neuquén?*

B. Con tu compañero(a), habla de las comidas, bebidas y postres del mapa. Digan cuáles comieron alguna vez.

— *¿Comiste alguna vez empanadas?*
— *No, pero comí cordero asado muchas veces.*

¿QUÉ OPINAS?

¿Qué fiestas celebran en tu casa con una comida especial? Pregunta a tres compañeros(as). Anota los resultados en la tabla. Usa el modelo.

Fiesta	yo	Mario	Marga	Nerea
Acción de Gracias		pavo		torta de manzana
4 de julio	asado			
Pesach			cordero asado	
Kwaanza				
Navidad				

¿SABES QUE...?

Argentina offers a great variety of traditional dishes. The popular **yerba mate** tea is made from the leaves of a bush that grows in the northeastern provinces. Other foods typical of the north are **locro**, a soup made with corn, beef, potatoes and other vegetables; **empanadas**, fried or baked turnovers stuffed with a variety of ingredients and **chipá**, a type of cheese bread.

The abundance of cattle and sheep as well as the influence of German, British, and Welsh cuisine, have produced dishes such as **chorizos** (a kind of sausage), **asado** (grilled meats), and **cordero asado** (roasted lamb).

Throughout the country, popular desserts include: **alfajores**, a dessert made of two layers of dough with a filling; **dulce de cayote**, a sweet spread similar in color and texture to orange marmalade, made from the **cayote** fruit (which is smooth and green on the outside and white on the inside).

191

Habla del mapa gastronómico

Pair Activities: Conversing
A. Talk about what dish, drink, or dessert is typical of each place.
B. Talk about the dishes, drinks, or desserts on the map. Say if you've ever eaten or drunk them.
Answers: See models on student page.
Extension: Suppose your partner is the owner of a gourmet store that sells products from Argentina. Create a dialog in which your partner recommends and you buy Argentinean products.

¿Qué opinas?

Group Activity: Taking a Poll
Form groups of four. What holidays do you celebrate in your home with a special meal? Record your answers in a chart like the model.

Class Activity: Evaluation
Have a volunteer write the holidays that students celebrate with a special meal. As the representative of each group reports its answers, have another volunteer write the foods served at those meals.
Decide which holidays are celebrated most often with a meal. Which holiday is celebrated with the greatest variety of food? What foods are most popular during holidays?

CHECK

- *¿Comiste alguna vez cordero asado? ¿Cuándo?*
- *¿Cuánto tiempo hace que comiste torta de manzana?*
- *¿Cómo cocinaron el último pavo que comiste?*

Para hispanohablantes

Tell the class what Argentinean foods on the map are or are not eaten at your home. For example: *No comemos cordero asado en mi casa.*

191

Communicative Objectives
- to talk about foods and kitchen utensils
- to talk about preparing a meal

Related Components

Activity Book p. 91-92	**Transparencies** Ch. 7: Palabras en acción Transparency 45
Cuaderno p. 55-56	**Tutor Page** p. 31

GETTING STARTED

Have students name their favorite foods. Are the people in the drawing preparing any of those things?

DISCUSS

Ask what several of the people in the drawing are doing and saying (for example, the little boy and his father by the table). Model the dialogs. Have students perform the dialogs.

Para hispanohablantes

If you use words or expressions other than the ones introduced in this chapter, share them with the class. A few variations:
el ají: el pimiento
la bolsa: la funda
las galletitas: las galletas
la olla: el caldero
el pepino: el pepinillo
la sandía: el melón de agua
las uvas pasas: las pasas
las verduras: los vegetales

PALABRAS EN ACCIÓN

¡ES HORA DE COMER!

la salsa de tomate
los fideos
¿Ya hierve el agua?
la olla
Yo creo que ya está hirviendo.
la sartén
Los platos ya están lavados.
Las verduras no están cortadas.
la botella de aceite
el ají
el pepino
las aceitunas
la cebolla

 ¿Qué ves en la cocina?

Haz una lista de las cosas que se necesitan para cocinar. Compara tu lista con la de tu compañero(a).

La olla, la sartén, el aceite...

 ¿Qué hicieron?

Escoge cuatro personas del dibujo. Pregúntale a tu compañero(a) qué hicieron.

— *¿Qué hizo el chico de la camiseta marrón?*
— *Cortó las verduras para la ensalada.*

 ¿Qué es?

Describe algo que ves en el dibujo. Tu compañero(a) tiene que adivinar qué es.

— *Es rojo y está en la mesa. ¿Qué es?*
— *¡Es un ají!*

4 Tu plato favorito

Habla con tu compañero(a) y di qué ingredientes tiene tu plato o postre favorito.

— *Mi plato favorito tiene fideos, aceite de oliva, queso y salsa de tomate.*
— *Mi postre favorito tiene nueces, azúcar, pasas, huevos y harina.*

192

For students having difficulty talking about preparing a meal, you might consider:
- **The tutor page:** Pair the student with a native speaker or a more able student, using the tutor page.

Optional activity: See page 186C: *Pruébalo*

 la bolsa

el molde

las pasas

la harina el azúcar

el vinagre la harina el azúcar

las nueces

el ventilador

la sandía

las galletitas

el mantel

¿Compraste las uvas?

No. El supermercado no estaba abierto.

¿Te lavaste las manos?

¿Trajiste las pasas y las nueces para la torta de Año Nuevo?

Sí, me lavé las manos y puse la mesa.

Hace mucho calor. ¿Pongo el ventilador?

Sí, aquí están.

Sí, por favor.

---

5 **¿Qué cocinaste?**

Habla con tu compañero(a) de lo que cocinaste la última vez que invitaste a tus amigos(as).

— *Yo cociné fideos con salsa de tomate y con verduras al vapor. ¿Y tú?*
— *Cociné pollo asado y papas fritas.*

6 **Miniteatro**

Imagina que tu compañero(a) y tú prepararon una cena especial. Creen un diálogo sobre lo que hicieron antes y después de comer.

— *Antes de comer yo barrí la cocina. Y tú, ¿qué hiciste?*
— *Puse la mesa. ¿Qué hiciste tú después de comer?*
— *Saqué la basura. ¿Y tú?*
— *Lavé los platos.*

7 **La cena del Club de Español**

Diseña un cartel para una cena de Reyes que va a preparar el Club de Español. Incluye cuándo va a ser, el precio por persona y el menú. Usa fotos o dibujos de revistas y periódicos.

8 **Tú eres el autor**

Escribe un párrafo sobre lo que te gustaba comer cuando eras niño(a).

> *Cuando era niño(a), mi comida favorita eran los huevos revueltos con cebolla y ají. También me gustaban muchísimo los fideos con salsa de tomate y los huevos fritos.*

193

Pair Activity
Choose four people from the drawing. Ask your partner what they did.

3. Pair Activity
Describe something you see in the drawing. Your partner guesses what it is.
Extension: Say two words associated with an object in the kitchen. Your partner guesses what it is. Example: *freír, huevos, (la sartén)*

4. Pair Activity
Talk about the ingredients in your favorite dish or dessert.
Extension: Name some ingredients that were in something you ate last night.

5. Pair Activity
Talk about what you cooked the last time you invited friends over.
Extension: Talk about what you would like to cook if your friends came to dinner again.

6. Roleplay Activity
You and your partner have prepared a special dinner. Create a dialog about what you did before and after eating.

7. Hands-On Activity
Classwork or homework for individuals or small groups. Design a poster for the Spanish Club's **Reyes** (Epiphany) dinner. Say when it is going to be, how much it will cost, and what will be on the menu. Use photos or drawings from magazines and newspapers.
Extension: Make a duty list. Who will set up before and clean up after the dinner?

8. Writing Activity
Write a paragraph about what you liked to eat when you were young.
Note: Copy the model on the board, underlining those words which students will replace. Elicit suggestions, write them on the board, and have students select items for their individual paragraphs.

ACTIVITIES

1. Individual and Pair Activity
Make a list of things you need in order to cook. Compare lists with your partner.
Extension: Tell the cooking method you use with each of the utensils.
Example: *la sartén: para freír*

CHECK

- *¿Quién puso el pollo en el horno? ¿Hace cuánto tiempo?*
- *¿Qué actividades ya están hechas en el dibujo?*
- *¿Qué van a hacer después de comer?*

LOG BOOK
Have students write down, step by step, things they do before and after dinner.

Communicative Objectives

- to talk about things you've been doing for a while, using **hace... que**
- to say what you did, using verbs with irregular stems in the preterite

Related Components

Activity Book p. 93-94	**Cuaderno** p. 57
Audio Book Script: Seg. 3 Activities: p. 48	**Transparencies** Ch. 7: Para comunicarnos mejor Transparency 46
Audio Chapter: 8A, Seg. 3	**Tutor Page** p. 32

☐ GETTING STARTED

Ask someone, "How long ago did you move here?" Then ask the same person, "How long have you been living here?" Ask what the difference is between these two questions. (One asks about when something happened in the past. The other asks about something that began in the past and is still going on.)

Language in Context

Hace... que: Give examples using both the present and present progressive tenses:
¿Cuántos meses hace que estudiamos español?
Hace más de un año, ¿verdad?
Hace (tiempo) que estoy hablando.
Hace (tiempo) que tú no me escuchas.
Encourage students to think of **hace** as meaning "it has been" rather than the literal "it makes." Point out that **hace** is used for both singular and plural nouns.
Irregular Preterites: Remind students that some verbs are simply irregular. The everyday verbs on this page are among them.

☐ DISCUSS

Review vocabulary from previous chapters and introduce some of this chapter's new vocabulary with questions and statements that use **hace... que** or verbs with irregular stem changes in the preterite.
Hace treinta y cinco minutos que estoy enseñando. ¿Cuánto hace que están estudiando?
¿Cuánto hace que estás estudiando en esta escuela?
¿Estuviste en la biblioteca ayer?

194

¡OJO!

The verbs **decir** *(to say)* and **traer** *(to bring)* are irregular in the preterite tense.

traje	trajimos
trajiste	trajisteis
trajo	trajeron

To talk about actions that began in the past but are still going on, use *hace* followed by an expression of time plus *que* and the verb in the present tense.

— *Hace dos meses que vivimos en Buenos Aires.*

We have been living in Buenos Aires for two months.

To tell what you or somebody else did, you may use verbs that have an irregular stem in the preterite.

— *Ayer estuve todo el día en la biblioteca.*

Yesterday I was at the library all day.

Here is the preterite of **estar** *(to be)* and other stem-changing verbs.

preterite	estar
yo	estuve
tú	estuviste
usted	estuvo
él/ella	estuvo
nosotros(as)	estuvimos
vosotros(as)	estuvisteis
ustedes	estuvieron
ellos/ellas	estuvieron

preterite of stem-changing verbs		
	stem	endings
poder	pud-	-e
poner	pus-	-iste
querer	quis-	-o
saber	sup-	-imos
tener	tuv-	-isteis
venir	vin-	-ieron

For students having difficulty talking about what they've been doing, using **hace... que,** or what they did, using verbs with an irregular stem in the preterite, you might consider:

- **The tutor page:** Pair the student with a native speaker or a more able student, using the tutor page.

Optional activity: See page 186C: *¿Cuánto tiempo hace?*

personales

¿Cuánto tiempo hace que...? Pregúntale a tu compañero(a).

— *¿Cuánto tiempo hace que vives en la misma casa?*
— *Hace cinco años que vivo en la misma casa.*

1. vives en la misma casa
2. estudias español
3. tienes correo electrónico
4. vienes a esta escuela
5. conoces a tu mejor amigo(a)
6. no tienes vacaciones

¿Qué hiciste?

Pregúntale a tu compañero(a) qué hizo durante las vacaciones.

— *¿Qué hiciste durante las vacaciones?*
— *Estuve en casa de mis primos.*

Un fin de semana especial

En grupo, hagan una encuesta entre sus compañeros para averiguar qué hicieron este fin de semana.

¿Qué más hiciste?
¿Pudiste ver a tus amigos?
¿Fuiste a algún lugar?
¿Dónde estuviste?
¿Tuviste mucho tiempo libre?
¿Te quedaste aquí?
¿Trajiste algún recuerdo?

¿Qué hiciste este fin de semana?

Yo	*fui al gimnasio*
Darío	*estuve en una fiesta*
Susana	*tuve que ir a la biblioteca*
Rosalía	*cociné una torta de cumpleaños*
Serafín	*fui al cine*

Presenta los resultados a la clase.

Yo fui al gimnasio. Darío estuvo en una fiesta. Rosalía cocinó una torta de cumpleaños. Susana tuvo que ir a la bibliotéca.

195

4. *¿Cuánto hace que vienes a esta escuela?*
Hace dos años que vengo a esta escuela.
5. *¿Cuánto hace que conoces a tu mejor amigo(a)?*
Hace seis años que lo(a) conozco.
6. *¿Cuánto hace que no tienes vacaciones?*
Hace un mes que no tengo vacaciones.
Extension: Start a sentence with **Hace... que.** Your partner finishes it.
A: *Hace dos años que...*
B: *...estoy en Dallas.*

2. Pair Activity
Ask your partner what he/she did during vacation.
Answers: See model on student page.
Extension: Say whether you did each activity your partner did.

3. Group Activity
In a group, take a poll to find out what people did last weekend. Report the results to the class.
Answers:
See model on student page.
Extension: Ask how long it has been since your partner did those activities.

CHECK

- *¿Cuánto hace que estudian español?*
- *¿Cuánto hace que viven en Estados Unidos?*
- *¿Vinieron temprano a la escuela?*
- *¿Estuvieron en la escuela ayer?*

LOG BOOK
Have students write one sentence for each of the verbs on these pages that has an irregular stem in the preterite.

ACTIVITIES

Students use **hace... que** and verbs with irregular stems in the preterite to say what people are doing or once did.

1. Pair Activity
Ask your partner how long he/she has been doing these activities.
Possible Answers:
1. See model on student page.
2. *¿Cuánto hace que estudias español?*
Hace un año y medio que estudio español.
3. *¿Cuánto hace que tienes correo electrónico?*
Hace dos meses que tengo correo electrónico.

Para hispanohablantes
Use **hace... que** to tell the class five things about your life.

195

Communicative Objectives
- to say how something is, using **estar** and a past participle
- to describe things, using a past participle as an adjective

Related Components

Activity Book p. 95-96	**Cuaderno** p. 58
Audio Book Script: Seg.4 Activities: p. 49	**Transparencies** Ch. 7 Para comunicarnos mejor Tranparency 46
Audio Chapter: 8A, Seg. 4	**Tutor Page** p. 33

GETTING STARTED

Ask students to say how they like their eggs. Write **fritos, hervidos,** and **revueltos** on the board. Show what verbs these adjectives come from.

Language in Context

The Past Participle: Point out that in English, past participles usually end in **-ed** (e.g., *finished* or *talked*), and that this form is the same as the past tense. Ask students to suggest past participles that are not the same as the past tense, and write *I___* and *I have ___* on the board to help them visualize it.
(A few: did/done, ate/eaten, saw/seen, sang/sung, spoke/spoken)

The Past Participle as Adjective: Return to the *Getting Started* list, and write down the corresponding English words. Point out that *fried* is both the past tense of *to fry* and an adjective that describes the state of an egg.

DISCUSS

Review vocabulary from previous chapters and introduce some of this chapter's new vocabulary with questions and statements that use **estar** with a past participle or past participles that are used as adjectives.
¡Libros abiertos!
¡Libros cerrados!
¿Quién está cansado?
¿La tarea está hecha?
¿Está cerrada la puerta?
¿La ventana está abierta o cerrada?
¿Prefieres los huevos fritos o revueltos?

PARA COMUNICARNOS MEJOR
¿ESTÁ PUESTA LA MESA?

To describe a condition, you may use *estar* followed by the past participle of a verb.

— *Sí, la mesa está puesta y la cena está servida.*

Yes, the table is set and dinner is served.

☐ To form regular past participles, drop the ending of the infinitive and add **-ado** to **-ar** verbs, and **-ido** to **-er** and **-ir** verbs.

past participles

-ar verbs	asar	as**ado** *(roasted)*
-er verbs	recoger	recog**ido** *(cleared)*
-ir verbs	hervir	herv**ido** *(boiled)*

☐ Some irregular participles are:

infinitive	past participle
abrir	**abierto** *(open)*
freír	**frito** *(fried)*
hacer	**hecho** *(done)*
poner	**puesto** *(put, set, turned on)*
revolver	**revuelto** *(stirred, scrambled)*

☐ The past participle can function as an adjective. As with all adjectives, past participles have the same gender and number as the nouns they refer to.

Necesito carne picada y huevos duros.

I need ground meat and hard-boiled eggs.

196

¿Te gustan las papas asadas?
¿Te gusta comer cebollas cortadas y fritas?

For students having difficulty describing things, using either **estar** with a past participle or past participles as adjectives, you might consider:
- **The tutor page:** Pair the student with a native speaker or a more able student, using the tutor page.

Optional activity: See page 186D: *¿Cómo está preparado?*

 Año Nuevo en Buenos Aires

Con tu compañero(a), habla de lo que hiciste para la cena de Año Nuevo.

— *¿Cortaste los pepinos para la ensalada?*
— *Sí, ya están cortados.*

1. ¿Cortaste los pepinos para la ensalada?
2. ¿Abriste la botella de aceite de oliva?
3. ¿Herviste los huevos?
4. ¿Compraste las almendras?
5. ¿Pusiste la mesa?
6. ¿Pusiste el aire acondicionado?
7. ¿Sacaste la basura?

 Todo listo

Tu compañero(a) y tú van a hacer un flan. Pero tu compañero(a) ya preparó casi todo. Pregúntale qué más tienen que hacer.

— *¿Abrimos el paquete de azúcar?*
— *Ya está abierto.*

1. ¿Abrimos el paquete de azúcar?
2. ¿Ponemos el azúcar?
3. ¿Hervimos la leche?
4. ¿Sacamos los huevos del refrigerador?
5. ¿Revolvemos los huevos con la leche?
6. ¿Calentamos el molde?
7. ¿Ponemos todo en el horno?

 ¿Cómo les gusta?

A. Pregúntale a un grupo de compañeros(as) qué comidas prefieren. Haz una tabla con los resultados.

B. Informen a la clase de los resultados.

Antonia prefiere los huevos fritos. A Lupe le gustan más los huevos duros. Marta prefiere los huevos revueltos.

		Antonia	Lupe	Marta
los huevos	duros		✓	
	fritos	✓		
	revueltos			✓
la carne	poco hecha	✓	✓	
	hecha			
	bien hecha			✓
las papas	hervidas			
	fritas			
	asadas			
	al horno			

197

Students use past participles to talk about holidays and food preparation.

1. Pair Activity
Discuss the preparations for a New Year's dinner with your partner.
Possible Answers:
1. See model on student page.
2. *Sí, ya está abierta.*
3. *Sí, ya están hervidos.*
4. *Sí, ya están compradas.*
5. *Sí, ya está puesta.*
6. *Sí, ya está puesto.*
7. *Sí, ya lestá sacada.*

2. Pair Activity
You get together to make a flan, but your partner has done almost everything. Ask what still has to be done.
Answers:
1. See model on student page.
2. *Ya está puesto.*
3. *Ya está hervida.*
4. *Ya están sacados.*
5. *Ya están revueltos.*
6. *Ya está calentado.*
7. *Ya está puesto.*

3. Group Activity
A. Talk about what foods you prefer. Make a chart like the model and record your answers on it.
B. Share your answers with the class.
Answers: See models on student page.
Extension: Make statements about the results. Others say if they are true or false.

 CHECK

• *¿Cómo prefieres los huevos?*
• *¿Tenemos que poner la mesa?*
• *¿Escribiste la tarea?*
• *¿Hiciste todas las actividades?*

LOG BOOK
Have students write sentences using past participles to describe the condition of five objects in their kitchens at home.

Para hispanohablantes

Tell the class about what you ate last night. Say if it was fried, boiled, stirred, scrambled, or roasted.

Objectives

Communicative:
• to say what you have done
• to talk about how long it has been since something happened

Cultural:
• to learn about cultural activities in Buenos Aires

Related Components

Assessment Oral Proficiency: p. 27	Conexiones: 17B **Conexiones** Chapter 7
Audio Book Script: Seg. 5 Activities: p. 50	**Magazine** Juntos en Argentina
Audio Chapter: 8A, Seg. 5	**Tutor Page** p. 34

GETTING STARTED

Students should now be able to correctly use **hace... que**, verbs with irregular stems in the preterite, past participles, and all of the chapter vocabulary.

Have students look at the **Guía** and locate events as you name them. Ask questions. Examples:

¿Cómo se llama la película en el Cine Gran Rex?

¿Qué especialidades ofrecen en el Restaurante La harina y el vinagre?

SITUACIONES
GUÍA PARA EL FIN DE SEMANA

Este fin de semana, en Buenos Aires...

Película: *Un lugar en el mundo*
Viernes y sábado, a las 23:00 horas
Cine Gran Rex

Conferencia: "Argentina y los escritores"
Viernes, a las 18:00 horas
Centro Cultural La Recoleta

Música: Concierto de la Orquesta de Cámara de Buenos Aires
Sábado, a las 20:00 horas
Galerías Pacífico

Teatro: *Escenas de la vida diaria*
Sábado, a las 20:30 horas
Domingo, a las 17:00 horas
Sala Blanca Podestá

Feria de libros de segunda mano
Sábado y domingo, de 12:00 a 17:00 horas
Plaza Italia

Mercado de pulgas en San Telmo
Sábado y domingo, de 11:00 a 18:00 horas

Fútbol: Boca Juniors contra River Plate
Domingo, a las 14:00 horas
Estadio del Club Boca Juniors

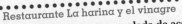

Restaurante La harina y el vinagre

Especialidades: Fideos con salsa de tomate, ensalada de aceitunas y pepinos, y cordero asado. *Excelentes postres:* torta de almendras, torta de chocolate, galletitas de nueces con helado de vainilla.

Almuerzo, de 12:00 a 16:00 horas / Cena, de 20:30 a 23:00 horas
Avenida 9 de Julio N° 123. Teléfono: 555-8793

198

For students having difficulty talking about what they have been doing or did in the past, you might consider:

• **The tutor page:** Pair the student with a native speaker or a more able student, using the tutor page.

Optional activity: See page 186D: *Del dicho al hecho*

Para hispanohablantes

Give the class examples of other uses of **hace... que.**

¿Dónde estuviste?

Con tu compañero(a), imaginen que pasaron un fin de semana en Buenos Aires. Hablen de dónde estuvieron.

— *El sábado por la mañana yo estuve en el mercado de pulgas. Por la noche, mis amigos y yo estuvimos en el cine Gran Rex. Y tú, ¿dónde estuviste?*
— *Yo estuve en la feria de libros. ¿Dónde estuviste el domingo?*

 ¿Qué hiciste?

Con tu compañero(a), habla de las actividades que hiciste en cada lugar.

— *¿Qué viste en el cine Gran Rex?*
— *Vi la película* Un lugar en el mundo *con unos amigos. Y tú, ¿qué hiciste en la feria de libros?*

 ¿Ya está hecho?

Tu compañero(a) y tú están preparando una cena especial de Navidad. Hagan un diálogo sobre las cosas que ya están hechas y las que tienen que hacer.

— *¿Pusiste la mesa?*
— *Sí, ya está puesta. Pero tenemos que comprar las nueces.*
— *No, ya las compré.*

 Entrevista

Tu compañero(a) es un(a) famoso(a) cocinero(a). Hazle una entrevista.

— *¿Cuánto tiempo hace que eres cocinero?*
— *Hace dos años que trabajo de cocinero, pero siempre me gustó cocinar para mis amigos.*

 Tu diario

Escribe un párrafo sobre la última fiesta que celebraste en tu casa. Di qué comida preparaste, cómo la preparaste y quién estuvo en la fiesta.

La última fiesta que celebré en mi casa fue el cumpleaños de mi hermano Marcelo. Compré una torta de chocolate y decoré toda la casa. Pero antes mi hermana y yo barrimos la casa, pusimos la mesa, trajimos un mantel con los colores favoritos de Marcelo...

PARA TU REFERENCIA

el/la cocinero(a) *cook*
el mercado de pulgas *flea market*
la Orquesta de Cámara *chamber orchestra*
de segunda mano *secondhand*

199

 APPLY

1. Pair Activity
Talk about where each of you was during your weekend in Buenos Aires.
Answers: See model on student page.
Extension: Say what time each of the events took place. Example: *El mercado de pulgas empezó a las 11:00.*

2. Pair Activity
Talk about what you did in each of the places in the **Guía.**
Answers: See model on student page.
Extension: Make a list of the things you did and rank them in order of preference. Say why you liked the one at the top of your list most.

3. Pair Activity
You're preparing a Christmas dinner. Create a dialog about what has been done and what needs to be done.
Answers: See model on student page.
Extension: Describe the foods. Example: *Las cebollas están fritas.*

4. Pair Activity
Interview your partner, a famous chef.
Answers: See model on student page.
Extension: Ask how long the cook has been preparing a particular food. Example: *¿Cuánto tiempo hace que estás cocinando la verdura? Hace veinte minutos que cocino la verdura.*

5. Homework or Classwork
Write a paragraph about the last party you had at your house. Say what foods you prepared, how you prepared them, and who was there.
Note: Copy the model on the board, underlining those words which students will replace. Elicit suggestions, write them on the board, and have students select items for their individual paragraphs.

Dictation
Read aloud your paragraph as your partner writes it down.

CHECK

- *¿Dónde estuviste el sábado?*
- *¿Escribieron sus apuntes?*
- *¿Cuánto hace que eres el/la mejor estudiante de la escuela?*

LOG BOOK
Have students write how long they have been doing certain weekend activities.

199

PARA RESOLVER

Objectives
Communicative: to talk about and write down recipes
Cultural: to learn how to make a traditional Hispanic dish

Related Components

Video: Tape/Book
Unit 4: Seg. 2

Scan to Chapter 7

GETTING STARTED

Ask students to talk about favorite dishes that are not traditional American foods.

APPLY

Form groups. Each will create a recipe for a cookbook.

PASO 1: ¿Plato principal o postre?
Make two lists: one for main dishes, another for desserts. Decide which type of recipe you would like to write.
Answers: See model on student page.
Extension: Write a list of ingredients for one of the dishes you did not choose.

PASO 2: Flan al caramelo
Decide how many people you want the recipe to serve. Make a list of ingredients and the necessary quantities of each.
Answers: See model on student page.
Extension: Find out how many grams are in a pound, and liters in a gallon.

PASO 3: Vamos a cocinar
Write the steps of your recipe.
Answers: See model on student page.
Extension: One partner reads each step of the completed recipe. The other says that it has been done. Example:
A: *Hervir el agua en una olla.*
B: *Está hervida.*

PASO 4: Nuestra receta
Take a picture of your dish and present it to the class.
Extension: Have volunteers read aloud their recipes as a partner writes them on the blackboard. Students may wish to copy them in their cookbooks.

PARA RESOLVER
¡ES HORA DE COMER!

La clase va a escribir un libro de recetas.

PASO 1 ¿Plato principal o postre?
En grupo, hagan una lista de diferentes platos según dos categorías: plato principal o postre. Decidan para qué categoría quieren escribir la receta.

> *Platos principales: arroz con pollo, fideos con salsa de tomate...*
> *Postres: arroz con leche, torta de nueces y pasas, flan al caramelo...*
> *Vamos a escribir la receta de un postre: flan al caramelo.*

PASO 2 Flan al caramelo
Decidan para cuántas personas va a ser la receta. Hagan una lista de los ingredientes y de las cantidades que necesitan.

> *La receta va a ser para cuatro personas.*
> *Ingredientes y cantidades: 150 gramos de azúcar, medio litro de leche y cuatro huevos.*

PASO 3 Vamos a cocinar
Escriban los pasos que tienen que seguir para cocinar su receta.

> 1. *Hervir la leche en una olla.*
> 2. *En un plato, batir los huevos...*
> 3. *Calentar el azúcar en un molde para flan...*
> 4. *Poner la mezcla en el molde y...*

PASO 4 Nuestra receta
Saquen una foto de su plato y preséntela a la clase.

PARA TU REFERENCIA

añadir *add*
el baño María *double boiler*
batir *to beat*
las cantidades *amounts*
cremoso(a) *creamy*
cubrir *to cover*
el fondo *bottom*
el horno *oven*
la mezcla *mixture*
la pared *side*
el plato principal *main course*
poco a poco *little by little*

200

Research Project

Have students research different cooking traditions in Latin America. Then have them organize the information according to the countries they have chosen, and the most common ingredients and typical dishes from each country.

MEETING INDIVIDUAL NEEDS

Reaching All Students

For Visual Learners
Make drawings of foods prepared in different ways. (e.g., *verduras a la parrilla*)

For Kinesthetic and Auditory Learners
Act out the steps of a recipe as someone else reads them aloud.

Hoy:
Flan al Caramelo

Para 4 personas

- 150 gramos de azúcar para el caramelo
- medio litro de leche
- 4 huevos
- 5 cucharadas de azúcar

- Calentar el azúcar en un molde para flan, hasta formar un caramelo cremoso. Cubrir bien el fondo y las paredes del molde con este caramelo. Déjalo enfriar.

- Hervir la leche en una olla. Añadir el azúcar a la leche.

- En un plato, batir los huevos. Después añadir los huevos, poco a poco, a la leche hervida, revolviendo todo hasta tener una mezcla.

- Poner la mezcla en el molde y cocinar al baño María en el horno a 350 °F de 40 a 50 minutos.

¿SABES QUE...?

A very popular dessert in Argentina is *dulce de leche*, milk cooked with sugar until it is thick. This dessert can be eaten as is or used as the base for other sweets. Other common desserts are *flan*, rice pudding, *almendrado* (ice cream rolled in crushed almonds), *dulce de batata* (a thick paste made of sweet potatoes, sliced and served with cheese), and *dulce de membrillo* (similar to *dulce de batata*, but made with quince).

201

CHECK

LOG BOOK
Have students write a family recipe in their Log Books.

Background

Cooking Words
Here are additional words that students may be interested in knowing:

au gratin *gratinado*
bake *hornear*
brown *dorar*
chop *cortar*
cook *cocer, guisar*
dice *cortar en dados*
dress (salad) *aliñar*
dressing (salad) *el aliño*
frozen *congelado(a)*
gallon *un galón*
grate *rayar*
grated cheese *el queso rayado*
marinate *marinar, escabechar*
measurements *las medidas*
medium *al punto, en el punto*
ounce *una onza*
pinch *una pizca*
pint *una pinta*
poach *escalfar*
poached egg *huevo escalfado*
pound *una libra*
quart *un cuarto de galón*
rare *crudo*
reheat *recalentar*
sauté *saltear*
season (salt & pepper) *salpimentar*
season *aderezar*
simmer *hervir (cocer) a fuego lento*
smoke *ahumar*
soft-boiled egg *huevo pasado (por agua)*
stew (a) *un estofado, un cocido*
stew (to) *estofar*
well-done *bien hecho*

Para hispanohablantes

Talk about a traditional recipe from your native country.

ENTÉRATE

Objectives

Communicative: to talk about different ways people speak Spanish
Cultural: to learn about words and phrases characteristic of Argentina

Related Components

Audio Conexiones: 17B	**Magazine** Juntos en Argentina
Conexiones Chapter 7	

☐ GETTING STARTED

If possible, show Segment 1 of the Unit 4 video. Ask students if they notice anything different about the way people from Argentina speak. Draw attention to the unique rhythms.

☐ DISCUSS

Using the Text

Have volunteers read aloud the text. Then ask questions. Suggestions:

¿Qué es el voseo?
¿De qué verbos son tenés, venís y podés?
¿Cómo le dices a un niño "come tu comida" si usas el voseo?
¿Cómo dices "es un regalo para ti" en Argentina?
¿En qué otros países usan el voseo?
¿Usan el voseo igual que en Argentina?
¿Qué otra palabra usan los argentinos?
¿Le dicen che a todas las personas?
¿Cómo sabes que una persona es de Argentina?

☐ CHECK

Te toca a vos
Possible Answers:
1. *Falsa. Los argentinos usan el che para dirigirse a sus amigos.*
2. *Falsa. Es fácil de reconocer, gracias al uso del voseo y del che.*
3. *Cierta.*
4. *Falsa. También se usa en Costa Rica, El Salvador, Nicaragua, Guatemala, Uruguay y Honduras.*

ENTÉRATE

¿CHE°, TENÉS HAMBRE?

> ¿Che, venís a mi fiesta?

Argentina es uno de los países de Hispanoamérica que usa el **voseo**. ¿Qué es el **voseo**? Es el uso de **vos** en lugar de° *tú*. Los argentinos dicen **vos tenés, vos venís** y **vos podés** en lugar de *tú tienes, tú vienes* y *tú puedes*. También los imperativos cambian: en lugar de *lava los platos* o *pon la mesa*, los argentinos dicen **lavá los platos** y **poné la mesa**. Y el **vos** también se usa en lugar del *ti*, como en la frase *Te toca a ti*, que en Argentina se dice **Te toca a vos**. Con variaciones según el país, el **voseo** también se usa en Costa Rica, El Salvador, Nicaragua, Guatemala, Honduras y Uruguay.

Además del° **voseo**, los argentinos usan la palabra **che** para dirigirse a° otra persona de una manera° familiar.

El español de Argentina es muy fácil de reconocer° debido al° uso del **voseo** y del **che**.

además del *in addition to* **che** *you (familiar)* **debido al** *on account of*	**dirigirse a** *to address someone* **en lugar de** *instead of*	**la manera** *way* **reconocer** *to recognize*

TE TOCA A VOS

Di cuáles de las siguientes oraciones son ciertas y cuáles son falsas. Corrige las falsas.

1. Los argentinos usan el *che* para dirigirse a todo el mundo.
2. El español de Argentina es difícil de reconocer.
3. El *vos* se usa en lugar de *tú* y de *ti*.
4. El *voseo* sólo se usa en Argentina y Uruguay.

202

Thinking About Language

Regional variations should not be a new idea for people who grew up in the United States, where many accents and words are specific to certain regions. Ask students to think about country and western singers or actors from New York or London. What about Southern actors on TV, like Jeff Foxworthy or Brett Butler? What do they say that tells us where they are from?
Point out that getting used to another accent can take time, but we can usually understand people with just a little effort.

PORTFOLIO

Have students make a map identifying countries that use **voseo**. Students should include at least three sentences that use the word **vos**.

Para hispanohablantes

Are there differences between the Spanish you speak and the way other people you know or see on TV speak Spanish? Explain to the class in English and Spanish.

VOCABULARIO TEMÁTICO

De compras
la caja *box*
el gramo *gram*
la lata *can*
el litro *liter*
el paquete *package*

La comida
el aceite de oliva *olive oil*
la aceituna *olive*
el ají *pepper*
la almendra *almond*
el asado *barbecue*
el azúcar *sugar*
la carne picada *ground meat*
la carne poca
hecha/hecha/bien hecha
rare/medium/well done meat
la cebolla *onion*
el cordero *lamb*
la empanada
small vegetable or meat pie
los fideos *noodles*
la galletita *cookie*
la harina *flour*
los huevos duros
hard-boiled eggs
los huevos fritos *fried eggs*
los huevos revueltos
scrambled eggs
la nuez/las nueces *walnut(s)*
la papa al horno *baked
potato*

la pasa *raisin*
el pavo *turkey*
el pepino *cucumber*
la salsa de tomate
tomato sauce
la sandía *watermelon*
la torta (Argentina) *pie*
la tortilla *omelette*
la uva *grape*
el vinagre *vinegar*

La receta
The recipe
asar *to roast*
calentar(e>ie) *to heat*
freír(e>i) *to fry*
hervir(e>ie) *to boil*
preparar *to prepare*
revolver *to stir, to scramble*

En la cocina
la olla *pot*
el mantel *tablecloth*
el molde *baking pan*
la sartén *frying pan*
el ventilador *fan*

Antes y después de comer
barrer la cocina
to sweep the kitchen
lavar los platos
to wash the dishes
limpiar la mesa
to clean off the table

recoger la mesa
to clear the table
sacar la basura
to take out the garbage

Las celebraciones
el 4 de julio *Fourth of July*
Acción de Gracias
Thanksgiving
Año Nuevo *New Year*
Navidad *Christmas*
Pesach *Passover*
Reyes *Epiphany*

Expresiones y palabras
¿Cuánto tiempo hace que...?
How long . . . ?
¡Es hora de comer!
It's time to eat!
abierto(a) (abrir) *opened*
a la parrilla *grilled*
al vapor *steamed*
calentar *to heat*
hace dos meses que...
for two months . . .
hecho(a) (hacer) *done*
medio(a) *half*
puesto(a) (poner) *put, set,
turned on*
revuelto(a) (revolver)
stirred, scrambled
traer *to bring*

LA CONEXIÓN INGLÉS-ESPAÑOL

There are often cognates for Spanish words that end in **-ro.** Sometimes they are easier to identify if you drop the **-ro** and add a silent **-e** or **-er.**

centro → *centr* → **center**

Find another word in the *Vocabulario temático* that closely follows this rule.

VOCABULARIO TEMÁTICO

Objective
• to review vocabulary

Related Components

Activity Book	Audio
Chapter Review: p. 97-98	Assessment: 15A
Assessment	**Cuaderno**
Listening Script: p. 15	p. 59-60
Chapter Test: p. 81-86	**Transparencies** Ch. 7: Dibujos y palabras Transparency 47

Vocabulary

Point out that this list is organized by themes. Use the headings to review vocabulary. You may wish to ask Spanish speakers to share variations on these words and phrases with the class.

LOG BOOK
Have students plan a menu of their meals for one day.

La conexión inglés-español
Students should be familar with several words that follow this rule: *metro* and *centímetro* (which become "meter" and "centimeter"), and also *teatro* (which becomes "theater").

	Objetivos page 205 *Una semana en una estancia*	Conversemos pages 206-207 *El campo y tú*	Realidades pages 208-209 *¡Estancias para todos los gustos!*	Palabras en acción pages 210-211 *Una estancia en La Pampa*
Comunicación	To talk about: • what products your state or region produces	Discuss products a state or region produces		Read cartoon, create dialog; make poster; write paragraph
	• typical activities in the countryside	Discuss typical activities in the country	Read text, make list, talk about preferences, choose activities, survey class	Read cartoon, discuss characters; animals; equipment; talk about life in the country; create dialog; make poster; write paragraph
	• farm animals in your area	Discuss farm animals in an area		Read cartoon, create dialog; make poster; write paragraph
Cultura	To learn about: • typical activities on an *estancia* in Argentina • the *gaucho* of Argentina • road signs in Latin America	Learn about *estancias* (Argentine *haciendas*)	Announcement for types of *estancias* in various regions of Argentina	
Vocabulario temático	To learn expressions for: • agricultural products	Talk about agricultural products	Read text, make list, talk about preferences, choose activities, survey class	Read cartoon, create dialog; make poster; write paragraph
	• domesticated farm animals	Talk about domesticated farm animals	Read text, make list, discuss activities, talk about preferences, choose activities, survey class	Read cartoon; talk about animals; create dialog; make poster; write paragraph
	• farm equipment	Talk about farm equipment	Read text, make list, discuss activities on *estancias,* talk about preferences, choose activities, survey class	Read cartoon, make list; discuss characters; animals; equipment; life in the country; create dialog; make poster; write paragraph
Estructura	To talk about: • activities and chores you will do: the present tense, the present form of *ir + a,* and the future tense	Use the present tense, the present form of *ir + a,* and the future tense to discuss work you will do on an *estancia*	Read cartoon, create dialog; write paragraph	Discuss work on an *estancia;* describe activities; interview classmates, report to class
	• when an event occurs, how it occurs, and an exchange: *por*		Read text, discuss activities on *estancias*	Read cartoon, create dialog; write paragraph
	• your intended purpose, destination, or schedule deadlines: *para*			Read cartoon, discuss equipment; create dialog; write paragraph

Para comunicarnos mejor (1) pages 212-213 ¿Visitaremos una estancia?	Para comunicarnos mejor (2) pages 214-215 ¿Por o para?	Situaciones pages 216-217 ¡Ven a la doma!	Para resolver pages 218-219 El mapa de nuestro pueblo	Entérate page 220 Los gauchos
			Choose place; draw map; present map to class	Discuss the history and culture of gauchos in Argentina
Discuss work on an estancia; describe activities	Discuss estancia photos	Read text, discuss rodeo; create dialog; make list of activities;	Choose place; draw map; discuss directions; present map to class	
Describe activities on an estancia		Read text, make list of activities; act out interview with estancia worker	Choose place; draw map; present map to class	
Discuss activities done on estancias	Photographs of estancias; create dialogs about taking vacation on an estancia	Announcement about the Gran doma de potros (horsebreaking festival)	Information about traffic awareness program in Argentina; traffic signs used in Argentina	
Discuss work on an estancia; describe activities	Discuss estancia photos			
Discuss work on an estancia; describe activities	Discuss estancia photos	**Re-entry of vocabulary**		**Extension of vocabulary**
Discuss work on an estancia; describe activities	Discuss estancia photos			
Discuss estancia photos	Express "for" using por and para			
Interview classmates, report to class	Talk about trip to Argentina; discuss estancia photos	**Re-entry of structure**		**Extension of structure**
Interview classmates, report to class				

Categóricamente

GAME

Objective
- to play a game of categories, using Chapter 8 *Vocabulario temático*

Use
after *Palabras en acción*, pages 210-211

Activity
- Select a scorekeeper/timekeeper and form two teams to play against each other in row order.
- Use the headings of the *Vocabulario temático* for the categories: *en el campo, los animales, en la estancia, actividades del campo, para trabajar en el campo.* Select one category at a time.
- The first players from the two teams, going alternately, have two minutes to name items that belong in that category. If one player is stumped, the other player goes again.
- No items can be repeated. At the end of two minutes, the team with the longer list of correct responses gets a point and the right to respond first when the next player and category are selected.
- Categories may be repeated, but not specific responses. Use vocabulary from other chapters if time permits.

Haré ésto y luego...

GAME

Objective
- to play a sequencing game, using the future tense and **ir a** with an infinitive

Use
after *Para comunicarnos mejor*, pages 212-213

Materials
- bilingual dictionary

Preparation
- Make a list of activities that can be done in steps. Use both review vocabulary and words and phrases from the Chapter 8 *Vocabulario temático: plantar un árbol, ordeñar las vacas, dar de comer a los animales, jugar a las damas, jugar al ajedrez, escribir un reportaje.*

Activity
- Divide the class into two teams. Team A is the **ir a** plus an infinitive team and Team B is the future tense team.
- Tell students which activity to describe. Teams have five minutes to jot down five steps.
- The teams present their steps in chronological order. For example, Team A might give the following steps for *plantar un árbol: Primero, voy a comprar un árbol. Luego voy a hacer un pozo*. Después voy a poner el árbol en el pozo y voy a cubrirlo con tierra. Y por último voy a regar el árbol.* Team B presents its list or borrows from Team A's steps, in either case using the future tense: *Compraré un árbol. Luego haré un pozo. Más tarde pondré el árbol en el pozo y lo cubriré con tierra. Finalmente regaré el árbol.*

* **pozo** *hole*

Ganaremos la copa*

LANGUAGE ARTS CONNECTION

Objective
• to talk about goals for the future, using the future tense

Use
after *Para comunicarnos mejor,* pages 212-213

Activity
• Have students list five goals that they have for the next year. They should use the future tense to write sentences that express those goals. Possible sentences may include: *Sacaré buenas notas. Compraré una moto nueva. Con el equipo de fútbol, ganaremos la copa.*
• Taking turns, students read aloud their phrases. They continue until everybody has read all their "goals."
• Select someone to keep track of the various goals mentioned and have students draw conclusions from the tally about what they think is important, necessary, etc.

Variation
• Volunteers name different places. For each place, their classmates brainstorm phrases using the future tense. For example, the place is *la escuela. No iré a la escuela mañana. Llevaré los libros a mi armario.*

* **copa** *cup, trophy*

¿Para mí? ¿Por qué?

WRITING CONNECTION

Objective
• to write original sentences, using the prepositions **por** and **para**

Use
after *Para comunicarnos mejor,* pages 214-215

Materials
• 3" x 5" index cards, one per student
• paper bag

Preparation
• Write or have a student write the following phrases on 10 index cards: due date=**para**, use=**para**, direction=**para**, recipient=**para**, purpose=**para**, exchange=**por**, period of time=**por**, by means of=**por**, time of day=**por**, through/around=**por**. Make as many sets as you need for each student to get one card.

Activity
• Decide on a playing order.
• Put all of the cards in the bag and mix.
• Each student picks a card and writes a sentence on the board that would use **por** or **para** as indicated. For example, Lisa picks: period of time=**por** and writes: *Juan vivió en Buenos Aires_____seis meses.*
• The first student presents his/her sentence to the next student, reading it without the preposition. If you feel the sentence doesn't demonstrate the construction properly, ask another student to furnish an example. Students answer in playing order only.
• The second student must repeat the sentence and fill in the preposition: *Juan vivió en Buenos Aires por seis meses.*

UNA SEMANA EN UNA ESTANCIA

Introduce the chapter and its theme by asking students to think of life in rural environments. Discuss the differences between life in the country and the city (population, transportation, lifestyle, and so forth). How do people who live in the country earn their living?

Related Components

Audio	**Video: Tape/Book**
Conexiones: 17B	Unit 4: Seg. 3
Conexiones	
Chapter 8	

Scan to Chapter 8

GETTING STARTED

Ask students to look at the photographs. What places do they associate with horseback riding? Ask questions. Suggestions: *¿Qué está haciendo el hombre de la foto? ¿Crees que lo hace para pasarla bien o que es su trabajo? ¿Qué crees que hará luego?*

Critical Thinking

Use the following activity to help students discover what they would need to know in order to talk about the countryside.

En el campo

Tell students to think about things they would find in the countryside and things that people do there. Have them form groups and make lists of:

- animals they expect to find in the countryside
- agricultural products of the United States
- what a farmer's schedule would be like
- buildings and places they would see in the countryside
- things people do at a farm

Have each group write its list on the board. Have the class discuss the lists and decide which items are essential.
Have each group submit a revised list. When you finish the chapter, have the class review their lists to see how they compare to what they learned in the chapter.

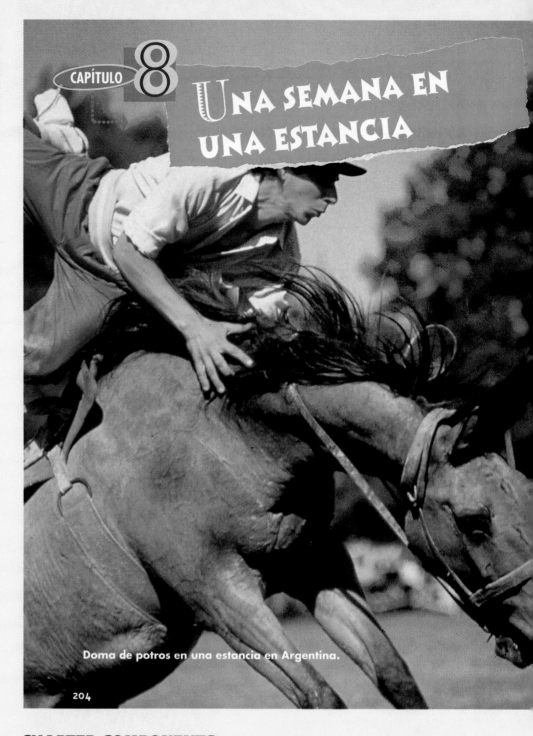

CAPÍTULO **8**

UNA SEMANA EN UNA ESTANCIA

Doma de potros en una estancia en Argentina.

204

CHAPTER COMPONENTS

Activity Book	**Audio Book**	**Conexiones**	**Transparencies**
p. 99-108	Script: p. 51-53	Chapter 8	Chapter 8
Assessment	Activities: p. 54-56	**Cuaderno**	Transparencies 48-52
Oral Proficiency:	**Audio**	p. 61-68	**Tutor Pages**
p. 28	Chapter: 8B	**Magazine**	p. 35-38
Listening Script:	Assessment: 15A	Juntos en Argentina	**Video: Tape/Book**
p. 16	Conexiones: 17B		Unit 4: Seg. 2
Chapter Test:			
p. 87-92			

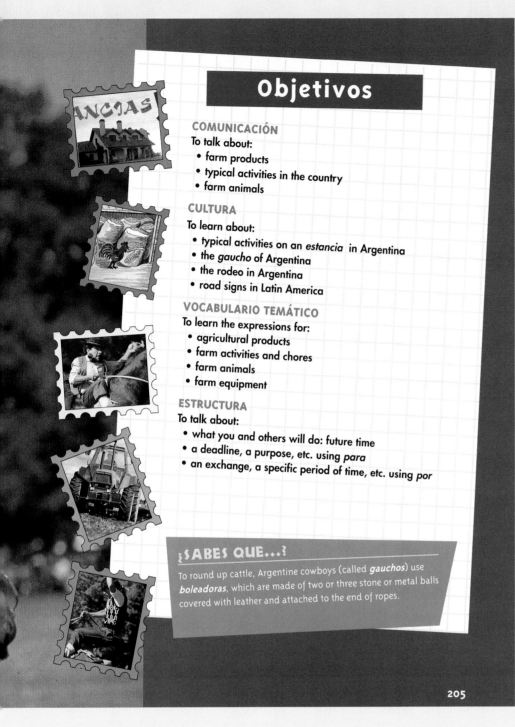

Objetivos

COMUNICACIÓN

To talk about:
- farm products
- typical activities in the country
- farm animals

CULTURA

To learn about:
- typical activities on an *estancia* in Argentina
- the *gaucho* of Argentina
- the rodeo in Argentina
- road signs in Latin America

VOCABULARIO TEMÁTICO

To learn the expressions for:
- agricultural products
- farm activities and chores
- farm animals
- farm equipment

ESTRUCTURA

To talk about:
- what you and others will do: future time
- a deadline, a purpose, etc. using *para*
- an exchange, a specific period of time, etc. using *por*

¿SABES QUE...?

To round up cattle, Argentine cowboys (called *gauchos*) use *boleadoras*, which are made of two or three stone or metal balls covered with leather and attached to the end of ropes.

205

Thinking About Language

Ask students to brainstorm any Spanish words or phrases they know for the words in the lists they created for the *Critical Thinking* activity on page 204. Are any of the words cognates? Ask speakers of other languages to share expressions related to farming and ranching with the class.

Here are some additional activities that you may wish to use as you work through this chapter with your students.

Communication

Encourage after-class activities that may enhance student interest and proficiency. For example:
- have students initiate an *intercambio* (an arrangement with a Spanish speaker to get together to practice speaking) with someone in your school or community
- ask students to request information on *estancias* in Spanish. One source: *La Casa de Turismo de Buenos Aires Callao 237, Buenos Aires, Argentina* Telephone: 40-7045 x47

Culture

To encourage greater cultural understanding:
- have students listen to tango music or attend a tango performance
- have students organize an Argentinian food festival with *mate* and *empanadas*
- decorate the classroom with posters of the *pampas,* Buenos Aires, and other regions of Argentina
- show the video that accompanies Unit 4 of this textbook

Vocabulary

To reinforce vocabulary, have students:
- play *Memoria,* a word-association game. Divide the class into groups of six. Make flashcards of ranch objects and activities. Shuffle the cards and lay them face down. Students take turns choosing two cards. The objective is to match an activity with its object counterpart. Example: *cepillo* and *cepillar los caballos*

Structure

To reinforce **por** and **para**:
- make a **por** and **para** bulletin board which shows the various uses of each word. Encourage students to add examples of the different uses, preferably together with forms of the future tense or **ir a** with an infinitive. Example: *Compraré un regalo para mi madre.*

▶▶▶**INTERNET LINK**

Photos from the Pampas http://www. cco.caltech.edu/~repetto/

Communicative Objectives
- to talk about farm animals, crops, and activities
- to talk about things in the country

Related Components

Activity Book p. 99	**Cuaderno** p. 61
Audio Book Script: Seg. 1	**Transparencies** Ch. 8: Conversemos Transparency 48
Audio Chapter: 8B, Seg. 1	

GETTING STARTED

Ask students to comment on the photo. Does this resemble any part of your state? How is it different?

ACTIVITIES

These activities give students an opportunity to begin communicating with each other and with you, focusing on the theme and objectives of the chapter. The activities can be used as oral class activities, or, if you prefer, you can pair students to achieve more interaction.

En tu estado, ¿qué animales hay en el campo?
Class activity to introduce farm animal vocabulary and review **haber.** Ask the title question and discuss the words. Have students describe each of the animals with words, sounds, or gestures.

¿Qué produce tu estado?
Class activity to introduce farm crops. Model the question and the crops. Help students figure out what the words mean. **(Trigo** may require such questions as: What is flour made of?) Discuss crops your state produces and encourage students to look up words they don't know in the dictionary.

¿Fuiste alguna vez al campo? ¿Qué viste?
Class activity to introduce things found in the country and to review the preterite of **ver.** Model the questions and answers. Define each word by mentioning things that are found or done there. Expand by comparing and contrasting city life with country life. For example:
En el campo no hay mucho ruido.
En la ciudad hay mucho ruido y tráfico.

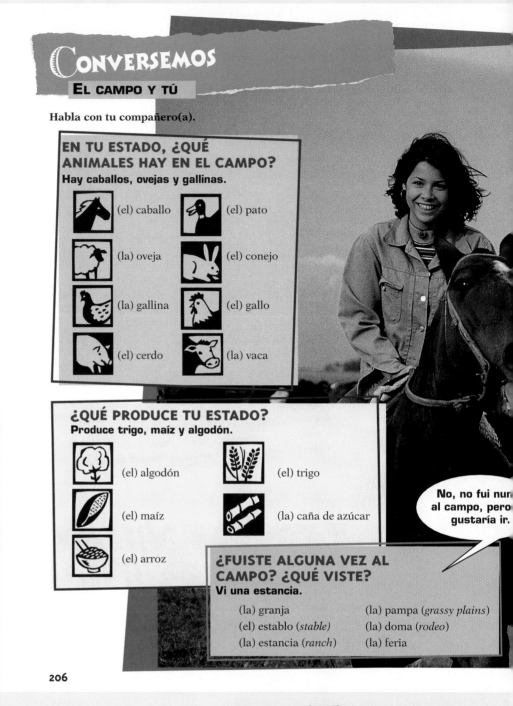

CONVERSEMOS
EL CAMPO Y TÚ

Habla con tu compañero(a).

EN TU ESTADO, ¿QUÉ ANIMALES HAY EN EL CAMPO?
Hay caballos, ovejas y gallinas.

(el) caballo
(el) pato
(la) oveja
(el) conejo
(la) gallina
(el) gallo
(el) cerdo
(la) vaca

¿QUÉ PRODUCE TU ESTADO?
Produce trigo, maíz y algodón.

(el) algodón
(el) trigo
(el) maíz
(la) caña de azúcar
(el) arroz

¿FUISTE ALGUNA VEZ AL CAMPO? ¿QUÉ VISTE?
Vi una estancia.

(la) granja
(la) pampa (*grassy plains*)
(el) establo (*stable*)
(la) doma (*rodeo*)
(la) estancia (*ranch*)
(la) feria

No, no fui nun[ca] al campo, pero [me] gustaría ir.

206

MEETING INDIVIDUAL NEEDS

Reaching All Students

For Auditory Learners
Imitate the sounds of farm animals and have others guess the names of the animals.

For Visual Learners
Make farm-product flashcards. Quiz each other in pairs.

For Kinesthetic Learners
Act out farm chores and have others say their names in Spanish.

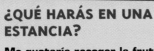

¿QUÉ HARÁS EN UNA ESTANCIA?

Me gustaría recoger la fruta.

dar de comer a los animales
(to feed the animals)

cepillar los caballos
(to brush the horses)

montar a caballo
(to go horseback riding)

recoger la fruta
(to pick fruit)

regar las plantas
(to water the plants)

plantar árboles
(to plant trees)

sembrar las semillas
(to sow seeds)

ordeñar las vacas
(to milk the cows)

¿QUÉ HAY QUE HACER EN UNA ESTANCIA?

Es importante levantarse temprano.
(It's important to get up early.)

Es mejor no acostarse tarde.
(It's better not to go to bed late.)

Hay que cultivar la tierra.
(One has to / must till the soil.)

Es necesario cuidar el ganado.
(It's necessary to take care of the cattle.)

Es práctico saber manejar un tractor.
(It's useful to know how to drive a tractor.)

Hay que recoger la cosecha.
(One has to / must harvest the crop.)

207

¿Qué harás en una estancia?
Class activity to introduce farm activities. Have students say what they would like to do. Encourage the use of alternative answers, including what they would not like to do. Review words and expressions by asking students to explain why they do or do not want to do each activity (for example, *me interesa, me aburre, ¡es bárbaro!*).

¿Qué hay que hacer en una estancia?
Class activity to introduce **hay que,** generalizations, and new vocabulary. Model the title question and expression. Extend with variations such as, *¿Qué hay que hacer para ser buen estudiante?*
Have students make statements about school, and discuss whether they are true or false. Example: *Es importante llegar tarde a la clase.*

CHECK

• *¿Qué animales hay en nuestro estado?*
• *¿Qué produce nuestro estado?*
• *¿Qué hay que hacer en una estancia?*

LOG BOOK
Have students write about four farm activities they would like to do.

Objectives
Communicative: to talk about what happens on a ranch
Cultural: to learn about ranches in Argentina

Related Components

Activity Book p. 100	Audio Chapter: 8B, Seg. 2
Audio Book Script: Seg. 2	Cuaderno p. 62

GETTING STARTED

Ask if anyone has ever been to a dude ranch. Ask what kinds of things were there. If no one has been to one, ask what they would expect to find there.

DISCUSS

Talk about the photographs and captions, and ask questions. Suggestions:

¡Estancias para todos los gustos!
¿Qué palabra es como gustos?
¿En qué es diferente la frase "para todos los gustos" de la frase "lo que nos gusta a todos nosotros"?
¿Qué puedes hacer al aire libre?
¿Qué es una estancia?
¿Qué puedes hacer en Argentina?

Estancia La Criolla
¿Qué puedes tomar en la Estancia La Criolla?
¿Qué haces en un asado?
¿Cuánto cuesta visitar la estancia por persona por día?

Estancia Sur
¿Qué puedes hacer en la Estancia Sur?
¿Qué actividades hay con los animales?
¿Cuánto cuesta visitar esta estancia por persona por día?
¿Qué hay que hacer si quieres más información?

REALIDADES

¡ESTANCIAS!
PARA TODOS LOS GUSTOS

¿Les gustaría pasar unas vacaciones lejos de la ciudad? ¿Les gustaría practicar sus deportes favoritos al aire libre? ¿Les gustaría participar en las actividades típicas del campo? ¡Vengan a una estancia!

En Argentina hay estancias para todos los gustos. En muchas regiones del país es posible visitar estancias. Pueden quedarse unos días pero es mejor quedarse todo un mes.

Estancia La Criolla
En La Criolla, pueden tomar mate, comer empanadas y también hacer un asado. Después de la cena, pueden cantar al son de una guitarra y bailar danzas criollas. (120 pesos por persona por día)

Estancia Sur
Si les gusta el campo y la naturaleza la van a pasar muy bien en la estancia Sur. Aquí pueden cuidar el ganado, montar a caballo, pasear en carruaje, dar de comer a los animales y recoger la fruta. (100 pesos por persona por día)

Para más información, llamen a la Secretaría de Turismo de la Nación. Teléfono 312-2232.

208

✓ CULTURE NOTE

Mate is an herbal tea that is very popular in Argentina. It is made by placing the leaves in a gourd and pouring hot water on them. The drinker sips the tea through a tube called a *bombilla* (because it has a rounded end that resembles a lightbulb).

MEETING INDIVIDUAL NEEDS

Reaching All Students

For Auditory Learners
Read aloud the brochure. Have your partner transcribe it. Correct mistakes.

For Visual Learners
Make a drawing of a ranch. Label each activity and object.

For Kinesthetic Learners
Pick one of these ranches and explain why visitors should go there.

HABLA DEL FOLLETO

A. Haz una lista de todas las actividades que puedes hacer en una estancia.

Comer empanadas, ver danzas criollas...

B. Con tu compañero(a), habla de lo que es posible hacer en cada estancia.

— *¿Qué se puede hacer en La Criolla?*
— *Se puede hacer un asado, tomar mate...*

C. Ahora, hablen sobre qué estancia les gustaría visitar y por qué.

— *Me gustaría visitar la estancia Sur porque allí es posible montar a caballo. ¿Y a ti?*
— *Yo prefiero ir a...*

¿QUÉ OPINAS?

Haz una lista de las actividades típicas de una estancia. Escoge tus tres actividades favoritas. Luego haz una encuesta. Usa el modelo.

Actividad	yo	la clase
pasear en carruaje	✓	|||
dar de comer a los animales		
montar a caballo		
hacer un asado	✓	✝✝✝
cantar y bailar danzas criollas		
comer empanadas		
recoger la fruta	✓	
cuidar el ganado		

Según la encuesta, ¿cuál es la actividad más popular? ¿Y la menos popular?

ACTIVITIES

Habla del folleto

Individual and Pair Activities: Analyzing and Discussing
A. Make a list of all the things you can do on a ranch.
B. Talk with your partner about what you can do on each of these ranches.
C. Talk with your partner about which ranch the two of you would like to visit and why.
Answers: See models on student page.

¿Qué opinas?

Group Activity: Taking a Poll
Make a list of typical ranch activities. Survey your group and choose the three favorite activities. Tally them on a chart like the one on page 209.
Class Activity: Evaluation
• Have a volunteer list the activities on the board.
• Have another volunteer write in the numbers as representatives report on their polls.
• Which are the most popular activities? Which are the least popular?

CHECK

• *¿Te gustaría pasar unas vacaciones en una estancia? ¿Por qué?*
• *¿Qué es lo más divertido que se puede hacer en la Estancia La Criolla?*
• *¿Qué prefieres hacer, dar de comer a los caballos o montar a caballo?*

LOG BOOK
Have students write five sentences about what they would like to do on a ranch.

Para hispanohablantes
Write a paragraph describing a ranch scene from a TV show or movie. Read your paragraph to the class.

Communicative Objectives

- to talk about things found on a ranch
- to talk about things you do on a ranch
- to talk about the names of animals

Related Components

Activity Book	Transparencies
p. 101-102	Ch. 8: Palabras en
Cuaderno	acción
p. 63-64	Transparency 49
	Tutor Page
	p. 35

GETTING STARTED

Write these animal sounds in the lefthand column on the board, and ask students to figure out what these "words" are.

beeee	**la oveja**
cloc, cloc	**la gallina**
cua, cua	**el pato**
guau, guau	**el perro**
jiiiii	**el caballo**
miau, miau	**el gato**
muuuu	**la vaca**
kikirikí	**el gallo**

If no one has a clue, ask volunteers to pronounce them. Once they understand that these are representations of animal sounds, have them match each sound with the appropriate animal. (Most of these animals are in the drawing.) Discuss why the sounds are written in such different ways in English and Spanish.

DISCUSS

Ask what the characters in the picture are saying, and model the dialogs. Have students act out the dialogs.

PALABRAS EN ACCIÓN
UNA ESTANCIA EN LA PAMPA

el granero

el establo

¿Cuántas veces por día es necesario dar de comer a los caballos?

Dos veces por día.

el cepillo

el maíz

¿Es difícil montar a caballo?

Sí, pero también es divertido.

la gallina

el pato

el caballo

1 ¿Qué ves en el dibujo?

Haz una lista de las cosas que ves en la estancia. Compara tu lista con la de tu compañero(a).

El tractor, la segadora...

2 ¿Qué hacen?

Escoge cinco personas del dibujo. Pregúntale a tu compañero(a) qué están haciendo.

— *¿Qué está haciendo el chico de la camisa verde?*
— *Está dando de comer a los animales.*

3 ¿Dónde están los animales?

Escoge cuatro animales del dibujo. Pregúntale a tu compañero(a) dónde están.

— *¿Dónde está el caballo negro?*
— *En el establo.*

4 ¿Para qué son?

Pregúntale a tu compañero(a) para qué son las cosas que hay en el campo.

— *¿Para qué es la segadora?*
— *La segadora es para recoger la cosecha.*

210

For students having difficulty talking about things found on or activities at a ranch or farm, you might consider:

- **The tutor page:** Pair the student with a native speaker or a more able student, using the tutor page.

Optional activity: See page 204C: *Categóricamente*

¿Qué sembraremos?

la oveja

el corral

el cerdo

la vaca

el conejo

el trabajador

el gallo

¿A qué hora se levanta?

la manguera

las semillas

la segadora

el granjero

Vamos a sembrar trigo.

la tierra

¿Qué vamos a comer hoy?

A las cinco. En el campo hay que levantarse temprano.

la jardinera

Voy a hacer un asado.

el huerto

el tractor

el capataz

el conejo

el cocinero

la parrilla

el camión

5 ¡Vamos al campo!

Pregúntale a tu compañero(a) qué le gustaría hacer en el campo.

— ¿Qué harás en el campo?
— Me gustaría plantar árboles.

6 Miniteatro

Imagina que eres un(a) trabajador(a) en una estancia y tu compañero(a) está de visita. Creen un diálogo.

— Generalmente, ¿a qué hora hay que levantarse?
— Es necesario levantarse a las cinco de la mañana.
— ¿Qué hay que hacer por la mañana?
— Es importante cuidar los caballos.

7 La estancia

Diseña un cartel sobre una estancia en Argentina. Describe qué animales puedes ver y qué actividades puedes hacer. Usa dibujos o fotos de revistas y periódicos.

8 Tú eres el autor

En un párrafo, compara la rutina diaria y las responsabilidades de la gente que vive en el campo con la rutina y las responsabilidades de la gente que vive en la ciudad.

En el campo, la gente se levanta y se acuesta antes que la gente en la ciudad. La gente en el campo tiene que cuidar el ganado, sembrar, regar...

211

ACTIVITIES

1. Pair Activity
Make a list of the things you see in the drawing. Compare lists with your partner.
Extension: Write lists for these categories: person, animal, thing, and activity.

2. Pair Activity
Choose five people from the drawing. Ask your partner what each is doing.

3. Pair Activity
Choose four animals from the drawing. Ask your partner where each is.
Extension: Ask your partner where each person is.

4. Pair Activity
Ask your partner what the farm equipment is used for.

5. Pair Activity
Ask your partner what he or she would like to do on the farm.

6. Roleplay Activity
Imagine that you work on a ranch and your partner comes to visit you. Create a dialog about things that have to be done on the ranch.
Extension: Memorize and act out other pairs' dialogs for the class.

7. Hands-On Activity
Homework for individuals or small groups. Design a poster about an Argentinean ranch. Describe the animals you can see and the activities you can do there. Use photos and drawings.
Extension: Exchange posters and write descriptions of them.

8. Writing Activity
Write a paragraph comparing the daily routines and responsibilities of country and city life.
Note: Help students get started by copying the model on the board and underlining the words which students will replace. Elicit suggestions, write them on the board, and have students choose some for their paragraphs.

CHECK

- ¿Qué te gustaría hacer en el campo?
- ¿Qué hay que hacer en una estancia?
- ¿Para qué se usa el tractor?

LOG BOOK
Have students write down what one must do on a ranch, using **hay que** or **es necesario**.

Communicative Objective
- to talk about what you will do on an *estancia,* using the present tense, **ir a,** and the future tense

Related Components

Activity Book p. 103-104	**Audio** Chapter: 8B, Seg. 3
Audio Book Script: Seg. 3 Activities: p. 54	**Cuaderno** p. 65
	Tutor Page p. 36

GETTING STARTED

Ask students how the future tense is expressed in English. Have them give examples.

Language in Context

Ask how these sentences differ:
I am going to milk the cows.
I will milk the cows.

Write the Spanish equivalents and discuss them:
Voy a ordeñar las vacas.
Ordeñaré las vacas.

Let students know that the future tense is used to refer to actions that take place in a more distant future; the structure **ir a** generally refers to the immediate future.

Refer students to the paradigm. For most verbs, the stem of the future is the infinitive. Have students note the accent marks on all endings except for **-emos.**

DISCUSS

Review vocabulary from previous chapters and introduce some of this chapter's vocabulary with questions and statements that use the future of **-ar, -er,** and **-ir** verbs.
¿Qué harás en la estancia?
¿Nos levantaremos temprano?
¿Qué cocinará el cocinero?
¿Dónde estará el ganado?
¿Habrá muchas vacas?
¿Cuándo trabajarán los granjeros, por la mañana, por la tarde o por la noche?

PARA COMUNICARNOS MEJOR
¿VISITAREMOS UNA ESTANCIA?

1. The present tense is often used in Spanish to express future time:
   - With a time expression that refers to future time or when it is understood from context.

   Miguel llama más tarde.   Miguel will call later.

2. The present form of the verb *ir + a* + infinitive is also used in Spanish to express future time.

   Voy a visitar una granja.   I am going to visit a farm.

3. The future tense is also used in Spanish, just as it is in English, to express future time.

   Llamaré más tarde.   I will call later.

The following chart shows how to form the future tense of regular -ar, -er, and -ir verbs.

FUTURE TENSE	
Regular Verbs	
INFINITIVE	ENDINGS
llamar comer subir	-é -ás -á -emos -éis -án

Some verbs are irregular in the future tense. The same endings are used, but they are added to an irregular stem instead of to the infinitive. The following verbs have irregular future stems.

decir: **dir-**	poner: **pondr-**	salir: **saldr-**
haber: **habr-**	querer: **querr-**	tener: **tendr-**
hacer: **har-**	saber: **sabr-**	venir: **vendr-**
poder: **podr-**		

212

For students having difficulty talking about what they will do in the future, you might consider:
- **The tutor page:** Pair a student with a native speaker or a more able student, using the tutor page.

Optional activities: See pages 204C: *Haré esto y luego...* and 204D: *Ganaremos la copa*

En una estancia

Pregúntale a tu compañero(a) quién hará las siguientes actividades en una estancia.

— *En una estancia, ¿quién recogerá la cosecha?*
— *El trabajador la recogerá.*

1. recoger la cosecha
2. llevar los animales a la feria
3. limpiar el establo

4. hacer el asado
5. cultivar la tierra
6. cepillar los caballos

 ¿Cómo es?

Pregúntale a tu compañero(a) si hará las siguientes actividades.

— *¿Montarás a caballo?*
— *Sí, montaré a caballo. Es divertido.*

1.
2.
3.
4.
5.
6.

es divertido
es necesario
es interesante
es fácil
es importante
es práctico

3 Actividades diarias

Haz una encuesta sobre las actividades diarias que harán tus compañeros(as) la próxima semana.

	Alicia	Jorge
Antes de ir a la escuela	prepararé el desayuno	me ducharé
Por la tarde		
Antes de comer		
Después de comer		
Antes de acostarse		

Informa a la clase de los resultados.

Antes de ir a la escuela, Alicia preparará el desayuno. Jorge se duchará.

213

ACTIVITIES

Students use the future tense to talk about who will do different chores on a ranch.

1. Pair Activity
Ask each other who will do the following ranch activities.
Possible Answers:
1. See model on student page.
2. *¿Quién llevará los animales a la feria?*
   El capataz los llevará.
3. *¿Quién limpiará el establo?*
   El trabajador lo limpiará.
4. *¿Quién hará el asado?*
   La cocinera lo hará.
5. *¿Quién cultivará la tierra?*
   La granjera la cultivará.
6. *¿Quién cepillará los caballos?*
   El trabajador los cepillará.

2. Pair Activity
Ask if your partner will do these activities.
Possible Answers:
1. See model on student page.
2. *¿Plantarás un árbol?*
   Sí, plantaré un árbol.
3. *¿Darás de comer a los animales?*
   Sí, daré de comer a los animales.
4. *¿Recogerás la fruta?*
   No, no la recogeré.
5. *¿Ordeñarás las vacas?*
   Sí, las ordeñaré.
6. *¿Cultivarás la tierra?*
   No, no la cultivaré.
Extension: Rewrite your sentences using **ir a.**

3. Group Activity
Survey your classmates about the daily activities they will do. Share with the class.
Answers: See model on student page.

CHECK

- *¿Cuándo iremos a la estancia?*
- *¿Qué harás allí?*
- *¿Te levantarás temprano?*

LOG BOOK
Have students write five sentences about what they will do and where they will be when they graduate.

213

Communicative Objective
• to express *for*, using **por** and **para**

Related Components

Activity Book p. 105-106	**Cuaderno** p. 66
Audio Book Script: Seg.4 Activities: p. 55	**Transparencies** Ch. 8: Para comunicarnos mejor Transparency 50
Audio Chapter: 8B, Seg. 4	**Tutor Page** p. 37

GETTING STARTED

Ask students to compare these sentences:
Compré el libro por diez dólares.
El libro es para Nancy.

Language in Context

Por and Para

It may help if students think of:
por as an action in the middle of a line (duration, through): *Paseamos por el parque.*
para as an action at the end of a line (deadline, recipient): *Tengo algo para ti.*

DISCUSS

Review vocabulary from previous chapters and introduce some of this chapter's new vocabulary with questions and statements that use **por** and **para**.
¿Estudias por la tarde o por la noche?
Este cuaderno es para mi clase de español.
Siempre salgo para la escuela a las ocho.
Gracias por tu ayuda.
¿Para qué es el camión?
¿Para qué es la manguera?
¿Te gusta vivir en el campo?
¡Claro! Por eso vivo aquí.

PARA COMUNICARNOS MEJOR

¿POR O PARA?

The prepositions *para* and *por* can both mean "for." However, in Spanish each one is used differently.

☐ Use *para* to indicate:

a deadline	**Necesito la segadora para mañana.** I need the mower by (for) tomorrow.
a function	**El tractor es para cultivar la tierra.** A tractor is used to till the soil.
a direction	**Vamos para el granero.** We are going towards the barn.
a recipient	**Esta comida es para los patos.** This food is for the ducks.
a purpose	**Van a la feria para comprar gallos.** They are going to the fair in order to buy roosters.

☐ Use *por* to indicate:

an exchange of one thing for another	**Pagué mucho dinero por esa vaca.** I paid a lot of money for that cow.
a specific period of time	**Me voy a quedar en la estancia por tres meses.** I am going to stay at the hacienda for three months.
by means of	**Hablamos por teléfono.** We spoke by phone.
the time of day	**Por la mañana monto a caballo.** In the morning I ride on horseback.
around, through	**Voy a caminar por la feria.** I am going to walk around the fair.

214

Language Note

The verbs **buscar, pedir,** and **esperar** do not require **por** or **para**, even though their English counterparts do. That is because *for* is "built into" these words.
For example:
Busco mi libro. I am looking for my book.
Los esperamos. We are waiting for them.
Ella pidió agua. She asked for water.

For students having difficulty distinguishing between the different uses of **por** and **para**, you might consider:
• **The tutor page:** Pair the student with a native speaker or a more able student, using the tutor page.
Optional activity: See page 204D: *¿Para mí? ¿Por qué?*

1 De viaje por Argentina

Tu compañero(a) viajará a Argentina. Hazle las siguientes preguntas.

— ¿Para qué irás a Argentina?
— Iré para visitar a unos amigos.

1. ¿Para qué irás a Argentina?
2. ¿Cuánto pagarás por el pasaje?
3. ¿Aprenderás a montar a caballo?
4. ¿Para quién comprarás regalos?
5. Desde allí, ¿hablarás con tu familia por teléfono?

2 Recuerdos de Argentina

Tu compañero(a) estuvo de vacaciones en Argentina. Hazle preguntas sobre las fotos que trajo.

— Y esta cosa, ¿para qué es?
— Es un tractor. Es para cultivar la tierra.

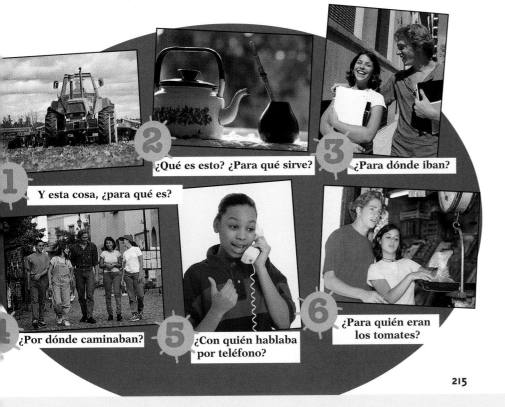

Y esta cosa, ¿para qué es?

¿Qué es esto? ¿Para qué sirve?

¿Para dónde iban?

¿Por dónde caminaban?

¿Con quién hablaba por teléfono?

¿Para quién eran los tomates?

215

ACTIVITIES

Students use **por** and **para** and the future tense to talk about a trip to Argentina.

1. Pair Activity
Your partner will travel to Argentina. Ask him or her these questions.
Possible Answers:
1. See model on student page.
2. *Pagaré trescientos dólares por el pasaje.*
3. *Sí, aprenderé a montar a caballo.*
4. *Compraré regalos para mi hermano.*
5. *Sí, hablaré por teléfono con mi familia.*
Extension: Say why you will do things.
Estudiaré mucho para sacar buenas notas.

2. Pair Activity
Your partner was on vacation at a ranch. Ask these questions about the photos.
Answers:
1. See model on student page.
2. *Esto es una pava de agua caliente y un mate. Sirven para tomar mate.*
3. *Íbamos para la escuela.*
4. *Caminábamos por la ciudad.*
5. *Hablaba por teléfono con mi amiga. Vive en Buenos Aires.*
6. *Los tomates eran para mi madre.*
Extension: Name objects. Your partner says how much he or she paid for them.
A: *¿Cuánto pagaste por tu vaca?*
B: *Pagué trescientos dólares por mi vaca.*

CHECK

- *¿Hablas por teléfono todas las noches?*
- *¿Cuánto pagaste por el disco compacto?*
- *¿Para quién es el regalo?*
- *¿Para qué vas a la tienda?*

LOG BOOK
Have students write one sentence for each use of **por** and **para**.

Para hispanohablantes

Think of phrases or expressions with **por** and **para** to share with the class.

215

Objectives
Communicative: to make plans to go somewhere
Cultural: to learn about rodeos in Argentina

Related Components

Assessment	Conexiones
Oral Proficiency: p. 28	Chapter 8
Audio Book	**Magazine**
Script: Seg. 5	Juntos en Argentina
Activities: p. 56	**Tutor Page**
Audio	p. 38
Chapter: 8B, Seg. 5	
Conexiones: 17B	

☐ GETTING STARTED

Students should now be able to correctly use **por** and **para, ir a** plus an infinitive, the future tense, and the chapter vocabulary. Have students look at the poster and try to figure out what type of event this is.

☐ APPLY

1. Pair Activity
Make plans to go to the Villaverde rodeo.
Answers: See model on student page.
Extension: Make up and write down directions to get to Villaverde.
Tomaremos la carretera Norte.

2. Pair Activity
Create a dialog with your partner about the activities you will see at the rodeo.
Answers: See model on student page.
Extension: Exchange your dialogs with other pairs. Check the text, and correct mistakes.

3. Pair Activity
Make a list of farm activities. Say whether they are easy or difficult, and how often each activity must be done.
Answers: See model on student page.
Extension: Using the model, make a class chart of the activities. Discuss the results with the class.

4. Pair Activity
Your partner works on a ranch. Interview him or her.
Answers: See model on student page.

5. Homework or Classwork
Write a paragraph about your daily routine, using **por** and **para.**
Answers: See model on student page.
Note: Help students get started by copying the model on the board and underlining the words which students will replace. Elicit suggestions, write them on the board, and have students choose some for their paragraphs.
Extension: Have volunteers dictate their paragraphs to the class. Then have students discuss and compare each other's daily routines.

For students having difficulty talking about ranch activities, you might consider:
• **The tutor page:** Pair the student with a native speaker or a more able student, using the tutor page.

SITUACIONES
¡VEN A LA DOMA!

GRAN doma DE POTROS EN VILLAVERDE

¡Vengan a ver a los domadores más expertos de La Pampa! Domingo, 27 de abril

◉ Concurso de doma
◉ Concurso de lazo
◉ Concurso de boleadoras
◉ Carreras de caballos

Y después, quédense a disfrutar de la fiesta en El Boliche, con asado, empanadas, mate, música, canciones y danzas criollas.

¡Un espectáculo para toda la familia!

Para más información, llamen a la estancia Villaverde: Tel. 555-0011

PARA TU REFERENCIA

disfrutar de *to enjoy*
el domador *horse-breaker*
el lazo *lasso*
el potro *colt*

216

¿Vamos a la doma?

Con tu compañero(a), haz planes para ir a la doma de Villaverde. ¿Qué día irán? ¿Qué ropa se pondrán? ¿Con quién irán?

— *Iremos a la doma el sábado.*
— *¿Invitaremos a Luis?*

 ¿Qué vamos a ver?

Con tu compañero(a), haz un diálogo sobre las actividades que verán en Villaverde.

— *¿Veremos una carrera de caballos?*
— *Sí, y también iremos al concurso de boleadoras.*
— *Y después tendremos que quedarnos para la fiesta en El Boliche.*

 ¿Es fácil o difícil?

Con tu compañero(a), haz una lista de actividades del campo y di si son fáciles o difíciles. Digan también con qué frecuencia hay que hacer estas actividades.

Actividades	Es fácil	Es difícil	Es necesario
dar de comer a los conejos	✓		todos los días
cepillar los caballos	✓		todos los días
ordeñar las vacas		✓	dos veces por día

 Entrevista

Entrevista a una persona que trabaja en una estancia.

— *¿Cuáles son las responsabilidades de su trabajo?*
— *Tengo que cuidar el ganado. Tengo que dar de comer a los animales, cepillar los caballos y ordeñar las vacas.*
— *¿También trabaja la tierra?*
— *Sí. Yo riego y recojo la cosecha.*

 Tu diario

Escribe un párrafo sobre tu rutina diaria usando *por* y *para.*

Por la mañana voy a la escuela por el parque. Por la tarde voy al gimnasio para nadar. Por la noche hago la tarea para la clase de español. Y para divertirme, generalmente salgo con mis amigos o hablo con ellos por teléfono.

217

- *¿Qué concurso te gustaría ver?*
- *¿Irás a la fiesta en El Boliche? ¿Por qué?*
- *¿De dónde son los domadores?*

LOG BOOK
Have students make a schedule of their daily routine.

Background

Argentina's Pampas
The *pampas* are flatlands located in the center of Argentina. They are very similar to the prairie lands of the midwestern US. Most of the country's agricultural production and cattle ranching occurs in the *pampas.* The topsoil is unusually deep. The nation's agricultural and cattle-ranching industries are located in the more humid parts of the *pampas.* Grains and grasses are grown there (year-round grass feeding gives Argentinian beef its distinctive flavor). Cattle ranching is a very important industry in Argentina. During the early 1970s, the average Argentinian consumed over 200 pounds of meat per year—a higher per capita rate than anywhere else in the world. Argentina exports large amounts of beef to Italy, Switzerland, and West Germany.

Para hispanohablantes

Write a poem about life in the country. Read it to the class.

Communicative Objectives
• to give and follow directions
• to understand and use traffic signs

Related Components

Transparencies	Video: Tape/Book
Ch. 8: Para resolver Transparency 51	Unit 4: Seg. 3

Scan to Chapter 8

GETTING STARTED

Ask why traffic signs are needed. Which ones are not essential? Are there any that do not exist that you believe should exist? What are they?

APPLY

Form groups. Each group will make a map with traffic signs of your town. Students may want to do some research in the library, or bring maps from home to use as reference. Ask them to create categories for the information they gather (e.g., traffic signs versus information signs).

PASO 1: Las señales
Look at the traffic signs in the drawing and say what each is for.
Answers: See model on student page.
Extension: Say what objects in the classroom are used for. Example:
El borrador es para limpiar la pizarra.

PASO 2: Nuestro pueblo
Choose the part of your town you wish to draw (e.g., downtown, the neighborhood around your school, roads in and out of your town). Think of a few places to include on the streets and highways.
Answers: See model on student page.
Extension: Ask other groups about the area they chose and the places they included.

PASO 3: El manual de manejar
Look at the driver's manual signs on page 219. Say which ones you'll need for your map.
Answers: See model on student page.
Extension: Explain why maps and traffic signs are important or necessary.

PASO 4: El mapa
Draw a map of the area you chose. Include traffic signs.

PASO 5: Las indicaciones
Choose two places on the map and say how to get from one place to the other.
Answers: See model on student page.
Extension: With another group, take turns dictating directions to each other. Then, exchange maps and practice giving and following directions.

PASO 6: El resultado final
Present your map to the class.

218

En grupo, harán un mapa de su pueblo o de su ciudad con señales de tráfico.

PASO 1   Las señales
Miren las señales de tráfico y digan para qué se usa cada una.

> *La señal de Dirección obligatoria se usa para decir que la calle o carretera sólo tiene una dirección.*

PASO 2   Nuestro pueblo
Escojan qué zona quieren dibujar: el centro comercial, el vecindario de la escuela, las carreteras que salen de su pueblo o ciudad... Decidan qué lugares incluirán en cada calle y cada ruta.

> *Vamos a dibujar un mapa de nuestro pueblo, de sus calles y de las rutas cerca de él. En la ruta 54 dibujaremos la Estancia Juanita...*

PASO 3   El manual de manejar
Miren las señales de tráfico en la página 219. Estas señales son del manual de manejar. Digan qué señales necesitarán para su mapa.

> — Hay que usar la señal de Escuela para la ruta 22.
> — Sí. También es importante usar la señal de Cruce para las rutas 54 y 22.

PASO 4   El mapa
Dibujen el mapa de la zona que escogieron. Incluyan las señales.

PASO 5   Las indicaciones
Escojan dos lugares del mapa y digan cómo llegar de un lugar a otro.

> *Para llegar a la estación de trenes desde la feria, hay que ir por la ruta 22 hasta la calle Peña. Allí, es necesario doblar a la izquierda.*

PASO 6   El resultado final
Presenten el mapa a la clase.

218

PARA TU REFERENCIA

la carretera resbaladiza *slippery road*
ceda el paso *yield*
el cruce *intersection*
la dirección obligatoria *detour*
pare *stop*
el paso a nivel *railroad crossing*
prohibido tocar la bocina *don't honk the horn*
la ruta *route*

MEETING INDIVIDUAL NEEDS

Reaching All Students

For Auditory/Kinesthetic Learners
Use commands to guide someone around the class to find a hidden object.

For Visual Learners
Quiz each other in pairs using traffic sign flashcards.

Señales de Tráfico

Prohibido circular en bicicletas	Prohibido tocar la bocina	Paso a nivel	
Aeropuerto	Gasolinera (1k m.)	Teléfono (100 m.)	Hospital
Semáforo	Cruce	Escuela	Carretera resbaladiza
Doble dirección	Prohibido el paso	Ceda el paso	Obras
Pare*	Prohibido girar en U	Dirección obligatoria	Rotonda

*In Argentina, they use *Pare*. In other countries, they use *Alto* or *Stop*.

¡SABES QUE...?

In an effort to lower the number of traffic accidents and to increase safety awareness, Argentina launched a campaign called **Luchemos por la vida** (Let's fight for life). The program educates students of all ages about the need to act responsibly to avoid accidents and save lives.

219

PORTFOLIO

Encourage students to include their maps in their Portfolios.

Background

Driving Words

Here are additional words that students may be interested in knowing:

cloverleaf *el cruce de trébol*
crossing signal *la señal de proximidad, la señal de cruce*
emergency brake *el freno de emergencia*
entrance ramp *la rampa de entrada*
exit ramp *la rampa de salida*
fire hydrant *la boca de incendios*
gas pump *el surtidor de gasolina*
highway *la autopista*
intersection *la intersección*
lane *la pista, el carril*
overpass *el paso superior*
parking meter *el parquímetro*
railroad crossing *el paso a nivel*
railroad track *la vía de ferrocarril*
right-of-way *el derecho de paso*
shoulder *el borde, el bordillo, el cordón*
sidewalk *la acera*
toll booth *la cabina de peaje*
traffic light *el semáforo*
underpass *el paso inferior*

Location Words Students Know

al norte, al noreste, al este, al sureste, al sur, al suroeste, al oeste, al noroeste (de)
a la derecha (de), a la izquierda (de), dobla a la, sigue derecho por, en el centro, entre, al lado de, delante de, detrás de, cerca de, lejos de

Para hispanohablantes

Think of other traffic signs and say their names in Spanish.

ENTÉRATE

Objectives
Communicative: to talk about *gauchos*
Cultural: to learn about an Argentine lifestyle

Related Components

Audio	Magazine
Conexiones: 17B	Juntos Argentina
Conexiones	
Chapter 8	

GETTING STARTED

Ask students if they have ever heard of *gauchos*. If not, have students look at the photos. Who do they think *gauchos* are?

DISCUSS

Using the Text

Have volunteers read the text. Ask some questions. Suggestions:
¿Qué representa el gaucho en Argentina?
¿Qué eran los gauchos en el siglo XVIII?
¿Cómo iban vestidos los gauchos?
Describan las bombachas.
¿Qué son las boleadoras?
¿Para qué eran?
¿Qué hicieron los propietarios privados?
¿Por qué perdieron los gauchos su espíritu libre y solitario?
¿Dónde trabajan los gauchos hoy?
¿Cuál es su responsabilidad?

CHECK

Te toca a ti
Possible Answers:
1. *Hoy los gauchos trabajan en el campo, generalmente en las estancias.*
2. *Escribió sobre el antiguo estilo de vida gauchesco.*
3. *Las usaban para inmovilizar a los animales.*
4. *La ropa típica del gaucho era el poncho, el sombrero y las bombachas.*
5. *Porque los propietarios privados compraron las tierras de las pampas.*

ENTÉRATE

LOS GAUCHOS

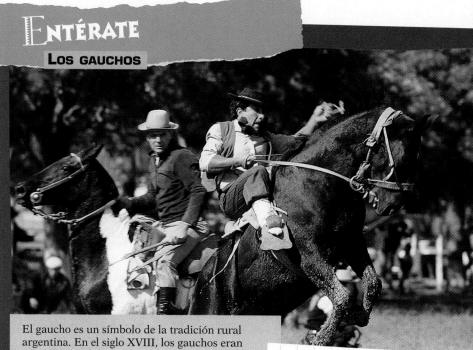

El gaucho es un símbolo de la tradición rural argentina. En el siglo XVIII, los gauchos eran nómadas que capturaban caballos salvajes° y ganado que se escapaba° en las pampas.

La ropa típica del gaucho era el poncho, el sombrero y las "bombachas", unos pantalones muy grandes. Los gauchos usaban lazos y "boleadoras", un instrumento hecho de cuerdas de cuero con tres bolas° en las puntas,° que se tiraba a las patas° del animal para inmovilizarlo.

En el siglo XIX, cuando propietarios privados° empezaron a comprar las tierras de las pampas, muchos contrataron° gauchos para trabajar en las estancias. Así los gauchos perdieron° su espíritu libre°. Muchos escritores argentinos de la época escribieron novelas sobre el antiguo estilo de vida gauchesco,° como José Hernández en *Martín Fierro* (1872).

Hoy, los gauchos son los trabajadores del campo en Argentina. Trabajan generalmente en las estancias y su responsabilidad es domar° potros y caballos, y cuidar los animales.

220

TE TOCA A TI

Contesta las preguntas.
1. ¿Qué hacen los gauchos hoy?
2. ¿Sobre qué escribió José Hernández?
3. ¿Para qué usaban los gauchos las boleadoras?
4. ¿Cuál era la ropa típica de los gauchos?
5. ¿Por qué cambió el estilo de vida de los gauchos en el siglo XIX?

(las) bolas *balls*
contrataron *they hired*
domar *to tame*
en las puntas *at the end*
el espíritu libre *free spirit*
gauchesco *of the guachos*
las patas *legs*
perdieron *they lost*
los propietarios privados *private owners*
salvajes *wild*
se escapaba *ran away*

CULTURE NOTE

The 19th-century *gauchos* were like the real cowboys of the old West, not the ones in the movies. Some were criminals. Most were homeless, and not interested in settling down. They camped out on the pampas.
The epic poem *Martín Fierro* by José Hernández (1834–86) is about the injustices that wiped out the original *gauchos*.

LOG BOOK

Have students write a few sentences about the North American cowhand.

Para hispanohablantes

In your own words, describe the lifestyle of the *gauchos*.

Vocabulario temático

En el campo
el algodón *cotton*
la caña de azúcar *sugar cane*
la doma *rodeo*
la estancia *ranch*
el maíz *corn*
la pampa *grassy plains*
la semilla *seed*
el trigo *wheat*

Los animales
el caballo *horse*
el cerdo *pig*
el conejo *rabbit*
el potro *colt*
la gallina *hen*
el gallo *rooster*
el ganado *cattle*
la oveja *sheep*
el pato *duck*
la vaca *cow*

En la estancia
el capataz *foreman*
el/la cocinero(a) *cook*
el corral *corral*
el establo *stable*
el granero *barn*
el/la granjero(a) *farmer*

el huerto
  fruit and vegetable garden
el/la jardinero(a) *gardener*
la tierra *land, soil*
el/la trabajador(a) *worker*

Actividades del campo
cepillar los caballos
  to brush the horses
cuidar el ganado
  to take care of the cattle
cultivar la tierra
  to till the soil
dar de comer a los animales
  to feed the animals
manejar el tractor
  to drive the tractor
ordeñar las vacas
  to milk the cows
plantar
  to plant
recoger la cosecha
  to harvest the crop
recoger la fruta
  to pick fruit
regar (e>ie)
  to water
sembrar (e>ie)
  to sow

Para trabajar en el campo
el camión *truck*
el cepillo *brush*
la manguera *hose*
la segadora *mower, harvester*
el tractor *tractor*

Expresiones y palabras
es difícil *it's difficult*
es fácil *it's easy*
es importante *it's important*
es mejor *it's better*
es necesario *it's necessary*
es posible *it's possible*
es práctico *it's useful*
hay que *one has to/must*
acostarse (o>ue)
  to go to bed
levantarse *to get up*
la parrilla *grill*
producir *to produce*
la responsabilidad
  responsibility
la rutina diaria *daily routine*
temprano *early*

LA CONEXIÓN INGLÉS-ESPAÑOL

Corral is spelled in Spanish as it is in English. Is there another word in the *Vocabulario temático* that is also spelled exactly the same way in both languages and has the same meanings?

Some cognates may be harder to identify than others. *Dormir,* for instance, does not sound anything like *sleep,* but when we compare it with the English word *dormitory* (a room for sleeping), the connection is easy to see. The Spanish word for "dormitory," or "bedroom," is *dormitorio.*

One-syllable words in English do not usually have a cognate in Spanish, but words consisting of two or more syllables often do: *tractor, plantar, importante, necesario.*

221

Objective
• to review vocabulary

Related Components

Activity Book	Audio
Chapter Review: p. 107-108	Assessment: 15A
Assessment	**Cuaderno**
Listening Script: p. 16	p. 67-68
Chapter Test: p. 87-92	**Transparencies** Ch. 8: Dibujos y palabras Transparency 52

Vocabulary

Point out that this section is organized by themes. Use the headings to review vocabulary. You may wish to ask Spanish speakers to share variations on these words and phrases with the class.

LOG BOOK

Have students write three sentences about one of the animals they learned about in this chapter.

La conexión inglés-español

Animal is spelled exactly as in English. Other cognates in the list that students may discover are: *maíz* (maize or corn), *establo* (stable), *fruta* (fruit), *posible* (possible), *producir* (to produce), *responsabilidad* (responsibility) and *rutina* (routine).

ADELANTE

Objectives

Prereading Strategy: to make use of previous knowledge
Cultural: to learn about Argentina's rich and varied terrain

Related Components

Magazine	Video: Tape/Book
Juntos en Argentina	Unit 4: Seg. 4

Scan to Adelante

GETTING STARTED

Ask students about the photographs here. What does the variety of pictures tell them about Argentina? What do students think this *Adelante* will be about?

Using the Video

Show Segment 4 of the Unit 4 video, an introduction to Argentina's geography.

Antes de leer

Have students read the first paragraph; ask questions. Examples:
Mira un mapa del mundo. ¿Hay países en América Latina que son más grandes que Argentina? (Brazil)
The following information can be found in the photos and captions:
¿Dónde están los picos más altos?
¿En qué parte del país hace calor? ¿Y frío?
Give students the directions on the student page.
Possible Adjectives:
bonito, diferente, emocionante, grande, hermoso, impresionante, increíble, larguísimo

About the Landscape

Argentina is divided into these regions:
1. the Andes mountain range, along the western border with Chile
2. the northern plains and Gran Chaco
3. the pampas, in central Argentina
4. the wind-swept steppes of Patagonia, in the south

ADELANTE

ANTES DE LEER

Argentina es un país de contrastes naturales: desde las inmensas llanuras hasta los picos más altos, con climas casi tropicales en el norte y temperaturas polares en el sur.

Piensa en lo que sabes de la geografía de América del Sur. ¿Hay algo que te llama la atención? Piensa en tres adjetivos para describir América del Sur.

222

ADELANTE COMPONENTS

Activity Book p. 109-112	Audio Adelante: 9A, 9B	Transparencies Unit 4: Adelante Transparencies 53-54	Video: Tape/Book Unit 4: Seg. 4-5
Assessment Portfolio: p. 39-40	Magazine Juntos en Argentina		

◀¿Te gustaría escalar uno de los picos más altos de América del Sur? El Fitz Roy está en la provincia de Santa Cruz y tiene 3.400 metros de altura.

◀Miles de elefantes marinos toman el sol en las playas de la península de Valdés, la única colonia de elefantes marinos de América.

◀Hoy en día los gauchos trabajan en las estancias. Su responsabilidad es domar° caballos y cuidar los animales.

domar *to tame*

223

Using the Photos

Los parques nacionales

Mount Fitz Roy is located in the southern-most part of Argentina, near the Chilean border. It is part of a national park. Other national parks in Patagonia include the Parque Nacional Nahuel Huapi, in the vicinity of San Carlos de Bariloche, and the Parque Nacional Los Arrayanes, in the province of Chubut.

¿Para qué van algunas personas al pico Fitz Roy?

¿Dónde está el pico?

Extension: *Más o menos, ¿cuántos pies equivalen a 3.400 metros?* (multiply by 3.3 to go from meters to feet: about 11,200 feet)

La península de Valdés

Sea elephants are one of two types of very large seals. The name comes from the long nose of the male sea elephant. Besides its large reserve of sea elephants, Península de Valdés is the largest reserve of sea lions, seals, penguins, and other exotic birds.

Estás en Argentina y quieres observar ele-fantes marinos. ¿Adónde puedes ir?

¿Puedes ver elefantes marinos en otros lugares de América del Sur?

Los gauchos del sur

Gauchos are not only expert horsemen. Some gauchos that live in Argentina's southeast are sheep breeders, herders and shearers.

Algunos argentinos tienen costumbres antiguas. ¿Cómo se llaman?

¿Dónde trabajan los gauchos hoy en día?

¿Cuáles son sus responsabilidades?

Para hispanohablantes

Tell the class about the climate and landscape of a country your family came from or has visited.

Objectives

Reading Strategy: to elicit meaning from context
Cultural: to learn about geographical features of Argentina

Related Components

Activity Book p. 109	Audio Adelante: 9A

GETTING STARTED

Ask if anyone has seen a large waterfall, a spectacular mountain, a petrified forest, or a glacier.

Background

Argentina is unusual among Latin American nations because it has a population of almost exclusively European origin. Spaniards and Italians were the most numerous immigrants, but waves of Britons and Germans have also left their mark. It is also one of the most highly urbanized countries in the Western Hemisphere; nearly all its inhabitants live in cities. Immigrants have tended to remain in the great port Buenos Aires, a city that is probably the most European-looking of any in the Western Hemisphere. Its population is about 12,000,000 people.
Argentina owes its name to the belief that it was rich in silver and to a poem called *La Argentina,* written by Barco Centenera, in 1602.

Identifying Main Ideas and Details

Have students notice that the subheadings in the text identify main ideas. With your students, construct a chart showing the main ideas and details of the passage.

Argentina
tierra de contrastes

Argentina está en el extremo sur del continente americano. Tiene fronteras con Chile, Bolivia, Brasil, Uruguay y Paraguay. Sus tierras inmensas van desde el trópico hasta la zona antártica.

Las cataratas del Iguazú

Las cataratas del Iguazú son las más impresionantes del mundo. Son más de 75 cataratas. Sus aguas caen desde 76 metros de altura.

Según una leyenda guaraní, un dios° del bosque se enamoró de una muchacha llamada Naipur. Un día, un guerrero° huyó° con Naipur por el río. El dios se enojó y hundió° el lecho del río.° Y así nacieron las cataratas del Iguazú. El dios convirtió° a Naipur en una roca y al guerrero en un árbol.

▲ El Aconcagua es uno de los picos más altos del mundo.

▲ Iguazú en guaraní significa *agua grande.*

convirtió *turned*	hundió *sank*
el dios *god*	huyó *fled*
el guerrero *warrior*	el lecho del río *riverbed*

224

DISCUSS

Suggestions for discussion:

Tierra de contrastes

Have students locate Argentina and its neighbors on a map. Ask:
¿En qué lugar de América del Sur está Argentina?
¿Qué países están al norte de Argentina? ¿Y al oeste?
¿Cuáles son los tres países más grandes de América? (Canadá, Estados Unidos, Brasil)

Las cataratas del Iguazú

¿Cuántas cataratas tiene el río Iguazú?
¿Qué quiere decir Iguazú?
Según lo que sabes del clima de Argentina, ¿piensas que Iguazú está en el norte o en el sur del país? ¿Por qué?
Según la leyenda guaraní, ¿cuál es el origen de las cataratas?

El centinela de piedra°

El Aconcagua es un pico de 6.959 metros de altura. Está en los Andes y es la montaña más alta de América. El nombre viene del quechua Ackon-Cahuac, y significa "centinela de piedra".

Araucarias gigantes

El Monumento Natural de Bosques Petrificados es un desierto volcánico de la era jurásica. Hace 150 millones de años esta región era húmeda y tenía bosques de araucarias, unos árboles de la familia de los pinos que sólo crecen en el hemisferio sur. La ceniza° de los volcanes de esta región cubrió° los bosques, que se fosilizaron lentamente.

▲ **El glaciar Perito Moreno.**

la ceniza *ash*
cubrió *covered*
las fogatas *fires*
se convierte en *becomes*
sigue creciendo *keeps on growing*

▲ **El explorador Fernando de Magallanes llamó a la región sur de Argentina *Tierra del Fuego* por las fogatas° que hacían los nativos.**

Los icebergs azules

El glaciar Perito Moreno es una masa de hielo de más de 60 metros de altura, que está en el lago Argentino, en la Patagonia. Es uno de los pocos glaciares del mundo que sigue creciendo.° Cada tres o cuatro años, una pequeña parte de este glaciar cae al lago Argentino y se convierte en° un iceberg. Muchos de estos icebergs son azules.

La misteriosa Tierra del Fuego

Tierra del Fuego es un archipiélago que está en el extremo sur de Argentina. Allí está Ushuaia, la ciudad más al sur del mundo.

Entre el continente y las islas de Tierra del Fuego está el estrecho de Magallanes. Los vientos son muy violentos y producen olas de muchos metros de altura.

> **DATOS SOBRE ARGENTINA**
>
> Es el octavo país más grande del mundo.
>
> Es el segundo país más grande y más poblado de América del Sur.
>
> Tiene el pico más alto de América: el Aconcagua, de 6.959 metros.
>
> Tiene la ciudad más al sur del mundo: Ushuaia.
>
> Tiene uno de los pocos glaciares del mundo que sigue creciendo: el glaciar Perito Moreno.

225

El centinela de piedra

¿En qué región está el Aconcagua? ¿Qué es? ¿De dónde viene su nombre? Más o menos, ¿cuántos pies son 6.595 metros?

Extension: At what time of the year do you think mountain climbers would climb Aconcagua? Why?

Araucarias gigantes

¿Qué es el Monumento Natural de Bosques Petrificados?
¿Cómo era la región hace 150 millones de años?
¿Qué son las araucarias?
¿Qué les pasó a estos árboles?

Los icebergs azules

¿Dónde está el glaciar Perito Moreno? ¿En qué región?
¿Por qué es diferente el glaciar Perito Moreno?
¿Cómo se forman los icebergs?
¿Viste un glaciar o un iceberg alguna vez? ¿Dónde?

La misteriosa Tierra del Fuego

¿Qué es Tierra del Fuego? ¿Dónde está?
¿Qué es Ushuaia?
¿Qué hay entre las islas de Tierra del Fuego y Argentina?
¿Es fácil navegar por el Estrecho de Magallanes?
¿Por qué se llama Tierra del Fuego este lugar de Argentina?

History Link: Who was Magallanes? (Ferdinand Magellan, c. 1480-1521, was a Portuguese navigator who led a Spanish expedition on the first circumnavigation of the globe. Although he was killed in the Philippines, his crew and ship, the Victoria, completed the voyage back to Spain.)

CHECK

- *¿Qué países están al lado de Argentina?*
- *¿Por qué es famoso el Aconcagua?*
- *¿En qué parte del país hay glaciares? A veces, ¿qué producen los glaciares?*
- *¿Cómo es Tierra del Fuego?*

LOG BOOK

Have students pretend they are visiting Argentina. Ask them to write three diary entries, telling about places they visited and things they saw.

Reading Aloud

Have volunteers take turns reading aloud different paragraphs from the passage.

These activities can be done as classwork or homework.

Objectives
Organizing Skills: to use lists to organize information
Communication Skills: to write questions and answers

Related Components

Activity Book	Assessment
p. 110	Portfolio: p. 39-40

ACTIVITIES

1. Juego de preguntas
Group Activity Write four questions about the reading for other groups to answer. Groups win one point for each correct answer and lose one turn for an incorrect answer.
Answers: Answers will vary.

2. Animales de Argentina
Group Activity Find out what kinds of animals there are in various regions of Argentina. Use encyclopedias, books, or magazines.
Possible Answers:
Iguazú: *tucanes, loros, monos, tapires, jaguares*
Tierra de Fuego: *elefantes marinos, pingüinos*
Los Andes: *guanacos, cóndores, zorros*
Las llanuras: *guanacos, vizcachas, pumas, zorros, chinchillas, armadillos, vicuñas*

3. Crucigrama
Individual Activity Create a crossword puzzle, using the places and vocabulary from the reading.
Answers: Answers will vary.

4. Compruébalo
Individual Activity Choose the correct ending for each sentence.
1. b **2.** c **3.** e **4.** d **5.** f **6.** a

DESPUÉS DE LEER

❶ Juego de preguntas
En grupo, escriban cuatro preguntas sobre Argentina. Hagan las preguntas a otro grupo. Anoten las respuestas.
• Los grupos ganan un punto por cada respuesta correcta.
• Si un grupo no sabe la respuesta, pierde su turno.

❷ Animales de Argentina
En grupo, busquen datos sobre los animales que hay en las diferentes regiones de Argentina. Pueden usar la enciclopedia, libros o revistas.

❸ Crucigrama
En una hoja de papel cuadriculado haz tu propio crucigrama, usando los lugares y el vocabulario del artículo.

❹ Compruébalo
Busca la descripción correcta.

1. La ciudad de Ushvaia está en...
2. Las cataratas del Iguazú caen desde...
3. El Aconcagua es un pico de...
4. El Monumento Natural de Bosques Petrificados es...
5. El Perito Moreno es...
6. Tierra del Fuego es...

a. un archipiélago en el sur de Argentina.
b. el extremo sur del continente americano.
c. 76 metros de altura.
d. un desierto volcánico de la era jurásica.
e. 6.959 metros de altura.
f. uno de los pocos glaciares del mundo que sigue creciendo.

TALLER DE ESCRITORES

1. UN CARTEL

Con tu compañero(a), diseña un cartel turístico sobre Argentina.
Incluye:

- datos de interés sobre el país
- lugares para visitar
- una descripción de los lugares
- comidas y bebidas típicas
- fotos de revistas y dibujos

2. CORREO ELECTRÓNICO

En grupo, preparen una lista de cinco preguntas para
enviar por correo electrónico a unos amigos en
Argentina. Tema: ¿Qué hacen los jóvenes en el campo y
en la ciudad?

- ¿Qué hacen los fines de semana?
- Cuando van al campo / a la ciudad, ¿qué les
  gusta hacer?
- ¿Cómo ayudan en la casa?
- ¿Qué platos saben cocinar?

Si no tienen correo electrónico, envíen una carta con estas preguntas.

3. UNA VIAJE

Pronto estarás de vacaciones en Argentina, tierra de grandes contrastes.
Usando el tiempo futuro, escribe un párrafo sobre lo que podrás ver allí:
gauchos, los Andes, la Patagonia...

227

Objectives
- to develop writing skills
- to use vocabulary and structures from this unit

Related Components

Activity Book	Assessment
p. 111	Portfolio: p. 39-40

ACTIVITIES

1. Un cartel
Pair Activity Students design a tourism poster for Argentina. Students may wish to use the library to gather additional information. They should include:
- historical and cultural facts
- places worth visiting
- descriptions of those places
- regional food and drink specialties
- photos and drawings

Edit: Pairs exchange posters and review and edit each other's work. They should make notes about possible errors, then work together to check spelling and grammar, and to prepare their final versions.

Present: Students show and explain their poster to the class.

Variation: You may wish to have students work in groups of five or ten; each student or pair chooses one topic and contributes to a group poster.

2. Correo electrónico
Group Activity Students will prepare five questions for a class in Argentina. The theme: what young people do in the city and the country. They should find out:
- what students do on weekends
- what they like to do in the city or the country
- what they do to help out at home
- what dishes they know how to cook
Send your questions by e-mail.

3. Un viaje
Individual Activity Students will use the future tense to write a paragraph about what they will see on a trip to Argentina.

PORTFOLIO
Suggest that students select one of these assignments to add to their Portfolios.

Objectives

Communicative: to listen to and understand directions

Cultural: to learn about *empanadas,* a popular meal in Argentina

• to make *empanadas*

Related Components

Assessment Portfolio: p. 39-40	**Video: Tape/Book** Unit 4: Seg. 5
Transparencies Unit 4: Project Transparency 53	

Scan to La obra

Ingredients and Utensils

- flour, 2 cups
- salt and pepper
- lard, 1 cup
- water, 1/4 cup
- ground beef, 1 lb.
- 1 large onion
- 5 hard-boiled eggs
- paprika, 1 tsp.
- 12 olives
- cumin, 1 tsp.
- raisins, 1/4 cup
- cooking oil
- rolling pin
- measuring cup
- fork
- frying pan
- bowl
- round cookie-cutter, 5" diam.

GETTING STARTED

Encourage students to use their eyes more than their ears. Rather than try to understand every word, they should concentrate on the actions and listen only for clues. If possible, show the *empanada*-making segment of the Unit 4 video.

DISCUSS

Read aloud the introductory text. Ask a few questions, such as:
¿En qué países se comen empanadas?
¿Quiénes introdujeron las empanadas en América?
¿De qué están hechas?

MANOS A LA OBRA

¡BUEN PROVECHO!

Las empanadas son un plato típico de Argentina y de otros países de América Latina. Llegaron a América con los españoles, que las adoptaron de los árabes.

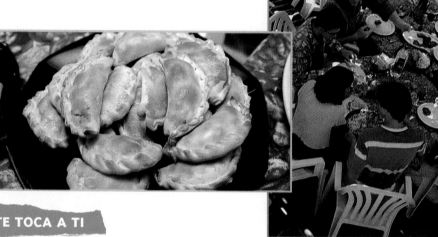

TE TOCA A TI

Hay muchos tipos de empanadas. En cada región de Argentina las hacen de una manera diferente. El relleno° puede ser de carne, de pollo, de pavo o de muchas otras cosas. Hoy prepararemos empanadas de carne.

Utensilios
un rodillo° y un tenedor
una tapa° de cinco pulgadas

Ingredientes

La masa°
dos tazas de harina
sal
una taza de manteca°
1/4 de taza de agua fría

El relleno
1/2 kilo de carne picada°
una cebolla grande,
  picada° fina
cinco huevos duros
una cucharadita° de
  pimentón°

doce aceitunas picadas
una cucharadita de comino
  molido°
1/4 de taza de pasas°
sal y pimienta°

aceite para freír

228

el comino molido *powdered cumin*
la cucharadita *teaspoon*
la manteca *lard*
la masa *dough*

las pasas *raisins*
picada *chopped*
el pimentón *red pepper*
la pimienta *pepper*

el relleno *filling*
el rodillo *rolling pin*
la tapa *lid*

Thinking About Language

Ask students to guess what Spanish work **empanada** could come from. They may need some hints to arrive at **pan.** Explain that an empanada is literally something "in" or "covered with" bread or dough.

1 Combina la harina, la sal y la manteca. Poco a poco,° añade° el agua. Mézclalo° todo bien y haz una masa. Con el rodillo, extiende° la masa.

2 Con la tapa o las manos, haz círculos de cinco pulgadas.

3 Fríe la carne durante un minuto. Después añade la cebolla picada, el pimentón, el comino, las pasas, las aceitunas, la sal y la pimienta. Fríe todo a fuego lento° durante 20 minutos.

4 Deja enfriar° el relleno. Después, pon un poco de relleno encima de cada círculo de masa. Añade también un poco de huevo duro en cada empanada.

5 Pon un poco de agua en los bordes° de cada círculo. Cierra la empanada. Une los bordes con un tenedor o con las manos.

6 Puedes cocinar las empanadas de dos maneras:° friéndolas en aceite (de 10 a 15 minutos) o poniéndolas en el horno a 375 °F durante 25 minutos. ¡Buen provecho!

a fuego lento *over a low flame*
añade *add*

los bordes *edges*
de dos maneras *in two ways*
deja enfriar... *let cool . . .*

extiende *extend*
mézclalo *mix it*
poco a poco *little by little*

HANDS-ON

Using the directions in the book, lead students through the creation of an *empanada*.
1. Act out the process as you or a volunteer read aloud the instructions.
2. After you have done this several times, invite volunteers to do it as you read aloud the directions.
3. Do this as TPR with the whole class.

CHECK

Have students perform the actions of *empanada*-making as you describe them, but give the instructions in a different order.

LOG BOOK

Have students write down the ingredients needed to make *empanadas*.

Para hispanohablantes

Ask a family member for the recipe of a typical dish from the country your family originally came from. Share with the class. If possible, prepare the dish and serve it to the class.

Research Project

Have students form groups to research national or regional variations for making **empanadas.** Encourage them to use a variety of sources—the library, videos, or interviews with friends, relatives, or other teachers. They may also want to search the Internet, if possible. Ask them to organize their information according to country or region.

Objectives

- to expand reading comprehension
- to relate the study of Spanish to other subject areas

Related Components

Activity Book	Transparencies
p. 112	Unit 4: Adelante
Assessment	Transparency 54
Portfolio: p. 39-40	**Video: Tape/Book**
Audio	Unit 4: Seg. 4
Adelante: 9B	

Scan to Adelante

El pato

About Pato

Why would a game be called "duck"? Because the original game was played with a duck in a basket. (The winners got to eat it.) Nowadays the *pato* is a leather ball with handles.

Possible Answers:

- *Es un deporte argentino muy antiguo.*
- *El polo, las carreras de caballos.*

Activity

Ask students to say whether the following statements are true or false.
1. *Para jugar al pato, tienes que saber montar a caballo.* (Cierto)
2. *Es un deporte que se juega en equipos.* (Cierto)
3. *El juego empieza cuando un jugador tira el pato a la meta.* (Falso)

Una bebida para compartir

About Mate

Mate is made from the holly leaf. It is considered a stimulant, yet is soothing to the stomach and nutritious.

Possible Answers:

- *Es una planta aromática.*
- *Se toma en una calabacita hueca, con una caña.*

Activity

Ask questions:
¿El mate se toma frío o caliente?
¿Qué contiene la infusión de mate?
¿Conoces otros rituales similares?
¿Cómo se prepara el mate?

DEPORTE

EL PATO

El pato es un deporte argentino muy antiguo. Dos equipos de cuatro jugadores a caballo tratan de agarrar° "el pato"— una pelota de cuero con asas.° El juego empieza cuando un jugador tira el pato al suelo.° Los otros jugadores tienen que ir a buscarlo y el jugador que lo agarra tiene que llegar a la meta° y marcar un gol. Antes, el pato se jugaba en el campo. Hoy día se puede jugar al pato en un estadio.

- ¿Qué es el *pato*?
- ¿Qué otros deportes conoces que se practican a caballo?

GASTRONOMÍA

UNA BEBIDA PARA COMPARTIR

El mate es la bebida nacional de Argentina. Tomar mate es un ritual que comparten las familias y los amigos. La *yerba mate* es una planta aromática que se cultiva en el norte del país. La infusión° de mate se hace poniendo yerba mate seca en una calabacita hueca,° que también se llama *mate*. Después se añade agua muy caliente y azúcar. Se toma con una caña° de metal o de plata, que se llama *bombilla*.

- ¿Qué es la yerba mate?
- ¿Cómo se toma el mate?

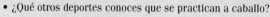

agarrar *to grab*		
las asas *handles*	**la caña** *straw*	
la calabacita hueca *hollow gourd*	**la infusión** *herb tea, infusion*	**tira ... al suelo** *throws ... on the ground*
	la meta *finish line*	**tratan de agarrar** *try to catch*

230

Reading Aloud

Have volunteers take turns reading aloud the selections in *Otras fronteras*.

Research Project

Ask students to form groups to do additional research on one of the topics in *Otras fronteras*. Encourage them to use a variety of sources: reference books, the Internet, interviews, etc. Have them organize their findings according to sources.

ARTE

LA BOCA Y SU ARTISTA

El barrio° de La Boca está en la costa al sur de la ciudad de Buenos Aires. Allí nació el artista Benito Quinquela Martín (1890-1977). Quinquela empezó a pintar en este barrio y le dedicó toda su vida.°

Quinquela decoró con murales y esculturas la calle Caminito, una de las calles más famosas de Buenos Aires. Los vecinos pintaron sus casas con los mismos colores vivos que Quinquela usó en sus obras. La calle Caminito es también famosa porque el cantante Carlos Gardel la inmortalizó en uno de sus tangos. Hoy, La Boca es uno de los lugares más pintorescos de toda América del Sur.

- ¿Qué hizo Benito Quinquela en La Boca?
- ¿Por qué es famosa la calle Caminito?

CINE

EL CINE ARGENTINO

Desde su comienzo° en 1897, el cine argentino tuvo reconocimiento internacional. Muchos directores argentinos consiguieron° fama mundial. Uno de ellos es la directora María Luisa Bemberg, quien dirigió:° *Camila, Miss Mary, Señora de nadie* y *Yo, la peor de todas;* ésta última sobre la vida de la escritora mexicana Sor Juana Inés de la Cruz. En 1986, *La historia oficial* de Luis Puenzo, ganó el Oscar a la mejor película extranjera.

- ¿Cuándo comenzó el cine argentino?
- ¿Qué directores argentinos conoces?

el barrio *neighborhood*
el comienzo *beginning*
consiguieron *achieved*

dirigió *directed*
le dedicó toda su vida *devoted his whole life to it*

231

La Boca y su artista

About Quinquela and La Boca

La Boca was originally a working-class suburb of Buenos Aires, a district of simple houses with corrugated iron roofs. The name refers to the mouth of the river. Quinquela Martín inspired other artists to move there. He also turned his studio into a free art school for needy children with a talent for the arts.

Possible Answers:

- *Decoró con murales y esculturas una calle de La Boca.*
- *Es famosa por el arte de Quinquela. También es el título de un tango de Carlos Gardel.*

Activity

Ask questions, such as:
¿Qué es La Boca? ¿Dónde está?
¿Cómo se llama un artista conocido que nació allí?
¿Cómo es el arte de Quinquela?
¿A los residentes de La Boca les gustó el trabajo de Quinquela?
¿Cómo lo sabes?
¿Quién es Carlos Gardel?

El cine argentino

About *La historia oficial*

In the film, an upper-class Argentinian couple adopts an orphaned child. The wife discovers, however, that the parents had been killed by a police death squad and the child stolen. The story was based on real-life events during the rule of a military junta. During this period, over 30,000 people "disappeared."

Answers:

- *Comenzó en 1897.*
- *María Luisa Bemberg y Luis Puenzo.*

Activity

Ask students to say whether the following statements are true or false.

1. *El cine argentino comenzó en el año 1986. (Falso)*
2. *María Luisa Bemberg es una directora de cine argentina. (Cierto)*
3. *Ninguna película argentina ha ganado un Oscar. (Falso)*

 Tell your students . . .

In this unit we travel to Spain, where high fashion and competitive sports play vital roles in the everyday life of young people. Spain's capital, Madrid, is a world center of clothing design (Chapter 9), while Barcelona has been associated with the best in sports since it played host to the 1992 Olympic Games (Chapter 10). In Madrid, we join a photo shoot of the latest in teen fashion, then visit a hair stylist before taking off on a clothes-shopping spree that leads to a chat with cutting-edge designer Agatha Ruiz de la Prada. In Barcelona, after a quick run-down of healthy do's and don'ts, we work out at a gym, watch a jai-alai game, and drive to a sports center where Spain's top athletes practice in ideal condi-tions. Then we take our places on the starting line for an exhilarating 42-kilome-ter marathon.

Before leaving Madrid and Barcelona, we take a quick survey of Spain's favorite sports. Would it surprise you to learn that soccer is Spain's most popular sport, with basketball coming in a not-so-close second? But Spaniards are also enthusi-astic about swimming, gymnastics, bicycling, golf, field hockey, judo, and volley-ball. Finally, we visit one of Spain's renowned leather craftsmen, who helps us make a leather belt pouch that's both stylish and sporting.

CULTURAL BACKGROUND: FOR THE TEACHER

Geography and Climate

Spain covers most of the Iberian peninsula in southwestern Europe. It shares borders with Portugal, France, and Andorra. Three bodies of water surround Spain: the Atlantic Ocean, the Mediterranean Sea, and the Bay of Biscay. The Meseta, Spain's largest geographic region, is a broad central plateau bordered by mountains on all sides. Madrid, the capital of Spain, is located in the middle of this region. Summers in the Meseta are hot and winters are cold. The entire northern region is rainy while the interior of southern Spain is exceptionally dry. Long beaches, a temperate climate, and mild sea breezes draw crowds of tourists to Spain's Mediterranean coast.

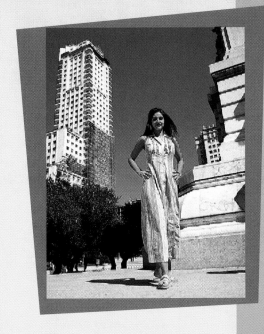

History and Government

Spaniards owe much of their cultural diversity to successive waves of foreign influences. Celts, Phoenicians, Carthaginians, Greeks, Romans, Visigoths, and Moors all inhabited the peninsula. By 1492, the Catholic Monarchs, King Ferdinand and Queen Isabella, had united many of Spain's kingdoms into one nation. The monarchy sent explorers to the New World and quickly annexed these newly discovered lands. Two generations later, under the reign of Philip II, Spain had the largest and most powerful empire in the world with colonies in four different continents. Spain's fortune declined during the 18th and 19th centuries, due partly to the loss of its profitable, colonial empire.

Long-simmering tensions among rivaling, political factions led to the Spanish Civil War in 1936. General Francisco Franco emerged as the leader of the Nationalist Party and defeated the Popular Front. What followed was a military dictatorship under Franco's rule until his death in 1975. After the death of Franco, King Juan Carlos became head of state. By 1978, Spain had become a constitutional monarchy. Since then, the country has embarked on a path of progressive economic, social, and political reform.

Languages of Spain

Four main languages are spoken in Spain. Spanish, often referred to by Spaniards as Castilian, is spoken by the country's 40 million inhabitants. The regional languages, Basque, Catalan, and Galician, are spoken in the Basque Country, Catalonia, and Galicia, respectively. All four are official languages of the country. They each have standardized grammar and their own literature.

Yo, Cristóbal Colón

HISTORY CONNECTION

Objective
- to write a diary entry in Christopher Columbus' journal

Use
any time during Unit 5

Materials
- TRB Activity Support Page 18, *Yo, Cristóbal Colón* (diary page)

Activity
- Share the FYI, and anything else you know about Columbus's first voyage to the New World. Distribute activity support page.
- Have students write an entry in Columbus' secret diary. They can make up as much as they like, but the entries should be based on facts from the FYI. One entry might begin: *6 de agosto de 1492. Hoy hace tres días que salimos de Palos. Todos los marineros están contentos. Hace buen tiempo.*
- Have students read their entries to the rest of the class. When all entries have been read, students vote for the most convincing, the most interesting, etc.

FYI
On August 3, 1492, Christopher Columbus and his fleet of three ships, *La Niña, La Pinta,* and *La Santa María,* set sail for the Indies from Palos in southern Spain. During the trip Columbus kept a journal, and in it he describes the crew's high spirits at the beginning of the journey, and their fear when they left Europe behind. To comfort them, he reported less progress each day than the ships actually made, but in his diary he kept secret calculations of their exact position. At the end of September, some crew members planned a mutiny which Columbus stopped by threatening the conspirators with death. On October 11, a sailor saw signs of land, and the next day the three ships dropped anchor in the New World.

¿Te gusta el gazpacho?

HANDS ON: COOKING

Objective
- to prepare and eat *gazpacho,* a cold vegetable soup from Andalusia

Use
any time during unit 5

Ingredients
- 4 bell peppers
- 2 cloves of garlic
- 2 lbs tomatoes
- 10 tbs olive oil
- 4 tbs vinegar
- 1/4 lb bread crumbs
- 4 cups cold water
- salt
- croutons

Supplies
- knife
- mortar and pestle
- bowl
- strainer
- small paper cups

Preparation
- Dice peppers. Crush garlic and diced peppers in mortar with a little salt. Put mixture in bowl.
- Cut tomatoes into little pieces and add to bowl.
- Add moistened bread crumbs and crush with pestle.
- When everything is well crushed, add olive oil little by little, stirring continuously.
- After oil has been absorbed, add cold water and then strain off until soup is as thick or thin as you want it.
- Add vinegar and salt to taste, and refrigerate. Serve the *gazpacho* very cold—with croutons, if you wish. Six servings should be enough to give 32 students a good taste.

FYI
The word *gazpacho* probably comes from the Etruscan word *caspa,* which means "piece" and may refer to cutting vegetables into little pieces. Olive oil and garlic are basic ingredients in Spanish cooking, as they are in the cooking of France, Italy, and Greece. At various times, parts of the Spanish peninsula were Greek and Roman colonies, and the influence of the two ancient civilizations can be seen not only in Spain's culinary traditions but also in many architectural ruins.

Ya somos políglotas*

CULTURAL CONNECTION

Objective
• to explore the three other languages spoken in Spain besides Castilian

Use
any time during Unit 5

Materials
• TRB Activity Support Page 19, *Ya somos políglotas*
• bilingual dictionaries

Activity
• Share the FYI and distribute the Activity Support Page.
• Ask students to look at List 1, with words in Castilian and their equivalents in French and Portuguese. Have them fill in the column provided for the English.
• Have students look at List 2, with words in Castilian, Basque, Catalan, and Galician. Then have them order the words in the Catalan and Galician columns so that the words and phrases match the Castilian and Basque columns, which are already matched. Students should order the two columns by comparing the Catalan expressions with Castilian and French, and the Galician expressions with Castilian and Portuguese.
(Answer key: *List 1* United States, you're welcome, goodbye, good, friend, yesterday *List 2* Catalan 2, 4, 1, 6, 3, 5 Galician 5, 3, 6, 1, 4, 2)

FYI
Four main languages are spoken in Spain: Castilian, Basque, Catalan, and Galician. Spaniards often refer to the Spanish language as Castilian, which is spoken by the country's 40 million citizens. Basque is spoken in the Basque country, located partly in northern Spain and partly in southwestern France. It is spoken by 600,000 people. Catalan is spoken by 6 million people who live in French Provence as well as Catalonia, Valencia, and the Balearic Islands. Catalan sounds like a cross between Spanish and French. Galician combines features of Spanish and Portuguese and is spoken by the 3 million inhabitants of Galicia.

*políglota someone who speaks several languages

Mi edificio modernista

ART CONNECTION

Objective
• to design a house modeled after a 20th-century masterpiece in Barcelona

Use
any time during Unit 5

Materials
• posterboard
• markers
• bilingual dictionaries
• TRB Activity Support Page 20, *Modernismo catalán*

Preparation
• Divide class into groups of four. Each group is a team of architects.

Activity
• Share the FYI and add anything else you know about *modernismo* or *art nouveau.*
• Distribute activity support page. Have each group choose their favorite building and discuss their preference. For example, an architect from one group might say: *Nuestro edificio favorito es el de Gaudí, porque tiene formas interesantes y muchos colores.* Someone from another group: *Nosotros preferimos la Casa Ametller de Puig i Cadafalch porque es simple.*
• After the discussion, ask each group to draw the front of another house, in the style of the architect whose house they prefer.
• Display the drawings and ask the class to vote for the new house they like the most. Why do they like it?

FYI
During the 19th century, the population and wealth of Barcelona skyrocketed as a result of the city's effective style of industrialization. Prosperity led to political and cultural innovation, exemplified at the end of the century by *modernismo,* the Catalan version of the sinuous organic art called *art nouveau* in France. A stroll through the streets of Barcelona's Eixample neighborhood brings you face-to-face with countless examples of modernist architecture. Nowhere is this more true than on the so-called "block of discord," in the Paseo de Gracia, where you can see extraordinary buildings by several of the era's finest architects. The most famous ones are Casa Ametller, by Puig i Cadafalch (1867-1957), Casa Batlló, by Gaudí (1852-1926) and Casa Lleó Morera, by Domènech Montaner (1850-1923).

ESPAÑA: ¡QUÉ BIEN TE SIENTA!

Unit Opener Goals
- to introduce Spain
- to talk about fashion and health

Related Components

Transparencies	Video: Tape/Book
Unit 5: Chapters 9-10	Unit 5: Seg. 1
Transparencies 55-67	

Scan to Unit 5

■ GETTING STARTED

Ask students to name cities they know in Spain. Ask questions that elicit Madrid and Barcelona as answers. Examples:
¿Qué ciudad es la capital de España?
¿En qué ciudad fueron los Juegos Olímpicos de 1992?
Have students locate these cities on a map.

Using the Video

Show Segment 1 of the Unit 5 video, an introduction to Spain.

Using the Transparencies

To help orient students to Spain, use the Locator Map Transparency. You may want to use other transparencies for Unit 5 at this time.

■ DISCUSS

Presenting Spain

For more information about Spain, refer to pages 232A–232D.

Using the Text

English: After students have read the introduction, ask questions. For example:
What large cities are you familiar with?
What do you think all cosmopolitan cities, like Madrid and Barcelona, have in common?

Spanish: Ask Spanish speakers to share with the class any words or phrases they associate with health, fitness, or fashion.

UNIDAD 5

ESPAÑA

¡QUÉ BIEN TE SIENTA!

En la unidad 5:

Capítulo 9	¿Qué está de moda?
Capítulo 10	¡Ponte en forma!
Adelante	**Para leer:** Fútbol y baloncesto en España
	Proyecto: Práctico y de moda
	Otras fronteras: Cine, arte y astronomía

Funicular de Montjuich, Barcelona.
Plaza de España, Madrid.

232

UNIT COMPONENTS

Activity Book p. 113-136	**Audio Book** Script: p. 57-59; 63-65	**Conexiones** Chapters 9-10	**Transparencies** Unit 5: Chapters 9-10 Transparencies 55-67
Assessment Oral Proficiency: p. 29-30 Listening Script: p. 17-18 Chapter Tests: p. 93-104 Portfolio: p. 41-42	Activities: p. 60-62; 66-68 **Audio** Chapter: 10A, 10B Adelante: 11A, 11B Assessment: 15A, 15B Conexiones: 18A	**Cuaderno** p. 69-84 **Magazine** Juntos en España	**Tutor Pages** p. 39-46 **Video: Tape/Book** Unit 5: Segments 1-5

What do you do to keep in shape? What clothes do you and your friends wear? These are questions asked by people your age all over the world. In this unit, you'll get some answers from teenagers of Madrid and Barcelona.

Madrid is the center of Spain's fashion industry. Here's where many of Spain's cutting-edge styles are designed and made. In this unit, you'll do some shopping, get a new hair style, and learn what's "in" for Spanish teens. In Barcelona, you'll work out at a gym, visit a school for athletes, and get a good look at how young *barceloneses* keep healthy and in shape.

After you've gotten into the swing of fashion and fitness, you'll learn something about sports in Spain. Soccer and basketball are very popular in Spain, and you'll learn why. Finally, you'll make a *riñonera*, or a small leather bag to wear around your waist to carry your money and other things for your visit to these two exciting Spanish cities. *¡Ponte en forma!*

233

INTERDISCIPLINARY CONNECTIONS

To provide other perspectives, have students research questions like these:

Dance

Encourage students to research dances and the countries each dance is associated with. A few examples from Spain: *jota, flamenco,* and *sardana.*

Social Studies

Spain is a member of the European Union (EU). What is the purpose of the EU and what other countries are members? (The nations of the EU—known as the European Community until 1994—are working toward establishing common defense and foreign policies, and, ultimately, a common currency. The Treaty of European Union went into effect on November 1, 1993. At the beginning of 1996, the other 14 member countries were Austria, Belgium, Denmark, Finland, France, Germany, Greece, Ireland, Italy, Luxembourg, Netherlands, Portugal, Sweden, and the United Kingdom.)

Geography

The rain in Spain falls mainly on the plain, doesn't it? (No. The high plains, or Meseta Central, are semiarid. Summer features hot, dusty winds, and winter cold, gusty ones. Most of the rain falls along the north coast, especially in Galicia, in the northwest.)

Politics

What kind of a government does Spain have? (Spain is a constitutional monarchy, like Great Britain. The king is head of state but has no direct role in the operations of the government. The prime minister directs the government's day-to-day operations, controlling the Cortes, Spain's two-house legislature.)

	Objetivos page 235 *¿Qué está de moda?*	Conversemos pages 236-237 *La moda y tú*	Realidades pages 238-239 *Moda joven*	Palabras en acción pages 240-241 *¡Vamos a las galerías!*
Comunicación	To talk about: • clothing and hair styles	Discuss clothing and hair styles	Read text, talk about shoe and clothing styles	Read cartoon, discuss characters; describe places; discuss current fashion
	• how clothes fit and look	Discuss how clothes fit and look	Read text, talk about choices in clothing, survey class	Read cartoon, create dialog
	• taking care of your personal appearance	Discuss caring for one's personal appearance	Read text, make list, talk about choices in clothing, survey class	Read cartoon, discuss appearance and hair style; create dialog
Cultura	To learn about: • clothing and hairstyles of Spanish teenagers • Spanish designers		Announcement for a Spanish shoe store; Spain's role in the history of shoe design	Information about *Las galerías* (shopping center in Madrid)
Vocabulario temático	To know the expressions for: • types of clothing and footwear	Talk about types of clothing and footwear	Read text, make list, talk about choices in clothing, survey class	Read cartoon, discuss characters; describe places; discuss fashion; design poster; write of clothing and weather
	• hairstyles	Talk about getting your hair styled	Read text, talk about shoe and clothing styles	Read cartoon, discuss appearance and hair style; design poster
	• getting ready to go out	Talk about getting ready for an event	Read text, talk about choices in clothing, survey class	Read cartoon, discuss characters; talk about current fashion; discuss appearance and hair style; write about clothing and weather
Estructura	To talk about: • specific clothes and other items: demonstrative pronouns	Use demonstrative pronouns to discuss particular clothes and other items	Read text, make list, talk about choices in clothing, survey class	Read cartoon, make list; discuss characters; describe places; discuss fashion; create dialog; write about clothing and weather
	• how to avoid repeating a noun: article + adjective		Read text, use article + adjective to talk about choices in clothing	
	• qualities of people, places, and things: the verb *ser*	Use the verb ser to discuss qualities of people, places, and things	Read text, talk about choices in clothing, survey class	Read cartoon, create dialog
	• temporary condition or qualities: the verb *estar*	Use the verb *estar* to discuss temporary conditions and qualities	Read text, talk about choices in clothing, survey class	Read cartoon, describe places; discuss current fashion

¿QUÉ ESTÁ DE MODA?

Para comunicarnos mejor (1) pages 242-243 *¿Ése es de lana?*	Para comunicarnos mejor (2) pages 244-245 *¿Es interesante Madrid?*	Situaciones pages 246-247 *¡A cortarse el pelo!*	Para resolver pages 248-249 *Una revista de modas*	Entérate page 250 *España: moda internacional*
Discuss purchases; create dialogs between customer and sales clerk	Discuss purchases; talk about clothing; make table	Read text, discuss hair salon, hair styles; role-play dialog between hairdresser and customer; interview famous hairdresser; write in diary	Choose name, specialty, and season for fashion magazine; discuss clothing design; choose pictures; present to class	Discuss the fashion industry in Spain
Discuss purchases	Discuss purchases	Read text, write in diary	Choose pictures; present magazine to class	
Discuss purchases	Discuss purchases	Read text, discuss hair salon; talk about hair styles	Choose name, specialty, and season for fashion magazine; talk about clothing design; choose pictures; present to class	
	Photograph of a statue in Madrid; converse about Madrid	Announcement for a hair cutting salon in Spain	Information about what Spanish teenagers wear	
Discuss purchases; create dialogs between customer and sales clerk	Discuss purchases; talk about clothing; make table			
	Make table	**Re-entry of vocabulary**		**Extension of vocabulary**
Discuss purchases	Talk about clothing; make table			
Discuss purchases; create dialogs between customer and sales clerk	Talk about things that don't change, using *ser* and an adjective			
	Talk about clothing; make table	**Re-entry of structure**		**Extension of structure**
Create dialogs between customer and sales clerk. Use demonstrative pronouns to refer to a specific person, place or thing	Discuss purchases; talk about clothing; make table			
Create dialogs between customer and sales clerk	Discuss purchases; talk about clothing; make table			

¿Qué llevo hoy?

GAME

Objective
• to play a game describing clothing, using Chapter 9 *Vocabulario temático*

Use
after *Palabras en acción,* pages 240-241

Materials
• foam ball

Preparation
• Review the *Vocabulario temático.*
• Remind students that an adjective's gender and number agree with those of the noun it modifies, and that most nouns precede their adjectives.

Activity
• Throw the ball to a student and ask: *¿Qué llevo hoy?*
• The student answers by describing your clothing. For example, he/she might say: *Hoy usted lleva pantalones a cuadros, una camisa blanca sin mangas y zapatos bajos negros.*
• The student then throws the ball to another student, repeating the question: *¿Qué llevo hoy?*
• The game is over when everyone has described his/her clothing.

Variation
• After playing the activity above, students write their names on slips of paper and mix them in a bag. A volunteer comes to the front of the class, faces the blackboard, picks a name from the bag, and describes from memory the clothing of the chosen student.

Dime quién es

HANDS ON: COLLAGE

Objective
• to make and identify collages, using Chapter 9 *Vocabulario temático*

Use
after *Palabras en acción,* pages 240-241

Materials
• news and fashion magazines
• scissors
• glue
• posterboard
• bilingual dictionary (one per group)

Preparation
• Hand out magazines, one per student, and have students form groups of four.
• Each group selects a picture of a famous person, without letting other groups know whom they pick.

Activity
• Have students use fashion magazines and newspapers to cut out items of clothing.
• Groups work together to make a fashion collage that represents an individual's personality.
• Other groups look at the collage and describe what the personality of the person who dresses in this type of clothing might be like. The group must work together to come up with reasons for their decision. Example: A collage showing sneakers, baggy pants, ripped jeans, a tee-shirt, a leather jacket, motorcycle boots. Possible answer: *Esta persona es muy deportiva porque le gusta la ropa cómoda, como los tenis, los pantalones anchos y las chaquetas de cuero.*

La moda de hoy

GAME

Objective
- to play a game about current fashions, using adjectives and articles

Use
after *Para comunicarnos mejor,* pages 242-243

Materials
- 3" x 5" index cards

Preparation
- Have students brainstorm adjectives that describe current fashions in clothing, such as *largo, corto, bonito, moderno, viejo, suave, de cuero, de algodón, de lana, de mangas largas/cortas,* etc. List them on the chalkboard.
- Write four categories on the chalkboard: *pantalones de hoy, zapatos de hoy, abrigos/chaquetas de hoy,* and *camisas/camisetas de hoy.*

Activity
- Pair students and give each pair a set of four index cards, asking them to write a different category on each card.
- Have the first pair do the activity in front of the room so the class learns how to play the game. For example: Student A mixes the cards, and Student B selects one. If it's the *abrigos/chaquetas* card, Student B asks a question such as: *¿Qué abrigos te gustan?* Student A looks at the list of adjectives on the chalkboard and answers in a way that explains his/her preference(s). For example: *Me gustan los de cuero porque son más modernos.* Make sure pairs replace each noun with an article followed by an adjective or adjectives.
- Partners reverse roles after each card, playing until both have selected adjectives for all categories.

Desfile de modas

FASHION CONNECTION

Objective
- to have a fashion show, using demonstrative pronouns and the verbs **ser** and **estar**

Use
after *Para comunicarnos mejor,* pages 244-245

Materials
- coats and jackets, or backpacks

Preparation
- Have students bring in different items of clothing to place in a box in the front of the room.

Activity
- Each group chooses several different items of clothing to model in front of the class.
- As they model the item, students describe what they are wearing. For example: *Esta chaqueta es de cuero. Es muy cómoda y popular. Es negra y tiene cremallera.*
- Other members of the group may make additional observations, using the *Vocabulario temático.*

¿QUÉ ESTÁ DE MODA?

Introduce the chapter and its theme by asking if students think that teenagers all over the world wear more or less the same styles. What factors probably influence how young people dress? Are these exactly the same everywhere?

Related Components

Audio Conexiones: 18A	**Video: Tape/Book** Unit 5: Seg. 2
Conexiones Chapter 9	

Scan to Chapter 9

GETTING STARTED

Have students look at the photograph and think about why these people are dressed as they are. Ask questions. Suggestions:

¿Adónde piensas que van estos jóvenes?
¿Están vestidos para ir a una fiesta?
¿Por qué piensas que sí o que no?

Critical Thinking

Use the following activity to help students discover for themselves what they need to know in order to talk about clothing, hairstyles, and footwear.

La ropa, el pelo y los zapatos
Tell students to think about fashion for clothing, hair, and shoes. Assign groups to make lists of:
- clothing styles
- clothing designs
- hairstyles
- shoe styles
- what they do to take care of their appearance
- words that describe clothing

Have each group write its list on the board. Have the class discuss the lists and decide which items are the most essential. Have each group submit a revised list. When you finish the chapter, have the class review the lists to see how they compare to what they learned in the chapter.

CAPÍTULO 9

¿QUÉ ESTÁ DE MODA?

De moda en Madrid.

234

CHAPTER COMPONENTS

Activity Book p. 113-122	**Audio Book** Script: p. 57-59 Activities: p. 60-62	**Conexiones** Chapter 9	**Transparencies** Chapter 9 Transparencies 56-60
Assessment Oral Proficiency: p. 29 Listening Script: p. 17 Chapter Test: p. 93-98	**Audio** Chapter: 10A Assessment: 15A Conexiones: 18A	**Cuaderno** p. 69-76 **Magazine** Juntos en España	**Tutor Pages** p. 39-42 **Video: Tape/Book** Unit 5: Seg. 2

Objetivos

COMUNICACIÓN
To talk about:
- clothing, shoes, and hairstyles
- taking care of your personal appearance

CULTURA
To learn about:
- what Spanish teenagers wear
- Spanish designers

VOCABULARIO TEMÁTICO
To know the expressions for:
- types of clothing and footwear
- hairstyles
- getting ready to go out
- going shopping and to the hairdresser's

ESTRUCTURA
To talk about:
- specific clothes and other items: demonstrative pronouns
- how to avoid repeating a noun
- permanent qualities: the verb *ser*
- temporary qualities: the verb *estar*

¿SABES QUE...?

Most people probably think of Italy or France as the center of European clothing design. However, fashion is also a thriving business in Spain. Some well-known Spanish designers include Adolfo Domínguez, Jesús del Pozo, Pedro del Hierro, Purificación García, and Sybilla. Spaniards like to keep informed about the latest fashion news. Spanish versions of *Vogue* and *Elle* are among the fashion magazines popular with many Spaniards. Most newspapers, such as *El País*, feature current trends, emerging designers, and seasonal shows in a special fashion section of their Sunday editions.

Here are some additional activities that you may wish to use as you work through this chapter with your students.

Communication
Encourage after-class activities that may enhance student interest and proficiency. Some ideas:
- organize a Spanish fashion show, with students as models, photographers, designers, reporters, and commentators. Videotape the show.

Culture
The written word can only hint at what life is like in other lands. To encourage greater understanding:
- rent videos of films from Spain to show what Madrid looks like and what people there wear
- show the video that accompanies Unit 5 of this textbook

Vocabulary
To reinforce vocabulary, have students:
- make sets of flashcards for these categories: shirts, pants, patterns and colors, hairstyles, footwear, personal appearance. Students take turns choosing one card from each pile and describe a person according to the cards.

Structure
To reinforce demonstrative pronouns and **ser** and **estar** with adjectives:
- have students look through a clothing catalog and describe the clothing they like. They should say which they would prefer to buy and compare various articles of clothing.

Thinking About Language
Ask students to use the lists from the *Critical Thinking* activity to brainstorm equivalent words in Spanish, or in other languages. Are there any cognates?

 INTERNET LINK

Spain http://www.odci.gov:80/cia/ publications/95fact/es.html

Communicative Objectives

To talk about:
• clothing and hairstyles
• personal appearance
• footwear

Related Components

Activity Book p. 113	**Cuaderno** p. 69
Audio Book Script: Seg. 1	**Transparencies** Ch. 9: Conversemos Transparency 56
Audio Chapter: 10A, Seg. 1	

GETTING STARTED

Ask students to give examples of the latest fashion trends. How long do they think these styles will be "in"?

ACTIVITIES

These activities give students an opportunity to begin communicating with each other and with you, focusing on the theme and objectives of the chapter. The activities can be used as oral class activities, or, if you prefer, you can pair students to achieve more interaction.

¿Qué tipo de ropa y diseños están de moda?

Class activity to introduce and review clothing items. Ask *¿Qué llevan Uds. hoy?* Have students use new and review words to say what they and others are wearing. Point out examples of clothing patterns in the class. Ask the title question. Ask what is not fashionable right now.

¿Cómo cuidas tu aspecto?

Class activity to introduce vocabulary related to grooming. Do a quick review of reflexive verbs and **por** (to express frequency). Have students use vocabulary from previous chapters to describe their morning routine. Examples: *bañarse, cepillarse los dientes, ducharse, lavarse el pelo, peinarse, ponerse la ropa, secarse.*

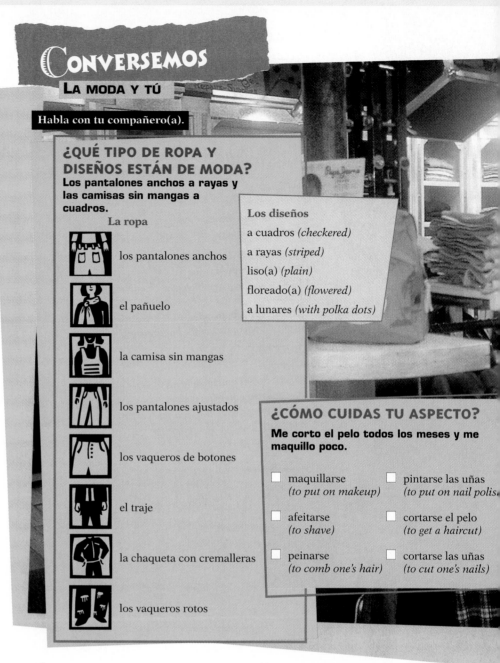

CONVERSEMOS

LA MODA Y TÚ

Habla con tu compañero(a).

¿QUÉ TIPO DE ROPA Y DISEÑOS ESTÁN DE MODA?
Los pantalones anchos a rayas y las camisas sin mangas a cuadros.

La ropa

los pantalones anchos

el pañuelo

la camisa sin mangas

los pantalones ajustados

los vaqueros de botones

el traje

la chaqueta con cremalleras

los vaqueros rotos

Los diseños

a cuadros *(checkered)*

a rayas *(striped)*

liso(a) *(plain)*

floreado(a) *(flowered)*

a lunares *(with polka dots)*

¿CÓMO CUIDAS TU ASPECTO?

Me corto el pelo todos los meses y me maquillo poco.

☐ maquillarse *(to put on makeup)*

☐ pintarse las uñas *(to put on nail polish)*

☐ afeitarse *(to shave)*

☐ cortarse el pelo *(to get a haircut)*

☐ peinarse *(to comb one's hair)*

☐ cortarse las uñas *(to cut one's nails)*

236

MEETING INDIVIDUAL NEEDS

Reaching All Students

For Auditory/Visual Learners
Describe what someone in class is wearing for others to guess who it is.

For Kinesthetic Learners
Mime all the actions in *¿Cómo cuidas tu aspecto?* The class writes down the order in which you acted them.

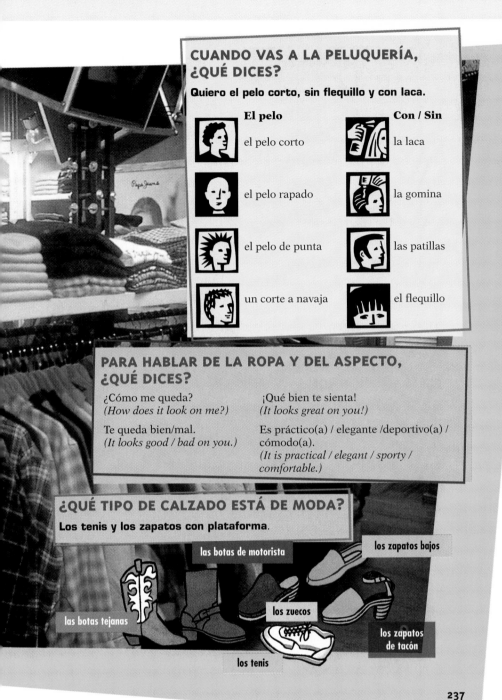

CUANDO VAS A LA PELUQUERÍA, ¿QUÉ DICES?

Quiero el pelo corto, sin flequillo y con laca.

El pelo		Con / Sin	
	el pelo corto		la laca
	el pelo rapado		la gomina
	el pelo de punta		las patillas
	un corte a navaja		el flequillo

PARA HABLAR DE LA ROPA Y DEL ASPECTO, ¿QUÉ DICES?

¿Cómo me queda?
(How does it look on me?)

Te queda bien/mal.
(It looks good / bad on you.)

¡Qué bien te sienta!
(It looks great on you!)

Es práctico(a) / elegante /deportivo(a) / cómodo(a).
(It is practical / elegant / sporty / comfortable.)

¿QUÉ TIPO DE CALZADO ESTÁ DE MODA?

Los tenis y los zapatos con plataforma.

las botas de motorista

los zapatos bajos

las botas tejanas

los zuecos

los zapatos de tacón

los tenis

237

Cuando vas a la peluquería, ¿qué dices?

Class activity to discuss hairstyles and hair products. Ask students about their own hairstyles. Use magazine photos to demonstrate the new vocabulary. Have two volunteers roleplay a scene between a **peluquero(a)** and a **cliente**.

Para hablar de la ropa y del aspecto, ¿qué dices?

Class activity to introduce phrases that describe how clothes fit and look. Put on a piece of clothing that does not fit well and ask *¿Cómo me queda?* Bring in magazine photos of people who seem well-dressed and others who don't. Incorporate the vocabulary from the first activity.

¿Qué tipo de calzado está de moda?

Class activity to introduce types of shoes. Ask: *¿Qué zapatos llevas hoy? ¿Están de moda?* Use TPR to expand this activity. Give commands such as: *Levanten la mano los chicos y las chicas que tienen botas tejanas.* Ask what kinds of shoes they would wear to parties, proms, and other affairs.

CHECK

- *¿Qué tipo de ropa llevas hoy?*
- *¿Cómo cuidas tu aspecto todos los días?*
- *¿Cómo llevas el pelo hoy?*

PORTFOLIO

Have students cut out some glossy magazine photos of people with different hairstyles and clothing. Students should label the photos and include them in their Portfolios.

Communicative Objectives
- to talk about shoe and clothing styles
- to say what kinds of clothing you like

Related Components

Activity Book p. 114	Audio Chapter: 10A, Seg. 2
Audio Book Script: Seg. 2	Cuaderno p. 70

☐ GETTING STARTED

Ask students what qualities they look for when buying a new pair of shoes. Is style more important than comfort?

☐ DISCUSS

Talk about the advertisement, and ask questions. Suggestions:

Calzados Dandy
¿Qué es "moda para los pies"?
¿Qué prefieres, las botas o los zapatos?
¿Cómo son los calzados Dandy?
¿Qué tipo de calzado Dandy te gustaría comprar? ¿Por qué?
Ask volunteers to draw the several models of Dandy footwear on the board.

REALIDADES

MODA JOVEN

CALZADOS DANDY

MODA PARA LOS PIES

Te presentamos unas botas Dandy. Te llevan a todos lados y están siempre contigo. Se llevan bien con los trajes y con los vaqueros rotos. Son deportivas, cómodas y prácticas. ¿Las quieres como amigas?

También tenemos:
botas de motorista
zapatos bajos
zuecos a lunares
zapatos de tacón
sandalias floreadas

238

MEETING INDIVIDUAL NEEDS

Reaching All Students

For Auditory Learners
Name a place, and have others say what type of shoes you should wear. Example:
La playa: Debes llevar sandalias.
La estancia: Debes llevar botas tejanas.

For Visual Learners
Design an ad for a shoe made in 2050. Create names for the brand and the model, describe the model, say how much the shoes cost, and why people should buy them.

HABLA DEL ANUNCIO

A. Haz una lista de la ropa que queda bien con el calzado del anuncio.

Los pantalones ajustados, los trajes...

B. Habla con tu compañero(a). Di por qué te gustaría o no, comprar zapatos o botas Dandy.

— *Me gustaría comprar las botas negras Dandy porque son deportivas. ¿Y a ti?*
— *A mí me gustaría comprar las botas marrones porque puedo llevarlas con mi traje nuevo.*

¿QUÉ OPINAS?

¿Por qué llevas esa ropa? Haz una lista de la ropa. Después, haz una encuesta en la clase. Usa el modelo.

Ropa	porque...	yo	la clase
la camisa a rayas	es cómoda	✓	//
el traje	es elegante		///
los vaqueros	son deportivos	✓	///
los vaqueros rotos	están de moda		

Según la encuesta, ¿cuál es la ropa más popular?
¿Y la menos?

¿SABES QUE...?

Footwear has a long history on the Spanish peninsula. Cave paintings found in Spain, dating back to 15,000 B.C., show a man wearing leather boots and a woman wearing fur boots. Throughout the ages, Spaniards have made significant contributions to shoe design. In fact, one of today's most influential shoe designers, Manolo Blahnik, was born and raised in the Canary Islands. His shoes are renowned for their originality and their fine materials.

239

Habla del anuncio

Individual and Pair Activities: Writing and Conversing
A. Make a list of clothes that would go well with the shoes you see in the ad.
B. With your partner, talk about why you would or would not like to buy a pair of Dandy shoes or boots.
Answers: See models on student page.
Extension: Describe the footwear you saw the last time you went shopping.

¿Qué opinas?

Group Activity: Taking a Poll
Why do you wear the kinds of clothes you wear? Make a list of clothing, and take a class poll. Make a chart like the one shown to record the reasons.
Answers: See model on student page.

Class Activity: Evaluation
- Have representatives of each group take turns reporting on their polls. Have volunteers go to the board and list the items of clothing, the reasons for wearing them, and the numbers.
- According to the poll, which are the most and least popular reasons for wearing certain clothes?
Extension: Write five sentences summarizing your results.

Extension: Find three fashion advertisements and analyze what each is trying to communicate. Share your findings with the class, and discuss how such advertising affects your lives.

CHECK

- *¿Cómo son los calzados Dandy?*
- *¿Qué tipos de zapatos tienen?*
- *¿Dónde compras tus zapatos?*

LOG BOOK
Have students make a list of the types of shoes they own.

Para hispanohablantes

Think of other expressions you would use to talk about fashion.

PALABRAS EN ACCIÓN

Communicative Objectives

To talk about:
- shopping malls
- clothing
- hair salons

Related Components

Activity Book p. 115-116	Transparencies Ch. 9: Palabras en acción
Cuaderno p. 71-72	Tutor Page p. 39

GETTING STARTED

Ask students to name some stores or chains that are popular with teenagers. How are these stores different from the ones their parents prefer?

DISCUSS

Name an object from the drawing and have students compete to find it. Comment on and ask questions about the drawing. For example:
¿En qué lugar cortan el pelo?
¿Cómo se llama la tienda de calzado?
¿Te gusta el nombre?

Para hispanohablantes

If you use words or expressions other than the ones introduced in this chapter, share them with the class. A few variations:

a rayas: de rayas
el aspecto: la pinta, la apariencia
el calzado: los zapatos
la camisa sin mangas: la camisa de manguillos
cortarse el pelo: recortarse
el corte: el recorte
la cremallera: el cierre
floreado: de flores
la gomina: la brillantina
la laca: el spray
a lunares: de puntitos, de topos
la máquina de afeitar: la rasuradora eléctrica
los pantalones ajustados: los pantalones apretados
el peluquero: el barbero, el estilista
la peluquería: el salón de belleza

PALABRAS EN ACCIÓN

¡VAMOS A LAS GALERÍAS!

1 **¿Qué ves en el dibujo?**

Haz una lista de los lugares y las cosas que ves en las galerías. Compara tu lista con la de tu compañero(a).

> *En la peluquería: las tijeras, el secador...*

2 **¿Qué hacen? ¿Qué llevan?**

Escoge cinco personas del dibujo. Pregúntale a tu compañero(a) qué están haciendo y qué ropa llevan.

> — *¿Qué está haciendo el peluquero?*
> — *Está cortando el pelo.*
> — *¿Qué ropa lleva el cliente en la peluquería?*
> — *Lleva unos pantalones lisos y una camisa a lunares.*

3 **¿Dónde estoy?**

Eres un(a) cliente o empleado(a) en los lugares del dibujo. Haz tres preguntas sobre cada lugar. Tu compañero(a) tiene que adivinar dónde estás.

> — *¿Dónde está el probador?*
> — *¿Están de rebaja las camisas sin mangas?*
> — *¿Cuánto cuestan los trajes a rayas?*
> — *Estás en la Boutique Mambo.*

4 **¿Qué está de moda?**

Pregúntale a tu compañero(a) qué está de moda este año.

> — *¿Qué está de moda?*
> — *Los pantalones anchos, las botas de motorista, los zapatos de tacón...*

240

For students having difficulty talking about clothing, shoes, or hairstyles, you might consider:
- **The tutor page:** Pair the student with a native speaker or a more able student, using the tutor page.

Optional activities: See page 234C: *¿Qué llevo hoy?* and *Dime quién es*

5. El pelo y el aspecto

Pregúntale a tu compañero(a) cómo le gusta llevar el pelo y cómo cuida su apariencia.

— ¿Cómo te gusta llevar el pelo?
— Me gusta el pelo de punta y con mucha gomina.
— ¿Cómo cuidas tu aspecto?
— Me maquillo todos los días.

6. Miniteatro

Imagina que tu compañero(a) y tú están en una tienda de ropa o en una zapatería. Hagan un diálogo.

— ¿Cómo me quedan estos pantalones?
— Te quedan muy bien. ¿Son cómodos?
— Sí. Y me gustan porque también son deportivos.

7. La peluquería

Diseña un cartel con un anuncio para una peluquería. Describe qué cortes de pelo hacen y cuánto cuesta cada uno. Usa dibujos o fotos de revistas y periódicos.

8. Tú eres el autor

Escribe un párrafo sobre la ropa que llevas cuando hace calor y cuando hace frío.

Cuando hace calor me pongo pantalones anchos lisos, una camisa sin mangas floreada y zuecos rojos. Cuando hace frío me pongo unos pantalones vaqueros ajustados, un suéter y una chaqueta de cuero.

241

ACTIVITIES

1. Pair Activity
Make a list of the places and things you see in the mall. Compare lists.
Extension: Write a word that describes each place or thing on your list.

2. Pair Activity
Choose five people from the drawing. Ask your partner what they are doing and wearing.
Extension: Say what your partner is wearing.

3. Pair Activity
Pretend you are a customer or an employee in one of the places in the drawing. Think of three questions you would ask in each place. Your partner guesses where you are.
Extension: Answer the questions that your partner asked.

4. Pair Activity
Ask what is fashionable this year.
Extension: Ask what was fashionable a year or two ago.

5. Pair Activity
Ask what hairstyles and personal grooming practices your partner prefers.
Extension: Report to the class. Example: *A Ramón le gusta llevar el pelo de punta y con mucha gomina.*

6. Roleplay Activity
Imagine that you are in a clothing store or a shoe store. Create a dialog.
Note: Students may want to use the "Sizes and Measurements" chart on page 247.

7. Hands-On Activity
Design an ad for a hair salon. Describe the haircuts and list the prices. Use drawings or photos from magazines or newspapers.
Extension: React to the prices. Example: *¡Qué caro!*

8. Writing Activity
Write a paragraph about the clothes you wear during hot or cold weather.
Note: Have students follow the model, changing words as necessary. Help students by copying the paragraph on the board, underlining the words to be changed.

CHECK

- ¿Cómo es la ropa que llevas hoy?
- ¿Cómo llevas el pelo hoy?
- ¿Qué calzado llevas en invierno?

LOG BOOK
Have students write a few sentences describing what they wore to school yesterday.

Communicative Objectives

- to refer to a specific person, place or thing, using demonstrative pronouns
- to avoid repeating a noun, using an article with an adjective
- to respond to a question in which the article **un** is used, using **uno(a)**

Related Components

Activity Book p. 117-118	**Cuaderno** p. 73
Audio Book Script: Seg. 3 Activities: p.60	**Transparencies** Ch. 9: Para comunicarnos mejor Transparency 58
Audio Chapter: 10A, Seg. 3	**Tutor Page** p. 40

GETTING STARTED

Review demonstrative adjectives before discussing demonstrative pronouns. Write sentences with examples of both on the board, and ask what looks different about the sentences. (Demonstrative pronouns carry an accent.)

Language in Context

Demonstrative Pronouns: Point out that pronouns in Spanish work in the same way as in English. For example, hold up a pencil and say something like: "Look at this six-inch tubular yellow wood-and-graphite writing instrument." Then hold up another object and say: "Look at this."
Point out that the second sentence was far less specific than the first. Was it any more difficult to understand than the first sentence? Are there advantages to simply saying *this* or *that* at times, rather than repeating *pencil* (or whatever the noun happens to be)?
Make sure that students realize that **éste** is used to refer to something that is close and **ése** to something further away. Also point out demonstrative pronouns and adjectives may be used in the same sentence. For example: *Esta camisa es más elegante que ésa.*

Using Adjectives and Articles: It may be easier to begin by demonstrating the structure in English: "Do you prefer the yellow pencil or the green?" How do we know that *green* refers to a pencil? Would adding *one* after *green* help? How?

¿ÉSE ES DE LANA?

To avoid repeating nouns, we use demonstrative pronouns. These agree in gender and number with the nouns they replace.

— ¿Ese traje es de lana?	Is that suit made of wool?
— No. Ése es de algodón.	No. That one is made of cotton.
— ¿Y de qué son estas camisas?	And what are these shirts made of?
— Éstas son de lana.	These are made of wool.

☐ Demonstrative pronouns are the same as demonstrative adjectives except that the pronouns have a written accent.

Estas botas me gustan, pero aquéllas me gustan más.	I like these boots, but I like those over there better.

demonstrative pronouns

	singular			plural		
masculine	éste	ése	aquél	éstos	ésos	aquéllos
feminine	ésta	ésa	aquélla	éstas	ésas	aquéllas
	this (one)	that (one)	that (one)	these	those	those

Another way to avoid repeating a noun is to use an article with an adjective. The adjective agrees in gender and number with the noun it replaces.

— ¿Te gustan los pantalones negros?	Do you like the black pants?
— Más o menos. Me gustan más los azules.	So-so. I like the blue ones better.

☐ When the article used in the question is **un,** it becomes **uno** in the answer.

— ¿Necesitas un secador grande?	Do you need a big hair dryer?
— No. Necesito uno pequeño.	No. I need a small one.

DISCUSS

Review vocabulary from previous chapters and introduce some of this chapter's new vocabulary with questions and statements that use **uno,** articles with adjectives, and demonstrative pronouns.
¿Cuál es mi libro, éste o aquél?
¿Qué libro te gusta más, éste o ése?
Quiero comprar pantalones como aquéllos.
¿Te gustan los nuevos discos de Hootie and the Blowfish?
Me gustan más los antiguos.
¿Quieres un traje elegante o uno deportivo?
Quiero uno deportivo.

For students having difficulty using demonstrative pronouns, articles with adjectives, or **uno,** you might consider:
- **The tutor page:** Pair the student with a native speaker or a more able student, using the tutor page.

Optional activity: See page 234D: *La moda de hoy*

1 ¿Éste o aquél?

Quieres comprar algo, pero no puedes decidir qué comprar.
Pregúntale a tu compañero(a).

— ¿Te gusta esta chaqueta de cuero con cremalleras?
— No mucho. Me gusta más aquélla con botones.

1.   3.   5.

2.   4.   6.

2 De compras

Es el cumpleaños de un(a) compañero(a). ¿Qué le van a comprar?
Pregúntale a tu compañero(a).

— ¿Le compramos una camisa floreada?
— No. Una lisa le gustará más.

1.   3.   5.

2.   4.   6.

3 En el centro comercial Isalo

Tu compañero(a) es empleado(a) en un centro comercial y tú eres
un(a) cliente. Hazle preguntas sobre las cosas que vende.

— ¿Es de lana ese pañuelo?
— ¿Qué pañuelo? ¿El rojo o el floreado?
— El rojo.
— Ése es de lana.

1. ¿Es de lana ese pañuelo?
2. ¿De qué talla es esa camisa sin mangas?
3. ¿Son de botones esos vaqueros?
4. ¿Esos secadores están en rebaja?
5. ¿Cuánto cuestan esas botas de motorista?
6. Ese traje, ¿es de algodón?

243

ACTIVITIES

Students use demonstrative pronouns,
articles with adjectives, and **uno** to talk
about shopping.

1. Pair Activity
You want to buy something, but can't
decide what. Ask your partner.
Possible Answers:
1. See model on student page.
2. ¿Te gustan los vaqueros de botones?
   No, me gustan más los rotos.
3. ¿Te gusta el traje a cuadros?
   No tanto. Prefiero éste a rayas.

4. ¿Te gusta la máquina de afeitar amarilla?
   No. Prefiero aquélla negra.
5. ¿Te gustan estos pantalones de color rosa?
   No. Ése no es mi color favorito.
6. ¿Te gustan los pantalones anchos lisos?
   No. Me quedan mejor los ajustados.

2. Pair Activity
It's a friend's birthday. What will you and
your partner buy him or her?
Answers:
1. See model on student page.
2. ...un secador grande?
   No. Ella necesita uno pequeño.
3. ...los zapatos a cuadros?
   Sí. Le gustan ésos más que las botas.
4. ...unos pantalones a lunares?
   No. Ésos no le gustan.
5. ...la gomina?
   Sí. También le compraremos aquella laca.
6. ...los zapatos de tacón?
   No. Unos bajos le van a quedar mejor.

3. Pair Activity
Practice these dialogs between a shopping
center employee and a customer.
Possible Answers:
1. See model on student page.
2. ¿Qué camisa? ¿La roja o la verde?
   La verde.
   Ésa es de talla mediana.
3. ¿Cuáles vaqueros? ¿Los negros o los
   azules?
   Los negros.
   Ésos son de cremallera.
4. ¿Qué secadores? ¿Los grandes o los
   pequeños?
   Los pequeños.
   Ésos no están en rebaja.
5. ¿Qué botas? ¿Las negros o las marrones?
   Las marrones.
   Ésas cuestan ochenta dólares.
6. ¿Qué traje? ¿El liso o el a lunares?
   El a lunares.
   Ése es de algodón.

CHECK

- ¿Son de talla mediana esos pantalones?
- ¿Te compramos unos zapatos a lunares?
- ¿Les gustaron aquellos zuecos que vieron ayer?
- ¿Necesitas una chaqueta de cuero?

Communicative Objectives
- to talk about things that don't change, using **ser** and an adjective
- to talk about things that might change, using **estar** and an adjective

Related Components

Activity Book p. 119-120	**Audio** Chapter: 10A, Seg. 4
Audio Book Script: Seg.4 Activities: p. 61	**Cuaderno** p. 74
	Tutor Page p. 41

GETTING STARTED

Review the explanation of the different uses of **ser** and **estar** in Chapter 12 of the Level 1 textbook.

Language in Context

Ser and **estar**: You might begin by showing students a piece of fruit and talking about it:
La manzana es una fruta deliciosa.
(Taste the apple.)
¡Esta manzana está deliciosa!
Ask what the difference is between these two sentences. How is "the fruit known as the apple" different from "the apple that I am eating"? Does the first statement mean that every apple in the world tastes delicious, even rotten ones?

DISCUSS

Review vocabulary from previous chapters and introduce some of this chapter's new vocabulary with questions and statements that use **ser** and **estar** and an adjective (or an expression that functions as an adjective).
¿Están de moda los vaqueros?
¿Son elegantes los vaqueros?
Y las botas tejanas, ¿están de moda?
¿Cómo son las botas tejanas, altas o bajas?
¿Están sucios tus zapatos?
¿Cómo es la ropa que te gusta?
¿Cuál es la ropa más cómoda?

PARA COMUNICARNOS MEJOR
¿ES INTERESANTE MADRID?

To talk about the permanent qualities of a person, place, or thing, use the verb *ser* followed by an adjective.

— *Sí. Madrid es interesantísimo.*	Yes. Madrid is very interesting.
Mi peluquero es muy simpático.	My hairdresser is very nice.
Ese abrigo es muy práctico.	That coat is very useful.

To express qualities that might be temporary, use *estar* followed by an adjective.

Los vaqueros de botones están de moda.	The buttoned jeans are in style.

☐ Many adjectives can be used with either *ser* or *estar*, depending on what the speaker intends to communicate. In general, when to be implies looks or appearances, *estar* is used. Compare the following pairs of sentences.

Daniel es guapo.	Daniel is handsome.
Daniel está muy guapo hoy.	Daniel looks very handsome today.
Esos vaqueros son ajustados.	Those jeans are tight.
Esos vaqueros están rotos.	Those jeans are torn.

244

For students having difficulty understanding the different uses of **ser** and **estar**, you might consider:
- **The tutor page:** Pair the student with a native speaker or a more able student, using the tutor page.

Optional activity: See page 234D: *Desfile de modas*

1 Ropa y calzado

Tu compañero(a) fue de compras. Pregúntale qué compró.

— *Ayer fui de compras y compré unos pantalones.*
— *¿Ah sí? ¿Cómo son?*
— *Son ajustados, azules y a rayas. ¡Y están de moda!*

1.
2.
3.
4.
5.
6.

2 ¿Está de moda?

Habla con tu compañero(a) sobre la ropa.

— *¿Cómo es la ropa que usas?*
— *Es práctica y muy cómoda.*

¿Cómo es la ropa que usas?
¿Está de moda?
¿Es cara o barata?
¿De qué es?
¿Está vieja?

3 ¿Cúal es su estilo?

Averigua qué estilo de ropa, de calzado y de pelo les gusta o no les gusta llevar a tus compañeros y por qué. Anota las respuestas.

¿Te gusta (n)...?	Sí	¿Por qué?	No	¿Por qué?	
los trajes	✓✓✓	son elegantes están de moda ✓	✓✓	✓✓	no son cómodos ✓ no están en rebaja ✓
los vaqueros de botones					
los zapatos bajos					
los zuecos					
el pelo rapado					
la gomina					

245

Para hispanohablantes

Describe the temporary and permanent qualities of the clothes you are wearing.

245

Communicative Objective
• to talk about getting a haircut

Related Components

Assessment Oral Proficiency: p. 29	**Conexiones** Chapter 9
Audio Book Script: Seg. 5 Activities: p. 62	**Magazine** Juntos en España **Tutor Page** p. 42
Audio Chapter: 10A, Seg. 5 Conexiones: 18A	

GETTING STARTED

Students should now be able to correctly use demonstrative pronouns, articles with adjectives, **uno,** and all of the chapter vocabulary.
Point out that numbers can be masculine or feminine, depending on the currency. *(Doscientos dólares/Doscientas pesetas)*
Note: Check your newspaper for the pesetas/dollars exchange rate. Do a quick review of numbers from 100 to 3,000.

APPLY

1. Pair Activity
Talk about the services and prices at *La Elegante.*
Answers: See model on student page.
Extension: Rank the services from most to least expensive. Create sentences about the price.

2. Pair Activity
You are going to *La Elegante.* Talk with your partner about the type of haircut that you want and why.
Answers: See model on student page.
Extension: Describe the hairstyles of people in magazine photos.

3. Pair Activity
Create a dialog between a customer and a salesperson for each of the following: a hair salon, a clothing store, and a shoe store.
Extension: Write down your dialog and dictate it to your partner. Then edit your partner's writing.

SITUACIONES
¡A CORTARSE EL PELO!

Salón unisex

Peluquería La Elegante

Precios para todos:

Corte de pelo	1.800 ptas.
Corte de puntas	900 ptas.
Corte de patillas	500 ptas.
Corte de flequillo	500 ptas.
Permanente	2.500 ptas.
Reflejos	2.500 ptas.
EXTRAS	
Gomina	200 ptas.
Laca	150 ptas.

Para los más exigentes:

Corte a navaja	1.300 ptas.
Pelo rapado	1.200 ptas.
Pelo de punta	2.000 ptas.
Maquillaje	700 ptas.
Hacerse las uñas	400 ptas.

1 En la peluquería La Elegante

Con tu compañero(a), habla de los servicios que ofrece la peluquería La Elegante y de los precios de cada uno.

— En la peluquería La Elegante te cortan el pelo a navaja.
— ¿Y cuánto cuesta?
— Cuesta 1.300 pesetas.

246

4. Homework or Classwork
Write a paragraph about what fashion will be like in the year 2050. Describe the types of clothing, designs, shoes, and haircuts that will be in style then.
Answers: See model on student page.
Note: Have students follow the model, changing words as necessary. Help students by copying the paragraph on the board, underlining the words to be changed.

For students having difficulty talking about hairstyles, or the prices of services at a hair salon, you might consider:
• **The tutor page:** Pair the student with a native speaker or a more able student, using the tutor page.

¿Qué corte quieres?

El lunes irás a la peluquería. Con tu compañero(a), habla del corte de pelo que quieres y por qué.

— Voy a cortarme el pelo.
— ¿Qué corte te harán?
— El pelo rapado, porque es muy cómodo y práctico.

 ¡Qué bien te queda!

Con tu compañero(a) haz tres diálogos para tres lugares: una peluquería, una tienda de ropa y una zapatería. Tu compañero(a) trabaja allí y tú eres un(a) cliente.

En la peluquería
— Buenos días, ¿cuánto cuesta maquillarse?
— Cuesta siete dólares.
— ¿Y hacerse las uñas?

En la tienda de ropa
— Hola, ¿cuánto cuesta esa camisa?
— ¿La floreada o la lisa?
— La lisa.
— Ésa cuesta 16 dólares.

En la zapatería
— Por favor, ¿están en rebaja estos zuecos?
— No. Éstos no están en rebaja, pero aquéllos sí.

4 Tu diario

Escribe un párrafo sobre la moda del año 2050. Explica qué tipo de ropa y diseños estarán de moda.

La moda en el año 2050 será unisex, deportiva y práctica. En ropa estarán de moda las chaquetas lisas con cremalleras y los pantalones ajustados a rayas. El pelo se llevará corto, sin patillas ni flequillo.

PARA TU REFERENCIA

exigente *demanding*
la permanente *permanent wave*
las puntas *ends*
los reflejos *highlights*
los servicios *services*

247

CHECK

• ¿Cómo es un corte de pelo rapado?
• ¿Cuánto cuesta una permanente?
• ¿Te pones gomina en el pelo?

LOG BOOK

Have students pretend they are going to Madrid as foreign exchange students. Each student should write a letter to the host family describing his or her appearance and the clothes he or she will be wearing.

Background

Sizes And Measurements

U.S.	Spain	U.S.	Spain
Women's Dresses			
6	36	12	42
8	38	14	44
10	40	16	46
Men's Suits			
34	44	40	50
36	46	42	52
38	48	44	54
Women's Shoes			
4	34	7	37
5	35	8	38
6	36	9	39
Men's Shoes			
8	40	10	43
8.5	41	11	44
9	42	12	45

Pair Activity

Have students imagine that they are in Madrid with a classmate and want to buy shoes and clothing for family members or friends. Have them develop a dialog about what they will buy and the sizes they need.

Para hispanohablantes

Tell the class other words or expressions you know to describe hairstyles.

Communicative Objective
• to use clothing words

Related Components

Video: Tape/Book
Unit 5: Seg. 2

Scan to Chapter 9

GETTING STARTED

Ask students to name a few men's and women's fashion magazines, such as *Vogue* or *GQ*. What do they expect to find in these magazines?

APPLY

Form groups. Each will design a fashion magazine for teens. Bring in a few fashion magazines to illustrate the objectives of this activity.

PASO 1: Nuestra moda
Decide:
• the name of your magazine
• what kinds of fashions it will include
• what season it will focus on
Answers: See model on student page.

PASO 2: Los diseños
Now talk about:
• the type of clothing
• the materials that will be in fashion
• the designs
• the colors in fashion
Answers: See model on student page.
Extension: Create an article on official school uniforms. Each group should choose a different style (conservative, eccentric, sporty), make a sketch, and write a long caption defending the style.

Dictation
Have students dictate their captions as students in other groups transcribe them.

PARA RESOLVER
UNA REVISTA DE MODAS

En grupos, harán una revista de modas para jóvenes.

PASO 1 Nuestra moda
Decidan:
• *cómo se llamará la revista*
• *cómo será la moda de la revista*
• *para qué estación del año va a ser la moda*

> *La revista se llamará Juvenalia.*
> *Nuestra moda será práctica y cómoda.*
> *Saldremos con la moda de otoño.*

PASO 2 Los diseños
Ahora hablen sobre:
• *el tipo de ropa*
• *los materiales que usarán*
• *los diseños*
• *los colores de moda*

> *Tendremos: vaqueros, chaquetas, pantalones ajustados... La ropa será de algodón y de cuero. Vamos a usar los cuadros, las rayas... Los colores serán los típicos del otoño: el marrón, el anaranjado y el rojo.*

PASO 3 Una moda muy práctica
Ahora escojan cuatro fotos o hagan cuatro dibujos para incluir en la revista. Describan la ropa, el calzado y el corte de pelo que llevarán los modelos en cada foto.

> *Foto 1 Ella: suéter negro. Falda de lana, a cuadros negros y rojos. Gorra roja. Lleva el pelo largo.*
>
> *Él: camisa a rayas azules y blancas, de algodón. Lleva el pelo corto.*

PASO 4 La revista
Presenten su trabajo a los otros grupos. Toda la clase decidirá el mejor nombre para la revista y si van a incluir todas las fotos o sólo la mejor foto de cada grupo.

248

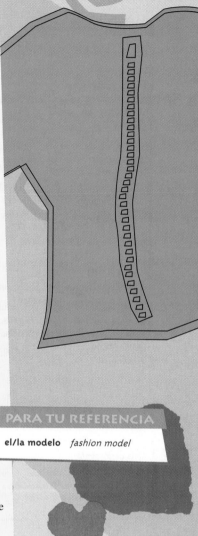

PARA TU REFERENCIA

el/la modelo   *fashion model*

PASO 3: Una moda muy práctica
Choose four photos or make four drawings for the magazine. Describe each model's clothing, shoes, and haircut.
Answers: See model on student page.
Extension: Make talk balloons for the people in the photos or drawings.

PASO 4: La revista
Present your work to the class. The class should decide on the name of a collective magazine, and determine which illustrations to include: all of them, or just the best from each group.
Answers: See model on student page.
Extension: Design an advertisement for your magazine that uses **ser** and **estar**.

249

CHECK

LOG BOOK
Have students make a *sopa de letras* (word search) with this chapter's vocabulary.

Background

Clothing Words
Here are additional words that students may be interested in knowing:

designer clothing *la ropa de diseñador*
discount clothing *la ropa con descuento*
fad *la novedad*
formal wear *la ropa formal*
trend *la tendencia (de la moda)*
gown *el vestido de noche, el vestido largo*
pantyhose *las pantimedias, las medias*
polo shirt *el polo, la camiseta*
shoelaces *los cordones de zapatos*
socks *los calcetines, los zoquetes*
sweatshirt *la camisa de entrenamiento, la sudadera, el jersey de chándal*
sweatpants *los pantalones de entrenamiento, los pantalones de chándal*
tie *la corbata*
tuxedo *el traje de etiqueta*
underwear *la ropa interior*
uniform *el uniforme*
wedding dress *el vestido de novia, el traje de novia*
denim *la mezclilla, vaquero(a), tela de jean*
linen *el lino*
polyester *el poliéster*
satin *el satén, el raso*
silk *la seda*
velvet *el terciopelo*

MEETING INDIVIDUAL NEEDS

Reaching All Students

For Auditory Learners
Name a situation *(un concierto de rock)* and have others say what you should wear *(botas de motorista, vaqueros rotos)*.

For Visual Learners
Draw or find pictures of people who are badly dressed. Write a few lines about what is wrong with their outfits.

Para hispanohablantes

Imagine you will spend a year in Madrid. List the items you'll take with you. Plan on trips to places like the beach on the Costa del Sol, and pack accordingly.

249

Objectives

Communicative: to speak and read about fashion designers

Cultural: to learn about the fashion industry in Spain

Related Components

Audio	Magazine
Conexiones: 18A	Juntos en España
Conexiones	
Chapter 9	

GETTING STARTED

Ask students to name designers they have heard of (e.g., Calvin Klein). Are products with designer labels better or just more expensive? Why are they expensive?

DISCUSS

Using the Text

Have volunteers read aloud each paragraph. Ask questions. Suggestions:

¿Cuáles son tres diseñadores españoles?
¿En qué trabaja Paloma Picasso?
¿Qué hace un diseñador?
Explica la frase "La arruga es bella".
¿Qué presentan los diseñadores?
¿Cómo se llaman los salones de moda más famosos de España?
¿Dónde están?
¿Cuál es la diferencia entre calzado y zapatos?
¿De qué materiales hacen zapatos y bolsos en España?
¿Qué otros productos de cuero hacen?

CHECK

Te toca a ti
Possible Answers:

1. *...muchas fábricas de ropa y muchos diseñadores muy conocidos.*
2. *...Paloma Picasso, Ágatha Ruiz de la Prada y Adolfo Domínguez.*
3. *...la calidad y los bellos diseños en calzado y en otros productos de cuero.*
4. *...de otros países.*
5. *...vanguardistas.*

ENTÉRATE

ESPAÑA: MODA INTERNACIONAL

En España hay muchas fábricas de ropa y muchos diseñadores° conocidos en todo el mundo. En joyería,° está Paloma Picasso, la hija del pintor Pablo Picasso. En ropa, están los diseños vanguardistas° de Ágatha Ruiz de la Prada. Y también está Adolfo Domínguez, quien refiriéndose a la ropa, hizo popular la frase "La arruga es bella".°

Los diseñadores españoles presentan sus colecciones en dos salones de moda:° el Salón Cibeles, en Madrid, y el Salón Gaudí, en Barcelona. A estos salones siempre vienen diseñadores de otros países.

España es también muy conocida por la calidad° y los bellos diseños de calzado y otros productos de cuero y piel, como° bolsos, cinturones y chaquetas.

TE TOCA A TI

Completa las oraciones.

1. En España hay...
2. Algunos nombres famosos son...
3. España es también muy conocida por...
4. A los salones de moda van diseñadores...
5. Los diseños de Ágatha Ruiz de la Prada son...

La arruga es bella. *Wrinkles are beautiful.*	**los diseñadores** *designers*
la calidad *quality*	**la joyería** *jewelry*
como *like*	**los salones de moda** *fashion shows*
	los vanguardistas *trend setters*

250

LOG BOOK

Domínguez said: *"La arruga es bella."* Have students write a few sentences that would describe the way they feel about fashion.

Vocabulario temático

La ropa
la camisa sin mangas
  sleeveless shirt
los pantalones ajustados
  tight pants
los pantalones anchos
  baggy pants
el pañuelo *scarf*
el traje *suit*
los vaqueros rotos *torn jeans*

Los diseños
Designs
a cuadros *checkered*
a lunares *with polka dots*
a rayas *striped*
floreado(a) *flowered*
liso(a) *plain*

El calzado
Footwear
las botas de motorista
  motorcycle boots
los zapatos bajos *flats*
los zapatos de tacón
  high heels
los zuecos *clogs*

El pelo
el corte a navaja *razor cut*
el flequillo *bangs*
las patillas *sideburns*
el pelo rapado *crew cut*
el pelo de punta *spiked hair*

En la peluquería
At the hairdresser's
el corte de pelo *haircut*
la gomina *styling gel*
la laca *hair spray*
la máquina de afeitar
  electric shaver
el/la peluquero(a) *hairdresser*
el secador *hair dryer*
las tijeras *scissors*

El aspecto
Appearance
afeitarse *to shave*
cortarse el pelo *to get a haircut*
cortarse las uñas
  to cut one's nails

cuidar *to take care of*
maquillarse *to put on makeup*
hacerse las uñas
  to have one's nails done

Expresiones y palabras
¿Cómo me queda?
  How does it look on me?
¡Qué bien te sienta!
  It's looks great on you!
¿Qué número usas? *What
  (shoe) size do you wear?*
Te queda bien/mal.
  It's looks good/bad on you.
Varias veces por...
  Several times a...
el botón *button*
la cremallera *zipper*
deportivo(a) *sporty, casual*
elegante *elegant*
la galería *shopping mall*
práctico *practical*
el probador *dressing room*
probarse(o>ue) *to try on*

LA CONEXIÓN INGLÉS-ESPAÑOL

The Spanish word ***pantalones*** is actually a cognate form for our present-day *trousers* because *trousers* were once called "pantaloons." The current English word "pants" probably comes from the same root as ***pantalones***.

How many cognates can you identify in the **Vocabulario temático**?

251

VOCABULARIO TEMÁTICO

Objective
• to review vocabulary

Related Components

Activity Book	Cuaderno
Chapter Review: p. 121-122	p. 75-76
Assessment	**Transparencies**
Listening Script: p. 17	Ch. 9: Dibujos y palabras
Chapter Test: p. 93-98	Transparencies 59-60
Audio	
Assessment: 15A	

Vocabulary

Point out that this section is organized by themes. Use the headings to review vocabulary. You may wish to ask Spanish speakers to share variations on these words and phrases with the class.

LOG BOOK

Have students make a list of the shoes and clothing they would wear for a special occasion.

La conexión inglés-español

Students may discover some less obvious cognates. For example: *raya* (in the expression *a rayas*) is related to the English word "ray," or line; *máquina* is a cognate of English "machine"; and *botón* and "button" are cognates.

	Objetivos page 253 *¡Ponte en forma!*	Conversemos pages 254-255 *Tu salud*	Realidades pages 256-257 *Gimnasio La pesa de oro*	Palabras en acción pages 258-259 *En el gimnasio*
Comunicación	To talk about: • ways to stay healthy	Discuss ways to maintain good health	Read text, make list, discuss physical training, talk about getting in shape, survey class, make table	Read cartoon, give and take advice on how to keep healthy; discuss getting in shape; create dialog; make poster; write exercise program
	• how to get in shape	Discuss how to get in shape	Read text, discuss staying healthy and in shape	Read cartoon, talk about characters; discuss getting in shape; write exercise program
	• how to deal with minor ailments	Discuss how to deal with minor ailments	Read text, talk about parts of the body	Read cartoon, create dialog; make poster
Cultura	To learn about: • Barcelona's largest sports center • the nutritional content of various food products		Spanish announcement for classes offered at a gymnasium	
Vocabulario temático	To learn the expressions for: • staying healthy	Talk about healthy living	Read text, make list, discuss physical training; talk about getting in shape, survey class, make table	Read cartoon, give and take advice on how to keep healthy; discuss getting in shape; create dialog; make poster
	• exercise and aerobics activities	Talk about exercise and aerobics activities	Read text, discuss staying healthy and in shape	Read cartoon, talk about characters; discuss getting in shape; write exercise program
	• parts of the body	Talk about parts of the body	Read text, make list, talk about parts of the body	Read cartoon, make list; create dialog; make poster
Estructura	To talk about: • what a friend should do: informal *tú* commands	Use informal *tú* commands to discuss what a friend should do		Read cartoon, give advice on how to keep healthy; create dialog
	• what a friend should not do: informal negative commands	Use informal negative commands to discuss what a friend should not do		Read cartoon, give advice on how to keep healthy; create dialog

¡PONTE EN FORMA!

Para comunicarnos mejor (1) pages 260-261 *¡Evita el estrés!*	Para comunicarnos mejor (2) pages 262-263 *¡No tomes mucho café!*	Situaciones pages 264-265 *Aliméntate bien*	Para resolver pages 266-267 *Mantente sano*	Entérate page 268 *Una escuela para deportistas*
Discuss getting in shape; talk about how to maintain good health; make table	Discuss how to stay healthy; talk about what not to do when sick; make table	Read text, answer questions; discuss healthy eating; act out interview with nutritionist; write in diary	Make list of health topics; choose one topic; give advice	Discuss the *CAR* sports center near Barcelona
Discuss getting in shape; make table	Discuss how to stay healthy	Read text, discuss healthy eating; write in diary	Make list of health topics; choose one topic and display poster	
Make table	Discuss how to stay healthy; talk about what not to do when sick; make table	Read text, discuss healthy eating	Make list of health topics; choose one topic; illustrate text	
		Nutrition labels from Spanish foods	Information about in-line skating in Barcelona	Article about the *Centro de Alto Rendimiento,* the athletic training center near Barcelona
Discuss getting in shape; talk about how to maintain good health; make table	Discuss how to stay healthy; talk about what not to do when sick; make table			
Discuss getting in shape; make table	Discuss how to stay healthy	**Re-entry of vocabulary**		**Extension of vocabulary**
	Make table			
Discuss getting in shape; talk about how to maintain good health; make table		**Re-entry of structure**		**Extension of structure**
	Discuss how to stay healthy; talk about what not to do when sick; make table			

252B

¡Salud!

ART CONNECTION

Objective
• to make posters about better life through better health, using Chapter 10 *Vocabulario temático*

Use
after *Palabras en acción,* pages 258-259

Materials
• encyclopedia
• bilingual dictionaries
• markers
• posterboard

Activity
• Each group of four students focuses on one area of the body. For example, Group A selects the eyes.
• Have them look for information about how daily life affects this body part.
• Have the group list five pieces of advice to correct or prevent danger to the body part chosen. For example, if the group chooses the eyes: *Come fruta y verdura, que contienen mucha vitamina A, descansa con frecuencia si usas la computadora, no mires la televisión de cerca, usa luz natural si es posible, si llevas gafas: úsalas, lleva gafas de protección al hacer trabajos peligrosos,* etc.
• Groups design health posters for the body parts they chose. They can also design logos modeled on the picture of a cigarette inside a red circle with a red line through it.
• Groups present their posters and ask the class for more suggestions.
• Display the posters.

¿Qué hago, doctor?

SCIENCE CONNECTION

Objective
• to explore new ways to solve health problems, using Chapter 10 *Vocabulario temático*

Use
after *Palabras en acción,* pages 258-259

Materials
• 3" x 5" index cards

Preparation
• Give one index card to each student.
• Have them write a real or imaginary health problem on it. For example: *No puedo dormir. Peso demasiado. Me duele la espalda.*

Activity
• Collect the cards and redistribute them, making sure no student has the card he/she wrote.
• Have students work in pairs and play the roles of patient and physician.
• The patient introduces him/herself and tells the physician his/her health problem.
• The physician gives the patient health advice, using two affirmative statements and two negative ones. For example, to a patient who can't sleep at night the physician might say: *Usted tiene que alimentarse bien y tiene que evitar el estrés. No debe tomar medicamentos para dormir y no debe tomar café antes de ir a dormir.*
• Then students reverse roles.
• As each pair finishes the activity, the patients repeat the physicians' advice to the class: *No puedo dormir y el doctor me dice que tengo que alimentarme bien,* etc.

Reglas de oro

SPORTS CONNECTION

Objective
• to talk about health and sports, using affirmative informal *(tú)* commands

Use
after *Para comunicarnos mejor,* pages 260-261

Materials
• sports magazines
• scissors
• glue
• markers
• posterboard

Preparation
• Hand out magazines to groups of four students. Each group decides on a favorite athlete, finds his/her picture in the magazines, cuts out the picture and glues it on the posterboard.

Activity
• Some group members write a short biography of their favorite athlete, while others write *Diez reglas para ser un gran atleta.* For example, a group that chose Michael Jordan might write: *Si quieres llegar a ser un buen jugador de baloncesto como yo, sigue estas reglas: Haz ejercicio cada día. No fumes. Aliméntate bien. Mantente sano. Duerme ocho horas cada noche,* etc.
• After the group decides what their poster will look like, some members work on the art and others figure out the best way to present the text.
• Display posters and ask class to vote for their favorite.

No salgas esta noche

GAME

Objective
• to play a role-reversal game, using negative informal *(tú)* commands

Use
after *Para comunicarnos mejor,* pages 262-263

Activity
• Young people often think that mustn'ts, don'ts, shouldn'ts, and won'ts are all that *they* hear from parents. Now they can tell authority figures in their lives what they shouldn't do.
• Students brainstorm negative commands they hear from adults, and write them on the chalkboard. For example: *No hables con la boca llena. No vuelvas muy tarde. No te pongas ese vestido tan corto. No salgas sin comer,* ect.
• Divide class into groups of five, and have each group write ten negative commands they would give to their parents.
• Select a scorekeeper.
• Groups share commands with the rest of the class, and students decide which ones are fair or unfair. Groups receive five points for each fair command.
• The group with the most points wins.

¡PONTE EN FORMA!

Introduce the chapter and its theme by asking students to think about their health. What decisions do they make to maintain good health and stay in shape?

Related Components

Audio	Video: Tape/Book
Conexiones: 18A	Unit 5: Seg. 3
Conexiones	
Chapter 10	

Scan to Chapter 10

GETTING STARTED

Ask students if they can identify what the young people in the photograph are doing. Ask questions:
¿Dónde están los chicos de la foto?
¿Qué piensas que van a hacer?
¿Por qué es importante hacer deporte?

Critical Thinking

Use the following activity to help students discover what they would need to know in order to talk about health.

¿Tienes buena salud?
Ask students to think about what makes us healthy. Then have them list:
• things they do to stay healthy
• things they do to stay in shape
• things they might say to a doctor when they feel ill
• what the doctor tells them to do
• advice for staying healthy

Have each group write their list on the board. Have the class discuss the lists and decide which items are the most essential. Have each group submit a revised list. When you finish the chapter, have the class review the lists to see how they compare to what they learned in the chapter.

CAPÍTULO **10**

¡PONTE EN FORMA!

Ir al gimnasio ayuda a ponerse en forma.

252

CHAPTER COMPONENTS

Activity Book	Audio Book	Cuaderno	Tutor Pages
p. 123-132	Script: p. 63-65	p. 77-84	p. 43-46
Assessment	Activities: p. 66-68	**Magazine**	**Video: Tape/Book**
Oral Proficiency:	**Audio**	Juntos en España	Unit 5: Seg. 3
p. 30	Chapter: 10B	**Transparencies**	
Listening Script:	Assessment: 15B	Chapter 10	
p. 18	Conexiones: 18A	Transparencies 61-65	
Chapter Test:	**Conexiones**		
p. 99-104	Chapter 10		

Objetivos

COMUNICACIÓN
To talk about:
- ways to stay healthy
- how to stay in shape
- dealing with minor ailments

CULTURA
To learn about:
- Spain's largest sports center and school
- the nutritional content of various foods

VOCABULARIO TEMÁTICO
To learn the expressions for:
- staying healthy
- exercise and aerobic activities
- parts of the body
- how you feel

ESTRUCTURA
To talk about:
- telling a friend to do something: informal *(tú)* affirmative commands
- telling a friend not to do something: informal *(tú)* negative commands

¿SABES QUE...?

Spanish teenagers enjoy outdoor activities such as skating, jogging, and mountain biking to stay in shape. In addition, joining health clubs and attending aerobics classes is becoming increasingly popular. After school, many students play basketball, swim, do gymnastics, or participate in *fútbol de sala* (a scaled-down version of soccer).

253

CONVERSEMOS

Communicative Objectives
- to talk about ways to stay healthy
- to talk about getting in shape
- to give advice

Related Components

Activity Book p. 123	**Cuaderno** p. 77
Audio Book Script: Seg. 1	**Transparencies** Ch.10: Conversemos Transparency 61
Audio Chapter: 10B, Seg. 1	

GETTING STARTED

Ask for a definition of good health. Is it more than simply never being sick?

ACTIVITIES

These activities give students an opportunity to begin communicating with each other and with you, focusing on the theme and objectives of the chapter. The activities can be used as oral class activities, or, if you prefer, you can pair students to achieve more interaction.

¿Cómo te mantienes sano(a)?
Class activity to introduce health vocabulary. Read aloud the title question. Use the statements to poll the class on their health habits. Where possible, ask additional questions, such as: *¿Es necesario hacer ejercicio todos los días?*

¿Cómo te mantienes en forma?
Class activity to introduce ways to stay in shape. Model the question, example, and answers. Ask individuals the question. Encourage the use of alternative answers. Ask how long it has been since they did these activities.

CONVERSEMOS
TU SALUD

Habla con tu compañero(a).

¿CÓMO TE MANTIENES SANO(A)?
[How do you stay healthy?]

Como muchas frutas y verduras y hago ejercicio.

	Sí	No
Como muchas frutas y verduras.	❑	❑
Tomo poco café.	❑	❑
Evito las grasas. *(I avoid fatty foods.)*	❑	❑
Me alimento bien. *(I eat healthy food.)*	❑	❑
Como poca sal. *(I eat little salt.)*	❑	❑
Duermo ocho horas al día. *(I sleep eight hours a day.)*	❑	❑
Hago ejercicio. *(I exercise.)*	❑	❑
Evito el estrés. *(I avoid stress.)*	❑	❑

¿CÓMO TE MANTIENES EN FORMA?
[How do you stay in shape?]

Juego al baloncesto y hago abdominales.

jugar al baloncesto	Hacer...	escalera
patinar	abdominales	pesas
saltar a la cuerda	flexiones	cinta

254

CUANDO NO TE SIENTES BIEN, ¿QUÉ DICES?
(When you don't feel well, what do you say?)

Tengo fiebre. *(I have a fever.)*

Tengo agujetas. *(I'm sore / I have sore muscles.)*

Me duele la cabeza. *(I have a headache.)*

Tengo catarro. *(I have a cold.)*

Me duele la garganta. *(My throat hurts.)*

Tengo gripe. *(I have the flu.)*

Y EL MÉDICO / LA MÉDICA, ¿QUÉ TE DICE?

Toma dos aspirinas. *(Take two aspirins.)*

No vayas a la escuela. *(Don't go to school.)*

Vete a casa y descansa. *(Go home and rest.)*

CONSEJOS PARA MANTENERSE SANO(A)

No tomes mucho café.

No fumes. *(Don't smoke.)*

Di no a las drogas. *(Say no to drugs.)*

No tomes bebidas alcohólicas.

Evita el estrés.

255

Cuando no te sientes bien, ¿qué dices?
Class activity to introduce things to say when you don't feel well. Model the question and answers. Use gestures and facial expressions to illustrate the meanings. Discuss the expressions and ask the question in the title. After reviewing, ask students to expand on these additional expressions. Example:
No puedo hablar. Me duele la garganta.

Y el médico/la médica, ¿qué te dice?
Class activity to introduce things doctors say. After modeling and discussing, combine this activity with the previous one by having pairs play doctor and patient.

Consejos para mantenerse sano(a)
Class activity to introduce commands that relate to staying healthy. Model the commands. Make simple statements that would elicit the advice. Example:
A: *Estoy muy nervioso.*
B: *No tomes mucho café.*

CHECK

- *¿Cómo te mantienes sano(a)?*
- *¿Qué haces cuando te duele la cabeza?*
- *¿Qué consejos das a alguien que quiere mantenerse sano(a)?*

LOG BOOK
Have students write things they do to stay healthy and fit.

Communicative Objective
• to talk about exercise classes

Related Components

| Activity Book
p. 124 | Audio
Chapter: 10B, Seg. 2 |
| Audio Book
Script: Seg. 2 | Cuaderno
p. 78 |

GETTING STARTED

Ask students what this page appears to be. Which of these offerings seems to be the most appealing form of exercise?

DISCUSS

Talk about the photographs and captions, and ask questions. Suggestions:

Gimnasio
¿Qué quiere decir "La pesa de oro"? (the golden weight)
¿Qué te ofrece este gimnasio?

Aerobic
¿Qué ejercicio es bueno para el corazón?
¿Qué puedes hacer en una clase de aerobic?

Escalera
¿Qué quiere decir "escalera"?
¿Con qué músculos trabajas en la escalera?
¿Qué haces al ritmo de la música?

Karate
¿Qué puedes aprender en esta clase?
¿Qué tipos de ejercicios puedes hacer en cada sesión?
¿Qué incluye esta clase?

Yoga
¿Qué ejercicios combina la clase de yoga?
¿Para qué es excelente?

Total
¿Qué incluye esta clase?
¿Por qué se llama "Total"?

Gimnasia acuática
¿Dónde haces estos ejercicios?
¿Te gusta el agua?

REALIDADES

GIMNASIO
La pesa de oro

Te ofrece clases con entrenadores especializados.
Escoge la más adecuada a tus necesidades.

Aerobic
Combina gimnasia y ejercicios para el corazón. Salta, corre y baila con la música, todo en una clase.

Escalera
Haz ejercicio con los músculos de las piernas subiendo y bajando la escalera al ritmo de la música.

Karate
Aprende defensa personal y ponte en forma con ejercicios de resistencia, fuerza, flexibilidad y coordinación en cada sesión. Esta clase incluye abdominales y flexiones.

Yoga
Combina ejercicios de respiración y relajación. Excelente para evitar el estrés.

Total
Haz ejercicio con todo el cuerpo. Esta clase incluye cinta, bicicleta, escalera y pesas.

Gimnasia acuática
Haz ejercicios en la piscina. Si te gusta el agua, ¡ésta es tu clase!

256

Language Note
Point out that **el gimnasio** means "gymnasium" and **la gimnasia** means "gymnastics."

MEETING INDIVIDUAL NEEDS

Reaching All Students

For Auditory Learners
Describe what is offered in one of the classes. Have others guess its name.

For Kinesthetic Learners
Pretend you are the *entrenador especializado* for one of the classes. Demonstrate how you would show people what to do.

HABLA DEL FOLLETO

A. Haz una lista de los ejercicios que puedes hacer en cada clase.

Clase de escalera: ejercicios con música para los músculos de las piernas.
Clase total: ejercicios de cinta, bicicleta, escalera y pesas para todo el cuerpo.

B. ¿A qué clases te gustaría ir? ¿Por qué? Habla con tu compañero(a).

— A mí me gustaría ir a la clase de gimnasia acuática.
— ¿Por qué?
— Porque me encanta el agua. Y a ti, ¿a qué clase te gustaría ir?

¿QUÉ OPINAS?

¿Qué haces para mantenerte en forma? Haz una encuesta. Usa la tabla.

¿Qué haces?	yo	la clase
nadar	✓	
pesas		
jugar al béisbol		|||
jugar al fútbol		||
aerobic		
correr		
patinar		

Según la encuesta, ¿cuál es la actividad más común? ¿Y la menos común?

257

ACTIVITIES

Habla del folleto

Individual and Pair Activities: Writing and Conversing

A. Make a list of exercises you can do in each class.
Possible Answers: See model on student page for *escalera* and *total*.
- *Clase de aerobic: ejercicios para el corazón, saltar, correr y bailar.*
- *Clase de karate: ejercicios de resistencia, fuerza, flexibilidad y coordinación para ponerse en forma.*
- *Clase de yoga: ejercicios de respiración y relajación para evitar el estrés.*
- *Clase de gimnasia acuática: ejercicios en la piscina.*

B. Speak with your partner about which classes you would like to go to, and why.
Answers: See model on student page.

¿Qué opinas?

Group Activity: Taking a Poll
What does your group do to stay in shape? Record their answers on a chart like the one on page 257.

Class Activity: Evaluation
- Have a volunteer list the activities on the board as representatives of each group name them.
- Have another volunteer write in the numbers for each activity as each group reports on its poll.
- Which are the most and least popular activities for staying in shape?
Extension: Write a paragraph summarizing the results.

CHECK

- *¿A qué clases te gustaría ir?*
- *¿Qué clase trabaja los músculos de las piernas?*
- *¿Qué clase combina ejercicios de respiración y relajación?*

LOG BOOK
Have students list the sports and exercises from their poll, and the season(s) they associate with each.

Para hispanohablantes

Explain to the class why it is important or necessary to stay in shape.

257

Communicative Objectives

To talk about:
- exercises and fitness activities
- staying healthy and in shape
- parts of the body

Related Components

Activity Book p. 125-126	Transparencies Ch. 10: Palabras en acción Transparency 62
Cuaderno p. 79-80	
	Tutor Page p. 43

GETTING STARTED

Ask students about their physical fitness. Do they feel they get enough exercise?

DISCUSS

Go over the page, pointing to the exercise machines and exercises, and asking what they are.

Para hispanohablantes

If you use words or expressions other than the ones introduced in this chapter, share them with the class. A few variations:

aerobic: ejercicios aeróbicos

alimentarse bien: comer bien

correr: hacer footing

el estrés: la tensión

las grasas: las comidas grasosas, las comidas grasientas

las flexiones: las lagartijas

ponerse en forma: tomar condición física

Tengo agujetas: Me duelen los músculos, Tengo dolor muscular

Tengo catarro: Estoy resfriado, Estoy constipado

PALABRAS EN ACCIÓN

EN EL GIMNASIO

¿Vienes a nadar después de hacer pesas?

No, hoy no puedo.

LOS MÚSCULOS DEL CUERPO

el músculo

el corazón

el cuello

las pesas

el hombro

Hacer aerobic es bueno para el corazón.

Sí. Y también es divertido.

1 ¿Qué ves en el dibujo?

Haz una lista de las partes del cuerpo que ves en el dibujo. Compara tu lista con la de tu compañero(a).

La cabeza, la rodilla...

2 ¿Qué hacen?

Escoge cinco personas del dibujo. Pregúntale a tu compañero(a) qué están haciendo.

— *¿Qué está haciendo el chico de la camiseta blanca y los pantalones azules?*
— *Está haciendo pesas.*

3 Para mantenerse sano(a)

Dile a tu compañero(a) qué debe o no debe hacer para mantenerse sano(a).

— *Evita el estrés. Aliméntate bien.*

4 La salud

Pregúntale a tu compañero(a) qué hace para mantenerse sano(a).

— *¿Qué haces para mantenerte sano(a)?*
— *Como verduras y frutas. ¿Y tú?*
— *Yo no tomo mucho café.*

258

For students having difficulty talking about exercises and staying in shape, you might consider:
- **The tutor page:** Pair the student with a native speaker or a more able student, using the tutor page.

Optional activities: See page 252C: *¡Salud!* and *¿Qué hago, doctor?*

5 El ejercicio

Pregúntale a tu compañero(a) qué hace para mantenerse en forma.

— ¿Qué haces para mantenerte en forma?
— Monto en bicicleta. ¿Y tú?
— Yo juego al baloncesto.

6 Miniteatro

Imagina que te sientes mal y estás en la oficina del/de la médico(a). Crea un diálogo con tu compañero(a).

— ¿Cómo te sientes?
— Mal. Creo que tengo fiebre.
— Sí, tienes fiebre. ¿Te duele algo?
— Sí, la garganta.
— Vete a casa y descansa.

7 Cartel

Diseña un cartel sobre el tema de la salud. Usa dibujos o fotos de revistas y periódicos.

8 Tú eres el autor

Haz un programa para ponerte en forma. Describe qué tipo de ejercicio harás cada día y durante cuánto tiempo. Presenta tu programa a la clase.

Lunes: hacer aerobic por media hora.
Martes: nadar en la piscina por una hora...

259

3. Pair Activity
Say what your partner should or should not do to stay healthy.
Extension: Change your advice from an informal command to a formal one.

3. Pair Activity
Say what your partner should or should not do to stay healthy.
Extension: Change your advice from an informal command to a formal one.

4. Pair Activity
Ask what your partner does in order to stay healthy.
Extension: Write down your partner's answers, then rewrite them in the **nosotros** form.

5. Pair Activity
Ask what your partner does in order to stay in shape.
Extension: Tell your partner what other exercises he or she should do and why.

6. Roleplay Activity
Imagine that you don't feel well and have gone to a doctor. Create a dialog with your partner, the doctor.
Extension: Record the dialog and exchange tapes with other pairs. Write down as much of their dialog as you can.

7. Hands-On Activity
Homework or classwork for individuals or small groups Design a poster with a health theme. Use drawings or photos.
Extension: Donate some of the posters to the school nurse's office.

8. Writing Activity
Develop a personal fitness program for getting in shape. Describe what type of exercise you are going to do each day, and for how long. Present your program to the class.
Note: Help students by eliciting a list of activities in infinitive form and writing them on the board.

CHECK

- ¿Qué ejercicio te gustaría hacer?
- ¿Cuántas veces por semana haces ejercicio?
- ¿Qué haces para mantenerte sano?
- Da tres consejos a alguien que quiere mantenerse en forma.

LOG BOOK
Have students write a short dialog between two of the people in the drawing.

ACTIVITIES

1. Individual/Pair Activity
Make a list of the parts of the body that you see in the drawing. Compare lists with your partner.

2. Pair Activity
Choose five people from the drawing. Ask your partner what each one is doing.
Extension: Say how many times a week a person should do these exercises.

PARA COMUNICARNOS MEJOR

Communicative Objective
- to tell someone to do something, using affirmative informal (**tú**) commands and pronouns

Related Components

Activity Book p. 127-128	**Transparencies** Ch. 10: Para comunicarnos mejor Transparency 63
Audio Book Script: Seg. 3 Activities: p. 66	**Tutor Page** p. 44
Audio Chapter: 10B, Seg. 3	
Cuaderno p. 81	

GETTING STARTED

Write the word **nada** on the board. Ask students what it means. See if they realize that it is also the informal command form of **nadar**.

Language in Context

Affirmative *Tú* Commands: Review commands using occupations discussed in this textbook. Have students make up commands for these people:

la bombera: *¡Apaga el fuego!*
el cocinero: *¡Cocina la comida!*
la estudiante: *¡Haz la tarea!*
el músico: *¡Toca una canción!*
el policía: *¡Ten cuidado!*
la peluquera: *¡Córtame el pelo!*

Pronouns and *Tú* Commands: Explain that when a pronoun (direct, indirect, and reflexive) is used with an affirmative command, it is pronounced (and written) as if it were part of the command.

DISCUSS

Review vocabulary from previous chapters and introduce new vocabulary with questions and statements that use informal **tú** commands:

Si quiero proteger el medio ambiente, ¿qué debo hacer?
Va a llover. ¿Qué debo hacer?
Viajo al extranjero. ¿Qué consejos me das?
Si tengo gripe, ¿debo ir a la escuela?
Quiero ponerme en forma. ¿Debo fumar?
Si alguien me ofrece drogas, ¿qué digo?

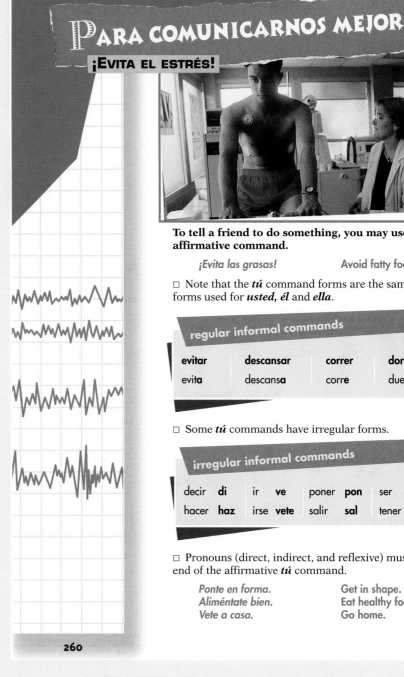

PARA COMUNICARNOS MEJOR
¡EVITA EL ESTRÉS!

To tell a friend to do something, you may use an informal *(tú)* affirmative command.

¡Evita las grasas!   Avoid fatty foods!

☐ Note that the *tú* command forms are the same as the present tense forms used for *usted, él* and *ella*.

regular informal commands			
evitar	descansar	correr	dormir
evita	descansa	corre	duerme

☐ Some *tú* commands have irregular forms.

irregular informal commands											
decir	**di**	ir	**ve**	poner	**pon**	ser	**sé**	venir	**ven**		
hacer	**haz**	irse	**vete**	salir	**sal**	tener	**ten**				

☐ Pronouns (direct, indirect, and reflexive) must be attached to the end of the affirmative *tú* command.

Ponte en forma.   Get in shape.
Aliméntate bien.   Eat healthy food.
Vete a casa.   Go home.

260

For students having difficulty using regular and irregular **tú** commands, or using pronouns with affirmative **tú** commands, you might consider:
- **The tutor page:** Pair the student with a native speaker or a more able student, using the tutor page.

Optional activity: See page 252D: *Reglas de oro*

1 ¡Ponte en forma!

Pregúntale a tu compañero(a) qué puedes hacer para ponerte en forma.

—¿Qué hago para ponerme en forma?
— Haz pesas.

1. 3. 5.

2. 4. 6.

2 ¡Mantente sano(a)!

Pregúntale a tu compañero(a) qué puedes hacer para mantenerte sano(a).

—¿Qué hago para mantenerme sano?
— Aliméntate bien. Come muchas verduras.

3 Consejos

En grupo, hagan una tabla de consejos para diferentes personas y situaciones.

Consejos para alguien que...	yo	Rebeca	Luis
quiere evitar el estrés	canta	baila	haz ejercicio
no puede dormir	lee un libro	pon música	toma leche
tiene catarro			
quiere evitar las grasas			
tiene agujetas			
tiene gripe			

261

ACTIVITIES

Students use informal **tú** commands to talk about staying healthy and in shape.

1. Pair Activity
Ask your partner what you can do to get in shape.
Answers:
1. See model on student page.
2. *Corre.*
3. *Haz abdominales.*
4. *Haz aerobic.*
5. *Haz flexiones.*
6. *Haz cinta.*
Extension: Use **tener que** to tell your partner how to stay in shape.

2. Pair Activity
Ask your partner what you can do to stay healthy.
Possible Answers:
1. See model on student page.
2. *Haz ejercicio. Haz aerobic todos los días.*
3. *No fumes. Corre todas las mañanas.*
4. *Aliméntate bien. Come muchas frutas.*
5. *Duerme ocho horas por día.*
Extension: Use **debes** to tell your partner how to stay healthy.

3. Group Activity
Make a chart with advice for different people and situations.
Possible Answers: (For the first two categories, see model on student page.)
catarro: toma sopa, vete a dormir
grasas: come frutas y verduras
agujetas: toma dos aspirinas, descansa
gripe: toma jugo de naranja, ve al doctor
Extension: Change your answers in the chart to include pronouns. Example:
Haz ejercicio. ¡Hazlo!

CHECK

• *¿Qué le dices a tu amigo(a) si...*
...le duele la cabeza?
...tiene fiebre?
...quiere ponerse en forma?
...quiere venir a tu casa?
...tiene que ir al doctor?
...no puede dormir?

LOG BOOK
Have students make sentences with irregular forms of **tú** commands.

Communicative Objective

• to tell someone not to do something, using negative **tú** commands and pronouns

Related Components

Activity Book p. 129-130	**Audio** Chapter: 10B, Seg. 4
Audio Book Script: Seg. 4 Activities: p. 67	**Cuaderno** p. 82
	Tutor Page p. 45

GETTING STARTED

Ask what the people in the pictures are probably doing and saying. What advice would you give them?

Language in Context

Negative *Tú* Commands: Give a series of negative commands using the health and exercise vocabulary. For example, lift an imaginary coffee cup toward your lips and slap down the offending hand while giving the command. *¡No tomes café!* (Not all commands need to refer to health.)

DISCUSS

Review vocabulary from previous chapters and introduce new vocabulary with questions and statements that use positive and negative **tú** commands.
¡Escucha!
No hables. No digas nada.
No llegues tarde a clase.
Siéntate aquí, no te sientes allí.
Ten cuidado.
No corras en el pasillo.
No uses aparatos electrónicos en la clase.
Aliméntate bien. No comas mucho chocolate.
No te acuestes tarde. Vete a dormir a las ocho.
No hagas abdominales. Haz flexiones.
No te preocupes. Evita el estrés.
No trabajes mucho.

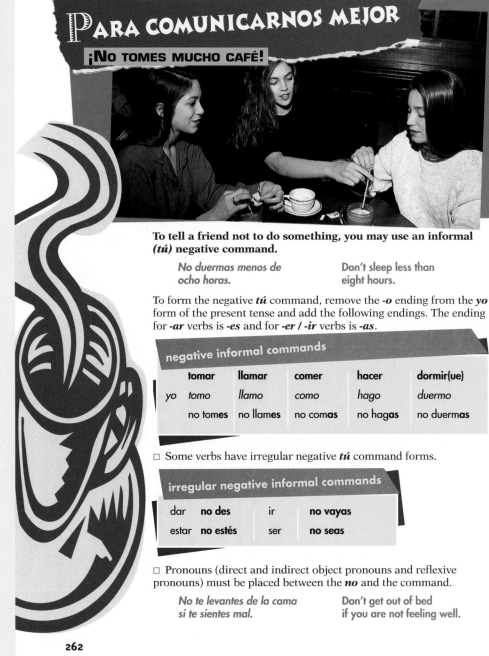

PARA COMUNICARNOS MEJOR

¡NO TOMES MUCHO CAFÉ!

To tell a friend not to do something, you may use an informal (*tú*) negative command.

No duermas menos de ocho horas.	Don't sleep less than eight hours.

To form the negative *tú* command, remove the *-o* ending from the *yo* form of the present tense and add the following endings. The ending for *-ar* verbs is *-es* and for *-er / -ir* verbs is *-as*.

negative informal commands

	tomar	llamar	comer	hacer	dormir(ue)
yo	tomo	llamo	como	hago	duermo
	no tom**es**	no llam**es**	no com**as**	no hag**as**	no duerm**as**

☐ Some verbs have irregular negative *tú* command forms.

irregular negative informal commands

dar	**no des**	ir	**no vayas**
estar	**no estés**	ser	**no seas**

☐ Pronouns (direct and indirect object pronouns and reflexive pronouns) must be placed between the *no* and the command.

No te levantes de la cama si te sientes mal.	Don't get out of bed if you are not feeling well.

262

For students having difficulty using regular and irregular negative **tú** commands, or using pronouns with negative **tú** commands, you might consider:
• **The tutor page:** Pair the student with a native speaker or a more able student, using the tutor page.
Optional activity: See page 252D: *No salgas esta noche*

1 No comas muchos dulces

Pregúntale a tu compañero(a) qué no debes hacer en cada situación.

— ¿Qué hago para alimentarme bien?
— No comas muchos dulces.

1. alimentarse bien
2. ponerse en forma
3. evitar el estrés
4. mantenerse sano(a)
5. dormir bien
6. evitar las grasas

No...
comer muchos dulces
poner mucha sal en la comida
tomar mucho café
comer muchas grasas
fumar
tomar bebidas alcohólicas

2 ¿Qué no debo hacer?

Pregúntale a tu compañero(a) qué no debes hacer cuando te sientes mal.

— ¿Qué no debo hacer cuando estoy enfermo?
— No hagas ejercicio.

1. estoy enfermo(a)
2. tengo catarro
3. tengo agujetas
4. me duele el estómago
5. tengo gripe
6. tengo fiebre

No...
hacer ejercicio
ir a esquiar
jugar al baloncesto
viajar
comer
ir a la escuela
salir de casa

3 Me duele...

En grupo, hagan una tabla de consejos para cuando les duele algo.

Me duele	Antonia	Claudia	Alfonso
el cuello	no salgas de casa		no vayas a la escuela
la garganta	no hables	no cantes	no tomes bebidas frías
el estómago		no comas dulces	
la rodilla la cabeza el hombro la pierna			

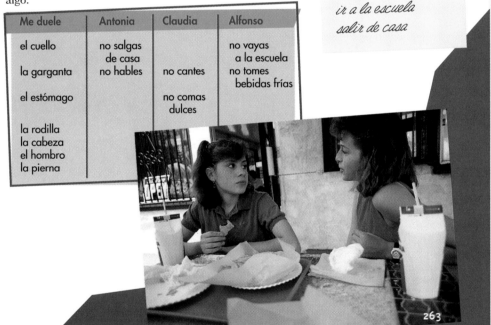

Para hispanohablantes

Pretend you are babysitting your little brother. Tell him what he cannot do.

Students use negative **tú** commands to talk about what one should avoid doing in order to stay healthy.

1. Pair Activity
Ask your partner what you should not do in these situations.
Possible Answers:
1. See model on student page.
2. *¿Qué hago para ponerme en forma?* No fumes.
3. *¿Qué hago para evitar el estrés?* No salgas todos los días.
4. *¿Qué hago para mantenerme sano(a)?* No tomes bebidas alcohólicas.
5. *¿Qué hago para dormir bien?* No tomes mucho café.
6. *¿Qué hago para evitar las grasas?* No comas grasas.
Extension: Offer advice with affirmative commands.

2. Pair Activity
Ask your partner what you should not do when you don't feel well.
Possible Answers:
1. See model on student page.
2. *No salgas de casa.*
3. *No hagas ejercicio.*
4. *No comas.*
5. *No vayas a esquiar.*
6. *No vayas a la escuela.*
Extension: Act out one of these ailments. Have others tell you what you should not do.

3. Group Activity
Make a chart with each person's advice for what to do when some part of you hurts.
Possible Advice: See model on student page for first three categories.
la rodilla: no juegues al baloncesto
la cabeza: no pongas música
el hombro: no vayas a esquiar
la pierna: no hagas ejercicio
Extension: Rewrite the best pieces of advice as affirmative commands.

CHECK

• *¿Qué le dices a un amigo cuando*
  ...está enfermo?
  ...quiere evitar el estrés?
  ...se siente mal?
  ...quiere mantenerse sano?
  ...le duele la garganta?

LOG BOOK
Have students write five sentences with advice for staying healthy.

263

SITUACIONES

Objectives
Communicative:
- to talk about diet and nutrition
- to give advice, using commands

Cultural:
- to look at food labels in Spanish

Related Components

Assessment	**Conexiones**
Oral Proficiency:	Chapter 10
p. 30	**Magazine**
Audio Book	Juntos en España
Script: Seg. 5	**Transparencies**
Activities: p. 68	Ch. 10: Situaciones
Audio	Transparency 64
Chapter: 10B, Seg. 5	**Tutor Page**
Conexiones: 18A	p. 46

GETTING STARTED

Students should now be able to correctly use affirmative and negative informal (**tú**) commands (with and without pronouns) and all of the chapter vocabulary.
Have students look at the food labels. Ask them to comment. If possible, bring in real cans and boxes that have labels in Spanish. Use the labels on this page to identify the components on the new labels.

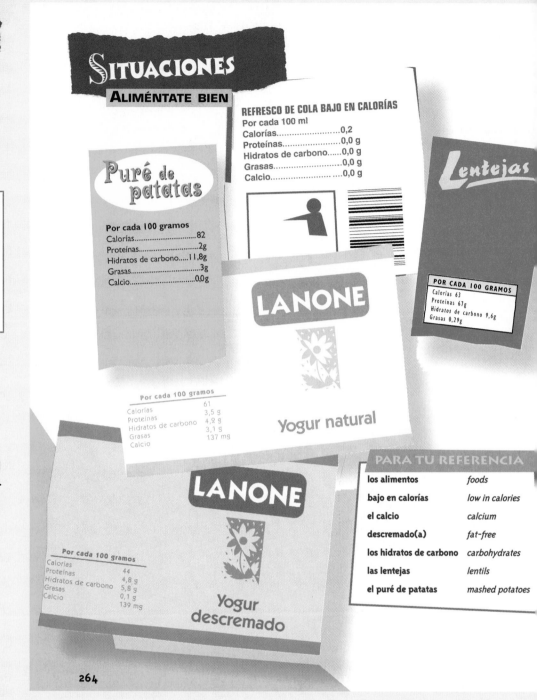

SITUACIONES

ALIMÉNTATE BIEN

REFRESCO DE COLA BAJO EN CALORÍAS
Por cada 100 ml
Calorías........................0,2
Proteínas.....................0,0 g
Hidratos de carbono......0,0 g
Grasas.........................0,0 g
Calcio..........................0,0 g

Puré de patatas

Por cada 100 gramos
Calorías.............................82
Proteínas............................2g
Hidratos de carbono.....11,8g
Grasas................................3g
Calcio..............................0,0g

Lentejas

POR CADA 100 GRAMOS
Calorías 63
Proteínas 67g
Hidratos de carbono 9,6g
Grasas 0,29g

LANONE

Por cada 100 gramos
Calorías | 61
Proteínas | 3,5 g
Hidratos de carbono | 4,2 g
Grasas | 3,1 g
Calcio | 137 mg

Yogur natural

LANONE

Por cada 100 gramos
Calorías |
Proteínas | 44
Hidratos de carbono | 4,8 g
Grasas | 5,8 g
Calcio | 0,1 g
 | 139 mg

Yogur descremado

PARA TU REFERENCIA

los alimentos	*foods*
bajo en calorías	*low in calories*
el calcio	*calcium*
descremado(a)	*fat-free*
los hidratos de carbono	*carbohydrates*
las lentejas	*lentils*
el puré de patatas	*mashed potatoes*

264

Para hispanohablantes

Borrow several Spanish-language magazines that have health columns or articles and bring them to class. Distribute them to your classmates and tell the class about the health tips they contain.

For students having difficulty giving advice about diet and nutrition, you might consider:
- **The tutor page:** Pair the student with a native speaker or a more able student, using the tutor page.

¿Cuál tiene más?

¿Cuál de los productos tiene más calorías? ¿Y más calcio? ¿Y más hidratos de carbono? ¿Y más grasas? ¿Y más proteínas?

El puré de patatas tiene más calorías.

 Come lentejas

Dile a tu compañero(a) qué quieres evitar y él/ella te va a aconsejar qué debes comer.

— *Yo quiero evitar las grasas.*
— *Pues come lentejas. Tienen poca grasa.*

 Para mantenerse sano(a)

Tu compañero(a) quiere mantenerse sano(a). ¿Qué le aconsejas?

Come yogur.
No le pongas mucha sal a la comida.
Duerme ocho horas al día.
Haz ejercicio.
Evita el estrés.

 Entrevista

Tu compañero(a) es un(una) experto(a) en nutrición. Hazle una entrevista.

— *¿Qué debo hacer para alimentarme bien?*
— *No tomes mucho café...*

 Tu diario

Escribe un párrafo explicando qué comes, qué ejercicio haces y cuántas horas duermes al día.

Desayuno: leche con cereales y fruta. Comida: hamburguesa con papas fritas, arroz con pollo o tacos. Cena: sándwiches de jamón o de queso, con lechuga y tomate. No voy al gimnasio, pero juego al béisbol con mis amigos. Y duermo ocho horas al día.

265

 APPLY

1. Individual Activity
Say which of the products have the most calories, calcium, carbohydrates, fat, and protein.
Answers:
See model on student page.
El yogur descremado tiene más calcio.
El puré de patatas tiene más hidratos de carbono.
El yogur natural tiene más grasas.
Las lentejas tienen más proteínas.
Extension: Scramble the letters of some words on these pages for your partner to unscramble. Example:
osahtidr ed rocoban—hidratos de carbono

2. Pair Activity
Tell your partner what you want to avoid. Your partner will advise you on what you should eat.
Answers: See model on student page.
Extension: Compare five foods you do and don't like using **más/menos...que.** Dictate your sentences to your partner.

3. Pair Activity
Advise your partner on how to remain healthy.
Answers: See model on student page.
Extension: Make a chart of the four food groups. *(Verduras y frutas, Carnes y pescados, Pan y cereales, Leche)* List five new foods under each heading.

4. Pair Activity
Interview your partner, who is a nutrition expert, about good health.
Answers: See model on student page.

5. Homework or Classwork
Write a paragraph explaining what you eat, what exercises you do, and how many hours you sleep each day.
Answers: See model on student page.
Note: Have students follow the model, changing words as necessary. Help students by copying the paragraph on the board, underlining the words to be changed.

 CHECK

- *¿Qué tiene más proteínas, el puré de patatas o el yogur natural?*
- *¿Qué quiere decir descremado?*
- *¿Qué debo hacer para alimentarme bien?*

LOG BOOK
Have students write the list of the four basic food groups in their Log Book.

Communicative Objective
• to talk about health and fitness

Related Components

Video: Tape/Book
Unit 5: Seg. 3

Scan to Chapter 10

GETTING STARTED

What are some excuses people make for not maintaining a healthy lifestyle?

APPLY

Form groups. Each will make a poster about staying fit and healthy. You may wish to assign a different theme to each group to avoid repetition.

PASO 1: La salud
Make a list of health themes.
Answers: See model on student page.
Extension: Ask other groups about the themes they chose.

PASO 2: Nuestro tema
Choose the theme of your poster.
Answers: See model on student page.

PASO 3: Consejos
Write five pieces of advice that have to do with your poster's theme.
Answers: See model on student page.
Extension: With another group, take turns dicating your pieces of advice.

Paso 4: Las ilustraciones
Take photographs, draw pictures, or use magazine photos to decorate the poster.

PASO 5: Nuestro cartel
Design the poster. Put your poster up in the classroom.

PARA RESOLVER
MANTENTE SANO

En grupo, van a hacer carteles con consejos para mantenerse sanos.

PASO 1 La salud
Hagan una lista de temas relacionados con la salud.

- *alimentarse bien*
- *no fumar*
- *hacer ejercicio*
- *evitar el estrés*

PASO 2 Nuestro tema
Decidan el tema del cartel que harán.

> *Nosotros haremos un cartel sobre cómo evitar el estrés.*

PASO 3 Consejos
Escriban cinco consejos relacionados con el tema que eligieron para su cartel.

- *Duerme ocho horas al día.*
- *Escucha música.*
- *Baila.*
- *Llévate bien con todo el mundo.*
- *Haz ejercicio.*

PASO 4 Las ilustraciones
Saquen fotos o hagan dibujos para ilustrar el cartel. También pueden usar fotos de revistas relacionadas con su tema.

PASO 5 Nuestro cartel
Diseñen el cartel. Decoren la clase con los carteles de todos los grupos.

PARA TU REFERENCIA

relacionados con	related to
elegir	to choose

¿SABES QUE...?

In addition to hosting marathon races, Spain became the world capital of in-line skating by sponsoring the first annual "Fiesta de Patín" in Barcelona in October of 1994. More than 15,000 people participated in the 9 km race (about 4 miles) through the city streets. The event, which was non-competitive, appealed mostly to young people. More than 90 percent of the participants were under 30 years of age.

266

MEETING INDIVIDUAL NEEDS

Reaching All Students

For Visual/Kinesthetic Learners
Use your poster and other visual aids to give a class presentation.

Evita el estrés

duerme ocho horas al día
escucha música●baila
llévate bien con todo el mundo
haz ejercicio

267

Have students copy one piece of advice from each of the posters in their Log Book.

Background

Exercise and Health Words
Here are additional words that students may be interested in knowing:

EXERCISE
cycling *el ciclismo*
diet *hacer (un) régimen, estar a dieta*
excercise bicycle *la bicicleta estática*
gain weight *engordar*
locker room *el salón de casilleros, la sala de taquillas, el camarín*
lose weight *adelgazar*
massage *masaje*
meditate *meditar*
running track *la pista*
sauna *el baño sauna, la sauna*
steamroom *el cuarto de vapor*
stopwatch *el cronómetro*
stretch *estirarse*
sweat (to) *sudar*
sweat *el sudor*
swimming *la natación*
swimming pool *la piscina*
trampoline *la cama elástica*

ILLNESSES
asthma *asma*
chicken pox *la varicela*
congestion *la congestión*
fever *la fiebre*
headache *el dolor de cabeza*
measles *el sarampión*
pneumonia *la pulmonía*
stomachache *el dolor de estómago*
strep throat *la garganta inflamada*
whooping cough *la tos ferina*

Para hispanohablantes

Explain why the advice from one of the posters is good advice.

Objectives

Communicative: to talk about training for sports
Cultural: to learn about the *CAR* sports center near Barcelona

Related Components

Audio	Magazine
Conexiones: 18A	Juntos en España
Conexiones	
Chapter 10	

GETTING STARTED

Ask students what kind of training a serious athlete must endure. Where does this type of training take place?

DISCUSS

Using the Text

Have volunteers read aloud the text. Ask questions. Suggestions:
¿Dónde está el Centro de Alto Rendimiento?
¿Quiénes van al CAR a entrenarse?
¿Qué pueden combinar los deportistas en esta escuela?
¿Para quién es este centro?
¿Qué deportes se pueden practicar allí?
¿Qué hace el equipo médico?
¿Cuáles son algunas de las enfermedades típicas de los deportistas?

CHECK

Te toca a ti
Answers:
1. *Falsa. El CAR tiene instalaciones para muchos deportes.*
2. *Cierta.*
3. *Falsa. El CAR está en Sant Cugat, a 30 kilómetros de Barcelona.*
4. *Falsa. Sólo los mejores atletas jóvenes pueden ir al CAR.*

ENTÉRATE

UNA ESCUELA PARA DEPORTISTAS

TE TOCA A TI

Di qué oraciones son ciertas y cuáles son falsas. Corrige las oraciones falsas.

1. El CAR no tiene instalaciones para muchos deportes.

2. El CAR tiene un centro de investigación de las enfermedades típicas de los atletas.

3. El Centro de Alto Rendimiento está en Barcelona.

4. Todos los atletas jóvenes pueden ir al CAR.

En Sant Cugat, a 30 kilómetros de Barcelona, está el Centro de Alto Rendimiento° (CAR). Aquí vienen a entrenarse° sólo los mejores atletas jóvenes. La escuela está especialmente diseñada para que los deportistas° puedan° combinar sus estudios con las sesiones de entrenamiento.° Es el único centro de España para deportistas de élite.

El CAR tiene instalaciones para tenis, gimnasia, baloncesto, natación, voleibol, taekwondo y muchos otros deportes. Hay un equipo médico que asiste° a los atletas lesionados.° También hay un centro de investigación para estudiar las enfermedades típicas de los deportistas, como el codo de tenista,° la tendonitis y las lesiones° de la rodilla.

asiste *takes care of*
el Centro de Alto Rendimiento *High Performance Center*
el codo de tenista *tennis elbow*
los deportistas *athletes*
entrenarse *to train*
el entrenamiento *training*
lesionados *injured*
las lesiones *injuries*
puedan *(they) can*

268

Thinking About Language

Acronyms don't always translate well. Ask what **CAR** stands for in Spanish and what it would be in English. (HPC—High Performance Center) In Spanish, as in English, acronyms are pronounced as if they were a word whenever possible. Ask students what they think these Spanish acronyms stand for:
ONU *Organización de las Naciones Unidas*
OTAN *Organización del Tratado del Atlántico Norte (NATO)*

LOG BOOK

Have students create acronyms for three imaginary Spanish organizations.
Example: **ONDA** *Organización Nacional de Deportes Acuáticos*

Para hispanohablantes

Tell the class about a place in your area that offers sports training.

VOCABULARIO TEMÁTICO

Para mantenerse sano(a)
To stay healthy
alimentarse bien
to eat healthy food
descansar *to rest*
dormir *to sleep*
evitar el estrés *to avoid stress*
evitar las grasas
to avoid fatty foods
hacer ejercicio *to exercise*
no fumar *not to smoke*
no tomar bebidas alcohólicas
not to drink alcoholic beverages

Para mantenerse en forma
To stay in shape
correr *to run*
hacer... *to do . . .*
   abdominales *sit-ups*
   aerobic *aerobics*
   bicicleta *stationary bicycle*
   cinta *treadmill*
   escalera *stair master*

flexiones *push-ups*
pesas *to lift weights*

Las partes del cuerpo
Parts of the body
la cabeza *head*
el corazón *heart*
el cuello *neck*
el estómago *stomach*
la garganta *throat*
el hombro *shoulder*
el músculo *muscle*
la pierna *leg*
la rodilla *knee*

¿Cómo te sientes?
How do you feel?
Me duele... *My . . . hurts.*
Me duele la cabeza.
I have a headache.
¿Qué te duele?
What's hurting you?
Tengo agujetas. *I'm sore. I have sore muscles.*

Tengo catarro. *I have a cold.*
Tengo gripe. *I have the flu.*
Tengo fiebre. *I have a fever.*

Expresiones y palabras
Di no a las drogas.
Say no to drugs.
la aspirina *aspirin*
la bebida alcohólica
alcoholic beverage
la droga *drug*
el ejercicio *exercise*
el estrés *stress*
evitar *to avoid*
la fiebre *fever*
la grasa *fat*
irse *to go*
la pesa *weight*
ponerse en forma
to get in shape
la sal *salt*
la salud *health*
sano(a) *healthy*
sentirse (e>i) bien/mal
to feel well/bad

LA CONEXIÓN INGLÉS-ESPAÑOL

The letter *x* in the word *exercise* corresponds with the letter *j* in the Spanish word *ejercicio*. There are other examples of cognates with this pattern:
ejecutivo → *executive*
ejemplo → *example*

Be on the lookout for other words in Spanish that include the letter *j*.

269

VOCABULARIO TEMÁTICO

Objective
• to review vocabulary

Related Components

Activity Book	Audio
Chapter Review: p. 131-132	Assessment: 15B
Assessment	**Cuaderno**
Listening Script: p. 18	p. 83-84
Chapter Test: p. 99-104	**Transparencies** Ch. 10: Dibujos y palabras Transparency 65

Vocabulary
Point out that this list is organized by themes. Use the headings to review vocabulary. You may wish to ask Spanish speakers to share variations on these words and phrases with the class.

LOG BOOK
Have students list five ways in which they try to stay fit and healthy.

La conexión inglés-español
There are a number of other words in which the Spanish **j** corresponds to English **x**. Students are likely to know at least two: *tejano* (English "Texan") and *relajante* (relaxing).

ADELANTE

Objectives
Prereading Strategy: to gain meaning from photographs and captions
Cultural: to learn about the popularity of soccer and basketball in Spain

Related Components

Magazine	Video: Tape/Book
Juntos en España	Unit 5: Seg. 4

Scan to Adelante

GETTING STARTED

Ask students if they have ever seen a professional soccer game. A World Cup game? Did anyone go to a game when the World Cup was held in the US in 1994? Now ask if anyone has seen or been to a professional basketball game. Why do students think certain sports are more popular in different countries?

Using the Video

Show Segment 4 of the Unit 5 video, an introduction to sports in Spain.

Antes de leer

Read aloud the first paragraph; ask questions. Examples:
¿Cuál es el rey de los deportes en España?
¿Cuál es el otro deporte más popular en España?
¿Entre quiénes es popular el baloncesto?
¿Cuál deporte piensas que es el más popular en Estados Unidos?
¿Hay otro deporte que cada día es más importante en Estados Unidos?

Have students look at the photos and captions on these pages and answer the question on the student page.
Answer: **a**

About Sports in Spain

Until the mid-20th century, bullfighting was the most popular spectator sport in Spain. Soccer was introduced by the British during the second half of the 19th century; by the 1950s it was the most popular sport. Although Spain's leading clubs have a distinguished record in international soccer circles, the national team has not fared as well.

ADELANTE

ANTES DE LEER

El fútbol es el rey° de los deportes en España. Durante décadas, el fútbol ha cautivado° a los aficionados,° domingo tras° domingo. Sin embargo, poco a poco, el baloncesto se está haciendo° más y más popular, especialmente entre los jóvenes.

Mira las páginas 270 a 273. Según las fotos y los títulos, ¿cuál es el tema principal del artículo?

    a. El fútbol y el baloncesto en España.

    b. Los españoles se ponen en forma.

    c. Los Juegos Olímpicos del 92.

El fútbol forma parte de la cultura española.

los aficionados *fans*	se está haciendo *is becoming*
ha cautivado *has captivated*	tras *after*
el rey *king*	

270

ADELANTE COMPONENTS

Activity Book	Audio Tapes	Transparencies	Video: Tape/Book
p. 133-136	Adelante: 11A, 11B	Unit 5: Adelante	Unit 5: Seg. 4-5
Assessment	**Magazine**	Transparencies	
Portfolio: p. 41-42	Juntos en España	66-67	

◄La selección española de fútbol es uno de los equipos más fuertes° de Europa.

◄Miles de españoles van a los estadios de fútbol cada domingo.

◄El equipo español de baloncesto ganó la medalla de plata en los Juegos Olímpicos de Los Ángeles en 1984. El baloncesto se hizo° muy popular en España. En la foto, Ferrán Martínez y Rafael Jofresa (de blanco) defienden° la selección española.

defienden *defend*
más fuertes *stronger*

se hizo *became*

271

DISCUSS

Using the Photos

Spanish National Soccer Team
¿Cómo es el equipo de fútbol español?

Extension: How has the Spanish soccer team done in World Cup competitions? Has it ever won the World Cup? (No)

Soccer Spectators
¿Qué día de la semana se juega al fútbol profesional en España generalmente?

Extension: What are some well-known or historic clubs in the Spanish National League? (In addition to the teams listed on page 272, some famous teams are: *Racing de Santander; Real Sociedad,* San Sebastian; *Deportivo de La Coruña; Tenerife,* Canary Islands; and *Betis,* Seville.)

Basketball
¿Qué hizo popular al baloncesto en España?

Extension: What are some of the better-known Spanish professional basketball teams? (Besides the teams listed on page 273, there are: *Taugrés,* Vitoria; *Estudiantes,* Madrid; and *Granollers,* Barcelona.)

Para hispanohablantes

Have students describe to the class a soccer or basketball game in Spanish.

▶▶▶INTERNET LINK

Soccer http://gnn.yahoo.com/gnn/ Regional/Countries/Spain/Sports/Football/

Objectives

Reading Strategy: to gain meaning from context
Cultural: to learn about the importance of soccer and basketball in Spain

Related Components

Activity Book p. 133	Audio Adelante: 11A

GETTING STARTED

Ask students to look at the list of sports that are popular in Spain (p. 273). Are these sports popular in your community? Have volunteers read aloud paragraphs from the article.

Soccer Words

POSITIONS AND EQUIPMENT

goalie *el arquero, el portero*
defenders *los defensas*
fullbacks *el (defensa) lateral izquierdo/ derecho, el centrocampista*
stopper *el defensa central*
sweeper *el líbero*
midfielder *el mediocampista central/ izquierdo/derecho, el centrocampista*
forwards *los delanteros*
striker *el delantero central*
wing *el puntero izquierdo/derecho, el delantero derecho/izquierdo*
coach *el entrenador, el míster*
linesman *el juez de línea, el linier*
referee *el árbitro, el colegiado*

PLAYS

corner kick *el tiro de esquina, el córner*
direct kick *el (tiro) directo*
dribbling *el dribling, el regate, el regateo*
foul *la falta*
free kick *el tiro libre*
goal *el gol*
goal kick *el saque de meta, el saque de puerta*
head the ball *cabecear*
header *el cabezazo*
indirect kick *el tiro indirecto*
kick *patear, chutar*
kickoff *el golpe/toque inicial*
offside *fuera de juego*
pass *el pase*
penalty *el penal, el penalty*
red card *la tarjeta roja*
substitution *el cambio*
throw-in *el saque lateral/de costado*
yellow card *la tarjeta amarilla*

El fútbol y el baloncesto en España

En España el fútbol es el deporte nacional. Todas las ciudades importantes tienen uno o más equipos de fútbol. Madrid, la capital, tiene tres equipos: el Real Madrid, el Atlético de Madrid y el Rayo Vallecano. Barcelona tiene dos: el Fútbol Club Barcelona y el Español.

El Español y el Atlético de Bilbao en un partido.▼

La Liga° y sus divisiones

Los equipos de fútbol compiten° en la Liga Nacional. Hay varias divisiones. La Primera División es la mejor. Generalmente cada equipo juega un partido por semana. Al final de la temporada, el equipo que queda primero° gana la Liga. Los dos equipos que quedan últimos bajan° a la división inferior. Los dos primeros equipos de las divisiones inferiores suben a la división superior.

▲**Después del fútbol, el baloncesto es el deporte más popular de España.**

El auge° del baloncesto

El baloncesto es cada día más popular, especialmente entre los jóvenes. En algunas ciudades, como en Vitoria (al norte, en el País Vasco), el equipo de baloncesto local es más importante que el de fútbol. Como en el fútbol, el baloncesto también tiene una liga nacional, que se llama ACB (Asociación de Clubs de

el auge *rise*
bajan *drop*
compiten *compete*

la Liga *League*
queda primero *in first place*

272

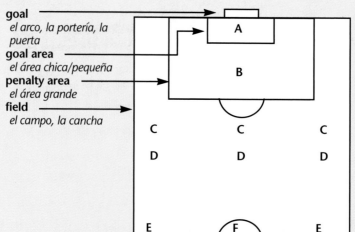

goal
   el arco, la portería, la puerta
goal area
   el área chica/pequeña
penalty area
   el área grande
field
   el campo, la cancha

KEY TO POSITIONS

A   arquero
B   líbero
C   defensas
D   mediocampistas
E   puntero
F   delantero central

Baloncesto). Tres de los equipos más fuertes de la ACB son el Barcelona, el Joventut de Badalona y el Real Madrid.

Los jugadores extranjeros

Cada equipo de fútbol puede tener hasta cuatro jugadores no europeos (no de la CEE),° pero sólo pueden jugar tres de ellos en cada partido. En baloncesto, cada club puede tener un máximo de tres jugadores no españoles. Muchos de los jugadores extranjeros de la Liga de Baloncesto española son estadounidenses. También hay muchos jugadores croatas y rusos.°

▲ Hay muchos jugadores extranjeros que juegan en las ligas españolas de fútbol y baloncesto. El danés° Michael Laudrup (a la izquierda) es uno de ellos. Juega con el Real Madrid.

▲ Los periódicos deportivos son muy populares en España. *El Mundo Deportivo* es el más antiguo. Se fundó a finales del siglo XIX.

Los periódicos deportivos

En España hay muchos periódicos de deportes. Muchos de estos periódicos venden más ejemplares° diariamente° que los demás periódicos. Los periódicos deportivos más famosos son *Marca* y *El Mundo Deportivo*.

la CEE *EC (European Community)*
danés *Danish*
diariamente *daily*

Los deportes en España

Aquí tienes una tabla de los deportes más populares en España.

1.	fútbol
2.	baloncesto
3.	balonmano
4.	hockey sobre patines
5.	ciclismo
6.	motociclismo
7.	tenis
8.	atletismo
9.	golf
10	voleibol
11.	judo
12.	gimnasia
13.	natación
14.	hockey sobre hierba°

los ejemplares *copies*
el hockey sobre hierba *field hockey*
rusos *Russian*

273

DISCUSS

Suggestions for discussion:

El fútbol y el baloncesto en España

¿Cuál es el deporte nacional de España?
¿Qué ciudades tienen equipos de fútbol?
¿Cómo se llaman los equipos de Madrid?
¿Y cómo se llaman los de Barcelona?

La Liga y sus divisiones

¿En qué compiten los equipos de fútbol?
¿Cuál es la mejor división?
¿Qué les pasa a los equipos que quedan últimos en la Primera División?
¿Qué les pasa a los dos primeros equipos de la Segunda División?

El auge del baloncesto

¿Cómo se llama la liga nacional de baloncesto?

Los jugadores extranjeros

¿Cuántos jugadores de países no europeos puede tener un equipo de fútbol español?
¿Pueden jugar todos los jugadores no europeos de un equipo en un partido?
¿De dónde son algunos jugadores extranjeros de baloncesto que juegan en equipos españoles?

Los periódicos deportivos

¿Cuáles son los dos periódicos deportivos más populares?
¿Hay periódicos o revistas en Estados Unidos que sólo tienen noticias deportivas? (Two: Sports Illustrated, The Sporting News.)

Los deportes en España

¿Cuál es el tercer deporte más popular en España?
¿Cuál es el menos popular?
¿Cuáles de estos deportes son populares en Estados Unidos?

CHECK

• ¿Dónde hay clubes de fútbol en España?
• ¿Es el fútbol más popular que el baloncesto en todas partes de España?
• ¿Qué periódico puedes leer para saber los resultados de un partido?

LOG BOOK

Have students write sentences about any of these sports in the US.

Identifying Main Ideas and Details

Have students notice that the subheadings in the text indentify main ideas. With your students, construct a chart showing the main ideas and details of the passage.

Para hispanohablantes

Ask friends and relatives to rank the sports they think are the most popular sports in Latin America. Tell the class.

These activities can be done as classwork or as homework.

Objectives
Organizing Skills: to use lists and tables to organize information
Communication Skills: to write questions and answers

Related Components

Activity Book	Assessment
p. 134	Portfolio: p. 41-42

ACTIVITIES

1. Los deportes aquí y allá
Individual Activity What differences are there between sports in Spain and in the US?
Possible Answers:
más popular: *el béisbol, el baloncesto, el fútbol americano, el hockey sobre patines*
varias divisiones: *sí*
la primera división es mejor: *sí*
extranjeros: *sí*

2. Todo tipo de deportes
Individual Activity List ten sports for each of two or more categories: for example, team sports and individual sports.
Possible Answers:
deportes de equipo: *el baloncesto, el béisbol, el fútbol americano, el hockey sobre patines, el voleibol*
deportes individuales: *el atletismo, el balonmano, el ciclismo, el golf, el tenis*

3. ¿Cuál es la pregunta?
Group Activity Write five questions and answers about the article. Read the answers to another group, which has to guess what the question is. Groups win one point for a correct answer and lose a point for incorrect answers.
Answers: Answers will vary.

4. Compruébalo
Individual Activity Say whether the following statements are true or false. Correct the false ones.
1. *Falsa. El fútbol es el deporte más popular.*
2. *Falsa. En España hay periódicos de deportes.*
3. *Cierta.*
4. *Falsa. En España el fútbol americano no es popular.*
5. *Cierta.*

274

---

❶ Los deportes aquí y allá
Según el artículo, ¿qué diferencias o similitudes hay entre los deportes de España y de Estados Unidos?
Haz una tabla; sigue el modelo.

	ESPAÑA	ESTADOS UNIDOS
el deporte más popular	el fútbol	
hay varias divisiones	sí	
la primera división es la mejor	sí	
los equipos tienen jugadores extranjeros	sí	

❷ Todo tipo de deportes
Haz una lista de los diez deportes que más te gustan. Piensa en una manera de organizarlos en categorías. Después, explica a tus compañeros qué tipo de deportes te gusta más y por qué.

❸ ¿Cuál es la pregunta?
En grupos, escriban cinco preguntas sobre el artículo. Anoten las respuestas en un papel. Lean las respuestas a otro grupo. Tienen que adivinar cuál es la pregunta.

- Los grupos ganan un punto cuando adivinan la pregunta.
- Si un grupo no la adivina, pierde un punto.

❹ Compruébalo
Según el artículo, di cuáles de las siguientes oraciones son ciertas o falsas. Corrige las oraciones falsas.

1. El baloncesto es el deporte más popular en España.
2. En España hay periódicos sólo de baloncesto y fútbol.
3. En teoría, los equipos de la primera división son mejores que los equipos de la segunda división.
4. En España el fútbol americano es muy popular.
5. En España algunos jugadores de los equipos de fútbol son extranjeros.

274

TALLER DE ESCRITORES

1. ENTREVISTA

Prepara una lista de ocho preguntas que te gustaría hacerle a tu deportista favorito(a). Después, con tu compañero(a), imaginen que son un(a) reportero(a) y un(a) deportista. Hagan la entrevista.

> R: ¿Cómo se mantiene usted en forma, señor Jordan?
>
> D: Todos los días hago ejercicio.
>
> R: ¿Hace abdominales?
>
> D: ¡No! ¡Nunca! No me gustan.

2. UNA FIESTA ORIGINAL

Imagina que irás a una fiesta de disfraces° muy especial: ¡el disfraz más horrible ganará un premio! Piensa en un diseño original y en colores que no están de moda. ¡No te olvides del peinado y del maquillaje! Describe tu disfraz en cinco oraciones (más o menos) y preséntalo a la clase.

> Llevaré un disfraz de los años sesenta. La camisa tendrá muchos colores...

3. ¿CÓMO PODEMOS AYUDAR?

Haz una lista de cuatro maneras de ayudar a otros a mantenerse sanos y ponerse en forma.

PROBLEMA	SOLUCIÓN
En la escuela, muchos estudiantes no están en forma.	hacer diez minutos de gimnasia con música todos los días, después de clase.
Algunos estudiantes fuman.	poner carteles en la escuela explicando por qué fumar es malo para la salud

el disfraz (los disfraces) costume(s)

275

Para hispanohablantes

Imagine that you are a coach and the class is your team. Tell them what to do to get ready for the next game.

TALLER DE ESCRITORES

Objectives
- to practice writing
- to use vocabulary and structures from this unit

Related Components

Activity Book	Assessment
p. 135	Portfolio: p. 41-42

ACTIVITIES

1. Entrevista
Individual and Pair Activity Students will prepare a list of eight questions they would like to ask their favorite sports star. In pairs, students act the roles of reporter and athlete and interview each other.
Extension: Use the library, the Internet, and other sources to do reseach on your favorite athlete. Organize the information you gather according to sources. Then write what answers you think your favorite athlete would give to the questions you created earlier.

2. Una fiesta original
Individual Activity Students will imagine they are going to a costume party. A prize will be given for the most horrible-looking costume. They should describe the costume in five sentences, including hair and makeup, and present it to the class.
Extension: Draw others' costumes as they describe them.

3. ¿Cómo podemos ayudar?
Individual Activity Students will identify four health problems and suggest solutions for people to maintain good health and stay in shape. Elicit suggestions from the class and write them on the board.
Edit: Discuss with the class questions about spelling and grammar. Pairs then exchange their work and review and edit each other's work, making notes about possible errors. Have them work together to check spelling and grammar, and to prepare final works.
Present: Students present their list of problems and solutions to the class.

PORTFOLIO
Suggest that students select their revision of Activity 3 for their Portfolios.

275

Objectives

Communicative: to listen to and understand directions
Cultural: to learn about leather in Spain
• to make a leather pouch

Related Components

Assessment	Video: Tape/Book
Portfolio: p. 41-42	Unit 5: Seg. 5
Transparencies	
Unit 5: Project	
Transparency 66	

Scan to La obra

Materials

• leather
• scissors
• leather hole puncher
• knife (to cut leather)
• hammer
• compass (drawing tool)
• paper
• colored pencil
• leather strings: two 18" and six 10"
• pattern (see student page)

GETTING STARTED

Encourage students to use their eyes more than their ears. Rather than try to understand every word, they should concentrate on the actions and listen only for clues. If possible, show the leather pouch-making segment of the Unit 5 video.

DISCUSS

Read aloud the introductory text, then ask a few questions. Examples:
¿Qué cosas se hacen de cuero? (Students have seen: *bolsa de mano, bota tejana, cinturón, chaqueta, falda, pelota de fútbol, maleta, mochila, sandalia, silla, zapatos.*)
¿Qué vamos a hacer hoy?
¿Para qué podemos usarla?

MANOS A LA OBRA

PRÁCTICO Y DE MODA

El cuero está en todas partes. Fíjate en° los zapatos, botas, chaquetas, bolsos, mochilas, riñoneras,° pulseras,... ¡los artículos más prácticos casi siempre son de cuero!

TE TOCA A TI

En los mercados y tiendas de España, puedes encontrar todo tipo de artículos de cuero. Muchos de estos artículos están hechos a mano. Con las herramientas° apropiadas° y un poco de imaginación, tú también puedes hacer algo para ponerte. Aquí haremos una riñonera para llevar tu dinero y tus cosas de una forma cómoda y segura.°

Materiales

• cuero
• tijeras
• un sacabocados°
• clavos gruesos°
• una cuchilla°
• un martillo°
• un compás
• un lápiz de color
• cuatro tiras° de cuero: dos de 18" y seis de 10" (puedes comprarlas o hacerlas tú)
• papel
• el patrón

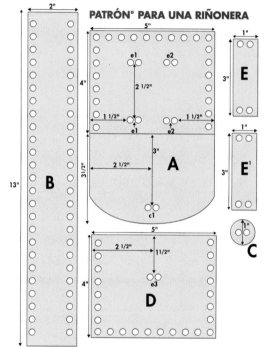

PATRÓN° PARA UNA RIÑONERA

apropiadas *appropriate*	las herramientas *tools*	las riñoneras *pouches*
los clavos gruesos *thick nails*	el sacabocados *hole puncher*	segura *safe*
la cuchilla *blade*	el martillo *hammer*	las tiras *strings*
fíjate en *pay attention to*	el patrón *pattern*	

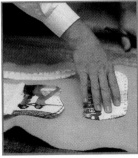

1 Con un papel haz el patrón. Copia las partes A, B, C, D, E y E¹ del modelo que ves en la página anterior (más grande, por supuesto). Pon el patrón sobre el cuero y márcalo con un lápiz. No te olvides de marcar todos los agujeros.°

2 Con las tijeras recorta el patrón de cuero. Marca todos los agujeros con un clavo y un martillo.

3 Con el sacabocados o el martillo y los clavos, haz los agujeros.

4 Si compraste las tiras de cuero, ve al paso 5. Si no las compraste, puedes hacerlas tú. Marca con el compás cuatro tiras en el cuero, dos largas (más o menos de 18") y seis cortas (de 10"). Después córtalas con la cuchilla.

los agujeros *holes*
el nudo *knot*

5 Pon C sobre A, haciendo que los aqujeros c queden sobre los agujeros c1. Pasa una de las tiras cortas por los agujeros y haz un nudo° en la parte de atrás. Pon E sobre A, haciendo que los aqujeros e queden sobre los agujeros e1. Pasa una de las tiras cortas por cada par de agujeros y haz un nudo en la parte de atrás. Repite e1 mismo procedimiento con F.

6 Con una de las tiras largas, une A y B. Con otra tira larga une AB y C. Para cerrar la riñonera, pasa una de las tiras cortas por los agujeros d, dejando suficiente tira libre para hacer un ojal por el que pasará C a manera de botón. ¡Ya tienes tu riñonera! Póntela en el cinturón.

277

Objectives

Communicative: to expand reading comprehension
Cultural: to relate the study of Spanish to other subject areas

Related Components

Activity Book p. 136	**Transparencies** Unit 5: Adelante Transparency 67
Assessment Portfolio: p. 41-42	**Video: Tape/Book** Unit 5: Seg. 4
Audio Adelante: 11B	

Scan to Adelante

Una joven actriz del cine español

About the Movie

Alfonso Arau is a Mexican director who has appeared as an actor in many Hollywood films. He gained international recognition with *Como agua para chocolate,* a film based on his wife's novel of the same name. *A Walk in the Clouds,* his first Hollywood film, takes place in the period following World War II. It is a love story about an ex-soldier (Reeves) and a young woman (Sánchez-Gijón) who is a member of an old Mexican-American wine-making family in northern California.

Answers:

• *Por su trabajo en la película* Un paseo por las nubes.
• *Empezó su carrera en una serie de televisión en España.*

Activity

Ask questions such as the following:
¿Quién es Aitana Sánchez-Gijón?
¿En qué medios ha trabajado?
¿Quién la dirigió en Un paseo por las nubes?
¿Viste Un paseo por las nubes? *¿Te gustó?*

Reading Aloud

Have volunteers take turns reading aloud the selections in *Otras fronteras.*

CINE

UNA JOVEN ACTRIZ DEL CINE ESPAÑOL

Aitana Sánchez-Gijón es una joven actriz española. Su primera aparición fue en una serie de televisión en España. Luego interpretó varias obras de teatro y empezó a trabajar en el cine con los mejores directores y actores españoles y europeos. En 1994, el director mexicano Alfonso Arau la escogió para actuar, junto a Keanu Reeves, en *Un paseo por las nubes.* Los expertos opinan que Aitana tiene un gran futuro en el cine norteamericano.

• ¿Por qué conoce el público americano a Aitana Sánchez-Gijón?
• ¿Dónde empezó su carrera como actriz?

ARTE

LA IMAGEN DEL TORO° EN LA PINTURA ESPAÑOLA

La imagen del toro aparece constantemente° en el arte español. Francisco de Goya, el gran pintor español del siglo XIX, pintó cientos de toros en sus cuadros. En el centro de *Guernica,* la gran obra de Picasso, también hay un toro. Hoy día, muchos jóvenes pintores españoles siguen esta tradición de incluir toros en sus obras. Ignacio Burgos es uno de ellos. Su pintura es expresionista.

• ¿Quién es Ignacio Burgos?
• ¿Conoces alguna obra de arte que incluye un toro? ¿De quién es?

aparece constantemente *appears constantly*
el toro *bull*

278

La imagen del toro en la pintura española

About the Bull Motif in Spanish Art

The image of the bull first appeared in prehistoric times, painted on the walls of caves in Altamira, Spain. Goya (1746-1828) created an important series of etchings and lithographs of bullfights. Picasso (1881-1973) was a major bullfight aficionado. Burgos (b. 1968) was inspired by prehistoric images in a natural history museum.

Possible Answers:

• *Es un pintor expresionista español.*
• *La obra* Guernica *de Pablo Picasso incluye un toro.*

Activity

¿Qué animal está en las obras de muchos artistas españoles?
¿Quién pintó muchos cuadros de toros?
¿Cómo se llama otro pintor que pinta toros?
¿Cómo se llama un pintor contemporáneo que pinta cuadros de toros?

LAS ISLAS CANARIAS Y SU OBSERVATORIO

ASTRONOMÍA

Las Islas Canarias están al oeste de la costa africana. Aunque están a 1.500 kilómetros de la Península Ibérica, forman parte de España. Este archipiélago° tiene siete islas principales, de origen volcánico. Durante todo el año el clima es primaveral.

La isla de La Palma está al noreste del archipiélago. Allí está el observatorio astronómico más grande del hemisferio norte. Este observatorio se construyó en la montaña más alta de la isla, el Roque° de los Muchachos.

- ¿Dónde están las Islas Canarias?
- ¿Qué hay en la isla de La Palma?

TECNOLOGÍA

UN LABORATORIO EN LAS ESTRELLAS

Llegaron los terrestres!

España es uno de los 13 países que están participando en la construcción de una estación en el espacio. Cada país construye una parte de esta estación en la Tierra y luego, cada parte se llevará al espacio.

En la estación habrá un laboratorio para hacer investigaciones médicas e industriales. El laboratorio funcionará con energía solar. En la estación también habrá habitaciones para seis astronautas de los países participantes. Esta estación espacial internacional se terminará de construir en el año 2002.

- ¿Cuántos países participan en la construcción de esta estación espacial?
- ¿Qué tiene que hacer cada país?

el archipiélago *archipelago (group of islands)*
el roque *rook, castle*

279

Research Project

Form groups and ask each group to do additional research on one of the selections on pages 278 and 279. Students should use the library, the Internet, documentaries, interviews (perhaps with science or art teachers), etc. Ask them to organize the information they gather by sources.

Las Islas Canarias y su observatorio

About the Islands
The Canary Islands lie west of Africa, at about the same latitude as southern Morocco and Miami. The volcanically-formed islands offer favorable resources for an observatory—high peaks and negligible amounts of cloud cover, pollution, artificial light at night, and rainfall.

Answers:
- *Están en la costa africana, a 1.500 kilómetros de la Península Ibérica.*
- *Allí está el observatorio astronómico más grande del hemisferio norte.*

Activity
Have students say whether the following statements are true or false.
1. *Las Islas Canarias están en África. (Falso)*
2. *Hay siete islas principales en el archipiélago. (Cierto)*
3. *El observatorio está en la isla Roque de los Muchachos. (Falso)*

Un laboratorio en las estrellas

About the Space Station
Space scientists from the US and twelve other countries—including Russia, France, Spain, Germany and Japan—are building an International Space Station known as ISS. It is the first permanent international space station, and will be used for at least ten years. Scientists are already preparing for their move up in space by living and working on a Russian space station.

Activity
Have students form groups and design their own space station. They should then explain to the class what it will be like, using the future tense of the verb *haber*. Example: *Habrá seis dormitorios, una cocina y un centro cultural. También habrá un centro para deportes...*
Also ask students to consider questions such as:
Which professions would be most useful on a space station? Why?
What are the advantages of multi-national collaboration on a project such as ISS?

Tell your students...

In this unit we visit different Spanish-speaking communities throughout the United States. First we take a look at how the Hispanic population contributes its time and resources to community service (Chapter 11). Across the country, young Hispanics are making the U. S. a better place by pitching in as volunteers at recycling centers, hospitals and clinics, senior citizen homes, libraries, and day care centers.

Then we explore some of the career opportunities available for people who can communicate effectively in both Spanish and English (Chapter 12). Many positions in government, business, and education, as well as in interpretation and translation, require strong Spanish language skills.

Before leaving these vibrant communities and completing our second year of **Juntos,** we explore the best ways to maintain our Spanish skills and prepare for a bilingual career. It's quite simple: read Spanish, speak Spanish, listen to Spanish, and have fun with Spanish.

VIDEO LINKS

Corresponding Video Segments

Text

Unit Overview
Unit Opener

1. Introduction to the Hispanic US

A brief glimpse of the Hispanic population

Chapter 11

2. Servicios a la comunidad

How to be a more responsible citizen; different ways to help others in the community

Grammar: **es** (adjective) **que** + present subjunctive; **nosotros** commands

Chapter 12

3. Las ventajas de ser bilingüe

Personal aptitudes and qualities, career goals, work conditions, bilingual careers in the US

Grammar: **recomendar** + **que** + present subjunctive; the present perfect

Adelante

4. Adelante

Reading Spanish, speaking Spanish, listening to Spanish, and having fun with Spanish

Manos a la obra

5. Manos a la obra

How to create a photo essay about someone with a bilingual career

Hispanic Success Story

Until the last third of the 20th century, relatively few immigrants to the US spoke Spanish. Emigrants from Spain tended to go to Latin America. On the other hand, many Hispanics found themselves living in US territories when Florida was annexed in 1821 and huge areas of Mexico were ceded to the US in 1847.

The number of Hispanics in the US began growing dramatically in 1965, when immigration laws were amended to allow a fairer distribution of quotas and a less restrictive policy toward political refugees. According to the 1990 census, 13,495,059 Hispanics of Mexican origin live in the US, representing 5.4% of the total population. The 2,727,754 Hispanics from Puerto Rico who live on the mainland represent 1.1% of the total. The total number of Hispanics, 22,354,059, was 9% of the total 1990 population.

The results of this subpopulation explosion can be seen on professional baseball teams, in bilingual classrooms, on bestseller lists, and in the President's Cabinet. But nowhere are they more pervasive or do they reach more non-Hispanics directly than in the food industry and related businesses. Mexican and Tex-Mex restaurants are facts of life in all 50 states, and Hispanic food specialties are now as easy to find in small-town supermarkets as in big-city bodegas.

Las conversiones

MATH CONNECTION

Objective
- to convert metric and US standard measurements

Use
any time during Unit 6

Materials
- TRB Activity Support Page 21, *Tabla de conversiones*
- TRB Activity Support Page 22, *Escenarios de conversión*
- Calculators
- Cloth tape measure (with US standard measurements)
- TRB Activity Support Page 23, *Respuestas para los escenarios de conversión*

Preparation
- Read FYI below.

Activity
- Divide the class into groups of five students.
- Distribute *Escenarios de conversión* and *Tabla de conversiones*
- Have each group select a scenario. The same scenario may be chosen by more than one group.
- Distribute one calculator per group and give the tape measure to the group(s) selecting scenario 1, *Tu abuela en la República Dominicana.*
- Have each group take about 15 minutes to read their scenario and calculate their conversions. Answers may be written on the chalkboard.
- Compare the responses and discuss the possible problems someone unfamiliar with a measurement system might face in day-to-day life.

FYI
The United States is the only country that uses a non-metric measuring system. People moving here or visiting must learn our system in order to do such basic tasks as buying clothes, shoes, and food, or judging temperature readings. In the same manner, Americans abroad may experience a similar frustration when trying to understand metric measurements. Adjusting to the new system takes time, and is an important part of acclimating to a new culture.

Tradiciones familiares

SOCIAL STUDIES CONNECTION

Objective
- to explore family backgrounds and traditions

Use
any time during Unit 6

Materials
- TRB Activity Support Page 24, *Tradiciones familiares en español*

Activity
- Divide the class into five groups and distribute *Tradiciones familiares en español.*
- Have each group choose a set of questions to discuss and make a table of the answers.
- Groups present their findings to the class.

Aló, ¿operadora?

WRITING CONNECTION

Objective
- to develop an advertisement for a long-distance telephone company

Use
any time during Unit 6

Preparation
- Tell students that they work in the advertising department of a long-distance telephone company. Their boss has told them that, according to various sources, Hispanic-Americans spend more money on long distance calls than the rest of the US population.

Activity
- Have students work in pairs to create a new service for the company's Hispanic customers. The service should show appreciation for the customers' loyalty and encourage them to make more telephone calls.
- Pairs write a short advertisement announcing a new service. The announcement will be targeted for the Spanish-speaking population of the United States. For example:

  ¡Usen Teléfono Latino!
  - *Llamen a su país.*
  - *Llamen entre las seis y las once de la noche y reciban una rebaja del cincuenta por ciento.*
  - *Denle las buenas noticias a sus amigos y parientes.*
- Have each pair read their annoucement to the class.

Traducción excelente

WRITING CONNECTION

Objective
- to write an itinerary in English for a weekend visit to your city or town and translate it into Spanish

Use
any time during Unit 6

Materials
- bilingual dictionaries

Preparation
- Tell the class that they will be visited for a weekend by Ana and Carlos, two friends from Mexico who are visiting the US for the first time. They want to see historic monuments, cultural sites, and other interesting places in your area.

Activity
- Share FYI, then divide class into groups of five.
- Have groups write an itinerary in English for a weekend visit. The itinerary should include times of arrival and departure, names and descriptions of places to visit, names and addresses of restaurants, descriptions of cultural and social events you've made plans for, etc.
- Collect the itineraries and hand them out to different groups to translate into Spanish.
- Have students read the translations out loud and discuss them. You might kick off the discussion by asking questions: *¿Era fácil hacer las traducciones? ¿Sería fácil traducir poemas o cuentos del inglés al español? ¿Crees que es posible capturar todo el significado cuando se hace una traducción?*

FYI
How would you like to translate a full-length novel or book of poems from Spanish into English? Some men and women have done it remarkably well: Helen Lane has translated many long novels by Peruvian Mario Vargas Llosa; Eliot Weinberger has translated almost all of Mexican Octavio Paz's poetry; and Gregory Rabassa's translation of *Cien años de soledad* Colombian novelist Gabriel García Márquez claims to prefer to his Spanish original.

ESTADOS UNIDOS: ESPAÑOL POR TODAS PARTES

Unit Opener Goal
• to talk about communities, volunteer work, and bilingual careers

Related Components

Transparencies	Video: Tape/Book
Unit 6: Chapters 11-12	Unit 6: Seg. 1
Transparencies 68-80	

Scan to Unit 6

GETTING STARTED

Ask students to think about the services offered in their community. Who provides them and where?

Using the Video
Show Segment 1 of the Unit 6 video, an introduction to bilingual communities in the United States.

Using the Transparencies
To help orient students, use the Locator Map Transparency. You may want to use other Unit 6 transparencies at this time.

DISCUSS

Presenting Bilingual Communities
For more information about bilingual communities, refer to pages 280A–280D.

Using the Text
English: After students have read the introduction, ask questions. For example: Has anyone worked part-time or as a volunteer?
Have you ever had to communicate with someone who did not speak a language you know? What did you do?
Spanish: Ask Spanish speakers to comment on the photos and share what they know about Hispanic communities and people they know who are bilingual.

UNIDAD **6**

ESTADOS UNIDOS

ESPAÑOL POR TODAS PARTES
En la unidad 6:

Capítulo 11	Servicios a la comunidad
Capítulo 12	Las ventajas de ser bilingüe
Adelante	**Para leer:** ¡Qué suerte ser bilingüe!
	Proyecto: Su vida en fotos
	Otras fronteras: Cultura, sociedad, teatro y arte

Desfile del Día de la hispanidad en Nueva York.

280

UNIT COMPONENTS

Activity Book p. 137-160	**Audio Book** Script: p. 69-71; 75-77	**Conexiones** Chapters 11-12	**Transparencies** Unit 6: Chapters 11-12
Assessment Oral Proficiency: p. 31-32 Listening Script: p.19-20 Chapter Tests: p. 105-116 Portfolio: p. 43-44	Activities: p. 72-74; 78-80 **Audio** Chapter: 12A, 12B Adelante: 13A, 13B Assessment: 15B Conexiones: 18B	**Cuaderno** p. 85-100 **Magazine** Juntos en Estados Unidos	Transparencies 68-80 **Tutor Pages** p. 47-54 **Video: Tape/Book** Unit 6: Segments 1-5

A community is like a family with a common goal—to help each other achieve a better life and brighter future. In the United States many young people use their ability to speak both Spanish and English to help their communities.

In this unit, you will meet some young bilingual volunteers who help at health clinics, summer camps, and day-care and senior citizen centers. From them, you can learn how to help your community and even plan for your future. Your growing ability to communicate in both English and Spanish will be a great asset.

There are many career choices for people who speak both Spanish and English. Self-evaluation will help you identify the ones that might suit you.

You will close the unit by getting some tips on how to become bilingual. Finally, you will create a photo essay about a day in the life of a bilingual professional. Perhaps this will inspire you to think about including Spanish in your own career goals. ¡Español por todas partes!

281

ACTIVITIES

INTERDISCIPLINARY CONNECTIONS

The following activity will help students develop both cross-cultural awareness and linguistic proficiency. It will also give them an opportunity to review what they have learned and to apply their skills in a communicative context.

Global Community

With a partner, choose one of the theme countries or cities in this book, and prepare an oral presentation.

- Research and present an overview of the geography, population, history, and culture of your country or city.
- Choose one of those topics to explore in depth, based on your personal interests.
- Use props and other visual aids: music, poems, photographs, maps, or drawings.

Note: If possible, pair native speakers or more able students with those having difficulty. Set aside time for the class to ask questions after each presentation.

✓ CULTURE NOTE

The *Día de la Hispanidad* is Latin America's alternative to Columbus Day. In New York, two parades and celebrations are held each October—on different Sundays.

	Objetivos page 283 *Servicios a la comunidad*	Conversemos pages 284-285 *La comunidad y tú*	Realidades pages 286-287 *¡Tu también puedes ayudar!*	Palabras en acción pages 288-289 *En el vecindario*
Comunicación	To talk about: • what services are offered in your community	Discuss what services are offered in your community	Read text, answer questions, discuss community services, survey class	Read cartoon, make list; discuss characters; talk about community centers
	• what you can do to help out in your community	Discuss what you can do to help out in your community	Read text, discuss volunteer work in the community	Read cartoon, discuss improvements, good citizen ship; create dialog; make poster; write paragraph
	• what the needs of your community are	Discuss what your community's needs are	Read text, survey class	Activities 4-8: Read cartoon, discuss improvements; talk about recycling; create dialog; make poster; write paragraph
Cultura	To learn about: • activities in typical community centers in the U.S. • special volunteer activities teenagers can perform		Pamphlet from *Acción Latina,* describing student community volunteers and volunteer positions available	
Vocabulario temático	To learn the expressions for: • types of community centers	Talk about types of community centers	Read text, answer questions, discuss community services	Read cartoon, make list; discuss characters, community centers improvements; create dialog; make poster; write paragraph
	• volunteer activities	Talk about volunteer activities	Read text, answer questions, discuss volunteer work in the community	Make lists; discuss characters, community centers improvements; create dialog, poster, paragraph
	• community residents who receive assistance	Talk about different kinds of people in the community	Read text, survey class	Read cartoon, make list; discuss characters; create dialog; make poster; write paragraph
Estructura	To talk about: • what needs to be done: expressions with the subjunctive		Read text, use the subjunctive to answer questions	Activity 7: Read cartoon, make poster
	• what everyone can do together to help out: *nosotros* commands	Use *nosotros* commands to discuss what everyone can do together to help out		Activity 7: Read cartoon, make poster

SERVICIOS A LA COMUNIDAD

Para comunicarnos mejor (1) pages 290-291 *Es importante que ayudemos*	Para comunicarnos mejor (2) pages 292-293 *¡Reciclemos!*	Situaciones pages 294-295 *Seamos mejores ciudadanos*	Para resolver pages 296-297 *¿Qué servicios ofrece tu comunidad?*	Entérate page 298 *Un café para poetas*
Discuss community centers	Make weekend plans; survey class, make table	Act out interview; write in diary	Make list and choose one community center; conduct interview; design poster, report to class	Discuss social gatherings and the Nuyorican Poet's Cafe
Discuss community centers; survey classmates	Make weekend plans; discuss improving your neighborhood through recycling	Discuss being a good citizen; talk about volunteer activities; write in diary	Make list and choose one community center; conduct interview; design poster	
Discuss community centers; survey classmates, report to class	Discuss improving your neighborhood; survey class, make table	Discuss being a good citizen; talk about volunteer activities; write in diary	Make list and choose one community center; conduct interview; design poster	
Photographs of teenagers doing volunteer work; discuss volunteer work to be done at a community center		Information about volunteer activities for teens		
Discuss community centers; survey classmates	Make weekend plans; discuss improving your neighborhood			
Discuss what to do at community centers; survey classmates	Activities 1-3: Make weekend plans; discuss improving your neighborhood through recycling	**Re-entry of vocabulary**		**Extension of vocabulary**
Discuss community centers; survey classmates, report to class	Discuss improving your neighborhood; survey class, make table			
Discuss statements that use *es...que* and the present subjunctive		**Re-entry of structure**		**Extension of structure**
	Activities 1-3: Make weekend plans; discuss improving your neighborhood; survey class, make table			

¿Qué palabra?

GAME

Objective
- to play a guessing game, using Chapter 11 *Vocabulario temático*

Use
after *Palabras en acción,* pages 288–289

Materials
- six 3 x 5 index cards, cut in half

Preparation
- Write 12 words or phrases from the *Vocabulario temático* on the card halves. For example: *guardería, centro de jubilados, contaminación, pintada, baile, música, adolescente, enfermos, ofrecer, plástico, traducción.*

Activity
- Select a scorekeeper to keep track of how many clues each player needs before guessing the right word or phrase.
- Ask a volunteer to go to the chalkboard and face the class.
- Call on another student and ask him/her to pick a card from the pile and write the word on the chalkboard behind the first student.
- The student who cannot see the word has to guess what it is by listening to clues given by the class. The first clue might be: *Es un lugar.* The volunteer guesses: *¿Residencia de ancianos?* Another student says: *Los ancianos no van a este lugar, van los niños.* The volunteer guesses again: *¿La guardería?*
- If the volunteer knows the word in English, but cannot remember the Spanish word, he/she may look it up in the *Vocabulario temático.*
- The game ends when all the words have been used, and the winner is the student who guesses his/her word or phrase after the fewest clues.

Variations
- Play another game with new words from the *Vocabulario temático.*

¿Qué pasa aquí?

SOCIAL STUDIES CONNECTION

Objective
- to discuss responsible citizenship, using **es** (adjective) **que** + the present subjunctive

Use
after *Para comunicarnos mejor,* pages 290–291

Materials
- bilingual dictionaries
- posterboard or large sheets of paper
- colored markers and/or pencils

Activity
- Divide students into groups of five.
- Each group writes ten sentences that describe responsible community citizenship, using the present subjunctive. Such a list might begin: *Es necesario que pongan más basureros en el vecindario. Es importante que las madres enseñen a sus hijos a echar basura en los basureros. Es increíble que algunas personas no reciclen.*
- Each group illustrates their ideas in a poster.
- Groups present their posters. The class votes on the one that does the best job of inspiring responsible citizenship.

¡Di con él!

GAME

Objective
- to play a bingo word game, using Chapter 11 *Vocabulario temático*

Use
after *Palabras en acción,* pages 288–289

Materials
- TRB Activity Support Page 25, *¡Di con él!* (grid)

Preparation
- Choose 25 words from the *Vocabulario temático.*

Activity
- Distribute the activity support page.
- Dictate the Spanish words you selected so students can fill in their grids—any way they want.
- Start the game by reading the English translations of the words. Keep track of the words you call.
- Students may use their copies of *Juntos* to look up words.
- Students draw an X through every word you call.
- The first student to get five words in a row calls *¡Di con él!* and wins.

¿Es así? ¡Qué horror!

SOCIAL STUDIES CONNECTION

Objective
- to talk about making positive changes in the community, using *nosotros* commands

Use
after *Para comunicarnos mejor,* pages 292–293

Preparation
- Divide class into groups of six.
- Tell students they are community leaders in a neighborhood that needs improvement.

Activity
- Have each group make a list of six things that they would like to improve in their community: *Las paredes no están muy limpias, los hospitales no atienden a todos los enfermos,* etc.
- Tell them that today is community cleanup day *(el día para mejorar la comunidad)* and that they have the power to make everything better.
- Have the groups change their lists by suggesting improvements. For example: *En nuestro vecindario las paredes no están limpias. ¡Qué horror! ¡Limpiemos las paredes con agua y jabón!*
- After each group presents its list, the rest of the class votes for the change they like most.
- Have the class discuss how different the community would be if their suggestions were put into effect, and how, as a group or individually, they could make some of the improvements themselves.

SERVICIOS A LA COMUNIDAD

Introduce the chapter and its theme by asking students what impact a neighborhood or community has on the individuals who live in it. Ask about local progams that are directed at teens, the elderly, and others. How important are they? Should there be more—or less? Do students feel that everyone should take care of themselves, or are community programs essential for a better life?

Related Components

Audio	**Video: Tape/Book**
Conexiones: 18B	Unit 6: Seg. 2
Conexiones	
Chapter 11	

Scan to Chapter 11

GETTING STARTED

Have students look at the photograph and discuss what the people are doing. Ask questions:
¿Dónde están los jóvenes de la foto?
¿Qué están haciendo?

Talking About Language

Use the following activity to help students discover what they need to know in order to talk about community services.

Ayudando a nuestra comunidad
Have students think about services their community offers. Then assign groups to make lists of the following topics:
• services that communities need
• places that offer services
• volunteer jobs
• things we can do to improve our neighborhoods

Have each group write its list on the board. Have the class discuss the lists and decide which are the most essential.
Have each group submit a revised list. When you finish the chapter, have the class review the lists to see how they compare to what they learned in the chapter.

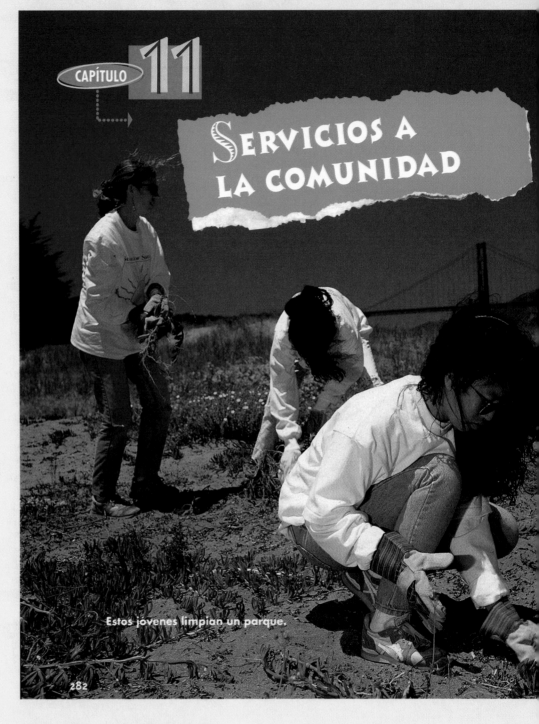

CAPÍTULO 11

SERVICIOS A LA COMUNIDAD

Estos jóvenes limpian un parque.

282

CHAPTER COMPONENTS

Activity Book	**Audio Book**	**Conexiones**	**Transparencies**
p. 137-146	Script: p. 69-71	Chapter 11	Chapter 11
Assessment	Activities: p. 72-74	**Cuaderno**	Transparencies 68-72
Oral Proficiency:	**Audio**	p. 85-92	**Tutor Pages**
p. 31	Chapter: 12A	**Magazine**	p. 47-50
Listening Script: p. 19	Assessment: 15B	Juntos en Estados	**Video: Tape/Book**
Chapter Test:	Conexiones: 18B	Unidos	Unit 6: Seg. 2
p. 105-110			

Objetivos

COMUNICACIÓN

To talk about:
- what services are offered in your community
- what you can do to help your community
- what the needs of your community are

CULTURA

To learn about:
- activities in typical community centers of the U.S.
- special volunteer activities that teenagers can perform
- the Nuyorican Poet's Café

VOCABULARIO TEMÁTICO

To learn the expressions for:
- types of community centers
- volunteer activities
- community residents who receive assistance

ESTRUCTURA

To talk about:
- what needs to be done: expressions with the subjunctive
- what we can do together to help out: *nosotros* commands

¿SABES QUE...?

Parks are natural treasures for recreational or aesthetic enjoyment. The U.S. National Park System administers 354 sites nationwide. In addition, there are about 3,300 state parks and thousands of local parks in towns and cities around the country. New York City alone has 1,700! Since parks are for everyone to use and enjoy, all visitors should do their part to preserve the beauty of these areas. Sometimes, volunteers are needed to help collect litter, sweep paths, trim weeds, or otherwise contribute to the well-being of these important community assets. Call your local parks commission if you want to help!

283

OPTIONAL CHAPTER ACTIVITIES

Here are some additional activities that you may wish to use as you work through this chapter with your students.

Communication

Encourage after-class activities that may enhance student interest and proficiency. For example:
- recommend movies about latino communities in the U.S. (e.g., *Stand and Deliver* or *The Milagro Bean Field War*)
- have students initiate an *intercambio* (an arrangement with a Spanish speaker to get together occasionally to practice each other's languages) with someone in their school or community

Culture

To encourage greater cultural understanding:
- look into services that are offered by local Hispanic groups
- report on community services that are listed on the internet
- show the video that accompanies Unit 6 of this textbook

Vocabulary

To reinforce vocabulary, have students:
- keep a log of problems they see in their community, and their suggestions for solving them
- find out what volunteer activities exist in the community and report to the class

Structure

To reinforce recommendations, suggestions, and the **nosotros** command:
- make a list of recommendations for the class to follow the rest of the year
- make banners with inspirational advice

Palabras de la comunidad
Have students use the lists from the previous activity as a springboard to brainstorm similar words in Spanish. Ask speakers of other languages to say the equivalent words in their native language.

 **INTERNET LINK**

Latino Community Organizations http://latino.sscnet.ucla.edu:80/community/commorg.html

Communicative Objectives
- to talk about community centers
- to say how you can volunteer
- to talk about what your neighborhood needs

Related Components

Activity Book p. 137	**Cuaderno** p. 85
Audio Book Script: Seg. 1	**Transparencies** Ch. 11: Conversemos Transparency 68
Audio Chapter: 12A, Seg. 1	

GETTING STARTED

Ask students to talk about what makes a neighborhood a community, instead of just a place to live.

ACTIVITIES

These activities give students an opportunity to begin communicating with each other and with you, focusing on the theme and objectives of the chapter. The activities can be used as oral class activities, or, if you prefer, you can pair students to achieve more interaction.

¿Qué hay en tu vecindario?
Class activity to introduce names for types of community centers. Ask students which of these their community has and does not have. What happens at these places? Who goes there?

¿Qué servicios ofrecen?
Class activity to introduce names of services that are provided by community centers and by the volunteers who work there. Ask students which community centers provide each of these activities. Ask them to suggest other activities that might take place there.

¿Cómo puedes ayudar en tu comunidad?
Class activity to reintroduce vocabulary and to introduce volunteer words. Ask students to say what they would prefer to do, and in what kind of center.

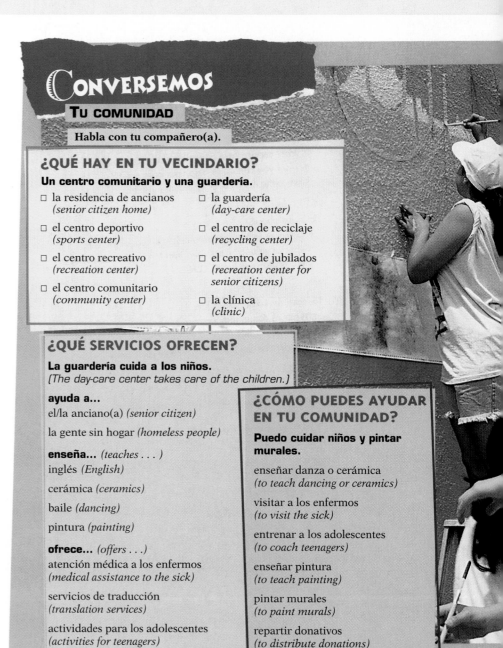

CONVERSEMOS

TU COMUNIDAD

Habla con tu compañero(a).

¿QUÉ HAY EN TU VECINDARIO?
Un centro comunitario y una guardería.

- ☐ la residencia de ancianos *(senior citizen home)*
- ☐ el centro deportivo *(sports center)*
- ☐ el centro recreativo *(recreation center)*
- ☐ el centro comunitario *(community center)*
- ☐ la guardería *(day-care center)*
- ☐ el centro de reciclaje *(recycling center)*
- ☐ el centro de jubilados *(recreation center for senior citizens)*
- ☐ la clínica *(clinic)*

¿QUÉ SERVICIOS OFRECEN?
La guardería cuida a los niños.
[The day-care center takes care of the children.]

ayuda a...
el/la anciano(a) *(senior citizen)*
la gente sin hogar *(homeless people)*

enseña... *(teaches . . .)*
inglés *(English)*
cerámica *(ceramics)*
baile *(dancing)*
pintura *(painting)*

ofrece... *(offers . . .)*
atención médica a los enfermos *(medical assistance to the sick)*
servicios de traducción *(translation services)*
actividades para los adolescentes *(activities for teenagers)*

¿CÓMO PUEDES AYUDAR EN TU COMUNIDAD?
Puedo cuidar niños y pintar murales.

enseñar danza o cerámica *(to teach dancing or ceramics)*
visitar a los enfermos *(to visit the sick)*
entrenar a los adolescentes *(to coach teenagers)*
enseñar pintura *(to teach painting)*
pintar murales *(to paint murals)*
repartir donativos *(to distribute donations)*

284

Reaching All Students

For Auditory Learners
Name a type of community center. Your partner says what services it offers.

For Visual Learners
Make cards. One should have a plus sign, another a minus sign, and the rest, the drawings from *¿Qué se necesita en tu vecindario?* Use them to form sentences for your partner to say or write.

¿QUÉ SE NECESITA EN TU VECINDARIO?

Se necesitan más basureros y menos pintadas.

Más...		Menos...	
	el basurero		la pintada
	la zona verde		el ruido
	el semáforo		la contaminación
	el mural		el tráfico
	el contenedor		

CUANDO QUIEREN AYUDAR EN SU COMUNIDAD, ¿QUÉ DICEN?

Reciclemos. *(Let's recycle.)*

Seamos buenos ciudadanos(as). *(Let's be good citizens.)*

Mantengamos los parques limpios. *(Let's keep the parks clean.)*

Trabajemos de voluntarios(as). *(Let's volunteer.)*

¿Qué se necesita en tu vecindario?
Class activity to introduce city vocabulary. Model the sentences and answers. Ask students to give reasons why the community might not need more of the items on the left side of the chart. For example:
No se necesitan basureros porque hay muchos.

Cuando quieren ayudar en su comunidad, ¿qué dicen?
Class activity to introduce **nosotros** commands. Model the sentences and answers. Try replacing *comunidad* with other words, such as *escuela, casa,* or *parque,* and asking for alternative answers.

CHECK

- *¿Qué centros hay en tu vecindario?*
- *¿Qué se necesita en tu vecindario?*
- *¿Cómo te gustaría ayudar en tu comunidad?*

LOG BOOK
Have students write three things they would tell their friends to do for the community.

285

REALIDADES

Objectives
Communicative: to talk about volunteer work in the community
Cultural: to learn about Latino teenagers who volunteer in their communities

Related Components

Activity Book p. 138	**Audio** Chapter: 12A, Seg. 2
Audio Book Script: Seg. 2	**Cuaderno** p. 86

GETTING STARTED

Ask students to name some volunteer jobs that exist or could exist in their community.

DISCUSS

Suggestions:

Los voluntarios
¿Cuál es el tema de la página del folleto Acción Latina?
¿Quiénes son los voluntarios más sobresalientes del mes?

Daisy García
¿Dónde trabaja Daisy?
¿Qué es importante para hacer este trabajo?
¿Y qué es necesario?

Sylvia Rodríguez
¿Dónde es voluntaria Sylvia?
¿Qué experiencia tiene Sylvia?
¿Qué cree Sylvia?

Rafael Díaz
¿Dónde es voluntario Rafael Díaz?
¿Por qué?
¿Qué consejo nos da Rafael?

Se necesitan voluntarios
¿Qué edad deben tener los voluntarios?
¿En qué trabajos deben tener experiencia?
¿Qué experiencia tienes tú?
¿A qué número de teléfono tienes que llamar?

REALIDADES
¡TÚ TAMBIÉN PUEDES AYUDAR!

LOS VOLUNTARIOS DEL MES
Éstos son algunos de los voluntarios más sobresalientes del mes.

Daisy García, 16 años. Trabaja en un campamento de verano para niños. Dice Daisy: "Me gusta mucho trabajar al aire libre. Es importante divertir a los chicos, pero también es necesario que te hagas respetar".

Sylvia Rodríguez, 15 años. Es voluntaria en un centro de jubilados. Dice Sylvia: "Yo antes ayudaba a mi abuela. Esta experiencia me sirve ahora para ayudar a los ancianos del centro. Yo creo que es muy importante que la gente se sienta útil".

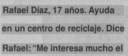

Rafael Díaz, 17 años. Ayuda en un centro de reciclaje. Dice Rafael: "Me interesa mucho el medio ambiente. Es necesario que lo cuidemos y que reciclemos el vidrio, el aluminio y el papel. Así me siento útil a mi comunidad".

Se necesitan voluntarios

Necesitamos jóvenes voluntarios(as), entre 14 y 18 años de edad, para que trabajen en la comunidad. Es necesario que hablen español. Es mejor que tengan experiencia en alguno de estos trabajos:

▶ cuidar niños

▶ enseñar inglés, informática, pintura o matemáticas

▶ organizar actividades para niños

▶ reciclar papel, aluminio, plástico y vidrio

▶ atender a los enfermos y a los ancianos

▶ repartir ropa y comida a la gente sin hogar

▶ enseñar deportes a niños

▶ plantar árboles

Si alguna vez trabajaste en alguna de estas cosas, llama al 555-0101. ¡Tú también puedes ayudar en tu comunidad!

HABLA DEL FOLLETO

A. ¿Qué dicen los(as) voluntarios(as) sobre sus trabajos?

Daisy dice que es importante divertir a los chicos y que...

B. Con tu compañero(a), habla de los trabajos de los voluntarios de Acción Latina. Di dónde te gustaría trabajar y por qué.

— *¿Dónde te gustaría trabajar?*
— *En un centro deportivo.*
— *¿Por qué?*
— *Porque me gusta entrenar a los niños.*

¿QUÉ OPINAS?

¿Qué se necesita en tu comunidad? ¿Qué opinas tú? ¿Qué opina la clase? Haz una encuesta. Usa el modelo.

Se necesita	yo	la clase
organizar actividades culturales	✓	////
entrenar a los adolescentes		XXX //
pintar murales		
reciclar		
repartir ropa y comida a la gente sin hogar		
ayudar a los enfermos y a los ancianos		
cuidar niños		
organizar actividades deportivas		

Según la encuesta, ¿qué es lo que más se necesita? ¿Y lo que menos se necesita?

ACTIVITIES

Habla del folleto

Individual and Pair Activities: Writing and Conversing
A. What do the volunteers say about their work?
Answers: See model on student page.
B. Talk with your partner about the work these volunteers do. Say in which of these places you would like to work and why.
Answers: See model on student page.

¿Qué opinas?

Group Activity: Taking a Poll
What does your community need? Record your group's answers on a chart like the one on page 287.

Class Activity: Evaluation
Have volunteers list the ideas and write the results on the board as representatives of the groups report them.
What does your community need the most? The least? Write a paragraph summarizing the results, and whether you agree with the class' decisions.

CHECK

- *¿Qué trabajos hacen los voluntarios?*
- *¿Qué trabajo te gustaría hacer? ¿Por qué?*
- *¿Qué se necesita en tu comunidad?*

LOG BOOK
Have students write down all examples of the subjunctive they find in the *folleto*.

Para hispanohablantes

Make a list of services or volunteer work your school needs and assign a classmate to each task. Tell each person why he or she received that task.

287

PALABRAS EN ACCIÓN

Communicative Objectives

- to talk about community and recreational centers
- to talk about recycling
- to talk about volunteering

Related Components

Activity Book p. 139-140 Cuaderno p. 87-88	Transparencies Ch. 11: Palabras en acción Transparency 69 Tutor Page p. 47

GETTING STARTED

Ask students to talk about community projects that would help make their community better.

DISCUSS

¿Qué centros hay en la comunidad del dibujo?
¿Qué se necesita en esta comunidad?
¿En qué lugar te gustaría ser voluntario?
¿Y en cuál no te gustaría?

Para hispanohablantes

If you use other words or expressions, share them with the class. A few variations:

el basurero: la basura, el cesto de basura, el zafacón, la papelera
el contenedor: el recipiente, el contáiner
el centro de jubilados: el centro de retirados
la guardería: el centro de cuidado diurno
el baile: la danza
la gente sin hogar: los desamparados

PALABRAS EN ACCIÓN

EN EL VECINDARIO

1 ¿Qué ves en el dibujo?

Haz una lista de las cosas que ves en el vecindario. Compara tu lista con la de tu compañero(a).

> *El contenedor para vidrio, el semáforo...*

2 ¿Qué hacen?

Escoge cinco personas del dibujo. Pregúntale a tu compañero(a) qué está haciendo cada una.

> — *¿Qué está haciendo la chica de la camisa verde?*
> — *Está pintando un mural.*

3 Los voluntarios

Lee los carteles en voz alta. Pregúntale a tu compañero(a) para qué necesitan voluntarios en cada lugar.

> — *¿Para qué necesitan voluntarios en el centro recreativo?*
> — *Para enseñar a bailar.*

4 En tu comunidad

Pregúntale a tu compañero(a) qué se necesita en su comunidad o en su escuela.

> — *¿Qué se necesita en tu comunidad?*
> — *Se necesitan más zonas verdes, más semáforos y menos pintadas.*

288

For students having difficulty discussing community centers, activities, or volunteer work, you might consider:

- **The tutor page:** Pair the student with a native speaker or a more able student, using the tutor page.

Optional activities: See page 282C: *¿Qué palabra?* and page 282D: *¡Di con él!*

5 Seamos buenos ciudadanos

Habla con tu compañero(a) sobre lo que hace para ser un(a) buen(a) ciudadano(a).

— ¿Qué haces para ser un buen ciudadano?
— Yo reparto ropa y comida a la gente sin hogar. ¿Y tú?

6 Miniteatro

Imagina que tu compañero(a) y tú quieren ser voluntarios en un centro recreativo para adolescentes. Hagan un diálogo.

— Me gustaría trabajar de voluntario en un centro recreativo.
— A mí también. ¿Cómo podemos ayudar?
— Podemos entrenar a los adolescentes para jugar al béisbol.

7 El centro comunitario

Diseña un cartel para un centro comunitario. Describe qué servicios ofrece y qué tipo de ayuda se necesita. Usa dibujos o fotos de revistas y periódicos.

8 Tú eres el autor

Escribe en un párrafo sobre lo que hace tu escuela para ayudar a la comunidad.

En mi escuela hay varios grupos de voluntarios. Un grupo recoge ropa y donativos para la gente sin hogar. Otro grupo visita a los enfermos de la clínica y otro enseña inglés. En mi escuela se recicla papel, vidrio, aluminio y plástico.

289

ACTIVITIES

1. Individual and Pair Activity
Make a list of the things you see in this neighborhood scene. Compare lists.

2. Pair Activity
Choose five people in the drawing. Ask your partner what each is doing.
Extension: Choose a place to volunteer and say why you are qualified to do it. For example:
Puedo trabajar en la guardería porque sé cuidar niños.

3. Pair Activity
Look at the posters in the drawing and read them aloud. Ask your partner why volunteers are needed in each place.
Extension: Write three more posters for this community.

4. Pair Activity
Ask your partner what is needed in your school or community.
Extension: Ask what is not needed in your partner's school or community. For example: *No se necesita basura.*

5. Pair Activity
Talk about the things that you do to be a good citizen.
Extension: Talk about who are the best citizens you know and why.

6. Roleplay Activity
You and your partner want to be volunteers at a recreational center for teenagers. Create a dialog.
Extension: You have an interview at the recreational center where you want to volunteer. Your partner, the director, asks what you think the community needs and why you want to volunteer.

7. Hands-On Activity
Homework or classwork for individuals or small groups. Design a poster for a community center that describes the services it offers and the kind of help it needs. Use drawings or photos.

8. Writing Activity
Write a paragraph about what your school does to help the community.
Extension: Exchange paragraphs with a partner and edit each other's work.

CHECK

- *¿Qué centros comunitarios o servicios hay en tu comunidad?*
- *¿Qué necesita tu comunidad?*
- *¿Cómo puedes ayudar en tu comunidad?*

LOG BOOK

Have students write a brief description of three community centers.

Communicative Objective

• to make suggestions or recommendations, using expressions with the present subjunctive

Related Components

Activity Book p. 141-142	**Cuaderno** p. 89
Audio Book Script: Seg. 3 Activities: p. 72	**Transparencies** Ch. 11: Para comunicarnos mejor Transparency 70
Audio Chapter: 12A, Seg. 3	**Tutor Page** p. 48

GETTING STARTED

Language in Context

The Present Subjunctive: Write the following sentences on the board:
Juan ayuda a José.
Es necesario que Juan ayude a José.

Ask students to discuss their meaning and structure.

Let students know that the subjunctive mood is used in Spanish much more than in English. It may be the most difficult part of the language to use correctly. For now, have students memorize some of the expressions to talk about suggestions, recommendations, and what needs to be done.

DISCUSS

Review and introduce vocabulary with questions and statements that use **es...que** and the present subjunctive.
¿Es importante que ayudemos a nuestros compañeros?
¿A qué otras personas es necesario que ayudemos?
¿Es mejor que atiendan o que no atiendan a los profesores?
¿Es necesario que yo recoja mi casa?
¿Es importante que ellos me ayuden?

290

PARA COMUNICARNOS MEJOR

ES IMPORTANTE QUE AYUDEMOS

To express what needs to be done, or to make suggestions or recommendations, you may use *es* and an adjective followed by *que* and a form of the present subjunctive.

> *Es necesario que ayudemos a los ancianos.*
> It is necessary that we help senior citizens.

☐ Common expressions with *es* and an adjective are:

es importante	*es necesario*
es increíble	*es mejor*

☐ Note that the subjunctive form is usually introduced by *que*.

> *Es importante que David nos ayude.*
> It is important that David help us.

☐ To form the present subjunctive, drop the *-o* of the *yo* form of the present indicative and add the appropriate endings.

	ayudar (to help)	comer (eat)	repartir (to deliver/to give out)
yo	ayud**e**	com**a**	repart**a**
tú	ayud**es**	com**as**	repart**as**
usted	ayud**e**	com**a**	repart**a**
él/ella	ayud**e**	com**a**	repart**a**
nosotros(as)	ayud**emos**	com**amos**	repart**amos**
vosotros(as)	ayud**éis**	com**áis**	repart**áis**
ustedes	ayud**en**	com**an**	repart**an**
ellos/ellas	ayud**en**	com**an**	repart**an**

¡OJO!

Verbs ending in **-car** (sacar), **-ger** (recoger) and **-zar** (organizar) have a spelling change in all forms of the subjunctive.

sacar → *saque...*
recoger → *recoja...*
organizar → *organice...*

☐ Note that verbs with irregular *yo* forms follow the same rule.

decir (yo digo) → **diga, digas, diga, digamos, digáis, digan.**
hacer (yo hago) → **haga...**
mantener (yo mantengo) → **mantenga...**

☐ Other verbs have irregular present subjunctive forms.

dar → **dé, des, dé, demos, deis, den.**
ser → **sea, seas, sea, seamos, seáis, sean.**

☐ The subjunctive form of *hay* is **haya.**

290

For students having difficulty making recommendations or suggestions, you might consider:

• **The tutor page:** Pair the student with a native speaker or a more able student, using the tutor page.

Optional activity: See pages 282C: *¿Qué pasa aquí?*

1 Las tareas de los voluntarios

Tú trabajas con los voluntarios de un centro comunitario. Diles qué tareas tienen que hacer según los días de la semana.

Los lunes es necesario que enseñen cerámica a los niños.

1. enseñar cerámica a los niños
2. repartir comida a la gente sin hogar
3. limpiar el parque
4. visitar a los enfermos que están en el hospital
5. atender a los ancianos
6. recoger donativos

2 ¡Es increíble!

Con tu compañero(a), haz una lista de actividades que algunas personas hacen o no hacen y que no son buenas para la comunidad.

> *Es increíble que algunas personas...*
> * *no reciclen*
> * *hagan pintadas*
> * *no usen los basureros*

3 En nuestro vecindario

En grupo hagan una encuesta sobre lo que se necesita en su vecindario.

Es importante que...

Alicia	Julio	Mabel
haya más zonas verdes	los centros recreativos organicen actividades deportivas para los adolescentes	todos mantengamos las calles limpias

Presenta los resultados a la clase.

Alicia dice que es importante que haya más zonas verdes. Julio piensa que es importante que los centros recreativos organicen actividades deportivas para los adolescentes. Mabel dice que es importante que todos mantengamos las calles limpias.

291

Para hispanohablantes

Write a letter to the class, telling them what is important or necessary in order to improve the community.

Students use **es...que** and the present subjunctive to say what needs to be done, or to make suggestions or recommendations.

1. Individual Activity
You work with volunteers at a community center. Tell the volunteers what they must do each day of the week.
Possible Answers:
1. See model on student page.
2. *Los martes es necesario que repartan comida a la gente sin hogar.*
3. *Los miércoles es necesario que limpien el parque.*
4. *Los jueves es necesario que visiten a los enfermos que están en el hospital.*
5. *Los viernes es necesario que atiendan a los ancianos.*
6. *Los sábados es necesario que recojan donativos.*
Extension: Think of other things that are important to do for the community.

2. Pair Activity
Make a list of things that some people do or don't do, which are not good for the community.
Possible Answers:
Es increíble que algunas personas:
* *no ayuden a los ancianos.*
* *no limpien el parque.*
* *contaminen.*
* *no mantengan las calles limpias.*
* *hagan tanto ruido.*
Extension: Say what people should do about each problem you named.

3. Group Activity
What does your neighborhood need? Record your answers on a chart like the model. Present your chart to the class.
Answers: See models on student page.

CHECK

* ¿Qué es importante que hagamos?
* ¿Qué es necesario que digamos?
* ¿Qué piensas que es increíble?

LOG BOOK
Have students write a paradigm of the present subjunctive for an **-ar, -er,** and an **-ir** verb.

Communicative Objectives
- to tell a friend to do something with you, using **nosotros** commands
- to use pronouns with **nosotros** commands

Related Components

Activity Book p. 143-144	**Audio** Chapter: 12A, Seg. 4
Audio Book Script: Seg.4 Activities: p. 73	**Cuaderno** p. 90
	Tutor Page p. 49

GETTING STARTED

Language in Context

Nosotros Commands: First tell students that **nosotros** commands are like **Ud.** commands—that is, -**ar** verbs shift to -**er** endings and -**er** and -**ir** verbs shift to -**ar** endings.

Next, give a series of **Ud.** commands to individuals, such as *levante la mano* or *cierre el libro*. Then begin to alternate the same actions with **nosotros** commands (*levantemos las manos*).

DISCUSS

Do a series of TPR exercises with **nosotros** commands:
¡Levantémonos!
¡Hablemos con nuestro compañero!
¡Digamos hola!
¡No hablemos!
¡Saquemos los libros de español!
¡Hagamos ejercicios!
¡No hagamos nada!

Tell your classmates to join you in three tasks that will make your classroom look better.

PARA COMUNICARNOS MEJOR
¡RECICLEMOS!

To tell a friend to do something with you, use a *nosotros* command.

¡Organicemos actividades culturales!	Let's organize cultural activities!

☐ The ***nosotros*** command uses the same form as the ***nosotros*** form of the present subjunctive.

-ar (verbs)	-er / -ir (verbs)
ayud**emos** (*let's help*)	dig**amos** (*let's say*)
recic**lemos** (*let's recycle*)	manteng**amos** (*let's keep*)

¡OJO!

Note that when ***nos*** is attached to the command form, the **-s** of the command is dropped and an accent is added.

Levantémonos antes de las siete.

☐ Pronouns (direct object pronouns, indirect object pronouns, reflexive pronouns) are attached to the end of an affirmative command.

Hablemos con los voluntarios y digámosles que queremos ayudar.	Let's talk to the volunteers and let's tell them that we want to help.

☐ With negative commands, the pronouns are placed directly before the verb.

No les digamos eso.	Let's not tell them that.

292

For students having difficulty using **nosotros** commands, you might consider:
- **The tutor page:** Pair the student with a native speaker or a more able student, using the tutor page.

Optional activity: See pages 282D: *¿Es así? ¡Qué horror!*

¡Ayudemos a todo el mundo!

Con tu compañero(a), haz planes para trabajar de voluntario durante el fin de semana.

— *Este fin de semana me gustaría visitar a los enfermos.*
— *¡Sí, visitémoslos!*

1. visitar a los enfermos
2. ayudar a la gente sin hogar
3. cuidar a los niños
4. entrenar a los adolescentes
5. atender a los ancianos
6. enseñar pintura a los niños

 ¡Mejoremos nuestro vecindario!

Con tu compañero(a), digan qué pueden hacer por su vecindario.

— *¡No hagamos pintadas!*
— *No, no las hagamos.*

1. no hacer pintadas
2. mantener las calles limpias
3. reciclar el aluminio, el papel, el plástico y el vidrio
4. pintar murales
5. visitar a los enfermos
6. cuidar las zonas verdes

 Los buenos ciudadanos

En grupo, hagan una encuesta sobre lo que dicen los buenos ciudadanos.

LOS BUENOS CIUDADANOS DICEN...

Darío	Trabajemos de voluntarios.
Ana	Repartamos ropa y comida a la gente sin hogar.
Manuel	Organicemos actividades para los niños.
María	
Marcelo	

293

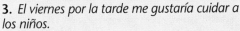 **ACTIVITIES**

Students use **nosotros** commands to say that they want others to do something with them.

1. Pair Activity
Make plans to work as a volunteer this weekend.
Possible Answers:
1. See model on student page.
2. *Este sábado me gustaría ayudar a la gente sin hogar.*
   ¡Sí, ayudémosla!

3. *El viernes por la tarde me gustaría cuidar a los niños.*
   ¡Sí, cuidémoslos!
4. *El domingo me gustaría entrenar a los adolescentes.*
   ¡Sí, entrenémoslos!
5. *El sábado por la mañana me gustaría atender a los ancianos.*
   ¡Sí, atendámoslos!
6. *Este fin de semana me gustaría enseñar pintura a los niños.*
   ¡Sí, enseñémosles!
Extension: Talk about other activities you would like to do this weekend. Example:
A. *¡Juguemos al fútbol americano!*
B. *¡Sí, juguemos!*

2. Pair Activity
Say what you can do to help improve the neighborhood.
Possible Answers:
1. See model on student page.
2. *¡Mantengamos las calles limpias!/*
   ¡Sí, mantengámoslas limpias!
3. *¡Reciclemos el aluminio, el papel, el plástico y el vidrio!*
   ¡Sí, reciclémoslos!
4. *¡Pintemos murales!*
   ¡Sí, pintémoslos!
5. *¡Visitemos a los enfermos!*
   ¡Sí, visitémoslos!
6. *¡Cuidemos las zonas verdes!*
   ¡Sí, cuidémoslas!
Extension: Design a flyer in which you tell Spanish students what you should do together.

3. Group Activity
Classwork or homework. Using a chart like the model, conduct a survey to find out what good citizens say should be done for the neighborhood.
Answers: See model on student page.

 CHECK

• *¿Qué debemos hacer en nuestro vecindario?*
• *¿Cómo podemos mantener limpio el medio ambiente?*
• *Queremos ser voluntarios. ¿Qué debemos hacer?*
• *¿Qué no debemos hacer?*

LOG BOOK
Have students write a few sentences about how to improve their neighborhood.

Communicative Objective
• to talk about being a good citizen

Related Components

Assessment Oral Proficiency: p. 31	**Conexiones** Chapter 11
Audio Book Script: Seg. 5 Activities: p. 74	**Magazine** Juntos en Estados Unidos
Audio Chapter: 12A, Seg. 5 Conexiones: 18B	**Tutor Page** p. 50

GETTING STARTED

Students should now be able to correctly use the present subjunctive, **nosotros** commands, and all of the chapter vocabulary. Have students read aloud *Las 10 reglas de oro de los buenos ciudadanos*. Have students raise their hands when they hear a rule they usually follow. Then, have them rate themselves as citizens, using the following scale:

10-7: Excellent citizen
6-4: Average citizen
3-0: A citizen who needs improvement

APPLY

1. Pair Activity
Discuss three things you should do to be good citizens.
Answers: See model on student page.
Extension: Say what we shouldn't do to our neighborhood.

2. Pair Activity
Discuss why it's important to volunteer.
Answers: See model on student page.
Extension: Suggest places where you can volunteer and what you will do there.

3. Pair Activity
Interview your partner, who is the director of a community center.
Answers: See model on student page.
Extension: Select one question and answer from the interview. Dictate them to a student other than your original partner.

SITUACIONES

SEAMOS MEJORES CIUDADANOS

LAS 10 REGLAS DE ORO DE LOS BUENOS CIUDADANOS

1 RECICLEMOS PAPEL, VIDRIO, ALUMINIO Y PLÁSTICO.
2 AYUDEMOS A NUESTRA COMUNIDAD.
3 MEJOREMOS NUESTRO VECINDARIO.
4 NO HAGAMOS PINTADAS.
5 RESPETEMOS LOS SEMÁFOROS.
6 NO CREEMOS CONTAMINACIÓN.
7 CUIDEMOS LAS ZONAS VERDES.
8 TRABAJEMOS DE VOLUNTARIOS.
9 NO HAGAMOS RUIDO INNECESARIO.
10 MANTENGAMOS LAS CALLES LIMPIAS.

294

For students having difficulty discussing what it means to be a good citizen, using the present subjunctive or **nosotros** commands, you might consider:
• **The tutor page:** Pair the student with a native speaker or a more able student, using the tutor page.
Optional activity: See page 282D: *¿Es así? ¡Qué horror!*

① Los buenos ciudadanos

Con tu compañero, digan tres cosas que deben hacer para ser buenos ciudadanos.

— *Debemos mantener las calles limpias.*
— *Sí, mantengámoslas limpias.*

② Los voluntarios

Con tu compañero(a), habla de por qué es importante que trabajen de voluntarios.

— *¿Por qué es importante que trabajemos de voluntarios?*
— *Porque es importante que nos sintamos útiles.*

③ Entrevista

Tu compañero(a) es el/la director(a) de un centro comunitario. Hazle una entrevista.

— *¿Qué servicios ofrece el centro?*
— *Nuestro centro organiza actividades culturales y deportivas. Ofrece servicios de traducción. También tiene una guardería.*

— *¿Cuántas personas trabajan en el centro?*
— *En el centro trabajan 55 personas.*

④ Tu diario

Escribe en tu diario sobre qué es necesario que hagan tus amigos y tú por el vecindario y la comunidad.

En nuestro vecindario es necesario que usemos más los basureros, que no creemos contaminación y que respetemos los semáforos.

En nuestra comunidad es necesario que seamos voluntarios en los centros comunitarios.

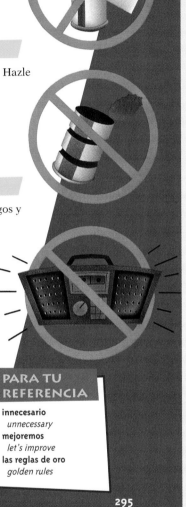

¿SABES QUE...?

You can do volunteer work at many places in your community. Parks, museums, day-care centers, libraries, hospitals, community centers, churches, and other places often need volunteers to help them serve the public. For information, you can ask the reference librarian at your local library, call your town or city administration offices, look at bulletin boards in churches or schools, or check the newspaper classified ads. If you live in an area with a large Hispanic population, you may want to practice your language skills by volunteering for an organization or group that works mostly with Spanish speakers.

PARA TU REFERENCIA

innecesario
unnecessary
mejoremos
let's improve
las reglas de oro
golden rules

295

---

4. Homework or Classwork
Write in your diary what you and your friends need to do for the community.
Answers: See model on student page.
Extension: Make up fortune-cookie messages about things to do to protect the environment. Put them in a basket. Take turns drawing messages from the basket and explaining how to carry them out.

CHECK

- *¿Cuáles son las reglas de los buenos ciudadanos?*
- *¿Qué es importante que hagamos para mejorar nuestra comunidad?*
- *¿Qué no debemos hacer?*

LOG BOOK
Have students write what *Las 10 reglas de oro de los buenos ciudadanos* are for their community or neighborhood.

Objectives

Communicative: to interview a community worker

Cultural: to learn about community centers and the services they offer

Related Components

Transparencies	Video: Tape/Book
Ch. 11: Para resolver	Unit 6: Seg. 2
Transparency 71	

Scan to Chapter 11

GETTING STARTED

Ask students to think of groups of people in any community who may have special needs, such as teenagers, elderly people, immigrants, or the handicapped. Does anyone know where these groups can go to obtain services?

APPLY

Form groups. Explain that each group will prepare a report on a local community center, including an interview with a community worker.

Note: If arranging for students to visit community centers is difficult, you may wish to obtain written information on those centers. Another possiblity: have some groups read the materials and act as informants for the others to interview.

PASO 1: ¿Qué centro estudiaran?

Make a list of community centers in your area. Choose one to study.

PASO 2: Las entrevistas

Prepare a list of questions for someone at the center you chose. Include:

- the name of the center
- how many people work there
- what services the center offers
- whether they have volunteers
- the number of volunteers
- what the volunteers do
- what others can do to help
- the name of the person to speak to if you wish to volunteer

---

PARA RESOLVER

¿QUÉ SERVICIOS OFRECE TU COMUNIDAD?

En grupo, van a hacer un estudio de los servicios que ofrecen los diferentes centros de su comunidad. Cada grupo escogerá un centro. Después dirán a los otros grupos por qué es importante que trabajen de voluntarios para el centro que han escogido.

PASO 1 ¿Qué centro estudiarán?
Hagan una lista de los centros que hay en su vecindario para ayudar a la comunidad. Decidan qué centro estudiarán.

Los centros que hay en nuestro vecindario son: un centro recreativo, una clínica...

Nuestro grupo ha decidido estudiar los servicios que ofrece el centro recreativo.

PASO 2 Las entrevistas
Preparen una lista de preguntas para un(a) empleado(a) del centro. Incluyan:

- ¿Cómo se llama el centro?
- ¿Cuántos empleados tiene el centro?
- ¿Qué servicios ofrece?
- ¿Hay alguien que trabaje de voluntario?
- ¿Cuántas?
- ¿Qué hacen los voluntarios?
- ¿Qué podemos hacer nosotros para ayudar?
- ¿Con quién tenemos que hablar si queremos trabajar de voluntarios?

PASO 3 Los resultados
Preparen un cartel con fotos para presentar a la clase los resultados de sus entrevistas. Expliquen por qué es importante que trabajen de voluntarios para el centro que escogieron.

296

Prepare a poster with photos to present what you learned to the class. Explain why it's important to volunteer for the center you chose.

Extension: Explain what citizenship rules are followed by good volunteers.

CHECK

PORTFOLIO

Have students include their best work from these activities in their Portfolios.

Para hispanohablantes

Suggest what you and your classmates can do to improve your school's environment.

297

Objectives

Communicative: to talk about social gatherings
Cultural: to learn about the Nuyorican Poet's Cafe

Related Components

Audio	Magazine
Conexiones: 18B	Juntos en Estados Unidos
Conexiones	
Chapter 11	

GETTING STARTED

Ask students why a common meeting place, such as a café, might be so important to writers and artists. Do they know of a place in their neighborhood that has poetry readings or art exhibitions, or where artists gather to exchange ideas and discuss their work?

DISCUSS

Using the Text

Have volunteers read the text of *Un café para poetas*. Ask questions. Suggestions:

El Nuyorican Poets' Café
¿Dónde está el Nuyorican Poet's Café?
¿Cuándo fue fundado?
¿Quiénes lo fundaron?

Un ambiente perfecto
¿Quiénes se encuentran en el café?
¿Para qué se encuentran?
¿Cómo imaginas el café? ¿Qué piensas que hay? ¿Qué es un escenario?
¿Quiénes hicieron famoso este café?
¿Qué busca Miguel Algarín?

CHECK

Te toca a ti
Answers:
1. *Falsa. Han sido los poetas puertorriqueños los que han hecho famoso este café.*
2. *Cierta.*
3. *Falsa. Está en Nueva York.*
4. *Cierta.*
5. *Cierta.*

ENTÉRATE

UN CAFÉ PARA POETAS

El Nuyorican Poet's Café está en Loisaida° en el sureste de Manhattan. Este café fue fundado a principios° de los años 70 por el dramaturgo° Miguel Piñero y el profesor puertorriqueño Miguel Algarín. Muchos poetas y escritores latinos se reúnen en este café. El Nuyorican Poet's Café ofrece el ambiente perfecto para conversar de literatura. También van a este café para leer su poesía, poetas no latinos y escritores de todo el mundo. Pero han sido los poetas puertorriqueños los que° han hecho famoso el café. Todavía hoy, Miguel Algarín sigue° buscando talentos jóvenes de la poesía contemporánea.

TE TOCA A TI
Di si las oraciones son ciertas o falsas. Corrige las oraciones falsas.

1. Las poesías de poetas no latinos hicieron famoso el Nuyorican Poet's Café.
2. Miguel Piñero fue uno de los fundadores del café.
3. El Nuyorican Poet's Café está en Puerto Rico.
4. Escritores y poetas de todo el mundo van al Nuyorican Poet's Café.
5. En este café se lee poesía y se conversa de literatura.

a principios *at the beginning*   **los que** *those who*
el dramaturgo *playwright*   **sigue** *continues*
Loisaida *Lower East Side*

298

LOG BOOK
Have students write a short, free-style poem in Spanish about anything they choose. Encourage them to have fun with the words.

Para hispanohablantes

Write a short poem in Spanish about friends or relatives who get together to talk about the things that interest them.

VOCABULARIO TEMÁTICO

En el vecindario
el centro comunitario *community center*
el centro deportivo *sports center*
el centro de jubilados *recreation center for senior citizens*
el centro de reciclaje *recycling center*
el centro recreativo *recreation center*
la clínica *clinic*
la guardería *day-care center*
la residencia de ancianos *senior citizen home*

En la calle
el basurero *garbage can*
la contaminación *pollution*
el mural *mural*
la pintada *graffiti*
el ruido *noise*
el semáforo *traffic light*
el tráfico *traffic*
la zona verde *green area*
los contenedores *trash containers*
  de aluminio *aluminum*
  de papel *paper*

de plástico *plastic*
de vidrio *glass*

¿Cómo puedes ayudar en tu comunidad?
How can you help in your community?
atender (e>ie) a los enfermos *to assist the sick*
enseñar *to teach*
  cerámica *ceramics*
  a bailar *dancing*
  pintura *painting*
entrenar a los niños(as) *to coach (to train) children*
mantener las zonas verdes limpias *to keep the park areas clean*
organizar actividades deportivas *to organize sport activities*
pintar murales *to paint murals*
repartir donativos *to distribute donations*
reciclar aluminio *to recycle aluminum*
trabajar de voluntario(a) *to volunteer*

¿A quién?
To whom?
el/la adolescente *teenager*
el/la anciano(a) *senior citizen*
el/la ciudadano(a) *citizen*
el/la enfermo(a) *sick person*
la gente sin hogar *homeless people*
el/la jubilado(a) *retired person*
los/las niños(as) *children*

Expresiones y palabras
¡Es increíble! *It is unbelievable!*
la actividad deportiva *sport activity*
la atención médica *medical assistance*
la escoba *broom*
ofrecer *to offer*
sentirse (e>ie) útil *to feel useful*
el servicio *service*
el trabajo *job*
la traducción *translation*

LA CONEXIÓN INGLÉS-ESPAÑOL

Sometimes finding the connection between words in Spanish and English requires a little detective work. How many cognates can you find in the ***Vocabulario temático*** for this chapter? Note that the Spanish word for a sick person ***(enfermo)*** is related to our English word *infirmary* (a place to care for the sick). The word *infirm* (weak, feeble) also exists in English.

299

Objective
• to review vocabulary

Related Components

Activity Book	Audio
Chapter Review: p. 145-146	Assessment: 15B
Assessment	**Cuaderno**
Listening Script: p. 19	p. 91-92
Chapter Test: p. 105-110	**Transparencies** Ch. 11: Dibujos y Palabras Transparency 72

Vocabulary

Point out that this list is organized by themes. Use the headings to review vocabulary. You may wish to ask Spanish speakers to share variations on these words and phrases with the class.

LOG BOOK
Have students describe the kind of community center that would best serve the needs of their community.

La conexión inglés-español
There are many recognizable cognates in this chapter, including *reciclaje*, *clínica*, *plástico*, *pintura*, *voluntario*, *increíble*, *violencia*, and others. Less obvious cognates are: *pintada* (related to English "painted" and meaning graffiti) and *ancianos* (cognate of English "ancient").

	Objetivos page 301 *Las ventajas de ser bilingüe*	Conversemos pages 302-303 *Tu futuro*	Realidades pages 304-305 *¿Qué aptitudes tienes?*	Palabras en acción pages 306-307 *Campamento de verano El Bosque*
Comunicación	To talk about: • personal aptitudes	Discuss personal aptitudes	Read text, make lists, discuss work preferences, recommend job, survey class, make table	Read cartoon, create dialogs; discuss summer camp
	• career interests, especially bilingual careers	Discuss career interests, especially bilingual careers	Read text, discuss personal qualities	Read cartoon, create dialogs; discuss being bilingual; write letter; write paragraph
	• future career goals and how to get a job	Discuss future career goals	Read text, make lists, discuss work preferences, and professions	Read cartoon, make list; create dialogs; talk about being bilingual; write letter; write paragraph
Cultura	To learn about: • typical U.S. aptitude surveys • types of bilingual careers available in the U.S.			Some different Spanish expressions having to do with jobs
Vocabulario temático	To learn the expressions for: • part-time and summer jobs for teens	Talk about part-time and summer jobs for teens	Read text, make lists, discuss work preferences, recommend job	Read cartoon, make list; create dialogs; discuss summer camp
	• work conditions	Talk about work conditions	Read text, make lists, discuss personal qualities	Read cartoon; discuss summer camp; create job dialog; write letter; write paragraph
	• important qualities of good workers	Talk about important qualities of good workers	Read text, make lists, discuss work preferences, and professions	Read cartoon, discuss summer camp; talk about aptitudes; write letter
Estructura	To talk about: • recommendations: expressions with a verb, followed by *que,* and the subjunctive of another verb	Use expressions with a verb, *que,* and the subjunctive of another verb to discuss recommendations	Read text, discuss work at a summer camp	Read cartoon, create job dialog
	• what you have done: the present perfect	Use the present perfect to discuss what you have done		Read cartoon, create dialogs; create job dialog; write letter; write paragraph

Para comunicarnos mejor (1) pages 308-309 *Te recomiendo que aprendas otro idioma*	Para comunicarnos mejor (2) pages 310-311 *¿Has buscado trabajo alguna vez?*	Situaciones pages 312-313 *Oportunidades de empleo para personas bilingües*	Para resolver pages 314-315 *Estudios y profesiones*	Entérate page 316 *¡Qué útiles son los idiomas!*
Discuss work preferences; survey class, give recommendation	Talk about looking for work	Read text, make lists, choose jobs; act out interview; write in diary	Make list, choose topic; discuss job opportunities; talk about aptitudes	Discuss how multilingual people learned languages
Survey class, make table, give recommendation	Talk about different jobs	Read text, make lists, choose jobs; talk about bilingual professions	Make list, choose topic; discuss job opportunities; talk about aptitudes; make and present poster	
Discuss work conditions; talk about work preferences; survey class, make table, give recommendation	Talk about looking for work and work preferences	Read text, make list; choose job, ask for advice, identify skills and qualities needed for various careers, choose jobs	Make list, choose topic; discuss job opportunities	
		Advertisements for bilingual employment opportunities	Advantages of knowing a second language in selecting a career	
Discuss work conditions; survey class, give recommendation	Discuss work experience; make survey, report to class			
Discuss work conditions; talk about work preferences	Talk about looking for work	**Re-entry of vocabulary**		**Extension of vocabulary**
Survey class, make table, give recommendation	Talk about looking for work and work preferences			
	Discuss what you have done, using *haber* and a past participle			
		Re-entry of structure		**Extension of structure**
Discuss statements that use *recomendar que* and the present subjunctive	Discuss work experience; talk about looking for work; make survey, report to class			

Trabajo, trabajo, trabajo

SOCIAL STUDIES CONNECTION

Objective
- to explore professions and jobs, using Chapter 12 *Vocabulario temático*

Use
any time after *Palabras en acción*, pages 306–307

Materials
- 3" x 5" index cards, cut in half

Preparation
- Using the *Vocabulario temático,* write three jobs or professions on each index card half. Prepare one card per student.
- Have students work in pairs.
- Tell the students that they have an uncle who has three jobs.

Activity
- Each student receives a card half. Make sure pairs have different words, and that they don't see each other's cards.
- Have students write several clues about each of their uncle's professions or jobs.
- One student asks: *¿Qué es tu tío?* The other student gives his/her clues. For example, if the student has the words: *abogado, intérprete, guía turístico,* the clues might be: *Mi tío tiene tres empleos: primero, trabaja para resolver problemas de sus clientes; segundo, sabe varios idiomas y traduce para otras personas; tercero, viaja mucho con grupos de turistas.* The other student guesses the professions: *¡Oh, ya sé! Tu tío es contador, telefonista, conductor de autobús.*
- If the first guesses are wrong, the student gives additional clues until the three professions have been correctly identified. Either student may use a textbook, if necessary.
- Have students reverse roles.

Se necesita...

WRITING CONNECTION

Objective
- to write a job advertisement

Use
any time after *Palabras en acción*, pages 306–307

Preparation
- Select five jobs or professions from the *Vocabulario temático* and write them on the chalkboard.

Activity
- Divide students into groups of five.
- Have each group select one job or profession from your list.
- Using their copies of *Juntos,* if necessary, students design job advertisements that include lists of qualities required for each job, as well as duties that the successful applicant will be expected to perform.
- Ask each group to read their advertisement to the class, which votes on the best ad.
- Then each group writes a letter to apply for the job.
- Groups read their letters of application to the class, which votes for which of them should get the job. No voting for your own group!

Algunos consejos

SOCIAL STUDIES CONNECTION

Objective
- to talk about successful careers, using *te recomiendo que* followed by present subjunctive

Use
any time after *Para comunicarnos mejor,* pages 308–309

Preparation
- Have students work in pairs.
- Each student asks partner: *¿Qué quieres ser en el futuro?* The other student selects a career and responds: *Quiero ser _____.*

Activity
- Students give five recommendations to help the other student excel in the chosen career. For example, if a student chooses to be a doctor, the other student could say: *Te recomiendo que estudies mucho. Te recomiendo que lo hagas por vocación, no por dinero. Te recomiendo que seas paciente.*
- Students reverse roles.
- Pairs tell class about the recommendations: *Yo quiero ser doctora y Andrés me recomienda que estudie mucho y...*

Y tú, ¿qué has hecho?

SOCIAL STUDIES CONNECTION

Objective
- to talk about on-the-job experience, using the present perfect

Use
any time after *Para comunicarnos mejor,* pages 310–311

Materials
- magazine pictures

Preparation
- Select six magazine pictures that show two people doing something together.
- Tape pictures to chalkboard, and label them 1, 2, 3, 4, 5, and 6.

Activity
- Divide class into groups of four and have each group select a picture without telling the rest of the class what it is.
- Groups write dialogs between the two people in their picture. The conversation should focus on work experience. For example, for a picture of two women seated in a restaurant: First woman: *Amanda, ¿has trabajado alguna vez de camarera?* Second woman: *¿Quién? ¿Yo? ¡No, nunca!*
- Have students read the conversations to the class. Other students try to match the dialogs to the pictures on the chalkboard. Which pictures are the hardest to match to their dialogs and which are the easiest? Why?

Introduce the chapter and its theme by asking who plans to continue studying Spanish and why. What advantages do these students think they'll have over someone who is not bilingual?

Related Components

Audio	Video: Tape/Book
Conexiones: 18B	Unit 6: Seg. 3
Conexiones	
Chapter 12	

Scan to Chapter 12

GETTING STARTED

Have students look at the photo. Ask questions. Suggestions:
¿Qué hace el señor de la foto?
¿Piensas que su trabajo es importante?
¿Por qué?

Talking About Language

You can use this opportunity to help students discover what words they need to know in order to look for a job.

¿Has buscado trabajo?
Ask students to think of words and phrases they associate with job-hunting. Then assign groups to make lists of:
• professions
• jobs for bilingual people
• what they most value about a job
• personal aptitudes
• jobs teenagers can get

Have each group write its list on the board. Have the class discuss the lists and decide which words from each list are the most useful.
Have each group submit a revised list. When you finish the chapter, have the class review the lists to see how they compare to what they learned in the chapter.

CAPÍTULO 12

LAS VENTAJAS DE SER BILINGÜE

300 **Aprender español tiene muchas ventajas.**

CHAPTER COMPONENTS

Activity Book	Audio Book	Cuaderno	Tutor Pages
p. 147-156	Script: p. 75-77	p. 93-100	p. 51-54
Assessment	Activities: p. 78-80	**Magazine**	**Video: Tape/Book**
Oral Proficiency:	**Audio**	Juntos en Estados	Unit 6: Seg. 3
p. 32	Chapter: 12B	Unidos	
Listening Script: p. 20	Assessment: 15B	**Transparencies**	
Chapter Test:	Conexiones: 18B	Chapter 12	
p. 111-116	**Conexiones**	Transparencies 73-78	
	Chapter 12		

Objetivos

COMUNICACIÓN
To talk about:
• career goals, especially bilingual careers
• work conditions
• personal aptitudes
• part-time or summer jobs
• job interviews

CULTURA
To learn about:
• typical US aptitude tests
• types of bilingual careers available in the US

VOCABULARIO TEMÁTICO
To learn the expressions for:
• part-time and summer jobs for teenagers
• careers
• work conditions
• personal aptitudes

ESTRUCTURA:
To talk about:
• recommendations and advice: use of the subjunctive
• what you have done: the present perfect

¿SABES QUE...?

More than 60 percent of the high school and college students in the United States who are studying a foreign language choose Spanish. Also, an increasing number of adults are learning Spanish, either on their own or through corporate programs. Knowing Spanish has many practical advantages, since there are over 300 million *hispanohablantes* in the world with whom to work, visit, and communicate. Besides, by the year 2010, Hispanics will be the largest minority group in the United States, making Spanish an even more important and useful language to learn.

301

Here are some additional activities that you may wish to use as you work through this chapter with your students.

Communication

Encourage class and after-class activities that may enhance student interest and proficiency. Some ideas:
• hand out the lyrics of a Spanish song, omitting simple or familiar words. Students listen to the song and figure out what should go in the blanks. Discuss the song's theme and lyrics.
• request information on bilingual careers from your guidance counselor or library

Culture

To encourage greater understanding:
• organize a Career Week—invite guest speakers to describe their jobs and talk about how knowledge of another language can be important and useful
• show the video that accompanies Unit 6 of this textbook

Vocabulary

To reinforce vocabulary:
• write the names of professions on flashcards and show them to the class. Ask students to say in English what those names bring to mind. Are there any cognates? Do they know any names of professions in other languages?
• have students use the flashcards to make simple one-line rhymes. For example:

El abogado es organizado.
El asistente es paciente.
El niñero quiere mi dinero.
El repartidor está en el ascensor.
Los traductores son buenos escritores.

Structure

To reinforce the subjunctive and present perfect:
• have pairs discuss how they have pre-pared for the future. They should make recommendations to each other.
• students take turns asking "Have you ever...?" questions and making recom-mendations. For example:

A: *¿Has comido paella alguna vez?*
B: *No.*
A: *Te recomiendo que comas paella.*

►►►INTERNET LINK

Bilingual Education http://education. indiana.edu:80/tched/ble/Bilingua.html

Communicative Objectives
• to talk about jobs and careers
• to talk about personal characteristics
• to talk about recommendations

Related Components

Activity Book p. 147	**Cuaderno** p. 93
Audio Book Script: Seg. 1	**Transparencies** Ch. 12: Conversemos Transparency 73
Audio Chapter: 12B, Seg. 1	

GETTING STARTED

Ask students what they think they will be doing ten years from now. Where will they work? Where will they live?

ACTIVITIES

These activities give students an opportunity to begin communicating with each other and with you, focusing on the theme and objectives of the chapter. The activities can be used as oral class activities, or, if you prefer, you can pair students to achieve more interaction.

¿Qué te gustaría ser?
Class activity to introduce professions. Ask individuals the title question. Encourage students to answer with other words. (A few words they know: *actor/actriz, agente de viajes, auxiliar de vuelo, cocinero(a), fotógrafo(a), granjero(a), músico(a), pescador(a), policía, profesor(a), reportero(a).*)

¿Qué oportunidades de empleo hay para las personas bilingües?
Class activity to introduce bilingual professions. Run through the list with students and ask for words they associate with each one. Ask again, *¿Qué te gustaría ser?*

Language Note
Point out that indefinite articles are not used in Spanish when talking about professions (*Soy maestra.*).

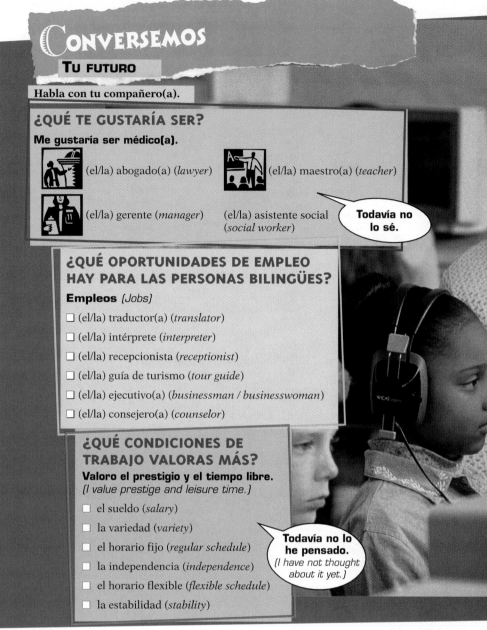

¿Qué condiciones de trabajo valoras más?
Class activity to introduce job vocabulary. Model the question and answer. Have students give an example or description for each (*sueldo: el dinero que recibes por trabajar*). Conduct a survey to see in what order students rank these conditions. Ask those who work part-time which of these are characteristics of their jobs.

MEETING INDIVIDUAL NEEDS

Reaching All Students

For Auditory Learners
You name a profession, your partner suggests a verb. *maestro, enseñar*

For Visual Learners
Choose three professions and list high school courses you need to succeed in them.

For Kinesthetic Learners
Take turns acting out professions for other students to guess.

¿QUÉ APTITUDES PERSONALES TIENES?

Soy una persona paciente y comunicativa.

- ☐ paciente (*patient*)
- ☐ comunicativo(a) (*communicative*)
- ☐ creativo(a) (*creative*)
- ☐ emprendedor(a) (*self-starter*)
- ☐ práctico(a) (*practical*)
- ☐ persuasivo(a) (*persuasive*)

- ☐ disciplinado(a) (*disciplined*)
- ☐ organizado(a) (*organized*)
- ☐ ambicioso(a) (*ambitious*)
- ☐ independiente (*independent*)
- ☐ honesto(a) (*honest*)

¿QUÉ EMPLEOS HAS TENIDO? ¿DÓNDE?

He trabajado de entrenador(a) en un campamento de verano.
[*I've worked as a coach in a summer camp.*]

(el/la) repartidor(a) (*delivery person*)

(el/la) cajero(a)
(*cashier*)

(el/la) niñero(a)
(*baby sitter*)

(el/la) conductor(a)
(*driver*)

No he trabajado nunca, pero estoy buscando trabajo.
[*I have never worked, but I am looking for a job.*]

UN(A) AMIGO(A) TIENE UNA ENTREVISTA DE TRABAJO. ¿QUÉ LE RECOMIENDAS?

Le recomiendo que sea paciente y que lleve una carta de recomendación.
[*I recommend that he/she be patient and bring a letter of recommendation.*]

que sea...	y que...
simpático(a)	cuide su aspecto
comunicativo(a)	llegue cinco minutos antes de la cita
honesto(a)	lleve su currículum

303

¿Qué aptitudes personales tienes?
Class activity to introduce personal attributes. Ask the title question and have volunteers read aloud the answers. Model the situation by asking yourself the question and describing yourself. Have students describe themselves and others in the class. Ask students to match these words with the professions from the first two activities.

¿Qué empleos has tenido? ¿Dónde?
Class activity to learn to talk about work experience. Model the questions and answers, and comment on each of the jobs. Have students look up the names of their jobs in the dictionary, or invent a job. Ask: *¿Cuánto tiempo trabajaste allí?*

Un(a) amigo(a) tiene una entrevista de trabajo. ¿Qué le recomiendas?
Class activity to review the subjunctive and recommendations. Model the answers, and remind students of the subjunctive forms they used in the last chapter.

CHECK

- *¿Qué te gustaría ser?*
- *¿Qué aptitudes personales tiene tu compañero?*
- *¿Qué le recomiendas a un amigo que quiere hablar español bien?*
- *¿Trabajaste en un restaurante alguna vez? ¿Qué hiciste?*

LOG BOOK

Have students write a short paragraph about the professions mentioned on these pages.

Communicative Objectives
- to talk about personal attributes
- to talk about personal aptitudes
- to talk about work conditions

Related Components

Activity Book p. 148	**Cuaderno** p. 94
Audio Script: Seg. 2	**Transparencies** Ch. 12: Realidades Transparency 74
Audio Chapter: 12B, Seg. 2	

GETTING STARTED

Ask students to look at the test and identify the words they know.

DISCUSS

Ask questions about the aptitude test. Suggestions:

¿Cómo eres?
¿Quién en la clase es organizado?
¿Quién es más paciente, Marta o Michael?
¿Cómo es una persona disciplinada?

¿Qué sabes hacer?
¿Quién sabe bailar? ¿Qué bailas?
¿Sabes cocinar? ¿Dónde aprendiste?
¿Quién sabe hablar otro idioma?

¿Qué te gusta hacer?
¿A quién le gusta hacer deportes? ¿Cuáles?
¿A alguien aquí le gusta viajar? ¿Adónde quieres ir?

Tu futuro
¿En qué trabajo puedes tener tiempo libre?
¿Vas a valorar un buen sueldo? ¿Por qué?
¿Qué es prestigio?
¿Qué otras condiciones prefieres?
¿Qué trabajo debes buscar si...
  te gusta trabajar al aire libre?
  quieres trabajar solo?
  no quieres trabajar en una oficina?

REALIDADES
¿QUÉ APTITUDES TIENES?

Prueba TUS APTITUDES

¿Cómo eres?
- [ ] creativo/a
- [ ] comunicativo/a
- [ ] disciplinado/a
- [ ] organizado/a
- [ ] persuasivo/a
- [ ] ambicioso/a
- [ ] emprendedor/a
- [ ] independiente
- [ ] práctico/a
- [ ] paciente
- [ ] honesto/a

¿Qué sabes hacer?
- [ ] cocinar
- [ ] hablar otro idioma
- [ ] usar la computadora
- [ ] cantar
- [ ] tocar un instrumento
- [ ] nadar
- [ ] bailar
- [ ] manejar un coche
- [ ] escribir bien

¿Qué te gusta hacer?
- [ ] dibujar
- [ ] leer
- [ ] enseñar a los niños
- [ ] cuidar animales
- [ ] hacer trabajos manuales
- [ ] trabajar en grupo
- [ ] ayudar a la gente
- [ ] escribir
- [ ] viajar
- [ ] hacer deporte

Tu futuro
¿Qué condiciones de trabajo crees que vas a valorar más?
- [ ] el tiempo libre
- [ ] la independencia
- [ ] la variedad
- [ ] la estabilidad
- [ ] el buen sueldo
- [ ] el prestigio

¿Qué otras condiciones prefieres?
- [ ] tener un horario fijo
- [ ] tener un horario flexible
- [ ] trabajar en una oficina
- [ ] trabajar al aire libre
- [ ] trabajar con los demás
- [ ] trabajar solo(a)

304

✓ CULTURE NOTE

In some Spanish-speaking countries, such as Argentina and Uruguay, students who wish to attend national universities take different types of college admissions tests, depending on what career they have chosen. Other countries have a system similar to the US with its SAT and ACT tests. In Spain, for example, all college applicants must pass the **examen de selectividad.** In Mexico, most students applying to the *Universidad Autóroma de Mexico* need to have completed special courses or have passed the **examen de ingreso.**

MEETING INDIVIDUAL NEEDS

Reaching All Students

For Auditory and Kinesthetic Learners
Dictate the descriptive words from the test in a random order, selecting three from each of the sections. Use voice and gestures to clarify wherever possible. Have students write down the words as you dictate them. Finally, say aloud the five categories, and have students decide which words belong in which categories.

MIRA LA PRUEBA

A. Haz tres listas: una de tus aptitudes personales, otra de las cosas que te gusta hacer y otra de las condiciones de trabajo que prefieres.

B. Según tus listas, ¿qué tipo de trabajo crees que te gustaría hacer en el futuro? ¿Por qué?

> *Creo que me gustaría trabajar para una revista o un periódico dibujando historietas porque soy una persona creativa. Me gusta dibujar y trabajar sola, y valoro la independencia.*

C. Pregúntale a tu compañero(a) qué le gusta hacer y para qué es bueno(a). Recomiéndale un trabajo.

> — ¿Qué te gusta hacer?
> — Me gusta hacer ejercicio y soy bueno para los deportes. ¿Qué me recomiendas?
> — Te recomiendo que busques un trabajo como entrenador.

¿QUÉ OPINAS?

¿Cuáles son las aptitudes personales que más se valoran en tu clase? Haz una encuesta. Anota los resultados en una tabla. Usa el modelo.

Valoro a las personas...	yo	la clase
creativas		
comunicativas	✓	//
disciplinadas		//////
organizadas		
persuasivas		
ambiciosas		
emprendedoras	✓	
independientes	✓	
prácticas		
pacientes		
honestas		

Según la encuesta, ¿cuáles son las aptitudes personales que más se valoran en la clase? ¿Y las que menos se valoran?

305

Mira la prueba

Individual and Pair Activities: Writing and Conversing
A. Make lists of: your personal aptitudes; things you like to do; and the type of working conditions you prefer.
B. Based on your answers, what type of work do you think you would like to do? Why?
C. Ask what your partner likes to do and thinks he or she does well. Recommend a career based on his or her answers.
Answers: See models on student page.
Extension: Say what career would not be good for your partner—and why.

¿Qué opinas?

Group Activity: Taking a Poll
Form groups. Discuss which qualities you value most. Record your answers on a chart like the one on page 305. (To make the poll more interesting, limit voters to the three qualities they rate most important.)

Class Activity: Evaluation
Have volunteers list personal aptitudes and add tally marks as representatives of each group call them out.
Add up the numbers for each and rank the qualities. Discuss the rankings.

CHECK

- *¿Quién en la clase...*
  es muy paciente?
  sabe tocar un instrumento?
  ha cuidado animales?
  valora la independencia?
  prefiere trabajar al aire libre?

LOG BOOK

Have students choose a profession, such as *bombero* or *policía,* and say what qualities a person needs to succeed in that career.

Para hispanohablantes

Think of four or five more useful qualities, jobs, and conditions to add to these lists. Explain them to the class.

305

Communicative Objectives
• to talk about personal qualities
• to talk about professions
• to talk about jobs at a summer camp

Related Components

Activity Book p. 149-150	**Transparencies** Ch. 12: Palabras en acción
Cuaderno p. 95-96	Transparency 75
	Tutor Page p. 51

GETTING STARTED

Ask if anyone in class has been to summer camp. Have them talk about the people who worked there.

DISCUSS

Comment on and ask questions about the people in the drawing. For example:
¿Cuántos trabajadores hay en el dibujo?
¿Quién cuida a los niños?
¿Qué hace el repartidor?
¿Dónde están los entrenadores?
¿Cuál es el trabajo del salvavidas?

Para hispanohablantes

If you use other words or expressions, share them with the class. A few variations:

el asistente social: el trabajador social
el campamento de verano: la colonia de vacaciones/de verano
el/la conductor(a): el chofer, el chófer
el curriculum: el resumé
el/la ejecutivo(a): el hombre/la mujer de negocios
el/la maestro(a): el/la profesor(a)
el/la niñero(a): la nana, el/la canguro
el sueldo: el salario, la paga

PALABRAS EN ACCIÓN
CAMPAMENTO DE VERANO *EL BOSQUE*

el salvavidas

¿Has traído las artesanías que hicimos ayer?

No, ¿las quieres ahora?

Sí, ya la he hecho.

¿Has hecho la ensalada?

el entrenador

la entrenadora

la cocinera

---

1 Los empleos

Haz una lista de los empleados que ves en el dibujo. Compara tu lista con las de tus compañeros(as).

El salvavidas, el entrenador...

2 Completa el diálogo

Escoge tres escenas del dibujo. Haz un diálogo para cada escena.

— *¿Has hecho la comida?*
— *No, no he tenido tiempo.*

306

3 ¿Qué trabajo te gustaría?

Con tu compañero(a), habla de qué trabajo te gustaría hacer en el campamento de verano *El Bosque* y por qué.

— *¿Qué trabajo te gustaría hacer?*
— *Me gustaría ser conductora.*
— *¿Por qué?*
— *Porque me encanta manejar.*

4 Las aptitudes personales

Pregúntale a tu compañero(a) qué aptitudes personales se necesitan tener para los empleos del dibujo.

— *¿Qué aptitudes personales necesita tener un entrenador?*
— *Necesita ser paciente y persuasivo.*

For students having difficulty discussing jobs or personal attributes, you might consider:
• **The tutor page:** Pair the student with a native speaker or a more able student, using the tutor page
Optional activity: See page 300C: *Trabajo, trabajo, trabajo*

el maestro

la consejera

la conductora

el repartidor

¿Les has escrito ya a tus padres?

No, no he tenido tiempo todavía.

el niñero

la directora

el currículum

la niñera

la niña

¿Qué empleos has tenido?

He trabajado de cajero.

1. Individual and Pair Activity
Make a list of the people's jobs in the drawing. Compare lists with your partner.
Extension: Divide your list into masculine and feminine nouns, and describe each.

2. Individual or Pair Activity
Choose three scenes from the drawing. Make a new dialog for each scene.
Extension: Read your dialogs to the class. Have them identify which people are speaking.

3. Pair Activity
Talk about what work you would like to do at *El Bosque* summer camp and why.
Extension: Say how your skills or interests relate to the position you chose.

4. Pair Activity
Ask your partner which qualities are necessary for each job in the drawing.

5. Pair Activity
Talk about advantages of being bilingual.
Extension: Say what you have to do to be bilingual. Use **hay que, es necesario,** and **es importante.**

6. Roleplay Activity
Imagine that you're in an employment office, and your partner is interviewing you. Create a dialog.

7. Writing Activity
Write a letter to the director of *El Bosque* summer camp asking for a job.
Extension: Pretend you are the director of the summer camp. Write a response.

8. Writing Activity
Write a paragraph about jobs you have had and the kind of work you would like to have in the future.

 Los idiomas

Con tu compañero(a), habla de las ventajas de ser bilingüe.

— ¿Por qué es bueno ser bilingüe?
— Porque tienes más oportunidades de trabajo.
— ¿Qué empleos hay para las personas bilingües?
— Intérprete...

 Miniteatro

Imagina que estás en una oficina de empleo y tu compañero(a) te está haciendo una entrevista. Creen un diálogo.

— ¿Qué empleos has tenido?
— He trabajado de recepcionista.
— ¿Dónde?
— En la oficina de un médico.

7 Una carta pidiendo empleo

Escribe una carta pidiendo empleo a la directora del campamento de verano *El Bosque*.

Señor director:
Me gustaría trabajar de maestra en el campamento de verano El Bosque. Hace dos años que enseño matemáticas a los niños de un centro comunitario de mi vecindario. Soy una persona paciente y muy comunicativa.

8 Tú eres el autor

Escribe un párrafo sobre los trabajos que hiciste y sobre qué profesión te gustaría tener en el futuro.

Trabajé en una guardería cuidando niños. Hice este trabajo en las vacaciones de verano. En el futuro me gustaría ser médica.

307

CHECK

• ¿Cómo es una persona emprendedora?
• ¿Quiénes han hecho la tarea?
• ¿Qué aptitudes personales necesita tener un maestro?

LOG BOOK
Have students write what qualities a good teacher should have.

PARA COMUNICARNOS MEJOR

Communicative Objectives
- to make recommendations
- to give advice

Related Components

Activity Book p. 151-152	**Cuaderno** p. 97
Audio Book Script: Seg. 3 Activities: p. 78	**Transparencies** Ch. 12: Para comunicarnas mejor Transparency 76
Audio Chapter: 12B, Seg. 3	**Tutor Page** p. 52

GETTING STARTED

Pair students and ask them to write job and career advice for their partners, starting with: "I recommend that..."

Language in Context

Remind students of two of the structures they learned in the preceding chapter: *es necesario que...* and *es importante que....* Point out that these statements are very similar to recommendations. Also point out that they share the "that" structure. For example:
Juan recommends that José exercise.
Juan recomienda que José haga ejercicio.

DISCUSS

Review vocabulary from previous chapters and introduce some of this chapter's vocabulary with questions and statements that use **recomendar que** and the present subjunctive.
¿Cómo eres? ¿Eres organizado?
Te recomiendo que busques trabajo de recepcionista.
¿Quién quiere ser intérprete?
Le recomiendo que estudie español.
¿Qué les recomienda a los estudiantes?
Yo les recomiendo que lleguen temprano a la clase de español.
Y ustedes, ¿qué me recomiendan a mí?

PARA COMUNICARNOS MEJOR

TE RECOMIENDO QUE APRENDAS OTRO IDIOMA

To make recommendations or give advice, use the verb *recomendar* followed by *que* and the present subjunctive form of a verb.

Te recomiendo que busques trabajo de abogada.	I recommend that you look for a job as a lawyer.
Le recomiendo que José estudie idiomas.	I recommend that José study languages.

¡OJO!

The endings to form the present subjunctive are added to the **yo** form of the present indicative after dropping the **-o.**

☐ Verbs ending in *-car*, *-zar*, and *-gar* have a spelling change in the present subjunctive.

present subjunctive	buscar	empezar	llegar
yo	bus**que**	empie**ce**	lle**gue**
tú	bus**ques**	empie**ces**	lle**gues**
usted	bus**que**	empie**ce**	lle**gue**
él/ella	bus**que**	empie**ce**	lle**gue**
nosotros(as)	bus**quemos**	empe**cemos**	lle**guemos**
vosotros(as)	bus**quéis**	empe**céis**	lle**guéis**
ustedes	bus**quen**	empie**cen**	lle**guen**
ellos/ellas	bus**quen**	empie**cen**	lle**guen**

For students having difficulty making recommendations, using **recomendar que** and the present subjunctive, you might consider:
- **The tutor page:** Pair the student with a native speaker or a more able student, using the tutor page.

Optional activity: See page 300D: *Algunos consejos*

Valores y profesiones

Dile a tu compañero(a) cuáles son las condiciones de trabajo que más valoras. Pregúntale qué trabajo te recomienda.

— *En un trabajo, yo valoro la variedad. ¿Qué me recomiendas?*
— *Te recomiendo que busques un empleo de intérprete.*

 Los estudios y el futuro

Dile a tu compañero(a) qué les gusta hacer a tus amigos(as). Pregúntale para qué profesión les recomienda estudiar.

— *A mi amiga le gusta ayudar a la gente con problemas.*
— *Le recomiendo que estudie para abogada.*

Le gusta...

1. ayudar a la gente con problemas
2. buscar palabras en el diccionario
3. conocer a personas famosas
4. hablar con personas de diferentes países
5. viajar
6. hacer deporte

Valoro...
la variedad
la independencia
la estabilidad
el sueldo
el tiempo libre
el prestigio

 Aptitudes personales

En grupo, pregúntales a tus compañeros cuáles son sus aptitudes personales.

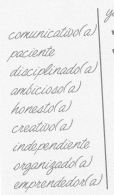

	yo	Eduardo	Teresa
comunicativo(a)	✓	✓	
paciente	✓	✓	
disciplinado(a)			
ambicioso(a)			
honesto(a)			
creativo(a)			
independiente			
organizado(a)			
emprendedor(a)			

Presenten los resultados. Una persona de otro grupo es consejera y les dice para qué trabajos son buenos.

— *Eduardo y yo somos comunicativos y muy pacientes.*
— *Les recomiendo que trabajen de asistentes sociales.*

309

Communicative Objective
• to talk about what you have done, using the present perfect

Related Components

Activity Book p. 153-154	Audio Chapter: 12B, Seg. 4
Audio Book Script: Seg.4 Activities: p. 79	Cuaderno p. 98
	Tutor Page p. 53

GETTING STARTED

Ask students what paid or volunteer work they have done.

Language in Context

Point out that this construction is very similar in Spanish and English. Example: I have worked as a cashier.
He trabajado de cajero.

DISCUSS

Review vocabulary from previous chapters and introduce some of this chapter's vocabulary with questions and statements that use the present perfect.

¿Has trabajado alguna vez?
¿Qué trabajo has hecho?
¿Qué trabajos han hecho tus amigos?
¿Quiénes han trabajado en una hamburguesería?
¿Quién ha tenido una entrevista de trabajo?
¿Quiénes han pensado en el sueldo que quieren ganar?
¿Qué trabajos no han hecho?

PARA COMUNICARNOS MEJOR

¿HAS BUSCADO TRABAJO ALGUNA VEZ?

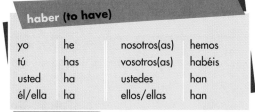

To say what you have done, use a present-tense form of *haber* followed by the past participle of another verb.

— *Sí, he buscado trabajo varias veces.*	Yes, I have looked for work several times.
— *¿Y has trabajado alguna vez?*	And have you ever worked?
— *Sí, he trabajado de cajera.*	Yes, I have worked as a cashier.

Here is the present tense of **haber**.

haber (to have)

yo	he	nosotros(as)	hemos
tú	has	vosotros(as)	habéis
usted	ha	ustedes	han
él/ella	ha	ellos/ellas	han

☐ To form the past participle, add the appropriate endings to the stem of the verb.

past participle

-ar verbs: -ado		-er / -ir verbs: -ido	
buscar	busc**ado**	repartir	repart**ido**
trabajar	trabaj**ado**	tener	ten**ido**

☐ Some verbs have an irregular past participle.

escribir	**escrito**	ir	**ido**
hacer	**hecho**	ser	**sido**

— *¿Has escrito tu currículum?*	Have you written your résumé?
— *Sí, ya lo he hecho.*	Yes, I have already done it.

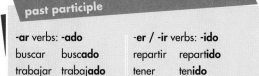

310

For students having difficulty using the present perfect to say what they have done, you might consider:
• **The tutor page:** Pair the student with a native speaker or a more able student, using the tutor page.
Optional activity: See page 300D: *Y tú, ¿qué has hecho?*

¿Qué trabajos has tenido?

Pregúntale a tu compañero(a).

— ¿Qué trabajos has tenido?
— He sido salvavidas.
— ¿Dónde?
— En una piscina.

1. ser salvavidas
2. cuidar niños
3. ser recepcionista
4. vender juguetes
5. hacer artesanías
6. escribir cartas en la computadora

En...
una piscina
un centro comunitario
una oficina de abogados
mi casa
una guardería
un campamento de verano
el parque

 El currículum

Tu compañero(a) está buscando trabajo. Hazle las siguientes preguntas.

— ¿Has escrito tu currículum?
— Sí, ya lo he escrito.
  (No, todavía no.)

1. escribir el currículum
2. pensar cuáles son tus aptitudes
3. buscar trabajo antes
4. tener alguna entrevista
5. pensar en el sueldo que quieres ganar
6. mirar los anuncios del periódico

3 Trabajos

En grupo, haz una encuesta para averiguar qué trabajos han hecho tus compañeros(as).

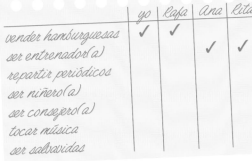

	yo	Rafa	Ana	Rita
vender hamburguesas	✓	✓		
ser entrenador(a)			✓	✓
repartir periódicos				
ser niñero(a)				
ser consejero(a)				
tocar música				
ser salvavidas				

Presenten los resultados a la clase.

Rafa y yo hemos vendido hamburguesas.
Ana y Rita han sido entrenadoras.

311

Students use the present perfect to say what they have done.

1. Pair Activity
Ask each other which of these jobs you have done and where you did them.
Possible Answers:
1. See model on student page.
2. *He cuidado niños.*
   En una guardería.
3. *He sido recepcionista.*
   En una oficina de abogados.
4. *He vendido juguetes.*
   En una juguetería.
5. *He hecho artesanías.*
   En un centro comunitario.
6. *He escrito cartas en la computadora.*
   En un campamento de verano.

2. Pair Activity
Your partner is looking for a job. Ask him or her the questions in the list.
Possible Answers:
1. See model on student page.
2. *¿Has pensado en cuáles son tus aptitudes?*
   Sí, ya lo he pensado.
3. *¿Has buscado trabajo antes?*
   Sí, ya lo he buscado.
4. *¿Has tenido alguna entrevista?*
   Sí, ya he tenido dos entrevistas.
5. *¿Has pensado en el sueldo que quieres ganar?*
   No, todavía no.
6. *¿Has mirado los anuncios del periódico?*
   Sí, ya los he mirado.
Extension: Use **voy a** to say you will do these things.

3. Group Activity
Ask members of your group what jobs they have had. Record the answers on a chart like the one on page 311. Present and explain your chart to the class.
Answers: See model on student page.

CHECK

• *¿Qué trabajos has hecho?*
• *¿Has buscado trabajo de vendedor?*
• *¿Has repartido periódicos?*
• *¿Qué trabajos no has tenido?*

LOG BOOK
Have students make a checklist of things that a person should do when looking for a job.

Objectives
Communicative: to talk about bilingual professions
Cultural: to discuss a Spanish classified ad section

Related Components

Assessment Oral Proficiency: p. 32	**Conexiones** Chapter 12
Audio Book Script: Seg. 5 Activities: p. 80	**Magazine** Juntos en Estados Unidos
Audio Chapter: 12B, Seg. 5 Conexiones: 18B	**Tutor Page** p. 54

GETTING STARTED

Students should now be able to use the subjunctive, the present perfect, and all of the chapter vocabulary correctly.
Have volunteers read aloud the classified ads as other students take turns transcribing them on the chalkboard. Ask students to identify all verbs that are in the subjunctive, and the infinitive of each of these.

APPLY

1. Individual Activity
Look at the classified ads and make a list of the jobs for bilingual people.
Answers: See model on student page.
Extension: Use **más/menos... que** to compare the ads. For example:
Ser traductor es más difícil que ser recepcionista.

2. Pair Activity
Choose a job from the list. Ask your partner to recommend what you should do.
Answers: See model on student page.
Extension: Make recordings of the classified ads, exchange with other pairs, listen to theirs, and write down as much as you can.

3. Individual Activity
Make a list of the work conditions you prefer, and another of your personal qualities. Decide which jobs you would be good at.
Answers: See model on student page.
Extension: Make an ad for your ideal job.

SITUACIONES

OPORTUNIDADES DE EMPLEO PARA PERSONAS BILINGÜES

Recepcionista bilingüe
Compañía internacional de ropa busca recepcionista con experiencia en computadoras. Es necesario que sea una persona comunicativa y organizada. Inglés y otro idioma (español, francés o japonés). Jornada completa. Se ofrece buen sueldo y estabilidad. P.O. Box 5574.

Bilingüe
Oficina busca abogado/a que hable inglés y español. Es importante que trabaje bien en grupo y que sea una persona emprendedora. Se ofrece buen ambiente de trabajo y horario flexible. P.O. Box 5575.

Profesor/a de español
Escuela de bachillerato necesita profesor(a) de español para segundo año. Es importante que sea una persona comunicativa. Jornada parcial. P.O. Box 5577.

Periodista
Conocida revista busca periodista para trabajar en Latinoamérica. Es necesario que hable español y que sea independiente y creativo(a). Se ofrece variedad.
P.O. Box 5578.

Traductores
La ONU busca traductores de español a inglés y viceversa. Excelente oportunidad de trabajo para personas disciplinadas. Horario flexible. P.O. Box 5579.

Ejecutivo/a
Compañía de importación y exportación necesita ejecutivo/a. Bilingüe: inglés y español. Es necesario que pueda viajar una vez por mes a Venezuela. Buscamos a una persona ambiciosa, persuasiva y práctica.
P.O. Box 5580.

PARA TU REFERENCIA

el ambiente *environment*
el bachillerato *high school education*
la compañía *company*
importación y exportación *import-export*
japonés *Japanese*
jornada completa *full-time*
jornada parcial *part-time*
ONU (Organización de las Naciones Unidas) *United Nations*

312

For students having difficulty talking about bilingual careers, or personal attributes and goals, you might consider:
• **The tutor page:** Pair the student with a native speaker or a more able student, using the tutor page.
Optional activity: See page 300C: *Se necesita...*

¿Eres bilingüe?

Mira los anuncios clasificados. Haz una lista de los trabajos que puedes encontrar si eres bilingüe.

Recepcionista...

 ¿Qué trabajo te gustaría?

Escoge un trabajo de la lista. Pregúntale a tu compañero(a) qué te recomienda que hagas.

— *Me gustaría trabajar de recepcionista. ¿Qué me recomiendas que haga?*
— *Te recomiendo que aprendas a usar bien la computadora y que estudies otro idioma.*

 Tus aptitudes

Escribe una lista de las condiciones de trabajo que más valoras y otra de tus aptitudes personales. Después decide qué trabajos son buenos para ti.

Condiciones de trabajo: *el tiempo libre, la variedad...*
Aptitudes: *comunicativa, creativa...*
Buenos trabajos para mí: *profesora...*

 Entrevista

Hazle una entrevista a una persona que busca empleo.

• *¿Qué ha estudiado? ¿Dónde?*
• *¿Ha trabajado antes? ¿En qué? ¿Dónde?*
• *¿Ha escrito su currículum?*
• *¿Ha pedido cartas de recomendación?*
• *¿Qué condiciones de trabajo valora más?*
• *¿Qué sueldo quiere ganar?*

 Tu diario

Escribe una carta explicando cuáles son tus aptitudes personales, tus valores y tu experiencia de trabajo.

Soy una persona persuasiva y práctica. Me gusta mucho trabajar en grupo. Sé usar la computadora. Las condiciones de trabajo que más valoro son el prestigio y la variedad. He repartido paquetes, he sido niñero y he trabajado de consejero en un campamento de verano.

313

4. Pair Activity
Interview a person who is looking for a job.
Answers: See model on student page.
Extension: Have your partner respond to your "ideal job" ad.

5. Homework or Classwork
Write a letter to a potential employer. Include your personal qualities, what work conditions you prefer, and your work experience.
Answers: See model on student page.

CHECK

• *¿Quién busca una recepcionista bilingüe?*
• *¿Adónde tienes que mandar una carta si quieres trabajar de profesor(a)?*
• *¿Has trabajado antes? ¿Dónde?*
• *¿Qué condiciones de trabajo valoras más?*

LOG BOOK
Have students write why they prefer a certain type of work environment.

Para hispanohablantes

Which of the countries in this book would you like to work in? Write a paragraph saying why.

Communicative Objective
- to talk about the advantages and disadvantages of various careers
- to identify skills and qualities needed for various careers

Related Components

Transparencies	Video: Tape/Book
Ch. 12: Para resolver	Unit 6: Seg. 3
Transparency 77	

Scan to Chapter 12

GETTING STARTED

Ask students what they used to answer when someone asked, "What are you going to be when you grow up?" Would they still give the same answer? Why or why not?

APPLY

Form groups. Each will design a poster about fields of study and career options.

PASO 1: Los estudios
Make a list of college majors. Choose one for your poster.
Answers: See model on student page.
Extension: Say what people whom you know are studying or have studied.

PASO 2: Las profesiones
Talk about the jobs that people who major in that area can probably get.
Answers: See model on student page.

PASO 3: Aptitudes personales
Describe the personal qualities that are necessary for each job.
Answers: See model on student page.
Extension: Choose two jobs you like from the list. Write a paragraph about each without mentioning the jobs' names, and dictate them to your partner. Then he/she guesses which jobs you wrote about.

PASO 4: Las condiciones de trabajo
Talk about the advantages and disadvantages of each job.
Answers: See model on student page.
Extension: Decide what you value in a job, and which of these jobs offers those advantages.

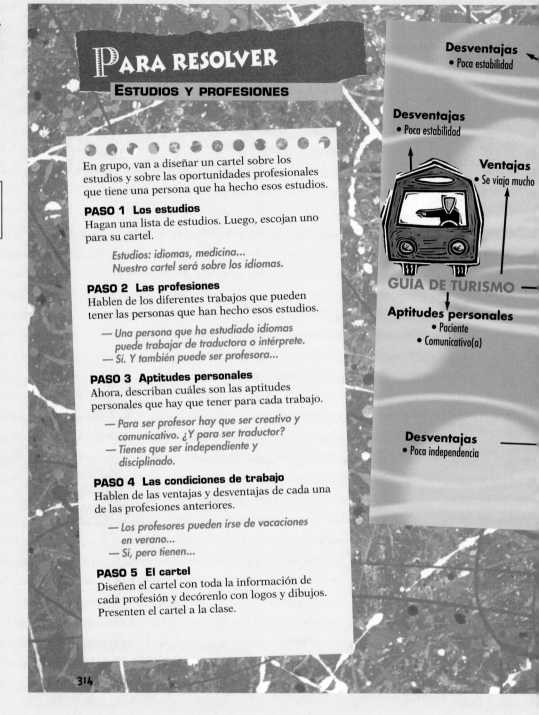

PARA RESOLVER
ESTUDIOS Y PROFESIONES

En grupo, van a diseñar un cartel sobre los estudios y sobre las oportunidades profesionales que tiene una persona que ha hecho esos estudios.

PASO 1 Los estudios
Hagan una lista de estudios. Luego, escojan uno para su cartel.

> *Estudios: idiomas, medicina...*
> *Nuestro cartel será sobre los idiomas.*

PASO 2 Las profesiones
Hablen de los diferentes trabajos que pueden tener las personas que han hecho esos estudios.

> — *Una persona que ha estudiado idiomas puede trabajar de traductora o intérprete.*
> — *Sí. Y también puede ser profesora...*

PASO 3 Aptitudes personales
Ahora, describan cuáles son las aptitudes personales que hay que tener para cada trabajo.

> — *Para ser profesor hay que ser creativo y comunicativo. ¿Y para ser traductor?*
> — *Tienes que ser independiente y disciplinado.*

PASO 4 Las condiciones de trabajo
Hablen de las ventajas y desventajas de cada una de las profesiones anteriores.

> — *Los profesores pueden irse de vacaciones en verano...*
> — *Sí, pero tienen...*

PASO 5 El cartel
Diseñen el cartel con toda la información de cada profesión y decórenlo con logos y dibujos. Presenten el cartel a la clase.

314

Desventajas
- Poca estabilidad

Desventajas
- Poca estabilidad

Ventajas
- Se viaja mucho

GUÍA DE TURISMO

Aptitudes personales
- Paciente
- Comunicativo(a)

Desventajas
- Poca independencia

PASO 5: El cartel
Design your poster, using your answers from *Pasos 1-4*. Present it to the class.
Answers: See model on student page.
Extension: Choose a career from any group's presentation. Write down the information and list any qualities you have that would make you good at it.

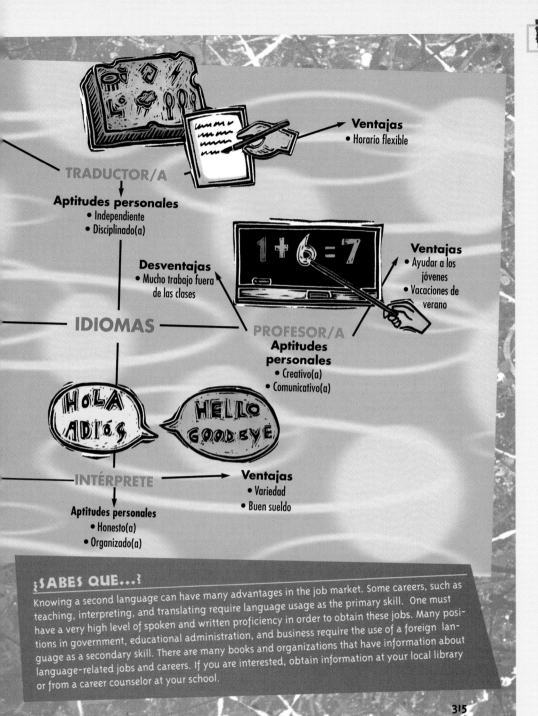

Ventajas
- Horario flexible

TRADUCTOR/A

Aptitudes personales
- Independiente
- Disciplinado(a)

Desventajas
- Mucho trabajo fuera de las clases

Ventajas
- Ayudar a los jóvenes
- Vacaciones de verano

IDIOMAS

PROFESOR/A

Aptitudes personales
- Creativo(a)
- Comunicativo(a)

INTÉRPRETE

Ventajas
- Variedad
- Buen sueldo

Aptitudes personales
- Honesto(a)
- Organizado(a)

¿SABES QUE...?

Knowing a second language can have many advantages in the job market. Some careers, such as teaching, interpreting, and translating require language usage as the primary skill. One must have a very high level of spoken and written proficiency in order to obtain these jobs. Many positions in government, educational administration, and business require the use of a foreign language as a secondary skill. There are many books and organizations that have information about language-related jobs and careers. If you are interested, obtain information at your local library or from a career counselor at your school.

315

Objectives
Commmunicative: to talk about studying languages
Cultural: to learn about a multilingual person

Related Components

Audio Conexiones: 18B **Conexiones** Chapter 12	**Magazine** Juntos en Estados Unido

GETTING STARTED

Ask students if they know anyone who speaks more than two languages. Discuss these people, the languages they speak, and how they learned those languages.

DISCUSS

Using the Text
Have volunteers read aloud the text. Ask questions. Suggestions:
¿Quién es Edward Powe?
¿De qué país es? ¿Cómo lo sabes?
¿Qué es el extranjero?
¿En qué partes del mundo ha estado Edward Powe?
¿Qué es el Cuerpo de Paz? ¿Qué hacen los voluntarios de esta organización?
¿En qué lugares del mundo están los trópicos de Cáncer y Capricornio?
¿Dónde se habla quechua? (Perú)

CHECK

Te toca a ti
Answers:
1. *Él ha viajado, ha recibido becas y ha tenido muchas oportunidades de empleo.*
2. *Su meta es completar una serie de siete tomos sobre la cultura de la gente que vive entre los trópicos de Cáncer y Capricornio.*
3. *Está estudiando quechua.*
4. *Ha trabajado en África, Estados Unidos y Colombia.*
5. *Ha viajado a Egipto, Brasil y Colombia.*

ENTÉRATE
¡QUÉ ÚTILES SON LOS IDIOMAS!

TE TOCA A TI
1. ¿Qué ventajas ha tenido Edward Powe por saber idiomas?
2. ¿Cuál es la meta del señor Powe?
3. ¿Qué está estudiando Edward Powe ahora?
4. ¿En qué países ha trabajado?
5. ¿A qué países ha viajado?

Edward Powe es un estadounidense muy interesado en los idiomas. Ha estudiado nueve idiomas, entre ellos el español. Empezó estudiando estos idiomas en Estados Unidos y después viajó a los países donde se hablan para practicarlos. Ha recibido varias becas° para estudiar idiomas en el extranjero. Ha viajado a Egipto, Brasil y Colombia.

Gracias a los idiomas que conoce, Powe ha tenido muchas oportunidades de empleo. Ha sido profesor universitario de idiomas africanos en África y en Estados Unidos. También ha vivido en Colombia, trabajando de voluntario para el Cuerpo de Paz.° Y ha trabajado en África como director adjunto° de esta organización.

Hoy Edward Powe es escritor. Su propósito° es completar una serie de siete tomos° sobre la cultura de la gente que vive entre el trópico de Cáncer y el trópico de Capricornio. Hasta ahora, ha completado dos tomos.

Ahora está estudiando un décimo° idioma, el quechua, mientras prepara un viaje de investigación a la región andina para escribir el tercer° tomo de la serie.

las becas *fellowships, grants*	**la meta** *goal*
el Cuerpo de Paz *Peace Corps*	**el propósito** *purpose*
décimo *tenth*	**tercer** *third*
el director adjunto *associate director*	**los tomos** *volumes*

316

Thinking of Language
Two ordinal numbers are introduced on this page (**tercer, décimo**). You may wish to introduce all of the first ten *números ordinales*. Ask students to name them in English, and write them on the board before you write the Spanish numbers.
1. *primero*
2. *segundo*
3. *tercero*
4. *cuarto*
5. *quinto*
6. *sexto*
7. *séptimo*
8. *octavo*
9. *noveno*
10. *décimo*

LOG BOOK
Have students find and write down sentences in this text that use the present perfect.

Para hispanohablantes
In Spanish, name as many languages as you can.

VOCABULARIO TEMÁTICO

Los trabajos
Jobs

el/la abogado(a) *lawyer*
el/la asistente social
  social worker
el/la cajero(a) *cashier*
el/la conductor(a) *driver*
el/la consejero(a) *counselor*
el/la ejecutivo(a)
  businessman/businesswoman
el/la entrenador(a)
  trainer, coach
el/la gerente *manager*
el/la guía de turismo *tour guide*
el/la intérprete *interpreter*
el/la maestro(a) *teacher*
el/la niñero(a) *baby sitter*
el/la recepcionista *receptionist*
el/la repartidor(a)
  delivery person
el/la traductor(a) *translator*

Las condiciones de trabajo
Work conditions

la estabilidad *stability*
el horario fijo *regular schedule*
el horario flexible *flexible
  schedule*
la independencia *independence*
el prestigio *prestige*
el sueldo *salary*
el tiempo libre *leisure time*
la variedad *variety*

Aptitudes personales
Personal qualities

ambicioso(a) *ambitious*
comunicativo(a) *communicative*
creativo(a) *creative*
disciplinado(a) *disciplined*
emprendedor(a) *self-starter*
honesto(a) *honest*
independiente *independent*

organizado(a) *organized*
paciente *patient*
persuasivo(a) *persuasive*
práctico(a) *practical*

Expresiones y palabras

la aptitud *quality*
bilingüe *bilingual*
el campamento de verano
  summer camp
la condición *condition*
el currículum *résumé*
el empleo *job*
el futuro *future*
la oportunidad *opportunity*
recomendar (e>ie) *to
  recommend*
valorar *to value*

LA CONEXIÓN INGLÉS-ESPAÑOL

There is a record number of cognates in the *Vocabulario temático* of this chapter. Do you think this fact has any relationship to the theme of the chapter? Note that all the personal qualities are cognates except one: *self-starter*. Can you think of an English word meaning "self-starter" that corresponds more closely to the Spanish word *emprendedor*?

In Spanish, an *emprendedor* is someone who takes on difficult tasks. (It is related to the English word *entrepreneur*, which comes from French.)

317

VOCABULARIO TEMÁTICO

Objective
• to review vocabulary

Related Components

Activity Book	Audio
Chapter Review: p. 155-156	Assessment: 15B
Assessment	**Cuaderno**
Listening Script: p. 20	p. 99-100
Chapter Test: p. 111-116	**Transparencies** Ch. 12: Dibujos y palabras Transparency 78

Vocabulary

Point out that this list is organized by themes. Use the headings to review vocabulary. You may wish to ask Spanish speakers to share variations on these words and phrases with the class.

La conexión inglés-español

There are at least 27 cognates in this chapter's *Vocabulario temático*. Divide the class into groups and have them compete to find as many as possible.

The word *currículum* may not be that obvious. In many English-speaking countries, such as England, Ireland, Scotland, and Australia, "curriculum vitae" is used instead of "resumé."

ADELANTE

Objectives

Prereading Strategy: to gain meaning from photographs and captions
Cultural: to discuss the extent to which Spanish is spoken in the world

Related Components

Magazine	Video: Tape/Book
Juntos en Estados Unidos	Unit 6 Seg. 4

Scan to Adelante

GETTING STARTED

Ask students to look at the photos on these pages. In what country do students think these scenes take place?

Using the Video

Show Segment 4 of the Unit 6 video, an introduction to Hispanics in the U.S.

Antes de leer

Have students read the first paragraph; ask questions. Examples:
¿Es posible ver ejemplos del español en Estados Unidos? ¿Dónde?
Have students look at the photos and captions and answer the questions.
Possible Answers:
• *Todas muestran ejemplos de la cultura hispana en Estados Unidos.*
• *Puedes encontrar español en los carteles de algunas tiendas, en periódicos y revistas, en canales de televisión y estaciones de radio.*

Hispanic Presence in the United States

In 1995, there were 22 million people of Hispanic origin in the U.S. That makes this country the fifth-largest Spanish-speaking nation in the world!
Mexicans, Puerto Ricans, and Cubans make up the majority of the nation's Hispanic population. The largest number of Hispanics (63%) reside in the southwestern states of Arizona, California, Colorado, New Mexico, and Texas—an area that was Mexican territory until around 1850. Of the rest of the Hispanic population, most live in New York, Florida, Illinois, and New Jersey.

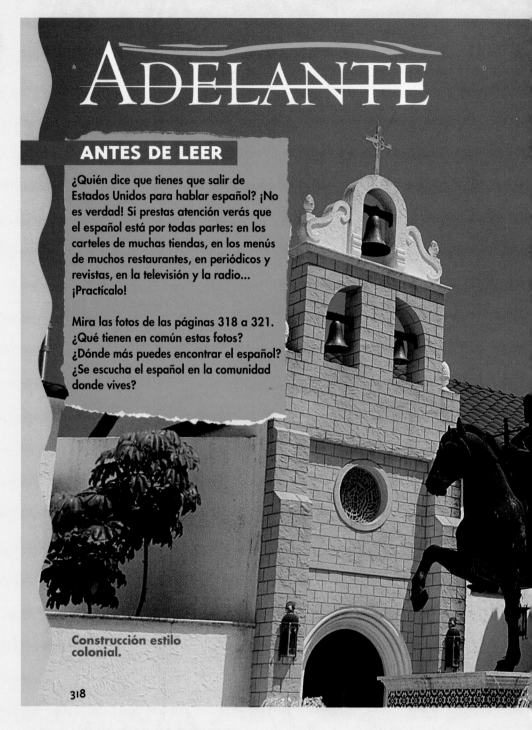

ADELANTE

ANTES DE LEER

¿Quién dice que tienes que salir de Estados Unidos para hablar español? ¡No es verdad! Si prestas atención verás que el español está por todas partes: en los carteles de muchas tiendas, en los menús de muchos restaurantes, en periódicos y revistas, en la televisión y la radio... ¡Practícalo!

Mira las fotos de las páginas 318 a 321. ¿Qué tienen en común estas fotos? ¿Dónde más puedes encontrar el español? ¿Se escucha el español en la comunidad donde vives?

Construcción estilo colonial.

318

ADELANTE COMPONENTS

Activity Book	Audio	Transparencies	Video: Tape/Book
p. 157-160	Adelante: 13A, 13B	Unit 6: Adelante	Unit 6 Seg. 4-5
Assessment	**Magazine**	Transparencies	
Portfolio: p. 43-44	Juntos en Estados Unidos	79-80	

◄En Estados Unidos hay muchos canales de televisión en español. Univisión es uno de ellos.

★ MENÚ DEL DÍA ★

CHAMPIÑONES CON CREMA

SOPA DE MÉDULA

NOPALITOS NAVEGANTES

O

TERNERA A LA NARANJA

POSTRE: GELATINA

CAFÉ O TÉ

◄¿No es divertido ir a un restaurante mexicano y saber qué dice el menú en español?

◄En el centro comunitario de Plaza de la Raza, en Los Ángeles, los chicos y las chicas pueden aprender bailes aztecas.

319

Using the Photos

Univisión
¿Cuál es el nombre de un canal de televisión en español?
¿Lo has visto alguna vez?
¿Has visto otros canales de televisión en español?
¿Qué programas tiene este canal?
¿De qué tipo de programa crees que es esta foto?

Mexican Restaurant Menu
¿Qué comida hay en este restaurante?
¿Sabes los nombres de algunos platos?
¿Has comido algunos de estos platos?
¿Los prepara tu familia?
¿Hay restaurantes mexicanos en nuestra comunidad?
¿Hay restaurantes que sirven comida de otros países hispanos? ¿Cuáles?

Aztec Dances
¿Qué hacen los jóvenes de la foto?
¿Has visto bailes aztecas? ¿Dónde?
¿De dónde eran los aztecas?
¿Están los jóvenes en México?
¿Conoces algunos bailes hispanos?

Objectives

Cultural: to learn about opportunities to hear, read, and speak Spanish in the US
Reading Strategy: to gain meaning from context

Related Components

Activity Book p. 157	Audio Adelante: 13A

GETTING STARTED

Ask students if they ever try to speak Spanish outside of school. Do they read, listen to, or watch any Spanish media?

Background

Hispanic Presence in the Media

Newspapers: There are more than 120 Spanish-language community papers published in the US, and nine major daily publications—three in San Antonio, two each in New York and Miami, and one each in Los Angeles and Chicago.
Magazines: There are more than 80 Spanish-language or Hispanic-theme magazines in the US.
Radio: Spanish-language radio in the US began back in the mid-1920s. Currently, there are 35 AM and 115 FM stations broadcasting full-time.
Television: The first Spanish-language television station in the US was San Antonio's KCOR, started in 1955. There are several Spanish "networks," notably Galavisión, which broadcasts continuously and reaches 28% of Hispanic households via 300 cable affiliations. A recent innovation in TV viewing among Spanish-speakers is HBO's *"Selecciones en español,"* which provides audio in Spanish for movies and sporting events.
It is believed that the growth of Spanish-language print and electronic media will strenghten the presence of the linguistic and cultural identity of Hispanics in the future.

DEL MUNDO HISPANO

¡Qué suerte ser bilingüe!

▲**Fíjate en los carteles y señales de la calle. En muchos lugares son bilingües, en inglés y español.**

Aprender español puede ser un poco duro° a veces, pero también puede ser divertido. Practicarlo sólo en clase no es suficiente°. Si de verdad quieres mejorar, tienes que aprovechar° todas las oportunidades para practicarlo. ¡Hay 300 millones de personas en el mundo con las que podrás comunicarte si hablas español!

¡Habla!

Seguro que° en tu comunidad hay alguien con quien puedes practicar tu español. Visita un centro comunitario hispano. Pide información sobre los programas que ofrece. Allí también puedes conocer chicos y chicas hispanos. Habla con ellos y no te preocupes si cometes errores: equivocarse° es una forma de aprender.

¡Escucha!

En Estados Unidos hay muchísimas estaciones de radio que tienen programas en español. Una de ellas es la KLAX, la estación número uno de Los Angeles. Escuchar la radio es una manera divertida de practicar español. Verás que, después de unos días, comprenderás muchas más cosas que al principio. Si te gusta la música, escucha canciones en español y presta atención a la letra.°

¡Lee!

¿Qué temas te interesan? ¿Te gusta la música, los deportes, el cine...? Si buscas un poco, encontrarás revistas en español sobre

▲**En Estados Unidos hay más de 120 periódicos en español. También hay cientos de revistas, de diferentes temas.**

aprovechar *to make the most of* duro *hard*	equivocarse *to make mistakes* la letra *lyrics*	seguro que *surely* suficiente *enough*

320

Identifying Main Ideas and Details

Have students notice that the subheadings in the text identify main ideas. With your students, construct a chart showing the main ideas and details of the passage.

Reading Aloud

Ask volunteers to take turns reading aloud the different sections of the article.

▲No importa la edad, ¡es emocionante poder leer una revista en español!

▲En Austin, Texas, el grupo de teatro Ánimo representa obras en inglés y en español.

tus temas favoritos. Además puedes estar informado de la actualidad leyendo uno de los más de 120 periódicos en español que hay en Estados Unidos. Visita cualquier° biblioteca. Leer te ayudará a aumentar° tu vocabulario y a comprender mejor las reglas de gramática sin que te des cuenta°.

¡Mira!

¿Te gusta el cine y la televisión? Hay cientos de películas en español que puedes alquilar en video o ver en el cine. Los subtítulos te ayudarán a entender las historias pero, muy pronto, verás que no necesitarás leerlos. Si te gusta el teatro, ve a ver alguna obra en español. Lee un poco sobre la obra antes de ir. Te ayudará a entender mejor la historia.° Si no quieres salir de casa, puedes poner uno de los más de 50 canales de televisión en español que tiene Estados Unidos, como MTV Latino, Telemundo, Univisión o Galavisión. ¡El español está siempre al alcance de tu mano!°

¡Toca!

Pon las manos sobre el teclado° de tu computadora y conéctate con todo un mundo en español. La Internet ofrece mucha información en español, especialmente a través de la World Wide Web. Prácticamente todos los países tienen información en línea. También puedes ponerte en contacto con chicos de países hispanohablantes mediante el correo electrónico. ¡Viaja por la Internet y deja que tus dedos te abran° las puertas de cualquier país!

al alcance de tu mano *within reach*
aumentar *to increase*
cualquier *any*
deja que tus dedos te abran
  let your fingers open

la historia *story line*
sin que te des cuenta *without realizing it*
el teclado *keyboard*

321

¡Escucha!
¿Dónde puedes escuchar español en Estados Unidos?
¿Dónde transmite la KLAX?
¿Es una estación popular?
¿Crees que es más fácil hablar o escuchar español?

¡Lee!
¿Cuántos periódicos en español hay en Estados Unidos?
¿Dónde puedes encontrar revistas y periódicos en español?
¿Has visto o leído un periódico o una revista en español? ¿Qué leíste?
¿Crees que es más fácil aprender español leyendo revistas o escuchando la radio y la televisión? ¿Por qué?

¡Mira!
¿Cómo puedes ver una película en español en Estados Unidos?
¿Cuántos canales de televisión en español hay en Estados Unidos?
¿Hay canales de televisión en español en nuestra comunidad?
¿Has visto algunos de sus programas?
¿De qué temas tratan?

¡Toca!
¿Cómo puedes usar tu computadora para practicar español?
¿Cómo puedes comunicarte directamente con chicos de países hispanohablantes?
¿Has usado el Internet para buscar información en español?
¿Te has comunicado por correo electrónico con chicos hispanohablantes?

CHECK

• Después de estudiar español en la escuela, ¿cómo puedes aprenderlo y practicarlo?

LOG BOOK
Have students list the communication verbs in this reading. For example: **hablar, practicar, comunicarse.**

DISCUSS

Suggestions for discussion:

Introducción
¿Dónde hay carteles bilingües?
¿Qué tienes que hacer para practicar español?
¿Viste un cartel? ¿Pudiste leerlo?
¿Cuántos hispanohablantes hay en el mundo?

¡Habla!
¿Has hablado alguna vez con un hispanohablante?
Si no, ¿te gustaría hacerlo?
¿Qué pasa si te equivocas?

Para hispanohablantes

Tell the class about the Spanish-language media that your friends and family watch, read, or listen to.

These activities can be done as classwork or as homework.

Objectives

Organizing Skills: to use lists; to do research, to organize information
Communication Skills: to make lists and to complete sentences

Related Components

Activity Book p. 158	Assessment Portfolio: p. 43-44

ACTIVITIES

1. Nuestro español

Pair Activity List ways you can improve your Spanish outside of the classroom.
Possible Answers: *escuchar la radio en español, leer periódicos en español, alquilar videos en español, ir al cine y ver películas en español, ver televisión en español, usar el Internet*

2. El español en mi vecindario

Individual Activity Do a study of places and media in your community where Spanish is spoken. Include local radio and TV, Spanish films from the video store, classified ads in Spanish, TV and radio guides, and papers and magazines in Spanish.
Answers: Information will vary.

3. Planes

Individual Activity Plan ways to improve your Spanish this summer.
Answers: See model on student text.

4. Ideas...

Individual Activity
Probable answers:
1. *conocer un mundo en español.*
2. *español.*
3. *una manera de aprender español.*
4. *aumentar tu vocabulario y comprender mejor la gramática.*
5. *aprender español viendo la televisión, escuchando la radio y usando el Internet y el correo electrónico.*

DESPUÉS DE LEER

❶ Nuestro español

Con tu compañero(a), haz una lista de las maneras de mejorar tu español fuera de la escuela.

-hablar con chicos y chicas hispanos
-leer revistas en español

❷ El español en mi vecindario

Haz una investigación sobre los lugares de tu vecindario donde te puedan ayudar a practicar español. Incluye además:
- estaciones de radio
- canales de televisión
- películas en español que hay en tu club de video
- revistas y periódicos en español que puedes comprar en el quiosco

❸ Planes

Haz un plan de las cosas que harás este verano para mejorar tu español. Usa la tabla como modelo.

EN CASA	FUERA DE CASA
leer	ir al cine

❹ Ideas...

Completa las oraciones según la información del artículo.
1. Con la Internet se puede...
2. Escuchando la radio se aprende...
3. Cometer errores es...
4. Leer en español ayuda a...
5. Sin salir de casa, puedes...

TALLER DE ESCRITORES

1 Tus metas

Escribe un párrafo sobre tus metas profesionales y personales. Explica qué quieres estudiar, por qué y dónde te gustaría trabajar.

Quiero estudiar química porque me gusta mucho hacer experimentos en el laboratorio. Después quiero trabajar en una farmacia.

2 Una carta

Con tu compañero(a) prepara una carta para pedir trabajo como voluntario en un centro comunitario de tu vecindario. Digan en qué han trabajado antes y qué aptitudes tienen.

Señor Director del
Centro Comunitario Latino:

Somos dos estudiantes de Abraham Lincoln High School. Queremos trabajar de voluntarios en el Centro comunitario latino. Antes hemos trabajado de niñeras y hemos sido consejeras en un campamento para jóvenes. Somos organizadas, responsables y serias. Nos gusta mucho trabajar y ayudar a otras personas. Le mandamos también nuestro currículum.

Muchas gracias por su atención.

Atentamente,

Laura López
Cristina Quiroga

3 Recomendaciones

Con tu compañero(a), haz un cartel con recomendaciones para prepararse para una entrevista de trabajo. Pueden decorar el cartel con fotografías de revistas y dibujos.

Para una entrevista es necesario que:

1 vayas bien vestido.

2

3

4

323

TALLER DE ESCRITORES

Objectives
- to practice writing
- to use vocabulary and structures from this unit

Related Components

Activity Book	Assessment
p. 159	Portfolio: p. 43-44

ACTIVITIES

1. Tus metas
Individual Activity Students will write a paragraph about what they would like to study, why, and where they would like to work. Encourage the use of the present subjunctive after impersonal expressions.
Extension: Collect papers and hand out at random. Students take turns reading the papers aloud without revealing the name of the writer. The class guesses the writer's identity.

2. Una carta
Pair Activity Students will write a letter asking for a chance to do volunteer work in a neighborhood community center. They should say what kinds of work they have done and what their aptitudes are.
Extension: Allow individuals the option of writing a letter of application for a job they are interested in.

3. Recomendaciones
Pair Activity Make a poster with recommendations for things to do before an interview.

PORTFOLIO
Suggest that students select one of these assignments for their Portfolios.

Para hispanohablantes

Do a variation of Activity 3: write about the best ways to learn a second language.

Objectives

Communicative: to listen to and understand directions
Cultural: to learn about the nature of some bilingual jobs

Related Components

Assessment	Video: Tape/Book
Portfolio: p. 43-44	Unit 6: Seg. 5
Transparencies	
Unit 6: Project	
Transparency 79	

Scan to La obra

Materials

- a camera
- a roll of film
- a pasteboard
- glue
- a labeler
- a tape recorder (optional)

GETTING STARTED

If possible, show the photo essay-making segment of the Unit 6 video.

DISCUSS

Read aloud the introductory text, then ask questions such as:
¿Qué son los reportajes fotográficos? ¿Cómo son?
¿Viste un reportaje fotográfico alguna vez? ¿Qué tema tenía?

Thinking About Language

Ask if students have thought about how many times we use familiar sayings or clichés instead of putting a thought in our own words. What are some of the more common ones in English?
Ask how the Spanish saying at the beginning of this reading differs from its English counterpart. (We say "a thousand words," they say "more than a thousand.")
Sayings can be a helpful way to learn Spanish.

They make it easier to remember how to say something, provide you with something to say when you don't know quite how to express yourself, and, because Spanish-speakers use them as much as anyone else, you will be able to understand people when they use them.

MANOS A LA OBRA

SU VIDA EN FOTOS

El refrán° dice que una imagen vale más que° mil palabras. Por eso muchas veces se usan fotografías para contar una historia, casi sin palabras. Los reportajes fotográficos son muy utilizados° en periódicos y revistas. En ellos las fotos son las protagonistas y el texto es muy corto.

TE TOCA A TI

Ahora tú harás tu propio reportaje fotográfico. El tema será un día de trabajo en la vida de una persona bilingüe. Piensa en alguien que tenga un trabajo relacionado con hablar dos o más idiomas y explica, con fotos, cómo es un día en su trabajo.

Materiales
- una cámara fotográfica
- un rollo de fotos
- una cartulina
- pegamento
- un marcador

1 Prepara una lista de preguntas relacionadas con el trabajo de tu personaje. Anótalas en un cuaderno.

2 Haz una entrevista a la persona escogida. Puedes grabar° sus respuestas o anotarlas.

3 Saca fotos de esa persona haciendo las diferentes actividades de su trabajo.

324

grabar *to record*
utilizados *used*
el refrán *saying*

vale más que *is worth more than*

HANDS-ON

Students will probably do this project as homework. To be sure they understand the directions, lead them through the various steps of the project.
1. As you act out each step, describe what you are doing.
2. After you have done this several times, invite volunteers to do it as you read.
3. Do this as TPR with the whole class.

CHECK

Have students perform the actions of photo essay-making as you describe them, but give the instructions in a different order.

LOG BOOK
Write down all the important action words used in this description of how to put together a photo essay.

Para hispanohablantes

Use your own words to demonstrate each step to the class.

4 Revela° las fotos y selecciona tus fotos favoritas.

5 Pega las fotos en una cartulina. Tienes que ponerlas en orden para explicar tu reportaje.

6 Escribe un pequeño párrafo° para cada foto.

párrafo *paragraph*
revela *develope*

OTRAS FRONTERAS

Objectives
- to expand reading comprehension
- to relate the study of Spanish to other subject areas

Related Components

Activity Book p. 160	**Transparencies** Unit 6: Adelante Transparency 80
Assessment Portfolio: p. 43-44	**Video: Tape/Book** Unit 6: Seg. 4
Audio Adelante: 13B	

Scan to Adelante

El Instituto Cervantes

About the Instituto Cervantes
The Instituto Cervantes, established in 1991, has centers in more than thirty cities. The first US center was in New York City, where the institute collaborates with universities and other institutions to organize film series, concerts, lectures, and other activities. Each institute has a library that includes books, videos, and other materials on Hispanic culture throughout the world.

The institute is named for Miguel de Cervantes (1547-1616), the author of *Don Quixote* and one of the most important figures in Spanish and world literature.
Note: The full title of the work commonly known as *Don Quixote* is *El ingenioso hidalgo Don Quijote de la Mancha.*

Activity
Have students say whether the following statements are true or false:
1. *En el Instituto Cervantes puedes encontrar libros en español. (Cierto)*
2. *El Instituto Cervantes fue fundado para enseñar español en Estados Unidos. (Falso; fue fundado para difundir la lengua y la cultura de España y otros países.)*
3. *El Instituto Cervantes sólo difunde la cultura de España. (Falso; también difunde la cultura de Hispanoamérica.)*
Ask the questions on the student page.
Possible Answers:
- *Es una organización fundada por el gobierno español para difundir la lengua y las culturas de España y de Hispanoamérica.*
- *Puedes encontrar películas, libros y música.*

CULTURA
EL INSTITUTO CERVANTES

¿Quieres ver una película en español? ¿Estás buscando alguna obra de la literatura española que no encuentras? ¿Quieres escuchar música de España? El Instituto Cervantes ofrece todas estas posibilidades y muchas más. Es una organización fundada por el gobierno español para difundir° la lengua y las culturas de España y también de Hispanoamérica. El Instituto prepara festivales de cine, conferencias y disertaciones° con escritores famosos. Hay delegaciones° del Instituto Cervantes en muchas ciudades de Estados Unidos.

- ¿Qué es el Instituto Cervantes?
- ¿Qué puedes encontrar en el Instituto Cervantes?

SOCIEDAD
LA CASA CENTRAL DE CHICAGO

La Casa Central es una agencia de servicios sociales. Es la más antigua de Chicago. Empezó como una institución de ayuda a los inmigrantes hispanos. Hoy tiene más de treinta programas, como guardería, residencia de ancianos y ayuda legal. La Casa Central también ofrece clases para niños y jóvenes, y tiene horarios nocturnos para la gente que trabaja de día. El objetivo de la Casa Central es que el inmigrante sea autosuficiente° dentro de la sociedad.

- ¿Qué ofrece la Casa Central?
- ¿Cuál es su objetivo?

las delegaciones *branches*
difundir *to spread*
las disertaciones *discussions*
autosuficiente *self-sufficient*

La Casa Central de Chicago

About Hispanic Chicago
The city of Chicago has over half a million people of Hispanic origin—more than San Antonio.
Ask the questions on the student page.
Possible Answers:
- *Ofrece servicios de guardería, residencia de ancianos y clases para niños y jóvenes.*
- *Su objetivo es que el inmigrante aprenda a ser autosuficiente.*

Activity
Have students say whether the following statements are true or false:
1. *La Casa Central ayuda a la comunidad. (Cierto)*
2. *Se ofrecen programas sólo para ancianos. (Falso; también ofrece clases para jóvenes, niños y adultos.)*
3. *La agencia cuida niños cuando sus padres trabajan. (Cierto)*

TEATRO

UN TEATRO SÓLO EN ESPAÑOL

En Nueva York hay un teatro que presenta obras en español. Se llama Repertorio Español y representa obras clásicas y contemporáneas de dramaturgos° hispanoamericanos y españoles. Allí podrás practicar tu español y aumentar tus conocimientos° sobre literatura, viendo obras como *Bodas de sangre* o *La vida es sueño.*

- ¿Qué presenta el Repertorio Español?
- ¿Cuál es la característica principal de este teatro?

ARTE RETRATOS° DE TEXAS

Carmen Lomas Garza es una artista *naïf* de Texas. El tema de sus cuadros es la vida cotidiana° y las tradiciones de Texas. En sus obras, Lomas Garza muestra° momentos de su vida y de la vida de su familia, como cumpleaños, ceremonias, fiestas tradicionales y escenas de la vida diaria. Ahora Carmen Lomas Garza vive en San Francisco pero viaja por todo el mundo mostrando a través de° sus cuadros cómo es la vida de los chicanos.

- ¿Cuál es el tema favorito de Carmen Lomas Garza?
- ¿Qué refleja la artista en sus obras?

a través de *through*
los conocimientos *knowledge*
los dramaturgos *playwrights*

muestra *shows*
los retratos *pictures*
la vida cotidiana *everyday life*

327

Un teatro sólo en español

About the Repertorio Español
The Repertorio Español is a small theater company, with a theater in a former townhouse on East 27th Street in New York. It was founded in 1968 and has produced more than 300 plays. On average, at least 12-14 plays are in repertory at any given time. One production, *Café con leche*, has run for eleven years.
Ask the questions on the student page.
Answers:
- *Representa obras clásicas y contemporáneas de dramaturgos hispanoamericanos y españoles.*
- *Presenta obras en español.*

Activity
As homework, have students research whether there are any Spanish-language performance groups in your area.

Retratos de Texas

About the Artist
Carmen Lomas Garza paints in a style reminiscent of Mexican primitive art.
Ask the questions on the student page.
Possible Answers:
- *La vida cotidiana y las tradiciones de Texas.*
- *Muestra momentos de su vida y de su familia.*

Activity
As classwork or homework, have students write a similar paragraph about their favorite artist.

Art Link: What types of events or scenes portray who you are? Draw one of these scenes.

Reading Aloud
Ask volunteers to take turns reading aloud the different articles in *Otras fronteras.*

VERBOS

Regular Verbs

Infinitive / Present Participle / Past Participle	Indicative Present	Imperfect	Preterite	Future	Subjunctive Present	Imperative
-ar verbs **comprar** comprando comprado	compro compras compra compramos compráis compran	compraba comprabas compraba comprábamos comprabais compraban	compré compraste compró compramos comprasteis compraron	compraré comprarás comprará compraremos compraréis comprarán	compre compres compre compremos compréis compren	compra / no compres compre compremos compren
-er verbs **comer** comiendo comido	como comes come comemos coméis comen	comía comías comía comíamos comíais comían	comí comiste comió comimos comisteis comieron	comeré comerás comerá comeremos comeréis comerán	coma comas coma comamos comáis coman	come / no comas coma comamos coman
-ir verbs **compartir** compartiendo compartido	comparto compartes comparte compartimos compartís comparten	compartía compartías compartía compartíamos compartíais compartían	compartí compartiste compartió compartimos compartisteis compartieron	compartiré compartirás compartirá compartiremos compartiréis compartirán	comparta compartas comparta compartamos compartáis compartan	comparte / no compartas comparta compartamos compartan

328

Irregular Verbs

Infinitive / Present Participle / Past Participle	Indicative Present	Imperfect	Preterite	Future	Subjunctive Present	Imperative
caer(se) cayendo caído	caigo caes cae caemos caéis caen	caía caías caía caíamos caíais caían	caí caíste cayó caímos caísteis cayeron	caeré caerás caerá caeremos caeréis caerán	caiga caigas caiga caigamos caigáis caigan	cae / no caigas caiga caigamos caigan
dar dando dado	doy das da damos dais dan	daba dabas daba dábamos dabais daban	di diste dio dimos disteis dieron	daré darás dará daremos daréis darán	dé des dé demos deis den	da / no dés dé demos den
decir diciendo dicho	digo dices dice decimos decís dicen	decía decías decía decíamos decíais decían	dije dijiste dijo dijimos dijisteis dijeron	diré dirás dirá diremos diréis dirán	diga digas diga digamos digáis digan	di / no digas diga digamos digan
destruir destruyendo destruido	destruyo destruyes destruye destruimos destruís destruyen	destruía destruías destruía destruíamos destruíais destruían	destruí destruiste destruyó destruimos destruisteis destruyeron	destruiré destruirás destruirá destruiremos destruiréis destruirán	destruya destruyas destruya destruyamos destruyáis destruyan	destruye / no destruyas destruya destruyamos destruyan
estar estando estado	estoy estás está estamos estáis están	estaba estabas estaba estábamos estabais estaban	estuve estuviste estuvo estuvimos estuvisteis estuvieron	estaré estarás estará estaremos estaréis estarán	esté estés esté estemos estéis estén	está / no estés esté estemos estén
hacer haciendo hecho	hago haces hace hacemos hacéis hacen	hacía hacías hacía hacíamos hacíais hacían	hice hiciste hizo hicimos hicisteis hicieron	haré harás hará haremos haréis harán	haga hagas haga hagamos hagáis hagan	haz / no hagas haga hagamos hagan

Verbos

Irregular Verbs

Infinitive / Present Participle / Past Participle	Indicative					Subjunctive	Imperative
	Present	Imperfect	Preterite	Future		Present	
ir(se) yendo ido	vas va vamos vais van	voy ibas iba íbamos ibais iban	iba fuiste fue fuimos fuisteis fueron	fui irás irá iremos iréis irán	iré vayas vaya vayamos vayáis vayan		vaya ve / no vayas vaya vayamos vayan
oír oyendo oído	oigo oyes oye oímos oís oyen	oía oías oía oíamos oíais oían	oí oíste oyó oímos oísteis oyeron	oiré oirás oirá oiremos oiréis oirán	oiga oigas oiga oigamos oigáis oigan		oye / no oigas oiga oigamos oigan
poner(se) poniéndo puesto	pongo pones pone ponemos ponéis ponen	ponía ponías ponía poníamos poníais ponían	puse pusiste puso pusimos pusisteis pusieron	pondré pondrás pondrá pondremos pondréis pondrán	ponga pongas ponga pongamos pongáis pongan		pon / no pongas ponga pongamos pongan
reír(se) riendo reído	río ríes ríe reímos reís ríen	reía reías reía reíamos reíais reían	reí reíste rió reímos reísteis rieron	reiré reirás reirá reiremos reiréis reirán	ría rías ría riamos riáis rían		ríe / no rías ría riamos rían
saber sabiendo sabido	sé sabes sabe sabemos sabéis saben	sabía sabías sabía sabíamos sabíais sabían	supe supiste supo supimos supisteis supieron	sabré sabrás sabrá sabremos sabréis sabrán	sepa sepas sepa sepamos sepáis sepan		sabe / no sepas sepa sepamos sepan
salir saliendo salido	salgo sales sale salimos salís salen	salía salías salía salíamos salíais salían	salí saliste salió salimos salisteis salieron	saldré saldrás saldrá saldremos saldréis saldrán	salga salgas salga salgamos salgáis salgan		sal / no salgas salga salgamos salgan

Irregular Verbs

Infinitive Present Participle Past Participle	Indicative					Subjunctive	Imperative
	Present	Imperfect	Preterite	Future		Present	
ser siendo sido	soy eres es somos sois son	era eras era éramos erais eran	fui fuiste fue fuimos fuisteis fueron	seré serás será seremos seréis serán		sea seas sea seamos seáis sean	sé / no seas sea seamos sean
tener teniendo tenido	tengo tienes tiene tenemos tenéis tienen	tenía tenías tenía teníamos teníais tenían	tuve tuviste tuvo tuvimos tuvisteis tuvieron	tendré tendrás tendrá tendremos tendréis tendrán		tenga tengas tenga tengamos tengáis tengan	ten / no tengas tenga tengamos tengan
traer trayendo traído	traigo traes trae traemos traéis traen	traía traías traía traíamos traíais traían	traje trajiste trajo trajimos trajisteis trajeron	traeré traerás traerá traeremos traeréis traerán		traiga traigas traiga traigamos traigáis traigan	trae / no traigas traiga traigamos traigan
venir viniendo venido	vengo vienes viene venimos venís vienen	venía venías venía veníamos veníais venían	vine viniste vino vinimos vinisteis vinieron	vendré vendrás vendrá vendremos vendréis vendrán		venga vengas venga vengamos vengáis vengan	ven / no vengas venga vengamos vengan
ver viendo visto	veo ves ve vemos veis ven	veía veías veía veíamos veíais veían	vi viste vio vimos visteis vieron	veré verás verá veremos veréis verán		vea veas vea veamos veáis vean	ve / no veas vea veamos vean

Verbos

331

Stem-Changing Verbs

Infinitive Present Participle Past Participle	Indicative				Subjunctive	Imperative
	Present	Imperfect	Preterite	Future	Present	
jugar (u > ue) jugando jugado	juego juegas juega jugamos jugáis juegan	jugaba jugabas jugaba jugábamos jugabais jugaban	jugué jugaste jugó jugamos jugasteis jugaron	jugaré jugarás jugará jugaremos jugaréis jugarán	juegue juegues juegue juguemos juguéis jueguen	juega / no juegues juegue juguemos jueguen
pedir (e > i) pidiendo pedido	pido pides pide pedimos pedís piden	pedía pedías pedía pedíamos pedíais pedían	pedí pediste pidió pedimos pedisteis pidieron	pediré pedirás pedirá pediremos pediréis pedirán	pida pidas pida pidamos pidáis pidan	pide / no pidas pida pidamos pidan
poder (o > ue) pudiendo podido	puedo puedes puede podemos podéis pueden	podía podías podía podíamos podíais podían	pude pudiste pudo pudimos pudisteis pudieron	podré podrás podrá podremos podréis podrán	pueda puedas pueda podamos podáis puedan	puede / no puedas pueda podamos puedan
querer (e > ie) queriendo querido	quiero quieres quiere queremos queréis quieren	quería querías quería queríamos queríais querían	quise quisiste quiso quisimos quisisteis quisieron	querré querrás querrá querremos querréis querrán	quiera quieras quiera queramos queráis quieran	quiere / no quieras quiera queramos quieran

Verbs with Spelling Changes

Infinitive / Present Participle / Past Participle	Indicative Present	Imperfect	Preterite	Future	Subjunctive Present	Imperative
conocer (c > zc) conociendo conocido	conozco conoces conoce conocemos conocéis conocen	conocía conocías conocía conocíamos conocíais conocían	conocí conociste conoció conocimos conocisteis conocieron	conoceré conocerás conocerá conoceremos conoceréis conocerán	conozca conozcas conozca conozcamos conozcáis conozcan	conoce / no conozcas conozca conozcamos conozcan
empezar (z > c) empezando empezado	empiezo empiezas empieza empezamos empezáis empiezan	empezaba empezabas empezaba empezábamos empezabais empezaban	empecé empezaste empezó empezamos empezasteis empezaron	empezaré empezarás empezará empezaremos empezaréis empezarán	empiece empieces empiece empecemos empecéis empiecen	empieza / no empieces empiece empecemos empiecen
leer (e > y) leyendo leído	leo lees lee leemos leéis leen	leía leías leía leíamos leíais leían	leí leíste leyó leímos leísteis leyeron	leeré leerás leerá leeremos leeréis leerán	lea leas lea leamos leáis lean	lee / no leas lea leamos lean
navegar (g > gu) navegando navegado	navego navegas navega navegamos navegáis navegan	navegaba navegabas navegaba navegábamos navegabais navegaban	navegué navegaste navegó navegamos navegasteis navegaron	navegaré navegarás navegará navegaremos navegaréis navegarán	navegaría navegues navegue naveguemos naveguéis naveguen	navega / no navegues navegue naveguemos naveguen
proteger protegiendo protegido	protejo proteges protege protegemos protegéis protegen	protegía protegías protegía protegíamos protegíais protegían	protegí protegiste protegió protegimos protegisteis protegieron	protegeré protegerás protegerá protegeremos protegeréis protegerán	proteja protejas proteja protejamos protejáis protejan	protege / no protejas proteja protejamos protejan

GLOSARIO ESPAÑOL-INGLÉS

The **Glossario Español-Inglés** contains almost all words from **Juntos Uno** and **Juntos Dos**, including vocabulary presented in the *Adelante* sections.

The number following each entry indicates the chapter in which the Spanish word or expression is first introduced. The letter *A* following an entry refers to the *Adelante* sections; the letter *E* refers to the *Encuentros* section in Level 1; a Roman numeral I indicates that the word was presented in **Juntos Uno**.

Most verbs appear in the infinitive form. Stem-changing verbs appear with the change in parentheses after the infinitive.

A

a *at; to, E*
  a la(s)... *at . . . (time), E*
  al (a+el=al) *to the, E*
  abajo *downstairs, I4*
el/la **abogado(a)** *lawyer, 12*
  abrazarse *to hug each other, 6*
el **abrigo** *coat, I6*
  abril *April, E*
  abrir *to open, I3*
  Abróchense los cinturones. *Fasten your seatbelts., 1*
el/la **abuelo(a)** *grandfather/ grandmother, E*
  aburrido(a) *boring, E*
  aburrirse *to get bored, 5*
  a.C. (antes de Cristo) *B.C. (before Christ), A2*
  acampar *to camp out, 2*
el **accidente** *accident, 3*
  los **accidentes geográficos** *topographical features, 2*
  Acción de Gracias *Thanksgiving 7*
el **aceite de oliva** *olive oil, 7*
la **aceituna** *olive, 7*
  aceptar *to accept, I10*
  acompañar *to accompany, A3*
  acostarse (o>ue) *to go to bed, 8*
  acostumbrarse *to get used to, A6*
la **actividad** *activity, E*
  la **actividad deportiva** *sports activity, 11*

activos(as) *active, A1*
el/la **actor/actriz** *actor/actress, 5*
las **actuaciones** *performances, 5*
  actuar *to act, 5*
  acuático(a) *aquatic, I5*
el **acuerdo** *treaty, A1*
  el **acuerdo de paz** *peace agreement, 3*
  adaptado(a) *adapted, I12*
  adecuado(a) *suitable, 10*
  además de *in addition to, 7*
  adiós *goodbye, E*
  admirar *to admire, I12*
el/la **adolescente** *teenager, 11*
  ¿Adónde? *Where?, I1*
  adquirir *to acquire, I11*
la **aduana** *customs, E*
la **aerolínea** *airline, 1*
el **aeropuerto** *airport, E*
  afeitarse *to shave, 9*
los/las **aficionados(as)** *fans, A5*
las **afueras** *suburbs, I4*
la **agencia** *agency, I11*
  la **agencia de intercambio estudiantil** *student exchange program agency, I11*
el/la **agente de aduanas** *customs officer, 1*
el/la **agente de migración** *immigration officer, 1*
  agosto *August, E*
el **agua mineral** *mineral water, I2*
el **aguacate** *avocado, I2*
el **agujero** *hole, A2*
  ahora *now, E*
el **aire** *air, I2*
  el **aire acondicionado** *air conditioner, 4*

  al aire libre *outdoors, I2*
el **ajedrez** *chess, I6*
el **ají (Argentina)** *pepper, 7*
  al alcance de tu mano *within your reach, A6*
  alegrarse *to be glad, 3*
la **alegría** *joy, A3*
el **alemán** *German (language), I7*
las **aletas** *flippers, I5*
la **alfombra** *rug, I4*
el **álgebra** *algebra, I7*
  algo *something, 3*
el **algodón** *cotton, 8*
  alguien *somebody; anybody, 3*
  algún *some; any, 3*
  alguno(a) *someone; anyone; some; any, 3*
la **alimentación** *feeding, A1*
  alimentarse bien *to eat healthfully, 10*
el **alimento** *food, A3*
el **almacén** *department store, I10*
la **almendra** *almond, 7*
la **almohada** *pillow, 1*
el **almuerzo** *lunch, E*
  alquilar *to rent, I5*
  alto(a) *tall; high, E*
  de alta competición *professional, A5*
la **altura** *height, I12*
el **aluminio** *aluminum, 11*
  amarillo(a) *yellow, E*
el **ámbar** *amber, A3*
  ambicioso(a) *ambitious, 12*
el **ambiente** *environment, 12*

la **ambulancia** *ambulance, 3*
América del Sur *South America, I11*
el/la **amigo(a)** *friend, E*
el **amor** *love, A2*
anaranjado(a) *orange, E*
ancho(a) *wide, A2*
el/la **anciano(a)** *senior citizen, 11*
el/la **anfitrión/anfitriona** *host, 3*
el **ángel** *angel, 5*
anidar *to nest, A1*
el **anillo** *ring, I10*
el **animal** *animal, 2*
el **aniversario** *anniversary, I3*
añadir *to add, 7*
el **año** *year, E*
el **Año Nuevo** *New Year, 7*
anoche *last night, I7*
antiguo(a) *ancient, I1*
el **anuncio** *advertisement; commercial, I9*
los **anzuelos** *hooks, A3*
apagar *to turn off, I9*
apagar un incendio *to put out a fire, 3*
el **aparato electrónico** *electronic appliance, I9*
aparecer *to appear, A5*
el **apellido** *last name, E*
aprender *to learn, I5*
aprovechar *to make the most of, A6*
la **aptitud** *quality, 12*
los **apuntes** *notes, I7*
aquí *here, E*
los **árabes** *Moors, A4*
el **árbol** *tree, I4*
el **archipiélago** *archipelago (group of islands), A5*
la **arena** *sand, I5*
los **aretes** *earrings, I10*
el **argumento** *plot, 6*
el **armario** *locker, I7*
el **aro** *ring, A2*
la **arquitectura** *architecture, 4*
arriba *upstairs, I4*
el **arroz** *rice, I2*
el **arte** *art, E*
las **artesanías** *arts and crafts, I1*
el **artículo** *article, I10*
el **asado** *barbecue, 7*
asar *to roast, 7*
las **asas** *handles, A4*
el **ascensor** *elevator, 4*
así *this way, A3*

el **asiento** *seat, 1*
el **asiento de pasillo** *aisle seat, 1*
el **asiento de ventanilla** *window seat, 1*
el/la **asistente social** *social worker, 12*
asistir *to take care of, 10*
el **aspecto** *appearance, 9*
la **aspiradora** *vacuum cleaner, 4*
la **aspirina** *aspirin, 10*
asustarse *to get scared, 3*
atar *to tie, A1*
la **atención médica** *medical assistance, 11*
atender (e>ie) *to assist, 11*
aterrizar *to land, 1*
atraer *to attract, A3*
el **atún** *tuna, I2*
los **audífonos** *headphones, 1*
el **auge** *rise, A5*
aumentar *to increase, A6*
aunque *even though, A3*
el **auto (Perú)** *car, I12*
el **autobús** *bus, E*
la **autopista** *expressway, 4*
la **autorización** *authorization; permission, I11*
autosuficiente *self-sufficient, A6*
el/la **auxiliar de vuelo** *flight attendant, 1*
la **avenida** *avenue, E*
averiguar *to find out, 1*
el **avión** *plane, I11*
en avión *by plane, I12*
ayer *yesterday, I7*
la **ayuda** *help, 4*
el **azúcar** *sugar, 7*
azul *blue, E*

B

el **bachillerato** *high school education, 12*
bailar *to dance, E*
el **baile** *dance, I8*
bajar *to turn down, I9; to drop, A1*
el **bajo** *bass, 5*
bajo(a) *short, E*
bajo en calorías *low in calories, 10*

el **baloncesto** *basketball, E*
la **balsa** *raft, 2*
la **banda de rock** *rock band, I8*
el **banquillo** *dugout, A3*
bañarse *to take a bath, I8*
la **bañera** *bathtub, I4*
el **baño María** *double boiler, 7*
barato(a) *inexpensive, I1*
la **barbacoa** *barbecue, I3*
bárbaro(a) (Argentina) *great; terrific, I11*
el **barco** *boat, I12*
barrer *to sweep, 7*
el **barrio** *neighborhood, A4*
de barro *made of clay, A2*
bastante *enough; quite, I5*
bastante bien *pretty well, I5*
la **basura** *trash, 2*
el **basurero** *garbage can, 11*
el/la **bateador(a)** *batter, A3*
la **batería** *drum set, 5*
el **batido** *milkshake, E*
batir *to beat, 7*
beber *to drink, I2*
la **bebida** *beverage, I2*
la **bebida alcohólica** *alcoholic beverage, 10*
las **becas** *fellowships, 12*
el **béisbol** *baseball, E*
el/la **benefactor(a)** *benefactor, 5*
besarse *to kiss each other, 6*
la **biblioteca** *library, I1*
la **bicicleta** *bicycle, I1*
bien *good; well; fine, E*
los **bienes manufacturados** *manufactured goods, 4*
¡Bienvenidos! *Welcome!, E*
bilingüe *bilingual, 12*
los **binoculares** *binoculars, 2*
la **biología** *biology, I7*
la **biomecánica** *biomechanics, A5*
el **bistec** *steak, I2*
blanco(a) *white, E*
la **blusa** *blouse, I8*
boca abajo *upside down, A2*
la **boda** *wedding, I3*
la **bodega** *grocery store, I10*
el **bolero** *bolero, I9*
el **boliche** *bowling alley, 5*
el **bolígrafo** *pen, E*
la **bolita** *marble, 6*
la **bolsa** *bag, I10*
el **bolso de mano** *handbag, I11*

el/la **bombero(a)** *firefighter, 3*
bonito(a) *pretty, E*
bordado(a) *embroidered, I10*
los **bordes** *edges, A4*
el/la **borinqueño(a)** *Puerto Rican, I5*
el **borrador** *eraser, E*
las **botas** *boots, I6*
   las **botas de montaña** *hiking boots, 2*
   las **botas de motorista** *motorcycle boots, 9*
   las **botas tejanas** *cowboy boots, I10*
el **bote a motor** *motorboat, I5*
la **botella** *bottle, 2*
el **botón** *button, 9*
el **broche** *pin, I10*
la **brújula** *compass, 2*
bucear *to (scuba) dive, I5*
el **buceo** *snorkeling, 2*
buen(o, a) *good, E*
   ¡Buen provecho! *Enjoy your meal!, I2*
   Buenas noches *Good evening; Good night, E*
   Buenas tardes *Good afternoon, E*
   Buenos días *Good morning, E*
buscar *to look for, I12*
los **buzos** *divers, 4*

C

el **caballero** *gentleman, E*
el **caballo** *horse, 8*
la **cabeza** *head, 3*
cada *each, I6*
la **cadena** *chain, 3*
las **caderas** *hips, A2*
caerse *to fall down; to collapse, 3*
el **café** *coffee, I2*
la **cafetería** *cafeteria, E*
la **caja** *box, 7*
el/la **cajero(a)** *cashier, 12*
el **calcio** *calcium, 10*
la **calcomanía (Rep. Dominicana)** *sticker, 6*
la **calculadora** *calculator, I7*
el **calendario** *calendar, E*
calentar *to heat, 7*
la **calidad** *quality, 9*

caliente *hot, I2*
la **calle** *street, E*
el **calzado** *footwear, 9*
la **cama** *bed, I4*
la **cámara** *camera, I10*
   la **cámara cinematográfica** *movie camera, 4*
   la **cámara de video** *video camera, 4*
cambiar *to exchange; to change, I10*
   cambiar dinero *to exchange money, I11*
   cambiar el canal *to change the channel, I9*
caminar *to walk, I1*
el **camión** *truck, 8*
la **camisa** *shirt, I8*
   la **camisa sin mangas** *sleeveless shirt, 9*
la **camiseta** *T-shirt, E*
el **campamento de verano** *summer camp, 12*
el **campeonato** *championship, 3*
el/la **campesino(a)** *peasant, 1*
el **campo** *countryside, I4*
la **caña** *straw, A4*
   la **caña de azúcar** *sugar cane, 8*
   la **caña de pescar** *fishing pole, 6*
el **canal** *channel, I9*
la **canasta** *basket (as in basketball), I7*
la **canción** *song, 5*
el **candelero** *candleholder, A2*
el **cañón** *canyon, I12*
cansado(a) *tired, I12*
el/la **cantante** *singer, 5*
cantar *to sing, I1*
las **cantidades** *quantities, 7*
la **cantimplora** *canteen, 2*
la **capa** *layer, A2*
el **capataz** *foreman, 8*
la **capital** *capital, E*
el **capítulo** *chapter, I7*
la **caravana** *trailer, I4*
caribeños(as) *Caribbean, 5*
la **carne** *meat, I2*
   la **carne picada** *ground meat, 7*
caro(a) *expensive, I2*
la **carpeta** *folder; binder, I7*
las **carreras** *races, 8*

la **carretera resbaladiza** *slippery road, 8*
el **carrito** *toy car, 6*
el **carro de bomberos** *firetruck, 3*
la **carta** *letter, I11*
el **cartel** *poster, E*
la **casa** *house, I3*
   en casa *at home, I4*
el **casco** *helmet, 2*
casi *almost, I10*
castaño(a) *brunette, E*
el **castillo** *castle, IA1*
las **cataratas** *waterfalls, I12*
el **catarro** *cold, 10*
la **catedral** *cathedral, I12*
catorce *fourteen, E*
el **caucho** *rubber, A2*
causar *to cause, 3*
   a causa de *because of, 4*
la **cebolla** *onion, 7*
ceder el paso *to yield, 8*
CEE *EC (European Community), A5*
la **celebración** *celebration, I3*
celebrar *to celebrate, I3*
el **cemento** *cement, 4*
la **cena** *dinner, I2*
la **ceniza** *ashes, A4*
el **centímetro** *centimeter, I12*
el **centro** *center, 2; downtown, I1*
   el **centro comercial** *shopping center, I1*
   el **centro comunitario** *community center, 11*
   el **centro cultural** *cultural center, 5*
   el **Centro de Alto Rendimiento** *High Performance Center, 10*
   el **centro de jubilados** *center for retired people, 11*
   el **centro de reciclaje** *recycling center, 11*
   el **centro deportivo** *sports center, 11*
   el **centro recreativo** *recreational center, 11*
cepillar *to brush, 8*
   cepillarse (los dientes) *to brush (one's teeth), I8*
el **cepillo** *brush, 8*
   el **cepillo de dientes** *toothbrush, E*

la **cerámica** *ceramics, 11*
cerca *nearby, I1*
cerca de *near, I4*
el **cerdo** *pig, 8*
el **cereal** *cereal, I2*
el **cero** *zero, E*
cerrar *to close, 4*
cerro *hill, 4*
el **certificado** *certificate, I11*
el **certificado de estudios** *school transcript, I11*
el **certificado médico** *health certificate, I11*
el **chaleco** *vest, I8*
el **chaleco salvavidas** *life jacket, I5*
el **champú** *shampoo, E*
la **chaqueta** *jacket, I8*
chau *bye, E*
¡ché! (Argentina) *hey!, 7*
el **cheque** *check, I10*
el **cheque de viajero** *traveler's check, I11*
chicano(a) *Mexican-American, IA5*
el/la **chico(a)** *boy; girl, E*
las **chinchetas** *tacks, A3*
el **chiste** *joke, 5*
chocar *to crash, 3*
el **chocolate** *chocolate, I2*
cien *one hundred, E*
los/las **científicos(as)** *scientists, A1*
la **cima** *top, A2*
cinco *five, E*
cincuenta *fifty, E*
el **cine** *movie, E*
el **cinturón** *belt, I10*
la **cita** *date, 6*
la **ciudad** *city, E*
el/la **ciudadano(a)** *citizen, 11*
¡Claro! *Of course!, I3*
la **clase** *classroom; class, E*
clavar *to nail, A3*
el/la **cliente/clienta** *client, I2*
la **clínica** *clinic, 11*
el **coche** *car, I1*
en coche *by car, I1*
la **cocina** *kitchen, I4*
cocinar *to cook, E*
el/la **cocinero(a)** *cook, 7*
el **código postal** *zip code, E*
los **codos** *elbows, A2*
el **codo de tenista** *tennis elbow, 10*
coger *to catch, 6*

la **colección** *collection, 6*
coleccionar *to collect, 6*
el **collar** *necklace, I10*
el **color** *color, E*
los **colores vivos** *vivid colors, A4*
el **colorido** *coloring, A2*
columpiarse *to swing, 6*
el **columpio** *swing, 6*
combinar *to combine, 10*
el **comedor** *dining room, I4*
comer *to eat, E*
cómico(a) *funny, I9*
el/la **cómico(a)** *comedian/comedienne, 5*
la **comida** *food; meal; dish, I2*
la **comida (México)** *lunch, I2*
la **comida rápida** *fast food, I2*
el **comienzo** *beginning, A4*
como *like, 9*
¿Cómo? *How?, E*
la **cómoda** *chest of drawers, I4*
cómodo(a) *comfortable, 4*
la **compañía** *company, 12*
comparar *to compare, 1*
el **compartimiento de arriba** *overhead bin, 1*
compartir (e>i) *to share, I2*
competir *to compete, A5*
la **composición** *composition, I7*
comprar *to buy, I1*
las **compras** *purchases, I10*
de compras *shopping, E*
comprender *to understand, I7*
la **computadora** *computer, E*
comunicativo(a) *communicative, 12*
la **comunidad** *community, 11*
con *with, E*
el **concierto** *concert, I1*
la **condición** *condition, 12*
el/la **conductor(a)** *driver, 12*
conectados(as) *connected, 4*
el **conejo** *rabbit, 8*
la **conferencia** *lecture, 5*
conmigo *with me, I1*
conocer *to know, I3*
los **conocimientos** *knowledge, A6*
el/la **consejero(a)** *counselor, I11*

el **consejo** *advice, I6*
conservar *to preserve, 2*
construir *to build, 3*
el **consulado** *consulate, I11*
la **contaminación** *pollution, 11*
contarse cuentos *to tell each other stories, 6*
contemporáneos(as) *contemporary, 5*
el **contenedor** *container, 11*
contento(a) *glad; happy, I12*
el **contestador automático** *answering machine, I8*
contestar *to answer, I1*
contigo *with you, I1*
continuamente *continually, 6*
contratar *to sign up, A3; to hire, 8*
el **control de seguridad** *security check, 1*
el **control remoto** *remote control, I9*
convertir(se) en *to become, A3; to turn into, A4*
la **coordinación** *coordination, 10*
el **corazón** *heart, A2*
la **corbata** *necktie, I10*
el **cordero** *lamb, 7*
la **cordillera** *mountain range, I12*
el **coro** *choir, I7*
la **corporación** *corporation, 5*
el **corral** *corral, 8*
el **correo** *post office, I4*
el **correo electrónico** *e-mail, 4*
el **correo urgente** *express/next-day mail, 4*
por correo *by mail, I4*
correr *to run, 10*
cortar *to cut, A2*
cortarse el pelo *to get a haircut, 9*
cortarse las uñas *to cut one's nails, 9*
No corte las flores. *Don't pick the flowers., 2*
el **corte de pelo** *haircut, 9*
el **corte a navaja** *razor cut, 9*
cortés *courteous, I11*

corto(a) *short, E*
la **cosa** *thing, E*
la **cosecha** *crop, 8*
costar (o>ue) *to cost, I8*
la **costumbre** *habit, 6; custom, I11*
crear *to create, I1*
creativo(a) *creative, 12*
crecer *to grow up, A1*
creer *to believe, A3*
la **cremallera** *zipper, 9*
cremoso(a) *creamy, 7*
criar *to breed, A2*
la **Cruz Roja** *Red Cross, 3*
el **cuaderno** *notebook, E*
a cuadros *checkered, 9*
¿Cuál(es)? *what; which, E*
cualquier *any, A6*
¿Cuándo? *When?, E*
¿Cuánto(a, os, as)? *How much?; How many?, E*
¿Cuánto cuesta(n)? *How much does it/do they cost?, E*
¿Cuánto mide(n)? *How tall is it/are they?, I12*
¿Cuánto tiempo hace que? *How long ago?, 7*
¿Cuántos años tienes? *How old are you?, E*
cuarenta *forty, E*
el **cuarto** *room, I4*
el **cuarto de baño** *bathroom, I4*
cuatro *four, E*
cuatrocientos(as) *four hundred, E*
cubano(a) *Cuban, I10*
cubrir *to cover, A1*
la **cuchara** *spoon, I2*
el **cuchillo** *knife, I2*
el **cuello** *neck, 10*
el **cuento** *short story, I7*
el **cuento de miedo** *scary story, 6*
la **cuerda** *rope, 6*
el **cuero** *leather, I10*
de cuero *made of leather, I10*
el **Cuerpo de Paz** *Peace Corps, 12*
cuidar *to take care of, 2*
cultivar la tierra *to till the soil, 8*
la **cultura** *culture, I11*
el **cumpleaños** *birthday, E*

cumplir... años *to turn ... years old, 6*
el **currículum** *resumé, 12*

D

la **dama** *lady, E*
danés/danesa *Danish, A5*
la **danza** *dance, 5; dancing, 11*
danzas criollas *Argentinian dance, 8*
dar *to give, I10*
dar de comer a los animales *to feed the animals, 8*
dar la bienvenida *to welcome, 3*
dar un discurso *to give a speech, 3*
d.C. (después de Cristo) *A.D. (after Christ), A2*
de *of; from, E*
¿De dónde eres? *Where are you from?, E*
¿De qué color es? *What color is it?, E*
¿De qué es? *What is it made of?, I10*
del (de+el=del) *of/from the, I1*
debajo de *under, I4*
deber (de) *to have (to); to ought (to), I6*
décimo(a) *tenth, 12*
decir (e>i) *to say; to tell, I11*
Di no a las drogas. *Say no to drugs., 10*
¡No me digas! *Is that so?, 3*
decorar *to decorate, I3*
los **dedos** *fingers, A2*
defender *to defend, A5*
la **defensa personal** *self-defense, 10*
dejar *to leave behind, 5*
delante de *in front of, I4*
las **delegaciones** *branches, A6*
delicioso(a) *delicious, I2*
dentro de *inside, I4*
el **deporte** *sport, E*
los/las **deportistas** *athletes, 10*
deportivo(a) *casual, 9*

la **derecha** *right (side), E*
derecho *straight, I1*
el **desayuno** *breakfast, I2*
descansar *to rest, 10*
descifrar *to decipher, 3*
descremado(a) *fat free, 10*
descubrir *to discover, I1*
el **descuento** *discount, 1*
desear *to desire; to wish, I2*
el **desfile** *parade, 5*
el **desierto** *desert, I12*
despegar *to take off, 1*
después *after, E*
destruir *to destroy, 3*
la **desventaja** *disadvantage, 4*
los **detalles** *details, 6*
detrás de *behind, I4*
devolver (o>ue) *to give back; to return, I10*
el **día** *day, E*
dibujar *to draw, E*
los **dibujos** *drawings, 5*
los **dibujos animados** *cartoons, I9*
el **diccionario** *dictionary, E*
diciembre *December, E*
diecinueve *nineteen, E*
dieciocho *eighteen, E*
dieciséis *sixteen, E*
diecisiete *seventeen, E*
los **dientes** *teeth, I8*
diez *ten, E*
diez mil *ten thousand, I8*
difícil *difficult, E*
la **difusión** *diffusion, 5*
el **dinero** *money, 5*
el **dinero en efectivo** *cash, I10*
los **dioses** *gods, A2*
la **dirección** *address, E*
la **dirección obligatoria** *detour, 8*
dirigir *to direct, A4*
dirigirse a *to address someone, 7*
disciplinado(a) *disciplined, 12*
el **disco compacto** *compact disc; CD, I1*
la **discoteca** *disco; dance club, I1*
los/las **diseñadores(as)** *designers, 9*
el **diseño** *design, 9*
las **disertaciones** *dissertations, A6*

338

el **disfraz (los disfraces)** costume(s), A5

la **diversidad biológica** biological diversity, 2

la **diversidad étnica** ethnic diversity, A1

divertido(a) fun; funny; amusing, E

divertirse (e>ie) to have fun, I11

doce twelve, E

el **documental** documentary, I9

el **documento** document, I11

el **dólar** dollar, E

doler to hurt, 10

Me duele la cabeza. I have a headache., 10

Me duele... My . . . hurts, 10

¿Qué te duele? What is hurting you?, 10

la **doma** rodeo show, 8

el/la **domador(a)** horse breaker, 8

domar to tame, 8

el **domingo** Sunday, E

el **donativo** donation, 11

¿Dónde? Where?, E

dormir (o>ue) to sleep, 10

dormirse (o>ue) to fall asleep, 5

el **dormitorio** bedroom, I4

dos two, E

dos mil two thousand, E

doscientos two hundred, E

el/la **dramaturgo(a)** playwright, 11

ducharse to take a shower, I8

dulce sweet, I2

la **duración** duration, I11

durante during, 1

durar to last, A2

duro(a) hard, A6

E

e and (before a word that starts with an i), 11

el **ecoturismo** ecotourism, 2

la **edad** age, 4

la **edad de oro** golden age, A2

---

el **edificio de oficinas** office building, 4

la **educación física** physical education, E

educativo(a) educational, I9

EE.UU. U.S., I10

el/la **ejecutivo(a)** business man/business woman, 12

los **ejemplares** copies, A5

el **ejercicio** exercise, 10

el **ejército** army, A1

ejemplo example, 3

el **the**, E

él he, E

la **elección** election, 3

los **elefantes marinos** elephant seals, A4

elegante elegant, 9

ella she, E

ellos(as) they, E

la **emergencia** emergency, 1

en caso de emergencia in case of an emergency, 1

emocionante exciting, I5

emocionarse to be moved, 3

la **empanada** small meat or vegetable pie, 7

empañarse to fog up, 4

empezar (e>ie) to begin, I7

empinado(a) steep, A2

el/la **empleado(a)** employee, 1

el **empleo** job, 12

emprendedor(a) self-starter, 12

en in/on/at, E

enamorarse to fall in love, 6

encantar to love; to delight, I5

Encantado(a). Nice to meet you., I3

¡Me encanta! I love it!, I5

encender (e>ie) to turn on, I9

encontrar (o>ue) to find, E

encontrarse (o>ue) to meet each other, I8

el **encuentro** meeting, 3

enero January, E

enfermo(a) ill; sick, I7

el/la **enfermo(a)** sick (person), 11

enojarse to get angry, 6

enormemente enormously, 6

la **ensalada** salad, I2

---

el/la **ensayista** essayist, 4

enseguida immediately; at once, 6

enseñar to teach, A1

enterarse to learn about, 3

entrar to enter, 4

entre between, I4

el/la **entrenador(a)** trainer; coach, 12

entrenar to train; to coach, 10

entretenido(a) entertaining, I9

la **entrevista** interview, E

envolver to wrap, A1

el **equipaje** baggage, 1

el **equipo de sonido** sound equipment, 5

equivocarse to make mistakes, A6

Es la.../Son las... It's . . . o'clock, E

la **escalera** stepaeorbics, 10

escaparse to run away, 8

escaso(a) rare, A3

la **escena** scene, 1

el **escenario** stage, 5

la **escoba** broom, 4

escoger to choose, E

esconder to hide, 6

escribir to write, I2

escribir un diario to keep a diary, I12

el **escritorio** desk, E

escuchar to listen to, E

la **escuela** school, E

la **escultura** sculpture, IA2

ese(a, o, os, as) that; those, I10

ése(a, o, os, as) that; that one; those, 9

las **esferas** spheres, A1

el **esnórquel** snorkel, I5

España Spain, I7

español(a) from Spain, E

el **español** Spanish (language), E

especial special, I3

especializados(as) specialized, 10

las **especies** species, 2

las **especies en peligro de extinción** endangered species, 2

espectacular spectacular, I12

el **espectáculo** show, I12

la **gente sin hogar**
homeless people, 11

la **geografía** *geography,* E

la **geometría** *geometry,* I7

el/la **gerente** *manager,* 12

el **gimnasio** *gym,* E

el **globo** *balloon,* I3

golpear *to hit,* 6

la **gomina** *styling gel,* 9

el/la **gorro(a)** *hat; cap,* I6

la **grabadora** *tape recorder,* A6

grabar *to record,* A6

gracias *thank you; thanks,* E
gracias a *thanks to,* 7

gracioso(a) *funny,* 5

el **grado** *degree
(temperature),* I6

la **graduación** *graduation,* I3

el **gramo** *gram,* 7

grande *large,* E

granero *barn,* 8

la **granja** *farm,* I4

el/la **granjero(a)** *farmer,* 8

la **grasa** *fat,* 10

gratis *free,* 1

la **gripe** *flu,* 10

gris *gray,* E

el **grupo musical** *musical
group ,* 5

los **guantes** *gloves,* I6

guapo(a) *handsome; pretty;
good-looking,* E

la **guardería** *day-care center,* 11

la **guerra civil** *civil war,* 1

el **guerrero** *warrior,* A4

el/la **guía de turismo** *tour
guide,* 12

la **guía turística** *travel guide,*
I12

la **guitarra** *guitar,* I3
la **guitarra eléctrica**
electric guitar, 5

gustar *to like; to be pleasing
to,* I2

H

hablar *to speak; talk,* E

hacer *to be (with weather
expressions),* I6

hace buen tiempo *the
weather is nice,* I6

hace calor *it's hot,* I6

hace fresco *it's cool,* I6

hace frío *it's cold,* I6

hace mal tiempo *the
weather is bad,* I6

hace sol *it's sunny,* I6

hace viento *it's windy,* I6

hace... que *it's been . . .
since,* 7

hacer *to do; to make,* I3

hacer abdominales *to do
sit-ups,* 10

hacer aerobics *to do
aerobics,* 10

hacer bicicleta *to do
stationary bicycle,* 10

hacer caminatas *to hike,* 2

hacer cinta *to treadmill,* 10

hacer cola *to wait on line,* 5

hacer ejercicio *to
exercise,* 10

hacer escalera *to do stair
climber,* 10

hacer flexiones *to do
push-ups,* 10

hacer el itinerario
to plan the itinerary, I11

hacer la maleta *to pack
the suitcase,* I11

hacer la reserva de avión
*to make plane
reservations,* I11

hacer los trámites *to do
the paperwork,* I11

hacer pesas *to lift
weights,* 10

hacer una reserva *to
make a reservation,* 1

hacerse las uñas *to do
one's nails,* 9

No haga fogatas. *Don't
make bonfires,* 2

hacia *toward,* 2

el **hambre** *hunger,* I2

la **hamburguesa** *hamburger,* E

la **harina** *flour,* 7

hasta *till,* 2
Hasta luego. *See you
later.,* E
Hasta mañana. *See you
tomorrow.,* E

hay *there is/there are,* E
Hay que... *One has
to/must . . . ,* 8

hecho(a) *done,* 7

el **helado (de vainilla)**
(vanilla) ice cream, I2

¡Hola! *Hi; Hello!,* E

la **herencia** *heritage,* I7

el/la **hermano(a)** *brother; sister,* E

los **hermanos** *brothers
and sisters; siblings,* E

hermoso(a) *beautiful,* I12

la **herramienta** *tool,* 1

hervir (e>ie) *to boil,* 7

hibernar *to hibernate,* A2

los **hidratos de carbono**
carbohydrates, 10

el **hielo** *ice,* I6

el/la **hijo(a)** *son/daughter,* I3

los **hijos** *children,* I3

hispano(a) *Hispanic,* I4

la **historia** *history,* E

las **historietas** *comics,* I9

las **hojas** *leaves,* A2

los/las **holandeses(as)**
Dutch, 4

el **hombre** *man,* I6

el **hombro** *shoulder,* 10

honesto(a) *honest,* 12

la **hora** *time; hour,* E
¿A qué hora? *At what
time?,* E
¿Qué hora es? *What time
is it?,* E

el **horario** *schedule,* E
el **horario fijo** *regular
schedule,* 12

el **horno** *oven,* 4
el **horno de leña** *wood
burning oven,* 4
el **horno microondas**
microwave oven, 4

horrible *awful; horrible,* I2

el **hospital** *hospital,* 3

la **hospitalidad** *hospitality,* I5

el **hotel** *hotel,* I4

hoy *today,* E

hubo *there was/there were,* 3

el **huerto** *fruit and vegetable
garden,* 8

los **huevos** *eggs,* I2
los **huevos duros**
hard-boiled eggs, 7
los **huevos fritos** *fried
eggs,* 7
los **huevos revueltos**
scrambled eggs, 7

humedecer *to dampen,* A2

húmedos(as) *humid,* A1

hundidos(as) *sunken,* 4

hundir *to sink,* A4

el **huracán** *hurricane,* I6

I

la **idea** *idea, E*
ideal *ideal, I4*
el **idioma** *language, I11*
la **iglesia** *church, I1*
el **imperio** *empire, I11*
el **impermeable** *raincoat, I6*
la **importación** *import, 12*
importante *important, 8*
impresionante *awesome; impressive, I12*
el **incendio** *fire, 3*
incluir *to include, E*
increíble *amazing; incredible, 12*
la **independencia** *independence, 12*
independiente *independent, 12*
las **indicaciones** *instructions, 2*
la **información** *information, E*
la **informática** *computer science, I7*
informativo(a) *informative, I9*
el **informe** *report, I7*
la **infusión** *herb tea; infusion, A4*
el **inglés** *English (language), E*
inmortalizar *to immortalize, A4*
innecesario *unnecessary, 11*
el **inodoro** *toilet, I4*
la **inscripción** *membership, 5*
el **instrumento** *instrument, IA2*
inteligente *intelligent, E*
intentar *to attempt to, 6*
interesante *interesting, E*
el/la **intérprete** *interpreter, 12*
introducir *to introduce, A3*
la **inundación** *flood, 3*
el **invento** *invention, A2*
el **invierno** *winter, I6*
la **invitación** *invitation, I3*
el/la **invitado(a)** *guest, I3*
invitar *to invite, I3*
ir *to go, I1*
ir al extranjero *to go abroad, I11*
ir de campamento *to go camping, 2*
ir de excursión *to go on an outing, 2*
ir de pesca *to go fishing, 6*
irse *to go away; to leave, 10*
la **isla** *island, I5*
el **italiano** *Italian (language), I2*
el **itinerario** *itinerary, I11*
la **izquierda** *left, E*

J

el **jabón** *soap, E*
el **jamón** *ham, I2*
el **japonés** *Japanese (language), 12*
el **jardín** *garden, I4*
el/la **jardinero(a)** *gardener, 8*
el **jazz** *jazz, I9*
los **jeroglíflicos** *hieroglyphics, 3*
la **jornada completa** *full-time, 12*
joven *young, E*
los **jóvenes** *young people, I1*
la **joya** *jewel, I10*
la **joyería** *jewelry store, I10*
el/la **jubilado(a)** *retired person, 11*
el **juego** *game, 6*
el **jueves** *Thursday, E*
las **jugadas** *plays, A3*
los/las **jugadores(as)** *players, A3*
jugar (u>ue) *to play, I6*
jugar al escondite *to play hide-and-seek, 6*
jugar al rescate *to play tag, 6*
el **jugo** *juice, I2*
julio *July, E*
junio *June, E*
junto a *next to; by, I1*
juntos(as) *together, E*

K

el **kilo** *kilo, I12*

L

la(s) *the, E; her/it/(them), I9*
los **labios** *lips, 3*
el **laboratorio** *laboratory, I7*
la **laca** *hair spray, 9*
el **lado** *side, I4*
a todos lados *everywhere, 9*
al lado de *next to, I4*
de lado a lado *from side to side, 5*
las **lagunas** *lagoons, A2*
la **lámpara** *lamp, I4*
la **lana** *wool, I12*
de lana *made of wool, I12*
el **lanzamiento** *throw, A3*
lanzar *to pitch; to throw, I5*
el **lápiz** *pencil, E*
largo(a) *long, E*
a lo largo (de) *along, I4*
lástima *shame, E*
la **lata** *can, 2*
latino(a) *of Latin descent, IA4*
el **lavaplatos** *dishwasher, I4*
lavar los platos *to wash the dishes, 7*
lavarse (el pelo) *to wash (one's hair), I8*
el **lazo** *lasso, 8*
le *to/for him, her, it, you, I10*
la **leche** *milk, I2*
el **lecho del río** *riverbed, A4*
los **lechones** *suckling pigs, 6*
la **lechuga** *lettuce, I2*
la **lectura de poesía** *poetry reading, 5*
leer *to read, E*
lejos *far, I1*
lejos de *far from, I4*
la **lengua** *language, IA1*
lentamente *slowly, 6*
las **lentejas** *lentils, 10*
los **lentes de sol** *sunglasses, I5*
lento(a) *slow, I9*
les *to/for them, you, I10*
lesionados(as) *injured, 10*
las **letras** *lyrics, 5*
levantarse *to get up, 8*
la **librería** *bookstore, I1*
el **libro** *book, E*
la **Liga** *League, A5*
la **limonada** *lemonade, E*
limpiar la mesa *to clean off the table, 7*
limpio(a) *clean, 4*
liso(a) *plain, 9*
la **lista** *list, I3*
listo(a) *ready, I8*
la **literatura** *literature, E*
el **litro** *liter, 7*
llamar *to call, I8*
llamar por teléfono *to phone, I8*

llamarse *to be named, E*
te llama la atención
attracts your attention, A4
las **llaves** *keys, I8*
la **llegada** *arrival, 1*
llegar *to arrive, I7; to reach, A2*
llenar *to fill out, I11*
lleno(a) de *full of, 2*
llevar *to carry; to bring, I5; to wear; to take, I6*
llevarse... *to get along . . . , 6*
llover (o>ue) *to rain, I6*
Llueve a cántaros. *It's raining cats and dogs., I6*
la **lluvia** *rain, I6*
lluviosos(as) *rainy, A1*
Lo siento, no puedo. *I'm sorry, I can't., I3*
lo(s) *him/it/(them), I9*
los **los** *the, E*
en lugar de *instead of, 7*
a lunares *polka dots, 9*
el **lunes** *Monday, E*
los **lunes (martes, etc.)** *on Mondays (Tuesdays, etc.), E*
la **luz** *light, A3*

M

la **madera** *wood, I12*
de madera *made of wood, I12*
la **madrastra** *stepmother, E*
la **madre** *mother, E*
la **madrina** *godmother, I3*
el/la **maestro(a)** *teacher, I2*
el **maíz** *corn, 8*
mal *badly, 6*
en mal estado *in bad shape, A1*
la **maleta** *suitcase, I11*
el/la **maletero(a)** *baggage handler, 1*
la **mamá** *mom, E*
el **mamey** *a tropical apricot-like fruit, I10*
mañana *tomorrow, E*
la **mañana** *morning, E*
de la mañana *in the morning, E*
mandar *to send, 4*

Mándalo por... *Send it by . . . , 4*
manejar *to drive, 8*
manejar el tractor *to drive a tractor, 8*
la **manera** *way, 7*
la **manguera** *hose, 8*
la **mano** *hand, E*
de segunda mano *second hand, 7*
la **manta** *blanket, I12*
la **manteca** *lard, A4*
el **mantel** *tablecloth, 7*
mantener *to keep, 11*
para mantenerse en forma *to stay in shape, 10*
para mantenerse sano(a) *to stay healthy, 10*
Mantenga limpio el océano. *Keep the ocean clean., 2*
la **mantequilla** *butter, I2*
la **manzana** *apple, I2*
el **mapa** *map, E*
el **maquillaje** *make up, I10*
maquillarse *to put on make up, 9*
la **máquina** *machine, 4*
la **máquina de afeitar** *electric shaver, 9*
la **máquina de escribir** *typewriter, 4*
la **máquina sacabocados** *hole puncher, A5*
las **máquinas de ejercicio** *exercise machines, I8*
el **mar** *sea, I5*
el **maratón** *marathon, 3*
maravillosamente *marvelously, 6*
los **mariachis** *members of a mariachi band, I1*
la **mariposa** *butterfly, 2*
marrón *brown, E*
el **martes** *Tuesday, E*
el **martillo** *hammer, A5*
marzo *March, E*
más *more, I5*
más... que *more . . . than, I9*
más o menos *so-so; more or less, I5*
más tarde *later, I8*
la **masa** *dough, A4*
la **máscara** *mask, I12*
la **máscara de bucear** *diving mask, I5*

la **máscara de oxígeno** *oxygen mask, 1*
las **mascotas** *pets, E*
matar *to kill, 6*
las **matemáticas** *mathematics, E*
la **materia** *subject, E*
mayo *May, E*
me *to/for me, E*
Me queda pequeño(a)/grande. *It's small/big on me., I10*
mediano(a) *medium, I10*
el/la **médico(a)** *doctor, 3*
las **medidas de seguridad** *security measures, 1*
el **medio ambiente** *environment, 2*
medio(a) *half, 7*
los **medios de comunicación** *media, I9*
por medios mágicos *with magic, A1*
mejor... que *better . . . than, I9*
mejorar *to improve, A5*
mejoremos *let's improve, 11*
el **melón** *melon, I2*
menos... que *less . . . than, I9*
el **menú** *menu, I2*
el **mercado** *market, I1*
el **mercado de pulgas** *flea market, 7*
meridional *southern, A4*
la **merienda** *afternoon snack, I2*
el **mes** *month, I7*
la **mesa** *table, I4*
la **mesa de noche** *night table, I4*
el/la **mesero(a)** *waiter/ waitress, I2*
mestizo(a) *mixed, A1*
la **meta** *finish line (as in a race), 3; goal, 12*
meter *to put, A2*
el **metro** *subway, E; meter, I12*
mezclar *to mix, A4*
la **mezcla** *mixture, 7*
mí *me, E*
mi(s) *my, E*
el **micrófono** *microphone, 5*
el **microscopio** *microscope, I7*
el **miércoles** *Wednesday, E*

la **migración** *immigration desk*, 1

mil *one thousand*, I8

mil cien *one thousand one hundred*, I8

mil quinientos *one thousand five hundred*, I8

mirar *to watch; to look at*, E

el/la **misionero(a)** *missionary*, I4

misterioso(a) *mysterious*, I12

la **mochila** *backpack; bookpack*, E

la **moda** *fashion; style; trend*, I8

de moda *in style*, I8

el **modelo** *model*, 4

el/la **modelo** *fashion model*, 9

moderno(a) *modern*, I1

mojar *to dampen; wet*, A1

el **molde** *baking pan*, 7

el **mole** *mole (a thick chili sauce)*, I2

No moleste a los animales. *Don't disturb the animals*, 2

el **momento** *moment*, I7

en este momento *right now*, I8

la **moneda** *coin*, 6

el **mono** *monkey*, 2

montar *to ride; mount*, E

montar a caballo *to horseback ride*, 2

montar en bicicleta *to ride a bike*, E

el **monte** *hill*, 1

morado(a) *purple*, E

el **mostrador** *counter*, 1

mostrar *to show*, A6

la **moto** *motorcycle*, I7

Mucho gusto. *Nice to meet you.*, E

mucho más *much more*, I1

mucho(a, os, as) *a lot (of); many*, E

los **muebles** *furniture*, I4

el **muelle** *dock*, 6

la **muerte** *death*, 3

la **mujer** *woman*, I6

el **Mundial de Fútbol** *World Cup*, 3

la **muñeca** *doll*, 6

el **muñequito** *action figure*, 6

el **mural** *mural*, 11

el **murciélago** *bat (animal)*, 2

el **músculo** *muscle*, 10

el **museo** *museum*, I1

el **musgo** *moss*, A1

la **música** *music*, E

la **música bailable** *dance music*, I9

la **música clásica** *classical music*, I9

la **pop music** *pop music*, I9

la **música tejana** *Texan (country) music*, I3

la **música Tex-Mex** *Tex-Mex music*, I9

el/la **músico(a)** *musician*, 5

muy *very*, E

Muy bien, gracias. *Very well, thank you.*, E

N

nacer *to be born*, 6

nada *nothing*, E

Nada especial. *Nothing special.*, I3

nadar *to swim*, I5

nadie *no one*, 3

la **naranja** *orange*, I2

la **naturaleza** *nature*, I11

la **navegación** *sailing*, 2

navegar *to sail*, I5

navegar los rápidos en balsa *to do white water rafting*, 2

la **Navidad** *Christmas*, 7

necesario(a) *necessary*, 8

las **necesidades** *needs*, 10

necesitar *to need*, E

negro(a) *black*, E

nervioso(a) *nervous*, I12

nevar (e>ie) *to snow*, I6

ni... ni *neither . . . nor*, 3

el/la **niñero(a)** *baby sitter*, 12

la **niñez** *childhood*, 6

ningún/ninguno(a) *none*, 3

los/ **niños(as)**

las *children*, 11

no *no; not*, E

la **noche** *evening; night*, E

de la noche *in the evening*, E

el **nombre** *name*, E

el **noreste** *northeast*, 2

el **noroeste** *northwest*, 2

el **norte** *north*, I6

nos *to/for us; ourselves*, I10

nosotros(as) *we*, E

la **nota** *grade*, I7

las **noticias** *news*, 3

la **noticia del día** *cover story*, 3

el **noticiero** *newscast*, I9

novecientos *nine hundred*, E

la **novela** *novel*, I7

noventa *ninety*, E

noviembre *November*, E

el/la **novio(a)** *boyfriend; girlfriend*, I3

el **nudo** *knot*, A5

nuestro(a) *our*, I4

nueve *nine*, E

nuevo(a) *new*, E

la/las **nuez/nueces** *walnut/walnuts*, 7

el **número** *number*, E

el **número de teléfono** *telephone number*, E

el **número de zapato** *shoe size*, I10

nunca *never*, I6

O

o *or*, I2

el **obispo** *bishop*, 4

la **obra** *play*, 5

observar *to watch; to observe*, 2

la **ocasión** *occasion*, I3

el **océano** *ocean*, I12

ochenta *eighty*, E

ocho *eight*, E

ochocientos *eight hundred*, E

octubre *October*, E

ocurrir *to take place*, 1

el **oeste** *west*, I6

la **oficina** *office*, E

la **oficina de cambio** *exchange office*, E

la **oficina de información** *information office*, E

la **oficina del director** *principal's office*, I7

el/la **oficinista** *office worker*, 4

ofrecer *to offer*, 11

oír *to hear*, 3

¡Oye! *Listen!*, I8

la **ola** *wave*, I5

la **olla** *pot*, 7

olvidarse *to forget*, 2

once *eleven*, E

ONU (Organización de las Naciones Unidas) *United Nations*, 12

la **oportunidad** *opportunity*, 12

ordeñar las vacas *to milk the cows*, 8

organizado(a) *organized*, 12

organizar *to organize*, 11

el **oro** *gold*, I10

la **orquesta de cámara** *chamber orchestra*, 7

la **orquídea** *orchid*, 2

os *to/for you (informal, pl.)*, I10

el **otoño** *fall/autumn*, I6

otro(a) *another; other*, E

la **oveja** *sheep*, 8

P

el/la **paciente** *patient*, 12

el **padrastro** *stepfather*, E

el **padre** *father*, E

los **padres** *parents*, E

el **padrino** *godfather*, I3

pagar *to pay*, I10

la **página** *page*, E

el **país** *country*, E

el **paisaje** *landscape*, I12

el **pájaro** *bird*, E

la **paleta** *paddle*, I5

la **palmera** *palm tree*, 2

la **pampa** *grassy plains*, 8

el **pan** *bread*, I2

los **pantalones** *pants*, I8

los **pantalones ajustados** *tight pants*, 9

los **pantalones anchos** *baggy pants*, 9

el **pañuelo** *scarf*, 9

la **papa** *potato*, I2

las **papas fritas** *French fries*, I2

el **papá** *dad*, E

el **papel** *paper*, E; *role*, I12

de papel *(made of) paper*, 11

el **papel carbón** *carbon paper*, 4

el **paquete** *package*, 7

para *for; in order to; to*, I2

el **paracaídas** *parachute*, I5

la **parada** *stop*, I1

el **paraguas** *umbrella*, I6

el **paraíso** *paradise*, A3

parar *to stop*, 8

sin parar *non-stop*, I9

parecido(a) *similar*, 5

la **pared** *wall*, I4

el/la **pariente(a)** *relative*, I3

el **parlante** *speaker*, 5

el **parque** *park*, I1

el **parque nacional** *national park*, 2

párrafo *paragraph*, A6

la **parrilla** *grill*, 8

a la parrilla *grilled*, 7

las **partes del cuerpo** *parts of the body*, 10

participar *to participate; to take part in*, I11

el **partido** *game (sport)*, I7

la **pasa** *raisin*, 7

el **pasaje** *airline fare*, I11

el **pasaje con descuento** *discount ticket*, 1

el **pasaje de ida** *one way ticket*, 1

el **pasaje de ida y vuelta** *round trip ticket*, 1

el/la **pasajero(a)** *passenger*, 1

el **pasaporte** *passport*, E

pasar *to spend; to happen; to pass*, I7

¿Qué pasó? *What happened?*, 3

pasar por *to go through*, 1

pasarla bien/mal *to have a good/bad time*, 5

la **Pascua** *Easter*, I3

pasear en bote *to take a boat ride*, 6

el **pasillo** *hallway*, I7

el **paso a nivel** *railroad crossing*, 8

la **pasta** *pasta*, I2

la **pasta de dientes** *toothpaste*, E

la **pasta de guayaba** *guava paste*, I10

el **pastel** *cake*, I2

las **patas** *legs*, 8

las **patillas** *sideburns*, 9

el **patinaje** *skating*, 5

patinar *to skate*, I1

patinar sobre hielo *to ice skate*, I6

los **patines** *skates*, 5

el **patio** *courtyard*, I7

el **pato** *duck*, 8

el **patrón** *pattern*, A5

el **pavo** *turkey*, 7

pedir (e>i) *to ask for; to order*, I11

pegar *to seal*, A3

peinarse *to comb one's hair*, I8

el **peine** *comb*, E

pelearse *to have a fight*, 6

la **película** *movie*, I9

pelirrojo(a) *redhead*, E

el **pelo** *hair*, E

el **pelo de punta** *spiked hair*, 9

el **pelo rapado** *crew cut*, 9

la **pelota** *ball*, I5

la **peluquería** *barber shop/hair dresser's shop*, 9

el/la **peluquero(a)** *barber/hairdresser*, 9

pensar *to think; to intend*, 1

peor (que) *worse (than)*, I9

el **pepino** *cucumber*, 7

pequeño(a) *small; little*, E

perder *to lose*, 8

¡Perdón! *Sorry!; Excuse me!*, E

el **perezoso** *sloth*, 2

perfectamente *perfectly*, I11

el **perfume** *perfume*, I10

el **periódico** *newspaper*, I1

el/la **periodista** *journalist*, 3

la **permanente** *permanent wave*, 9

permitir *to allow*, A1

pero *but*, E

el **perro** *dog*, E

la **persona** *person*, E

la **persona mayor** *elderly person*, A2

los **personajes** *characters*, 6

persuasivo(a) *persuasive*, 12

la **pesa** *weight*, 10

Pesach *Passover*, 7

la **pesca** *fishing*, 2

el **pescado** *fish*, I2

el/la **pescador(a)** *fisherman/fisherwoman*, 6

pescar *to fish*, 2

la **peseta** *Spain's currency unit, E*

el **peso** *Mexican currency unit, E*

los **pesos y medidas** *weights and measures, I12*

petrificado(a) *petrified, A4*

el **petróleo** *oil (petroleum), 3*

picado(a) *ground, 7*

picante *spicy, I2*

el **picnic** *picnic, I3*

los **picos** *peaks, A4*

el **pie** *foot, I12*

  a pie *on foot, I1*

  el **pie de foto** *caption, 3*

la **piedra** *stone, I11*

la **pierna** *leg, 10*

la **pintada** *graffiti, 11*

pintar *to paint, 11*

la **pintura** *painting, 4*

la **piña** *pineapple, I2*

la **piñata** *piñata, I3*

la **pirámide** *pyramid, I1*

la **piscina** *swimming pool, I5*

los **pisos** *floors, I4*

la **pizarra** *chalkboard; blackboard, E*

la **pizza** *pizza, E*

la **planta** *plant, I7*

plantar *to plant, 8*

el **plástico** *plastic, 11*

la **plata** *silver, I10*

el **plátano** *banana, I2*

el **plato** *plate, I2*

  el **plato del día** *daily special, I2*

  el **plato principal** *main course, 7*

la **playa** *beach, I5*

la **plaza** *square, I1*

las **plumas** *feathers, A1*

poco(a, os, as) *a little; not much; few, E*

poco a poco *little by little, 7*

poder (o>ue) *can; to be able to, I8*

  ¡No puede ser! *It can't be!, 3*

los **poderes** *powers, A3*

poderoso(a) *powerful, A2*

el **poema** *poem, I7*

la **poesía** *poetry, A2*

el/la **poeta** *poet, 4*

el/la **policía** *police officer, 3*

el **pollo** *chicken, I2*

ponchar *to strike out, A3*

el **poncho** *rain poncho, I12*

poner *to put, IA1*

  poner música *to play music, I9*

  ponerse *to put on; to wear, I8*

  ponerse en forma *to get in shape, 10*

  Pongan su equipaje debajo del asiento. *Put your luggage under the seat, 1*

  Pongan sus asientos en posición vertical. *Put your seats in the upright position, 1*

popular *popular, I3*

por *by; for; through, I1*

por favor *please, E*

¿Por qué? *Why?, E*

porque *because, E*

la **portada** *front page, 3*

posible *possible, 8*

el **postre** *dessert, I2*

el **potro** *colt, 8*

practicar *to practice, I5*

práctico(a) *practical, 9*

el **precio** *price, 1*

precolombino(a) *pre-Colombian, 5*

preferir (e>ie) *to prefer, I9*

la **pregunta** *question, E*

preguntar *to ask, E*

el **premio** *award, 3*

  el **premio Nobel** *Nobel Prize, I11*

preocupado(a) *worried, I12*

preocuparse *to worry, 3*

preparar *to prepare, 7*

  prepararse *to get ready, I8*

presentar a *to introduce someone to, 5*

  ¿Me puedes presentar a...? *Can you introduce me to . . . ?, 5*

el/la **presidente(a)** *president, 3*

prestar *to lend, 5*

  prestar atención a *to pay attention to, I6*

el **prestigio** *prestige, 12*

la **primavera** *spring, I6*

primero(a) *first, A2*

el/la **primo(a)** *cousin, I3*

a principios *at the beginning, 11*

la **probabilidad** *probability, I6*

el **probador** *dressing room, 9*

probar (o>ue) *to taste, I2*

  probarse (o>ue) *to try on, 9*

el **problema** *problem, I7*

producir *to make, 4; to produce, 8*

el/la **profesor(a)** *teacher, E*

profundo (a) *deep, I12*

el **programa** *TV show; program, I9*

  el **programa de concursos** *game show, I9*

  el **programa de intercambio** *exchange program, I11*

  el **programa de intercambio estudiantil** *student exchange program, I11*

la **programación** *programming, I9*

prohibido tocar la bocina *don't honk the horn, 8*

pronombre *pronoun*

el **pronóstico del tiempo** *weather forecast, I6*

pronto *soon, 18*

los/las **propietarios(as) privados(as)** *private owners, 8*

el **propósito** *purpose, 12*

la **prosa** *prose, A2*

el **protector solar** *sunscreen, I5*

proteger *to protect, 2*

las **pruebas de esfuerzo** *exercise tests, A5*

el **pueblo** *town, I4*

  el **pueblo costero** *beach village, 6*

  el **pueblo de montaña** *mountain village, 6*

  el **pueblo pesquero** *fishing village, 6*

el **puente** *bridge, A1*

la **puerta** *door, I4*

  la **puerta de embarque** *boarding gate, 1*

el **puerto** *seaport, 6*

el **puesto** *booth, I10*

puesto(a) *put, 7*

la **pulgada** *inch, I6*
la **pulsera** *bracelet, I10*
las **puntas** *ends, 9*
  en las puntas *at the ends, 8*
el **punto** *point (in a game), I*
  los **puntos de interés** *sights, I12*
  ¡Pura vida! (Costa Rica) *Cool!; Great!, 2*
el **puré de patatas** *mashed potatoes, 10*

Q

que *that, E*
¿Qué...? *What . . . ?*
¿Qué tal? *What's up?*
¡Qué bien te sienta! *It looks great on you!, 9*
¡Qué horror! *How awful!, 3*
quedar *to fit, I10*
  ¿Cómo me queda(n)? *How does it/do they look on me?, 9*
  quedar primero *to take first place, A5*
quedarse *to stay, 1*
  quedarse hasta tarde *to stay late, 5*
¿Quién? *Who?, E*
querer (e>ie) *to want, I5*
quererse (e>ie) *to love each other, 6*
el **queso** *cheese, I2*
el **quetzal** *quetzal, 2*
  ¿Con quién? *With whom?, I1*
la **química** *chemistry, I7*
quince *fifteen, E*
quinientos *five hundred, E*
el **quiosco** *newsstand, I1*

R

la **radio** *radio, I4*
las **raíces** *roots, 5*
el **rancho** *ranch, I4*
el **rap** *rap, I9*
  rápido(a) *fast, I9*
el **rascacielos** *skyscraper, 4*
los **rasgos** *traits, 7*

el **ratón** *mouse, E*
  a rayas *striped, 9*
la **razón** *reason, 4*
  reabrir *to reopen, 3*
la **reacción** *reaction, 3*
  reaccionar *to react, 3*
  reaparecer *to reappear, 3*
la **rebaja** *sale, I10*
el/la **recepcionista** *receptionist, 12*
la **receta** *recipe, 7*
  recibir *to receive, 3*
el **recibo** *receipt, I10*
  reciclar *to recycle, 11*
  recoger *to pick up, 7*
  recoger la cosecha *to harvest the crop, 8*
  recoger la fruta *to pick fruit, 8*
  recoger la mesa *to clear the table, 7*
  recomendar (e>ie) *to recommend, 12*
  reconocer *to recognize, 7*
el **recuerdo** *memory, 6*
la **red** *net, I5*
  en referencia a *in reference to, A1*
los **reflejos** *highlights, 9*
el **refrán** *saying, A6*
el **refresco** *soft drink; soda, E*
el **refrigerador** *refrigerator, I4*
  regalar *to give a present, I10*
el **regalo** *gift, I3*
  regar *to water, 8*
  regatear *to bargain, I10*
el **reggae** *reggae music, I9*
la **región** *region, I11*
las **reglas de oro** *golden rules, 11*
  regular *so-so, E*
  reírse (e>i) *to laugh, 5*
la **relación** *relationship, 6*
  relacionar *to relate, A3*
la **relajación** *relaxation, 10*
  relajante *relaxing, I9*
el **relleno** *filling, A4*
el **reloj** *watch; clock, I10*
  remar *to row, I5*
los **remos** *oars, I5*
el/la **repartidor(a)** *delivery person, 12*
  repartir *to deliver; to distribute, 11*
el **repelente de insectos** *insect repellent, 2*

el/la **reportero(a)** *reporter, 3*
el/la **representante de...** *representative of . . . , I11*
la **reserva** *reservation, I11*
  la **reserva natural** *natural reserve, 2*
  las **reservas de petróleo** *oil (petroleum) reserve, 3*
la **residencia de ancianos** *senior citizen home, 11*
la **resina fosilizada** *fossilized resin, A3*
  resistente *resistant, 4*
  respetar *to respect, I11*
  te hagas respetar *you get respect, 11*
la **respiración** *breathing, 10*
la **responsabilidad** *responsibility, 8*
el **restaurante** *restaurant, I2*
  el **restaurante al aire libre** *outdoor restaurant, I2*
  el **restaurante de comida rápida** *fast food restaurant, I2*
los **restos** *remnants, 4; remains, A3*
  retrasado(a) *delayed, 1*
  retratos *pictures, A6*
  revelar *to develop, A6*
la **revista** *magazine, E*
  la **revista de espectáculos** *entertainment magazine, I9*
  la **revista de moda** *fashion magazine, I9*
  revolver (o>ue) *to stir; to scramble, 7*
el **rey** *king, A2*
los **Reyes** *Epiphany, 7*
  rico(a) *tasty, I2*
el **rincón** *corner, 4*
la **riñonera** *pouch, A5*
el **río** *river, I4*
las **riquezas** *riches, A1*
el **ritmo** *rhythm, A3*
el **rock duro** *hard rock, I9*
  rodear *to surround, 2*
la **rodilla** *knee, 10*
  rojo(a) *red, E*
los **rollos** *rolls, A2*
  romper *to break, I3*
la **ropa** *clothing, I5*
el **ropero** *closet, I4*
  rubio(a) *blond, E*
las **ruedas** *wheels, A2*
el **ruido** *noise, 4*

ruidoso(a) *noisy, I9*
las **ruinas** *ruins, I11*
la **ruta** *route, 8*
la **rutina diaria** *daily routine, 8*

S

el **sábado** *Saturday, E*
saber *to know, I5*
sacar *to take; get, A1*
sacar el pasaporte *to get a passport, I12*
sacar fotos *to take pictures, I1*
sacar la basura *to take out the garbage, 7*
sacar una buena/mala nota *to get a good/bad grade, I7*
el **sacerdote** *priest, A2*
el **saco de dormir** *sleeping bag, 2*
la **sal** *salt, 10*
la **sala** *living room, I4*
la **sala de espera** *waiting room, 1*
la **salida** *exit, E; departure, 1*
salir *to go out, I8*
salir a mochilear (Chile) *to go backpacking, I11*
salir temprano *to leave early, 11*
el **salón de actos** *auditorium, I7*
el **salón de clase** *classroom, I7*
los **salones de moda** *fashion shows, 9*
la **salsa de tomate** *tomato sauce, 7*
saltar a la cuerda *to jump rope, 6*
la **salud** *health, 10*
saludar *to greet, I6*
salvaje *wild, 8*
el/la **salvavidas** *lifeguard, I5*
las **sandalias** *sandals, I10*
la **sandía** *watermelon, 7*
el **sándwich** *sandwich, E*
sangriento(a) *bloody, A1*
sano(a) *healthy, 10*
el **sarape** *shawl; blanket, 11*
la **sartén** *frying pan, 7*
el **saxofón** *saxophone, 5*

el **secador** *hair drier, 9*
secarse *to dry oneself, I8*
la **sección** *section, I9*
seco(a) *dry, A1*
la **sed** *thirst, I2*
la **segadora** *mower; harvester, 8*
seguir *to follow, 2*
Siga el sendero. *Follow the path., 2*
Siga las indicaciones/las señales. *Follow the instructions/the signs., 2*
la **segunda (tercera) base** *second (third) base, A3*
segura(o) *safe, A5*
seguro *most definitely, A6*
seis *six, E*
seiscientos *six hundred, E*
seleccionar *to choose, I3*
el **sello** *stamp, 6*
la **selva** *jungle, I1*
el **semáforo** *traffic light, 11*
la **semana** *week, E*
semanal *weekly, E*
sembrar (e>ie) *to sow, 8*
el **semestre** *semester, E*
la **semilla** *seed, 8*
el/la **senador(a)** *senator, 3*
la **señal** *sign, 2*
sencillo(a) *simple, A3*
el **sendero** *path, 2*
el **señor** *Mr.; Sir, E*
la **señora** *Mrs.; Maam, E*
las **señoras** *ladies, E*
la **señorita** *Ms.; Miss, E*
sentirse (e>ie) *to feel, 11*
sentirse bien/mal *to feel well/bad, 10*
sentirse útil *to feel helpful, 11*
septiembre *September, E*
ser *to be, E*
ser de... *to be from . . . , E*
la **serpiente** *snake, 2*
el **servicio** *service, 9*
la **servilleta** *napkin, I2*
servir (e>i) *to serve, 5*
sesenta *sixty, E*
setecientos *seven hundred, E*
setenta *seventy, E*
las **sevillanas** *typical dance of Seville, I7*
siempre *always, IA2*
la **sierra** *saw, A3*
siete *seven, E*

el **siglo** *century, A2*
significar *to signify; to mean, IA4*
la **silla** *chair, E*
el **sillón** *armchair, I4*
simpático(a) *nice, E*
sin *without, I6*
sin embargo *however, A1*
situado(a) *located, 4*
sobre *about, I1*
sobresalientes *outstanding, 11*
¡Socorro! *Help!, I5*
los/las **socios(as)** *members, 5*
el **sofá** *sofa, I4*
la **soledad** *solitude, A2*
la **solicitud** *application, I11*
sólo *only, I8*
solo(a) *alone, I8*
el **sombrero** *hat, I12*
la **sombrilla** *beach umbrella, I5*
el **son** *tune, 8*
la **sopa** *soup, I2*
sorprenderse *to be surprised, 3*
el **sótano** *basement, I4*
su(s) *your/his/her/their, I4*
el **sueldo** *salary, 12*
el **suelo** *ground, 6*
el **sueño** *dream, A3*
la **suerte** *luck, I7*
el **suéter** *sweater, I6*
suficiente *enough, A6*
la **sugerencia** *suggestion, A2*
el **sumario** *news summary, 3*
la **superficie** *surface, A3*
el **supermercado** *supermarket, I1*
el **sur** *south, I6*
el **sureste** *southeast, 2*
surgir *to arise, A2*
el **suroeste** *southwest, 2*

T

la **tabla a vela** *sailboard, I5*
la **tabla de surf** *surfboard, I5*
tal vez *perhaps, E*
la **talla** *clothing size, I1*
el **taller** *workshop, I1*
también *also; too, E*
tampoco *neither, 3*
tanto(a)... como *as much . . . as, 4*

tantos(as)... como *as many . . . as,* 4

tan... como *as . . . as,* 4

la **tapa** *lid,* A4

el **tapiz** *tapestry; carpet,* I12

la **taquería** *taco shop,* I2

tarde *late,* I8

la **tarde** *afternoon; evening,* E

de la **tarde** *in the afternoon; evening,* E

la **tarea** *homework,* I7

la **tarjeta** *(greeting) card,* E

la **tarjeta de crédito** *credit card,* I10

la **tarjeta postal** *postcard,* E

las **tarjetas identificadoras** *identification cards,* 4

la **tarjeta de embarque** *boarding pass,* 1

el **taxi** *taxi; cab,* E

la **taza** *cup,* I2

el **té** *tea,* I2

te *to/for you (informal sing.),* I10

el **teatro** *theater,* I1

el **teclado** *keyboard,* A6

la **tecnología** *technology,* 4

el **tejado** *roof,* 4

el **teléfono** *telephone,* E

el **teléfono celular** *cellular phone,* 4

el **telegrama** *telegram,* 4

la **teleguía** *TV guide,* I9

la **telenovela** *soap operas,* I9

la **televisión** *television,* E

el **tema** *topic,* I11

la **temperatura máxima/ mínima** *high/low temperature,* I6

la **temporada** *season,* A3

temprano *early,* 8

el **tenedor** *fork,* I2

tener (que) *to have (to),* E

Ten cuidado. *Be careful.,* I6

tener agujetas *to be sore,* 10

tener catarro *to have a cold,* 10

tener fiebre *to have a fever,* 10

tener gripe *to have the flu,* 10

No tengo ganas. *I don't feel like it.,* I8

Tengo mucha hambre/sed. *I'm very hungry/thirsty.,* I2

Tengo... años *I am . . . years old.,* E

No tiene miedo. *He/She isnt afraid.,* I5

los **tenis** *sneakers,* I8

tercer(o, a) *third,* I2

el/la **tercero(a)** *third,* 4

la **terminal de equipaje** *baggage claim,* 1

terminar *to finish; to terminate,* IA4

la **terraza** *terrace,* I3

el **terremoto** *earthquake,* 3

el **terreno montañoso** *mountainous terrain,* I12

el **territorio** *territory,* 2

los **tesoros** *treasures,* 4

los **testimonios** *evidence,* A2

ti *for/to you,* E

la **tía** *aunt,* I3

los **tiburones de agua dulce** *fresh-water sharks,* 1

el **tiempo** *weather,* I6

a tiempo *on time,* 1

el **tiempo libre** *leisure time,* 12

tiempo parcial *parttime,* 12

tiempo presente *present tense,* 7

la **tienda** *store,* E

la **tienda de artesanías** *craft shop,* I1

la **tienda de discos** *record store,* I1

la **tienda de campaña** *tent,* 2

la **tierra** *land/soil,* 8

las **tierras bajas** *lowlands,* A1

el **tiesto** *flowerpot,* A1

las **tijeras** *scissors,* 9

el **tío** *uncle,* I3

el **tipo** *kind; type,* I9

tirar *to throw,* 6

No tire basura. *Don't litter.,* 2

el **titular** *headline,* 3

la **tiza** *chalk,* E

la **toalla** *towel,* I5

el **tocacintas** *cassette player,* I9

tocar *to play (an instrument),* I3; *to touch,* 6

todavía *still,* I4

todavía no *not yet,* I7

todo(a) *all,* IA1

todos(as) *everyone; all,* I2

todos los días *everyday,* I4

tomar *to drink,* I2

tomar el sol *to sunbathe,* I5

el **tomate** *tomato,* I2

los **tomos** *volumes,* 12

la **tormenta** *storm,* I6

el **tornado** *tornado,* 3

los **toros** *bulls,* 6

la **torre** *tower,* I4

la **torta** *pie,* 7

la **tortilla** *tortilla,* I2

la **tortilla francesa** *omelette,* 7

la **tortuga** *turtle,* E

el/la **trabajador(a)** *worker,* 3

trabajar *to work,* I6

trabajar de voluntario(a) *to volunteer,* 11

el **trabajo** *job,* 11

el **tractor** *tractor,* 8

tradicionales *traditional,* 5

la **traducción** *translation,* 11

el/la **traductor(a)** *translator,* A2

traer *to bring,* 7

el **tráfico** *traffic,* 4

el **traje** *suit,* 9

el **traje de baño** *bathing suit,* I5

los **trámites** *paperwork,* 11

las **trampas metálicas** *metallic traps,* A3

transparente *transparent,* I5

el **transporte** *transportation,* I1

el **transporte público** *public transportation,* 4

tras *after,* A5

tratar de agarrar *to try to catch,* A4

a través de *through,* A6

trece *thirteen,* E

treinta *thirty,* E

el **tren** *train,* I1

trepar *to climb,* A1

tres *three,* E

trescientos *three hundred,* E

las **tribus** *tribes,* A3

el **trigo** *wheat,* 8

triste *sad,* I12

la **trompeta** *trumpet,* 5

tu *your (sing.),* E

tú *you,* E

los **tubos de ensayo** *test tubes, I7*
el **tucán** *toucan, 2*
tus *your (pl.), E*

U

último(a) *last, I7*
un/una *a, E*
el/la **único(a)** *only, 5*
unir *to join, E*
uno *one, E*
usar *are used, 1*
usted (Ud.) *you (formal sing.), E*
ustedes (Uds.) *you (formal pl.), E*
la **uva** *grape, 7*

V

vaciar *to empty, A3*
vacío(a) *empty, A3*
la **vainilla** *vanilla, I2*
¡Vale! (Spain) *Sure!; OK!, I8*
vale más que *it's worth more than, A6*
el **valle** *valley, I12*
valorar *to value, 12*
la **vanguardia** *van-guard, 5*
los/ **vanguardistas**
las *avant-gardists, 9*
los **vaqueros** *jeans, I8*
 los **vaqueros rotos** *ripped jeans, 9*
la **variedad** *variety, 12*
el **vaso** *glass, I2*
el **vecindario** *neighborhood, I4*
el/la **vecino(a)** *neighbor, I3*
vegetariano(a) *vegetarian, I2*
veinte *twenty, E*
veintiuno(dos...) *twenty one(two . . .), E*
la **vela** *candle, I3*
el **velero** *sail boat, I5*
el/la **vendedor(a)** *salesperson, I1*
vender *to sell, I1*
venir (e>i) *to come, I1*
la **venta** *sale, I5*

la **ventaja** *advantages, 4*
la **ventana** *window, I4*
el **ventilador** *fan, 4*
ver *to watch; to see, I9*
el **verano** *summer, I6*
¿verdad? *isn't it? aren't they? right?, I2*
verde *green, E*
las **verduras** *vegetables, I2*
el **vestido** *dress, I8*
vestirse *to get dressed, I7*
la **vez (pl. veces)** *time, IA2*
 a veces *sometimes, I6*
 a la vez que *at the same time as, 5*
 varias veces por... *several times a . . . , 9*
vía satélite *via satellite, 4*
viajar *to travel, I1*
el **viaje** *trip, I1*
la **víctima** *victim, 3*
la **vida** *life, A2*
 la **vida cotidiana** *everyday life, A3*
la **videocasetera** *video cassette recorder; VCR, I9*
el **videojuego** *videogame, E*
el **vidrio** *glass, 11*
viejo(a) *old, E*
el **viento** *wind, I6*
el **viernes** *Friday, E*
el **vinagre** *vinegar, 7*
la **violencia** *violence, 11*
la **visa** *visa, I11*
los/las **visitantes** *visitors, I4*
visitar *to visit, I1*
vivir *to live, I4*
el **vocabulario** *vocabulary, I7*
el **volcán** *volcano, 2*
voleibol *volleyball, E*
el/la **voluntario(a)** *volunteer, 3*
volver (o>ue) *to return, I8*
vosotros(as) *you (plural), E*
el **vuelo** *flight, 1*
 el **vuelo con escala** *stopover flight, 1*
 el **vuelo sin escala** *non-stop flight, 1*
vuestro(a) *you (informal pl.), 4*

Y

y *and, E*
ya *already, E*

la **yerba** *herb, A4*
yo *I, E*
el **yogur** *yogurt, I2*

Z

la **zapatería** *shoe store, I1*
los **zapatos** *shoes, I8*
 los **zapatos bajos** *flat shoes, 9*
 los **zapatos de tacón** *high-heel shoes, 9*
la **zona** *zone; area, I1*
 la **zona verde** *green area, 11*
 las **zonas arqueológicas** *archaeological areas, I1*
el **zoológico** *zoo, 5*
los **zuecos** *clogs, 9*

GLOSARIO INGLÉS-ESPAÑOL

The **English-Spanish Glossary** contains almost all vocabulary from **Juntos Uno** and **Juntos Dos.**

The number following each entry indicates the chapter in which the word or expression is first introduced. The letter *A* following an entry refers to the *Adelante* sections; the letter *E* refers to the *Encuentros* section in Level 1; a Roman numeral I indicates that the word was presented in **Juntos Uno.**

A

a, an *un; una, E*
able: to be able *poder (o>ue), I8*
about *sobre, I1*
to **accept** *aceptar, I10*
accident *el accidente, 3*
to **accompany** *acompañar, A3*
aquatic *acuático (a), I5*
to **acquire** *adquirir, I11*
to **act** *actuar, 5*
action figure *la figurita; (el) muñequito, 6*
active *activo(a), A1*
activity *la actividad, E*
actor *el actor, 5*
actress *la actriz, 5*
to **add** *añadir, 7*
address *la dirección, E*
to **admire** *admirar, I12*
advantage *la ventaja, 4*
advertisement *el anuncio, I9*
advice *el consejo, I6*
after *después, E*
afternoon *la tarde, E*
age *la edad, 4*
agency *la agencia, I11*
air *el aire, I2*
  air conditioner *el aire acondicionado, 4*
  airline *la aerolínea, 1*
  airline fare *el pasaje, I11*
airport *el aeropuerto, E*
aisle *el pasillo, 1*
algebra *el álgebra, I7*
all *todo(a), IA1*
to **allow** *permitir, A1*

almost *casi, I10*
alone *solo(a), I8*
along *a lo largo (de), I4*
already *ya, E*
also *también, E*
aluminum *el aluminio, 11*
always *siempre, IA2*
ambitious *ambicioso(a), 12*
ambulance *la ambulancia, 3*
ancient *antiguo(a), I1*
and *y, E*
angel *el ángel, 5*
animal *el animal, 2*
anniversary *el aniversario, I3*
another *otro(a), E*
to **answer** *contestar, I1*
answering machine *el contestador automático, I8*
any *cualquier, A6*
anybody *alguien; nadie, 3*
to **appear** *aparecer, A5*
appearance *el aspecto, 9*
apple *la manzana, I2*
application *la solicitud, I11*
April *abril, E*
architecture *la arquitectura, 4*
armchair *el sillón, 14*
army *el ejército, A1*
arrival *la llegada, 1*
to **arrive** *llegar, A2*
art *el arte, E*
article *el artículo, I10*

arts and crafts *las artesanías, I1*
as *tan; como, 4*
  as . . . as *tan... como, 4*
  as many . . . as *tantos(as)... como, 4*
  as much . . . as *tanto (a)... como, 4*
to **ask** *preguntar, E*
to **ask for** *pedir (e>i), I11*
aspirin *la aspirina, 10*
to **assist** *atender (e>ie), 11*
at *a; en, E*
  at home *en casa, 14*
  at the same time as *a la vez que, 5*
  at . . . (time) *a la(s)..., E*
athlete *el/la deportista, 10*
to **attract** *atraer, A3*
auditorium *el salón de actos, 17*
August *agosto, E*
aunt *la tía, I3*
authorization *la autorización, I11*
autumn *el otoño, I6*
avenue *la avenida, E*
avocado *el aguacate, I2*
to **avoid** *evitar, 10*
award *el premio, 3*
awful *horrible, I2; fatal, I7*

B

baby sitter *el/la niñero(a), 12*
backpack *la mochila, E*
bad *mal(o,a), 6*

351

bag *la bolsa, I10*
baggage *el equipaje, 1*
 baggage claim *la terminal de equipaje, 1*
 baggage handler *el/la maletero(a), 1*
ball *la pelota, I5*
balloon *el globo, I3*
banana *el plátano, I2*
bangs *el flequillo, 9*
barbecue *el asado, 7; (la) barbacoa, I3*
bargain *la ganga, I10*
to **bargain** *regatear, I10*
barn *el granero, 8*
baseball *el béisbol, E*
basement *el sótano, I4*
basket *la canasta, I7*
basketball *el baloncesto, E*
bass *el bajo, 5*
bat *el murciélago, 2*
bathing suit *el traje de baño, I5*
bathroom *el cuarto de baño, I4*
bathtub *la bañera, I4*
batter *el/la bateador (a), A3*
to **be** *estar; ser, E*
beach *la playa, I5*
beans *los frijoles, I2*
beautiful *hermoso(a), I12*
because *porque, E*
 because of *a causa de , 4*
bed *la cama, I4*
bedroom *el dormitorio, I4*
to **begin** *empezar (e>ie), I7*
beginning *el comienzo, A4*
behind *detrás de, I4*
to **believe** *creer, A3*
belt *el cinturón, I10*
better (than) *mejor (que), I9*
between *entre, I4*
beverage *la bebida, I2*
bicycle *la bicicleta, I1*
bilingual *bilingüe, 12*
binoculars *los binoculares, 2*
biology *la biología, I7*
bird *el pájaro, E*

birthday *el cumpleaños, E*
bizarre *extravagante, 6*
black *negro(a), E*
blanket *la manta, I12*
blond *rubio(a), E*
blouse *la blusa, I8*
blue *azul, E*
boarding gate *la puerta de embarque, 1*
boarding pass *la tarjeta de embarque, 1*
boat *el barco, I12*
to **boil** *hervir (e>ie), 7*
book *el libro, E*
bookcase *el estante, I4*
bookstore *la librería, I1*
booth *el puesto, I10*
boots *las botas, I6*
border *la frontera, I1*
boring *aburrido(a), E*
born: to be born *nacer (c>zc), 6*
bottle *la botella, 2*
bottom *el fondo, 7*
bowling alley *el boliche, 5*
box *la caja, 7*
boy *el chico, E*
boyfriend *el novio, I3*
bracelet *la pulsera, I10*
bread *el pan, I2*
to **break** *romper, I3*
breakfast *el desayuno, I2*
bridge *el puente, A1*
to **bring** *traer, 7*
brochure *el folleto, E*
broom *la escoba, 4*
brother *el hermano, E*
brothers and sisters *los hermanos, E*
brown *marrón, E*
brunette *castaño(a), E*
brush *el cepillo, 8*
to **brush** *cepillar, 8*
 to **brush (one's teeth)** *cepillarse (los dientes), I8*
to **build** *construir, 3*
bus *el autobús, E*
but *pero, E*
butter *la mantequilla, I2*
butterfly *la mariposa, 2*

button *el botón, 9*
to **buy** *comprar, I1*
by *por; en, I1*

C

cafeteria *la cafetería, E*
cake *el pastel, I2*
calculator *la calculadora, I7*
calendar *el calendario, E*
to **call** *llamar, I8*
camera *la cámara, I10*
to **camp** *acampar, 2*
can *poder (o>ue), I8*
can (metal) *la lata, 2*
candle *la vela, I3*
canteen *la cantimplora, 2*
capital *la capital, E*
car *el coche, I1; auto (Perú), I12*
to **carry** *llevar, 15*
cartoons *los dibujos animados, I9*
cash *el dinero en efectivo, I10*
cashier *el/la cajero(a), 12*
cassette player *el to cacintas, I9*
cat *el gato, E*
to **catch** *coger, 6*
cathedral *la catedral, I12*
to **cause** *causar, 3*
to **celebrate** *celebrar, I3*
celebration *la celebración, I3*
center *el centro, 2*
 cultural center *el centro cultural, 5*
 day-care center *la guardería, 11*
 recreational center *el centro recreativo, 11*
 recycling center *el centro de reciclaje, 11*
 shopping center *el centro comercial, I1*
 sports center *el centro deportivo, 11*
centimeter *el centímetro, I12*

century *el siglo, A2*
cereal *los cereales, I2*
certificate *el certificado, I11*
chair *la silla, E*
chalk *la tiza, E*
chalkboard *la pizarra, E*
championship *el campeonato, 3*
to **change** *cambiar, I9*
channel *el canal, I9*
chapter *el capítulo, I7*
character *el personaje, 6*
check *el cheque, I10*
to **check luggage** *facturar, 1*
cheese *el queso, I2*
chemistry *la química, I7*
chess *el ajedrez, I6*
chicken *el pollo, I2*
childhood *la niñez, 6*
children *los niños, 11*
chocolate *el chocolate, I2*
to **choose** *escoger, E*
Christmas *la Navidad, 7*
church *la iglesia, I1*
citizen *el/la ciudadano(a), I1*
city *la ciudad, E*
class *la clase, E*
clean *limpio(a), 4*
to **clean** *limpiar, 7*
to **climb** *subir, I12*
clock *el reloj, I10*
to **close** *cerrar, 4*
closet *el ropero, I4*
clothing *la ropa, I5*
coat *el abrigo, I6*
coffee *el café, I2*
coin *la moneda, 6*
cold (illness) *el catarro, 10*
cold *frío(a), I2*
to **collect** *coleccionar, 6*
collection *la colección, 6*
color *el color, E*
comb *el peine, E*
to **comb one's hair** *peinarse, I8*
to **come** *venir (e>i), I1*
comedian *el cómico, 5*
comedienne *la cómica, 5*
comfortable *cómodo(a), 4*
comics *las historietas, I9*

commercial *el anuncio, I9*
communicative *comunicativo(a), 12*
compact disc (CD) *el disco compacto, I1*
company *la compañía, 12*
to **compare** *comparar, 1*
compass *la brújula, 2*
composition *la composición, I7*
computer *la computadora, E*
  computer science *la informática, I7*
concert *el concierto, I1*
condition *la condición, 12*
Congratulations! *¡Felicidades!, I3*
container *el contenedor, 11*
cook *el/la cocinero(a), 7*
to **cook** *cocinar, E*
cookie *la galleta, I3*
corn *el maíz, 8*
corporation *la corporación, 5*
to **cost** *costar (o>ue), I8*
cotton *el algodón, 8*
country *el país, E*
countryside *el campo, I4*
courteous *cortés, I11*
cousin *el/la primo(a), I3*
to **create** *crear, I1*
creative *creativo(a), 12*
credit card *la tarjeta de crédito, I10*
crop *la cosecha, 8*
cucumber *el pepino, 7*
culture *la cultura, I11*
cup *la taza, I2*
customs *la aduana, E*
to **cut** *cortar, A2*
  to **cut one's nails** *cortarse las uñas, 9*

dad *el papá, E*
dance *la danza, 5; (el) baile, I8*
to **dance** *bailar, E*
date *la fecha, E; cita, 6*

daughter *la hija, I3*
day *el día, E*
death *la muerte, 3*
December *diciembre, E*
deep *profundo(a), I12*
degree *el grado, I6*
delicious *delicioso(a), I2*
to **deliver** *repartir, 11*
delivery person *el/la repartidor(a), 12*
demanding *exigente, 9*
department store *el almacén, I10*
desert *el desierto, I12*
design *el diseño, 9*
to **desire** *desear, I2*
desk *el escritorio, E*
dessert *el postre, I2*
to **destroy** *destruir, 3*
detail *el detalle, 6*
dictionary *el diccionario, E*
difficult *difícil, E*
dining room *el comedor, I4*
dinner *la cena, I2*
to **direct** *dirigir, A4*
disadvantage *la desventaja, 4*
disciplined *disciplinado(a), 12*
disco *la discoteca, I1*
discount *el descuento, 1*
to **discover** *descubrir, I1*
dishwasher *el lavaplatos, I4*
to **do** *hacer, I3*
  to **do aerobics** *hacer aerobic, 10*
  to **do push-ups** *hacer flexiones, 10*
  to **do sit-ups** *hacer abdominales, 10*
  to **do paperwork** *hacer los trámites, I11*
dock *el muelle, 6*
doctor *el/la médico(a), 3*
document *el documento, I11*
documentary *el documental, I9*
dog *el perro, E*
doll *la muñeca, 6*
dollar *el dólar, E*

353

donation *el donativo*, 11
door *la puerta*, I4
downstairs *abajo*, I4
downtown *el centro*, I1
to draw *dibujar*, E
drawing *el dibujo*, 5
dream *el sueño*, A3
dress *el vestido*, I8
dressing room *el probador*, 9
to drink *beber; tomar*, I2
to drive *manejar*, 8
driver *el/la conductor(a)*, 12
drums *la batería*, 5
dry *seco(a)*, A1
duck *el pato*, 8
during *durante*, 1

E

e-mail *el correo electrónico*, 4
each *cada*, I6
early *temprano*, 8
earrings *los aretes*, I10
earthquake *el terremoto*, 3
east *el este*, I6
Easter *la Pascua*, I3
easy *fácil*, E
to eat *comer*, E
ecotourism *el ecoturismo*, 2
educational *educativo(a)*, I9
egg *el huevo*, I2
eight *ocho*, E
eight hundred *ochocientos*, E
eighteen *dieciocho*, E
eighty *ochenta*, E
elbow *el codo*, A2
election *la elección*, 3
elegant *elegante*, 9
elevator *el ascensor*, 4
eleven *once*, E
emergency *la emergencia*, 1
employee *el/la empleado(a)*, 1

end *el fin*, A2
endangered *en peligro de extinción*, 2
English (language) *el inglés*, E
enormously *enormemente*, 6
enough *bastante*, I5; *suficiente*, A6
to enter *entrar*, 4
entertaining *entretenido(a)*, I9
environment *el medio ambiente*, 2
equipment *el equipo*, 5
eraser *el borrador*, E
evening *la tarde; noche*, E
every day *todos los días*, I4
everyone *todos(as)*, I2
everywhere *a todos lados*, 9
exam *el examen*, I7
example *ejemplo*, 3
exciting *emocionante*, I5
excursion *la excursión*, I7
excuse *la excusa*, I7
exercise *el ejercicio*, 10
to exercise *hacer ejercicio*, 10
exit *la salida*, E
expensive *caro(a)*, I2
experience *la experiencia*, I12
experiment *el experimento*, I7
to explain *explicar*, E
to explore *explorar*, 2
expressway *la autopista*, 4
extracurricular *extraescolar*, I7

F

fabulous *fabuloso(a)*, I5
factory *la fábrica*, 4
fall *el otoño*, I6
to fall *caerse*, 3
  to fall asleep *dormirse (o>ue)*, 5
  to fall in love *enamorarse*, 6
family *la familia*, E

famous *famoso(a)*, I3
fan *el ventilador*, 4
fantastic *fantástico (a)*, I9
far (from) *lejos (de)*, I1
farm *la granja; finca*, I4
farmer *el/la granjero(a)*, 8
fashion *la moda*, I8
  fashion magazine *la revista de moda*, I9
  fashion model *el/la modelo*, 9
  fashion show *el salón de moda*, 9
fast *rápido(a)*, I9
father *el padre*, E
favorite *favorito(a)*, E
fax *el fax*, 4
feather *la pluma*, A1
February *febrero*, E
to feel *sentirse (e>ie)*, 11
fever *la fiebre*, 10
fifteen *quince*, E
fifty *cincuenta*, E
to find *encontrar (o>ue)*, E
  to find out *averiguar*, 1
finger *el dedo*, A2
to finish *terminar*, IA4
fire *la fogata*, 2; *(el) incendio*, 3
firefighter *el/la bombero(a)*, 3
firetruck *el carro de bomberos*, 3
fireworks *los fuegos artificiales*, 6
first *primero(a)*, A2
fish *el pescado*, I2
to fish *pescar*, 2
five *cinco*, E
five hundred *quinientos*, E
flamingo *el flamenco*, 2
flexible *flexible*, 12
flight *el vuelo*, 1
  flight attendant *el/la auxiliar de vuelo*, 1
flood *la inundación*, 3
floor *el piso*, I4
flour *la harina*, 7
flower *la flor*, I3
flu *la gripe*, 10
to follow *seguir*, 2
food *la comida*, I2; *(el) alimento*, A3
foot *el pie*, I12

football *el fútbol americano*, E

footwear *el calzado*, 9

for *para; por*, I2

foreman *el/la capataz*, 8

to **forget** *olvidarse*, 2

fork *el tenedor*, I2

formula *la fórmula*, I7

forty *cuarenta*, E

four *cuatro*, E

four hundred *cuatrocientos*, E

fourteen *catorce*, E

free *gratis*, 1

French (language) *el francés*, I7

French fries *las papas fritas*, I2

frequently *con frecuencia*, 6

fresh *fresco(a)*, I2

Friday *el viernes*, E

friend *el/la amigo(a)*, E

from *de*, E

front page *la portada*, 3

fruit *la fruta*, I2

to **fry** *freír (e>i)*, 7

frying pan *la sartén*, 7

full *lleno(a)*, 2

  full-time *la jornada completa*, 12

fun *divertido(a)*, E

funny *gracioso(a)*, 5; *cómico(a)*, I9

furniture *los muebles*, I4

future *el futuro*, 12

G

game *el juego*, 6; *partido*, I7

  game show *el programa de concursos*, I9

garage *el garaje*, I4

garbage *la basura*, 11

  garbage can *el basurero*, 11

garden *el jardín*, I4

gardener *el/la jardinero(a)*, 8

gas station *la gasolinera*, I4

gentleman *el caballero*, E

geography *la geografía*, E

geometry *la geometría*, I7

German (language) *el alemán*, I7

to **get** *recibir*, IA2

  to **get a good/bad grade** *sacar buena/mala nota*, I7

  to **get a haircut** *cortarse el pelo*, 9

  to **get a passport** *sacar el pasaporte*, I12

  to **get along** *llevarse*, 6

  to **get angry** *enojarse*, 6

  to **get bored** *aburrirse*, 5

  to **get dressed** *vestirse*, I7

  to **get in shape** *ponerse en forma*, 10

  to **get ready** *prepararse*, I8

  to **get scared** *asustarse*, 3

  to **get up** *levantarse*, 8

  to **get used to** *acostumbrarse*, A6

gift *el regalo*, I3

girl *la chica*, E

girlfriend *la novia*, I3

to **give** *dar*, I10

  to **give a present** *regalar*, I10

  to **give a speech** *dar un discurso*, 3

  to **give back** *devolver (o>ue)*, I10

glad: to be glad *alegrarse*, 3

glass *el vaso*, I2; *vidrio*, 11

gloves *los guantes*, I6

to **go** *ir*, I1

  to **go abroad** *ir al extranjero*, I11

  to **go away** *irse*, 10

  to **go backpacking** *salir a mochilear (Chile)*, I11

  to **go camping** *ir de campamento*, 2

  to **go out** *salir*, I8

  to **go to bed** *acostarse (o>ue)*, 8

godfather *el padrino*, I3

godmother *la madrina*, I3

gold *el oro*, I10

good *buen(o,a)*, E

  Good afternoon *Buenas tardes*, E

  Good evening *Buenas noches*, E

  Good morning *Buenos días*, E

  Good night *Buenas noches*, E

goodbye *adiós*, E

grade *la nota*, I7

graduation *la graduación*, I3

graffiti *la pintada*, 11

gram *el gramo*, 7

grandfather *el abuelo*, E

grandmother *la abuela*, E

grape *la uva*, 7

gray *gris*, E

green *verde*, E

to **greet** *saludar*, I6

greeting card *la tarjeta*, E

grill *la parrilla*, 8

grocery store *la bodega*, I10

ground *el suelo*, 6

to **grow up** *crecer*, A1

guest *el/la invitado(a)*, I3

guitar *la guitarra*, I3

  electric guitar *la guitarra eléctrica*, 5

gym *el gimnasio*, E

H

hair *el pelo*, E

  hair drier *el secador*, 9

  hair spray *la laca*, 9

haircut *el corte de pelo*, 9

hairdresser *el/la peluquero(a)*, 9

  hairdresser's shop *la peluquería*, 9

half *medio(a)*, 7

hallway *el pasillo*, I7

ham *el jamón*, I2

hamburger *la hamburguesa*, E

hammer *el martillo*, A5

hand *la mano*, E

handbag *el bolso de mano, I11*

handsome *guapo, E*

to **happen** *pasar, I7*

Happy Birthday! *¡Feliz cumpleaños!, I3*

hard *duro(a), A6*

hard rock *el rock duro, I9*

hat *el/la gorro(a), I6; (el) sombrero, I12*

to **have** *tener, E*

to **have to** *tener que, E*

to **have a cold** *tener catarro, 10*

to **have a good/bad time** *pasarla bien/mal, 5*

to **have fun** *divertirse (e>ie), I11*

he *él, E*

head *la cabeza, 3*

headline *el titular, 3*

headphones *los audífonos, 1*

health *la salud, 10*

healthy *sano(a), 10*

to **hear** *oír, 3*

heart *el corazón, A2*

to **heat** *calentar, 7*

height *la altura, I12*

Hello! *¡Hola!, E*

helmet *el casco, 2*

help *la ayuda, 4*

Help! *¡Socorro!, I5*

to **help** *ayudar, 4*

hen *la gallina, 8*

her *su/sus, I4; la, I9*

to/for her *le, I10*

herb *la yerba, A4*

here *aquí, E*

Hi! *¡Hola!, E*

to **hide** *esconder, 6*

high *alto(a), E*

high-heel shoes *los zapatos de tacón, 9*

hiking boots *las botas de montaña, 2*

hill *el monte, 1; cerro, 4*

him *lo, I9*

to/for him *le, I10*

to **hire** *contratar, 8*

his *su/sus, I4*

Hispanic *hispano(a), I4*

history *la historia, E*

hole *el agujero, A2*

homeless people *la gente sin hogar, 11*

homework *la tarea, I7*

honest *honesto(a), 12*

horse *el caballo, 8*

to **horseback ride** *montar a caballo, 2*

hose *la manguera, 8*

hospital *el hospital, 3*

hospitality *la hospitalidad, I5*

host *el/la anfitrión/anfitriona, 3*

hot *caliente, I2*

hotel *el hotel, I4*

hour *la hora, E*

house *la casa, I3*

How? *¿Cómo?, E*

How awful! *¡Qué horror!, 3*

How does it look on me? *¿Cómo me queda?, 9*

How long ago . . . ? *¿Cuánto tiempo hace que...?, 7*

How much does it/do they cost? *¿Cuánto cuesta(n)?, E*

How much? *¿Cuánto(a)?, E*

How many? *¿Cuántos(as)?, E*

How old are you? *¿Cuántos años tienes?, E*

How tall is it/are they? *¿Cuánto mide(n)?, I12*

however *sin embargo, A1*

to **hug (each other)** *abrazar(se), 6*

humid *húmedo(a), A1*

hunger *el hambre, I2*

hurricane *el huracán, I6*

to **hurt** *doler, 10*

I

I *yo, E*

ice *el hielo, I6*

ice cream *el helado, I2*

idea *la idea, E*

ideal *ideal, I4*

ill *enfermo(a), I7*

immediately *en seguida, 6*

important *importante, 8*

impressive *impresionante, I12*

to **improve** *mejorar, A5*

in *en, E*

in order to *para, I2*

inch *la pulgada, I6*

to **include** *incluir, E*

incredible *increíble, 12*

independence *la independencia, 12*

independent *independiente, 12*

inexpensive *barato(a), I1*

information *la información, E*

insect *el insecto, 2*

insect repellent *el repelente de insectos, 2*

inside *dentro de, I4*

instructions *las indi caciones, 2*

instrument *el instrumento, IA2*

intelligent *inteligente, E*

interesting *interesante, E*

interpreter *el/la intérprete, 12*

interview *la entrevista, E*

to **introduce** *presentar, 5*

invention *el invento, A2*

invitation *la invitación, I3*

to **invite** *invitar, I3*

island *la isla, I5*

it *lo; la, I9*

Italian (language) *el italiano, I2*

itinerary *el itinerario, I11*

J

jacket *la chaqueta, I8*

January *enero, E*

Japanese (language) *el japonés, 12*

jazz *el jazz, I9*

jeans *los vaqueros, I8*

ripped jeans *los vaqueros rotos, 9*

jewel *la joya, I10*

356

jewelry store la joyería, I10

job el trabajo, 11; empleo, 12

joke el chiste, 5

journalist el/la periodista, 3

joy la alegría, A3

juice el jugo, I2

July julio, E

June junio, E

jungle la selva, I1

K

key la llave, I8

to kill matar, 6

king el rey, A2

to kiss (each other) besar(se), 6

kitchen la cocina, I4

knee la rodilla, 10

knife el cuchillo, I2

to know conocer, I3; saber, I5

knowledge el conocimiento, A6

L

laboratory el laboratorio, I7

lady la señora, E

lamb el cordero, 7

lamp la lámpara, I4

land la tierra, 8

to land aterrizar, 1

landscape el paisaje, I12

language la lengua, IA1; (el) idioma, I11

large grande, E

last último(a), I7

late tarde, I8

later más tarde, I8

to laugh reírse (e>i), 5

lawyer el/la abogado (a), 12

to learn aprender, I5

leather el cuero, I10

to leave salir, I1

leaf la hoja, A2

lecture la conferencia, 5

left la izquierda, E

leg la pierna, 10

lemonade la limonada, E

to lend prestar, 5

lentils las lentejas, 10

less menos, I9

less . . . than menos ... que, I9

less than (with number expressions) menos de, I10

letter la carta, I11

lettuce la lechuga, I2

library la biblioteca, I1

life la vida, A2

lifeguard el/la salvavidas, I5

light la luz, A3

like como, 9

to like gustar, I2

lips los labios, 3

list la lista, I3

to listen to escuchar, E

liter el litro, 7

literature la literatura, E

little poco(a, os, as); pequeño(a), E

to live vivir, I4

living room la sala, I4

locker el armario, I7

long largo(a), E

to look for buscar, I12

to lose perder, 8

lot (of) mucho(a, os, as), E

love el amor, A2

to love each other quererse (e>ie), 6

luck la suerte, I7

lunch el almuerzo, E; (la) comida (México), I2

M

machine la máquina, 4

magazine la revista, E

mail el correo, I4

main principal, 7

to make hacer, I3

to make mistakes equivocarse, A6

to make a reservation hacer la reserva, I11

makeup el maquillaje, I10

man el hombre, I6

manager el/la gerente, 12

many muchos(as), E

map el mapa, E

marathon el maratón, 3

March marzo, E

market el mercado, I1

mathematics las matemáticas, E

May mayo, E

me me; mí, E

to/for me me, I10

to mean significar, IA4

meat la carne, I2

media los medios de comunicación, I9

medium mediano(a), I10

meeting el encuentro, 3

melon el melón, I2

member el/la socio(a), 5

memory el recuerdo, 6

menu el menú, I2

microphone el micrófono, 5

microscope el microscopio, I7

milk la leche, I2

to milk the cows ordeñar las vacas, 8

milkshake el batido, E

mineral water el agua mineral, I2

mirror el espejo, I4

to mix mezclar, A4

mixture la mezcla, 7

model el modelo, 4

modern moderno(a), I1

mom la mamá, E

moment el momento, I7

Monday el lunes, E

money el dinero, 5

monkey el mono, 2

month el mes, I7

more más, I5

more . . . than más ... que, I9

more than (with number expressions) más de, IA1

more or less más o menos, I5

morning la mañana, E

in the morning de la mañana, E

mother la madre, E

motorboat el bote a motor, I5

motorcycle *la moto, I7*
mountain range *la cordillera, I12*
mouse *el ratón, E*
movie *la película, I9*
movie theater *el cine, E*
mower *la segadora, 8*
Mr. *el señor (Sr.), E*
Mrs. *la señora (Sra.), E*
Ms.; Miss *la señorita (Srta.), E*
much *mucho, I1*
mural *el mural, 11*
muscle *el músculo, 10*
museum *el museo, I1*
music *la música, E*
  dance music *la música bailable, I9*
  pop music *la pop music, I9*
musician *el/la músico(a), 5*
my *mi; mis, E*
mysterious *misterioso(a), I12*

N

name *el nombre, E*
name: to be named *llamarse, E*
napkin *la servilleta, I2*
national park *el parque nacional, 2*
natural reserve *la reserva natural, 2*
nature *la naturaleza, I11*
near *cerca (de), I4*
necessary *necesario(a), 8*
neck *el cuello, 10*
necklace *el collar, I10*
necktie *la corbata, I10*
to **need** *necesitar, E*
neighbor *el/la vecino(a), I3*
neighborhood *el barrio, A4; vecindario, I4*
neither *tampoco, 3*
  neither . . . nor *ni... ni, 3*
nervous *nervioso(a), I12*
net *la red, I5*
never *nunca, I6*
new *nuevo(a), E*
  New Year's *el Año Nuevo, 7*

news *las noticias, 3*
newscast *el noticiero, I9*
newspaper *el periódico, I1*
newsstand *el quiosco, I1*
next to *al lado de, I4*
nice *simpático(a), E*
  Nice to meet you. *Mucho gusto., E; Encantado(a)., I3*
night table *la mesa de noche, I4*
nine *nueve, E*
nine hundred *novecientos, E*
nineteen *diecinueve, E*
ninety *noventa, E*
no *no, E*
no one/nobody *nadie, 3*
noise *el ruido, 4*
noisy *ruidoso(a), I9*
non-stop *sin parar, I9*
  non-stop flight *el vuelo sin escala, 1*
none *ningún; ninguno(a), 3*
north *el norte, I6*
northeast *el nordeste, 2*
northwest *el noroeste, 2*
not *no, E*
  not yet *todavía no, I7*
notebook *el cuaderno, E*
notes *los apuntes, I7*
nothing *nada, E*
novel *la novela, I7*
November *noviembre, E*
now *ahora, E*
number *el número, E*

O

occasion *la ocasión, I3*
ocean *el océano, I12*
October *octubre, E*
of *de, E*
  Of course! *¡Claro!, I3*
to **offer** *ofrecer, 11*
office *la oficina, E*
oil *el petróleo, 3*
old *viejo(a), E*
olive *la aceituna, 7*
  olive oil *el aceite de oliva, 7*
omelette *la tortilla francesa, 7*
on *en, E*

on foot *a pie, I1*
on Mondays (Tuesdays, etc.) *los lunes (martes, etc.), E*
on time *a tiempo, 1*
one *uno, E*
one way ticket *el pasaje de ida, 1*
one hundred *cien, E*
one thousand *mil, I8*
one thousand five hundred *mil quinientos, I8*
one thousand one hundred *mil cien, I8*
onion *la cebolla, 7*
only *el/la único(a), 5; sólo, I8*
to **open** *abrir, I3*
opportunity *la oportunidad, 12*
or *o, I2*
orange *anaranjado(a), E; (la) naranja, 12*
orchid *la orquídea, 2*
to **order** *pedir (e>i), I11*
to **organize** *organizar, 11*
other *otro(a), E*
our *nuestro(a, os, as), I4*
outdoors *al aire libre, 12*
outside (of) *fuera (de), I4*
outstanding *sobresaliente, 11*
oven *el horno, 4*
  microwave oven *el horno microondas, 4*
overhead bin *el compartimiento de arriba, 1*
oxygen mask *la máscara de oxígeno, 1*

P

package *el paquete, 7*
page *la página, E*
to **paint** *pintar, 11*
painting *la pintura, 4*
palm tree *la palmera, 2*
pants *los pantalones, I8*
  baggy pants *los pantalones anchos, 9*
paper *el papel, E; I12*
paperwork *los trámites, 11*

358

parachute *el paracaídas, I5*

parade *el desfile, 5*

paradise *el paraíso, A3*

paragraph *el párrafo, A6*

parents *los padres, E*

park *el parque, I1*

part-time *el tiempo parcial, 12*

to participate *participar, I11*

party *la fiesta, I3*

passenger *el/la pasajero(a), 1*

Passover *Pesach, 7*

passport *el pasaporte, E*

pasta *la pasta, I2*

path *el sendero, 2*

patient *el/la paciente, 12*

pattern *el patrón, A5*

to pay *pagar, I10*

   to pay attention to *prestar atención a, I6*

peace *la paz, 3*

   Peace Corps *el Cuerpo de Paz, 12*

peasant *el/la campesino(a), 1*

pen *el bolígrafo, E*

pencil *el lápiz, E*

people *la gente, 11*

pepper *el ají (Argentina), 7*

perfectly *perfectamente, I11*

performance *la actuación, 5*

perfume *el perfume, I10*

perhaps *tal vez, E*

person *la persona, E*

persuasive *persuasivo(a), 12*

pet *la mascota, E*

pharmacy *la farmacia, E*

photocopying machine *la fotocopiadora, 4*

photograph *la foto, I1*

photographer *el/la fotógrafo(a), 3*

physical education *la educación física, E*

physics *la física, I7*

picnic *el picnic, I3*

picture *el retrato, A6*

pie *la torta, 7*

pig *el cerdo, 8*

pillow *la almohada, 1*

pin *el broche, I10*

pineapple *la piña, I2*

plain *liso(a), 9*

plane *el avión, I11*

plant *la planta, I7*

to plant *plantar, 8*

plastic *el plástico, 11*

plate *el plato, I2*

play *la obra, 5*

to play *jugar (u>ue), I6*

   to play (an instrument) *tocar, I3*

player *el/la jugador(a), A3*

playwright *el/la dramaturgo(a), 11*

please *por favor, E*

plot *el argumento, 6*

poem *el poema, I7*

poet *el/la poeta, 4*

poetry *la poesía, A2*

   poetry reading *la lectura de poesía, 5*

point *el punto, I*

police officer *el/la policía, 3*

polka dots *a lunares, 9*

pollution *la contaminación, 11*

popular *popular, I3*

possible *posible, 8*

post office *el correo, I4*

postcard *la tarjeta postal, E*

poster *el cartel, E*

pot *la olla, 7*

potato *la papa, I2; patata (España), 10*

power *el poder, A3*

powerful *poderoso(a), A2*

practical *práctico(a), 9*

to practice *practicar, I5*

to prefer *preferir (e>ie), I9*

to prepare *preparar, 7*

present *el presente, 7*

president *el/la presidente(a), 3*

prestige *el prestigio, 12*

pretty *guapa, E*

price *el precio, 1*

programming *la programación, I9*

pronoun *pronombre*

to protect *proteger, 2*

public *público(a), 4*

purchase *la compra, I10*

purple *morado(a), E*

purpose *el propósito, 12*

put *puesto(a), 7*

to put *poner, IA1*

   to put on *ponerse, I8*

   to put out a fire *apagar un incendio, 3*

Q

quality *la calidad, 9*

quantity *la cantidad, 7*

question *la pregunta, E*

R

rabbit *el conejo, 8*

radio *la radio, I4*

rain *la lluvia, I6*

to rain *llover (o>ue), I6*

raincoat *el impermeable, I6*

raisin *la pasa, 7*

ranch *la estancia, 8; (el) rancho, I4*

reaction *la reacción, 3*

to read *leer, E*

ready *listo(a), I8*

reason *la razón, 4*

receipt *el recibo, I10*

to receive *recibir, 3*

receptionist *el/la recepcionista, 12*

recipe *la receta, 7*

to recognize *reconocer, 7*

to recommend *recomendar (e>ie), 12*

to recycle *reciclar, 11*

red *rojo(a), E*

   Red Cross *la Cruz Roja, 3*

redhead *pelirrojo(a), E*

reference *la referencia, A1*

   in reference to *en referencia a, A1*

refrigerator *el refrigerador, I4*

region *la región, I11*

relationship *la relación, 6*

relative *el/la pariente(a), I3*

relaxation *la relajación, 10*

remote control *el control remoto, I9*

to rent *alquilar, I5*

report *el informe, I7*

reporter *el/la reportero(a),* 3

representative *el/la representante, I11*

reservation *la reserva, I11; reservación,* 1

resistant *resistente,* 4

responsibility *la responsabilidad,* 8

to **rest** *descansar,* 10

restaurant *el restaurante, I2*

resumé *el currículum, 12*

rice *el arroz, I2*

to **ride** *montar, E*

right *la derecha, E*

ring *el anillo, I10*

river *el río, I4*

rock band *la banda de rock, I8*

rodeo show *la doma,* 8

room *el cuarto, I4*

rooster *el gallo,* 8

roots *las raíces,* 5

rope *la cuerda,* 6

round trip ticket *el pasaje de ida y vuelta,* 1

rug *la alfombra, I4*

ruins *las ruinas, I11*

to **run** *correr,* 10

to **run away** *escaparse,* 8

S

sad *triste, I12*

safe *seguro(a), A5*

sailboat *el velero, I5*

sailing *la navegación,* 2

salad *la ensalada, I2*

salary *el sueldo, 12*

sale *la venta, I5; rebaja, I10*

salt *la sal,* 10

sand *la arena, I5*

sandals *las sandalias, I10*

sandwich *el sándwich, E*

Saturday *el sábado, E*

saxophone *el saxofón,* 5

to **say** *decir (e>i), I11*

scarf *la bufanda, I6; (el) pañuelo,* 9

scene *la escena,* 1

schedule *el horario, E*

school *la escuela, E*

scientist *el/la científico(a), A1*

scissors *las tijeras,* 9

to **scuba dive** *bucear, I5*

sea *el/la mar, I5*

seaport *el puerto,* 6

season *la temporada, A3; estación del año, I6*

seat *el asiento,* 1

aisle seat *el asiento de pasillo,* 1

window seat *el asiento de ventana,* 1

second *segundo(a), A3*

section *la sección, I9*

security *la seguridad,* 1

security check *el control de seguridad,* 1

security measures *las medidas de seguridad,* 1

to **see** *ver, I9*

seed *la semilla,* 8

to **sell** *vender, I1*

semester *el semestre, E*

senator *el/la senador(a),* 3

to **send** *mandar,* 4

senior citizen *el/la anciano(a),* 11

senior citizen home *la residencia de ancianos,* 11

September *septiembre, E*

to **serve** *servir (e>i),* 5

service *el servicio,* 9

seven *siete, E*

seven hundred *setecientos, E*

seventeen *diecisiete, E*

seventy *setenta, E*

shame *la lástima, E*

shampoo *el champú, E*

to **share** *compartir (e>i), I2*

to **shave** *afeitarse,* 9

she *ella, E*

sheep *la(s) oveja(s),* 8

shirt *la camisa, I8*

sleeveless shirt *la camisa sin mangas,* 9

shoe *el zapato, I8*

shoe size *el número de zapato, I10*

shoe store *la zapatería, I1*

shopping *de compras, E*

short *bajo(a); corto(a), E*

shoulder *el hombro,* 10

show *el espectáculo, I12*

to **show** *mostrar, A6*

sick *enfermo(a),* 11

side *el lado, I4*

sideburns *las patillas,* 9

sights *los puntos de interés, I12*

sign *la señal,* 2

to **sign** *firmar, A1*

similar *parecido(a),* 5

simple *sencillo(a), A3*

to **sing** *cantar, I1*

singer *el/la cantante,* 5

sink *el fregadero, I4*

sister *la hermana, E*

six *seis, E*

six hundred *seiscientos, E*

sixteen *dieciséis, E*

sixty *sesenta, E*

size *la talla, I1*

to **skate** *patinar, I1*

skates *los patines,* 5

skating *el patinaje,* 5

to **ski** *esquiar, I6*

skirt *la falda, I8*

skyscraper *el rascacielos,* 4

to **sleep** *dormir (o>ue),* 10

sleeping bag *el saco de dormir,* 2

sloth *el perezoso,* 2

slow *lento(a), I9*

small *pequeño(a), E*

snack (afternoon) *la merienda, I2*

snake *la serpiente,* 2

sneakers *los tenis, I8*

to **snow** *nevar (e>ie), I6*

soap *el jabón, E*

soap opera *la telenovela, I9*

soccer *el fútbol, E*

social worker *el/la asistente social, 12*

sofa *el sofá, I4*

soft drink *el refresco, E*

some *algún; alguno (a,os, as),* 3

somebody *alguien,* 3

something *algo,* 3

sometimes *a veces, I6*

son *el hijo, I3*

song *la canción,* 5

soon *pronto, I8*

Sorry! *¡Perdón!, E*

sound *el sonido,* 5

soup *la sopa, I2*

south *el sur, I6*

South America *América del Sur, I11*
southeast *el sureste, 2*
southwest *el suroeste, 2*
spaghetti *los espagueti, 7*
Spain *España, I7*
Spanish (language) *el español, E*
to **speak** *hablar, E*
speaker *el parlante, 5*
special *especial, I3*
species *las especies, 2*
spectacular *espectacular, I12*
spicy *picante, I2*
spiked hair *el pelo de punta, 9*
spoon *la cuchara, I2*
sport *el deporte, E*
spring *la primavera, I6*
stability *la estabilidad, 12*
stable *el establo, 8*
stadium *el estadio, I1*
stage *el escenario, 5*
stamp *el sello, 6*
star *la estrella, A3*
station *la estación, I1*
to **stay** *quedarse, 1*
steak *el bistec, I2*
stepfather *el padrastro, E*
stepmother *la madrastra, E*
stereo *el estéreo, I9*
sticker *la calcomanía (Rep. Dominicana), 6*
still *todavía, I4*
stomach *el estómago, 10*
stone *la piedra, I11*
stop *la parada, I1*
to **stop** *parar, 8*
store *la tienda, E*
storm *la tormenta, I6*
stove *la estufa, I4*
straight *derecho, I1*
straw *la caña, A4*
street *la calle, E*
strength *la fuerza, 10*
stress *el estrés, 10*
striped *a rayas, 9*
strong *fuerte, A5*
student *el/la estudiante, E*
studies *los estudios, I11*
to **study** *estudiar, I7*
subject *la materia, E*
suburbs *las afueras, I4*
subway *el metro, E*

sugar *el azúcar, 7*
suggestion *la sugerencia, A2*
suit *el traje, 9*
suitcase *la maleta, I11*
summer *el verano, I6*
summer camp *el campamento de verano, 12*
to **sunbathe** *tomar el sol, I5*
Sunday *el domingo, E*
sunglasses *los lentes de sol, I5*
sunscreen *el protector solar, I5*
supermarket *el supermercado, I1*
surprise: to be surprised *sorprenderse, 3*
sweater *el suéter, I6*
to **sweep** *barrer, 7*
sweet *dulce, I2*
to **swim** *nadar, I5*
swimming pool *la piscina, I5*
swing *el columpio, 6*

T

T-shirt *la camiseta, E*
table *la mesa, I4*
tablecloth *el mantel, 7*
to **take** *llevar, I6; sacar, A1*
  to **take off** *despegar, 1*
  to **take out the garbage** *sacar la basura, 7*
  to **take pictures** *sacar fotos, I1*
to **talk** *hablar, E*
tall *alto(a), E*
tape recorder *la grabadora, A6*
tasty *rico(a), I2*
tea *el té, I2*
to **teach** *enseñar, A1*
teacher *el/la profesor(a), E; maestro(a), 12*
technology *la tecnología, 4*
teenager *el/la adolescente, 11*
teeth *los dientes, I8*
telegram *el telegrama, 4*
telephone *el teléfono, E*

cellular phone *el teléfono celular, 4*
telephone number *el número de teléfono, E*
television *la televisión, E*
to **tell** *decir (e>i), I11*
temperature *la temperatura, I6*
ten *diez, E*
ten thousand *diez mil, I8*
tent *la tienda de campaña, 2*
tenth *décimo(a), 12*
territory *el territorio, 2*
test tube *el tubo de ensayo, I7*
thank you (thanks) *gracias, E*
Thanksgiving *Acción de Gracias, 7*
that *que, E; ese(a, o), I10*
the *el; la; los; las, E*
theater *el teatro, I1*
their *su; sus, I4*
them *los; las, I9*
  to/for them *les, I10*
these *estos(as), I10*
they *ellos(as), E*
thing *la cosa, E*
to **think** *pensar, 1*
third *tercero(a), 4*
thirst *la sed, I2*
thirteen *trece, E*
thirty *treinta, E*
this *este(a, o), I10*
  this way *así, A3*
those *esos(as), I10*
three *tres, E*
three hundred *trescientos, E*
throat *la garganta, 10*
through *por, I1; a través de, A6*
Thursday *el jueves, E*
to **till the soil** *cultivar la tierra, 8*
time *la hora, E; vez, IA2; (el) tiempo, I5*
tired *cansado(a), I12*
to *a, E*
today *hoy, E*
together *juntos(as), E*
toilet *el inodoro, I4*
tomato *el tomate, I2*
tomorrow *mañana, E*
too *también, E*

tool *la herramienta, 1*
toothbrush *el cepillo de dientes, E*
toothpaste *la pasta de dientes, E*
topic *el tema, I11*
tornado *el tornado, 3*
toucan *el tucán, 2*
to **touch** *tocar, 6*
tour guide *el/la guía de turismo, 12*
toward *hacia, 2*
towel *la toalla, I5*
tower *la torre, I4*
town *el pueblo, I4*
tractor *el tractor, 8*
traditional *tradicional, 5*
traffic *el tráfico, 4*
  traffic light *el semáforo, 11*
train *el tren, I1*
trainer *el/la entrenador(a), 12*
translation *la traducción, 11*
translator *el/la traductor(a), A2*
transparent *transparente, I5*
transportation *el transporte, I1*
trash *la basura, 2*
to **travel** *viajar, I1*
treasure *el tesoro, 4*
treaty *el acuerdo, A1*
tree *el árbol, I4*
trip *el viaje, I1*
truck *el camión, 8*
trumpet *la trompeta, 5*
to **try** *intentar, 6; tratar, A4*
  to **try on** *probarse (o>ue), 9*
Tuesday *el martes, E*
tuna *el atún, I2*
tune *el son, 8*
turkey *el pavo, 7*
to **turn off** *apagar, I9*
to **turn on** *encender (e>ie), I9*
turtle *la tortuga, E*
twelve *doce, E*
twenty *veinte, E*
twenty one(two . . .) *veintiuno(dos...), E*
two *dos, E*
two hundred *doscientos, E*

two thousand *dos mil, E*
type *el tipo, I9*
typewriter *la máquina de escribir, 4*

U

U.S. *EE.UU., I10*
ugly *feo(a), E*
umbrella *el paraguas, I6*
uncle *el tío, I3*
under *debajo de, I4*
to **understand** *comprender, I7*
United Nations *ONU (Organización de las Naciones Unidas), 12*
unnecessary *innecesario(a), 11*
until *hasta, 2*
upside down *boca abajo, A2*
upstairs *arriba, I4*
us *nos, I9*
  to/for us *nos, I10*
to **use** *usar, 1*
usually *generalmente, I1*

V

vacuum cleaner *la aspiradora, 4*
valley *el valle, I12*
vanguard *la vanguardia, 5*
vanilla *la vainilla, I2*
variety *la variedad, 12*
vegetables *las verduras, I2*
vegetarian *vegetariano(a), I2*
very *muy, E*
victim *la víctima, 3*
video camera *la cámara de video, 4*
video cassette recorder (VCR) *la videocasetera, I9*
videogame *el videojuego, E*
vinegar *el vinagre, 7*
violence *la violencia, 11*
visa *la visa, I11*
to **visit** *visitar, I1*
visitor *el/la visitante, I4*

vocabulary *el vocabulario, I7*
volcano *el volcán, 2*
volleyball *el voleibol, E*
volunteer *el/la voluntario(a), 3*
to **volunteer** *trabajar de voluntario(a), 11*

W

waiter *el mesero, I2*
waitress *la mesera, I2*
waiting room *la sala de espera, 1*
to **walk** *caminar, I1*
wall *la pared, I4*
walnut *la nuez, 7*
to **want** *querer (e>ie), I5*
warrior *el/la guerrero(a), A4*
to **wash** *lavar, 7*
  to **wash (one's hair)** *lavarse (el pelo), I8*
watch *el reloj, I10*
to **watch** *mirar, E*
waterfalls *las cataratas, I12*
watermelon *la sandía, 7*
wave *la ola, I5*
way *la manera, 7*
we *nosotros(as), E*
to **wear** *llevar, I6*
weather *el tiempo, I6*
weather forecast *el pronóstico del tiempo, I6*
wedding *la boda, I3*
Wednesday *el miércoles, E*
week *la semana, E*
weekend *el fin de semana, E*
weekly *semanal, E*
weight *la pesa, 10*
Welcome! *¡Bienvenidos!, E*
west *el oeste, I6*
to **wet** *mojar, A1*
What? *¿Qué...?, E*
  What happened? *¿Qué pasó?, 3*
  What's up? *¿Qué tal?, E*
wheat *el trigo, 8*

362

wheel *la rueda,* A2
When? *¿Cuándo?,* E
Where? *¿Dónde?,* E
  Where are you from?
  ¿De dónde eres?, E
  Where to? *¿Adónde?,* I1
Which? *¿Cuál(es)?,* E
white *blanco(a),* E
Who(m)? *¿Quién(es)?,* E
Why? *¿Por qué?,* E
wild *salvaje,* 8
to **win** *ganar,* I7
wind *el viento,* I6
window *la ventana,* I4
winter *el invierno,* I6
to **wish** *desear,* I2
with *con,* E
  with me *conmigo,* I1
  with you *contigo,* I1
without *sin,* I6
woman *la mujer,* I6
wood *la madera,* I12
wool *la lana,* I12
to **work** *trabajar,* I6

worker *el/la trabajador(a),* 3
workshop *el taller,* I1
World Cup *el Mundial de Fútbol,* 3
worried *preocupado (a),* I12
worse (than) *peor (que),* I9
to **write** *escribir,* I2

Y

year *el año,* E
yellow *amarillo(a),* E
yesterday *ayer,* I7
yogurt *el yogur,* I2
you *tú; vosotros(as); Ud.; Uds.,* E
  to/for you *te; os; le; les; ti,* I10
young *joven,* E
your *tu; tus,* E

Z

zero *el cero,* E
zip code *el código postal,* E
zipper *la cremallera,* 9
zone *la zona,* I1
zoo *el zoológico,* 5

English-Spanish Glossary

ÍNDICE

ÍNDICE

ÍNDICE

CREDITS

Contributing Writers
Pilar Álamo, Luisa N. Alfonso, Adrián Collado, Eva Gasteazoro, Ron Horning, Saskia Gorospe-Rombouts, Stephen McGroarty, Daniel Montoya, Nela Navarro-LaPointe, Mariana Pavetto, Candy Rodó, Isabel Sampedro, Jeff Segall, Tanya Torres, Pedro Valiente, Walter Vega

Contributing Editors
Inés Greenberger
José Luis Benavides, Raquel Díez, Claudia DoCampo, Richard deFuria, Eva Garriga, Andrea Heiss, Elvira Ortiz, Margaret Maujenest, Sharon Montoya, Andrés Palomino, Timothy Patrick, Mercedes Roffé, Vincent Smith, Marta Vengoechea

Design/Production
Design: Rhea Banker,
Chuck Yuen, Patty Harris
Production Management: Helen Breen, Jo Ann Hauck
Electronic Production: Gwen Waldron, Lynne Torrey
Photo Research: Rory Maxwell, Elisa Frohlich, Omni-Photo Communications

Text Credits
Grateful acknowledgment is made to the following for permission to reprint copyrighted material:
El Museo del Barrio
Logo and information concerning membership and cultural mission of El Museo del Barrio, New York City used with permission.
Note: Every effort has been made to locate the copyright owner of material reprinted in this book. Omissions brought to our attention will be corrected in subsequent printings.

Art Credits
045 Nancy Doniger; 045 Rita Lascaro; 048 Tim Egan; 049 Tim Egan; 051 Aaron Koster; 051 Nancy Doniger; 054 Frank Ferri; 062 Rita Lascaro; 063 Nancy Doniger; 065 Neverne Covington; 066 Jim Deigan; 067 Jim Deigan; 074 Anne Stanley; 075 Anne Stanley; 092 Nancy Doniger; 093 Nancy Doniger; 096 André Labrie; 097 André Labrie; 110 Nancy Doniger; 111 Nancy Doniger; 111 Rita Lascaro; 114 Susan Greenstein; 115 Susan Greenstein; 117 Nancy Doniger; 141 Nancy Doniger; 144 Debbie Tilley; 145 Debbie Tilley; 148 Neverne Covington; 149 Neverne Covington; 158 Nancy Doniger; 159 Nancy Doniger; 159 Rita Lascaro; 162 Rodica Prato; 163 Rodica Prato; 168 Steve Henry; 170 Joey Art; 171 Joey Art; 188 Nancy Doniger; 189 Nancy Doniger; 190 Abe Gurvin; 192 Tim Egan; 193 Tim Egan; 203 Patty Harris; 206 Nancy Doniger; 210 Rodica Prato; 211 Rodica Prato; 213 Nancy Doniger; 218 Anne Stanley; 219 Anne Stanley; 236 Nancy Doniger; 237 Nancy Doniger; 237 Susan Blubaugh; 238 Gayle Kabaker;

240 Tim Egan; 241 Tim Egan; 243 Nancy Doniger; 245 Nancy Doniger; 247 Susan Blubaugh; 254 Nancy Doniger; 258 Jim Deigan; 259 Jim Deigan; 261 Nancy Doniger; 285 Nancy Doniger; 288 Susan Hunt Yule; 289 Susan Hunt Yule; 294 Josie Yee; 295 Josie Yee; 296 Robin Hotchkis; 297 Robin Hotchkis; 302 Nancy Doniger; 303 Nancy Doniger; 306 Rodica Prato; 307 Rodica Prato; 314 Jannine Cabossel; 315 Jannine Cabossel

Photo credits
cover Paul Loven/The Image Bank; cover James Marshall/The Stock Market; cover Ken Karp; cover Henry Cordero; cover Grace Davies/Omni-Photo Communications
xxx bottom The Granger Collection; xxx center David Stoecklein/The Stock Market; xxx top Peter Morgan/Matrix; xxxi center Stephen Ogilvy; xxxi top Byron Augustin/DDB Stock Photo; xxxi bottom Donald Dietz/Stock Boston
xxx bottom The Granger Collection; xxx center David Stoecklein/The Stock Market; xxx top Peter Morgan/Matrix; xxxi center Stephen Ogilvy; xxxi top Byron Augustin/DDB Stock Photo; xxxi bottom Donald Dietz/Stock Boston
002 Michael Krasowitz/FPG; 008 bottom Henry Cordero; 008 center Henry Cordero; 008 top Robert Frerck; 012 bottom Michal Heron; 012 center Lou Bopp; 012 top Lou Bopp; 020 bottom Paco Elvira; 020 center Colin Fisher; 020 top Rocio Escobar; 022 Runk/Schoenberger/Grant Heilman Photography; 024 bottom James Davis/International Stock; 024 center R. Walker/H. Armstrong Roberts; 024 top Bachmann/PhotoEdit; 028 Monkmeyer/Collins; 031 Rocio Escobar; 032 bottom Ken Karp; 032 center Ken Karp; 032 top Barbara Alper/Stock Boston; 034 Ken Karp; 035 bottom Lou Bopp; 035 top Anna Elias; 036 bottom Lou Bopp; 036 top Michal Heron; 037 bottom Marcos Lopez; 037 top Lou Bopp; 040-041 Courtesy of Costa Rica Tourist Bureau; 041 bottom right Mike & Carol Werner/Comstock; 042-043 John F. Mason/The Stock Market; 043 bottom Rocio Escobar; 043 center Wil Blanche/Omni-Photo Communications; 043 top Comstock; 043 top center Rocio Escobar; 044-045 John F. Mason/The Stock Market; 050 Rocio Escobar; 053 Jeff Greenberg/Leo de Wys Inc.; 056-057 Comstock; 057 Wil Blanche/Omni-Photo Communications; 058 Rocio Escobar; 060-061 Rocio Escobar; 061 bottom Rocio Escobar; 061 bottom center John Elk III/Bruce Coleman Inc.; 061 center Rocio Escobar; 061 top Gregory G. Dimijian/Photo Researchers, Inc.; 062-063 Rocio Escobar; 064 bottom left Gregory G. Dimijian/Photo Researchers, Inc.; 064 bottom right Rocio Escobar; 064 top Rocio Escobar; 069 bottom Mike & Carol Werner/Comstock; 069 top Rocio Escobar; 070 Rocio Escobar; 071 Rocio Escobar; 072 left Rocio Esobar; 072 right Paul Gerda/Leo de Wys Inc.; 073 John Elk III/Bruce Coleman Inc.; 077 Rocio Escobar; 078-079 Art Gingert/Comstock; 079 bottom Louisa Preston/Photo Researchers, Inc.; 079 center Superstock; 079 top Rocio Escobar; 080 bot-

tom left David W. Hamilton/The Image Bank; 080 bottom right Rocio Escobar; 080 top Roy Morsch/The Stock Market; 081 bottom Byron Augustin/DDB Stock Photo; 081 top left Gregory G. Dimijian/Photo Researchers, Inc.; 081 top right Rocio Escobar; 083 Rocio Escobar; 084 bottom Lou Bopp; 084 top Lou Bopp; 085 bottom left Lou Bopp; 085 bottom right Lou Bopp; 085 top left Lou Bopp; 085 top right Lou Bopp; 086 bottom Tom Boyden; 086 top Rocio Escobar; 087 bottom Rocio Escobar; 087 top A.F.P. Photo; 088 MNAM; 088-089 Robert Frerck/The Stock Market; 089 Markova/The Stock Market; 090-091 Focus on Sports; 091 bottom Bill Hickey/Allsport USA; 091 bottom center D. Donne Bryant; 091 center Robert Frerck/Odyssey/Chicago; 091 top Henry Cordero; 091 top center Focus on Sports; 092-093 Comstock; 094 bottom center J.P. Courau/DDB Stock Photo; 094 bottom left RobertFrerck/Odyssey/Frerck/Chicago; 094 bottom right Focus on Sports; 094 top Michal Heron; 094 top center left The Bettmann Archive; 094 top center right Keith Dannemiller/SABA; 095 MNAM; 098 J.P. Courau/DDB Stock Photo; 099 A & J Verkaik/The Stock Market; 100 Peter Menzel/Stock Boston; 101 Henry Cordero; 102 D. Donne Bryant; 103 Robert Frerck/Odyssey/Chicago; 104-105 Bill Hickey/Allsport USA; 105 bottom Bob Daemmrich/Stock Boston; 106 J.P. Courau/DDB Stock Photo; 107 Robert Frerck/Odyssey/Chicago; 108-109 Keith Dannemiller/SABA; 109 bottom Eric Kroll/Omni-Photo Communications; 109 bottom center Giuliano du Portu; 109 center Emory Kristof/National Geographic Society; 109 top Bob Daemmrich ; 109 top center Peter Morgan/Matrix; 110-111 Joel Greenstein/Omni-Photo Communications; 112 bottom Arturo Rubio/DDB Stock Photo; 112 bottom center Chip and Rosa Maria Peterson; 112 top Markova/The Stock Market; 112 top center Peter Morgan/Matrix; 113 Bob Daemmrich; 118 Bob Daemmrich ; 119 Giuliano du Portu; 120-121 Steve Ogilvy; 123 Eric Kroll/Omni-Photo Communications; 124 Emory Kristof/national Geographic Society; 125 Jonathan Blair/National Geographic Society; 126-127 Carl Frank/Photo Researchers, Inc.; 127 bottom Odyssey/Frerck/Chicago; 127 center D. Donne Bryant; 127 top D. Donne Bryant; 128 bottom John V. Cotten/DDB Stock Photo; 128 top Robert Frerck/Odyssey/Chicago; 129 Robert Frerck/Odyssey; 131 David Madison; 132 bottom Stephen Ogilvy; 132 top Alyx Kellington/DDB Stock Photo; 133 bottom center Stephen Ogilvy; 133 bottom left Stephen Ogilvy; 133 bottom right Stephen Ogilvy; 133 top center Stephen Ogilvy; 133 top left Stephen Ogilvy; 133 top right Stephen Ogilvy; 134 bottom Suzanne L Murphy/DDB Stock Photo; 134 top Andres Palomino; 135 bottom Jeff Foott/Bruce Coleman Inc.; 135 top Grace Davies/Omni-Photo Communications; 136-137 Lou Bopp; 138-139 Lou Bopp; 139 bottom The Stock Market; 139 bottom center Lou Bopp; 139 top Lou Bopp; 139 top center

Eric Guttelwitz/Museo del Barrio/Omni Photo Communications; 140-141 Lou Bopp; 142 left "Portrait of Klavia". Rosa Ibarra/Courtesy of Museo del Barrio; 142 right "Spring in Paris". Oil on canvas, 1976, Pedro Villarini/Courtesy of Museo del Barrio, Omni Photo Communications; 143 bottom Museo del Barrio; 143 top Eric Guttelwitz/Museo del Barrio/Omni Photo Communications; 146 Lou Bopp; 149 Comstock; 150 bottom Stephen Ogilvy; 150 top Jeff Greenberg/Photo Researchers; 151 Stephen Ogilvy; 152-153 Stephen Ogilvy; 153 bottom Lou Bopp; 153 top left M. Lopez; 153 top right James McLoughlin/FPG International; 154 The Stock Market; 156-157 Lou Bopp; 157 bottom Lou Bopp; 157 bottom center Lou Bopp; 157 center Martha Cooper/Viesti Associates, Inc.; 157 top Lou Bopp; 157 top center Lou Bopp; 158-159 Lou Bopp; 160 bottom left Lou Bopp; 160 bottom right Lou Bopp; 160 top left Lou Bopp; 160 top right Lou Bopp; 161 1995 PhotoDisc, Inc.; 165 Lou Bopp; 167 bottom left Shelley Rotner/Omni Photo Communications; 167 bottom right Shelley Rotner/Omni Photo Communications; 169 C.D. Gordon/The Image Bank; 172 Martha Cooper/Viesti Associates, Inc.; 173 Stephen Ogilvy; 174-175 Rob Tringali Jr./Sportschrome East/West; 175 bottom Lou Bopp; 175 center Chip & Rosa Maria Peterson; 175 top Lou Bopp; 176 Rob Tringali/Sportschrome East/West; 176-177 Wide World Photos, Inc.; 177 Lou Bopp; 179 1995 PhotoDisc, Inc.; 180 bottom Lou Bopp; 180 top Lou Bopp; 181 bottom center Lou Bopp; 181 bottom left Lou Bopp; 181 bottom right Lou Bopp; 181 top center Lou Bopp; 181 top right Lou Bopp; 181 top right Lou Bopp; 182 bottom Dr. Paul A. Zahr/Photo Researchers, Inc.; 182 top Lou Bopp; 183 bottom Lou Bopp; 183 top Charles Seaborn/Odyssey/Chicago; 184-185 Mark Newman/International Stock; 185 Carlos Sanuvo/Bruce Coleman; 186-187 Marcos Lopez; 187 bottom Marcos Lopez; 187 bottom center Marcos Lopez; 187 top Stephen Ogilvy; 187 top center Robert Frerck/Odyssey/Chicago; 188-189 Joe Viesti; 194 Robert Frerck/Odyssey/Chicago; 196 Marcos Lopez; 197 Stephen Ogilvy; 199 Stephen Ogilvy; 200-201 Stephen Ogilvy; 202 Marcos Lopez; 204-205 Michael Moody/DDB Stock Photo; 205 bottom Michael Moody/DDB Stock Photo; 205 bottom center Marcos Lopez; 205 center Robert Frerck/Woodfin Camp; 205 top Carlos Goldin/Focus -Stock Fotografico; 206-207 Marcos Lopez; 208 bottom left Carlos Goldin/Focus -Stock Fotografico; 208 bottom right Marcos Lopez; 208 top Marcos Lopez; 212 Marcos Lopez; 214 Marcos Lopez; 215 bottom center Stephen Ogilvy; 215 bottom left Marcos Lopez; 215 bottom right Marcos Lopez; 215 top center Marcos Lopez; 215 top left Marcos Lopez; 215 top right Marcos Lopez; 216-217 Michael Moody/DDB Stock Photo; 220-221 Robert Frerck/Woodfin Camp; 222-223 Jose Fuste Raga/The Stock Market; 223 bottom The Stock Market; 223 center George D. Lepp/Comstock; 223 top Alex Stewart/The Image Bank; 224 bottom

367